Wayne F. Cooper

# Claude McKay
## Rebel Sojourner in the Harlem Renaissance

A Biography

Louisiana State University Press
Baton Rouge and London

*To Jean*

Designer: Laura Roubique
Typeface: Primer
Typesetter: G & S Typesetters, Inc.
Printer and binder: Thomson-Shore, Inc.

921
McKAY

Louisiana Paperback Edition, 1996

05 04 03 02 01 00 99 98 97 96   5 4 3 2 1

Library of Congress Cataloging-in-Publication Data

Cooper, Wayne F.
   Claude McKay: rebel sojourner in the Harlem
Renaissance.

   Revision of thesis (Ph.D.)—Rutgers University,
New Brunswick.
   Bibliography: p.
   Includes index.
   1. McKay, Claude, 1890–1948—Biography.  2. Authors,
American—20th Century—Biography. 3. Authors, Jamaican
—20th Century—Biography. 4. Harlem Renaissance.
5. Afro-American arts.  6. Afro-Americans—Intellectual
life. I. Title.
PS3525.A24785Z63   1987   818'.5209 [B]   86-18505
ISBN 0-8071-1310-7 (cloth)   ISBN 0-8071-2074-X (pbk.)

The paper in this book meets the guidelines for permanence
and durability of the Committee on Production Guidelines for
Book Longevity of the Council on Library Resources. ∞

# Contents

# Illustrations

following page 200

Claude McKay in 1920

Claude McKay and Max Eastman

Carl Cowl

Arthur A. Schomburg

Countee Cullen

Eulalie Imelda Lewars McKay

U'Theo McKay

Hope McKay Virtue

McKay country, Clarendon Parish

# Preface and Acknowledgments

In this biography of Claude McKay I have attempted two things. One is to make clear McKay's importance as a pioneer in twentieth-century black literature in the West Indies, the United States, and Africa. The second is to portray as accurately as possible the man and the artist from his birth in 1890 to his death in 1948. The first objective was more easily accomplished than the second.

There can be no doubt of McKay's importance as a pioneering black writer. In 1912 he produced two volumes of Jamaican dialect poetry that have long been recognized as unique and important contributions to a distinctive West Indian literature. Throughout McKay's career, Jamaica occupied a central, unifying place in his poetry and fiction, and he is today generally recognized as one of the earliest and most important black voices in the new West Indian literature that has developed in this century, largely since World War II.

His place as a forerunner to recent West Indian literature remains secure despite the fact that McKay left Jamaica in 1912 at the age of twenty-two and never returned. Like several other articulate West Indians in this century, he achieved his best work and won his largest audiences in the United States and Europe. During a lifetime of travel and observation, he produced penetrating commentaries on modern colonialism in which he clearly anticipated such later West Indian expatriates as George Padmore, C. L. R. James, Frantz Fanon, Derek Walcott, and V. S. Naipaul.

McKay also played an important role in the development of modern black American literature in the United States. In New York City, his militant protest poetry after World War I inaugurated a decade of intense black literary activity known as the Harlem Renaissance or the New Negro movement. His forthright declarations of alienation, anger, and rebellion after World War I gave early expression to themes that have since figured prominently in black American writing. And in his novels published in the late 1920s and early 1930s, he joined the other black writers of the 1920s who had begun to explore the continued relevance of their folk roots in Africa, the West Indies, and the rural South—a preoccupation that has by no means disappeared from recent black American literature.

McKay's novels, particularly his second, *Banjo*, published in 1929, also exerted a profound catalytic influence upon certain young French West Indians and West Africans, notably Léopold Sédar Senghor from Senegal and Aimé Césaire from Martinique. These two men would later acknowledge McKay's strong influence in their development of the literary doctrine of *Nègritude*, which dominated black French writing in the years after World War II.

Finally, it must be said that McKay's political and social commentary, embodied in his numerous articles over three decades (1918–1948) and in such books as *A Long Way from Home* (1937), *Harlem: Negro Metropolis* (1940), and *The Negroes in America* (1923), contained often prophetic statements on issues that later became increasingly important to black Americans and to the nation in general. In his articles and essays, McKay dealt at length with crucial black issues: the debate over traditional, civil rights–oriented integration versus strong, black, community-based ethnic development; and the importance of ethnic pluralism in American and world development. In addition, he commented intelligently on a range of historical problems associated with European imperialism, Western democracy, anticolonialism, and the rise of Russian communism.

In his essays, McKay came closest to developing a consistent stylistic excellence; in poetry and fiction he was never a stylistic innovator. But in all his works, he seized intuitively upon those themes of identity, alienation, rebellion, and community development that have dominated black literature—and much of Western literature in general—in this century.

In this study I have concentrated a good deal of attention on McKay's literary works, because most of his adult life was concerned with their production, and they remain in fact the chief reason for his enduring importance. Nevertheless, this is primarily a biography, not a work of literary analysis; its central focus is McKay's life, not simply his literature.

As an individual and as a literary artist, McKay was to an extraordinary degree deeply involved in the action and passion of his times. As a young Jamaican colonial, as an immigrant poet and political radical in the United States after World War I, as a doubly expatriated writer in Europe and North Africa from 1922 until 1934, as a politically conscious member of the Federal Writers' Project in New York City in the 1930s, and finally as a disillusioned secular idealist and world-weary convert to Catholicism in the 1940s, he participated in and wrote about some of the major historical events of this century. At the same time, he maintained a curious detachment and stubborn independence that ultimately left him isolated and lonely.

In many ways, his was a paradoxical personality, characterized always by a deep-seated ambivalence. Yet, despite years of wandering and personal isolation in many lands, he remained always securely anchored to a positive identity as the proud son of Jamaica's independent black peasantry. This self-confidence in his essential identity existed side by side with his ambivalence and his need for support and reassurance from a succession of patrons. And coloring both was an ever-present ironic awareness that his humanity could never be defined entirely by the simple boundaries of color and race.

Personally he was a complex and often exasperating man, alternately charming and spiteful, noble and petty, wise and self-deceptive. Through all his moods, he tried to the very end of his life to maintain in his political and social criticism a dispassionate objectivity and intellectual honesty that would transcend whatever weaknesses he had as a man. This very attitude, however, often led to profound misunderstandings and bitter conflicts.

On the whole, of course, it must be remembered that writers and artists, especially in the rootless turmoil of recent times, have often had difficult personalities and lonely lives. Judged in relation to such contemporaries as Robert Frost, Ezra Pound, and Ernest Hemingway (to name only three), McKay's personality was complex but stable, even engaging in its flexibility.

One contention of this study is that McKay's personality, as well as the major elements of his creative life and aesthetic tendencies, were already formed by the time he left Jamaica in 1912 at the age of twenty-two. In his adult life he tended to repeat certain fundamental behavioral patterns that had been established during his early years in Jamaica. As he grew older his literary art became more sophisticated and his social perceptions more acute, but on a personal level, his private life remained fixed within a cycle of dependence upon a succession of father figures. All his life, McKay remained trapped within a pattern set early as his mother's pampered youngest son. He always depended to a remarkable extent upon others to take care of his most elemental human needs. This is not stated to minimize the enormous obstacles McKay had actively to face and overcome as an independent black writer in a largely indifferent, even hostile white environment. In this respect, he displayed throughout his life great integrity and singleness of purpose. But often his genuine achievements were accomplished only after great difficulties because of basic patterns of immaturity that persisted until his death.

The ultimate focus of this work, however, is neither on McKay's character nor on his literature alone. It is, rather, on his reaction to the great social forces that impinged upon him from birth. Studies of literary figures do not normally come within the purview of the historian; such works are usually the special competence of literary critics. There are, however, individuals whose writings and actions have influenced many of the significant social movements of the age; they not only contribute to the literary scene, but in a larger part they mirror many of the basic trends and conflicts of their time. Claude McKay, black poet and novelist, was one of these people. And it is for this reason, above all, that he deserves the historian's attention.

For better or worse, this work is the result of many years of effort, during which time I have all too often engaged in other, more mundane work that provided a livelihood. As a consequence, the time required to produce this biography must have often seemed wholly unreasonable to many whose support was essential to its completion. For this reason, I would like to say a hearty thanks to all those who have nevertheless always said yes to this project. They include my family in Mobile, Hope McKay Virtue in California, and Carl Cowl and Frances Witlin in Brooklyn. That does not exhaust the list. Many more are acknowledged by their presence in the notes and the bibliography. At Rutgers, the State University of New Jersey in New Brunswick, I thank William L. O'Neill, Tilden Edelstein, Seth Scheiner, and Donald Gibson. My thanks also to Professor Gwendolyn Hall, who first encouraged me to enroll in the Afro-American program at Rutgers.

Barbara O'Neil Phillips and the other editors at Louisiana State University Press who shaped my manuscript into finished form must certainly be thanked. Finally, I must express my thanks to my wife, Carol Petillo. Her thoughtful analyses of my tendencies toward procrastination often turned what seemed like mountains into mere molehills, and her unfailing companionship, assistance, and example as a scholar in her own right enabled me to see this project through to the end.

Claude McKay

# 1
# The Jamaican Family Background

In 1921, Claude McKay wrote an article on the Irish revolution in which he declared that neither the British government nor the British Left really understood the Irish. But, he said, he thought he did. "My belonging to a subject race entitles me to some understanding of them," he explained. "And then I was born and reared a peasant; the peasant's passion for the soil possesses me, and it is one of the strongest passions in the Irish revolution." The remark provided insight into both the Sinn Fein movement for Irish independence and McKay's own background and character. It also illustrated McKay's limitations as a communist theoretician. "For my part," he remarked, "I love to think of communism liberating millions of city folk to go back to the land."[1] Although this statement may have betrayed an incurable romanticism, McKay's roots did, indeed, run deep in Jamaica's black peasantry. Its history, in fact, largely defined the place of Claude McKay's immediate family in nineteenth-century Jamaica. Theirs was the story of transplanted Africans forced to cultivate an alien soil. They survived to claim it as their own. Their history became Claude McKay's most basic legacy.

The McKay family had its origin in almost the exact geographical center of Jamaica, in upper Clarendon Parish. The mountains that dominated the environment would later be celebrated by Claude McKay in his earliest poetry. It was a pleasant land, whose seasons varied between the drier spring and summer months and the wet period, which began in October and lasted through March. The environment of Claude's boyhood—its mountain streams, its lush richness of soil and vegetation, its bright sunshine and variegated natural colors, the very sounds of tropical country life—would always remain vivid in his memory. At the end of his life, he fondly recalled the great fertility of the land of his birth: "There grow in abundance, as if spilled straight out of the Hand of God—bananas, oranges, coco, coffee, pimento, breadfruit, ackee, mangoes, sugar cane and all the lesser varieties of edibles such as various kinds of beans and peas, okra, cashews, cabbages, sweet potatoes, cassava and arrow-root."[2]

Claude McKay's parents had emerged from the black peasantry of upper Clarendon. By his birth in 1890, the free peasantry formed the majority there. Although this black peasantry was of relatively recent origin, its roots reached far back into slavery. Long before legal emancipation, Jamaica's slave population had been striving toward independence. In the nearly inaccessible interior, several maroon communities in the seventeenth and eighteenth centuries had won their freedom and a degree of autonomy within the colonial structure. On the plantations, slave revolts had been frequent, but the desire for freedom also expressed itself in other ways. Over the years, slaves had gained certain customary rights and privileges into which they poured their energy and ingenuity. By the 1830s, for example, from their own traditional provision grounds (garden plots), Jamaican slaves had devised an islandwide system of Sunday produce markets upon which the colony had come to depend for much of its food. From this system of provision grounds and slave markets, the freed slaves moved naturally toward acquiring land and expanding their economic opportunities.

With the end of slavery in the 1830s, many former slaves left the sugar plantations on the coastal plains and in the valleys and occupied the largely uncultivated mountainous interior. Some obtained clear title to their land; most simply claimed ownership by right of possession and cultivation. As a result, during the first three decades after emancipation, a significant proportion of Jamaica's African population transformed itself into a free black peasantry.[3] The road to independence proved a hard one. For decades, the blacks' interests remained subordinated to those more favorably placed in the island's complex social hierarchy. Between the blacks at the bottom and the traditional white-planter class at the top (who dominated the island's oppressive legislative assembly), there existed a small mulatto elite, the mixed-blood class also known as colored, whose interests as property owners did not always coincide with those of their darker kinsmen. In addition, after emancipation Chinese and East Indians were imported as contract laborers to replace those blacks who had left the sugar fields. They, too, soon deserted the plantations. Many left Jamaica, but those who remained soon competed with the tiny Jewish and Lebanese commercial communities in Jamaica. Their collective small-scale retail trade squeezed every available penny of profit from the struggling black peasantry.[4]

By the mid-1860s, chronic economic depression, drought, crop failures, famine, long-standing discriminatory legislation, and an antiquated judicial system combined to bring peasant discontent to a boil. At Morant Bay on October 11, 1865, black peasants attacked the parish courthouse and killed eighteen officials, planters, and their subordinates. British troops dispatched to the scene by the royal governor, Edward Eyre, speedily and brutally suppressed this rebellion. At the governor's behest, among those summarily executed was a mulatto politician from Kingston, George William Gordon, whose chief offense was his outspoken airings of small peasant grievances in the Jamaican assembly and his attacks on Governor Eyre's leadership.

The Morant Bay Rebellion and its outcome—largely random execution of black males in the vicinity, together with Gordon's martyrdom—led in Britain to a temporary revival of old abolitionist concern for the welfare of blacks in the British colony. A royal inquiry resulted in the removal of Governor Eyre and, most important, the abolition of the discredited, bankrupt Jamaican assembly. It was replaced by direct crown-colony rule in 1866. In the last third of the nineteenth century, crown-colony government at last brought order, some social reform, and a measure of stability, if not prosperity, to the colony's economy.[5]

During Claude McKay's boyhood in the 1890s, the acute troubles of slavery and the postemancipation period had been left behind, but certain legacies of those years remained vividly alive within the McKay family. Claude's parents had both grown up in the postemancipation period. Although the details of their early lives remain sketchy and often uncertain, some important facts are clear. Both families had experienced slavery, and both retained a clear memory of its harshness.

On Claude's mother's side, tradition told of an origin in Madagascar (a few slaves did in fact enter Jamaica from East Africa). That same tradition also told of a family bond so strong that, when faced with the slave auction block, they had agreed upon death before disunity. "And this fact solemnly announced in the market by the oldest white-haired Negro among them, had such an effect upon prospective buyers that it was impossible to sell them as individuals, and so they were all taken away together to those hills at Clarendon which their descendants still cultivate."[6] In Claude's boyhood, a mulatto planter clan, the Woolseys, which had perhaps owned his mother's family, still lived nearby in their decaying plantation home. Although greatly reduced in circumstances, if not in numbers, they still clung precariously to a slightly higher status than their peasant neighbors. The oldest among them often recalled the troubles she had had in disciplining her slaves.

Claude believed his father to be of Ashanti origin. He remembered that his father knew certain Ashanti customs and remembered stories of Africa, which he related to his children. Whenever his sons' behavior or cocky self-assurance angered him, he would remind them that their grandfather had been a slave and "knew how cruel the white man could be. You boys don't know anything."[7]

Although such memories remained alive within them, McKay's parents had also been molded by missionary influences and by the deep attachments of a newly independent peasantry to the soil. From their youth, both had made profound and permanent commitments to Christianity and to the cultivation and improvement of their own land. Upon these bedrocks they based their marriage and their lives.[8]

Claude's father, Thomas Francis McKay, was born around 1840 in the vicinity of Staceyville, a little community near the great Bull Mountain in upper Clarendon.[9] Little is known about Thomas' parents. At some point in his youth, Thomas Francis came under the decisive influence of a British missionary, who converted him to Christianity, instructed him in the fundamentals of reading and writing, and helped mold in him a rigidly fundamentalist, Old Testament cast of mind that absolutely forbade smoking, drinking, dancing, swearing, extramarital sex, or dishonesty in any form. Thomas Francis quite early chose a straight and narrow path and never deviated from it.[10]

Few of his neighbors, perhaps even few of his fellow churchmen, adopted so wholeheartedly the puritanical Christianity of noncon-formist England. One of the constant complaints of missionaries throughout the nineteenth century was the ease with which professing Christians in the hill country of Jamaica both joined the church and broke its moral codes. More than a few (some said a majority) continued also to believe in Obeah, the evil magic of African origin, and consulted Obeahmen on the sly. The random beliefs and practices, as well as the spirit, of African religions suffused black Jamaica. Many broke away from orthodox Protestant churches. They were constantly forming and re-forming native church sects whose unlettered pastors, the missionaries knew, allowed free vent to practices and doctrines of non-Christian origin.[11] Most black peasants had eagerly accepted the flexible spirit of Christianity but had left its rigid doctrinal orthodoxy to the anxious guardianship of the European missionaries. Thomas Francis McKay, however, grasped both spirit and doctrine in a tight embrace. Even more surprising, he actually practiced what he preached. In a region of syncretistic Afro-Christian religious beliefs, he stood as a clear exception to the rule.[12]

In *My Green Hills of Jamaica,* a late memoir of his boyhood, Claude stated that the missionary who had converted his father had been a Scotch Presbyterian. But others dispute this, maintaining that Thomas had from the first been a Baptist. This seems more likely. Upper Clarendon apparently had no Presbyterian mission churches in the mid-nineteenth century but did have numerous Congregationalist and Baptist missions, and there was a Baptist church at Staceyville during the elder McKay's youth. Without question, Thomas McKay did spend his adult years as a senior deacon in the Baptist church.[13]

The Baptists had by far the greatest respect and the largest following among the black peasantry. The first Baptist missionaries to Jamaica had been black men, former slave preachers from the United States. In the years after the American Revolution, they had filtered one by one into the island and had immediately won converts. Two of these men, George Lisle and Moses Baker, proved particularly successful. Eventually, Baker felt the need for help. He appealed to the Baptist Missionary Society in London, which sent its first missionaries to Jamaica in 1814. More soon followed.

In the tradition of Baptist ministers, more than one of these early missionaries identified completely with their congregations. They became so absorbed in defending the interests of their black followers that they were eventually accused of fomenting discontent and at least one major slave revolt. After emancipation, Baptist missionaries, along with other Protestant denominations, accompanied the freedmen into the interior, where they laid out villages, built churches, established schools, and educated future leaders like Thomas Francis McKay.[14]

Although the white missionaries of Jamaica fostered a mid-Victorian morality that few Jamaicans ever accepted as completely as Thomas McKay, the effects of their labors were not negligible. One black Jamaican clergyman later wrote that the early Baptist pioneers like

George Lisle and Moses Baker had been "pathfinders," men who had made an important contribution "in the making of a people." Because of their efforts, he concluded, "we who were no people, are now a people."[15] Thomas McKay would have undoubtedly concurred with such sentiments.

At the end of the 1860s, though serious and upright, Thomas was as yet unsettled. As a young man, he had farmed and worked as a laborer on local road maintenance crews. As he approached his thirtieth year, he was still unmarried. Around 1869, he found himself in the small community of Sunny Ville, about twelve miles from Staceyville. He had been lured there to court a local girl who a friend thought would make Thomas a good wife. The friend's matchmaking proved errant but not futile. In the way of love, the unexpected happened. Attending church in Sunny Ville, he chanced upon another who interested him more: Hannah Ann Elizabeth Edwards, the lithe young daughter of a local farmer. Not more than fifteen or sixteen at the time, Hannah had a bright smile and a gentle, gracious manner, which no doubt helped the intense stranger feel at ease in her presence. Equally important, she had a good Christian upbringing and she excelled in her letters. Thomas was stirred. He became a regular Sunday visitor.[16]

In her turn, perhaps, Hannah was pleased to be courted by such a mature and serious man, so unlike the local gay blades. Her father also liked him; he even gave Thomas a bit of land down the hill from his own home. Events moved swiftly. Thomas and Hannah Ann married in 1870, and they began their life together in a three-room thatched cottage Thomas constructed on his new land.[17]

Thomas Francis quickly proved himself an able, productive farmer. In addition to his own piece, he soon began to cultivate all the land owned by his father-in-law, who could no longer work because of infirmities. Through diligent labor and alert management, Thomas Francis eventually expanded his properties far beyond those of the average small landholder. Claude recorded years later that "in a short while he had acquired a dray with mules by which he would take his produce and his neighbors' to the far off markets, [and] by the time I left for America in 1912, . . . my father had acquired at least one hundred fertile acres."[18]

For years both Thomas Francis and Hannah Ann worked "grimly hard" to achieve prosperity. Thomas labored incessantly in the fields with hoe, cutlass, and pickax. His wife did the household chores, cultivated the gardens adjacent to their home, managed the small stock—chickens and goats and perhaps a pig or two—and all the while cared for an ever-expanding family.

During the first two years of marriage they had no offspring. Then between 1872 and 1890, Hannah Ann gave birth to eleven children, eight of whom (seven boys and one girl) lived to maturity. Uriah Theodore, their oldest son, was born March 23, 1872. There followed Matthew, Rachel (the only girl), Thomas Edison, Nathaniel, Reginald, and Hubert. Finally, on September 15, 1890, their last child was born. He was named Festus Claudius, after a Roman governor and an emperor mentioned in the New Testament Book of Acts. As Claude McKay, poet and novelist, he would celebrate the hills of Clarendon and the black peasantry of Jamaica.[19]

McKay's family was not unique in its relative prosperity, its strictly Christian profession, its literacy, and its upwardly mobile thrust, but such families were in the minority. They were to be found sprinkled among the great majority of poorer small landholders, whose limited acreage, meager education, common-law marriages, and Afro-European religious beliefs consigned them to an existence outside and clearly subordinate to the dominant, English-oriented island culture, whose ruling elite controlled Jamaica's politics, economy, and education system. By virtue of their superior economic position and Christian education, the dark-skinned McKays could claim a social position in Jamaican society akin to that of the traditional mulatto elite. They certainly distinguished themselves from their poorer neighbors and felt equal in every way to the colored elite, whose pretensions of superiority they scorned. As aspiring members of the middle class, the McKays were sensitive to any class discriminations based on skin color and were particularly critical of any such distinctions in Jamaican society. Claude would grow up suspicious and resentful of light mulattoes.[20]

While the McKays sought to compete socially and economically within the dominant culture, they nevertheless remained, by virtue of their origins, color, and location, firmly tied to the black peasantry. Nestled in the mountainous center of the island, Sunny Ville was a black community of small farmers remote from the larger towns and more than fifty miles from Kingston, the capital and commercial center. About twelve miles below Sunny Ville, down a steep, winding road, lay Chapelton, the principal town of upper Clarendon. Still farther south, twenty-two miles away, was the nearest rail center, the crossroads town of May Pen. Thirty-three miles from May Pen on the southeast coast lay Kingston.

In the small, largely self-contained world of Sunny Ville, the Mc-
Kays early assumed the role of community leaders. Thomas Francis
served as senior deacon in the Mt. Zion Baptist Church, which he
helped to build and which overlooked his home from a summit about
one-quarter mile away. Over the years, he befriended a succession
of British missionaries who pastored the church. He became fast
friends with the first English missionary there, William F. Hathaway,
who arrived in 1875. Together they made the Mt. Zion Church and
mission school the center of community life. It was Hathaway, too,
who tutored Thomas' eldest son, U'Theo, and helped prepare him for
Mico Teacher's College in Kingston, which he entered in 1891.[21]

Claude's father was one of the few black peasant cultivators of his
day who acquired enough property to qualify to vote in the island's
limited electoral system. It was a responsibility he assumed with his
usual probity. As Claude remembered him, "he was something of a
village leader, as they have in Africa." As "a patriarch of the mountain
country," the elder McKay often judged the petty disputes brought to
him by his neighbors, who preferred such informal proceedings to
the more distant and expensive processes of the colonial legal system.[22] By such informal but well-established customs, the black
peasantry of the area maintained a community existence. Their agricultural practices also ensured a common outlook and a degree of
unity. From the earliest days, they devised a system of mutual aid and
regularly borrowed one another's labor to clear land or harvest crops.[23]

During Claude McKay's formative years, his family maintained a
strong tie to Sunny Ville's black peasantry. But they also differed from
the average in important respects. Thomas and Hannah Ann had
been legally married in a Christian ceremony. This alone set them
apart from many who simply existed in common-law unions or who
had a series of partners before settling down with one. The elder
McKays spurned the relaxed morality of the typical Jamaican peasant. They had totally rejected any belief in Obeah. In a society where
the woman often managed her household alone, Thomas McKay
ruled like a mid-Victorian patriarch, more intense, more single-
minded, and more socially ambitious than most of his neighbors. Nor
did he neglect to educate his children for leadership. By Claude's
birth, the oldest son, U'Theo, was ready for college. By virtue of his
relatively large landholdings, the elder McKay had clearly elevated
himself above the subsistence farming practiced by his poorer neighbors. Unlike them, he could be classified as a small-scale commercial
farmer who produced such staples as coffee, bananas, and sugar both
for local markets and for external trade.

Claude McKay was thus born into an atypical, well-established black farm family. In a society where general poverty and distinct cultural cleavages, as much as racial identity, stood between the ruling elite and the masses, the McKays were striving with some success for upward mobility. In this setting, Claude McKay, the youngest son and the future poet, grew and developed.

Claude McKay spent his first seven years with his parents at Sunny Ville. The youngest child in a large family, he never lacked security or attention. In fact, he may have been somewhat pampered, especially by his mother. He later maintained that as the baby of the family he became her favorite, and certainly he developed early a strong identity with her that persisted throughout his life.

He always remembered his mother as unfailingly warm and loving. Hannah Ann Elizabeth McKay was a good and generous soul. Though a leader in church affairs, she did not let her religious scruples stand between her and the direct appreciation of other people's humanity, whatever their morals. For example, she always befriended the local girls who became pregnant out of wedlock. "From the time she was a young woman," her neighbors called her "Mother Mac." In the hill country around Sunny Ville, such a term was not used lightly. It betokened "real respect and endearment." McKay probably had his mother in mind in the dialect poem "Ribber Come-Do'n," when he wrote of the "kind district mother" who feeds a house full of neighboring children when she learns they have no food because their parents have been prevented from returning home. The eldest child in the poem refers to the "kind district mother" as "cousin Anna."[24]

"My mother," McKay maintained, "didn't care very much about what people did and why and how they did it. She only wanted to help them if they were in trouble. . . . She loved all people. It was a rich, warm love." In this regard she was quite the opposite of her husband. "All of us preferred my mother who was so much more elastic and understanding. She was a virtuous woman too. My father . . . was a Presbyterian Calvinist. A real black Scotchman. We boys wondered how his education could have made him that way. He was so entirely different from all our colored neighbors with their cockish-liquor drinking and rowdy singing. . . . So top-lofty, one might say. Yet everybody liked and respected him." His mother provided an effective counterbalance to his father's pious authoritarianism. Claude wrote that "she always took the children's side in dealings with my father who was strict and stern."[25]

McKay's devotion to his mother was no doubt heightened by the fact that after his birth she became ill and suffered for the remainder of her life from heart disease. In *My Green Hills of Jamaica,* he began the chapter titled "The Death of My Mother" by trying to recall his earliest childhood memory, but he decided that he could not distinguish between the actual remembrance of an accident at age two and the later telling of it. Then, abruptly, he stated, "One thing I do remember sharply is that my mother was ill and it was generally said that she became ill right after I was born."[26] Such knowledge must have been a heavy burden for young Claude, too easily translated into a sense of personal responsibility. In McKay's novel of Jamaican country life, *Banana Bottom,* the mother had died at the heroine's birth, and "the village folk said that she had killed her mother. That was the way the black peasants referred to a child that survived when the mother had died giving birth to it."[27]

Compared to the utter devotion with which he always referred to his mother, McKay's attitude toward his father was ambivalent, to say the least. In his mature years, Claude remembered with pride that his father had had a wonderful store of African tales.[28] He also acknowledged his father's integrity, his strength, and his actual accomplishments as a dedicated, conscientious parent and community leader. On the other hand, he never identified with the harsh disciplinarian and dour Old Testament moralist who towered over his childhood. To his youngest son, Thomas McKay would always remain a remote, austere, and ultimately unsympathetic authority figure. He may have been respected, but he was never unreservedly loved.

Claude grew into a strong, energetic boy who greatly enjoyed the simple pleasures of childhood. In the surrounding community, he found plenty of playmates. Together they enjoyed the usual children's games—chase, hide and seek, and "rounders, a mild form of American softball." On bright moonlit nights, he and the neighboring children delighted in making "moonshine babies" out of bits of broken crockery. One child would lie on his back with arms and legs outstretched while the others would outline his body with the pieces of glass. Then they would carefully lift their companion off the ground and stare in wonder at the shiny outline.[29]

Around his fourth year, Claude began to attend school at Mt. Zion, which crowned the hill above his home. The church was the largest building in the area, and its spacious sanctuary served as a school for the children from several adjacent communities. In *My Green Hills of Jamaica,* Claude recalled that its Sunday benches served as dividers to separate the various classes. Thus transformed, Mt. Zion had its own magic. "I remember," McKay wrote, "sitting there rapt with attention. . . . It was from this little school room in which I first learned about the history and geography of Jamaica that my interest in the history and geography of the world started."[30] Claude also enjoyed the special programs on holidays and at the close of term. In an isolated rural village like Sunny Ville, they provided one regular form of community entertainment.

In retrospect, however, Claude delighted most in the natural, spontaneous play of childhood. His earliest years became in his memory a kind of Eden, gone forever yet always accessible in imagination. To the mature poet, these became the years of peace, of balance, of freedom from conscious tension, a time when the imagination itself awoke to the world about it and he discovered the "wonder" that "clings" to life's commonplaces.[31] McKay's first seven years at Sunny Ville were not entirely free of the usual crises of childhood, but they were not unhappy. They were most poignantly remembered, perhaps, because they ended so abruptly.

Around 1897, Claude's eldest brother, Uriah Theodore (known as U'Theo), made one of his infrequent visits home. Only a year or two before, he had graduated from Mico Teacher's College in Kingston and had found a good position as a schoolteacher in a little town near Montego Bay. While he was home his parents decided that his youngest brother's education should be entrusted to him. So Claude bid farewell to Sunny Ville and returned with U'Theo. From the available evidence, it is not clear at exactly what age McKay left Sunny Ville and began to live with U'Theo. In *Pearson's* magazine in 1918 he stated he went to live with his brother at the age of nine. In 1923, the translator of his Soviet book wrote that "as an eight-year-old [McKay] was sent to school in a small town, where his brother was a teacher. Four years later he returned to his native village." Finally, in *My Green Hills,* McKay leaves the impression that he was six when he left Sunny Ville and that he stayed with U'Theo for seven years, "more or less." In *A Long Way from Home,* he stated that the time he spent with U'Theo was "spanned by the years between the Diamond Jubilee of Queen Victoria [in 1897] and her death [in 1901]." From these varying accounts, it seems safe to conclude that McKay left home around 1897 or shortly thereafter and remained away from the Sunny Ville area for at least four years.[32]

His parents' confidence in U'Theo as an educator and surrogate parent was not misplaced. He had received his grammar school education under the tutelage of William Hathaway and other churchmen in Clarendon Parish. And in his four years at Mico, U'Theo received a broad academic education in the natural sciences, mathematics, music, and the humanities, including a grounding in Latin and French. For the time and place, it was the best education available.[33]

U'Theo took full advantage of his opportunity. In late-nineteenth-century Jamaica, teaching or the ministry often proved only the first steps upward for young black men who desired to raise themselves out of the peasantry. In rural Jamaica, the village schoolteacher and the local preacher enjoyed a status and authority far above their roles as mere educators or ministers. They were often the individuals around whom the common social life of their communities revolved, and their influence frequently extended into economic and political spheres.[34]

Unlike the United States in this same period, Jamaica had no formal, racially based restrictions or rigid, castelike barriers between the black masses and the white and colored elite. An exceptionally able and well-placed black such as U'Theo could reasonably expect to rise in the island's social structure. A tall, broad-shouldered, well-built young man with a keen mind, irrepressible self-assurance, and abundant energy, U'Theo in the late 1890s stood on the threshold of a long and brilliant local career. He would eventually emerge as a highly successful planter, politician, and civic leader well known throughout Jamaica.[35]

After his mother and father, U'Theo easily ranked as the dominant adult in Claude McKay's childhood. In *My Green Hills of Jamaica,* McKay maintained that during those years with U'Theo, he never visited his parents or heard from them except for brief messages in their letters to U'Theo. Whether this was true or not, U'Theo during this time did exert a primary influence on Claude's life. Many of his basic ideas and intellectual attitudes, if not his purely emotional responses to the world, certainly developed under U'Theo's guidance.[36]

For Claude, the move from Sunny Ville to the outskirts of Montego Bay, already a fashionable resort area, meant a dramatic change. From barefoot country child, he suddenly became the schoolteacher's little brother, very conscious of his higher station in life. Now, he wore shoes to school and lived in a very neat little cottage with U'Theo and his new wife. Fortunately for Claude, the new sister-in-law was, like his mother, a warm and attentive woman, and he soon grew fond of her. Besides, she had wondrous things in her home, such as a highly polished whatnot table in the parlor on which sat intriguing glass and porcelain figurines. With such novel furnishings, and with the attention he received from U'Theo and his wife, Claude had no trouble accepting his new surroundings.[37]

U'Theo did occasionally whip his little brother. Once, for instance, he discovered some startlingly mature love notes that had passed between young Claude and his classmate, Agnes. U'Theo did not know that an older boy had written them for Claude. From the evidence, it appears that U'Theo's use of corporal punishment was neither exceptionally harsh nor frequent. "Beatings," as they were called in Jamaica, and, more commonly, the threat of beatings, formed a normal part of the Jamaican child's upbringing, a standard punishment in and out of school. But Claude never accepted such punishment without deep resentment and loud protests. And as he remarked in reference to the whipping he and Agnes received because of their little affair, "the beating did not change us."[38]

Although certainly a formidable figure, U'Theo apparently was not the forbidding presence Claude had discovered in their father. The youngster had little trouble relating to U'Theo. As the baby of the family, he may have already developed in Sunny Ville certain lasting habits of dependence. If anything, his move to the Montego Bay area only increased his appetite for security and attention. "There was one thing that gave me a great deal of physical and mental joy," he later wrote. "That was the fact that I was my brother's brother and because of this received so many little privileges." Even though under age, he was placed in "all the important school clubs" and was advanced to older classes. Everyone helped him. "They were all willing to do it," he recalled. "Then I soon discovered that except for figuring I had a good brain. I was good in geography and history, reading and writing and the natural sciences."[39] This may have been the beginning of that peculiar combination of dependence on others and aggressive independence that would eventually cause him much anguish.

During these early years, there was no thought of such eventualities. Claude was growing in body and mind. Under U'Theo's charge, his education went considerably beyond the normal elementary courses. A precocious child, Claude easily mastered his classroom assignments. Before long, he began to tackle the weightier volumes in his brother's small library. U'Theo was both surprised and pleased, and he imposed no restrictions on his brother's learning. When his wife once discovered the youngster wading through a decidedly antireligious work, she protested to her husband, who replied firmly, "Let the child read what he wants."[40]

During his years with U'Theo, Claude awoke to the unlimited pleasures of literature and undoubtedly enjoyed many happy days with books. Reading even began to supplant play as a major activity.

In fact, reading became a form of play. During this period, McKay discovered in literature broad new worlds of romance and thought. "These were . . . the indelible years of my first reading of anything . . . thrilling just for the thrill." He read Dickens "in small, sardine-packed words," Scott's Waverley novels, and a host of lesser Victorians. He also read Shakespeare from a set that the missionary William Hathaway had once given to U'Theo. All contributed to the awakening of a creative imagination.[41]

Of equal importance to the development of his youthful mind was the "free-thought" literature in his brother's library. The great debate that raged between science and theology, Darwinist and Christian, in nineteenth-century England had not failed to reach the most insignificant British colonies. It was heard in the remote hill country of Jamaica, and it played an influential role in Claude McKay's education. In U'Theo's home, Claude read before his fourteenth birthday such evolutionist works as Thomas Huxley's *Evidence as to Man's Place in Nature* and Ernst Haeckel's *The Riddle of the Universe at the Close of the Nineteenth Century.*[42]

U'Theo had probably become acquainted with Darwinist ideas as a student in Kingston. By the time he assumed responsibility for Claude, he had long since rejected his father's belief in revealed religion and considered himself an agnostic. It was a bold stance, but U'Theo took care to see that his beliefs did not threaten his professional standing. He did not proselytize, nor did he reject the Christian church as a useful social institution. He could have hardly afforded the personal consequences of such a stand. After all, he taught in a mission school and regularly invited the minister into his home for dinner. His job depended upon the good will of the church, and U'Theo was a practical man. Besides, he loved the traditional church music. Throughout Claude's boyhood U'Theo served enthusiastically as a highly successful and innovative choir leader. "It was said," Claude recalled, "that my brother was the first person in the country to stage the 'Hallelujah Chorus' of the great German musician Handel. As I remember, it was surely marvelous singing."[43]

Despite his compromises with the social realities of his time and place, U'Theo valued intellectual independence, and he communicated his Victorian rationalism to his younger brother with the proviso that "an agnostic should so live his life that Christian people would have to respect him."[44] As a teacher, U'Theo accepted that peculiar Darwinian educational paradox that sought "to expel the preternatural element from Christianity, to destroy its dogmatic structure, yet to keep intact its moral and spiritual results."[45]

Encouraged by U'Theo and by his own discovery of "the romance of science," Claude soon decided that he, too, was a freethinker. He read "Matthew Arnold's 'Literature and Dogma,' . . . Draper's 'The Conflict Between Religion and Science,' and a number of Herbert Spencer's works." U'Theo told Claude "about the lives of the great freethinkers of the times such as Thomas Huxley, Bradlaugh, the great parliamentarian, Mrs. Annie Besant and Mr. John M. Robertson also a parliamentarian."[46] Following U'Theo's lead, Claude in a short while moved far from the religion of his father.

U'Theo probably never dreamed that he was supplying his sensitive and romantic younger brother with ideas that would later serve as springboards for more sweeping attacks on other bulwarks of Western civilization. As a social and political radical, McKay would go far beyond his older brother's lack of belief in Christianity. In 1929, U'Theo wrote McKay, who was then in North Africa, and informed him that a local newspaper had stated he had been refused reentry into the United States because of his Bolshevik activities. Then he added, "I am quite certain, however, that you would do nothing to justify being debarred from the United States for it is not in our blood to be revolutionists."[47] After a hot reply from McKay, who apparently defined his position as something less than a murderous revolutionary, U'Theo wrote reassuringly, "I believe in independence, especially intellectual independence. . . . I still stand a free man where revealed religion is concerned. Try as I may, I cannot regard the teachings of priest and prophet as anything but superstition."[48]

As a growing boy, Claude did not dwell continuously on matters of faith. He experienced many of the good times enjoyed by boys everywhere. U'Theo had horses, and Claude loved to ride. His sister-in-law, however, felt it was too "common" for him to ride wildly across the pastures bareback. For a time, she arranged for him to ride properly with the children of the "local gentry."[49] During these years, Claude also enjoyed swimming, ball games, school and church picnics, and other affairs.

While under U'Theo's guidance, Claude also began to write poetry. According to his autobiography, his first effort was "a rhymed acrostic for [a] . . . school gala" written at the age of ten.[50] After that beginning, versemaking apparently became a habitual diversion. His earliest influences were varied. They included the lyrics of the local folk and church music. "All were singularly punctuated by meter and rhyme," Claude once explained, "and nearly all my own poetic thought has run naturally into these regular forms."[51] Although undoubtedly influenced by native verse and speech, McKay's school English was British, and the major and minor English poets were early set before him as examples worthy of imitation. As a youngster, he was attracted away from dialect and toward conventional English expression, which he accepted as the "correct" way to speak and write. He would later observe that "the direction of our schooling was of course English, and it was so successful that we really believed we were little black Britons."[52] The personal ambivalence that resulted from such training would be apparent in McKay's first volumes of dialect poetry.

By McKay's fourteenth birthday in 1904, U'Theo had quit his position near Montego Bay and had returned to Clarendon Parish. After a few years of teaching, he had acquired enough money to lease Palmyara, a large estate near Sunny Ville. He was beginning to move up in the world. U'Theo's decision, however, displeased his wife. She preferred to remain in St. James Parish, where she had grown up and where most of her friends and relatives lived. And she knew that the hills of upper Clarendon possessed few of the amenities of Montego Bay. There, for example, she lived on the main rail line to Kingston. At Sunny Ville the nearest railroad station lay twenty-two miles away in May Pen.

Claude may have also had misgivings about the move. He certainly sympathized with his sister-in-law. During his years with U'Theo, he had grown into a bright, sensitive, high-spirited teenager; he enjoyed his books and his highly developed independence of mind. He also relished his position as the only child in the household. U'Theo and his wife had no children of their own. In all his writings about his years with U'Theo, Claude never mentioned any visits from any of his other brothers or his sister. He especially enjoyed being privy to all his brother's plans and activities in the school and church. Each week U'Theo and his wife exchanged dinner visits with the minister and his wife. Claude particularly enjoyed these dinners, with their long, adult conversations and good desserts.[53]

On the whole, these had been happy, secure years. In 1918, Claude described them as "a great formative period in my life—a time of perfect freedom to play, read, and think as I liked."[54] Those days ended with U'Theo's decision to return to his native parish. In the end, his wife packed her belongings and accompanied him. Claude returned with them. For a while, he continued to live in U'Theo's new home. Around age fourteen, however, he returned to his parents' home and once again became a part of the larger family at Sunny Ville.

He faced some difficulties in the transition: "I had become used to the life of a small town child. I loved the grey macadamized roads, the better houses and my chic schoolmates. . . . I found a new world on my return to Sunny Ville. I had scarcely known my father and mother when I left with my brother about seven years previous. Now I had to become acquainted with my own family."[55] That reacquaintance was not wholly pleasant. One of Claude's major difficulties was his relationship with his father, who expected total obedience. In his turn, Claude no longer considered himself a child and resented his father's strict, old-fashioned attitudes. Never one to suffer in silence, he displayed increasing impertinence. Claude had arrived at that difficult age when a healthy male adolescent's natural aggressiveness often masks painful anxieties about his manhood. His father no doubt touched a raw nerve by viewing him as still a child, and he woefully underestimated the depth of Claude's resentment and the explosive volubility of his emotions. A confrontation between the two was not long in coming.

After some unrecorded incident that offended the elder McKay, he threatened Claude with a sound thrashing. According to Claude, the following scene then occurred:

> I was very impertinent and said to him . . . "you cannot whip me, sir. I am a man." He promptly tied me to a post and dropped my pants. He went to get his strap. When I saw him coming I started to curse and used every swear word a small boy could think of. My father who was a deacon of the church was so shocked he said: "I can't whip the boy. Why he's gone crazy." He left me tied there and went off to the fields. It was the last time he ever tied me up or laid a hand on me.[56]

One can only wonder if Thomas McKay ever recognized that Claude possessed in his own way that same fierce commitment to righteousness and justice that was such a prominent part of his own character. Although neither may have ever recognized it, their confrontation revealed their similarities as well as their differences. Theirs was in truth a difficult and painful relationship.[57]

Claude also found upon his return that his mother's health had grown worse. For that reason, perhaps, he more than ever treasured their relationship. In her he saw what he perceived to be his own best qualities. She loved books, she reacted spontaneously and warmly to the simple pleasures of life, and she set no artificial barriers between herself and others. Upon her alone he centered his love.

From the evidence, Claude resented the intrusion of his other brothers into the solitary, imaginative world he had created and sustained for himself under U'Theo's roof. At home in Sunny Ville, he had to fight hard to win a cot and a tiny space of his own in the room he shared with two older brothers.[58] Despite the inevitable tensions of family life, Claude did find pleasures at Sunny Ville. U'Theo generated a whirlwind of excitement by energetically plunging into the management of his new estate. He rented much of it to the local peasants. For once, his father abandoned his scruples against such practices and rented ten acres himself, planting it all in sugarcane. Soon there was much work to be done in the fields, and all the McKays shared in it. Despite his newly acquired status as a planter, U'Theo still found it necessary to teach, and he soon located a school near his new property. Claude continued his education with U'Theo and finished his regular grammar school course as his brother's junior teaching assistant. If not always happy and harmonious, the McKays were an intelligent, literate, and productive clan.[59]

In *My Green Hills of Jamaica,* Claude stressed that the country around Sunny Ville had its full share of bright and active individuals whose intelligence equaled, if it did not surpass, the supposedly more sophisticated urban dwellers of Europe and America. As much as possible, the McKays and their neighbors kept abreast of local and world affairs. If Claude's recollections were accurate, their access to the larger world came from a surprisingly large and varied number of journals, books, and newspapers published in Kingston, Great Britain, and the United States.

His sister, Rachel, had long kept up with the latest fashions in *Weldon's* and other women's magazines. A few neighbors subscribed to the weekly *Jamaica Times,* and all who were literate and ambitious read that important journal. Its editor, Thomas H. MacDermot, understood and identified completely with the needs and aspirations of those blacks from the lower and middle classes who wished to get ahead in life. U'Theo counted MacDermot as a friend and served as his country correspondent in the upper Clarendon area. McKay's long list of magazines and newspapers found in Clarendon (no doubt on an irregular and haphazard basis) included "*The Spectator, The Nineteenth Century, Answers, The Windsor,* the weekly edition of *The Times* (London), many English papers as well as *The Outlook, The Argosy,* the famous *New York Herald,* the *Deadwood Dick* detective stories and other magazines and newspapers which I don't remember from America."[60]

Claude also had access to much of the sentimental fiction characteristic of the late Victorian period. Some of it came from the mission school library, "to which," McKay wrote, "every intelligent barefoot boy had access, and there were many of us." The rest he no doubt found at home or in U'Theo's library. Like the journals, the fiction available was a mixed lot: "They were all good and bad thrown together and we young people read indiscriminately. We had Marie Corelli, Mrs. Humphry Ward, Miss Braddon, Mrs. Gaskell, Sheldon's *In His Steps,* which was a very wonderful book for us kids who were being trained to be model colonial Christians. Most famous of all the books was Mrs. Henry Wood's *East Lynn.* I remember that I read passages from it to my mother and cried in her lap and she cried too."[61] The impression of such literature on McKay's mind would later be clearly reflected in his dialect verse, where in one poem he would write of his desire to visit England and "watch de fact'ry chimneys pourin' smoke up to de sky . . . An' see de matches-children, dat I hear 'bout passin' by."[62]

During his teenage years at Sunny Ville, more tangible pleasures also presented themselves. Claude did not lag behind in the pursuit of the local girls. The daughters of the mulatto Lewars family in particular attracted Claude, who was fascinated by their "lovely soft skins."[63] His father naturally objected to his sons' uninhibited interest in the opposite sex. He earnestly exclaimed that he had "never known another woman" besides their mother, "and God helping me, I never will."[64] He had not, he said, educated his sons to be ensnared by any of the ignorant village girls, no matter how pretty they were. At the close of his life, McKay noted in a typed manuscript fragment that none of Thomas McKay's boys had been like their father: all would do the things that he would not, and in a handwritten insert he defiantly added, "without any regrets." He carefully noted that only his sister "lived up" to her father's ideals.[65]

If less respectful of Christian virtues than their parents, the younger McKays nevertheless exerted a positive influence within their community. As the eldest, U'Theo took an active and progressive lead in agricultural, educational, and musical affairs. After his arrival in the Sunny Ville area, he organized an exceptionally fine choir and decided to give in concert some of the great European choral pieces he had learned as a student at Mico. He drew upon the support of the local "gentry," attracted a favorable press in Kingston, and wound up touring all of Clarendon and parts of adjacent parishes with his group. U'Theo then persuaded a choir from Kingston, which had successfully toured England, to give a weekend of concerts in the Clarendon hills. His name quickly became synonymous with good music.

As his brother's confidant and a member of his choir, young Claude was at the center of events, and proud to be. The music uplifted him, and he eventually drew upon his experiences with his brother's choir to create one of his best short stories, "The Agricultural Show," which he wrote in the early 1930s.[66] Claude greatly admired the ease with which his brother brought together all elements of the local society, and over the years, he invested his brother's activities with great symbolic importance. They became a part of that pastoral childhood that existed in the Eden of his mind.

In actuality, Eden had its tensions. Around 1906, a fervent storm of revivalism, which had started in distant Wales, descended upon upper Clarendon. Throughout 1905 the Kingston *Daily Gleaner* tracked its course to Jamaica.[67] In Claude's village, it apparently arrived in the form of a small, fiery Welsh evangelist, who soon had the hill folks vibrant with the spirit of repentance. U'Theo and young Claude quickly became conspicuous by their resistance to the Holy Ghost. Some concluded that the Devil had guided U'Theo's education and that he in turn had corrupted his youngest brother. "All the people were angry with my brother. They prayed for him in church. . . . But in their prayers there was a menacing tone as if they would like to lynch him."[68] Claude always fondly remembered that he had responded with a little revival of his own among his youthful companions; soon, he had organized "ten . . . boys in a free-thought band, and most of them were heathen from their own primitive thinking, without benefit of books."[69]

U'Theo's reputation suffered no lasting damage. The revival spirit soon passed. Claude mischievously recalled that it had left in its wake more than one pregnant village girl. Such had been its power, however, that several guilty paramours confessed their misdeeds and married.[70]

By 1906, Claude faced another transition. He had finished grammar school and had to decide upon a career. At sixteen, he had grown into a strikingly handsome, quick-witted youth of average height and slim, muscular physique. He possessed the exceptionally quick mind and the direct, highly intuitive capabilities of a poet. But these were gifts one spent spontaneously and freely in the hills of Clarendon— he could not earn a living as a poet. Claude thought a great deal about the choices open to him. At least two of his other brothers had followed U'Theo into the teaching profession. Thomas Edison was preparing for the ministry. Another, Reginald, seemed content simply to farm as his father had done before him. None of these choices appealed to young Claude. He would try something different.

In an age when Booker T. Washington had already established his reputation as a practical educator in the American South, it appeared logical to the young poet to learn a craft and become a skilled tradesman. The colonial government was encouraging vocational education, and learning the secrets of a skilled craft may have appealed to Claude's sense of romance. In 1906, he took the junior teacher's yearly test and the government's "trade scholarship examination." He passed both and elected to accept the trade scholarship, although he could not decide what trade actually interested him. He was fortunately spared the necessity of choice when the government informed him that he would first spend a year studying at a trade school in Kingston. The prospect of a year in Kingston delighted him.[71]

Claude learned in the summer or fall of 1906 that his term would begin in January, 1907. In the interim, he enjoyed himself. The people of upper Clarendon took pride in those among their children who won any sort of scholarship. At parties he received many small gifts and was elaborately toasted by his friends and neighbors. His mother and his sister, meanwhile, took care to buy him the proper clothes for a year in Kingston. Finally, sometime after Christmas, he journeyed one morning before daybreak to May Pen, where he caught an early train to the capital.

An older cousin in the postal service met Claude in Kingston, introduced him to his circle of friends, and found for him a good rooming house near the trade school. It was not Claude's first visit to the city. As a small boy, he had accompanied his sister-in-law on a few shopping trips. Now he happily looked forward to remaining a whole year.

He had hardly settled in his new quarters, however, before disaster struck. School had not yet started, and Claude was lying in bed one afternoon reading a "wild west thriller" when his room suddenly buckled and crumpled, "as if some giant had crushed in the walls of the house." He managed to dash uninjured into the street, where he experienced a chaos of trembling earth and collapsing buildings. People ran wildly about him; flames soon engulfed parts of the city. Some looting occurred, but the people quickly began the frantic and gruesome task of digging the injured and dead from underneath the rubble. It was the worst earthquake to hit the Kingston area since 1696, when the buccaneer town of Port Royal slid beneath the sea.[72]

Along with most of Kingston, the trade school lay in ruins. That evening, Claude joined a long line of refugees streaming out of the city, back to their native villages. In *My Green Hills of Jamaica*, he recalled that the night lay beautiful, clear, and peaceful upon the countryside. He also remembered that "there were others coming toward the city."

> It was around May Pen that I met my father. It was night and he had been calling out to the different drays to see if I was on any of them. Finally he spotted the one which carried me. I remember the drayman stopped and I got off. My father hugged and kissed me. It gave me the strangest feel-

ing—my father's beard against my face because I had never before been kissed by him. He was always a very stern man; but now he must have felt that I'd escaped from something terribly tragic as he held me in his arms.[73]

The moment might have led to reconciliation between father and son, but by now Claude's estrangement from his father ran deep. At the end of his life, he recorded the exceptional event with feeling and understanding.

With the trade school destroyed, the government directed Claude to find a master craftsman willing to accept him as an apprentice. His relatives eventually found for him a tradesman in Brown's Town, just north of Clarendon in neighboring St. Ann's Parish. Claude was disappointed: the glamour of city life fascinated him, and he had also hoped to find in Kingston a trade that appealed to him. Now he found himself apprenticed to "Old Brenga, a light mulatto, kind of crabbed, yet kindly in a way. He was a jack-of-all-trades—a wheelwright, a carriage builder and an excellent cabinet maker."[74] Claude remained in his employ for about two years, from 1907 to 1909.

It was an odd but not wholly unsatisfactory arrangement. Claude's disinclination to learn matched the craftsman's reluctance to teach. "It was a fairly good arrangement because he was one of those men who wanted to guard his trade secrets and was not eager to teach me anything."[75] Claude happily learned nothing of consequence during his stay in Brown's Town.

He did, however, have some good times. For one thing, he enjoyed his new environment. Unlike Clarendon, St. Ann had a dry climate and rocky soil. Pimento and coffee trees grew in abundance. Brown's Town itself was one of the most attractive towns in the region. His employer often sent him around the countryside collecting debts. Claude particularly enjoyed visiting the larger estates and seeing the interiors of the old mansions. Sometimes he and his employer's young son, who often accompanied him on these trips, "would leave the highway and go into the fields and sit under the pimento trees, just talking and reading poetry while the John-tu-whits feasted and twitted on the ripe blue pimento fruit."[76] It was not a demanding existence, and his sojourn in St. Ann nourished Claude's development as a poet. For here, late in 1907 he met Walter Jekyll, an English gentleman resident in Jamaica, who over the next five years would give Claude the encouragement and direction he needed to emerge as a creative, productive, and recognized poet.

Despite the personal obscurity that he cultivated during his lifetime and that has since persisted, Walter Jekyll surely ranked among the more interesting Englishmen found in Queen Victoria's far-flung possessions. Jekyll had come from an old, upper-class family. His father, Edward Joseph Hill Jekyll, a former captain in the Grenadier guards, originally came from Wargrave Hill, Berkshire. Walter, his youngest son, had been born at Bramley House in Surrey on November 27, 1849. Educated at Harrow and Trinity College, Cambridge, where he graduated with honors in 1872, Jekyll excelled in music, literature, languages, and philosophy. After receiving an M.A. at Cambridge, he entered the Episcopal ministry, but in the great debate between religion and science he decided against the faith and renounced Christianity, probably around 1880. He next went to Italy and studied singing in Milan with the great master, Francesco Lamperti. Afterward, Jekyll returned to England and lived in various places, including London, Birmingham, Bournemouth, and Devonshire. He himself taught music; in Birmingham he gave penny singing lessons to the poor. In 1884 he published in London his own translation of Lamperti's *The Art of Singing According to Ancient Tradition and Personal Experiences,* a book his brother reported still had a sale in 1929, the year of Jekyll's death.[77]

While in Bournemouth in the early 1890s, Jekyll had become friendly with Robert Louis Stevenson, who at the time wrote a story that had been incubating in his mind for several years. Stevenson entitled his new story "The Strange Case of Dr. Jekyll and Mr. Hyde." Although Walter Jekyll may not have been in fact Stevenson's fictional Dr. Jekyll, he almost certainly lent his name to that author's famous character.[78]

Jekyll scorned notoriety (especially the sort that may have threatened to come his way as a result of Stevenson's work). He loved simplicity and solitude and felt uncomfortable in the ordinary roles expected of English gentlemen. During these years, he and an intimate friend, Ernest Boyle, spent several summers trout fishing deep in the mountains of Norway. His brother, Herbert, who in no way shared Walter's taste for the simple life in the open spaces, recounted that "the place they went to was very remote, and they had to walk the last fifty miles of the journey, taking with them a man and a cow. . . . The last thing they did on coming away was to make hay for next year's beds."[79]

Besides his distaste for the conventions of upper-class society, Jekyll sometimes suffered from asthma in the long, damp English winters, which he grew to dread increasingly with the passing years. Finally in 1895, after his mother's death, he settled permanently in Jamaica, whose climate he had enjoyed on several previous visits. After Jekyll had settled comfortably at Mavis Bank in the Blue Mountains northeast of Kingston, he was joined by Ernest Boyle, who moved into a home of his own in the same locality.[80]

In Jamaica, Jekyll maintained his old interests and developed new ones. He took great pleasure in tropical horticulture and became a close friend of the director of the famous Hope Gardens outside Kingston. All the while, he maintained his interest in the new criticisms of Christianity and found time to write on the subject. In 1904 he contributed his own attack upon traditional Christianity in a book entitled *The Bible Untrustworthy: A Critical Comparison of Contradictory Passages in the Bible.*[81]

These subjects hardly exhausted Jekyll's varied interests. As the independent scion of an old, aristocratic family, Jekyll looked askance at the rise of the middle class and bemoaned the deleterious effects of industrialism and urbanization in the modern world. He looked nostalgically upon the traditional peasantry as the source of every nation's real strength, and he mourned the destructive disregard for traditional ways in modern England. For the same reasons, he was highly critical of American life, which seemed to him to be based entirely on the material values of the middle classes. Once in Jamaica, he became fascinated by the folk music of its black peasants and by their wonderful stories of Annancy, the trickster spiderman of West African origin. He began to collect systematically the native Jamaican songs and stories. When Claude first met him in Brown's Town, the Folk-lore Society in England had just recently published his collection, *Jamaican Song and Story: Annancy Stories, Digging Sings, Ring Tunes, and Dancing Tunes.*[82]

The white man who had entered the shop of Claude's employer sometime in 1907 appeared to be in his late fifties. He was short and wiry, and his casual dress suggested a man not at all concerned with fashion. On his weatherbeaten face he wore a small goatee, and his confident stride betrayed the directness and self-possession of one sure of his place and purpose. Despite the eccentricity of his appearance, Jekyll remained an English gentleman.[83]

He had come to "old Brenga's" shop in Brown's Town from the resort town of Moneague in the eastern part of St. Ann to get a carriage wheel repaired. Claude's employer had heard that Jekyll was an author and sarcastically remarked that he had a poet in his employ and introduced the two. Unlike the wheelwright, Jekyll expressed genuine interest in McKay's poetry and asked to see it. Claude demurred, claiming that he had left his best poems at home in Sunny Ville. He liked Jekyll, however, and promised to send his poems to him. Claude kept his word, and the two began a regular correspondence. Over the next two years, their relationship developed slowly. "His interest in me was general at first," McKay recalled. "I was merely a literate phenomenon among the illiterate peasants whose songs and tales he was writing. Then in time there was a subtle change from a general to an individual interest and he became keen about my intellectual development and also in my verse as real poetry."[84]

During 1908, Claude had a more pressing concern than his developing friendship with Jekyll. His mother's health was steadily growing worse. By 1909, her heart disease had advanced beyond repair. She had begun to suffer from dropsy, a condition characterized by an abnormal retention of body fluids and progressive fatigue and weakness; she needed constant nursing. Claude felt impelled to return home. It meant giving up his apprenticeship, but that was easy: he had never developed any genuine interest in learning a trade. Once home, he encountered little criticism. "As I was the baby of the family and the favorite of my mother," he later explained, "there was little objection from the rest of the family about my giving up a government trade which in Jamaica was an important thing."[85]

The family had long since left the three-roomed thatched cottage where Thomas Francis and Hannah Ann had begun their married life. They now lived in a new, larger, more solidly built five-room house "with cedar floors and broadleaf shingles, mahogany chairs and a porch." For Hannah Ann, the climb upward had taken a heavy toll. The accumulated burdens of farm work, domestic chores, and childrearing had placed greater demands on her constitution than it could bear. In the end, she found no comfort, even in "the great carved mahogany, four poster bed which had belonged to her father." She asked to be placed on a mattress on the floor of her daughter Rachel's room. The move brought scant relief. She lingered awhile; finally, on December 19, 1909, she quietly died.[86]

Her slow decline had been exceedingly painful for all the family. For Claude, her death held special significance. His devotion to her had been complete, even excessive. Upon her he had concentrated all his familial affections, and he had projected upon her all those sensitive, romantic qualities he himself possessed. Over the years, he memorialized his mother in several highly emotional poems in which he expressed with precision the totality of his identification with her.

In one early dialect poem, he portrayed his mother as a warmly human individual who at the end had been far more concerned with the living world around her than with thoughts of what might lie beyond the grave. At the same time he revealed his own alienation from his father.[87] Much later, in a sonnet entitled "Heritage," McKay almost certainly had his mother in mind when he wrote

> I know the magic word, the peaceful thought,
>    The song that fills me in my lucid hours,
> The spirit's wine that fills my body through,
>    And makes me music-drunk, are yours, all yours.
> I cannot praise, for you have passed from praise,
>    I have no tinted thought to paint you true;
> But I can feel and I can write the word:
>    The best of me is but the least of you.[88]

When McKay decided to publish some of his first poetry in the United States under a pseudonym, he chose the name Eli Edwards, an abbreviated, masculinized version of his mother's maiden name, Hannah Ann Elizabeth Edwards.[89]

In the first of a two-part sonnet sequence published in 1921, Claude stated explicitly the significance his mother's death had for him within the family circle: "The only one I loved was gone."[90] In the second sonnet of this sequence, he fused his childhood, his mother, and Jamaica itself into a unity and re-created in miniature that imaginary refuge to which he again and again returned for solace.

> The dawn departs, the morning is begun,
> The Trades come whispering from off the seas,
> The fields of corn are golden in the sun,
> The dark-brown tassels fluttering in the breeze;
> The bell is sounding and children pass,
> Frog-leaping, skipping, shouting, laughing shrill,
> Down the red-road, over the pasture grass,
> Up to the schoolhouse crumbling on the hill.
> The older folk are at their peaceful toil,
> Some pulling up the weeds, some plucking corn,
> And others breaking up the sun-baked soil.
> Float, faintly-scented breeze, at early morn
> Over the earth where mortals sow and reap—
> Beneath its breast my mother lies asleep.[91]

After his mother's death, Claude had little desire to remain at home. His thoughts turned persistently to Kingston and the possibility of living closer to his new-found mentor, Walter Jekyll. Sometime after their initial meeting in Brown's Town, they had met again. The circumstances of that meeting were never recorded, but Claude had given Jekyll several poems. As he was reading them Jekyll suddenly began to laugh. Claude was stunned and angry. Jekyll hastened to explain that he had not been laughing at Claude's serious poetry, all of which had been written in standard English, but at the single humorous piece, written in the local dialect. Jekyll said he found Claude's poems in straight English too "repetitious. . . . 'But this,' said he, holding up the [dialect] poem, 'This is the real thing.'" Jekyll went on to say that except for himself no one had ever put the Jamaican dialect into literary form. He urged Claude, "as a native boy," to seize the opportunity. He assured him that his poems would sell.[92]

Claude hardly knew how to respond to such a suggestion. As he later explained, "I was not very enthusiastic about this statement, because to us who were getting an education in the English schools, the Jamaican dialect was considered a vulgar tongue. It was the language of the peasants. All cultivated people spoke English, straight English." After much thought, Claude eventually followed Jekyll's advice. After all, he did know "many pieces in the dialect which were based on our local songs of the draymen, the sugar mills, and the farm land." Besides, poems in the dialect were "so much easier to write than poems in straight English."[93] McKay did not elaborate on why dialect poems proved easier for him to write. Louise Bennett, who has written only in the dialect, once stated that because the "Jamaican language" was her native tongue, it was naturally the medium in which she thought and wrote best as a poet.[94] This might have also been true of McKay. Claude spoke the Jamaican dialect peculiar to the upper Clarendon area. In a recording made near the end of his life, he still retained, after an absence of more than thirty years, the "quaint" accent of a Jamaican hill countryman.[95]

After a brief visit with Jekyll in his home at Mavis Bank, Claude "one day . . . packed a few things in a battered old suitcase and went off to Kingston." This was probably late in 1909 or early in 1910, a few months after his mother's death. At the age of twenty, he still had "no special objective." He even felt unsure about his relationship with Jekyll. "I didn't want to tell Mr. Jekyll," he recalled, "that I had run away from home to be near him."[96] He obviously felt the need for guidance. He had rejected the paths followed by U'Theo and his older brothers but had developed no alternative path of his own. Jekyll offered him the opportunity to nourish his talent as a poet. Without quite admitting it, even to himself, he hastened to place himself under the older man's guidance. He wanted to proceed along the poet's path, but thirsted for the reassurance and approval of an older, authoritative voice. It was a pattern McKay would repeat with other men in other places to the very end of his life.

Although Claude felt unsure about his long-range career choices, he never timidly retreated from new experiences. On the contrary, he welcomed them. And like most young men fresh from the country, he hungered for the fabled good times to be found in the city. In Kingston, he soon found new friends, "chiefly waiters in the big hotels and cabarets . . . who lived very fast lives."[97] The little money

he had brought to Kingston did not last long, and he faced the necessity of earning a livelihood. For a while, he worked in a local "match
factory," but quickly grew bored by the long hours and the monotony
of his tasks.[98] He then impulsively chose a way out taken by many
similarly placed young men both before and after him: he joined the
constabulary. A disastrous love affair may also have been responsible:
an early newspaper account reported that it was rumored that McKay
joined the constabulary in the aftermath of a "pitiable love story." Mc-
Kay neither confirmed nor denied this, saying only, "I cannot touch the
public with my heart. . . . It would be of no interest to them."[99]

Patterned after the Irish constabulary, the Jamaican police had
been created in 1867 as part of the administrative reforms established after the Morant Bay Rebellion. It served as an efficient islandwide police force and functioned as a quasi-military institution. Men
enlisted for five years and received "military training and civil instruction in Spanish Town at the Old Military Barracks," before going
on regular duty. Like the British police, they carried only batons and
handcuffs, but in emergencies they could be issued firearms.[100]

Claude joined in June, 1911.[101] All the while he continued writing
dialect poems and regularly visited Jekyll, who had by this time become deeply involved with Claude's writing and his education. In addition to the encouragement and advice Jekyll gave him as a poet, he
had also begun to tutor Claude in language, literature, philosophy,
and history. With his wider knowledge and larger, more varied library,
Jekyll advanced Claude's education far beyond the point U'Theo had
taken him. Jekyll "loved good books and their makers more than anything else," and in Claude he found an apt and willing pupil.[102] For
Claude, their hours together proved wholly absorbing. In 1918, he
wrote that Jekyll

> opened up a new world to my view, introduced me to a greater, deeper
> literature—to Buddha, Schopenhauer and Goethe, Carlyle and Browning,
> Wilde, [Edward] Carpenter, Whitman, Hugo, Verlaine, Baudelaire, Shaw
> and the different writers of the rationalist press—more than I had time to
> read, but nearly all my spare time I spent listening to his reading choice
> bits from them, discussing the greatness of their minds, and telling of
> their lives, which I must confess I sometimes found even more interesting
> than their works.[103]

Some writers naturally proved of greater interest than others. As a
naïve child of British colonialism, Claude devoured with pleasure the
works of the social Darwinist, Herbert Spencer. Early in their friendship, Jekyll had given McKay a membership in the Rationalist Press
Association (RPA), an organization founded by the publisher Charles
Albert Watts in 1899 to promote scientific rationalism. As a member,

McKay received the RPA reprints.[104] But Jekyll also introduced him to the works of Hume and Berkeley, as well as to the great German philosophers—Kant, Schopenhauer, Spinoza and Nietzsche. Claude became well acquainted with Schopenhauer, whom Jekyll had only lately translated and published in a new book entitled *The Wisdom of Schopenhauer as Revealed in Some of His Writings*. Jekyll had also translated (but not published) selections from the great German romantics—Goethe, Schiller, and Heine. Their poetry enthralled McKay. "I loved German poetry," he wrote in *My Green Hills of Jamaica*. "Mr. Jekyll always read the German deep and sonorous before he translated it into English for me."[105]

In Jekyll's home, Claude also deepened his knowledge of the great English and other European poets. "With this man's excellent library at my disposal, I read poetry: *Childe Harold, The Dunciad, Essay on Man, Paradise Lost*, the Elizabethan lyrics, . . . the lyrics of Shelley and Keats and . . . of the late Victorian poets. . . . He translated and we read together pieces out of Dante [and] Leopardi."[106]

Jekyll knew six languages, and Claude asked that he teach him French, one of the languages U'Theo had studied at Mico. For the time, Jekyll's language instruction was unorthodox. He insisted that Claude begin by repeating aloud the French as it was read to him. He had been taught in that manner and thought it the best way to learn a language; Claude could study the grammar later.[107]

As Jekyll's protégé, Claude also became acquainted with some of Jamaica's social elite. Many were Jekyll's near neighbors in the healthier mountain parishes above the hot, dry Liguanea plain where Kingston sat, perpetually sweltering in the heat. Much to his delight, Claude was present one day when the colony's governor, Sidney Olivier, visited Jekyll's modest two-bedroom cottage. Olivier enjoyed his visit so much, he asked if he might not stay the night. Much to Claude's astonishment, Jekyll curtly refused the governor's request. When Olivier pointed out that Claude was staying, Jekyll told him there was a difference; Claude was his "special friend."

Jekyll was irate that Olivier had even made the request. He considered it a typical example of the bad manners displayed by England's aggressive middle class. Taken aback by this unusual outburst of intolerance, Claude asked how Jekyll could stand him, the mere son of a black peasant. "'Oh,' said he, 'English gentlemen have always liked their peasants; it's the ambitious middle class that we cannot tolerate.'" In retrospect, Claude confessed that he had perhaps been "a little snobbish myself because I admired Mr. Jekyll for pulling the governor down a step."[108]

One can only guess at the exact nature of the relationship between

Jekyll and McKay. Although it was never explicitly stated, the evidence suggests that Jekyll was homosexual. He never married; he had a long, intimate relationship with Ernest Boyle; and his own writing suggests a strong preference for the company of men and boys. In *Jamaican Song and Story*, he concluded his introductory discussion about the Jamaican dialect with these highly ambiguous remarks: "The men's voices are of extraordinary beauty. To hear a group chatting is a pure pleasure to the ear, quite irrespective of the funny things they say; their remarks are accompanied by the prettiest little twirks and turns of intonation, sometimes on the words, sometimes mere vocal ejaculations between them. The women's voices have the same fine quality when they speak low, but this they seldom do, and their usual vivacious chatter is anything but melodious."[109]

The evidence about Claude's sexual orientation is much more clear-cut. Although McKay had sexual relations with women, he also had many homosexual affairs, particularly in the United States and Europe. The evidence indicates his primary orientation was toward the homosexual on the spectrum of human sexual inclinations, not too surprising in view of the difficulties he had in relating to his father and the strong identification with his mother.[110] A homoerotic component most likely underlay the relationship Claude developed with Jekyll. This did not necessarily mean they developed a physical relationship. Nothing in Claude's writings ever hinted that their friendship took such a turn, but he did once indirectly suggest that Jekyll introduced him to the reality and to the moral legitimacy of homosexual love.

In 1918, *Pearson's* magazine published an essay in which McKay discussed Jekyll's great influence on his career. Among the famous authors he listed as having read and discussed with Jekyll, he significantly grouped together Oscar Wilde, Edward Carpenter, and Walt Whitman. Oscar Wilde's tragic self-exposure and imprisonment occurred the same year Jekyll settled in Jamaica, and although there was no connection between the two events, Jekyll would have undoubtedly been familiar with the Wilde affair, the most infamous case of homosexual persecution in nineteenth-century England. Edward Carpenter was a British author whose studies and commentaries on human sexuality would be much discussed in the 1920s. In 1894 he had published a work entitled *Homogenic Love and Its Place in a Free Society*, in which he defended homosexuality and "developed the thesis that the bisexually endowed were specially fitted for progressive leadership in a democratic society." He elaborated upon these ideas two years later in his best-known work, *Love's Coming of Age*.

Carpenter was a great admirer of Whitman, whom he visited in America and whom he imitated in his own poetry. In 1906 he published an account of his encounter with Whitman, which he titled *Days with Walt Whitman,* a well-known source on the Good Grey Poet's old age and reminiscences. If Jekyll introduced McKay to Carpenter's work, they almost certainly discussed his defense of homosexuality and his opinions of Whitman, whose own homoerotic passages in *Leaves of Grass* were well known. For those in 1918 who were possessed by "the love that dared not speak its name," the stringing together of the names Wilde, Carpenter, and Whitman would have left no doubt about McKay's meaning. It was there, so to speak, written between the lines.[111]

Claude was not the only young man befriended by Jekyll during his long residence in Jamaica. In the 1920s he met a young musician named Johnny Lyons, tutored him in singing, and helped launch his career. Like McKay before him, Lyons left Jamaica. He moved to London, where he won some success on the musical stage before settling down to a prosperous career as an accountant. After Jekyll's death in 1929, U'Theo disdainfully noted in a letter to Claude that Jekyll had left his library to an "ignorant" fellow in Hanover Parish.[112] Perhaps the "ignorant" fellow was Johnny Lyons, or a similar young man Jekyll was attempting to assist.

Ronald Hyam has speculated on the sexual dynamics that underlay Great Britain's nineteenth-century imperial exploits. According to Hyam, the wanderlust of Englishmen much more famous than Walter Jekyll could at least in part be explained by their homosexuality, which could not be freely expressed in Britain itself. Among them he included some of the principal architects of Victoria's empire, explorers, generals, and administrators: Sir Richard Burton, Lord H. H. Kitchener, General Charles Gordon, Cecil Rhodes, and Sir Matthew Nathan, the governor of the Gold Coast, Hong Kong, and Natal. Not all these men were sexually active; some apparently buried their strong homoerotic impulses beneath an almost demonic concentration on their work.[113]

Walter Jekyll can hardly be ranked with these fervid colonizers. On the contrary, Claude remembered that he "hated" the British Empire but feared German imperial expansion even more. As a rule, Claude stressed Jekyll's "gentleness and otherworldliness."[114] For a young man fresh from the country, Jekyll could not have been easy to understand. McKay remembered that "he was disillusioned with British liberalism, yet he did not believe in socialism or any of the radical parties of the day. He always said to me that the British upper class would know how to handle radicals and that Lloyd George who was the famous liberal radical then, would finish up as a lord. . . . He was . . . something of a Buddhist and did not think that the world could be reformed."[115]

Jekyll, in his lonely self-exile, reflected one isolated response to the doubts, tensions, and stress that had been engendered in Victorian England by the commingling of disparate social and intellectual elements. The conflict between science and religion, the personal repressiveness of middle-class manners and conventions, the decline of the landed aristocracy, the stubborn persistence of romanticism, industrialism, the awakening of working-class consciousness, and the demands of empire—all weighed upon the minds of sensitive Victorians.[116] Personal considerations had dictated that Jekyll seek a simpler, healthier, and less demanding existence in Jamaica, but he had brought his awareness of the complexities of modern life with him. In part romantic, in part a Spencerian rationalist, Jekyll had found in Jamaica a safe retreat from which to look upon the world with a measure of detachment.

Within Jamaica itself, he found satisfaction in its climate and great natural beauty, and also in its people, their language, customs, and songs. He also derived much satisfaction from the association of young men such as Claude McKay and Johnny Lyons, whose psychological uncertainties he perhaps understood and whose talents he could definitely help develop. It is probable that Jekyll's admiration and love for such young men expressed itself wholly in his role as mentor and friend. During this period, homosexual "passion" often expressed itself in this manner.[117] Whatever Jekyll's behavior in this regard, the relationship that developed between him and McKay had been actively sought by both, and in it each strongly fulfilled personal needs. At no time did Claude ever deprecate Jekyll's influence on his own life. In *Banana Bottom,* his novel of Jamaica at the turn of the century, McKay created Squire Gensir as Jekyll's fictional prototype. He dedicated the novel to Jekyll and memorialized him in the following passage, in which the novel's heroine, Bita Plant, looked back upon Gensir after his death and pondered the significance of his life:

> This man was the first to enter into the simple life of the island Negroes and proclaim significance and beauty in their transplanted African folk tales and in the words and music of their native dialect.
> Before him it had generally been said the Negroes were inartistic. But he had found artistry where others saw nothing, because he believed that wherever the imprints of nature and humanity were found, there also

were the seeds of creative life, and that above the dreary levels of existence everywhere there were always the radiant, the mysterious, the wonderful, the strange great moments whose magic may be caught by any clairvoyant mind and turned into magical form for the joy of man.[118]

Jekyll's insistence on the value and beauty of the Jamaican dialect and the folk traditions it embodied enabled Claude McKay to accept the dialect as a legitimate poetic medium; his acceptance of it enabled him to give voice to his own heritage and expose the problems he found within it and within himself. It was an unprecedented and difficult challenge. Because of his education, he had sentimentally regarded himself a part of the great British Empire. From his earliest years, he had accepted the English language and its literary traditions as his own. His use of the dialect might conceivably have turned into a mere academic exercise, an inconsequential diversion. But McKay always wrote directly from the deepest levels of his own personal feelings, and his experience in the constabulary propelled him into a direct confrontation with the limited alternatives and painful contradictions inherent for all blacks in the British Jamaican colonial situation.

McKay's enlistment in the constabulary might have ended disastrously had it not been for Jekyll's intercession. As an idealistic recruit fresh from the country, he was revolted by the constant brutality and duplicity, seemingly normal parts of the policeman's lot. He disliked with equal intensity the unending discipline of a semimilitary life and the policeman's preoccupation with "making cases."[119] Many who ran afoul of the law were simple peasants newly arrived from the country, and he often sympathized with their troubles.

He had not told his officers or fellow enlistees that he visited Jekyll or wrote poetry. After his initial training at the Old Military Barracks in Spanish Town, he had been assigned to regular clerical duty in the constabulary office there. Spanish Town was twelve miles west of Kingston and even farther from Jekyll's home at Mavis Bank. As long as he remained in Spanish Town, his visits to Jekyll had to be confined to weekends. Much to his surprise and embarrassment, Jekyll one day appeared in Spanish Town and spoke directly to the head of the constabulary. Shortly afterward, Claude was transferred to the constabulary office in Half-Way Tree, just north of Kingston proper, much closer to Jekyll. Moreover, although he "was supposed to do duty there about once a month . . . sometimes for three months I didn't go because the sergeant in the office was so indulgent."[120] No doubt, too, it helped to have friends in high places.

Before long, some of McKay's verse, along with an account of

Jekyll's role in his discovery and development as a poet, appeared in Jamaica's largest newspaper, the Kingston *Daily Gleaner*.[121] Jekyll thought the article full of exaggeration about himself, but he correctly surmised it would help the sale of Claude's first volume of dialect poetry, which the two were then putting together. About that time, Jekyll one day calmly announced that he was going to get Claude out of the constabulary. About two months later, Claude obtained his discharge; he had served less than a year of his five-year term. He would no longer have to place himself in opposition to those he regarded as his kin; an intolerable burden had been lifted from his shoulders. "So now I was happy as a golden finch. . . . I was writing my poetry. . . . I had the very best friend in the world. Oh, Jamaica was a happy place for me then. I thought I was walking always with flowers under my feet."[122] While Jekyll made arrangements for the publication of his poems, Claude returned to Sunny Ville, moved into a small thatched cottage near the family home, and farmed for several months.

In his twenty-first year, Claude McKay was on the verge of achieving considerable local success as a poet. He was a handsome, slim, dark brown young man of medium height. He had the ready smile and the rollicking laugh of a Jamaican countryman. Upon his broad, expressive face his "eyebrows arched high up and never came down, and his finely modeled features wore in consequence a fixed expression of ironical and rather mischievous scepticism."[123] He possessed a poet's keen sensibility and knew well his environment and its people. He understood himself less well. As the youngest child of a large family, he secretly doubted his ability to make his way alone in the world and remained unsure about his future. (Jekyll had already reminded him that he could not expect to earn a living as a poet.)[124] He still needed guidance but felt uncomfortable with his father. He greatly admired his older brother, U'Theo, but never wished to emulate him. He had not developed strong attachments to his other brothers, but did seem fond of his sister, Rachel. He had idolized his mother.

Now he once again found himself back home in Sunny Ville. He made clear his reasons for returning to Sunny Ville in the two volumes of Jamaican dialect poetry that finally appeared in 1912. Together they revealed the mind, moods, achievements, and limitations of the young poet, Claude McKay.

# 2
# The Jamaican Poetry as Autobiography: Claude McKay in 1912

In 1912, Claude McKay produced two volumes of poetry. *Songs of Jamaica* appeared early in January, and *Constab Ballads* became available locally in late November. That year he also published a significant number of poems in the island's two major newspapers, the Kingston *Daily Gleaner* and the weekly *Jamaica Times*.[1]

No black West Indian educated in the British imperial tradition had ever before attempted to use a local island dialect as his primary poetic medium. Ever since the eighteenth century, British West Indian poets, black and white, had with few exceptions striven to duplicate in language and form the traditions of English verse. They had also proclaimed in their poetry their loyalty as British imperial subjects. They had celebrated the great beauty of their New World homes, but in the tradition of British pastoral verse and the nature poetry of the romantic period.

From time to time a few blacks among them had expressed an awareness of their people's grievances as the descendants of exploited and abused black African slaves. But their exploration of the dilemmas inherent in their marginal position as the stepchildren of British culture remained for the most part submerged beneath a derivative pastoral tradition and respect for British literary forms and themes.[2]  35

In McKay's day, this imitative literary tradition still persisted in Jamaica. With the exception of Walter Jekyll, almost no one regarded the Jamaican dialect as a fit vehicle for serious literary expression. Even McKay had initially rejected it, and in *Songs of Jamaica* and *Constab Ballads,* many of his poems still reflected his attachment to standard nineteenth-century British literary modes and themes. At the same time, however, McKay wrote from the perspective of a black Jamaican of rural, peasant origins. To a greater degree than prior West Indian poets, he clearly revealed in his dialect poetry the intellectual, social, and cultural contradictions that faced a perceptive black artist in British colonial Jamaica.

Written with a naïve and disarming candor, these early poems can be read today as autobiography, as social documents of historical value, and as linguistic and artistic creations of pioneering importance in the development of modern West Indian literature. They are also of fundamental importance in understanding McKay's later work. In the dialect poems he developed certain basic themes and stylistic tendencies that persisted in all his subsequent writings. In short, McKay's dialect poetry provides insight into the mind and feelings of the young poet and into some of the hard realities of black life in Jamaica during the first two decades of the twentieth century.[3]

*Songs of Jamaica* contained fifty poems, *Constab Ballads* only twenty-eight. The first collection included many poems that dealt with various aspects of Jamaican country life as McKay had known it, and others that reflected McKay's intellectual convictions and commitments. It also had its share of love poems. Although written in dialect about Jamaican country youth, the love songs told conventional stories of lovers and their tribulations and contained little that was original or exceptionally striking, either in content or style. As its title implied, *Constab Ballads* consisted of poems that generally focus on McKay's experiences and impressions as a policeman in urban Kingston and Spanish Town. There was, however, an overlapping of themes in the two works; *Constab Ballads* actually elaborated on topics first introduced in *Songs of Jamaica.*[4]

In both volumes, the style, content, length, and overall quality of the individual poems varied enormously. Some were very short, little more than sentimental jingles. Others possessed considerable artistic merit. A few were sustained efforts of over a hundred lines. The individual poems also varied greatly in language. Although most were written in Jamaican dialect, several of the poems contained only a limited number of dialect words and usages. A few were written entirely in standard English. Throughout both volumes, McKay wavered between the use of a pungent, wholly colloquial Jamaican dialect and a standard English patterned upon the stereotyped Victorian romanticism of his day. *Songs of Jamaica* and *Constab Ballads* were the uneven first products of McKay's apprenticeship, and they frequently echoed the standardized, cliché-ridden themes of his West Indian literary predecessors and contemporaries.[5]

Although McKay's uniqueness and importance lay in his intense celebration of his rural, specifically black, Jamaican origins, he also affirmed in his poetry his attachment to the lyrical traditions of England and to Western civilization itself. The direction of his schooling had ensured his identity with Western intellectual traditions. On the other hand, his experiences in urban Kingston's constabulary had awakened in him an acute realization of the wide gap that separated most black Jamaicans from their British rulers. There consequently developed in McKay an intellectual and emotional tension that the dialect poems clearly reflected, not only by their curious and naïve mixture of styles and themes, but also by the consistently autobiographical thread that ran through both volumes.

On one very basic level, he remained in the dialect poetry the idealistic, if disillusioned, pupil with a sentimental conception of English cultural and intellectual achievements. Nowhere was this provincial, long-distance infatuation more evident than in the poem "Old England," where he confessed that for as long as he could remember he had longed "just to view de homeland England" and to see its famous sights. This relatively long poem of seven stanzas revealed not only McKay's English orientation but also the anti-Christian bent it had taken, for in it he elaborated upon the crumbling structure of Christian faith and indicated his preference for the new scientific rationalism that seemed likely to replace it.[6]

"Old England" contained abundant examples of McKay's dialect verse at its worst—painfully forced rhymes, worn poetic clichés ("to sail athwart the ocean an' to hear de billows roar"), and an overriding sentimentality.[7] Despite his nominal use of dialect, in "Old England" McKay did not advance far beyond the derivative traditions of earlier West Indian versifiers.

Other poems, particularly those that reflected his involvement with late Victorian intellectual issues, proved more successful. In one such poem, "Cudjoe Fresh from de Lecture," a Jamaican peasant ruminated on the implications for blacks of Darwin's evolutionary theory, which he had just heard expounded by a British lecturer. Cudjoe's remarks provided some subtle amendments to the orthodox social Darwinist doctrines of the day, which invariably placed the

black man last on the human evolutionary scale. Although he did not
have the scientific knowledge to reject outright the white man's de-
rogatory image of Africa, in general Cudjoe conceded little to the racism implicit in social Darwinist theory. In fact, he concluded that
there was little difference between the two races in the evolutionary
scheme.[8]

"Cudjoe Fresh from de Lecture" also revealed that neither McKay
nor his peasant persona had any effective image of Africa to counter
the one foisted on them by the white man. Because this image was
one of naked barbarism, Africa tended to be rejected throughout Mc-
Kay's dialect poetry. In one poem, for example, he said instead that

> Jamaica is de nigger's place,
>     No mind whe' some declare;
> Aldough dem call we "no land race,"
>     I know we home is here.[9]

While Africa may have been only an uncomfortable place from which
one long ago escaped, there could be no question about Jamaica. It
was home, a place known, accepted, and loved. McKay knew from
experience that Jamaica could provide blacks the subsistence needed
for them to stand upon their own feet, and what he knew from direct
experience he could write about with confidence and authority.

Both *Songs of Jamaica* and *Constab Ballads* included engaging
dialect poems that portrayed black Jamaican peasant life in realistic
detail. One such poem is "Quashie to Buccra," in which the black
peasant farmer complains to the white buyer that he offers little for
his sweet potatoes because he has no notion about the labor involved
in their production. Their cultivation, he maintains, "Is killin' some-
t'ing for a naygur man."[10] The sun is hot "like when fire ketch a
town," but the farmer "caan' lie down" until his work is finished. The
potato plant will yield in great quantity only if it is given lavish care.
The farmer notes that Buccra thinks his field pretty. He then re-
minds him that with all the attention it has gotten, it could not look
otherwise. "Yet still de hardship always melt away / Wheneber it come
roun' to reapin' day."[11] Although the price may not always be fair, an
abundant crop brings its own satisfactions.

It must be noted that Quashie is very much his own man. Although many blacks still labored on sugar plantations and cattle pens
in turn-of-the-century Jamaica, they made no appearance in McKay's
dialect poetry. When writing of country life, he invariably took the
point of view of the small, independent farmer who produced for both
the local and the export markets. Quashie's potatoes were for the
local market.

In McKay's boyhood, bananas provided the small farmer's chief revenue on the export market. In "King Banana," he celebrated its central place in the black farmer's life.[12] The "king banana" was a Martinique variety, known as "mancha" in Jamaica. The poem begins by noting that "Green mancha mek fe naygur man" (that is, blacks liked to eat them green, roasted or baked) while "A buccra fancy when it ripe."[13] In succeeding stanzas, he describes the steps in its cultivation. The underbrush is burned to clear the land and to kill insect pests. The land is then prepared with rake and hoe. These traditional methods produce big strong bunches. After they are cut, the bunches are wrapped in dried banana leaves and are firmly packed in drays to prevent bruising on the way to market. At market, they can always be sold. A few farmers may spend the money thus earned on rum, but others on the return trip home "hab money in t'read bag well." Whether the money is squandered or saved, the poem concludes, it nevertheless remains true that

> Green mancha mek fe naygur man,
>    It mek fe him all way;
> Our islan' is banana lan',
>    Banana car' de sway.[14]

Despite their independence, most Jamaican peasants had to struggle just to make ends meet. The demands of large families, the vagaries of weather, and the fluctuations of market prices made life uncertain and often harsh for the average small farmer. Central to his prosperity were the intensely active local markets where he went year round to dispose of his surplus produce. In "Two-an'-Six," McKay tells the story of Cous' Sun's trip to market in a rented dray packed with sugar he had refined at a hired mill. At the market, he finds that "sugar bears no price te-day." He has to sell his load for a mere "two-an'-six a tin," far below its normal price. He returns home ashamed and dispirited, with none of the usual treats for the children. His wife consoles him, and together they sit down to count up their profit and loss.

> So day k'lated eberyt'ing;
>    An' de profit it could bring,
> A'ter all de business fix',
>    Was a princely two-an'-six.[15]

"Two-an'-Six" contains its share of sentimentality, but it describes in realistic detail the bare margin upon which most Jamaican small farmers of McKay's day existed.

Abject poverty was a reality, or at least a constant threat, to every

Jamaican peasant. Those who owned sufficient land to gain a modest livelihood never knew when a disastrous drought, flood, hurricane, or other natural catastrophe might reduce them to misery. Resources and economic development were limited in Jamaica, and the hard-pressed peasant often resigned himself to an unending struggle for subsistence. In "Hard Times," the peasant protagonist proclaims that

> De peas won't pop, de corn can't grow,
> Poor people face look sad;
> Dat Gahd would cuss de lan' I'd know
> For black naygur too bad.[16]

Resignation did not appeal to all. Many Jamaicans migrated to Panama during this period. Others tried their luck elsewhere—on the plantations of nearby Cuba or more distant Costa Rica and Colombia. In all these places, they could earn more than on the local Jamaican plantations, where the presence of imported "coolie" laborers from India had helped drive wages below the subsistence level. A steady trickle of Jamaicans was also leaving for the United States during these years.[17]

Kingston offered a closer alternative, but few found anything better there than work as unskilled laborers, domestic servants, petty clerks, or small traders. Such jobs generally offered limited opportunities for advancement. Lack of hope sometimes turned women toward prostitution and men toward petty crime and dissipation. In McKay's youth, most of the grave social problems that today beset the giant, sprawling, run-down metropolis of Kingston could already be seen as growing elements in the city's daily life.[18]

As a constab, McKay saw the wide gulf that separated the comfortable social elite from the mass of country folk constantly coming and going in Kingston's crowded streets. As a young recruit, he had also become aware that the constabulary itself was composed of many young men, not unlike himself, who had joined the police force at least in part to escape the isolation and economic limitations of country life. McKay incorporated these insights into some of his most starkly realistic and effective dialect verse. In "Flat-Foot Drill," for example, the impatient drill instructor declares he is "boun' fe swea'"

> Dealin' with you' class all day,
> Neber see such from a barn
> "Right tu'n, you damn' bungo brut'!
> Do it so, you mountain man."[19]

The idea that joining the constabulary was a way of escaping rural poverty received even more elaborate treatment in "A Midnight

Woman to the Bobby." One of McKay's most accomplished dialect pieces, it is in the form of an irate monologue delivered by a street prostitute who has just been accosted by a young black policeman on his nightly beat in Spanish Town. The poem is remarkable for its vigorous, forthright use of authentic Jamaican language, as well as for its bitterly ironic commentary on the rural conditions that sometimes forced young men into the constabulary. The "midnight woman" clearly has no respect for a black man in what she perceives as a white man's uniform, and throughout the poem she heaps scorn upon his African physiognomy, his rural origins, and the abject poverty from which he fled.

> An' when de pinch o' time you feel
> A 'pur you a you' chigger heel,
> You lef' you' district, big an' coarse,
> An' come join buccra Police Force.[20]

The black policemen of McKay's day were, in fact, highly conscious of their ambiguous status as the enforcers of British colonial law.

In 1910, H. G. DeLisser, a white Jamaican author, described the way a black Jamaican policeman would typically intervene in a public argument that threatened to get out of hand. As spectators and participants all tried at once to give their versions of the altercation, the policeman would listen for a moment and then would "inform all and sundry with severity that 'although I am a black man, I am not a fool.' . . . He is conscious he is a black man: he tells you so. But he does that in order to let you know that you must not presume too much upon that fact." DeLisser went on to comment on the black Jamaican's "real attitude toward the government and the law."

> He regards them as something outside of and apart from himself. They are something imposed upon him which he is obliged to respect, but which he does not consider himself identified with, and which he is sometimes inclined to think of as oppressive. The laws are "backra laws." . . . He doubts the absolute impartiality of the law. He is quite satisfied that the policeman will readily arrest him while leaving his master to go free, though their offense may be the same. Consequently he is no stalwart admirer of the laws or defender of the government; he accepts them as he does the other inevitables of life, . . . [but] he would like to see less of the policeman.[21]

McKay's dialect poetry confirms DeLisser's observations. In his poems of rural life, the white man appears as an intrusive, though not absolutely dominant, presence; he is an annoyance more than an outright oppressor.[22] In his poems of black street life in Spanish Town and Kingston, the white presence, ironically acting indirectly through black policemen, becomes more constant and directly oppressive. In "The Apple-Woman's Complaint," for instance, a street peddler, informed that she must carry her tray of apples and not place it upon the sidewalk, receives this information as just another example of police harassment.

> Black nigger wukin' laka cow
> An' wipin' sweat-drops from him brow,
> Dough him is dyin' sake o' need,
> P'lice an' dem headman boun' fe feed.
>
> . . . . . . . . . . . . . .
>
> Ah son-son! dough you're bastard, yah,
> An' dere's no one you can call pa,
> Jes' try to ha' you' mudder's min'
> An' Police Force you'll neber jine.[23]

McKay's best dialect poems by far are those that vividly portray the island's poor and the difficulties under which they lived. There can be no doubt he sympathized and identified with them. Although his own family had achieved a measure of prosperity, he could not ignore the sea of human poverty around him. McKay's stint with the constabulary had brought him face to face with the injustices of Jamaican social life and the daily tensions, frustrations, and pain they engendered. In a preface to *Constab Ballads,* he recorded his reactions in a remarkably candid self-analysis:

> Let me confess it at once. I had not in me the stuff that goes to the making of a good constable; for I am so constituted that imagination outruns discretion, and it is my misfortune to have a most improper sympathy with wrongdoers. . . . Moreover, I am, by temperament, unadaptive; by which I mean that it is not in me to conform cheerfully to uncongenial usages. We blacks are all somewhat impatient with discipline, and to the natural impatience of my race there was added, in my case, a peculiar sensitiveness which made certain forms of discipline irksome, and a fierce hatred of injustice. Not that I ever openly rebelled; but the rebellion was in my heart, and it was fomented by the inevitable rubs of daily life—trifles to most of my comrades, but to me calamities and tragedies. To relieve my feelings, I wrote poems, and into them I poured my heart in its various moods.[24]

McKay's duties as a constab led him to emphasize in his dialect poetry his fundamental identity as a black man and to reaffirm his peasant origins. In one poem, a bobby declines to arrest a servant girl simply because her employer, "the sneering lady," is angry with her for some minor offense. In another poem, a constab is threatened with dismissal and the return to farm labor. He defiantly replies that such a prospect would be infinitely preferable to the life he had found in the constabulary.[25] And, in yet another poem, McKay exclaimed that

> Tis grievous to think dat, while toilin' on here,
>     My people won't love me again,
> My people, my people, me owna black skin,—
>     De wretched t'ought gives me such pain.[26]

No island poet had ever spoken so directly or at such length of his basic identity as a black man, a peasant, and a Jamaican. As he was to do so often in his life, McKay addressed himself directly in this early poetry to the deeply personal problems of alienation and identity. By donning the uniform of a constab, he separated himself from his black kinsmen in a more obvious way than the separation he experienced as a developing poet and intellectual. The peasants' lives were deeply rooted in self-sufficient rural folk patterns that enabled them to survive natural catastrophes, the fluctuations of market economics, and decades of governmental neglect. They experienced little benefit from British colonial government and often resented its interference in their lives. Government benefited "high people," and policemen were their tools.[27]

To be in such direct conflict with his fellow blacks was intolerable to McKay, and in the dialect poetry he bewailed his enlistment and melodramatically pledged a return to the rural environment of his birth. "For 'tis hatred without an' 'tis hatred within, / An' how can I live 'doubten heart?"[28]

McKay's best dialect poems are those in which he allowed black Jamaicans such as Quashie, Cudjoe, the "midnight woman," and the "apple-woman" to speak for themselves. Their rapier wit, ironic awareness, and telling phrases conveyed the real vitality of the Jamaican dialect and the Jamaican common folk. In their monologues, McKay created believable characters and fine poetry. In addition to these dramatic monologues, McKay also used the dialect effectively in such poems as "King Banana" and "Two-an'-Six" to describe various aspects of Jamaican country life. In still other narrative poems, such as "Pay-Day," "Knutsford Park Races," and "Papine Corner," he successfully depicted life in Kingston and its environs. In all these poems, McKay's use of the dialect remained unequaled until Louise Bennett in the 1940s dedicated herself wholly to Jamaican dialect poetry and drama.[29]

Less successful, however, were those poems in which McKay attempted to come to terms with his own situation as a man and a poet. Here his use of the dialect faltered under the weight of his peculiar

European intellectual inheritance; his personal role confusion as a black intellectual became evident, and he reacted with despair and disillusionment.

To some degree, too, the pessimism that pervaded both *Songs of Jamaica* and *Constab Ballads* was accentuated by McKay's infatuation with the ideas contained in *The Wisdom of Schopenhauer,* which Walter Jekyll had edited for the Rationalist Press Association in 1911.[30] Jekyll's translation of selections from Schopenhauer's writings offered McKay the idea that an impersonal, all-encompassing, and self-aggrandizing will pervaded the world and determined the human situation and human actions. According to Schopenhauer, a man became aware of the existence of will by recognizing its dominance within himself and by then observing its manifestations in nature. In the individual, thought itself served as an instrument of this blind will. Only through withdrawal from the actions of the world could man overcome the insatiable need of this omnivorous force for active dominance. Schopenhauer considered scientific thought ultimately subservient to the will, but he held a different view of art, through which he believed man could achieve knowledge of an archetypal reality that existed independently of the will.[31]

For a sensitive young man such as McKay, still very unsure of the direction his life should take, Schopenhauer's bleak and gloomy view of the human situation held a definite romantic appeal. After all, much had happened in his own experience that seemed to confirm the philosopher's ideas. His father's unbending Christian morality, his mother's agonizing death, the strife of constabulary life, the poverty around him, and even the logic of evolutionary theory—all seemed to confirm Schopenhauer's dreary world view and justify McKay's own melancholy.[32]

The only solution obvious to McKay was retreat from the world's inevitable strife: he would return to the mountains. In the poem "To W.G.G.," he appealed for a companion to accompany him.

> Come to de hills; dey may be drear,
> But we can shun de evil here.
> . . . . . . . . . . .
> De helpless playt'ing of a Will,
> We'll spend our short days here; an' still,
> Though prisoners, feel somehow free
> To live our lives o' misery.[33]

Schopenhauer's reverence for childhood also no doubt appealed to McKay. The old pessimist had written that "childhood was the time of innocence and happiness, the paradise of life, the lost Eden, on which we look longingly back through the whole remaining course of our life."[34] McKay could not have agreed more, and in his dialect poems the blessedness of childhood emerged as a fully developed theme. "Childhood pain could neber las',"[35] but he had wandered far from home and had turned his back on the satisfactions that flowed from the independent existence of the mountain peasantry.

> Fool! I hated my precious birthright,
>     Scornin' what made my father a man;
> Now I grope in de pitchy dark night,
>     Hate de day when me poo' life began.[36]

In one long poem, appropriately entitled "A Dream," McKay painted an idyllic picture of a typical childhood day in rural Jamaica and bemoaned its irrecoverable loss. "Gone now those happy days when all was blest / . . . The pains, the real in life, I've now to bear."[37]

Although there was much youthful self-indulgence and sentimental breast-beating in McKay's development of these themes, his personal dilemma was real. While remaining fundamentally loyal to the black peasantry, he had embraced uncritically the language and themes of European romanticism, the pessimism of Schopenhauer, and the scientific rationalism of late Victorian England. Within the context of their own cultures, the great romantics had attempted to transcend the mechanistic rationalism and the impersonal, laissez-faire materialism of the early industrial age. Their concerns were not without relevance to McKay and the Jamaica of his day, but in his dialect poetry he often failed to translate their preoccupations into terms truly applicable to his own situation as a deracinated black intellectual who wished to relate in a meaningful way to his people.

McKay did learn from his European predecessors certain techniques that he put to good use in his Jamaican dialect poetry. The dramatic monologues of the "midnight woman" and the "apple-woman," for instance, almost certainly reflect Robert Browning's influence. In *My Green Hills*, he wrote that in Jamaica "there were 'Browning Clubs' where the poetry of Robert Browning was studied but not understood. I had read my poems before many of these societies and the members used to say: 'Well, he's very nice and pretty you know, but he's not a real poet as Browning and Byron and Tennyson are poets.'" Another obvious influence in McKay's *Constab Ballads* was Rudyard Kipling's *Barrack-Room Ballads*. At least one English review noted the "Kiplingesque" influence in *Constab Ballads*.[38]

In general, however, McKay's dual heritage as a child of black Jamaica and imperial British culture required more than an unsophisticated incorporation of a clichéd English romanticism into Jamaican dialect. Nor would a simple retreat to the countryside of his youth resolve his problems, as he himself recognized.

> Tis home again but not the home of yore;
> Sadly the scene of bygone days I view,
> And as I walk the olden paths once more,
> My heart grows chilly as the morning dew.[39]

These lines are from "A Dream," McKay's paean to lost innocence. It was written entirely in standard English. Despite his facility with the dialect, at a most basic level he had also assimilated as his own the language of the dominant culture. He had not yet, however, learned to use its literary traditions to explore thoroughly the nature of his fundamental estrangement. The experience necessary for such an exploration would come later. Meanwhile, one can already see in the dialect poetry certain themes and stylistic responses that would persist in McKay's later poetry, all of which would be written in standard English. The basic insistence upon the innocence of childhood and a nostalgia for the countryside of his youth would remain. The note of protest present in the dialect poetry would grow stronger, too, and would sound more insistently in his later work. Even in the dialect volumes, the deeply personal expressions of anger, alienation, and rebellion that would characterize his later poetry sometimes broke through. In "Strokes of the Tamarind Switch," for example, McKay expressed his revulsion at the practice of flogging, which was still inflicted upon Jamaicans convicted of certain crimes.

> The cutting tamarind switch
> Had left its bloody mark,
> And on his legs were streaks
> That looked like boiling bark.[40]

Despite his genuine achievements in *Songs of Jamaica* and *Constab Ballads*, these volumes too often betrayed McKay's literary inexperience, emotional confusion, and intellectual immaturity. In "Bennie's Departure," a long description of his affection for and emotional dependence on a fellow recruit in the early days of their enlistment—a description, not incidentally, that bordered upon a passionate declaration of homosexual love—McKay observed that Bennie "was always quick and steady, / Not of wav'rin' min' like me."[41] McKay's "wav'rin' min'" can in part be attributed to his youthful inexperience and in part to the deep-seated psychological insecurity with which he viewed his future. But his uncertainty was made even more acute by his ambivalent suspension at this stage of his life between the peasant culture and the literate colonial society. All these factors contributed to the stylistic problems and contradictory emotional and intellectual stances in his dialect poetry.

Despite his emotional loyalty to the Jamaican peasantry, his commitment to the dialect was not total because he could not adequately express through his dialect persona all those aspects of his own intellectual and literary experiences that he had assimilated as an educated colonial. His education claimed a part of his being as surely as did his peasant heritage and could not be denied expression, as its awkward manifestation in the dialect attested. Although tied emotionally and racially to the uneducated peasantry, he no longer fully shared their necessarily restricted world view. On the other hand, while sharing the literate consciousness of the race from whom he had acquired his education, he could not identify with it at the deepest levels of his emotions.

Given this dual estrangement, the wonder is not that so much of McKay's dialect poetry was bad but that he achieved in it as much as he did. In his later poetry and novels, he would handle the problems of alienation and identity with greater self-consciousness and with more sophistication.[42]

Late in 1911, while awaiting the publication of *Songs of Jamaica*, McKay returned to Sunny Ville and attempted to assume the role of peasant-poet he had projected for himself in the dialect poetry. He moved into a small thatched cottage on his father's land and cultivated "peas and corn and yams." They were, he explained, "mostly light crops which gave me quick returns." But just as before, and to an even greater degree, he found he could not fit comfortably into the life around him. "The old embarrassment was always there. People knew that I was a poet, and that made me different, although I wanted so much to be like them. Even my closest friends at home were never the same. I tried to be as simple as simple, but they would never accept me with the old simplicity. Truly I must admit that I was much happier in Kingston where I went with the crowd and nobody knew me; or when I was up at Mr. Jekyll's where it was not at all embarrassing to be known and accepted as a poet."[43] His stay in Sunny Ville proved a brief, unsatisfactory interlude and lasted only a few months. Far from finding contentment, McKay in 1912 began to move inexorably toward active involvement in island economic and social controversy. He also began to plan a career for himself that would involve further education outside Jamaica.

Although *Songs of Jamaica* and *Constab Ballads* clearly revealed McKay's general concern for the extreme poverty and social disadvantages of the colony's black peasantry, neither of these volumes contained his poetry of social commentary, which appeared in the local newspapers after he left the constabulary. Late in 1911 and periodically throughout 1912, the *Daily Gleaner* and the *Jamaica Times* published poems by McKay in which he dealt with historically specific occurrences and situations of concern to Jamaica's government and population.

One of these poems, "Christmas in de Air," appeared in the *Jamaica Times* on December 16, 1911. In the form of a monologue uttered by a penniless Jamaican farmer, it commented extensively upon the wretched economic conditions of poor Jamaicans and the indifference of the colonial government to their plight. Typically, the farmer has an ailing wife and several children. They are facing drought, general crop failure, a lack of cash, and actual hunger. The farmer looks at the possibility of wage labor but finds nothing adequate to support his family.

> Wuk is shet do'n 'pon de road,
> An' plantation pay no good.
> Whole day ninepance for a man!
> Wha' dah come to dis ya lan'?

Meanwhile, he observes, the government does nothing about the high price of food. And furthermore, "Not a single wud is said / 'Bouten taxes to be paid." They have to be paid every year, even "though dere's hunger in the air." The government, the merchants, and the large planters are not hurt. Their profits must come before the desperate needs of the island's poor.

> While we're sufferin' in pain
> Dem can talk 'bout surplus gain;
> O me God! de sad do'n-care,
> An' dere's *Hard Times* in de air.[44]

The references to "surplus gain" and to *Hard Times*, Charles Dickens' novel of capitalist greed, are clear proof of McKay's early conviction that Jamaica's poverty had to be understood within the context of an economic system whose profitability for merchants and plantation owners was ultimately derived by denying the laboring masses any chance for a decent living.

McKay's Christmas complaint reflected actual economic hardships. Throughout 1911 and 1912, the *Jamaica Times* reported upon rural conditions and periodically ran a page-one letters-to-the-editor section entitled "The People's Parliament," in which the causes of Jamaica's poverty were frequently debated by its readers. The staid

*Daily Gleaner* also reported extensively upon adverse economic conditions throughout the island, but to a much greater degree, the *Times* reflected the frustrations and aspirations of Jamaica's struggling black majority.[45]

In March and April of 1911, for example, the *Times* reported upon the depressed economic condition of upper Clarendon and described the hopes of the people there that an extension of the railroad from May Pen to Chapelton would bring prosperity to the region. As work proceeded on the railway, the *Times* and the *Gleaner* duly noted the laborers' complaints of extremely low wages and contractors' deceptions about wage agreements.[46] One of the most interesting protests came from Claude's brother, U'Theo McKay. In a letter to the *Times*, he confirmed that the road laborer was sometimes being cheated out of his just wages. Because his work was vital to progress, U'Theo stated, "a man like this should get the reward of his labor. . . . The work on the New Roads and on the new rail line in Clarendon furnishes many cases in which he has not been rewarded for his toil. Surely it won't be long before the horny handed sons of toil are given ample protection for every day the world is awakening more and more to their great importance."[47] In part, U'Theo's remarks reflected his reading of Lord Sidney Olivier's *Capital and Labor in the West Indies,* in which Jamaica's new Fabian Socialist governor had argued against the traditional plantation system and for the small peasant landholder as the future backbone of a more equitable economic system in the West Indies. U'Theo may have also remembered his own father's beginnings as a road mender.[48]

It was against such a background of public concern and controversy that *Songs of Jamaica* appeared in early January, 1912. The *Jamaica Times* editor, Thomas H. MacDermot, gave it a glowing review. He complimented its local publisher, Aston W. Gardner, for competence in producing the book. He also paid tribute to Walter Jekyll's concise introductory remarks on the nature of the Jamaican dialect and "in passing" praised "the tactful and able help [Jekyll] had given in guiding these poems into publication in a form so creditable to all concerned."[49]

MacDermot's praise of McKay was heartfelt and bountiful. He noted McKay's rich lyric gift and predicted that the young poet was "destined" like "one of our mountain springs . . . to yield a great deal more of work as excellent as this, and still more so. . . . We venture to say it; here we have a poet." While MacDermot admitted that the poems in *Songs of Jamaica* varied in quality and that some might have "more wisely been left out," he nevertheless maintained that "as a whole, and speaking of the great majority of the poems, we have here outstanding merit. It is absolutely correct to say that the publication of this volume is an event of note in Jamaican literature." MacDermot went on to point out the variety found in McKay's poems, their "humour and pathos," their "spontaneity of feeling, and the facility with which feeling finds varied forms of expression." He took special note of the realism of many of the poems and asserted that they "give us genuine pictures of life in the countryside as it can be seen today by those who have eyes to see." A few poems he found too didactic; others had obviously forced rhyme schemes that led to a lack of "lyric ease and flow." These flaws, he predicted, would be overcome with practice. All in all, McKay had clearly found an ally in MacDermot, who in closing extended "a hearty sincere welcome to *Songs of Jamaica*. . . . It does its author credit; it does Jamaica credit, Jamaica who has produced him. We shall look forward to his future . . . with confidence."[50] The book also received favorable, if more restrained, notice in the *Daily Gleaner* and in other newspapers and journals in more distant parts of the empire. For the rest of the year, McKay received fairly frequent notice in both the *Times* and the *Gleaner*, and published poems in them with fair regularity.[51]

The *Daily Gleaner* of January 27, 1912, published a long poem (124 lines) by McKay entitled "Peasants' Way O' Thinkin'," which again described the economic bind faced by Jamaica's poor. This time the peasant narrator begins by commenting at length on whether import tariffs should be lowered or removed, a question that had been debated extensively for months in the Jamaican press. He asserts that the question has been debated too long by the government. Why not, he maintains, listen to the poor? After all, they know their own interests, and they most certainly know that a reduction of duties upon food imports would benefit them, not to mention reductions on other items such as clothes.

> We wouldn' mind ef dem could try
> Mek calico cheaper fe buy;
> Tek duty off o' we blue shirt
> An also off o' we t'atch hut.

Mention of the house tax signals an expansion of view. The peasant narrator proceeds to question whether tariff reduction would in fact lead to prosperity for the poor. After all, wages are extremely low. Furthermore, the East Indian, the Chinese, and above all, the petty Syrian merchants on the island squeeze the peasants for every possible penny and keep them in debt by selling them "fripp'ries an' de fin'ries" on trust. And to top it all, he continues, we are always reading "in dese ya modern days / Wha' foreigners think of our ways." In some respect, he says, their comments are funny and even flattering "an' giv to life a bit o' spice." But, he adds, the things written about us do not really reveal the way we think.

> For hardly can de buccra find
> What passin' in de black man's mind;
> He tellin' us we ought to stay,
> But dis is wha' we got to say:

> "We hea' a callin' from Colon,
> We hea' a callin' from Limon.
> Let's quit de t'ankless toil an' fret
> Fe where a better pay we'll get."

Although they may miss Jamaica and its free and easy ways, they will at least be able to make a decent living abroad, "And dere'll be cash fe sen' back home." [52]

Having stated the case for migration, the narrator then observes that since Jamaica is home, "we're boun' to come back here some day." And then with bittersweet irony, he concedes what the rest of the poem explicitly denies, namely that the poor peasant will then be stereotypically contented with his lot.

> We may n't be rich like buccra folk'
> For us de white, for dem de yolk;
> Da's de way dat the egg divide.
> An' we content wi' de outside.

> .   .   .   .   .   .   .   .   .   .

> A piece o' lan' fe raise two goat,
> A little rum fe ease we t'roat,
> A little cot fe res' we head—
> An' we're contented tell we dead. [53]

In "Peasants' Way O' Thinkin'" McKay used the dialect with irony and restraint to present the authorities and the literate public a serious message: that Jamaican blacks were far from naïvely contented with their lot.

By late February, 1912, popular discontent surfaced in Kingston in a well-organized campaign of direct action against an increase in streetcar fares. The Canadian-owned streetcar firm in the city had long been losing public confidence because of its failure to provide the adequate and reliable services promised in its public franchise. Public dissatisfaction became militant during the last week in February when the company decided to reduce the number of tickets that could be purchased for a shilling from seven to six. The price increase amounted to little more than a farthing, or a fourth of a penny.

Opposition to the fare increase took the form of a campaign of "passive resistance." The public was urged to stop buying groups of tickets ahead of time. Organized groups instead began to board the trolley cars, each individual insisting on paying the individual two-pence fare in farthings, which he would slowly and deliberately count out to the harassed conductor. Then he would demand a voucher, or receipt, which the company by law was obliged to provide upon request. From the first, the "passive resisters" appeared well organized, determined, and good-natured. By Friday, February 23, they had succeeded in blocking all services. On that same day, two men among the demonstrators were finally arrested for refusing to pay the fare without first obtaining vouchers, which the conductors had refused to issue. The arrests excited public anger and resulted in even larger crowds along the streetcar lines the following day. On Saturday, demonstrators packed the cars and more surrounded them on the outside, effectively disrupting all service.[54]

On Sunday, service resumed until about four in the afternoon, when "the resisters" returned, this time followed by "hooligans" and "more ignorant and wilder" elements who precipitated violence. Many cars were damaged and one was burned. Once again service was brought to a standstill. In desperation, the streetcar company appealed to the government for additional protection. On Monday night, a peaceful demonstration by the "passive resisters" in downtown Kingston attracted a large crowd. Once again, violence erupted, despite efforts by the "passive resisters" to contain the crowd. In the midst of the ensuing pandemonium, Governor Olivier arrived on the scene and attempted to address the mob. Wading into the crowd in an effort to restrain passions, he was stoned by a few before cooler heads could stop them. He escaped the indignity without serious injury, the riot act was read, and the crowd was dispersed by police gunfire and batons. One rioter was shot and killed.[55]

While deploring mob violence and looking with apprehension and disfavor upon the tactics of the "passive resisters," neither the *Daily Gleaner* nor the *Times* supported the streetcar line in the dispute. They instead appealed for restraint on all sides and urged the government and the courts to take steps to correct the tangled problems of public transportation in Kingston. The *Jamaica Times* believed that the only solution lay in government ownership of the streetcar lines. In the aftermath of the rioting, the *Times* also cautioned "the country people" that the dispute in Kingston was between the people and the streetcar company, *not* between the people and the government.[56]

For a while, it appeared that the passive resistance movement against the streetcar line had been killed by the violence of its less restrained supporters, but late in March the passive resisters staged a surprising comeback and threatened once again to shut down the line. This time they were effectively contained by arrests and lawsuits. They did not bow out, however, without a strong fight and a final, militant assertion of defiance in the form of a strongly worded poem by Claude McKay, which appeared in the *Gleaner* on April 6, 1912. Although there exists no evidence to indicate that McKay actually participated in any of the demonstrations in February, March, and April, his poem provides proof enough of his total support of the passive resisters. Although entitled "Passive Resistance," the poem ended on a note of defiance that threatened to match blow for blow, if violence should be visited upon the demonstrators.

> There'll be no more riotin',
> Stonin' p'lice an' burnin' car;
> But we mean to gain our rights
> By a strong though bloodless war.
>
> We will show an alien trust
> Dat Jamaicans too can fight
> An' dat while our blood is hot,
> They won't crush us wi' deir might.
> . . . . . . . . . . . .
> We'll keep up a bloodless war,
> We will pay the farthings-fare
> An' we send the challenge forth,
> "Only touch us if you dare!"[57]

McKay's passionate assertion of the right of self-defense anticipated in tone and substance the militant protest poetry he would later write in the United States. McKay's highly developed sensitivity to injustice made him a potential rebel in Jamaica, long before he became aware of American racial prejudice.

Jamaican history abounded with stories to spark his rebellious imagination. In the late fall of 1911, he recalled one famous island rebellion against injustice in a poem he submitted to *T.P.'s Weekly* of London, which solicited entries for an empire poetry competition. On May 3, 1912, the *Gleaner* announced that McKay had been awarded one of the prizes given by the London weekly for his poem "Gordon to the Oppressed Natives," a celebration of the 1865 Morant Bay Rebellion. In the poem, the mulatto politician George Gordon exhorts the "oppressed natives" to rise and crush those in Jamaica who would hold them in semiservitude and undo the great work of the

English abolitionists who had freed them. In fact, Gordon never urged rebellion, but McKay obviously needed to believe in him as a Jamaican hero who courageously led black men in revolt against grave injustices. Thus, we hear McKay speaking through his mythical hero.

In the poem, the Morant Bay rebels are addressed as "sons of Afric soil," who are "Dyin' in a foreign land." They are urged to crush the few who would deny them their legitimate freedom. The great abolitionists are invoked by name, and the rebels are reminded that no Englishman would ever bow beneath the kind of tyranny that oppresses them. A final appeal is then made:

> Rise, O people of my kind
> . . . . . . . . . . .
> Fight for freedom's rights you blacks,
> Ring de slaves' old battle-song![58]

In an unpublished fragment of *My Green Hills of Jamaica,* McKay maintained that in Jamaica, Gordon was a legendary hero whom "the peasants always talked about." He recalled that when "Gordon to the Oppressed Natives" was republished in Jamaica, "it was denounced by the leading ministers of various denominations as inciting to riot; but Mr. Jekyll wrote the *Daily Gleaner* that it was only a poet's way of expressing his appreciation of a great personality."[59] Gordon had long held a special fascination for McKay. Another Jamaican newspaper, the *Jamaican Tribune,* had published a prize-winning essay he had written as a schoolboy on Gordon and the Morant Bay Rebellion.[60]

McKay's outpouring of verse critical of Jamaican social and economic conditions might have caused concern in such conservative bastions as the established church and government circles, but he received no criticism from the leading newspapers of the day. Even the conservative *Daily Gleaner* welcomed McKay's verse. The only extended controversy he aroused occurred after the Jamaica Institute's decision in late April to award its Musgrave Silver Medal for distinguished achievement to Maxwell Hall, an English meteorologist who had studied the aftereffects of the great Kingston earthquake in 1907. The decision prompted T. H. MacDermot in a *Jamaica Times* editorial on March 9 to question the institute's judgment. He said that McKay had been recommended for the award and maintained that the institute might have been better advised to seize the opportunity to recognize the talents and accomplishments of a native Jamaican writer. "However," he concluded, "it is some honour for Mr. McKay that his work should have been proposed for the medal though it did not get it—this time."[61]

In an anonymous letter to the *Gleaner,* a writer who signed himself "Truth" showed much more animosity to the institute's board of governors, whom he accused of passing McKay over because of snobbery and ignorance of genuine literature.[62] At the end of March, another anonymous writer, "Jamaican," in a letter to the *Times* defended the institute's decision. He noted that *Songs of Jamaica* was only McKay's first book. Though "a very creditable first," he asked if it was "not a little hasty on the strength of this alone to give him such a prize?" Some of the poems in the volume, he pointed out, were indeed good, others were only passable. "Then," he continued, "we must remember that he had in preparing the volume for press, the help of a scholar like Mr. Jekyll." The writer surmised that Mr. Jekyll had recommended McKay for the award. But wasn't it reasonable, he wondered, to ask if *Songs of Jamaica* was McKay's best work? In future works, perhaps, he would grow as a poet. In this light, the board's decision not to give the award to McKay appeared reasonable. "Surely," the writer concluded, "the Board of Governors must be credited with independence of judgment and a resolve not merely to toady to the opinion of even so good a scholar as Mr. Jekyll, when they reached the decision they did."[63]

In his reply, MacDermot stated that in his original editorial on the subject, he had "recalled previous mistakes by the Board (or its Secretary Frank Cundall) in recognizing island talent to suggest that the opportunity might well have been seized to mark a complete break with old, unhappy far-off things, 'even' we may now add, if it did go a little too far in the other direction."[64] MacDermot's campaign on McKay's behalf brought results. A short item in the *Daily Gleaner* on May 4 reported that "Mr. De Lisser gave notice that at the next meeting of the Jamaica Institute's Board of Governors he would move that Mr. Claude McKay's claim for a Musgrave Silver Medal be considered."[65] At the end of 1912, after the appearance of *Constab Ballads,* the institute relented and awarded McKay, along with Hall, a medal.[66]

By then, however, McKay had left Jamaica. While the controversy over the Musgrave medal was developing, Claude was deciding to seek further education abroad. He had long since discovered he could not simply reintegrate himself into the community life of Sunny Ville as a poet-farmer. His family background, education, talent, and accomplishments obviously set him apart as one destined for a higher station in life. If he wished to remain among the peasantry, he must prepare to relate to them in a professional capacity both he and they could respect as natural and progressive.

Booker T. Washington's Tuskegee Institute had been much in the news ever since the *Daily Gleaner* had first announced in October,

1911, that the International Conference on the Negro would be held there in April, 1912.[67] In succeeding months both the *Gleaner* and the *Times* covered in detail the selection of Jamaican and other West Indian delegates to the conference. The *Times* in particular took a great interest in the event. As the conference date drew nearer, its editor advised Jamaica's delegates not to feel inferior in their accomplishments vis-à-vis American blacks. Although smaller, Jamaica had also produced eminent men. Americans, he observed, needed to be educated about the realities of life in Jamaica. Earlier, the *Times's* "The People's Parliament" had printed a long letter from a union of West Indian students attending Tuskegee, describing the school, its courses and costs, and explaining the steps necessary to gain admission.[68]

The conference coincided with the arrival in Jamaica of Miss Henrietta Vinton Davis, a black American "elocutionist," who toured the island with another black American entertainer, Madame Naomi Bailey Hardy, an accomplished contralto. McKay persuaded Walter Jekyll to attend one of their performances in Kingston. Afterward, McKay met Miss Davis, who spoke in glowing terms of the wonderful work being done at Tuskegee. Her personal friendship with Booker T. Washington no doubt made her description of his school even more appealing to the troubled young poet, who had not yet found a way to support himself in Jamaica.[69]

Thus in the spring of 1912, McKay saw a way to further himself professionally and to remain in intimate touch with his origins: he would study agronomy at Tuskegee.

Walter Jekyll was horrified at the idea. So was T. H. MacDermot, who had by then become friends with McKay. They both reminded him that in the United States he would face a harsh, unrelenting white racism very different from the color-graded class consciousness found in Jamaica. Knowing his sensitivity and emotional vulnerability, they feared the harshly restrictive conditions of black American life would damage him emotionally, if not actually endanger his life. In *My Green Hills of Jamaica,* McKay recalled that MacDermot had said to him, "Claude, we hate to see you go because you will be changed, terribly changed by America."[70]

At the time, such warnings meant little to McKay. He had been assured by Miss Davis and later by Dr. W. H. Plant, one of Jamaica's delegates to the 1912 conference, that he would feel safe and well protected amid Tuskegee's large student body. Washington's careful management of the school had won him and his students a measure of respect in the larger community. Despite the generally deplorable state of race relations in the United States, McKay was assured he would have little to fear at Tuskegee. This was just what he wished to hear.[71]

In his mind's eye, Booker T. Washington and Tuskegee loomed as beacons of black hope and accomplishment. As a symbol of progress in a progressive age, Washington's achievements at Tuskegee, real and imaginary, obscured from McKay's distant gaze the hard realities of American race relations. Besides, just as Washington symbolized hope for every black man the world over who knew of him, America held special significance for mankind in general, including black Jamaicans. As McKay later recalled, "Going to America was the greatest event in the history of our hills; America was the land of education and opportunity. . . . It was a new land to which all people who had youth, and a youthful mind turned. Surely there would be opportunity in this land even for a Negro."[72] Were not Booker T. Washington and Tuskegee Institute proof?

Having resolved in his own mind the dilemma of what to do with his future, McKay returned to Sunny Ville full of hope. He continued farming. He also organized a James Hill Literary Society, which by June had thirty-five members. On June 5, 1912, the society sponsored "An Evening with Present Day Jamaican Writers." MacDermot of the *Times* did not let the occasion pass without notice. In reporting the event, he stressed that it was "so much in a line" with the *Times*'s own policy over the years of "trying to bring Jamaica literary talent to the front" that he felt compelled to "give up space to an account of it, though our columns are hard pressed. We must have such a meeting fully on record." MacDermot printed the entire program, which consisted of twenty-seven recitations from the works of various contemporary Jamaicans, including McKay, DeLisser, and MacDermot, as well as lesser lights, most of whom have been long since forgotten. McKay read from DeLisser's works; other members of the society recited McKay's poems and the works of the other authors represented. Besides Claude, U'Theo, Hubert, and Nathaniel McKay participated in the recitations. An "unusually large turn-out of members and visitors" attended, and the *Times* reported that "a very enjoyable evening was spent[;] although a select literary treat, it was nowhere behind in laughter and fun. The humorous side was much in evidence."[73]

As the society's secretary and the one who planned the event, Claude opened the evening's entertainment. After the recitations, the society's president, one E. A. Haynes, remarked "in a neat speech . . . that it was a great thing for Jamaica when such a fine literary treat could be given exclusively by her writers all [save two] native born.

The descendants of slaves and their masters equally taking their place in the field of literature." He went on to urge all Jamaicans to support their writers by buying and reading their books. "Who would have thought," he concluded, "that say two decades back, such an enjoyable time could be spent without going to English and American books for the necessary pieces?" [74]

To MacDermot, such an occasion deep in the remote hills of Clarendon must have seemed miraculous proof that his long campaign to promote a specifically Jamaican literary consciousness had begun at last to bear fruit. For those who had staged the event, it represented one more step away from the shadows of slavery toward a new sense of island unity and purpose. More than thirty years later, U'Theo would invite the young dialect poet Louise Bennett to participate in yet another evening of Jamaican song and story in his native Clarendon. [75]

Claude, almost certainly, derived satisfaction from the success of the 1912 event. But he was already looking forward, a little nervously perhaps, to bigger successes. *Constab Ballads* was already in production and would be published in the late fall. He had accomplished much in 1912, but he still harbored doubts about the path he had taken as a poet. He knew his dialect verse was good as dialect verse. He still believed, however, along with other Jamaicans of his day, that to prove himself a real poet he would have to produce poems in standard English that reflected the great traditions of English verse. During the course of the year he had recited his dialect poetry before several island literary groups. They had all received him politely and had even praised his verse, but their reservations disturbed him. He remained too much a product of his time and place not to feel that he had yet to prove himself as a poet.

As he recalled in *My Green Hills of Jamaica,* "I used to think I would show them something. Someday I would write poetry in straight English and amaze and confound them because they thought I was not serious, simply because I wrote poems in the dialect which they did not consider profound." [76] In Jamaica he had found neither a suitable career nor that exact poetic voice he could indisputably call his own. In the United States, perhaps, he could find both. In many respects, he fit into an easily recognizable mold. He had become the talented provincial, restless to explore the metropolis and, despite all his uncertainties, ready to test his mettle in the larger world. As he afterward confessed to Frank Harris, at the back of his mind in 1912 "there had really been the dominant desire to find a bigger audience. Jamaica was too small for high achievement. There one was isolated, cut off from the great currents of life." In *Banana Bottom,* McKay wrote of one character, a hill country musician, that "the peasants took Crazy Bow as a fine fiddler for the hill country, but laughed at the idea of greatness in him. Greatness could not exist in the back-woods. Nor anywhere in the colony. To them and to all islanders greatness was a foreign thing."[77]

Jekyll had become reconciled to McKay's going to Tuskegee. Always a great proponent of a prosperous, independent peasantry, he responded positively to McKay's decision to study agronomy. Jekyll envisioned McKay returning to Jamaica to become a government agricultural instructor. Such a position would enable him to remain in touch with his sources as a dialect poet. Although McKay never specified the exact sum, Jekyll paid a significant portion of his school expenses. By the early summer, all arrangements had been made for McKay to enter Tuskegee in the fall. Until his departure in August, he had only to enjoy himself.[78]

The local folk helped him with his crops in return for a share of the proceeds. He had plenty of time to swim, party, and relax with friends. He always remembered that last summer in Clarendon as a time of almost idyllic pleasure. He grew especially close to Eulalie Imelda Lewars, a young daughter of a large neighboring clan. Her mellow brown skin and pretty face enchanted him, and she was bright, too, with every chance to win a scholarship when she finished her local education. On the whole, the Lewars were not inclined to scholarship. They were simple, warmhearted people who lacked the driving intensity of the darker McKays. They were nonetheless proud of Eulalie and thought it perhaps a good thing that such an accomplished young man as Claude should take an interest in her.[79]

Aside from their budding romance, Claude enjoyed above all else the local tea meetings, many of which he attended as a guest of honor. A major form of entertainment among the peasants, tea meetings were, in fact, not teas at all but dances that went on until late in the night. Staged in the open yards of their host, tea meetings followed a well-defined pattern of eating, drinking, and dancing, interspersed with deliberately exaggerated, ritual speech-making and climaxed by the auctioning off of pieces of specially baked bread. Symbolically, the bread represented the "crown" or "gate" of the village where the tea meeting was being held. The young men of the village were expected to protect their village gate by banding together and collectively outbidding all who would buy it at auction. To lose their gate to rivals from other villages meant some loss of face and rarely occurred. The crown, once bought, usually went to the successful bidder's favorite girl. The money spent for crown and gate amply covered the host's expenses for the evening's entertainment. Claude loved the homey pageantry, excitement, and warm community intimacy of these events. For the young men of the hill country, tea meetings also provided opportunities to attract and win new lady friends.[80]

Good church members, of course, frowned upon tea meetings, with their drinking, dancing, flirtatious courting, and general atmosphere of irreverent hilarity. Claude recalled in *My Green Hills of Jamaica* that "my father did not like these affairs and thought they were bad for me, but as I was going away to America I was privileged to do anything."[81] The summer sped quickly along, and soon the parties were over. McKay had arranged to leave from Port Antonio on Jamaica's northern coast in a United Fruit Company passenger-cargo ship, but late in July he first went to Kingston to say goodbye to all his friends there.

Walter Jekyll declined to see him off when he left Kingston for Port Antonio. "Mr. Jekyll did not come to see me off. He said he couldn't stand it and might possibly break down and cry in public which he didn't want to do. So I went up to his place to say farewell." There he saw again all the people he had met over the years in his visits to Jekyll's home at Mavis Bank. Many, he later recalled, "thought I would have been better off if I had gone to Europe but everybody wanted me to go someplace."[82]

Returning to Kingston, he visited friends there, including T. H. MacDermot, and then went to Port Antonio to meet his girlfriend for "three glorious days" of "bathing on the beach and eating fried fish." Very likely, his girl was Eulalie Imelda Lewars, for she told him upon his departure, "Remember to send for me when you're settled in America and I will go anyplace where you are because I love you."[83] Two years later he would send for her.

In early August, at the age of twenty-one, McKay left from Port Antonio for the United States. After his departure, two farewell poems, both written in standard English, appeared in the local papers. Both were highly revealing confessions of his feelings on leaving his birthplace. "To a Friend" appeared in the *Jamaica Times*. It was both an admission of weakness and fear and a vow to overcome such shortcomings within himself. In the poem he bid an emotional farewell and confessed that his friend knew full well the personal uncertainties and fears that had beset him in the weeks before his departure. His comrade had sustained him but "henceforward . . . I must depend upon myself alone."

> . . . comrade true,
> The boy you know
> Will come back home a man:
> He means to make you proud of him,
> He'll breast the waves and strongly swim
> And conquer,—for he can.[84]

Obviously a bad poem, it nonetheless revealed those qualities of hesitancy and dependency, paradoxically combined with ambition and audacity, that would always characterize McKay's personality. The other valedictory poem, "Clarendon Hills, Farewell," which the *Gleaner* published, contained an equally revealing message, one that implied his trip might be much more than a temporary departure for educational purposes. In it, he confessed his estrangement from Clarendon. In returning there, he had "hoped to find repose" but instead found "old sad woes," which led him to conclude that

> 'Tis you that cause them, for in those day-dreams
> Wherein I chiefly live I find of late
> My love for you is turning into hate.

He then hears his reader accuse him of being fickle. Will he love one day and hate the next? Is that not breaking "faith with your old associates"? To which the poet slyly replies that "hills have no heart . . . / And taking love from them, to make amends, / I give a double portion to my friends."[85] The hills McKay had loved had been the soft, comforting hills of infancy where "childhood pain could neber las'."[86] Now that he was an adult, the hard realities of life in Clarendon were apparent to him. He meant to escape.

T. H. MacDermot truly appreciated McKay's potential as a poet, and he wished to see that potential realized in Jamaica. McKay's departure left him with uneasy forebodings and a distinct sense of loss. In the *Jamaica Times* of August 10, 1912, he described his final meeting with McKay.

> We parted in Kingston and our surroundings were dust, hot zinc roofs, noise and other city horrors. But I think we felt we were away in the woods listening to some quietly murmuring brooklet and catching the notes of the John-to-whit concerning which that very week this paper printed a song, by McKay. He is off to a training center in America, to study agriculture and he is not likely to be back within three years. My heart smites me at the thought. Change he must in some things, still I feel pretty confident that the inner man of native modesty and simple beauty is going to defy "the world's coarse finger and thumb." [His] is a lovable disposition and after we [parted] I felt that Jamaica was suddenly a lonely place.[87]

Although he could not have known it when he left in August of 1912, McKay was destined never to return to Jamaica. In the future, the Jamaica he would recall would not be the class-ridden colony of hard poverty and limited opportunities he had written about in his socially conscious dialect poems. It would be the proud, lovely, independent island land he had enshrined forever as part of that lost, idyllic childhood of his imagination. It would be this ideal Jamaica of childhood memory that would nourish him through the restless adventures that lay ahead.

# 3
# The Early American Years, 1912–1919

The apprehension Thomas MacDermot felt on the eve of Claude McKay's departure from Jamaica arose from the sure knowledge that the sensitive young poet would face in the United States a system of race relations that differed radically from his island experience. In Jamaica, there existed a legal structure that theoretically allowed civil equality to all while effectively maintaining a class system that masked a continued discrimination based on race.

Over the years, blacks with education, ability, and property had slowly joined the traditional white and mulatto elites as part of a ruling gentry that subordinated racial differences in the interests of class harmony. While the great black majority remained fated by poverty, illiteracy, and governmental neglect to a permanently inferior status, they suffered few of the brutal denials of legal rights that characterized American race relations during this same period. No elaborate system of formal racial segregation daily reminded black Jamaicans of the social disabilities that in fact still crippled their chances of upward mobility. Along with Jamaicans of all complexions, blacks enjoyed normal civil liberties and a social intercourse largely unfettered by legal restrictions based on race.[1]

By contrast, blacks in the United States, who constituted at most only about 12 percent of the country's population, lived amid a large white majority whose racial prejudices imposed severe limits on black participation in every aspect of national existence. In fact, the status of Afro-Americans in the early twentieth century had reached its lowest level since the Civil War. By legal and illegal means, the Reconstruction amendments guaranteeing them full citizenship had been largely circumvented, especially in the South, and blacks had once again been pushed by the combined forces of law and popular prejudice into a permanently inferior color caste. The white majority that towered over them was by turn benevolently paternalistic and viciously repressive. In such a system, Afro-Americans were at best looked upon as creatures to pity and, at worst, as objects of contempt.[2]

Nothing in Claude McKay's life could have prepared him for the harsh realities he would face upon his arrival in the United States. In Jamaica he had experienced life at all levels of the social structure. And although he had ardently championed the black peasantry and poor city folk in his dialect poetry, he himself had been spared the personal humiliations experienced by those at the very bottom of the island's social structure, no matter how much he recognized their suffering as his own. The McKays were a proud, independent, black Jamaican family who expected to be judged by their ability and achievements. As the youngest McKay, Claude inherited in full measure his family's social aggressiveness and sensitivity to class and racial nuances.[3]

At the age of twenty-one, Claude McKay remained a young man still unsure of his proper role in life. He combined a bold and adventurous mind with a certain need for personal support from an authority figure he could trust and respect. In Jamaica, U'Theo and Walter Jekyll had successively assumed this role for him. In the United States, he looked to Booker T. Washington and Tuskegee Institute for similar support. When he left Jamaica, he did not know that Washington's leadership was already being seriously challenged within black America by new leaders who scorned his compromises with southern segregationists and northern paternalists.[4]

When McKay disembarked in Charleston, South Carolina, in the late summer of 1912, he encountered a system of racial segregation that effectively denied blacks any social or civil intercourse with the white majority except as menials or supplicants. Any deviation from this pattern by blacks in the American South exposed them to severe rebuke, imprisonment, or even death at the hands of a lynch mob.

McKay later wrote of the surprise, horror, and anger he experienced when he discovered for himself the nature of American racial prejudices. "I had heard of prejudice in America but never dreamed of it being so intensely bitter; for at home there is also prejudice of the English sort, subtle and dignified, rooted in class distinction—color and race being hardly taken into account. . . . At first I was horrified, my spirit revolted against the ignoble cruelty and blindness of it all. Then I soon found myself hating in return but this feeling couldn't last for to hate is to be miserable." McKay tried to avoid being consumed by bitterness. "I ceased to think of people and things in the mass—why should I fight with mad dogs only to be bitten and probably transformed into a mad dog myself?" He instead turned to "the individual soul, the spiritual leaders, for comfort and consolation."[5] In times of great stress this type of contemplative retreat would not prove sufficient; in his poetry, McKay would eventually deal much more completely and thoroughly with his hatred of American racial prejudices.

In Charleston, he found white restaurants, water fountains, restrooms, and other public facilities closed to him. And where their black counterparts existed, he almost invariably found them inferior to those for whites. For the black traveler, public conveniences that whites took for granted often simply did not exist. On the train from Charleston to Tuskegee, for example, McKay probably rode with others of his race jammed into a dingy segregated coach with no dining-car service. There must have been moments on that journey through the cool pine woods and hot cotton fields of South Carolina, Georgia, and Alabama when he simply sat in stunned silence. Then, as later, he no doubt found relief in the matter-of-fact vitality and human warmth with which so many native blacks coped with their everyday humiliations. After all, he was not alone. In America, people of his race numbered in the millions. From the common man among them, as well as from their leaders and intellectuals, he would learn much.

Tuskegee, however, proved a disappointment. He noted in 1918 that he had been repelled by the "semi-military, machinelike existence there," but he never elaborated upon his dissatisfaction in any subsequent writings.[6] One can only conclude that McKay found the regimentation of student life personally intolerable. He had always resented discipline imposed upon him by others, whether by members of his family or by the Jamaican constabulary; he had enjoyed the pleasures of independence in Jamaica and had probably looked forward to even more in the United States. The student regulations and

much of the curriculum at Tuskegee must have seemed to him designed for children. He was, after all, twenty-two and could discipline himself. He would not be told how to order his life.

More important, perhaps, Tuskegee provided him with few intellectual challenges. The school emphasized vocational training and the development of character and habits presumably acceptable to the great American middle class. Booker T. Washington's goals were survival, acceptance, and economic success. And as Tuskegee's ruler made clear, his program sought to take students from the poorest and most unpromising environments in the Deep South and recondition them into model citizens through a combination of hard work, discipline, moral training, and a basic education that usually did not go beyond the high school level. For a mature student such as McKay, whose literary education already equaled, perhaps exceeded, that of his teachers, the limited academic program at Tuskegee could not have provided much challenge. There were well-trained teachers at Tuskegee, but their classroom efforts were generally aimed at students much less well prepared than McKay.[7]

Whatever the reasons for his disenchantment at Tuskegee, McKay in 1912 remained awed by Washington's commanding presence. After Washington's death in 1915, McKay movingly evoked the reverence he had felt in the presence of Tuskegee's leader:

> I vividly recall the noon-day hour
> You walked into the wide and well-filled hall;
> We rose and sang, at the conductor's call,
> Dunbar's Tuskegee hymn. A splendid tower
> of strength, as would a gardener on the flower
> Nursed tenderly, you gazed upon us all
> Assembled there, a serried, sable wall
> Fast mortared by your subtle tack and power.

"In Memoriam: Booker T. Washington" was a splendid tribute. It also clearly revealed McKay's initial desire to follow Washington's leadership and to win the older man's approval:

> O how I loved, adored your furrowed face!
> And fondly hoped, before your days were done,
> You would look in mine too with paternal grace.
> But vain are hopes and dreams!—gone: you are gone,
> Death's hand has torn you from your trusting race,
> And O! We feel so utterly alone.[8]

Despite McKay's unquestioning acceptance of the great Tuskegeean's leadership, soon after his arrival at Tuskegee he began to make preparations to leave. For reasons he never chose to explain, he decided to transfer to Kansas State College in Manhattan, Kansas. The move appears to have been made amicably, without any unpleasant confrontation with anyone in Tuskegee's administrative system. McKay simply concluded he could not fit into Tuskegee's system of education. By October, arrangements had been made for his transfer. McKay arrived in Manhattan on October 30 and immediately settled down to "a special" two-year course at Kansas State.

For a Jamaican countryman with a romantic turn of mind, the Great Plains of distant Kansas must have seemed as foreign and exciting as Outer Mongolia. His first impressions were certainly favorable. On November 16, 1912, he wrote to J. H. Palmer, the registrar at Tuskegee: "I registered and took up my studies on the 31st. I like the place very much. The agricultural teaching given although, in some cases, of a very practical nature does not tend to alienate one's mind from the farm, but is never kept longer than two hours at one subject. I have registered for a special course of two years."* McKay thanked Palmer for his kindness to him while at Tuskegee and then noted in a postscript that "board here is high, costing sixteen dollars per month."[9]

McKay remained at Kansas State for almost two years, from the fall of 1912 through the spring term of 1914. His transcript listed Walter Jekyll as his "guardian" and "means of support." McKay designated Jekyll's occupation as "gentleman," a term that undoubtedly had a more specific meaning to McKay than it did to the Kansas State registrar.[10]

Over the years, McKay wrote surprisingly little about his experiences in Kansas. In *McClure's Magazine* in 1928, he implied that Kansas had ultimately bored him, that he could not enjoy there much companionship with members of his own race, and that his eventual move to New York City had, among other things, brought him once again into welcome contact with a large and active black community. These remarks were written in Europe after the first flush of success with his novel *Home to Harlem* and almost certainly exaggerated the sterility of his sojourn in Kansas. In actuality, his two years there proved intellectually stimulating and far from dull, despite the harshly cold winters and long hot summers on the Great Plains. And McKay did associate while there with members of the

*Claude McKay to J. H. Palmer, November 16, 1912, © 1987 by Hope McKay Virtue, 1110 Olive Avenue, Long Beach, Calif. 90813, and used by her permission. This letter is in the Booker T. Washington Papers (Container 459) at the Library of Congress.

small black bourgeoisie that then existed in the cities of the West; during holidays and summer vacations he visited Kansas City, Wichita, and Denver.[11]

It was probably in Kansas, too, that he first began his involvement with radical American politics. According to the Soviet translator of his Russian-language book, *Negroes in America,* McKay while at Kansas State became "a member of a small group of white students with a socialist bent. They were all sons of poor people, and, while studying at the college, took various odd jobs to support themselves."[12] McKay certainly had plenty of opportunity to hear politics discussed in Kansas. Progressive reform was at the moment triumphant in America. Woodrow Wilson had been elected president in 1912 on a reform platform. On the Left, the Socialist Party of America had also reached a peak of influence, as had the militantly active labor union, the Industrial Workers of the World (IWW). The union's insistence on absolute racial equality in all its organizing campaigns especially appealed to McKay. On matters of race, the IWW was clearly well ahead of both the other labor movements and the general society. The Socialist presidential candidate in 1912, Eugene V. Debs, had received almost 900,000 votes. In the very recent past, Kansas had been an important center of populist agitation, and although it never became a Socialist stronghold, in 1912 the most popular Socialist newspaper in the history of the United States, the weekly *Appeal to Reason,* was published in Girard, Kansas.[13]

Of greater importance to his self-understanding, McKay learned from a sympathetic English teacher at Kansas about W. E. B. Du Bois's *The Souls of Black Folk,* which had first appeared in 1903. His curiosity aroused, McKay had to journey to the Topeka Public Library to read the book. It proved an important event in his intellectual development. "The book," McKay later reported, "shook me like an earthquake."[14]

In *The Souls of Black Folk,* Du Bois first publicly criticized Booker T. Washington's accommodationist racial strategy and thereby launched his own career as a major spokesman for militant integrationist forces in America. The book was equally significant for its discussion of the problem of self-identification, which Du Bois maintained gnawed at the heart of the Negro's "spiritual" life in America. Du Bois stated that in the United States, blacks had "no true self-consciousness" but could see themselves only "through the revelation of the other world," that is, through the dominant white society's conception of the Negro. Such a situation, he ventured, created a "double consciousness," a sense of always seeing oneself through foreign eyes, "of measuring one's soul by the tape of an alien world that looks on in amused contempt or pity." As a result, Du Bois declared, "One ever feels his twoness—an American, a Negro; two souls, two thoughts, two unreconciled stirrings: two warring ideals in one dark body, whose dogged strength alone keeps it from being torn asunder." For Du Bois as for many after him, this psychological struggle was of central importance for the Negro in America. In fact, he wrote, "The history of the American Negro is the history of this struggle,—this longing to attain self-conscious manhood, to merge his double self into a better and truer self. In this merging he wishes neither of the older selves to be lost." [15]

Du Bois's message, written with great candor and passion, struck McKay with the force of revelation. In *The Souls of Black Folk,* Du Bois had clearly analyzed not only a central psychological dilemma of American blacks but a problem Claude himself had not been consciously able to confront and resolve in his dialect poetry. *The Souls of Black Folk* forced him to confront his own deepest ambivalence as a black colonial reared in both the folk and the British imperial traditions. The shock he felt upon reading it was the shock of self-recognition.

McKay was not the only black writer to be stirred by Du Bois's book. Langston Hughes wrote that "my earliest memory of any book . . . except a school book, is *The Souls of Black Folk.*" [16] Another black writer, James Weldon Johnson, considered it "a work which . . . has had a greater effect upon and within the Negro race in America than any other single textbook published . . . since *Uncle Tom's Cabin.*" [17] Reading Du Bois's book in lonely isolation all over America, young black intellectuals such as McKay and Hughes saw, perhaps for the first time, a vital part of their own personal problems clearly, passionately, and reasonably discussed. Certainly the problem of black self-integration and self-image was of central importance in McKay's own writing, and it has remained a major theme in American Negro literature.

Kansas State provided McKay time for learning, personal growth, and reflection. But his academic and applied agricultural courses kept him busy. In his *McClure's* article of 1928, McKay wrote that "there were too few Negroes in the college town for any lively social life and for two years I lived austerely and wrote no poetry." [18] An examination of his academic records shows that there would, indeed, have been little time for poetry. His transcripts reveal a full schedule of classes in applied agriculture and a considerable number of academic courses.

McKay entered as a subfreshman. By the spring term of 1913, he had proved himself a capable student. He did his best work in traditional classroom subjects. In his first year at Kansas State, he received Es (for excellence) in zoology and advanced grammar. In ancient history, college rhetoric, elementary botany, elementary math, and English literature he did well (G). McKay did fail two courses—Woodwork I and Stock Judging I—but in the remainder, including public speaking, at which he never excelled, he got Ps (for passing). By the fall of 1913, he had achieved the status of freshman and had scheduled a full course in agriculture—dairying, principles of feeding, sociology, agricultural education, and general entomology. He did excellently in agricultural education but merely passed the rest. In the spring term, his grades improved noticeably: five Gs (in poultry, soils, soils lab, "inter. law," and agricultural economy) and three Ps (pork and meat products, general geology, and insects and spraying).[19] His courses presented him with no serious problems.

But despite his best intentions, McKay had concluded by the summer of 1914 that he would not become an agronomist and that he therefore had no reason to stay at Kansas State. In *A Long Way from Home,* he wrote that after two years in Kansas he had been "gripped by the lust to wander and wonder. The spirit of the vagabond, the daemon of some poets, had got hold of me." He had no desire to return home. "What I had previously done was done," he noted. Just as he had earlier abandoned his wheelwright's apprenticeship in Jamaica, he once more drew back from a practical vocational commitment and dreamed again of writing poetry. "Against [America's] mighty throbbing force, its grand energy and power and bigness, its bitterness burning in my black body, I would raise my voice to make a canticle of my reaction."[20]

This account of his decision to leave Kansas State was, of course, written in retrospect; what McKay omitted was as significant as what he included. He had not left Kansas empty-handed or without plans. For two years, he had corresponded with his Jamaican sweetheart, Eulalie Imelda Lewars, and in the spring of 1914 an unusual gift made it possible for them to plan a reunion and wedding in New York City during the summer. A person whom he later identified only as "an English admirer" of his Jamaican dialect poetry sent McKay "a few thousand dollars."[21] McKay never identified the donor or explained why he proved so generous. At one point, he did write that the money was "a legacy";[22] it almost certainly came from Walter Jekyll. At any rate, whether the money came as a wedding gift or whether its receipt enabled McKay to propose marriage, with it McKay abandoned Kansas for New York City and marriage.

After he spent two years in school and only occasionally visited Topeka and other western cities, the lure of the sophisticated and bustling metropolis in the East no doubt exerted its own powerful attraction upon McKay, as it did upon many other restless and creative writers and artists of the time. But New York seems initially to have attracted McKay for reasons other than art. As the child of an upwardly mobile Jamaican peasant farmer, he knew that with his newly acquired capital he should seek a proper investment. He and an otherwise unidentified "friend," who had decided to accompany him, knew good business opportunities abounded in New York City.[23] With its large, growing black population, including a considerable number of Jamaicans and other West Indians, New York seemed the perfect place to try one's hand in business. In the forefront of his mind there remained the necessity of earning one's way, so, shortly after arriving in New York, McKay invested the greater portion of his money in a business venture: he became a restauranteur.

His bride joined him in New York. On July 30, 1914, at five in the afternoon they were married in Jersey City, New Jersey, just across the river from Manhattan. It was a quiet ceremony, with the Reverend Charles H. Benselar officiating, and attended by only two other people, D. Della Hope and Ambrozine Nelson (perhaps the companion who had accompanied McKay to New York from Kansas), who signed the marriage license as witnesses.[24] Claude McKay was twenty-three years old; his bride was younger but, as it turned out, much more ready for marriage than was her handsome young groom.

McKay had yet to come to terms with himself, his ambitions, and his personal sexual inclinations. As the child of a rising bourgeois family, he clung stubbornly but tenuously to certain standard symbols of respectability—an education, the pursuit of a financially secure career, marriage, and the family. At the same time, he remained unfulfilled by the pursuit of these objectives. A certain unappeased restlessness continued to propel him away from the comforts of middle-class life.

Although he did not fully realize it when he arranged to meet his bride there, New York would provide more than enough stimulation to distract Claude from conventional pursuits and compel him toward his true career as a man of letters. The city overwhelmed him with its size, energy, and variety; above all, he was delighted to find in Harlem, fast becoming New York's principal Negro section, a refuge among his own people where he could at last relax and relieve his pent-up emotions completely. He later wrote that "Harlem was my first positive reaction to American life. . . . After two years in the blue-sky-law desert of Kansas, it was like entering a paradise of my

own people. . . . I gave myself entirely up to getting deep down into
. . . [the] rhythm of Harlem life which still remains one of the most
pleasurable sensations of my blood."[25] In 1914, Harlem did not yet
have the frightfully congested and desperately frustrated population
of its later years. The people were generally poor but hopeful. A fine
new section of town filled with broad avenues, large, spacious apartment buildings, and tree-lined streets had become available to them.
The bright, clear air of Harlem inspired an optimism, a certain in-
definable freedom and exuberance. Despite the problems that remained, and they were many, it was a great time to be young, black,
and ambitious. In Harlem, hope filled the air.[26]

In addition to being the financial and artistic capital of America,
New York City was also well on its way to becoming the center of
black American protest against racial injustices and the focal point of
black artistic and intellectual endeavors. By 1914, the newly organized National Association for the Advancement of Colored People
(NAACP) had established its headquarters in New York. The National
Urban League, also in its infancy, likewise had its parent offices
there. These two groups were rapidly emerging as the two principal
black reform organizations in the country.

In contrast to Booker T. Washington's counsels of patience and ac-
commodation, the NAACP had from its inception in 1907 pushed toward a frontal challenge on constitutional grounds to the system of
legal racial segregation that had grown up in the South and the less
rigid, but no less real, system of discrimination that characterized
the rest of the nation.[27] Since its founding in 1911, the National Urban League had been dedicated to opening new economic opportunities for blacks, largely through the piecemeal method of individually
persuading private businesses in the North to hire blacks in positions
previously closed to them. As its name implied, the Urban League
concerned itself with the social welfare of the growing black popula-
tions in the nation's cities.[28] The presence of the national offices of
the NAACP and the National Urban League ensured that in the years
ahead New York would become the focal point of a veritable Renaissance of black social protest, intellectual rejuvenation, and artistic
activity. Viewed in this larger perspective, Claude McKay was only
one of many young black men of ability, ambition, and social awareness who were for any number of reasons attracted to New York in
the years around World War I.

Despite the rapidly accelerating movement of Manhattan's black
population northward to Harlem, McKay chose (perhaps because it
was cheaper) to take over a small restaurant in one of the city's older

black neighborhoods. He later claimed his restaurant was located in "a tough district of Brooklyn," but James Weldon Johnson in 1928 wrote that it had been located on West Fifty-third Street in the infamous Tenderloin area of mid-Manhattan.[29] This would have placed it in the center of Manhattan's older black area on a street that Johnson fondly remembered "was still a center of New York Negro life" in 1914. McKay denied the accuracy of Johnson's statement.[30] From McKay's own vague testimony and from circumstantial evidence, it seems his restaurant was most probably located somewhere in the vicinity of Myrtle Avenue, adjacent to the downtown Borough Hall section of Brooklyn. In *Home to Harlem,* one character remembers that the black cabarets and gambling joints along Myrtle Avenue during the prewar era were exciting places, but another concludes, "Myrtle Avenue . . . pretty name, all right, but it stinks like a sewer. Legs and feet! Come take me outa it back home to Harlem."[31]

Wherever McKay's restaurant was located, one thing we know is that vice of all kinds flourished around it. His venture carried with it risks both financial and physical. To protect himself, he bought a revolver.[32] As it turned out, financial problems proved far greater than the physical dangers, and after a few months, his restaurant failed. McKay lacked the steady patience and single-minded dedication to business required for even minor success. As he later remembered, "high living" and "bad business" soon swallowed all his money.[33] In 1918, he confessed in one of his only published references to his restaurant that it "proved a failure because I didn't put all my time and energy into it." His marriage was next to go. "My wife," McKay wrote in 1918, "wearied of the life [in New York] in six months and returned to Jamaica."[34] After her return, she gave birth to their only child, Rhue Hope McKay, whom Claude, as it turned out, would never see.

Thus, although the city and its people proved exciting to McKay, his first year in New York ended with bitter failures in business and marriage. Both involved pain for himself and others. He seldom spoke of either in any of his published writings. He became especially secretive about his business failure; unresolved litigation or the threat of it, together with bad memories and perhaps a lingering sense of guilt, drove him to silence on the matter. After the publication of *Home to Harlem* in 1928, McKay wrote James Weldon Johnson, who had submitted a biographical sketch of McKay to Harper, that it would be better not to air the details of his old business venture. Johnson replied that the publisher had fortunately not mentioned anything about the restaurant in its publicity.[35]

But McKay's marriage could not be so discreetly passed over. A child was involved, and despite McKay's belated recognition that for him marriage was really out of the question, his wife had already sacrificed the possibility of further education in Jamaica to join him in New York. Her commitment had been total. She could not understand his warring emotions—his ardor and indifference, his ambitions and his reckless abandon, his gaiety and sudden, inexplicable periods of bitterness, his utter self-assurance and restless, uncertain questing. He bewildered as well as hurt her, and their brief, intense, and ultimately impossible relationship in New York embittered her life. She felt betrayed and abandoned and would in succeeding years try to reestablish a relationship Claude had long since dismissed.[36]

Some have considered the short story "Truant" a straightforward, thinly fictionalized account of McKay's marriage. While it does accurately reflect McKay's personal rejection of marriage, its details do not conform to his actual experience. In the story the character Barclay Oram is working for the Pennsylvania Railroad. His wife is an American black woman; they have a small child and live together in post–World War I Harlem. He had abandoned an education at a leading Negro university to marry her when she became pregnant. He later concludes that his job and marriage represent a dead end for him and quietly abandons his wife and child. McKay's own marriage had taken place under other circumstances and much earlier, and had ended when Eulalie returned in disillusionment to Jamaica. The story nevertheless does project with emotional accuracy, if not factual detail, the personal circumstances of his marriage. He writes that Barclay's wife, Rhoda, had entered marriage "at that vague age when some women feel that marriage is more than the grim pursuit of a career," and that Barclay himself "did not fully realize the responsibility, perhaps could not, of marriage. Never fully understood its significance."

> Barclay remembered now that he was as keen as Rhoda for the marriage. Carried away by the curiosity to take up a new role, there had been something almost of eagerness in his desire to quit the university. And it had seemed a beautiful gesture. . . . He remembered all, regretting nothing, since his life was a continual fluxion from one state to another. His deepest regret was always momentary, arising from remaining in a rut after he had exhausted the experience.
>
> Rhoda now seemed just another impasse into which he had drifted. Just a hole to pull out of again and away from the [rail]road, that arena of steel rushing him round and round in the same familiar circle. He had to evade it and be irresponsible again.

Like McKay, Barclay ultimately decides he is not subject to conventional moral law, "the cold white law. . . . Spiritually he was subject to another law. Other gods of strange barbaric glory claimed his allegiance and not the grim frock-coated gentleman of the Moral Law of the land." Barclay (read McKay) accepts isolation as a necessary condition of his existence. "Maybe," he concluded, "his true life lay in eternal inquietude."[37]

At the heart of McKay's own marriage dilemma, of course, lay his homosexuality. New York, with its great concentration of population and teeming impersonality, tolerated the existence of a large though officially repressed homosexual community whose members found regular, if illicit, outlets for the exercise of their sexual and social tastes. McKay enjoyed this almost clandestine aspect of New York life, and after the dissolution of his marriage he pursued a love life that included partners of both sexes.[38] Most of his affairs were brief but passionate. McKay mentioned at least one of his homosexual relationships in verse. In the commemorative poem "Rest in Peace," he stated explicitly that the person whose unexpected death is reflected upon was "my friend and lover." In other poems, he celebrated brief affairs with partners whose sex is never explicitly stated. They could well have been either men or women.[39] Aside from the occasionally daring reference to homosexual love buried in his poetry, McKay rarely discussed homosexuality in his writings. An exception was one chapter in the unpublished novel "Romance in Marseille," in which he sympathetically portrayed aspects of gay life in Marseilles.[40] In general, however, McKay never openly explored or publicly acknowledged homosexuality as an aspect of his personal life. Although it inevitably emerged indirectly in his published novels and short stories, McKay, like many homosexual writers of his day, did not seriously challenge the rule that such subjects were not to be discussed openly in creative literature. Even if the rule had been relaxed, McKay may not have chosen to identify himself as explicitly homosexual. As in other areas of his life, he remained to the end highly ambivalent about his sexual preferences and probably considered bisexuality normal for himself, if not all mankind.

By 1915, after the failure of his business and his marriage, McKay had begun to move toward his chosen position as iconoclast and rebel. He would go his own way and by trial and error discover which paths best suited him. He abandoned altogether the idea of returning to school. In "Truant," McKay through Barclay Oram hinted at his own gradual liberation from the spell of formal learning: "He had been enchanted by the words: University, Seat of Learning. He had seen young men of the insular island villages returned from the native colleges. They all brought back with them a new style of clothes, a different accent, a new gait, the exciting, intoxicating smell of the city—so much more intriguing than the ever-fresh accustomed smell of the bright-green hill-valley village. . . . For Barclay then the highroad to wisdom led necessarily by way of a university. It had never occurred to him that he might have also attained his goal in his own free, informal way."[41]

In 1915, this realization had become a necessity for McKay. He had exhausted all funds, and no more were forthcoming. He had to find a job. As he explained in *Pearson's Magazine* in 1918, pride, if nothing else, pushed all thoughts of returning to Jamaica from his mind. "I hated to go back after having failed at nearly everything so I just stayed here and worked desultorily—porter, houseman, janitor, butler, waiter—anything that came handy."[42] He also finally decided to write and to discover once and for all the extent of his literary talents. "I was determined to find expression in writing. . . . I took my menial tasks like a student who is working his way through a university. . . . If I would not graduate as a bachelor of arts or science, I would graduate as a poet."[43]

McKay was not the only young man in America intent upon finding his voice in the years just before World War I. As the Irish painter John Butler Yeats had remarked in 1908, the fiddles were beginning to tune up all over America. The historian Henry May has made clear that by 1914 the new "music" from these fiddles had begun to contribute to the breakdown of the old basic assumptions about morality, progress, and Western civilization that the Victorian "custodians of American culture" had established.[44]

World War I and its disruptive aftermath, according to May, completed this process. Between 1912 and 1917—McKay's arrival in the United States and the year he first published in America—there was occurring in literature and art what May has termed the "Innocent Rebellion." In contrast to the less innocent, more thoroughgoing literary upheaval that developed after World War I and in the 1920s, the Innocent Rebellion between 1912 and 1917 was characterized by gaiety, optimism, and cheerful irreverence. Although it did not dislodge the "custodians of culture" from their seats of power in academia, publishing, and the arts, it did prepare the way for their eventual displacement.[45] It was thus a time of great transition, both in the life of Claude McKay and in the history of American thought and art. The old, fundamental assumptions that had dominated American intellectual life since the Civil War—the belief in a universal morality, the inevitability of progress, and the sanctity of inherited Anglo-Saxon cultural norms—were all beginning to be questioned and undermined.

From the small towns and villages of the Midwest, Sherwood Anderson, Carl Sandburg, Floyd Dell, and others had begun to gravitate toward Chicago, where new literary magazines of significance, such as *Poetry* and the *Little Review,* supported their rebellion against nineteenth-century formalism. By 1915, the Chicago rebellion had acquired allies in New York, where younger critics and editors such as Walter Lippmann, Van Wyck Brooks, Lewis Mumford, Waldo Frank, Max Eastman, and Joel Oppenheim added their cosmopolitan outlook and critical acuity to the Innocent Rebellion. Of particular importance were such new magazines as the *New Republic,* the *Masses,* and *Seven Arts.* Their editors and contributors generally felt that they were witnesses to the end of an era and participants in the shaping of a new one. In the process, they rejected what they considered America's repressive Puritan heritage and began a search for a "usable past" upon which to build a brighter, freer, and more equitable future.[46]

Their efforts did not escape the notice of Claude McKay. Although his specific path to rebellion had been different from that of most of his white American counterparts from the East or Midwest, he had much in common with them. Like the young rebels of the prewar years, he had imbibed from infancy the literary culture of England. While Americans were intent upon searching for a usable national past, McKay had begun once again to think about the significance of the black experience in both Jamaica and the United States, to question his relation to it, and to ponder its larger meaning for black people everywhere. Like the young American rebels, McKay had early rejected a repressive Calvinist heritage, had eagerly embraced the more radical European critics of society and culture as they had been presented to him in Jamaica, and had simultaneously attempted in his dialect verse to create a specifically Jamaican poetry. After 1914, he moved toward participation in the larger literary rebellion then gathering strength in America.[47]

At first, his progress was not rapid. McKay had to work for a living, and the jobs he found were the traditional ones open to black men in American cities—"porter, fireman [to coal-burning boilers], waiter, bar-boy, houseman. I waded through the muck and scum," he later wrote, "with the one objective dominating my mind." He would become a poet and writer. "My leisure was divided between the experiment of daily living and the experiment of essays in writing." The years from 1914 until his first big success in 1919 "sped by—five of them—like a rivulet flowing to feed a river." The simile was apt. These years of labor in New York and other cities of the Northeast proved to be a crucial period from which he drew much material for his later stories, novels, and poems. In many of his future writings he would remember his work experiences in both their rich and barren days. During the winter of 1915–1916, he added to his initial restaurant experience by working briefly in a resort hotel in Hanover, New Hampshire. A little later, he found a position as waiter in a fashionable women's club in New York. Finally he entered into the hectic rush and bustle of a job as a dining-car waiter on the Pennsylvania Railroad during the height of America's participation in World War I.[48]

All the while, he was writing and dreaming of finding an appreciative American audience. In his early American verse, he dropped dialect altogether and reverted in part to a stilted imitation of German and English romantic models he had first read in Jamaica. These verses, full of outmoded poetic diction and romantic clichés, often revealed the painful role confusion that still beset him. In some of these poems, McKay addressed himself directly to race and racial conflicts; he already spoke with an originality, directness, and obvious depth of feeling that contrasted oddly with the orthodoxy of his poetic forms and diction.

In January, 1916, while in Hanover, McKay sent samples of his current efforts to William Stanley Braithwaite, the poetry editor of the Boston *Evening Transcript* and the lone light-mulatto pillar of literary respectability among Boston's surviving "custodians of culture."[49] In addressing this well-known critic, McKay adopted an almost girlish tone of shyness and hesitancy and even concealed his real name behind the pseudonym of Rhonda Hope. He explained that he had previously submitted his poetry to several newspapers but they had shown an interest only in those poems that bore directly upon racial themes. "This had set me to wondering," he wrote, "whether Fine Arts is not beyond nation or race—if one's mind can be limited to one's race and its problems when Art is as sublime as He who gave it to man."[50] McKay surely knew of Braithwaite's conservatism. He had been reading his annual anthologies of magazine verse since 1913; after his arrival in New Hampshire, he had also read Braithwaite's columns on poetry every Wednesday and Saturday in the *Transcript*.[51] In part he was attempting to strike a tone that would elicit Braithwaite's sympathy and a response from him. But in part, too, he still had doubts about his literary gifts. If he sought to use Braithwaite by adopting a tone of somewhat hypocritical supplication, it was because at base he needed the older man's reassurance and advice. "I do not write because I am over anxious to win recognition and appreciation," he explained, "but I have often thought that, if my gift is genuine, I should strive for that which might enable me to do yet better work than I can at present."[52] Braithwaite apparently gave him the warm response he sought. In reply McKay thanked him and added that "as a rule the race problem does not inspire me very much to poetic efforts. Of the many things I have written very few are of racial themes, but sometimes my emotions are stirred by something above the ordinary, I feel the urge to write and the thought will not down."[53]

McKay sent Braithwaite seven poems. Three dealt with the inevitable disillusionments of love. One, entitled "Remorse," may well have reflected the pain he experienced after the breakup of his marriage and his wife's return to Jamaica: "I wail, 'I love you, I repent, / Forgive me,'—all in vain." A longer poem in this group, "My Ethiopian Maid," may also have been at least partly inspired by his relationship with Eulalie. He describes his "Ethiopian maid's" fair, creamy brown skin, her sunny round face, her passionate eyes, and beautiful voice but concludes that he can love her only "from afar . . . . ne'er shall I touch you, o beautiful star, / With hands that can only defile." In "My Werther Days," McKay evoked the memory of Goethe's famous character and sang of his own disillusionment and of his inability to rise, like some, above a preoccupation with earthly love and set his heart on "things of heaven."

> I have not faith to turn mine eyes above,
> The strongly-whirling world I but see through
> The splintered window of my house of love.[54]

Despite his wholly justified concern that he not be categorized simply as a black poet writing narrowly on black themes, the best poems he submitted to Braithwaite did, in fact, explore most intimately his emotions as a black in an overwhelmingly hostile world. One of these was "In Memoriam: Booker T. Washington"; the other was an early version of "To the White Fiends," which he later published with the modern forms of "you" substituted for the original "ye" and "thee."[55]

Despite his use of clichés and forced rhyme schemes, McKay was already exploring the almost primeval horrors implicit in American race relations. Although he may have still questioned the legitimacy of such themes as subjects for poetry, they stirred in him emotions and thoughts that, as he noted in his second letter to Braithwaite, de-

manded expression. McKay fully shared his people's deepest emotional reactions to their plight as a suppressed and brutalized race.
Their feelings were, moreover, as "universal" as those of all races and
nationalities. McKay would shortly put aside any doubts about the
appropriateness of racial themes in poetry.[56]

His immediate problem was to find an editor who would publish
his work. His earliest American poems were apparently rejected by
both black and white journals, but he persisted in sending his poems
to those he judged might be most receptive. He wanted the widest
possible audience. Although he would later publish in black newspapers and journals, McKay from the first also sought acceptance
in national publications whose readers were predominantly white.
From childhood he had immersed himself in the literary traditions of
the English-speaking world; now he wanted to be recognized as a legitimate heir to those traditions. The fact that an increasing number
of his poems dealt with the joys, sorrows, and pain of his race did not
mean he felt estranged from those European and American poets
whose works had provided him with his earliest literary inspiration
and models. On the contrary, "I felt more confidence in my own way
because, of all the poets I admire, major and minor, Byron, Shelley,
Keats, Blake, Burns, Whitman, Heine, Baudelaire, Verlaine, and
Rimbaud and the rest—it seemed to me when I read them—in their
poetry I could feel their race, their class, their roots in the soil, growing into plants, spreading and forming the backgrounds against which
they were silhouetted. I could not feel the reality of them without that.
So likewise I could not realize myself writing without conviction."[57]

In reality, few white editors in 1915 and 1916 ever considered giving blacks equal representation in their publications. Black writers as
a rule only occasionally appeared in white publications, and almost
none wrote regularly for journals. William Braithwaite was a rare exception among Afro-American journalists of his day. Had he been as
frank as McKay on matters concerning race relations, even he would
not have survived as a practicing journalist on a large metropolitan
daily.

By 1916, however, certain influential critics and editors had already begun to challenge the national indifference toward black writers. Among the charter members of the NAACP, there were several
prominent editors, journalists, and critics. They included Oswald
Garrison Villard, soon to be editor of the *Nation*, a leading progressive
weekly; the journalists William English Walling and Charles Edward
Russell; and the Columbia University scholar and critic, Joel Spingarn.[58] McKay especially admired the *Nation* and held Villard in high

esteem. A grandson of the great abolitionist William Lloyd Garrison, he carried forward into the twentieth century the highest standards of the nineteenth-century reformists. McKay sent Villard some of his verses in 1916. Although Villard expressed an interest in them, he never published any.[59]

A year later, he had better luck with Joel Spingarn. A central figure during these early years of the NAACP, Spingarn had already distinguished himself in the history of American literary criticism by introducing to the United States the aesthetic ideas of Benedetto Croce, the Italian philosopher and historian, and by the publication in 1917 of his book *Creative Criticism,* which in its essentials anticipated the critical principles in the New Criticism of T. S. Eliot, Allen Tate, John Crowe Ransom, and R. P. Blackmur.[60] McKay read Spingarn's book and wrote to him. Spingarn was sufficiently impressed by McKay's poems to recommend them to the youthful editors of *Seven Arts,* Joel Oppenheim and Waldo Frank.[61]

During its brief existence between 1916 and 1917, *Seven Arts* served as an important platform for the young men of the Innocent Rebellion. Its editors revived Walt Whitman's call for a regeneration of American civilization through literature. They proclaimed their faith "that we are living in the first days of a renascent period, a time which means for America the coming of that national self-consciousness which is the beginning of greatness." By and large, the staff of and the contributors to *Seven Arts* formed the cutting edge of the critical rebellion then in progress against the dead weight of an expiring genteel tradition. They included Paul Rosenfeld, H. L. Mencken, Theodore Dreiser, Amy Lowell, Robert Frost, Van Wyck Brooks, John Dos Passos, and Randolph Bourne. Oppenheim and Frank sought to publish new voices in fiction, poetry, and criticism. They believed literary spontaneity was a necessity if the dying hand of an empty gentility was ever to be removed from the living body of American literature. "We have no tradition to continue; we have no school of style to build up. What we ask of the writer is simply self-expression without regard to current magazine standards. We should prefer that portion of his work which is done through a joyous necessity of the writer himself."[62]

Editors with such standards could hardly refuse the work of a young black man whose lyric forms, though traditional, expressed the spirit and consciousness of black America and uncovered the muffled voice of ancient Africa. In October, 1917, *Seven Arts* published two sonnets by McKay, "Invocation" and "The Harlem Dancer." For these poems McKay used the pseudonym Eli Edwards, which, as he noted in *A Long Way from Home*, "was adapted from my mother's name." He went on to explain that at the time he was working as a waiter at a fashionable women's club in New York. Because its "members were students of the arts" and often discussed "the new and little magazines," McKay believed that he should use a pseudonym in *Seven Arts* so that his job as a waiter would not be compromised.[63]

Both poems suggested that blacks had been cut off from their African roots and placed in false positions by white civilization and the circumstances of modern life. In the sonnet "Invocation," McKay made clear the obstacles that stood between the poet and his ancestral spirit. Foremost among them were the distractions of "modern Time's unnumbered works and ways." But his awe and wonderment before contemporary life could not compensate for the eclipse of that ancient spirit that in the past had itself raised mighty civilizations "in the curtained days / Before the white God said: Let there be light!" Having suggested that the rise to hegemony of European civilization had thrown the African spirit into darkness, he appealed for it once again to

> Bring ancient music to my modern heart,
> Let fall the light upon my sable face
> That once gleamed upon the Ethiopian's art,
> Lift me to thee out of this alien place
> So I may be, thine exiled counterpart,
> The worthy singer of my world and race.[64]

In "Invocation," McKay first clearly revealed his comprehension of a dilemma common to the Western black intellectual: feeling a part of contemporary European civilization, possessing a "modern heart," while remaining fundamentally "exiled" in "this alien place." The dilemma was an old one and had most recently been given classic expression in Du Bois's *The Souls of Black Folk*. McKay would continue to explore its complexities and its ironies in other sonnets published over the next few years. The centrality of this problem in his poetry would place him near the beginning of a long line of twentieth-century black authors who would examine the same problem, each in his own way. Richard Wright would later describe it in *Black Boy* as being "somehow in Western Civilization but not of it." Ralph Ellison after World War II would liken it to invisibility, and in the 1960s, James Baldwin would conclude that "nobody knows my name." In each case, different metaphors, styles, and literary forms would be employed to explore the highly personal yet broadly representative problems of black identity and alienation that Claude McKay began to face during World War I.[65]

In "The Harlem Dancer," the other sonnet published by *Seven Arts*, McKay meditated upon a scene, perhaps in a Harlem bordello, of a woman gracefully singing and dancing before an aroused audience of young men and prostitutes. The poet-observer, however, looked upon the event with detachment. He perceived that the woman, too, was similarly detached. For the poet, half-hypnotized by her voice and the sway of her "perfect, half-clothed body," she became a symbol of another, more distant, bucolic life he sensed still held her allegiance. Momentarily she swept him back to his own tropical past:

> Her voice was like the sound of blended flutes
> Blown by black players upon a picnic day.
>
> . . . . . . . . . . . . . .
>
> To me she seemed a proudly-swaying palm
> Grown lovelier for passing through a storm.
>
> . . . . . . . . . . . . . .
>
> The wine-flushed, bold-eyed boys, and even the girls,
> Devoured her shape with eager, passionate gaze;
> But looking at her falsely-smiling face,
> I knew her self was not in that strange place.[66]

McKay must have been pleased to publish in *Seven Arts*. He shared its pages with some distinguished names, as well as with other young men and women whose reputations would grow in succeeding years. In the same October, 1917, issue in which his work appeared, there also appeared poems by Amy Lowell and Jean Starr Untermeyer, an antiwar essay by Randolph Bourne, and another statement on the war by Bertrand Russell, who questioned whether old-fashioned nationalism could or should survive the great bloodbath in Europe. The issue also contained a statement on black music and its critics by Carl Van Vechten, who, like McKay, was to play a prominent role in ushering in the Negro Renaissance of the 1920s. But McKay's first appearance in *Seven Arts* was his last. The magazine ceased publication with the October issue. The uncompromising antiwar essays of Randolph Bourne, which *Seven Arts* insisted upon publishing in the face of rising governmental and public intolerance of such criticism, frightened away the magazine's wealthy sponsor.[67]

McKay probably would not have continued his association with *Seven Arts* had it survived. His personal involvement with the magazine, its editors, and chief contributors was slight. McKay in 1917 was moving toward a commitment to actual political, as well as literary, rebellion. The editors of and contributors to *Seven Arts*, with few exceptions, never went so far. Their protest remained largely literary and theoretical. Although some considered themselves socialists, they were white, middle-class, college-educated artists and critics whose participation in the radical political movements of their times would never go beyond their roles as critical observers. McKay certainly understood the chasms of class and color that prevented them from ever identifying completely with him and his race. Despite the real appreciation of men like Carl Van Vechten and Waldo Frank for the vitality of the popular Negro arts and music, their identity with it could never be complete. Their exceptional interest aside, the white world to which they belonged generally thought little of Negroes or their accomplishments. Bertrand Russell, for example, in the same issue of *Seven Arts* in which McKay's poems appeared, concluded his essay on the lessons of World War I with the following observation: "Mankind cannot afford to risk another great war. Every advance in technical civilization must make war more deadly, and a great war a hundred years hence might well leave the world in the exclusive possession of negroes [*sic*]. If we wish to avert this calamity we must be bold, constructive, and not afraid to be revolutionary."[68]

McKay's appearance in *Seven Arts* did not change his life—he remained a waiter. Sometime in 1917, he left his position at the women's club to take a job as a dining-car waiter on the Pennsylvania Railroad. It proved to be a memorable experience. In April, the United States entered the tragic conflict in Europe on the side of Great Britain, France, and the new provisional government of Russia. A great democratic world alliance against Germany and Austria, it seemed, had been formed. Using the latest techniques of mass advertising and propaganda to spur patriotism and a united war effort, the United States entered a period of unprecedented national mobilization of men, matériel, and manufacturing. An Allied victory could be assured only by quick action, and on the home front the nation's railroads had to be operated at maximum efficiency to handle the increased flow of men and materials. The traditional private operation of the national railway systems quickly proved incapable of attaining the coordination and economy of command required by the circumstances, and the government soon took over the railroads for the duration of the war. Claude McKay was thus swept by the rush of events into a critical wartime industry. Along with other blacks who had begun during the war years to move in record numbers from the South into northern cities, McKay found all the work he could handle. With the great European immigration of previous years cut off, labor was in short supply everywhere.

Because of their vital role in the war effort, railroad workers were draft-exempt. McKay's new job took him regularly from New York through Newark, Philadelphia, and Harrisburg to Pittsburgh, the very center of America's industrial heartland. Sometimes he also made the Washington run through Baltimore. From 1917 through 1919, he became a regular visitor to the Black Belt neighborhoods of the principal cities of the industrial Northeast and a witness to the enormous energy, chaos, and tensions unleashed during America's first great crusade for democracy abroad.

> We are out in the field, . . .
> Thundering through from city to city
>
> . . . . . . . . . . . .
> Through Johnstown glowing like a world aflame,
> And Pittsburgh, Negro black, brooding in iron smoke,
> Philly's Fifteenth street of wenches, speakeasies, and cops.
>
> . . . . . . . . . . . . . . . . . .
> And darkly we wonder, night-wrapped in the light.[69]

His new job demanded energy and quick wit. McKay had both. He also possessed a decided restlessness and a desire not to linger too long in one place or with one person. The railroad seemed made to order for him. His brief encounters with diners, the constant travel, and his adventures with fellow railway men in the various cities along their route—all provided the challenge, variety, and adventure that suited McKay's temperament. The hectic pace of wartime America complemented the tumult and rush of his own nervous energy. Both seemed at times compressed to bursting in the buzz of a crowded dining car rushing headlong across the eastern countryside.

The hours were in truth often long and tiring, but the pay and tips were good, and McKay stayed with the railroad longer than any similar job he ever had. He did not stick it out, however, for the pay alone. What he wrote of his character Ray, in the novel *Home to Harlem,* had been equally true of his own experience: "If the railroad had not been cacophonous and riotous enough to balance the dynamo roaring within him, he would have jumped it long ago."[70] He did not particularly mind the diners. In fact, he saw in them a certain romance that provided compensation for their occasional unpleasantness. "It was often a pleasure," he once wrote, "something of an anticipated adventure each day to meet new passengers, remark the temperature of their looks and sometimes make casual conversation with a transient acquaintance."[71]

McKay did his job well. He was promoted rapidly over others with longer service and in three months became a first pantryman, the dining-car equivalent of headwaiter. As he later explained to Max

Eastman, "It was no easy assignment, for my associates were tough and conscienceless and I had to see that they did not steal all the supplies to take home. I did my job thoroughly and made them respect and like me."[72]

During the next three years, from 1917 through most of 1919, Harlem remained McKay's home base. He had a spacious furnished room on 131st Street in a rooming house owned by a "Mr. Morris," a southern black man who also owned a saloon McKay frequented while in Harlem. For at least two of these years McKay also had a steady friend in Manda, a homely, wholly unpretentious young black woman recently removed from the South, whom McKay had picked up one night in LeRoy's, an infamous cellar cabaret on the corner of 135th Street and Fifth Avenue, referred to by locals as "The Jungle." As McKay described her in *A Long Way from Home,* Manda was plump, plain, and undemanding. "She was a real peasant type and worked as a laundress in a boarding house." She appreciated McKay's interest in her, and he appreciated her self-sufficiency and uncomplaining acceptance of his "little eccentricities." It became her habit to drop by McKay's room when he was in town. In the course of her stay, she would always tidy up his living quarters. If she found him reading or writing, she would leave him alone and go to the basement kitchen and cook them a meal. In short, she took care of McKay while demanding very little in return. As he would later remember it, they never had "a lot to say to each other" but nevertheless "sailed smoothly along for a couple of years. Manda was a good balance to my nervous self."[73]

One eccentricity that did raise Manda's eyebrows was the friendship McKay developed during these years with a young white man named Michael. Although McKay passed him off as the wayward son of a wealthy businessman, Michael was in reality a small-time crook who blackmailed respectable types after maneuvering them into compromising positions in parks, washrooms, and lavatories around the city. In appearance, this unsavory Irish lad possessed "a disarming cleanliness and wholesomeness" and looked "like a nice college student." As McKay described it, their initial meeting might well have served as material for a scene in a silent "cops and robbers" melodrama. Late one night after a card game, McKay had stopped in a midtown restaurant for a meal when "a young fellow came in, sat down at my table, and taking my cap from the chair, put it on. Before I could say a word about such a surprising thing, he said in a low, nervous voice: 'It's all right, let me wear your cap. The bulls are right after me. . . . They won't recognize me sitting here with you, for I was bareheaded.'" Michael accompanied McKay home that night. For a long time afterward, he made periodic visits to Harlem, where he sometimes in McKay's absence used his room to hide from the police. McKay liked Michael. He was "refreshingly frank" about his exploits, and McKay never felt personally threatened by his new friend, "although I had some dandy suits in my closet and three Liberty Bonds in my trunk." Michael, it seemed, "was profoundly sentimental about friendship, the friends of his friends, and anyone who had befriended him." He hated only the police and the priests of the Catholic church, in whose orphanages he had been reared.[74]

When the mood struck him, McKay made friends easily, and he spent part of his spare time participating in the social life that centered around Harlem's black cabarets. In them, he found others who were, like himself, expatriated countrymen and women, single, often alone, and out for a good time before returning to their rooms or the boring routines of their menial jobs. In the few brief hours of their socializing, they lived with an intensity and abandon that McKay found intoxicating: "The cabarets in Harlem in those days enthralled me more than any theater downtown. They were so intimate. If they were lacking in variety they were rich in warmth and native excitement."[75]

These years proved the decisive period in McKay's life, the crucial turning point, when he broke through the inhibitions that had previously restrained him and discovered a milieu more congenial to his temperament.

> It was not until I was forced down among the rough body of the great serving class of Negroes that I got to know my Aframerica. I was perhaps then at the most impressionable adult age and the warm contact with my workmates, boys and girls, their spontaneous ways of acting on and living for the moment, the physical and sensuous delights, the loose freedom in contrast to the definite peasant patterns by which I had been raised—all served to feed the riotous sentiments smoldering in me and cut me finally adrift from the fixed moorings my mind had been led to respect, but to which my heart had never held.[76]

It was probably during this period, too, that McKay experimented with cocaine and opium. Years later a friend from his railroad days wrote McKay and reminded him of the time they had gone to New York's Chinatown in search of "Chinese tobacco."[77] In *Home to Harlem*, a chapter entitled "Snow Storm in Pittsburgh" relates how the characters Jake and Ray sniff cocaine one night during a layover of their dining-car crew. Jake remarks he doesn't have the habit but is willing to try anything "once again." One of the dealers who sells them the cocaine reminisces about a group he used to know who "hed no use foh nothing but the pipe . . . the Chinese stuff."[78] McKay's flirtation with drugs never developed into habitual use, nor does he ever seem to have developed a serious drinking problem; his finely tuned nervous system needed little of the added stimulation drugs or alcohol provided. But like most everyone else in his social milieu, he did drink and smoke, sometimes to excess. As he grew older, he curbed both habits for health reasons.

All the while, McKay continued to write, to read, and to dream of future literary triumphs. His rushed and harried railroad experiences, the intense if confined vitality of the burgeoning Black Belts of the Northeast, the mounting tensions between blacks and whites as the war threw them into unfamiliar intimacy, his growing understanding that the Great War in Europe represented the death throes of a vanishing era, and his corresponding sense that his old literary idols could provide no sure guidance along the uncertain way ahead— all these varied forces only stimulated his creativity and contributed to a restless output of poetry. Once while waiting tables on a busy train he was seized with such lyrical desire that he could not function. He told the steward he had "unbearable" stomach pains and locked himself in the lavatory, where he wrote out his work on a "scrap of paper."[79]

His appearance in *Seven Arts* had been a fleeting triumph. After its demise, he continued to seek publication in other magazines. At last, in 1918 he received a note from a boyhood idol: the great Irish editor Frank Harris, who had published *Pearson's Magazine* in New York since 1916. Harris informed McKay that he desired to publish some of his poems in *Pearson's* and asked if they could not meet to discuss McKay's work. McKay felt that at last his chance had come. His talent had been recognized by a man who had earlier, as editor of the *Fortnightly Review* and the *Saturday Review* in London, published such talents as Oscar Wilde, George Bernard Shaw, and H. G. Wells. These men and others, whom McKay had idolized from afar, had been befriended at various points in their career by Harris. Now, it seemed to McKay, his own turn had come. Through *Pearson's* he would gain a readership much larger than the one he had enjoyed in Jamaica. His long struggle would be rewarded. After six years in the United States, he felt at last on the verge of success.[80]

To McKay, Harris was "a romantic luminary of the writing world." He had read Harris "avidly" since he had assumed the editorship of *Pearson's* during the war, and had taken personally Harris' first editorial in which he had stated that "the purpose of *Pearson's* was to reach and discover the obscure talents of America who were perhaps discouraged, engaged in uncongenial labor when they might be doing creative work."[81]

McKay's first meeting with Harris took place in Harris' apartment on Waverly Place in Greenwich Village. Harris offered McKay wine, and the two relaxed. McKay reviewed his career in Jamaica, showed Harris scrapbooks full of literary mementos he had brought from Jamaica, and told him of Walter Jekyll, his move to Tuskegee and then to Kansas, and his life in New York. Harris listened with interest. McKay's story set off within the aging man an explosion of memories and opinions. He expounded on the intellectual dishonesty of Herbert Spencer, talked of his own sojourn to Kansas as a young man, and assured McKay he could teach him more in one evening than Jekyll had over several years. As the evening wore on and the wine continued to flow, Harris talked; his wife returned from the theater and went upstairs to bed. Harris continued to talk, reviewing his own career and expounding on the men and events he had known. McKay sat enthralled. He later stated that Harris had launched into his long monologue "like a perfect little boat riding the great waves."[82]

Alone with one of the great conversationalists of the age, McKay witnessed a sterling performance. Harris was in the twilight of a great, if checkered, career, and McKay noted that his "hand had grown shaky as we drank, and he spilled some of the wine as he poured. But it seemed to me that it was more with memories and words that he was intoxicated; that the wine was a tonic only to them." McKay finally took his leave in the early morning hours, "uplifted by Frank Harris' grand voice, roaring like a waterfall in my head." As he later wrote, it had been "nearly an all-night seance," an altogether "unforgettable experience" of a man "talking for the beauty of talking, talking exquisitely, talking sensibly."[83]

The talk resulted in McKay's appearance in the September, 1918, issue of *Pearson's Magazine*. Along with five of his poems, *Pearson's* also printed a short autobiographical statement in which McKay succinctly reviewed his career up to 1918. In it, he included his reaction to the Great War. For him, as for many others around the world, it had swept away many illusions. The old assumptions about the natural superiority of European civilization, which he had incorporated into his early dialect poetry, had already been severely shaken by what he had seen of American racism. "And now," he wrote, "this great catastrophe has come upon the world proving the real hollowness of nationhood, patriotism, racial pride and most of the things which one was taught to respect and reverence."[84] Although he did not mention it in the article, the war also swept away McKay's unquestioned acceptance of European rationalism. In 1944 he noted in a letter to an old friend that "I used to have great faith in agnosticism, up until World War I, when the German and British agnostics or rationalists lost all sense of reason, became rabid nationalists and began denouncing one another."[85]

The statement in *Pearson's* provided important clues to why McKay would eventually turn to religion, but it gave little hint that within a few short months he would embrace international communism. In his most desperate moments he may have sought comfort from the great spiritual counselors of world literature, but in his more hopeful moods he still believed in progress and the efficacy of collective action in human affairs. In Jamaica, he had become well acquainted with Fabian socialism through his brother's interest in the ideas of Sir Sidney Olivier and through his own love of George Bernard Shaw's works. In the United States, particularly in New York, he became acquainted with more radical variants of socialist thought and action.

In addition to the American Socialist party, whose dominant reformist wing most closely resembled the English Fabians, the United States also harbored more extreme adherents to socialist theory. These included revolutionary Marxists and members of the IWW, an anarcho-syndicalist offshoot of the Socialist party, which reached its peak of activity and influence during McKay's first years in the United States. In New York, and perhaps earlier in Kansas, McKay had readily available to him the literature of all these groups. The dramatic strikes, revolutionary zeal, and unadulterated idealism of the IWW certainly aroused McKay's sympathies. If the Translator's Note in McKay's Russian book *Negroes in America* (1923) can be taken at its face value (McKay was in 1923 trying to convince the Russian authorities he was in fact a revolutionary), after he left the railroad sometime in 1919, he took for a brief time a factory job in New York and while there joined the "Wobblies," as IWW members were called. In his book, McKay devoted considerable space to the IWW and lauded its work. In all likelihood, it was in 1918 the one revolutionary organization he most admired, for it was uncompromisingly active and militantly egalitarian in respect to blacks.[86]

McKay's interest in the IWW was almost certainly reinforced, too, by his growing friendship with Hubert H. Harrison, one of Harlem's pioneering black Socialists. In 1913 and 1914, Harrison had, in defiance of Socialist party directives, become an outspoken defender of

IWW activities. When the Socialists suspended him from membership for three months, he left the party.[87] Harrison was the first black intellectual in New York whom McKay got to know really well, and he trusted Harrison's political opinions, which were grounded in a sound knowledge of men and events.[88] Born in the Virgin Islands and educated in New York public schools, Harrison became one of the first and greatest in a long line of Harlem street-corner orators. He also contributed articles and book reviews to a number of newspapers and magazines through the years. A man of imposing physique, encyclopedic knowledge, and rare oratorical ability, Harrison became something of a legend in his lifetime, though he has since been largely forgotten. Henry Miller has described him as a soapbox orator without peer:

> There was no one in those days, . . . who could hold a candle to Hubert Harrison. With a few well-directed words he had the ability to demolish any opponent. He did it neatly and smoothly too, "with kid gloves," so to speak. . . . He was a man who electrified one by his mere presence. . . . Harrison . . . , no matter what the provocation, always retained his self-possession, his dignity. He had a way of placing the back of his hand on his hip, his trunk tilted, his ears cocked to catch every last word the questioner, or the heckler put to him. Well he knew how to bide his time! When the tumult had subsided there would come that broad smile of his, a broad, good-natured grin, and he would answer his man—always fair and square, always full on, like a broadside. Soon everyone would be laughing, everyone but the poor imbecile who had dared to put the question.[89]

Another major influence that steered McKay toward a commitment to political radicalism was the *Masses,* the one literary magazine in New York that gave consistent coverage and support to IWW activities. Quite aside from its position on the IWW, however, the *Masses* could have hardly failed to attract McKay's attention. Described by Daniel Aaron as "that spectacular organ of socialism, anarchism, paganism, and rebellion," it combined concern for artistic expression with a deep social consciousness and an abiding commitment to revolutionary change. The *Masses* printed a broad spectrum of radical opinion and never adopted a rigidly doctrinaire line in politics or art. It proclaimed its certainty that life, spontaneous creativity, and true social justice stood above any particular dogma.[90]

In its very organization and in its every issue, the *Masses* tried to put into practice its professed principles. Its masthead proclaimed: "THIS MAGAZINE IS OWNED AND PUBLISHED COOPERATIVELY BY ITS EDITORS. IT HAS NO DIVIDENDS TO PAY, AND NOBODY IS TRYING TO MAKE MONEY OUT OF IT. A REVOLUTIONARY AND NOT A REFORM MAGA-

ZINE; A MAGAZINE WITH A SENSE OF HUMOR AND NO RESPECT FOR THE
RESPECTABLE; FRANK, ARROGANT, IMPERTINENT, SEARCHING FOR THE
TRUE CAUSES; A MAGAZINE DIRECTED AGAINST RIGIDITY AND DOGMA
WHEREVER IT IS FOUND: PRINTING WHAT IS TOO NAKED OR TRUE FOR A
MONEY-MAKING PRESS; A MAGAZINE WHOSE FINAL POLICY IS TO DO AS
IT PLEASES AND CONCILIATE NOBODY, NOT EVEN ITS READERS—THERE
IS A FIELD FOR THIS PUBLICATION IN AMERICA."[91]

The *Masses* had made its first appearance in 1913, the year of the
IWW-led strike by textile workers in Paterson, New Jersey. It continued to publish until the government banned the November-
December, 1917, issue from the mails because of the magazine's
militantly revolutionary criticism of the American war effort. In February, 1918, the *Masses* reappeared as the *Liberator,* with an editorial
staff now toughened by two wartime trials for sedition and immea-
surably heartened by the recent example of the Bolshevik Revolution
in Russia.[92]

Like others who had been moved by the magazine's commitment
to social justice, McKay had especially liked the *Masses'* superb illustrations and cartoons.

> I liked its slogans, its make-up, and above all, its cartoons. There was a
> difference, a freshness in its social information. And I felt a special inter-
> est in its sympathetic and iconoclastic items about the Negro. Sometimes
> the magazine repelled me. There was one issue particularly which car-
> ried a powerful bloody brutal cover drawing by Robert Minor. The drawing
> was of Negroes tortured on crosses deep down in Georgia. I bought the
> magazine and tore the cover off, but it haunted me for a long time. There
> were other drawings of Negroes by an artist named Stuart Davis. I thought
> they were the most superbly sympathetic drawings of Negroes done by an
> American. And to me they have never been surpassed.[93]

Davis and Minor were only two of the artists whose talents illuminated each issue of the *Masses*. Others included John Sloan, George
Bellows, Art Young, Boardman Robinson, Maurice Becker, and John
Barber. Together they constituted a unique gallery of the period's
noteworthy artists, even though their emphasis on social realism was
soon to be eclipsed by "the advent of modernism" from Europe.[94]

McKay had submitted poems to the *Masses*, but none had been
accepted for publication. In April, 1919, however, the *Liberator* finally printed one of his poems, "The Dominant White," and at least
one person on the magazine's editorial staff took a special interest in
him. Sometime in the spring of 1919, McKay received a note from
Crystal Eastman, the older sister of Max Eastman, the chief editor
who had guided the journal's progress from its inception. In March,

1918, Crystal had joined Max as the co-owner and editor of the new *Liberator*. While Frank Harris evoked for McKay the literary heroes of his colonial boyhood, Crystal and Max Eastman seemed to him the living embodiments of the revolutionary present.[95]

Crystal had liked his poems and his autobiographical statement in *Pearson's*, as well as the latest batch of poems he had submitted to the *Liberator*. She invited McKay to discuss his work with her in the *Liberator* offices on Fourteenth Street. There he met her, a solid woman almost six feet tall, whose handsome face and easy, yet dynamic, grace commanded respect. A labor lawyer who had drafted New York State's first workmen's compensation law, she had also in 1917 cofounded with Roger Baldwin and Norman Thomas the American Civil Liberties Union. As a suffragist, radical feminist, antimilitarist, and socialist, Crystal Eastman had, throughout the recent war, waged unceasing battle against the hysterical repression that had swept the home front and that had not yet receded. Like her brother, she had survived the reactionary climate of the war determined to advance the cause of socialist revolution. In addition she continued to demand equal rights for women. Her hard work, dedication, and achievements as a social reformer and revolutionary, in fact, equaled her brother's.[96]

McKay immediately recognized in Crystal a kindred spirit. Their conversation was easy and relaxed. He told Crystal about his life on the railroad and of that day when his urge to write had forced him into the cramped privacy of the dining-car washroom. When she observed that the retreat had enabled him to produce a poem and thereby rid him of his "birth pains," they had a hearty laugh. From the first, they established a friendship McKay would treasure the rest of his life. "The moment I saw her and heard her voice," McKay wrote in his memoirs, "I liked Crystal Eastman. I think she was the most beautiful white woman I ever knew." For McKay, the essence of her beauty lay "in her magnificent presence." And, he added, "she had a way of holding her head like a large bird poised in a listening attitude." Crystal arranged for him to meet Max, who served as chief editor of the new *Liberator* and who "had final word on all contributions."[97]

Shortly afterward, McKay spent an afternoon with Eastman, who subjected McKay's poems to a close critical examination. What he saw impressed him, and McKay left assured that the *Liberator* would soon publish a whole page of his poetry. As with Crystal, McKay's first meeting with Max Eastman had gone well. While Crystal had surprised and delighted him, Max had seemed to him "the composite personality of *The Masses* and *The Liberator*" he had always imagined him to be: "colorful, easy of motion, clothes hanging a little loosely or carelessly, but good stuff with an unstylish elegance."[98] Max was also without doubt one of the handsomest public figures of his generation. At thirty-six he possessed, like his older sister, the same combination of height, unconscious grace, and striking features that commanded attention and admiration. In addition, Max's distinctive hair, already prematurely silver white, accentuated his distinguished air. Unlike his sister, however, he did not exude an aura of dynamism but appeared very relaxed and attentive, winning those around him by enveloping them in his own apparent self-confidence and objective conviction.[99] To McKay, he appeared the very embodiment of reasonableness and good sense. He would always look upon Eastman as a man whose critical opinions he trusted. Although they would later have differences over politics and religion, McKay usually accepted Eastman's literary judgments, especially his critical evaluations of poetry. Their friendship was to grow, deepen, and survive even those occasionally bitter disagreements that led to temporary silences between them. Eastman was to become a friend to whom McKay would turn in moments of greatest need. Few of his relationships would prove so durable.[100]

In 1919, of course, McKay was not the only young writer who looked upon Max Eastman as a heroic defender of revolutionary truth and justice against a rising capitalist reaction in postwar Europe and America. Since he first assumed the *Masses* editorship in 1913, he had inspired many others with the courage to act upon their own socialist convictions. "Your place," he had written, "is with the working people in their fight for more life than it will benefit capital to give them; your place is in the working-class struggle; your word is Revolution." Joseph Freeman later wrote that "these words were not merely an expression of opinion; they were absolute truth. We remembered them for years, and cited them verbatim to convert others."[101]

After the outbreak of the war, Eastman had spoken courageously against American intervention. In 1918, he and several other staff members of the *Masses* had twice stood trial in federal courts accused under the terms of the wartime Espionage Act with conspiracy to obstruct the draft. In both trials, Eastman's eloquence as a defendant had resulted in hung juries, and the charges were dropped. When McKay met him in 1919, Eastman was at the height of his fame as a militant hero of the American Left, still very much absorbed as the editor of the *Liberator* in battling the mounting Red Scare at home and publicizing the accomplishments of the Bolshevik Revolution in Russia.[102]

Eastman's courageous editorship of the *Liberator,* combined with his good looks and relaxed presence, explain in part why McKay from the first accepted his leadership and critical opinions. But other, less obvious factors were equally important. Despite clear differences in their backgrounds, the two had much in common. Eastman had been born in upstate New York in 1882. Both Eastman's mother and father had been Congregationalist ministers. Like McKay, he had rejected his parents' religion but had remained strongly influenced by his mother, the stronger, more innovative, more aggressive of his parents. Eastman went to Williams College and did graduate work in philosophy at Columbia under John Dewey. Like McKay, he had early acquired a naïve faith in science. Unlike McKay, however, Eastman's uncritical belief in the broad efficacy of the scientific method persisted through most of his life. This blind faith that the methods of science were generally applicable to all areas of human endeavor made the "scientific" socialism of Marx and Lenin especially attractive to Eastman. In 1919, both he and McKay had become convinced that socialism was "an experiment that ought to be tried." [103]

Eastman and McKay also generally shared the same ideas about the arts, especially poetry. Neither was a stylistic innovator; both adhered stubbornly to classical forms in their verse. Although McKay had earlier achieved moments of genuine innovation and originality in his dialect verse, he had abandoned such experiments in the United States and never returned to them. McKay applauded Eastman's attacks on the modernists in art and literature, even though he would eventually be more inclined than Eastman to tolerate such innovators as T. S. Eliot. [104]

Eastman was not obviously egomaniacal like Harris. He represented to McKay all that was finest in the American, Anglo-Saxon Protestant intellectual tradition. Then, too, there was something undeniably aristocratic in Eastman's appearance, apparent self-assurance, and way of life that appealed enormously to McKay. In one of his earliest surviving letters to Eastman, McKay wrote, "I was glad to see how you live—so unaffectedly free—not striving to be like the masses like some radicals, but just yourself. I *love* your life—more than your poetry, more than your personality." [105]

Eastman took the place that Jekyll had occupied in McKay's life: patron, friend, confidant, and sympathetic critic. Although he was McKay's senior by only eight years, in many respects he became, like Jekyll before him, a father figure for McKay. This situation had its inevitable ironies. As William O'Neill has made clear in his biography, Eastman harbored deep insecurities of his own, despite his outward calm. His relationship with his own father had never been intimate and he himself had a series of father substitutes. As the youngest child in his family, Eastman, like McKay, always had doubts about his personal adequacy. Like McKay, too, he had always been a "mama's boy." Unlike McKay, he never allowed whatever homosexual inclinations he may have had to surface. He instead became a practicing advocate of free love between men and women and had innumerable affairs. In his forties, he did eventually establish a stable, though nonmonogamous, union with his second wife.[106]

From the first, the friendship between Eastman and McKay went beyond a mere patron-client bond, even though this would always be an undeniable element in their relationship. This aspect of their friendship resulted partly from their initial acquaintance as editor and author, partly from Eastman's far more secure position as a middle-class white man in a white society, and finally from the fact that McKay never succeeded as well as Eastman in making and keeping money. No matter how precarious Eastman's finances were at any given time, he usually had more money than McKay and was always willing to help him. On his side, Eastman sincerely admired and respected McKay as a man and a writer. He was convinced that McKay had something he feared he himself lacked—lyric genius. He always insisted that McKay remain true to his vocation as creative artist and writer. Naïvely and with a wholly unconscious condescension, he believed he had discovered in McKay the greatest lyric poet the Negro race had ever produced. Eastman soon came to appreciate, too, McKay's company—his quick wit and ready laugh, his sharp, intuitive political judgment, and his alertness to social and intellectual nuances. Eastman also quickly learned that McKay could be moody and remote or bitingly sarcastic and bitter. At such times, he left McKay alone. Eastman knew McKay as a black had cause for bitterness most white Americans could only imagine. Their friendship had, after all, begun during a time of extreme tension throughout the nation and the world.[107]

In the transition to peace, the nation in 1919 was reacting with fear and violence toward the unsettling changes the war had wrought at home and abroad. The specter of Communist revolution had already become a reality in Russia, and from there threatened all of Europe. Now, at the war's end, it seemed that a Communist leader might also gain control of Hungary. A Communist attempt to seize power in Germany had been temporarily thwarted, but the newly created Third Communist International had already announced its intentions to spread its revolutionary activities to every capitalist nation, including the United States. In the spring of 1919, unknown terrorists in America had almost succeeded in mailing packages containing bombs to several important government officials. The crusade to make the world safe for democracy had evidently not made the United States immune to the radical consequences of the Great War in Europe.[108]

In the United States a rising tide of disillusionment and reaction had set in against the consequences of the war and against President Wilson's efforts to effect through American acceptance of the Versailles treaty the machinery to avert another world war. A hurried demobilization of troops, fears of a severe economic recession, a rapidly rising rate of inflation, and an outbreak of labor-management disputes in industry had all combined to exaggerate the fear that revolution threatened the internal stability of the United States. These events enabled those who sought scapegoats to direct the nation's aggression from the German Hun to foreign-born political radicals within the United States. They were perceived as diabolical carriers of the new Bolshevik plague. The resulting Red Scare in the spring and summer of 1919 led to mob action against radicals and to police raids on radical organizations and their meetings. Mass arrests eventually resulted in the deportation of several hundred East Europeans from the United States to Russia.[109]

This rising nativist reaction to distant events in Europe represented only half of the domestic hysteria unleashed in 1919. America's black population also suffered as a result of the reactionary dementia that seized the nation. The demands of wartime industry for labor had led to an accelerated migration of blacks to urban industrial areas of the North. In addition, 200,000 black soldiers had served in France. Everywhere the traditional patterns of race relations appeared threatened. In the South, blacks on the move, blacks in the army, blacks with any initiative whatsoever were all looked upon as potential troublemakers. Lynchings rose dramatically and in 1919 reached a crescendo of primal savagery. Several blacks were tortured and burned at the stake in ritualistic mass exorcisms of southern communal fears.[110]

In the North, events took a different turn. There blacks had moved into urban milieus different from those in the South and had entered jobs traditionally held by white European immigrants. As in the past, blacks also occasionally allowed themselves to be used as strikebreakers in fiercely bitter industrial disputes. Some were unwittingly hustled into these positions by agents promising high salaries and steady jobs. Others knowingly undercut the collective efforts of white laborers because they knew these same workers had often barred blacks from their unions. In the rising labor turmoil of 1919, blacks became easy targets for many disaffected urban whites in the North, who already felt threatened by rising inflation, an uncertain job market, and the social changes of the war years. The new black migrants further threatened them with more job competition and inexplicable cultural differences. Differences in skin color only accentuated all the other sources of conflict between blacks and whites in 1919. By the war's end, Negroes had come to embody for the northern industrial worker many of his worst frustrations and fears. As a consequence, the Red Scare became for blacks the Red Summer of 1919, a nightmare of bloody riots and violent death. From May until January, there occurred no less than twenty-five racial riots in urban centers throughout the country. The Chicago riot in July was perhaps the worst. When it was over, authorities counted 38 Negroes and whites dead, more than 520 injured, and many more homeless.[111]

Black hopes for a better life had been raised by the changes World War I had brought to their lives and by the Wilsonian rhetoric extolling America's role as a defender of democracy. They had expected a larger share of justice at home, and at the end of the war they were in no mood to acquiesce meekly in the destruction of their limited gains.[112] It was against this background of international change and domestic reaction that Claude McKay first met Crystal and Max Eastman.

Through the spring and summer of 1919, McKay still held his job as a dining-car waiter on the Pennsylvania Railroad. Since his arrival in the United States he had suffered great anguish over the cruel inequalities of American race relations. His emotions ranged from horror through gloomy depression and self-pity to forthright anger. Outbreaks of mob violence against blacks never left him indifferent. McKay's description of the character Ray in *Home to Harlem* was equally true of himself: "Any upset—a terror-breathing, Negro-baiting headline in a metropolitan newspaper or the news of a human bonfire in Dixie—could make him miserable and despairingly despondent like an injured child. While any flash of beauty or wonder might lift him happier than a god."[113]

Because his job carried him constantly from city to city, McKay traveled during the first half of 1919 with an almost constant dread of imminent danger. He remembered those days most vividly in *A Long Way from Home:* "Traveling from city to city and unable to gauge the attitude and temper of each one, we Negro railroad men were nervous. We were less light-hearted. We did not separate from one another gaily to spend ourselves in speakeasies and gambling joints. We stuck together, some of us armed, going from the railroad station to our quarters. We stayed in our quarters all through the dreary ominous nights, for we never knew what was going to happen."[114]

As McKay suggested, blacks in the summer of 1919 were prepared to strike back when attacked.[115] Although McKay abhorred violence, he believed in self-defense and hated the injustices around him. Like Ray in *Home to Harlem,* he was a "reservoir of intense emotional energy. Life touched him emotionally in a thousand vivid ways. Maybe his own being was something of a touchstone of the general emotion of his race."[116]

In the face of gathering violence, he began to write poems filled with hatred for those who would drown in blood all black hopes and aspirations. After the heavy clouds had gathered and the storm of racial turbulence had broken across the nation, he carried these new poems to Crystal and Max Eastman. Max did not hesitate to publish them. As early as 1912, he had advised blacks in a *Masses* editorial to arm themselves, and when attacked, to fight back: "We believe there will be less innocent blood and less misery spread over the history of the next century if the black citizens arise and demand respect in the name of power than there will be if they continue to be niggers (that is to say, servile), and accept the counsel of those of their own race who advise them to be niggers."[117]

By the spring of 1919, McKay at last stood ready to proclaim his own political militancy and to plunge into the turbulent, exhilarating waters of revolutionary politics and art. His previous life seemed but a slow preparation for such commitment. With the *Masses* and the *Liberator* he could both serve the cause of social justice and find himself as writer and artist.

In the July, 1919, *Liberator,* Eastman printed seven poems by McKay in an explosive two-page spread. With heavy sarcasm and devastating irony, McKay contrasted the nobly expressed ideals of America at war and the actual conditions of mob violence and primitive passions that prevailed within its borders:

> Black Southern men, like hogs await your doom!
> White wretches hunt and haul you from your huts,
> They squeeze the babies out of your women's wombs,
> They cut your members off, rip out your guts!
> It is a Roman Holiday: and worse:
> It is the mad beast risen from his lair,
> The dead accusing years eternal curse,
> Reeking of vengeance, in fulfillment here—
> Bravo Democracy! Hail greatest power
> That saved sick Europe in her darkest hour![118]

After "A Roman Holiday," there followed "If We Must Die," an exhortation to black men not to go meekly:

If we must die, let it not be like hogs
Hunted and penned in an inglorious spot,
While round us bark the mad and hungry dogs,
Making their mock at our accursed lot.
If we must die, O let us nobly die,
So that our precious blood may not be shed
In vain; then even the monsters we defy
Shall be constrained to honor us though dead!
O kinsmen! we must meet the common foe!
Though far outnumbered let us show us brave,
And for their thousand blows deal one deathblow!
What though before us lies the open grave?
Like men we'll face the murderous, cowardly pack,
Pressed to the wall, dying, but fighting back![119]

Frank Harris the previous summer had urged McKay not to hold back his real feelings when writing of mob violence against his race but to rise and storm the heights, "like Milton when he wrote 'On the Late Massacre in Piedmont.'" Harris had pointed specifically to McKay's sonnet "The Lynching" as an example of a poem whose expressed sentiments did not really plumb the horror of racial repression in the United States. In it McKay had compared the mutilated black victim of a lynching to a Christ figure and had commented upon the satanic, unearthly "glee" with which men, women, and children went through the rites of his crucifixion. Harris had objected that "a sonnet like this, after reading the report of the St. Louis Massacre in 1917 . . . sounds like an anti-climax." He had then quoted Milton: "Avenge O Lord! thy slaughtered Saints whose bones / Lie scattered on the Alpine mountains cold." Those lines, Harris had stated, "have the sublime human cry of anguish and hate against man's inhumanity to man. Some day you will rip it out of your guts."[120]

In the summer of 1919, McKay at last responded to the desperate conditions of his people with an unsparing, unapologetic condemnation of those responsible for the violence against them. In "If We Must Die," he appealed directly to his people to resist with courage and determination those who would murder them. The poem eloquently expressed black America's mood of desperation and defiance that summer. McKay had first read the poem to the men of his dining-car crew. They had reacted with intense emotion. Even the irresponsible fourth waiter, a man afflicted with "a strangely acute form of satyriasis," had wept.[121]

Whatever flaws one may find in the construction and diction of "If We Must Die," whatever echoes one may hear in it of the heroic sentimentalism of Victorian England, McKay had written a poem that immediately won a permanent place in the memory of a beleaguered people. Because of it, American blacks embraced him and have ever since claimed him as their own. "Indeed," McKay eventually concluded, "that one grand outburst is their sole standard of appraising my poetry."[122] White America has remained less impressed. As late as September, 1971, *Time* magazine could report that rebellious black inmates at Attica State Prison in upstate New York had "passed around clandestine writings of their own: among them was a poem by an unknown prisoner, crude but touching in its would-be heroic style, entitled 'If We Must Die.'"[123]

McKay's dramatic appearance in the July, 1919, *Liberator* marked his definitive break with the status quo. In his poems he did not merely condemn racial injustices; he renounced the entire social, economic, and political order that had allowed these injustices to occur. In so doing, he joined other American radicals, black and white, who after World War I looked to the Bolshevik Revolution in Russia as an example of how to achieve the unfulfilled democratic promises of the "old regimes" throughout Europe and America. Like other radicals, McKay yearned for a restructured Western civilization in which Negroes, along with all men, could live in dignity and freedom. McKay's denunciation of white America was thus qualified by his belief that in a future social system dedicated to the worker, not the capitalist, black and white laborers would no longer have to compete for the "almighty dollar" but could work together for a classless society. Only by a communist reordering of society could either blacks or whites achieve true freedom.

It should be emphasized that the most important and enduring ideological aspect of McKay's rebellion was the fierce, unswerving loyalty he demonstrated toward the "common people" of his race, a loyalty that amounted at times to an incipient black nationalism and that seemed to contradict other aspects of his thought. In the four years following World War I, McKay would reveal in clear, unmistakable terms his disgust with the American system of race relations. Against a system apparently bent on depriving blacks of their basic human dignity, McKay lashed out in his poetry with a virile and unabashed hatred rarely equaled by any American writer, black or white. In the process, he did not refrain from criticizing the more conservative members of his own race for what he considered their timidity and neglect of duty.

Almost all the poems in his July, 1919, *Liberator* appearance dealt directly with racial themes. One exception was a sardonic portrait entitled "The Capitalist at Dinner." In the best cartoon tradition of the period, "the capitalist" is depicted as a disgustingly fat man with a pimply bald head, seated before an overladen table:

> The entire service tries its best to please
> This overpampered piece of broken health,
> Who sits there thoughtless, querulous, obese,
> Wrapped in his sordid visions of vast wealth.
> Great God! If creatures like this money-fool,
> Who hold the services of mankind so cheap,
> Over the people must forever rule,
> Driving them at their will like helpless sheep—
> Then let proud mothers cease from giving birth;
> Let human beings perish from the earth.[124]

In a poem entitled "The Little Peoples," McKay noted that in Europe "the big men of the world" had met and decreed that "the little nations that are white and weak" should henceforth be free. Then observing that the position of black men had not changed, despite the great events of Europe, he taunted them for their apathy:

> But we, the blacks, less than the trampled dust,
> Who walk the new ways with the old dim eyes,—
> We to the ancient gods of greed and lust
> Must still be offered up as sacrifice!
> Oh, we who deign to live but will not dare
> The white man's burden must forever bear![125]

In the context of its presentation, "If We Must Die" was a veritable call to arms. By appearing in the *Liberator,* McKay willingly cast his lot with those despised radicals who were defiantly announcing the death of Western capitalism and the birth of an international proletariat revolution. At the age of twenty-nine, he had made his commitment.

Since his arrival in the United States in 1912, McKay's inability to fit into the conventional order had led successively to his leaving college, failure in business, and a broken marriage. Even in Jamaica, where racial handicaps had been less pressing, his social sensitivity had made adjustment difficult. Once he was in the United States, his being a Negro undoubtedly added enormously to the problems created by his intense emotional life. He was made forcefully aware of the harsh ambiguities involved in being a Negro in America and, indeed, throughout the Western world. His tendency to rebel, already evident in Jamaica, only increased as the reasons for rebellion multiplied. When his rebellion finally burst forth on the pages of the *Liberator,* he was prepared for full-fledged participation in radical politics.

# 4
# McKay in England, 1919–1921

McKay's July, 1919, appearance in the *Liberator* signaled the beginning of his life as a professional writer. Although he would sometimes find it necessary to seek other work, by and large he would spend the rest of his life as a writer—poet, journalist, novelist, and essayist. Approaching his thirtieth birthday, he had finally arrived at his life's work as a man of letters. The years immediately ahead would be fruitful, exciting, and often joyous. They would also be a time during which McKay's literary development and political commitments would mature together in a tense, unstable conjunction.

A warm editorial endorsement by Max Eastman accompanied McKay's explosive midsummer appearance in the *Liberator*. Eastman wrote that "his attitude toward life is like Shelley's, free and yet strenuously idealistic. . . . I wish he would write more poems as mettlesome and perfectly chiselled throughout as some of his stanzas are. And I think he will, for he is young and has arrived at the degree of power and skill revealed in these poems practically without encouragement or critical help. To me they show a fine clear flame of life . . . not to be forgotten."[1]

In the long Red Summer of 1919, McKay also evoked favorable responses in the nation's black newspapers. "If We Must Die," in particular, was widely reprinted. It provided yet another indication that black Americans had begun to pass beyond the reach of white terror into a new age of self-assertive independence and ideological innovation. In New York, the Jamaican journalist and radical W. A. Domingo perhaps best summarized the mood of many American blacks. "New Negroes are determined to make their dying a costly investment for all concerned. If they must die, they are determined that they shall not travel the valley of the shadow of death alone, but that some of their oppressors shall be their companions. . . . [Their] creed is admirably summed up in the poem of Claude McKay."[2]

Although segregation and racial exploitation still remained throughout the American South, many black Americans nevertheless saw hope for the future. They were encouraged by the consequences of the Great War, by the black man's continued northward migration, by the aggressive civil rights militancy of the NAACP, and by the collective possibilities opening to them as a result of all these changes. As Alain Locke wrote in 1925, "The mind of the Negro seems suddenly to have slipped from under the tyranny of social intimidation and to be shaking off the psychology of imitation and implied inferiority. . . . The multitude perhaps feels as yet only a strange relief and a new vague urge, but the thinking few know that in the reaction the vital inner grip of prejudice has been broken."[3]

Appearing during a month of major riots in Washington and Chicago, McKay's poems in the July *Liberator* articulated this determination of black Americans to be free in the fullest sense, even in the face of terror. Although his voice came from a new and unexpected quarter, most American blacks welcomed its message as their own. Afro-Americans were growing used to diversity. Booker T. Washington's behind-the-scenes attempts to corral all black leaders had never succeeded. By 1919, the NAACP had clearly taken the lead among black organizations, but other groups and viewpoints contested its leadership. While the NAACP pushed insistently for fair play and equal rights as the constitutional guarantees of all American citizens, other blacks were already rejecting its legalistic, middle-class, integrationist goals for more extreme solutions to the injustices confronting them.

Since 1918, the African Zionism of Marcus Garvey's Universal Negro Improvement Association and African Communities League had been attracting increasing numbers, both in the United States and abroad. Like Claude McKay, Garvey was a Jamaican immigrant who had been attracted to the United States by Booker T. Washington's Tuskegee program. Garvey had dreamed of emulating Washington and leading Jamaicans out of their poverty. Once he was in the United States, his dreams of black redemption grew to encompass all blacks everywhere. Garvey's ambitions were limitless. He planned to lead a triumphant return of his people to Africa and there resurrect the glory of black civilization. But blacks in the New World, he believed, had first to be awakened, organized, and led toward the ultimate goal of Pan-African nationhood. In New York during World War I, Garvey had begun his great crusade. A squat, powerful figure, he communicated his message with eloquence and passion. He preached racial pride and a positive assertion of black initiative to free the race from its subservience to white standards and goals. He soon created an organizational apparatus of pageantry and power to complement his demagogic talents. Among unsettled blacks throughout the nation, especially those in racially tense cities North and South, he recruited many devoted followers and an even larger number of sympathizers. Garvey had a ready answer to the white racist reaction of the postwar period: blacks would create their own nation and leave white America to its own devices.[4]

McKay early recognized the impractical, dangerously utopian nature of Garvey's goals, even as he envied his fellow Jamaican's ability to stir the masses. When McKay had read "If We Must Die" to his fellow railroad men, one had immediately suggested that he recite the poem in Liberty Hall, Garvey's headquarters in New York. The suggestion had made McKay uncomfortable. "As I was not uplifted with his enthusiasm for the Garvey Movement," McKay remembered, "yet did not like to say so, I told him truthfully that I had no ambition to harangue a crowd."[5]

McKay belonged neither to the middle-class protest tradition of the NAACP nor to the grass-roots black nationalist camp of Garvey's Back to Africa movement. He was ideologically closest to a small but articulate group of black intellectuals, then only just emerging in Harlem, who were convinced that black interests would be best served in the kind of world advocated by international socialism.

In 1919, the only member of this group McKay knew well was Hubert Harrison, who had lately turned to Garvey in an effort to steer him closer to his own broadly socialistic ideas. Harrison was the eldest of Harlem's black socialists, the most experienced, and the most eclectic. He had already tried life in the American Socialist party and the IWW, and had concluded that blacks needed to organize themselves more effectively if they were to exert any influence on modern reform. He therefore sought to use his ability and experiences within Garvey's UNIA to steer blacks toward more effective participation in the socialistic and nationalistic struggles for self-determination that agitated peoples around the globe in the years after World War I.[6]

There were younger intellectuals, however, who, like McKay, were only just emerging as left-wing essayists, editors, and political activists in Harlem. Chief among them were A. Philip Randolph and Chandler Owen. Their new monthly magazine, the *Messenger*, presented to the black community in 1919 a socialist alternative to the reformism of the NAACP. Randolph and Owen were so articulate that many thought them better read than, in fact, they were. Some even mistakenly believed Randolph to be a Harvard graduate. Under their leadership, the *Messenger* quickly emerged as an exciting black monthly. Randolph and Owen were American blacks, and Randolph in particular brought to their joint endeavors the magnificent presence and self-possession of the southern black religious orator.[7]

Several other young men in Harlem were also struggling in 1919 to organize politically and to articulate their positions in other new magazines. These included Cyril Briggs, Richard B. Moore, and W. A. Domingo, all West Indians. Briggs came originally from Nevis and, until 1918, had been an editor of the New York *Amsterdam News*, the Negro weekly. He had started his own monthly, the *Crusader,* and an independent Crusader News Service, which supplied news items to black newspapers across the country.[8]

Like Garvey, Briggs believed in black self-determination and in the eventual establishment of a black nation in the American West or elsewhere. Unlike Garvey, Briggs was a socialist. He recognized that Garvey's extreme black nationalism placed him on the same footing with the most extreme white racists, and he also knew that the UNIA's Back to Africa program was mostly fantasy. In 1919, Briggs founded a semisecret revolutionary organization, the African Blood Brotherhood, which dedicated itself to "a liberated race; absolute race equality—political, economic, social; the fostering of race pride; organized and uncompromising opposition to Ku Kluxism; rapprochement and fellowship within the darker masses and with the class conscious revolutionary workers; industrial development; higher wages for Negro labor, lower rents; a united Negro front."[9]

Briggs was a capable polemicist and organizer, despite a severe stutter, which limited his effectiveness as a speaker. A sprinkling of thoughtful young blacks in the urban North joined his brotherhood. Among them was Richard B. Moore from Barbados, who shared leadership responsibilities with Briggs. Moore developed into an orator of electrifying passion and clarity. Others who joined the brotherhood included Claude McKay, Lovett Fort-Whiteman, Otto Hall, and his younger brother Harry Haywood in Chicago. Within two years the African Blood Brotherhood would merge with the Communist party to form the first sizable group of black American Communists.[10]

Another notable West Indian radical in New York was W. A. Domingo. Domingo had been the first editor of Garvey's newspaper, the *Negro World*, but he had soon found it impossible to deal with Garvey's egomania. In 1919, he wrote for the *Messenger,* and in 1920 established his own short-lived magazine, the *Emancipator.* Domingo eventually established a successful import business in New York City. In the 1930s he would emerge as a spokesman for Jamaican nationalism.[11]

McKay shared many of the political ideas of this new generation of black intellectuals and political activists, but as a literary artist he had succeeded in gaining publication in a revolutionary magazine that addressed itself to the widest possible American audience.[12] Although no less race conscious, McKay moved aggressively onto the center stage of American literary radicalism. Although alert to racial slights and slurs, he assumed his rights as a literary artist to move among his equals and to present through his writings a black perspective on contemporary life.[13]

McKay had only just established his new association with the *Liberator* when an unexpected opportunity arose for him to visit England. Like the money that had enabled him to leave Kansas, the offer of a free trip to Europe came from wealthy admirers of his Jamaican dialect poems. In *A Long Way from Home,* McKay identified his patrons as "the Grays," a brother and sister of uncertain European origin whom he never otherwise explicitly described. They were utopian idealists. Before 1912, the brother had corresponded from Singapore with Walter Jekyll about the possibility of establishing in the Far East "an international utopian colony for intellectuals and creative talents." When *Songs of Jamaica* appeared in 1912, McKay had received a letter of congratulations from Gray. Six years later in 1918, after his poems appeared in *Pearson's,* McKay again heard from him. Gray announced that he and his sister would be coming through New York on their way from Japan to Europe and would like to meet McKay. After the outbreak of World War I, their international colony had been broken up by the host government. Its members, unable to resolve their differences over the war, had gone their separate ways.

McKay found the Grays nice but colorless. Mr. Gray in particular surprised him. He appeared "lank and limp and strangely gray-eyed and there was a grayness in his personality like the sensation of a dry sponge." His sister was stronger and more prepossessing. McKay thought Gray's vanity must have been "vastly greater than his intelligence" for him ever to have imagined "himself capable of being the inspirer of an international colony of happy humanity." He nevertheless showed the two around Harlem, introduced them to Frank Harris, and generally tried to be a gracious host. Much to his surprise, they responded by offering him the opportunity to live with them in Spain. After much soul-searching, McKay said that although he appreciated their offer and wanted very much to visit Europe, he did not think it would be possible for him to live with them for any extended period of time. Although they were surprised by McKay's refusal, they appreciated his candor. As an alternative, they offered him a vacation abroad. McKay accepted and arranged a trip to England.[14]

It seemed time for a change. He had already left his railroad job. He had no personal commitments that tied him to New York, and, perhaps most important, he wanted some respite, however brief, from the pressure-cooker tensions of living black in white America. McKay left for England in the early fall of 1919. In the past, he had capitalized upon the publication of his dialect poetry to escape from Jamaica to the United States. Later he had used money from Walter Jekyll to flee Kansas State for New York City. Now, having just gained fresh notoriety as a militant black poet in New York, he was once again, with the help of admirers, leaving for new adventures. Armed at last with revolutionary hope and zeal, the idealistic "black Briton" of former days was finally going home.[15]

When he arrived, he found a drabness in the land and the people, a remoteness of spirit, along with unconscious assumptions of superiority on the part of Britons toward their colonial subjects that altogether destroyed whatever vestiges still remained of his schoolboy love of England. He even had a hard time finding a room. He wanted to live near the British Museum but found that blacks were considered unsuitable tenants. After much searching, he finally found temporary quarters in the home of a French family residing in London. This experience left him embittered and wary.[16]

McKay's British "vacation" nevertheless turned into a lengthy sojourn. He was abroad for over a year and a half. And except for brief visits across the Channel to Holland and Belgium, he remained in England, settling in London. Like any visitor, he saw the sights, went to lectures, museums, and theaters, and tried during his first weeks in London to orient himself in his new environment. It proved difficult. He disliked its dampness and air pollution, not to mention its citizenry, whom as a rule he found to be "a strangely unsympathetic people, as coldly chilling as their English fog."[17]

Despite his adverse reactions to London and Londoners, he did find friends and soon began to divide his time among several diverse groups. One consisted of black West Indians and Africans, a varied lot of soldiers, sailors, students, struggling professionals, and athletes, most of whom did not share McKay's enthusiasm for international communism. Within Britain itself they had discovered among all classes a general ignorance and indifference (even hostility) toward colonial peoples and their problems, which tended to draw them together. In fact, peoples of Africa, the West Indies, the Middle East, and Asia who met in Great Britian after World War I discovered that they shared many problems.[18]

A West Indian student from Oxford introduced McKay to a club for colored soldiers in London, located in a basement on Drury Lane. McKay became a regular visitor. There he met many Africans, West Indians, and "a few colored Americans, East Indians, and Egyptians." He listened with interest to their accounts of personal "war experiences in France, Egypt, and Arabia." They in turn were curious about black life in the United States; McKay hastened to acquaint them with black American newspapers and magazines. "I brought to the club copies of . . . *The Crisis, The Messenger, The Negro World,* the Pittsburgh *Courier* and the Chicago *Defender*." McKay enjoyed the camaraderie of the soldiers' club and the friends he met there. One Jamaican soldier took him on "a holiday trip" to an army camp in Winchester, and there he undoubtedly met others with whom he could share memories of home. In the larger perspective, of course, this was a seed time for the anticolonial revolts and independence movements that would come to fruition in Africa, Asia, and the Caribbean after World War II. During the 1920s and 1930s, many future leaders from these areas would live and study in the great metropolitan capitals of Europe. During McKay's residence in London, for example, the future Chinese Communist leader and diplomat, Chou En-lai, arrived in Paris as a student. There over the next four years, he met other future Chinese Communist leaders, as well as Ho Chi Minh, the future leader of the Vietnamese Communist party.[19]

Before McKay left New York, Hubert Harrison, the new editor of Garvey's *Negro World*, had asked him to submit articles from England. He now obliged by writing a series on the colored soldiers' club. Only random copies of the *Negro World* from the 1919–1920 period have survived, and none includes McKay's articles. In *A Long Way from Home,* however, McKay noted that when they appeared, the white matron who managed the soldiers' club had been offended by his description of her "patronizing white maternal attitude toward her colored charges."[20] After this, McKay appeared less often at the club. But he had already gained there a circle of friends and acquaintances, some of whom he introduced to another club he frequented.

This was the International Socialist Club, an old establishment that dated from 1849. Located in East End, Shoreditch, it had become by 1919 a hotbed of "dogmatists and doctrinaires of radical left ideas: Socialists, Communists, anarchists, syndicalists, one-big-unionists, and trade unionists, soap-boxers, poetasters, scribblers, editors of little radical sheets which flourish in London."[21] There, McKay met Jewish intellectuals from Russia, Poland, and Germany and left-wing nationalists from Czechoslovakia, Italy, and Ireland. The International Club lacked the irreverent bohemianism of Greenwich Village and the romantic lyricism of the *Masses* and the *Liberator*. McKay instead discovered there men and women totally absorbed in revolutionary theory and politics. "There was an uncompromising earnestness and seriousness about those radicals that reminded me of an orthodox group of persons engaged in the discussion of a theological creed." At this point, McKay's own commitment to revolutionary socialism was firm. Marxists predominated at the International Club, and their debates soon revealed to McKay how little he actually knew about socialist theory.

To hold his own in such serious company, he had no recourse but to read Karl Marx, the great theoretician of communist revolution. After his long absorption in English literary traditions, he found Marx difficult. As he later remembered, "Much of it was like studying subjects you dislike, which are necessary to pass an examination. However, I got the essential stuff. And a Marx emerged from his pages different from my former idea of him as a torch-burning prophet of social revolution. . . . I marveled that any modern system of social education could ignore the man who stood like a great fixed monument in the way of the world." McKay perceived that Marx had outlined "a new social system for the world"; he accepted this system, even rejoiced in its possibility.[22] But McKay never really substituted Marxist analysis for his own highly romantic, intuitive grasp of the necessity for socialism. Intellectually, his roots remained in Victorian and Edwardian England, and he would later assert that John Stuart Mill had been a greater economist than Marx. One suspects he actually learned more from the wit of George Bernard Shaw and the flaming intensity of his new socialist companions than from Marx's writings.[23]

At the International Socialist Club, McKay heard "most" of England's "outstanding extreme radicals." They included "Walton Newbold, the first Communist Member of Parliament; Saklatvala, the Indian Parsee and first unofficial Communist Member of Parliament; A. J. Cook of the Miner's Federation . . . ; Guy Aldred, an anarchist editor; Jack Tanner, a shop steward committee leader; Arthur McManus and William Gallacher, the agitators from the Clyde; [and] George Lansbury, the editor of the *Daily Herald*." As the only black visitor to the club, McKay added to its international atmosphere by bringing along some of his West Indian and African friends, including "three soldiers from the Drury Lane Club, and a couple of boxers." In due course, the boxers even staged an exhibition at the club, much to the wonderment of its members. The International Club also offered other social activities, mainly dances, that provided McKay with opportunities to become well acquainted with many of its regulars.[24]

The club gave McKay an entrée into the passionate, frustrating world of England's extreme political Left, which stood in 1919 in embattled opposition to the dominant Labour party. For some time, there had existed in Britain an extremely vocal, though very small, number of Marxist socialists who considered parliamentary democracy a sham and the traditional Labour party leaders servants of the establishment. They were convinced that a revolutionary proletariat was necessary if capitalism was ever to be replaced by a socialist system.[25]

The end of the Great War once again meant confrontation between capital and labor on the home front, and with the example of the Bolshevik Revolution in Russia before them, the Marxist Left in England, though miniscule, stood poised to seize its chance. The Marxists did not, however, present a united front. Although their total numbers probably never exceeded ten thousand, they had never united in one party. Aside from those independent souls who existed in lonely isolation within the Labour party and among rank-and-file unionists, revolutionary Marxists were in 1919 split into three rival organizations. The largest of these was the British Socialist Party (BSP), an outgrowth of the original Social Democratic Federation. Over the years it had grown less militant and more electoral-minded. By 1919, it had even affiliated with the Labour party and had become the least revolutionary of the three major Marxist groups.[26]

Unlike the BSP, the rival Socialist Labour Party (SLP), originally inspired by Daniel De Leon's party in the United States, had not compromised with existing electoral politics. Like the Bolsheviks in Russia, it had instead sought to maintain a hard core of strictly disciplined revolutionists dedicated to preparing the masses through propaganda and industrial organization for the coming struggle for power. Being elitist and austerely ideological, it had never attracted as many members as the more fraternal BSP.[27]

The third notable Marxist faction in Great Britain in 1919 was the Workers' Socialist Federation. Its guiding spirit was Sylvia Pankhurst of the suffragist Pankhurst family. Before the war, Sylvia, her two sisters, Adela and Christabel, and their mother, Emmeline, had led an army of militant British suffragettes in a determined quest for the right to vote. Sylvia had also been concerned with the plight of the poor and the broader questions of social justice. Even before World War I, she had begun to train and organize women in London's slum-ridden East End for participation in both the suffragette and socialist movements. During the war, women's suffrage was at last accepted as inevitable, but the larger injustices within the social system remained. Sylvia, therefore, transferred all her passion and energy to the cause of social revolution. Her weekly, the *Women's Dreadnought,* became the *Workers' Dreadnought* and her East London Federation of Suffragettes was transformed into the Workers' Socialist Federation (WSF). A "self-giving fury" had joined the thin, scattered ranks of Britain's Marxist revolutionaries. Sylvia Pankhurst's commitment to the socialist cause was total and unsparing, and her tiny band of suffragettes and revolutionary idealists soon added Claude McKay to its numbers.[28]

McKay almost certainly had heard of Sylvia Pankhurst before he left the United States. The Pankhurst family's militancy in the cause of social justice for women was legendary, and Sylvia's adherence to revolutionary socialism was also well known. Whether McKay was familiar with her activities or not, she knew of him. In mid-September, 1919, the *Workers' Dreadnought* reprinted a column of McKay's poems from the July *Liberator,* along with an explanation that they were written by "a negro [sic] of Jamaica, who, when he wrote them, was a waiter in an American dining car."[29] Once he arrived in London, McKay soon became more intimately acquainted with the activities of Pankhurst's Workers' Socialist Federation. The organization was active at the International Socialist Club. WSF members, including Pankhurst, spoke before it; they also held some of their organizational meetings and social fund-raisers there. It was probably at the International Club that McKay first met members of the *Workers' Dreadnought* staff, who invited him to contribute to their weekly.[30]

In his memoirs, McKay stated that he heard Pankhurst speak at the club but that he did not meet her until April, 1920. At that time she published a letter that McKay had originally written to George Lansbury, editor of the *Daily Herald,* London's only socialist daily. The *Herald* had been engaged in a propaganda campaign to stop French occupation of the Ruhr Valley in Germany. The *Herald* feared the French action might topple the shaky Weimar Republic and pave the way for a return to power of German reactionaries and extreme nationalists. Hoping to arouse public opinion against the French, the *Daily Herald* played upon the racial fears of its readers by publishing a front-page article on April 10, 1920, entitled "Black Scourge in Europe: Sexual Horror Let Loose by France on Rhine." The piece contained numerous tales of sexual atrocities committed by French African troops in Germany. By its unfounded insinuations of black hypersexuality and gross sexual anatomy, the article slandered the black race in general with racist smears of the worst kind. Written by E. D. Morel, a left-liberal champion of blacks in Africa who had earlier exposed King Leopold II's infamous regime in the Congo, the article touched off international protests against French intervention, which Morel nourished for more than a year with further racist charges. The *Herald*'s editor, George Lansbury, a prominent socialist and Labour politician, declined to print McKay's letter of protest. The letter subsequently appeared in the *Workers' Dreadnought* on April 24, 1920, the only substantial reply to Morel's racial allegations from the British radical press.[31]

In his letter, McKay rejected Lansbury's editorial explanation that he was not seeking to encourage racial prejudice by printing Morel's article. In fact, McKay maintained, the false statements about black sexual anatomy and ungovernable lust contained in Morel's article would do incalculable harm to the cause of racial understanding that Lansbury professed to champion. McKay confessed himself "quite ignorant of the well-known physiological reasons that make the raping of a white woman by a negro resultful of serious and fatal injury." Violent rape, he reminded Lansbury, often entailed injury or death, no matter the perpetrator's race. "Why all this obscene, maniacal outburst about the sex vitality of black men in a proletarian paper?" Certainly blacks were no more lustful than those European colonials abroad who had produced the countless "mulattoes, octoroons, and eurasians disowned of the Caucasian race." The charge that blacks were "sexually unrestrainable" he dismissed as "palpably false. I, a full-blooded Negro, can control my sexual proclivities when I care to, and I am endowed with my full share of the primitive passion." McKay went on to say that the substantial issues involving French exploitation of Germany and the true facts of French conscription of black African troops were "clearly" matters "upon which the French Socialists should take united action. But not as you have done. I write," McKay concluded, "because I feel that the ultimate result of your propaganda will be further strife and blood-spilling between the whites and the many members of my race, boycotted economically and socially, who have been dumped down on the English docks since the ending of the European war. . . . The Negro-baiting Bourbons of the United States will thank you, and the proletarian underworld of London will certainly gloat over the scoop of the Christian-Socialist-pacifist *Daily Herald.*"[32]

In *A Long Way from Home,* McKay stated it was only after Pankhurst received this letter that she invited him to her office and offered him steady employment as a member of the *Dreadnought* staff. McKay also left the impression in his autobiography that his letter to the *Herald* was his first contribution to the *Dreadnought.*[33] Such was not the case. As early as January 10, 1920, the *Dreadnought* published two poems by McKay; other poems and articles followed throughout January, February, and April. Despite this discrepancy, McKay may have been correct about his first meeting with Pankhurst. During the fall and early winter of 1919, she had been abroad in Italy and Germany, and did not return to England until January, 1920.[34] By then McKay had almost certainly met other members of the *Dreadnought* staff at the International Socialist Club. They probably passed on McKay's initial *Dreadnought* contributions to Pankhurst, who accepted them without having actually met their author. If this supposition is correct, his fiery letter to Lansbury, often the target of *Dreadnought* barbs, may well have prompted Pankhurst to meet McKay and offer him employment.[35]

Regardless of how McKay first met Pankhurst and her followers, his involvement in their newspaper and party activities placed him squarely in the middle of Britain's revolutionary Left. From its inception in October, 1917, Pankhurst had actively defended the Bolshevik seizure of power in Russia. Like other revolutionary idealists, she had hoped working-class reaction against the war would soon bring similar revolutions to western Europe and Great Britain. She had given up on British parliamentary democracy. Despite labor representation, Parliament remained firmly in the hands of the ruling class. Time after time, official labor leaders and politicians had proved willing to compromise when they should have militantly pressed for fundamental changes in class relations.[36]

In July, 1918, Sylvia had founded the Russian People's Information Bureau to disseminate the truth about the course of the Russian

Revolution and to help combat the reactionary forces arrayed against it in Britain. In September, 1919, she attended the Italian Socialist Party Congress in Bologna. From there, she traveled to a sectional meeting of the newly formed Third Communist International (Comintern) held in Amsterdam and then went to Germany, where she met with leaders of Spartacus, revolutionary German Communists whose dynamic leaders, Rosa Luxemburg and Karl Liebknecht, had been murdered early in 1919. Pankhurst returned to England in January, 1920, fully aware of the renewed strength of conservative reaction throughout western Europe. In England, she redoubled her efforts to prevent the shipments of munitions to Polish and other anti-Bolshevik forces in eastern Europe. The WSF daily picketed the gates and harangued the workers on the East India Docks, urging them to refuse to load ships with arms bound for Poland.[37]

The WSF's other major concern in 1920 revolved around the Third International's order that Great Britain's divided revolutionary socialists unite into a single Communist party capable of collaborating with the Labour party. The Pankhurst organization had early declared its allegiance to the Third International, but had balked at the idea of participating with the Labour party in electoral politics.[38]

When in early January, 1920, Claude McKay cast his lot with Pankhurst's Workers' Socialist Federation, all the groups involved in the controversy about the nature and direction of the future Communist party of Great Britain were claiming allegiance to the Comintern and all felt that their policies would eventually receive its vindication and blessings. In *A Long Way from Home,* McKay gave no indication of how deeply he became involved in these complicated proceedings, although he did discuss some of the reasons he joined the WSF and the *Workers' Dreadnought* staff. Foremost among them was his admiration for Sylvia Pankhurst, whom he remembered as "a personality as picturesque and passionate as any radical in London." Here was a woman who lived her socialist convictions and expected others to do the same. McKay recalled that she was "a plain little Queen-Victoria sized woman with plenty of long unruly bronze-like hair. There was no distinction about her clothes, and on the whole she was very undistinguished. But her eyes were fiery, even a little fanatic, with a glint of shrewdness. . . . And in the labor movement she was always jabbing her hat pin into the hides of the smug and slack labor leaders. . . . And wherever imperialism got drunk and went wild among native peoples, the Pankhurst paper would be on the job." In April, when Pankhurst offered him enough money for room and board in exchange for "some work for the *Workers' Dreadnought,*" he jumped at the chance. No doubt he needed the money—the Grays' generosity could not have supported McKay for long—and besides, "the opportunity to practice a little practical journalism was not to be missed."[39]

By April, he had in fact already contributed five poems and three articles to the *Dreadnought*. In these early pieces, McKay proclaimed his allegiance to international communism, attempted to explain the American racial situation to British readers, and declared his abiding conviction that "socialism should step in to bridge the gulf that has been created between the white and coloured workers by Capitalism and its servant, Christianity."[40] For McKay, communism provided a secular faith to which he could devote himself and a practical program of revolutionary action that blacks could follow to free themselves from racial oppression and place themselves in a position of true equality with white Europeans. McKay expressed both his ardent faith and his deep longing for black self-assertion and independence in his initial contributions to the *Workers' Dreadnought*, two poems entitled "Travail" and "Samson," which appeared January 10, 1920. In "Travail," he revealed the truly religious intensity with which he (and many others of his generation) embraced the new Communist internationalism that had emerged out of World War I and the Russian Revolution. For him, as for many others, international communism quite simply represented "the grandest purpose, noblest path of life / There—where high passion swells is my heart's desire."[41] At the same time, in "Samson," McKay spoke in purely biblical and racial terms while addressing his fellow blacks:

> O sable Samsons, in white prisons bound,
> Wounded and blinded, in your hidden strength
> Put forth your swarthy hands; the pillars found,
> Strain mightily at them until at length
> The accursed walls, reared of your blood and tears,
> Come crashing, sounding freedom in your ears.[42]

The high tension displayed in these two poems between hopes for international brotherhood and a more narrow but equally fervent racial loyalty remained characteristic of McKay. In numerous poems and articles during his Communist years, he freely expressed both sentiments.

After January 10, other poems and articles by McKay quickly followed. For a number of reasons many of his *Dreadnought* contributions appeared under pseudonyms. McKay had first used his pseudonym Rhonda Hope back in 1916 when he wrote to the critic

William Stanley Braithwaite.[43] His reasons then were probably shyness and fear of rebuff. Now he had more serious reasons for wishing to hide his identity. Pankhurst's group and her newspaper were under constant police scrutiny. One member of the WSF had already been sentenced to six months' imprisonment for inciting rebellion in the army. Pankhurst's right to travel abroad had long been denied; her fall trip through western Europe had been made illegally. Given the legal uncertainties and tensions that surrounded each issue of the *Dreadnought,* many of its contributors understandably chose to remain anonymous or to use pseudonyms.[44]

While all this was in the time-honored tradition of European radicals, McKay may also have had additional reasons for signing many of his *Dreadnought* poems with a pseudonym. While his *Dreadnought* verses were obviously expressions of deep emotions and firm convictions, many could only be characterized as proletariat doggerel. Because they were clearly inferior to his best efforts and overtly propagandistic, McKay was very likely relieved to acknowledge only a few as his own. After he became regularly involved in the weekly production of the *Dreadnought* in the summer and fall of 1920, he began to use pseudonyms for almost all his contributions; the only exceptions were a few book reviews. By contrast, the first three articles he wrote in January and February, 1920, had all been signed "Claude McKay," an indication that his involvement with the *Dreadnought* was at first casual. McKay's pseudonyms for his later articles were Hugh Hope, E. Edwards, C. E. Edwards, Ness Edwards, and Leon Lopez. All these "contributors" disappeared from the *Dreadnought,* never to reappear, after McKay left England at the end of 1920.[45]

McKay's first *Dreadnought* article, "Socialism and the Negro," appeared at the end of January, 1920. In it, he summarized the racial situation in the United States and surveyed from a radical perspective the diverse efforts of reformers, socialists, and Garveyites to resolve the racial problems besetting the country. Most significantly, he revealed that "although an international Socialist, I am supporting the [Garvey] movement, for I believe that for subject people, at least, Nationalism is the open door to Communism." McKay then chided those English Communists who turned their backs on the Irish and Indian independence movements simply because they were nationalistic. In his opinion, their position was myopic, perhaps even self-serving.[46]

By reminding British revolutionaries of their anti-imperialist duties, McKay aided Pankhurst in twisting the tails of laggard British revolutionary lions. In 1920, McKay wanted revolution and was impatient with anything less. In "Song of the New Soldier and Worker," he concluded a description of "the hungry, hideous huge machine" of capitalism by exclaiming:

> O pull the thing to pieces! O, wreck it all
>     and smash
> With the power and the will that only holy hate
>     can give;
> Even though our broken bodies may be caught in
>     the crash—
> Even so—that children yet unborn may live.[47]

This poem appeared in the *Dreadnought* in early April under the pseudonym Hugh Hope. After his letter to George Lansbury on April 24, however, McKay published nothing more in the *Dreadnought* until July 3.

This break occurred because during this period he became involved in preparing a large group of his poems for publication in another journal. C. K. Ogden, the critic and editor of the prestigious *Cambridge Magazine,* had decided to publish a generous sampling of McKay's best lyrics. McKay never explained how his friendship with Ogden had begun; he only stated in *A Long Way from Home* that Ogden had steered him "round the picture galleries" and had been generally kind.[48] McKay had very likely submitted his poems for Ogden's consideration, along with letters of introduction from the United States, for Ogden said in *Cambridge Magazine* that McKay "came to England with introductions from three of the leading editors in America, and a collection of unpublished manuscripts."[49]

Ogden, whose reputation as a literary theorist grew enormously in the 1920s and 1930s, had, during World War I, been a consistent advocate of peace and international understanding. Toward these ends, he had instituted in *Cambridge Magazine* a monthly digest of news gleaned from the press of all the belligerent countries. As an advocate of international understanding and justice, he was not at all intimidated by McKay's Bolshevism. He certainly liked McKay's poetry. In fact, Ogden stated that with "the exception of Siegfried Sassoon's 'Base Details,'" he had "seen nothing of equal literary interest from a young poet since Rupert Brooke sent us his essay on Tchekov."[50] In Ogden, McKay had once again found an influential and effective ally, who eagerly set about winning for McKay the widest possible audience.

In June, 1920, Ogden included in the summer issue of *Cambridge*

*Magazine* twenty-three of McKay's sonnets and other short lyrics. Although none was propagandistic verse from the *Dreadnought,* a few did contain bitterly ironic commentaries on the racial problem, the stress of working-class life, and the spiritual emptiness experienced by many in New York and other large cities of the capitalist world. These themes would always be present in McKay's work, and he combined them in *Cambridge Magazine* with two of his other basic poetic concerns—the inevitability of love and its disillusionment, and a pervasive nostalgia for the Jamaica of his childhood.[51]

These were all subjects McKay had first developed in his Jamaican dialect poetry, and he now expressed them in the conventional, even anachronistic style of late-nineteenth-century Victorian neoromanticism. Despite his political radicalism, McKay in his poetry remained firmly attached to the poetic forms, if not always the themes, accepted by the literate elite of late-nineteenth-century Jamaica. He had far surpassed the expectations of his Jamaican critics, but to a greater extent than he ever acknowledged, their stylistic tastes in poetry had, in the process, become his own.[52]

Since his first letters to William Stanley Braithwaite back in 1916, McKay had been seeking a publisher for the poems he had written since leaving Jamaica. In Ogden, he had found an influential friend who aided him in his search. By the time McKay's verses appeared in *Cambridge Magazine,* Ogden was already helping arrange the fall publication of his poetry by the London firm of Grant Richards. A long-standing ambition had at last been achieved.

In July, McKay once again turned his full attention to the *Workers' Dreadnought* and to Sylvia Pankhurst's Workers' Socialist Federation. The Pankhurst group continued to resist the directive of the Comintern that all of Great Britain's Marxist parties and factions unite into a single Communist party willing to affiliate with the Labour party. On June 19, 1920, the WSF met in convention with a few like-minded allies, principally the tiny South Wales Socialist Society. Together, the two groups unilaterally transformed themselves into the Communist Party (British Section of the Third International) [CP (BSTI)].[53] Pankhurst immediately set out for Moscow to present her case in person before the Second World Congress of the Third Communist International scheduled to begin in July.[54]

During Pankhurst's absence, McKay resumed writing for the *Dreadnought* and began in earnest his duties as a regular member of its staff. Pankhurst expected him not only to contribute poems and book reviews but also to report on developments in the London dock area and elsewhere that were of particular interest to him as a black colonial. Finally, he was to cull regularly from the foreign press those items he deemed of interest to *Dreadnought* readers. In this latter activity, McKay worked with a young Finn named Erkki Veltheim. Veltheim also used the cover name of Andersen, but to McKay and those who worked with him on the *Dreadnought,* he was Comrade Vie. Pankhurst's secretary hinted to McKay that, although he was only twenty-two, Comrade Vie had an important role to play in the international Communist movement. In *A Long Way from Home,* McKay stated that they divided the task of surveying the world's press between them. McKay "read foreign newspapers from America, India, Australia, and other parts of the British Empire . . ."; "Comrade Vie read the foreign-language papers, mainly French and German." They also collaborated as writers. McKay corrected his English and Comrade Vie "criticized" McKay's articles in an effort to make them "more effectively radical."[55]

The *Dreadnought* continued to pursue an aggressively revolutionary course. It kept up its "Hands Off Russia" campaign, supported the Irish rebellion, reported upon revolutionary events in Russia and elsewhere, and argued against any compromise with Britain's parliamentary establishment. Its pages were filled with the wrongs suffered by the poor of England and the colonies.[56]

From July through November, McKay contributed his full share to the *Workers' Dreadnought.* During this five-month span, he wrote a total of twenty-four articles, poems, and reviews, in addition to performing his editorial duties. In his articles, McKay tried to apply his growing knowledge of Marxist theory to the political problems that confronted the Pankhurst organization and the working class in general. Although not always profoundly original, these articles revealed the extent of McKay's involvement in revolutionary Marxism in 1920, and they also provide some insight into the reasons for his eventual retreat from it.[57]

Like his contemporary Ezra Pound, though from a radically different perspective, McKay was fascinated by the monetary problems of the postwar period. In several articles, he reviewed the efforts of the Allied powers to piece together an international monetary system that would best allow the dominant classes in their respective societies to reconstruct and maintain their old privileges. As McKay saw it, they had a difficult task that could only be accomplished at the expense of the defeated nations and the workers of all countries. And in the process new rivalries were emerging among Great Britain, Japan, and the United States. New York now supplanted London as the financial center of the capitalist world, a fact that clearly signaled an approaching end to British imperial dominance around the world.[58]

Besides his reviews and articles on international finance and Marxist strategy and tactics, McKay also wrote other articles of topical interest. He attended the Communist Unity Conference held on July 31 and August 1, 1920, which established the Communist Party of Great Britain (CPGB). It had won the backing of Lenin and the Third International and put Pankhurst's CP (BSTI) in the uncomfortable position of minority opposition. For this reason, perhaps, McKay cynically reported in the *Dreadnought* that "what impressed me most as I followed the dreary and strict parliamentary routine of the Unity Conference was how so many of the speakers delighted in dialectical oratory and how others seemed enamoured with the melody of their own voices."[59]

In the remainder of his article, he summarized the views of Tom Watkins, a radical Welsh miner, on Robert Smillie, the leader of the Miners' Federation. In 1918, Smillie had achieved great prominence because of his skillful representation of the miners' case for public ownership and workers' control of the coal mining industry on the Sankey Commission, which had, in fact, recommended the nationalization of mining. The government had not acted on this recommendation, and many on the Left felt that Smillie had been duped into accepting far less than the commission had recommended. As Tom Watkins told McKay, "Smillie was fooled and now his obsession is to redeem himself."[60]

Aging, thoroughly upright and honest, a labor leader from the days of Keir Hardie's prime, Smillie was a self-made man who, despite his ideological conservatism, tried to remain faithful to the best interests of the miners. Smillie fascinated McKay, perhaps initially because of Crystal Eastman's interest in him, and later because of the charisma of the man himself. In September, McKay traveled to Portsmouth, where he reported the deliberations of the official Trade Union Congress. Although generally very critical of the rank-and-file trade union apathy displayed there and of the skillful suppression of meaningful debate by the labor officials who dominated the proceedings, McKay once again singled out Smillie as the honorable exception. He later wrote that "Smillie was like a powerful ash which had forced itself up, coaxing nourishment out of infertile soil, and towering over saplings and shrubs. . . . When he stood forth to speak the audience was shot through with excitement, and subdued. . . . I remember his passionate speech for real democracy in the Congress. . . . You felt Smillie had convinced the delegates, but when the vote was taken it went against him." At the congress, McKay sought out the radical Welsh delegates from the Rhondda Valley in south Wales. They received him warmly, and one of their leaders, A. J. Cook, talked at length about the British labor movement. Smillie, McKay later wrote, also "said a few wise words to me about the necessity of colored labor being organized, especially in the vast European colonies, for the betterment of its own living standard and to protect that of white organized labor." McKay returned to London highly pleased with his visit to Portsmouth, but when Pankhurst came back from Russia she "sharply reproved" him for praising Smillie, who, after all, was an official labor leader.[61]

McKay smarted at the rebuff; he was especially resentful because Pankhurst had earlier suppressed an article he had written about a large lumber mill near the *Dreadnought* offices. The workers at the mill had struck for better pay, and in the ensuing struggle, as McKay learned from the strikers, William Lansbury, the owner, had employed nonunion workers. Writing with Comrade Vie, McKay had exposed this practice, emphasizing William Lansbury's family connections with the editor of the socialist *Daily Herald*.

Pankhurst had declined to print the exposé. Years before, as a militant suffragist and social reformer, she had twice avoided arrest because William Lansbury had smuggled her out of town hidden beneath bundles of wood on the floor of his lumber wagon. Besides, she owed his relative, George Lansbury, twenty pounds, not to mention money she had borrowed from the *Daily Herald* in order to print the *Dreadnought*. McKay ruefully concluded that "after all, . . . there are items which the capitalist press does not consider fit to print for capitalist reasons and items which the radical press does not consider fit to print for radical reasons."[62]

McKay learned more about the strange twists and turns of human loyalties from Pankhurst's trip to Russia. She had gone determined to press upon Lenin and the Comintern the correctness of her position concerning the future direction of British communism. Once in Russia, however, her fierce resolve gave way before the skillful persuasion of Lenin and the spectacle of the new Bolshevik government's heroic struggle for survival. The best interests of international communism, she decided, dictated the British Communists should follow the course laid down by the Comintern. She consequently returned to England and persuaded her group to prepare to unify with the CPGB. For a time, at least, Sylvia Pankhurst had subordinated her quixotic zeal for truth to Lenin's policy of Communist *realpolitik*.[63]

This process had hardly begun when a new storm descended upon Pankhurst, the *Dreadnought*, and her embattled group. And McKay found himself at its center.

Despite Pankhurst's occasional vetoes and criticisms of his articles, McKay remained alert for items and events of unusual interest and significance. In early September he discovered a story of unrest and disaffection in the Royal Navy, which Pankhurst eagerly seized upon and developed into a series of articles whose repercussions resulted in her imprisonment and the eventual breakup of her party.

Before McKay left for the Trade Union Congress in Portsmouth, he had made the acquaintance of a young sailor named David Springhall, whose youthful enthusiasm for communism made him eager to contribute to the *Dreadnought*. At the time, there was restlessness in the navy over low pay and lack of dependents' benefits. Springhall told McKay he would send him some articles on these and other topics. The *Dreadnought* subsequently published three articles, all presumably by Springhall. The first appeared under the fictitious name of R.000 (Stoker), HMS *Reliance*; the second was signed S.000 (Gunner), HMS *Lucie*; and the third, S.000 (Gunner), HMS *Hunter*. Only McKay and Pankhurst knew the identity of the author. The first two (on September 4 and 25, respectively) were autobiographical, relating Springhall's experiences with the British navy in Russian waters during World War I. On October 16, however, the *Dreadnought* featured the third article, "Discontent on the Lower Deck." It contained a detailed list of enlisted men's grievances and a ringing call for all sailors to stand by the working class in its struggles against the ruling establishment. Along with a magnificent center picture of Karl Marx taken from the czarist archives in Moscow, the article covered the entire front page.[64]

Using the wartime Defence of the Realm Act, still in effect, the British government responded to the article by arresting Sylvia Pankhurst, charging her with publishing articles "calculated and likely to cause sedition amongst His Majesty's forces, in the Navy, and among the civilian population."[65] To bolster its case, the government cited three other such articles in the *Dreadnought* of October 16: "How to Get a Labour Government" by H. Rubenstein, "The Datum Line" by Pankhurst herself, and "The Yellow Peril and the Dockers" by Leon Lopez.

Lopez was very likely another pseudonym for Claude McKay, who had been asked by Pankhurst when he originally accepted his *Dreadnought* job to "dig up something along the London docks from the colored as well as the white seamen and write from a point of view that would be fresh and different."[66] In "The Yellow Peril and the Dockers," as in the other articles cited, militant calls had been made for working-class solidarity in the war against capitalism and the established government. H. Rubenstein had quoted William Morris to the effect that Parliament after the revolution could possibly be used as a manure dump, and Leon Lopez had ended his article (on the prejudices shown by the East End dockers toward the Chinese in the area) by declaring that "the dockers, instead of being unduly concerned about the presence of their coloured fellow-men, who like themselves, are the victims of capitalism and civilizaton, should turn their attention to the huge stores of wealth along the water-front. The country's riches are not in the West End, in the palatial houses of the suburbs; they are stored in the East End, and the jobless should lead the attack on the bastilles, the bonded warehouses along the docks to solve the question of unemployment."[67] This, indeed, was goading the imperial lion in a most sensitive area.

Besides arresting Pankhurst, the government raided the *Dreadnought* offices on Fleet Street. McKay happened to be descending from the small office he occupied on the top floor when he encountered Pankhurst's secretary coming upstairs.

> She whispered that Scotland Yard was downstairs. Immediately I thought of Springhall's article and I returned to my rooms, where I had the original under a blotter. Quickly I folded it and stuck it in my sock. Going down, I met a detective coming up. They had turned Pankhurst's office upside down and descended to the press-room, without finding what they were looking for.
> "And what are you?" the detective asked.
> "Nothing, Sir," I said, with a big black grin. Chuckling, he let me pass. (I learned afterward that he was the ace of Scotland Yard.) I walked out of that building and into another, and entering a water closet I tore up the original article, dropped it in, and pulled the chain.

Springhall's identity remained hidden, but Scotland Yard had not been entirely satisfied with McKay's "big black grin." That night when he returned to his quarters on Bow Road, he found another detective waiting for him. McKay had no incriminating evidence in his room, only poems. As he later wrote, the detective "was very polite and I was more so. With alacrity I showed him all my papers, but he found nothing but lyrics."[68]

Even so, the beleaguered little group around Pankhurst now found itself subjected to intolerable strains. A week after Pankhurst's arrest, the police arrested Comrade Vie as he was leaving the home of a radical member of Parliament. They discovered in his possession letters from Pankhurst to Lenin and other Bolshevik officials, ciphered messages to the Comintern, and information about British industrial centers, armed forces, and Ireland. He even had "a manual for the officers of the future British Red Army and statements about the distribution of money" by the Comintern to the CP(BSTI) and other Communist groups and sympathizers in Great Britain. Comrade Vie was revealed as a Bolshevik courier who had entered England illegally. He had been preparing to leave the country when the police arrested him. The British historian Walter Kendall has suggested that Veltheim may have influenced the CP(BSTI) in its attempts to propagandize among the enlisted men of the British armed services.[69]

His arrest threw the Pankhurst organization into turmoil. Edgar Whitehead, secretary of the CP(BSTI), was convinced that Veltheim had been betrayed by a spy within the party ranks. Everyone, even Pankhurst, became a suspect. McKay had to give an account of himself.[70] Whitehead's suspicions that Veltheim had been betrayed were correct, but the police agent eventually revealed himself to be Jacob Nositvitsky, not a member of Pankhurst's group but a Russian-American Communist in London.

Considering the evidence presented at his trial, Veltheim was given a remarkably light sentence—six months' imprisonment for alien nonregistration. At the end of his term, he was deported.[71] Early in November, Sylvia Pankhurst also was convicted of the charges against her and sentenced to six months' imprisonment—but not before using her trial for a full exposition of her communist beliefs. As in the old suffrage campaigns, Sylvia once again stood undaunted before the British bar to defend the justice of her cause. Among other things, she declared that

> although I have been a socialist all my life, I have tried to palliate this capitalist system. . . . I saved £400 and went to work in the East End, just before the war. At the beginning of the war, there were no separation allowances for the women. Many and many a time they have brought their children dying to me. I started four clinics for dying children, and I have set up night after night with the little ones who were brought to me. I also set up a day nursery, but all my experience showed it was useless trying to palliate an impossible system. This is a wrong system and has got to be smashed. I would give my life to smash it. You cannot frighten me with any sentence you may impose. . . . I have just returned from Soviet Russia. There the children are not left to starve.[72]

In the middle of all these trials and party troubles, McKay's first book of verse since 1912 was published. Although *Spring in New Hampshire* was only a slim volume of forty pages, it represented for

McKay proof of his growth as a poet. He had left his Jamaican dialect verse behind and could now be judged within the larger traditions of English poetry. His publisher asked George Bernard Shaw to write an introduction to his poems, but Shaw declined. He stated that McKay's poetry "should stand on its own." An introduction by Shaw might have boosted sales, but McKay decided that, after all, Shaw was not a poet or even "a subtle appreciator of the nuances of profound poetry."[73] He turned instead to C. K. Ogden, who persuaded his friend and collaborator I. A. Richards to write a short introduction to *Spring in New Hampshire.*

Richards would shortly gain a reputation as one of England's most innovative and influential literary critics; his introduction to *Spring in New Hampshire* may have given McKay the assurance he needed that he had at last proved himself as a poet. But in fact, Richards wrote his preface only at Ogden's behest. In it, he stated that "the poems here selected may, in the opinion of not a few who have seen them in periodical form, claim a place beside the best work that the present generation is producing in this country." Forty-six years later Richards was less equivocal: "I never met McKay and I haven't read his poetry since."[74] His endorsement nevertheless gave McKay satisfaction and probably helped win the book a wider audience among reviewers.

In the fall of 1920, however, McKay had become so upset by the troubles of the CP(BSTI) that he scarcely followed the book's reception. After Veltheim's arrest, the air had become thick with accusations of police spying. One evening at the International Socialist Club, Whitehead showed him an anonymous letter that accused McKay of being a spy. "I declare," McKay later remembered, "that I felt sick and was seized with a crazy craving to get quickly out of that atmosphere and away from London."[75] He had no money. He had long ago used the little provided by the Grays for his trip abroad. Pankhurst's organization provided him with just enough to cover his room and board. He had to depend upon friends in England to raise enough money for a return voyage to New York.

Early in 1921, he sailed for the United States, disillusioned with England and the English.[76] McKay had also found racism interwoven with England's postwar conservatism. Even British socialists, he discovered, often displayed a gross insensitivity to the nuances of race relations that sometimes matched the verbal blunderings of the most blatant imperialists. This blindness in matters of race and national prejudices alternately bemused and angered him. The *Daily Herald*'s campaign against the use of African troops on the Rhine was only the most flagrant example of racism on the British Left. Of equal concern to him were the resentments displayed by English dockers and others along the London waterfront toward blacks and Asians who had to compete with them for scarce jobs. Only the *Dreadnought*, it seemed to him, fought consistently against the spread of such working-class prejudices.[77]

Others on the Left, such as his old idol, George Bernard Shaw, exhibited sympathy for the problems that confronted blacks in English society, but from McKay's point of view the great satirist had a shallow understanding of the world's racial problems; he did not seem to see how fully blacks and Asians the world over were awakening to the challenge presented by European domination.

Some weeks after his arrival in England, McKay had, on the strength of Frank Harris' letter of introduction, spent an evening with Shaw at his home in Adelphi Terrace. Everything about Shaw intrigued McKay. He had often studied Shaw's photographs and admired the "elegant" appearance and youthful face beneath his fine white beard and hair. He had also been impressed by Shaw's athletic appearance and had heard of his interest in boxing. Face to face, however, McKay found that "Shaw looked healthy, but not like the ordinary healthy rugged man. Under his fine white hair, his complexion was as soft and rosy as a little child's. And there was something about him that reminded me of an evergreen plant grown indoors. As an animal he suggested an antelope to my mind. And his physique gave an impression of something brittle and frail that one would want to handle with care, like chinaware. I thought that perhaps it was his vegetarian diet that gave him that remarkably deceptive appearance." Over the course of the evening, they discussed (among other things) Frank Harris, the current London stage, and Shaw's trip to Jamaica back in 1912 during Lord Olivier's governorship. For both McKay and Shaw, those days must have reminded them of an innocence forever lost. "Once," McKay recalled, "[Shaw] mentioned the World War, and let out a whinny which sounded exactly like a young colt in distress or like an accent from his great drama, *Heartbreak House*. I felt at once," McKay continued, "that in spite of his elegant composed exterior, the World War must have had a shattering effect on him. Perhaps, prior to 1914 he had thought, as did other Fabian Socialists, that a wholesale war of slaughter and carnage between civilized nations was impossible; that the world was passing gradually from the cutthroat competitive to a co-operative stage. I myself, under the influence of the international idealistic thought of that period, used to think that way." For all his admiration for the man and his accomplishments in the theater, McKay sensed Shaw's limitations as a student of contemporary world politics. Once Shaw said, laughing, that "a Chinese intellectual . . . had come all the way from China to visit him, and wanted to talk only about Irish politics." McKay shared Shaw's amusement, even while resenting his obtuseness. Shaw also told McKay about an Indian who had brought him an interesting play, which Shaw had judged good but not adaptable to the modern theater. He then observed that "it must be tragic for a sensitive Negro to be a poet. Why didn't you choose pugilism instead of poetry for a profession?" [78]

Several weeks later McKay had occasion to remember Shaw's remarks. He went to see one of the West Indian boxers he had introduced to the International Socialist Club fight an Englishman in Holborn. It was a tough, evenly matched bout, which McKay's friend won by a knockout in a late round. Afterward, the boxer's friends from the colored soldiers' club gathered around him in congratulation. To celebrate, they suggested he accompany them to a "colored restaurant off Shaftesbury Avenue." At that moment an Englishman pushed through the little group and also congratulated the boxer, praising him lavishly for his skills. The boxer, "a modest type of fellow," shook the man's hand and then turned to introduce him to his wife, who happened to be a white woman. Much to everyone's surprise, the Englishman ignored the woman's proffered hand and turned on the boxer, exclaiming in outrage, "You damned nigger." The boxer dropped the man with a single blow, and they all hurried away to dinner. "We sat around, the poor woman among us, endeavoring to woo the spirit of celebration. But we were all wet. The boxer said: 'I guess they don't want no colored in this damned white man's country.' He dropped his head on the table and sobbed like a child. And I thought that that was *his* knockout." McKay then remembered Shaw's remark to him about choosing pugilism for a profession. "He no doubt imagined that it would be easier for a black man to win success at boxing than at writing in a white world. But looking at life through an African telescope, I could not see such a great difference in the choice." [79]

In England, McKay saw the white racist's obsessive fear of black sexuality displayed in the most unlikely places—in George Lansbury's socialist *Daily Herald,* among the dockers of the East End, and even in a review of his new book of poems. The critic of the London *Spectator,* an upper-class organ of impeccable English taste, wrote that "*Spring in New Hampshire* is extrinsically as well as intrinsically interesting. It is written by a man who is a pure-blooded

Negro. . . . Perhaps the ordinary reader's first impulse in realizing
that the book is by an American Negro is to inquire into its good taste.
Not until we are satisfied that his work does not overstep the barriers
which a not quite explicable but deep instinct in us is ever alive to
maintain can we judge it with genuine fairness. Mr. Claude McKay
never offends our sensibilities. His love poetry is clear of the hint
which would put our racial instinct against him, whether we would
or not."[80]

The white man's fear of black male sexuality, cropping up repeatedly in just those places within white society where McKay most consistently sought support, made him recoil into himself, to remember
with startling clarity his own difference, his blackness. It reminded
him of the psychological gulf that he bridged each time he made a
white friend or responded positively to white achievements. In the
midst of all the racially integrated activities of his year in England, a
part of him remained black and alone.

By and large, it was just this aspect of his English experience
he chose to emphasize in the mid-1930s when he wrote *A Long
Way from Home*. By then, McKay had abandoned international communism and was instead stressing that blacks should concentrate
upon organizing themselves as a more cohesive ethnic group for self-
protection and the promotion of their own best interests within the
American nation.[81] While he told of his involvement with Sylvia
Pankhurst's organization, he did not bother to explain in detail the
context and the extent of his own commitment to communist revolutionary activity in 1920. In the 1930s, he had other points he wished
to make, and a full exposition of his association with the WSF, Pankhurst, and the other members of Britain's revolutionary Left would
have meant a different emphasis. In reality, McKay in England lived
more intensely and learned more than he conveyed seventeen years
later in *A Long Way from Home*.

As a member of Pankhurst's small Communist sect, McKay experienced firsthand the realities of international Communist politics at a
critical time when the newly formed Comintern and Lenin himself
were bringing pressure to bear on the CP(BSTI) to merge with other
groups into a single Communist party of Great Britain whose tenets
conformed strictly to Comintern policy. Because of this experience,
McKay very early began to doubt the wisdom of an international
Communist movement based so firmly upon a Russian leadership
whose interests could not always be identical with those of Communists in other countries.

From his work on the *Dreadnought*, McKay gained practical experience as a working journalist. Altogether, from September, 1919 (when Pankhurst first reprinted his poetry from the *Liberator*), to November, 1920, McKay published in the *Dreadnought* sixteen poems, twenty articles and letters, and five book reviews. In addition, he brought to Sylvia Pankhurst's attention the series of articles on the navy by the sailor David Springhall. If McKay had allowed Springhall's manuscript to fall into the hands of Scotland Yard, Springhall (and McKay himself) would probably have also been arrested. As it turned out, Springhall was soon discharged without penalties and subsequently played an active role in the CPGB.[82]

Besides Pankhurst, McKay also met many of the prominent British Communists and left-wing labor leaders active in 1920, some of whom he counted among his friends while in England. Two of these were Frank Budgen and his future wife, Francine, whom he met at the International Socialist Club. Besides being active in the Socialist Labour Party, Frank Budgen was also an artist. His friendship with James Joyce eventually led him to write a major study of Joyce and the writing of *Ulysses*.[83]

There survives from 1920 a very revealing letter from McKay to Francine Budgen in which he discussed his British experience and his relationship to his radical compatriots at the club. The letter substantiates that McKay did, in fact, encounter much overt racism in England. It also reveals that despite his commitment to communism in 1920, he viewed himself as first a writer and artist and felt that he was in a class apart from his purely political comrades.

In response to a letter from Francine in which she obviously had expressed discouragement about an article, perhaps written by a socialist, which did not reflect well upon the movement, McKay wrote

You're a brave girl, but you mustn't be downhearted. . . . I am not a bit downhearted. I am merely doing my bit of propaganda to offset that of the anti-Negro Americans, the colonial whites, and prejudiced Englishmen. I can afford to ignore them at the International Socialist Club. I go when I want for relaxation. I've always been on my guard for I know white men only too well. . . . But I never had much to do with the lower orders until I went to America. In spite of the prejudices they are much finer in the North than the horrid Cockney type like Field that I met at the Club. . . . Will you come tomorrow (Wednesday)? I shall have to meet Field in Committee about the charges I have made against him for trying to stir up race prejudice in the club.

Yes: I agree with you. Too much time should not be wasted at the club. It is nice to drop in for an hour or more once or twice a week but hardly oftener. I go merely because I haven't money to go to good concerts, plays, etc. if you didn't live so far out we could go out once in a while, but it is too far to take you back and my district is rough and dangerous. One must not deliberately invite trouble. It doesn't help any cause. Then I find it so difficult to get rooms on account of my colour! It's rather funny.

McKay turned again to the subject of the International Club and observed that many there were mere "hangers on to the movement," not serious revolutionaries. "They have no idea of what constitutes practical socialism. They talk, but never try to live. I have no doubt you could teach some of them much as you say. I approach the whole crowd from the critical artistic standpoint—only to measure and weigh and discount them."*

Forty-six years later, the Budgens could not remember the article McKay referred to in the letter or if any action had been taken against Billy Field at the club for stirring up racial prejudices. But they did retain a vivid memory of McKay—handsome, somewhat dandified, quaint of speech, and nondogmatic in his politics. Budgen, who painted McKay's portrait, remembered his face was "illuminated by real intelligence." He also knew how to make fine cocktails (a skill learned during his railroad days). Both remembered McKay was openly homosexual but not at all effeminate. To the Budgens, McKay was outgoing and pleasant. They did not consider him particularly anti-British or bitterly antiwhite. The Budgens had not been a part of the Pankhurst group. They remembered little about his work with Pankhurst except that he eventually grew somewhat waspish and cynical in his remarks about her movement. Neither felt that McKay knew much about Marxism. They instead remembered his wit, intelligence, and friendly, outgoing personality.[84]

Although McKay left England thoroughly disillusioned with the British in general, he left behind good friends and carried with him many positive experiences. While he understood Sylvia Pankhurst's limitations as a revolutionary leader, he respected her personal integrity, her dedication to the cause of social justice, and her passionate willingness to act upon her conviction, "to live" and not just "talk" revolutionary Marxism. Pankhurst's group, he later concluded, "was perhaps more piquant than important." And although "Pankhurst was a good agitator and fighter, . . . she wasn't a leader. She possessed the magnetism to attract people to her organization, but she did not

*Claude McKay to Francine [Budgen], [ca. August, 1920], © 1987 by Hope McKay Virtue, 1110 Olive Avenue, Long Beach, Calif. 90813, and used by her permission. This letter is in the possession of Mrs. Francine Budgen, widow of Frank Budgen, London; copy in my possession.

have the power to hold them. . . . It was a one-woman show, not broad-based enough to play a decisive role in the labor movement."[85] Not long after her release from prison, she broke with her own Communist movement when it demanded control of her newspaper. Pankhurst remained on the Left but she rejected dominance by the Comintern and became critical of Soviet Russia. As the 1920s progressed, the antifascist crusade claimed most of her energy.[86] When McKay himself visited Russia in 1922, the example of Pankhurst's disappointment with Comintern policy in England must have constantly reminded him that wholehearted acceptance of international communism would entail a real loss of freedom to think, plan, and act independently as an artist and individual.

Finally, because of another unusual Englishman, C. K. Ogden, McKay found a publisher for the best poetry he had written since leaving Jamaica. *Spring in New Hampshire* represented an expansion and maturation of the central themes first developed in his dialect poetry. Verses of love, lost innocence, and nostalgia for Jamaica alternated with poems in which McKay expressed anger, alienation, and rebellion against the racial oppression he had faced since leaving Jamaica. The heightened poetic creativity that had begun in 1919 continued during his year in England and would culminate within two years in *Harlem Shadows*, his most important collection of verse.

McKay's visit to England only reinforced his conviction that the world that had shaped his youth, the prewar world of his pastoral childhood, as well as the rational, progressive world envisioned by his late Victorian intellectual mentors, had been irrevocably shattered by the Great War. From it, there had emerged the great struggle between world capitalism and Communist revolution.

In part, perhaps, because the England he saw after World War I differed so radically from the one he had envisioned during his youth, McKay experienced there an especially intense nostalgia for Jamaica. The England he had once hoped to see had been the idealized, faraway kingdom of his lost tropical childhood. Now, only the childhood itself remained inviolate, deep within the recesses of memory:

> . . . I have embalmed the days,
> Even the sacred moments when we played,
> All innocent of passion, uncorrupt,
> At noon and evening in the flame-heart's shade.
> We were so happy, happy, I remember,
> Beneath the poinsettia's red in warm December.[87]

It was in England that McKay composed "Flame-Heart," and it was there, too, that he first published "Exhortation," his fervent call for black men to seize the opportunities presented by the death of the old order in Europe and the birth of the new in Russia. In such poems, and in his numerous articles, reviews, and letters, McKay during his visit to England was among the first to signal the beginnings of a black colonial revolt against British imperialism that would peak after World War II. Other disillusioned colonials would follow. But McKay must be reckoned the first black socialist to write for an English periodical. He was, chronologically at least, a predecessor of what in the 1930s and 1940s became, to use George Shepperson's expression, the "Hampstead School of African Socialism." Thus, McKay, twenty years before Kwame Nkrumah, Julius Nyerere, and Jomo Kenyatta, argued that socialism and black nationalism were interdependent.[88]

But McKay claimed no following in Jamaica, much less in Africa. He was a literary artist, not a political leader. By the end of 1920, he was eager to return once more to New York, to Harlem, and to the literary and political ferment of Greenwich Village and the *Liberator*.

# 5
# With the *Liberator,*
# 1921–1922

While in England, McKay had maintained his connection with the *Liberator,* which had published during his absence four of his poems. His friendship with Max and Crystal Eastman was firmly established, and he looked forward to seeing them again.[1] When he arrived in New York in the winter of 1921, however, he did not immediately contact the Eastmans. He went instead to Harlem, where he stayed for a time with an old friend from Jamaica, a bewitching woman whose solid business instincts and personal allure had enabled her to succeed in New York, first as the operator of an intimate "buffet flat" and then, with the advent of Prohibition, as the owner of an equally cozy speakeasy. In *A Long Way from Home,* McKay characteristically identified her only by a pseudonym, Sanina, but he dropped some suggestive if vague hints about her identity. She was "an attractive quadroon . . . who could pass as white," and her family evidently was closely allied to the McKays, for "her dominating octoroon grandmother" had been McKay's "godmother." He wrote, "I felt a congeniality and sweet nostalgia for her company, for we had grown up together from kindergarten. Underneath all her shrewd New York getting-byness there was discernible the green bloom of West Indian naïveté. Yet her poise was a marvel and kept her there floating like an imperishable block of butter on the crest of the dark heaving wave of Harlem."[2] Sanina may have been one of the "Woolsey clan" mentioned by McKay in *My Green Hills of Jamaica.*[3] Whatever her origins or her attractions, she did not hold McKay for long. After ten days, he began to grow restless. He had spent the fifty dollars he had managed to bring back from England and had to think once again about a livelihood. Fortunately, Max Eastman made him an offer he joyfully accepted.

While relaxing at Sanina's, McKay had informed the Eastmans of his return and Max had invited him to spend a weekend in his home at Croton-on-Hudson, just north of New York City. While McKay was there, Eastman invited him to join the *Liberator* staff as an associate editor.[4]

Both Crystal and Max had long been anxious to devote less time to editorial duties and more time to their own writing. In February, 1921, Crystal had resigned as editor. Max, who had himself previously resigned, now returned to inform *Liberator* readers that he, Floyd Dell, Robert Minor, and Claude McKay would share editorial duties. "It is our purpose," he wrote, "to make the *Liberator* in spirit more like its honorably annihilated predecessor, *The Masses*, on subject-matter a little more closely related to the American labor movement. We wish our contributors—and especially those rare and obstreperous geniuses who contributed to *The Masses*—would take note of this fact." Claude joined the *Liberator* at a high point in its fortunes. The U.S. Post Office Department had recently restored its second-class mailing privileges and had refunded more than eleven thousand dollars paid in first-class postage while the second-class application was pending. With this unexpected bonanza, the new *Liberator* editorial staff could for the next year look forward to adequate operating funds.[5] Thanks to Crystal Eastman's editorship, they also had a very capable business manager in Margaret Lane, who had previously been active in the management of the Women's Peace party. Crystal had also hired an excellent secretary and several good stenographers. At least for a while, the *Liberator*'s future seemed secure.[6]

For Claude, the magazine's new stability meant he could look forward to a regular salary, small but adequate for room and board. From the beginning, McKay's role involved substantial editorial responsibilities. Eastman had agreed to return as editor only if McKay assumed the editorial duties previously handled by Floyd Dell, who was currently writing a book. As McKay put it, "I responded with my hand and my head and my heart. . . . My experience with the *Dreadnought* in London was of great service to me now."[7]

Although in effect still editor-in-chief, Eastman during this period left all but the final assembly of the *Liberator* to Minor, McKay, and Dell. Eastman depended on them to give him the free time he needed for his writing, and he appeared at the *Liberator* offices only to prepare the monthly issues for printing. "Then," McKay remembered, "he worked with devilish energy, sifting and scrapping material, titling articles and pictures. And the magazine was always out on time."[8] Eastman wrote many, if not most, editorials while Dell continued to write his reviews and social criticisms. Despite the editorial input of Robert Minor, who was rapidly evolving into a fully committed Communist party functionary, and of McKay, whose contributions ranged across a broader spectrum of concerns, the *Liberator* still bore the decisive imprint of Max Eastman's editorship.

Still spellbound by the cataclysmic transformations occurring in Russia, Eastman and his staff devoted a great deal of space in 1921 to a discussion of events there. They tried to understand and faithfully report Lenin's strategy and tactics and to help fashion in the West a similar Marxist-Leninist approach to change. They were attempting to infuse into the idealistic "lyrical" Left of the old *Masses* a more serious revolutionary realism, seemingly exemplified by the Bolsheviks under Lenin's leadership. In this effort, Eastman led the way, but the metamorphosis was never complete. The *Liberator*, after all, was not a party magazine. Its contributors were a varied lot of artists, writers, social reformers, and revolutionary zealots whose commitments to socialism as yet conformed strictly to no party line. Some, such as Robert Minor, Joseph Freeman, and Irwin Granich (Michael Gold), were in the process of transforming themselves into advocates of the Comintern's emerging revolutionary orthodoxy. For others, such complete adherence to the cause never occurred. They retained the old libertarianism and individualism displayed in the *Masses*. To maintain such a stance, however, inevitably led to conflict, and one of the prices of this conflict was a gradual erosion of the carefree spirit, the optimistic naïveté, and the spontaneous humor that had characterized the *Masses*. When McKay joined the *Liberator* staff in March, 1921, these tensions had not grown intolerable, but they were there, working within and among the individuals who composed the magazine's inner circle. Eastman gave them indirect, perhaps unconscious expression in his March editorial assertion that the new editorial group intended to bring the *Liberator* closer to the spirit of the old *Masses* while also drawing closer ideologically to the revolutionary wing of the labor movement. In Eastman's case, and surely with many others, the conflict between ideology and individuality was an inner conflict well before it developed into a public controversy between opposing individuals and groups.[9]

When McKay assumed his new duties, the differences that existed among the *Liberator* staff members had not yet disrupted the informal union that united them around Eastman and the monthly production of his magazine. Many artists who had worked with him on the *Masses* still contributed their wonderfully vivid, almost naïvely absurd drawings and cartoons of bloated capitalists and embattled workingmen. Floyd Dell still wrote earnestly of youth, marriage, and changing social values. And a wide variety of talented contributors still lent excitement to the *Liberator*.

Above all, however, the question that dominated its pages was the future of the Bolshevik experiment in Russia and of international socialism. The two now seemed inextricably linked. Revolutionary changes had been thwarted in central and western Europe and in the United States since the war. Only in Russia had significant change occurred. Counterrevolution had not succeeded in toppling the new government there. The civil war between White Russians and Red seemed to be drawing to a close with the Red flag triumphant everywhere. The magazine's position was that the new Union of Soviet Socialist Republics must be understood, encouraged, and supported, and its example must be followed by serious revolutionaries if socialism was ever to be realized in the West.

One co-worker on the old *Masses* had already sacrificed his life to the cause of the Russian Revolution, the youthful and energetic John Reed, whose sympathetic reportage of events in Russia had early won the confidence of Lenin. Reed had recently died of fever in Moscow and had been given a hero's burial in the Kremlin wall. His death had only intensified the concern, sympathy, and commitment the *Liberator* displayed toward the Communist cause of revolutionary Russia.[10]

For McKay, a commitment to Communist revolution and life as an artist as yet posed no insurmountable contradictions. He thoroughly enjoyed his new position. Like Joseph Freeman, who was also contributing poems and occasional reviews to the *Liberator*, Claude had begun as an outsider, as an admiring reader of the *Masses*. Now, he had at last arrived on the inside. For the first time since boyhood, he had found, no matter how briefly, a home. As Max Eastman declared in his editorial announcing the new composition of his staff, "Floyd Dell, Robert Minor, and Claude McKay naturally belong to the editorial staff of *The Liberator,* and everybody will be pleased to see them where they belong."[11]

For McKay, one of the pleasures of the job was the unexpected, often unusual, and sometimes famous people who constantly turned up at the *Liberator* offices. Many of them were women. Some, like the statuesque English artist Clare Sheridan, were friends of Crystal Eastman's. Others, like Elinor Wylie, came to discuss their poetry. A few were Greenwich Village characters and hangers-on, like the exotically maniacal Baroness von Freytag-Loringhoven. She visited McKay often, "always," he remembered, "gaudily accoutered in rainbow raiment, festooned with barbaric beads and spangles and bangles, and toting along her inevitable poodle in gilded harness. She had such a precious way of petting the poodle with a slap and ejaculating, 'Hund-bitch!'" Many of the women who visited the *Liberator* offices came to meet its handsome chief editor. For Max Eastman, McKay believed, "was an ikon for the radical women." But Eastman was seldom there, "and so I acted like a black page, listening a lot and saying very little, but gratefully acknowledging all the gifts of gracious words that were offered to *The Liberator.*"[12] McKay was being unduly modest. Some of the women also became his friends. Clare Sheridan expressed admiration for him in her American diary, and the youthful and earnest Dorothy Day, who would later found her own weekly, also befriended him from time to time.[13]

In his capacity as editor, McKay also became acquainted with some notable men. E. E. Cummings one day dropped by the office and engaged McKay in a long discussion about some poems he had submitted. McKay wished to publish several in a prominent spread, but Robert Minor emphatically refused. He maintained that Cummings' verse contained nothing to advance the revolutionary consciousness of *Liberator* readers. McKay "protested that the verses were poetry, and that in any work of art my natural reaction was more for its intrinsic beauty than for its social significance." While he argued that his "social sentiments were strong, definite and radical," they were different from his "esthetic emotions . . . and should not be mixed up." Despite Minor's objections, McKay managed to insert a few of Cummings' poems in the *Liberator.*[14]

Everyone on the *Liberator* staff respected one celebrated visitor, the great silent-film star, Charlie Chaplin. Chaplin sympathized with the *Liberator*'s radical politics, and by chance he also shared for a while with Max Eastman the same mistress, the actress Florence Deshon. Their tangled affairs ended tragically with Deshon's death by suicide in 1922.[15]

During his tenure with the *Liberator,* McKay several times enjoyed Chaplin's company. Chaplin liked McKay's poetry and quoted it in his early travelogue, *My Trip Abroad.* He also remembered McKay in his autobiography.[16] One day at the *Liberator,* Chaplin also met and liked Hubert Harrison. Later, he asked McKay to invite Harrison to a party at the Greenwich Village home of Eugen Boissevain, who was shortly to marry the poet Edna St. Vincent Millay. Besides Chaplin, Max and Crystal Eastman were there, along with the civil liberties lawyer Dudley Field Malone, Doris Stevens, "a leader of the woman's movement," and McKay's friend William Gropper. Harrison knew many women and McKay had suggested he bring a date to the party. Harrison arrived late with "an old brown girl who was neither big nor little, short nor fat, or anything." McKay concluded that "erotically he was very indiscriminate and I suppose that descending from the soap-box, he remembered the party and invited the first pick-up he met to accompany him." As it turned out, the woman and everyone else had a grand time. For McKay, the party turned into one of those rare, memorable occasions when "no white shadow and no black apprehension, no complexes arising out of conscious superiority or circumstantial inferiority" intruded to spoil the "spirit of happy relaxation."[17]

Such contacts between whites and blacks in New York would grow as the decade advanced and would play an important role in launching the black literary and artistic awakening known as the Harlem Renaissance. Informal gatherings smoothed the way to publishers, editors, and theatrical producers and directors. McKay had been among the first to take full advantage of this new development, which in itself had been encouraged and promoted by the officials—black and white—of the NAACP and the National Urban League. As early as 1917, through the intercession of the NAACP's Joel Spingarn, McKay had succeeded in publishing two poems in *Seven Arts.* Now, as an associate editor of the *Liberator,* he was in an even better position to advance his literary career.[18]

McKay had returned to New York determined to find a publisher for an expanded American edition of *Spring in New Hampshire.* As early as September, 1919, he thought he had received from the young publisher Alfred A. Knopf a firm commitment to publish his poems, but over a year later he wrote William Stanley Braithwaite from London that he still was looking for an American publisher, "Knopf having failed me at the last moment."[19]

Assistance in finding a publisher eventually came, once again, from Joel Spingarn. In the fall of 1921, Spingarn persuaded Harcourt, Brace and Company to accept McKay's poems for publication in the spring of 1922. The certainty of an American book of verse meant much to McKay. On the advice of his English publishers, he had omitted from *Spring in New Hampshire* his most militantly racial poems, including "If We Must Die." This had bothered him at the time, and it upset him even more when, upon his return to New York, Frank Harris had discovered the omission and had indignantly called him a "traitor" to his race and to his "own integrity. That's what the English . . . have done to your people," Harris exclaimed, "emasculated them. . . . You were bolder in America. The English make obscene sycophants of their subject peoples. I am Irish and I know. But we Irish have guts the English cannot rip out of us. I'm ashamed of you, sir. It's a good thing you got out of England. It is no place for a genius to live." [20]

McKay left Harris' "uncomfortable presence" thoroughly castigated but determined to see the publication of all his poems in an expanded American edition. He had not hesitated to seek Spingarn's assistance, even though he had never felt completely at ease in his company. McKay thought Spingarn disapproved of his radicalism, and he resented what he saw as Spingarn's presumptuous role as strategist and spokesman for the black race within the NAACP. On the other hand, he admired the man's personal integrity and his dedication to the cause of racial justice. Above all, he could not deny Spingarn's usefulness to himself. McKay's attitude to Spingarn remained ambivalent, though the relationship proved to be of personal benefit. In general, however, ambivalence could be said to characterize his attitude toward most of the national NAACP leadership in New York. [21]

Before his trip to England, McKay had not had a chance to get to know the officials and staff at the NAACP's national headquarters. After his return, his successes as a poet and a radical journalist soon enabled him to meet the leaders of black protest and black "society" in New York City. Among the leaders of the NAACP, only its executive secretary, James Weldon Johnson, won McKay's unqualified admiration. As a former teacher, U.S. consul, lawyer, musician, poet, and novelist, Johnson moved with self-possession and dignity among blacks and whites. Like Claude's elder brother, U'Theo, he was clearly a superior man among men, who had never allowed his aspirations or interests to become limited and ingrown because of his race. Among Afro-American leaders, Claude admired and trusted Johnson alone without reservation. [22]

McKay's relations with the other NAACP leaders during this pe-

riod were cordial but not close. He appreciated the passionate dedication of W. E. B. Du Bois, who, as editor of the NAACP's *Crisis* magazine, pushed relentlessly for the advancement of blacks in every area.
He had himself been profoundly influenced by Du Bois's writings,
but like many who met him, McKay found Du Bois too aloof and formal for any genuine friendship to develop between them. Besides,
during this period, they were ideologically at odds. Du Bois had
briefly joined the Socialist party in 1912, but he had soon left it to
support Woodrow Wilson's first candidacy. With the advent of the
Russian Revolution, he had reserved judgment about the future of
revolutionary socialism. On this point, Du Bois revealed his differences with McKay in an exchange of opinion in the July, 1921, *Crisis*. In a letter to the editor, McKay criticized Du Bois for "sneering"
at the Russian Revolution, which he ardently defended as "the greatest event in the history of humanity." McKay readily admitted that the
NAACP had done great work and should be supported by all "progressive Negroes," but it was doing nothing to bring black and white
labor together in a revolutionary front. Du Bois replied by calmly
questioning whether blacks should or could place as much trust in
the working-class struggle as McKay seemed to be doing.[23]

McKay's ideological differences with NAACP leaders did not prevent them from associating with him on a social basis, and during
1921 and 1922 he met Walter White, Johnson's young assistant from
Atlanta; Jessie Fauset, the literary editor of *Crisis;* and Mary White
Ovington, one of the founding members on the NAACP's board of directors. All proved friendly and helpful. Although middle-class herself, Jessie Fauset enjoyed socializing with young bohemian writers
and artists and did not object to McKay. Neither did Walter White,
whose extensive connections with white writers, publishers, and
journalists in New York would later prove helpful to McKay.[24]

While outwardly friendly, McKay harbored reservations about
most of the NAACP group. Like Spingarn, Ovington was white and
not completely to be trusted as a spokesperson for a Negro organization. Walter White presented another problem, one deeply rooted in
McKay's background. In Jamaica, he had grown up resentful of those
mulattoes and octoroons whose self-advancement compelled them to
identify with the white elite. Walter White, blond-haired and blue-
eyed, came from a long-established, light-complexioned Atlanta family. McKay had trouble identifying him as a Negro. He nevertheless
soon found he liked Walter White, whose natural ebullience and
charm put McKay at ease. The stories of White's "undercover" investigations of lynchings in the Deep South, where discovery of his true

identity might have meant death, also inspired respect. While none of the other Negro leaders in the national offices of the NAACP was as pink-cheeked as Walter White, neither (with the exception of William Pickens) were they as dark as McKay. Even the racially obsessed W. E. B. Du Bois had Caucasian features and an olive complexion. And James Weldon Johnson, who was darker, had once passed as a Latin American on a southern train.[25]

McKay's ambivalence toward the NAACP persisted, as did his in-grained suspicion of light-skinned racial leaders. In Jamaica, such an elite had formed a class apart. They considered themselves superior to the black peasantry and aspired to equality with the British ruling class. In pursuit of this end, they had time and again acted contrary to the interests of the black majority. McKay was never convinced that the integrationist policies of the NAACP did not encourage the development of a similar situation in the United States. By the 1930s, he would articulate a comprehensive criticism of the NAACP's ra-cial integration policies, but in 1921 he only criticized the NAACP's middle-class orientation and lack of sympathy with Bolshevism.[26]

Although the NAACP certainly adopted no official policy of support for socialism, McKay may have exaggerated the leadership's opposi-tion to it. Several NAACP leaders published articles and book reviews in the militantly socialist *Liberator.* James Weldon Johnson, Walter White, and Mary White Ovington had all contributed articles and re-views on the contemporary racial situation before McKay joined the editorial staff.[27]

Interestingly, while these NAACP leaders all appeared in the *Lib-erator,* none of McKay's black radical associates in Harlem ever wrote for it, though all were articulate, well read, and much further to the left than Johnson, White, or Ovington. After McKay became associate editor, he twice invited (at Hubert Harrison's suggestion) Harlem's black socialists to discuss with Robert Minor how they might effec-tively influence Garvey's Back to Africa movement. "Besides Har-rison," McKay later recalled, "there were Grace Campbell, one of the pioneer Negro members of the Socialist Party; Richard Moore and W. A. Domingo, who edited *The Emancipator,* a radical Harlem weekly; Cyril Briggs, the founder of the African Blood Brotherhood and editor of the monthly magazine, *The Crusader;* Mr. Fanning, who owned the only Negro cigar store in Harlem; and one Otto Huiswoud, who hailed from Curaçao, the birthplace of Daniel De Leon. Perhaps there were others whom I don't remember."[28] The meetings were in-tense and lively, but nothing came of them. Garvey and his chief lieu-tenants had no intention of espousing socialism. They were more interested in enshrining themselves as the reigning imperial aristocracy of a resurgent Pan-African nationalism and had no patience with socialist ideas.

By chance, Eastman dropped by the *Liberator* offices while the second meeting of Harlem's "black Reds" was in progress. Although he greeted them cordially, he was alarmed by the prospect that such gatherings might inspire the government once again to take action against him and his fellow editors. Having twice faced trial as editor of the *Masses,* he did not wish to provoke a third indictment and cautioned against any more meetings by the group in the *Liberator* offices.[29]

McKay's association with the individual members of this group, of course, continued; but none became contributors to the *Liberator.* They remained uptown and tried to develop their own organs of expression. When they did reach out for white contact, it was toward the newly formed American Communist party, in the case of Briggs's African Blood Brotherhood, or toward the Socialist party, in the case of A. Philip Randolph and Chandler Owen. On the whole, they must have felt that the literary and artistically inclined group at the *Liberator* had little to offer them. They may have enjoyed the magazine, but unlike McKay's, their primary orientation was toward politics and labor organization, not art and literature.[30]

While McKay contributed an occasional poem, article, or letter to their various periodicals, and while he joined Briggs's African Blood Brotherhood and almost certainly encouraged its affiliation with the American Communist party, his center of focus remained with the *Liberator* group. He sought to contribute as an individual and as a poet to the Communist cause, but aside from his involvement with Pankhurst's Workers' Socialist Federation, he never really became a disciplined, working member of any political organization inside or outside Harlem. Although he joined the IWW during the war, the WSF in London, and Briggs's brotherhood and the underground Communist Party of America once he returned to New York, he never subordinated his own ideas or ambitions to any party program. In this sense, his later assertion that he never joined any Communist party was half true but hardly the whole story.[31]

Although McKay maintained connections with Harlem's small, diverse band of socialists and made a few friends among the moderate NAACP leadership, he had little success with the members of Harlem's status-conscious, middle-class social set. He disliked reciting his poetry before their organizations, and they were offended by his casual attire, bohemian air, and lack of polish as a public speaker. He complained to Hubert Harrison about the invitations he received to perform before such audiences, but Harrison, an excellent public speaker himself, chided McKay and advised him that "he owed it" to his race to make such appearances. From his experiences, McKay concluded that "poets and novelists should let good actors perform for them." McKay did not lack sophistication, wit, or even social pretensions of his own, but these all seemed to fail him when confronted by black middle-class social consciousness, which he felt was at base only a tragic, futile imitation of its white counterpart. What he loved about Harlem was the richly textured, complex, and emotionally charged social life of its working class, whom he had discovered in his early days in New York. "And now that I was legging limpingly along with the intellectual gang, Harlem for me did not hold quite the same thrill and glamor as before. Where formerly in saloons and cabarets and along the streets I received impressions like arrows piercing my nerves and distilled poetry from them, now I was often pointed out as an author. I lost the rare feeling of a vagabond feeding upon secret music singing in me." Despite his love for its folk culture, McKay never really learned to function in black American society. As a dining-car waiter he had managed well enough, but in his vocation as writer, poet, and intellectual he never found a comfortable niche. A part of him remained always the outside observer and critic. As a West Indian, he had encountered some resentment, suspicion, and hostility among the black working class, but it never seemed serious enough to bother him. He recognized that, like most Americans, blacks knew very little of their ancestors and kinsmen elsewhere in the world. That did not, however, lessen their decided sense of superiority over West Indians, whom they were prone to dismiss contemptuously as "monkey-chasers." To McKay, this only proved their need of education. He reserved his real resentment for the black middle class and the direction and thrust of its civil rights movement, whose goal seemed to him to be assimilation for the few at the expense of any advancement for the majority of their fellow blacks.[32]

During McKay's tenure with the *Liberator,* Hubert Harrison remained his closest friend among New York's black intelligentsia, most of whom were, like himself, precariously situated, both economically and socially. Harrison's views about black American society, its civil rights leadership, and its relationship with the larger white society coincided with and had a lasting influence upon McKay's social thought. After passing through the Socialist party and the IWW, and after working briefly with Garvey's UNIA, Harrison had by 1921 come "to the conclusion that out of the purgatory of their own social confusion, Negroes would sooner or later have to develop their own leaders, independent of white control." In this regard, he had a certain contempt for the NAACP, which he liked to call the "National Association for the Advancement of Certain People." He once remarked to McKay "that the NAACP was the progeny of black snobbery and white pride, and had developed into a great organization, with Du-Bois like a wasp in Booker Washington's hide until the day of his death." Harrison combined an "ebony hard" sense of humor with clarity of intellect and immense learning. And he laughed in a "large sugary black African way, which sounded like the rustling of dry bamboo leaves agitated by the wind." McKay delighted in his company. Harrison's tragedy was that he, too, never really found a secure place in the upper echelons of Afro-American society. In his day, there was no leadership position available to accommodate his large, egocentric personality.[33]

While McKay agreed with Harrison about the limitations of the NAACP, he was never ready, as was Harrison, to ridicule its leaders publicly. He respected their genuine accomplishments, and they had, after all, been good to him. Consequently, when Harrison in the *Negro World* reported that McKay had told of dining recently with certain "pseudo intellectuals" from the NAACP, McKay responded by castigating Harrison in a letter, copies of which he sent to Walter White and James Weldon Johnson, along with a cover letter in which he disassociated himself from Harrison's remarks. To Harrison, he wrote:[34]

> I have just noticed your reference to me in the "Negro World" of today which, in my opinion, is in extraordinary bad taste. You are simply hurting me personally by such methods. . . . I could not dream of referring to people who have had me as their private guest in such an indecent and uncalled for public way, nor have I given you any reason to make such a covert attack on them.
>
> You have by your action, violated the simplest proprieties of social intercourse that even a kindergartener or an idiot would respect, and it is your duty as a newspaperman, if you have any moral obligation to your profession, to correct your statement in the next issue of the "Negro World."
>
> You are very wrong to think that you can praise my work by a personal attack on intelligent minds, that whatever their faults, are working for the common cause in their own way.*

McKay's letter revealed that Harrison had probably not engaged in any blatant untruths in reporting his conversation with McKay, but he had committed a serious indiscretion. Despite his haste in cor-

*Claude McKay to Hubert Harrison, January 7, 1922, © 1987 by Hope McKay Virtue, 1110 Olive Avenue, Long Beach, Calif. 90813, and used by her permission. This letter is in the James Weldon Johnson Papers, NAACP Collection, at the Library of Congress.

recting Harrison and in apologizing to Johnson and White, McKay's entrée into Harlem's inner circle of civil rights leaders (not to mention into Harlem society) was, in fact, limited by his own ambivalence and iconoclasm.

In addition, as an editor of an influential radical magazine downtown, McKay had access to the literary bohemia of Greenwich Village. This aspect of his social life had its own satisfactions and frustrations. For the most part, he enjoyed the friends and acquaintances he made while serving with the *Liberator*. He was often surprised, flattered, and pleased by their generosity. "Friends vied with friends in giving me invitations to their homes for parties and car rides and in offering tickets for plays and concerts." The *Liberator* still had a few wealthy supporters. One of them, Elizabeth Sage Hare, thought enough of McKay's accomplishments to present him a check for five hundred dollars. His less affluent friends introduced him to those "Village tearooms and gin mills which were not crazy with colorophobia." McKay "reciprocated by inviting some of them up to the cabarets and cozy flats of Harlem."

Despite such amiability, McKay, unlike his white friends, could never forget the color bar that still imposed itself between him and the larger American society. In New York, the color bar lacked formal sanctions or any consistent pattern, which made it all the more treacherous when it suddenly confronted the unwary black, like a hidden trap in a flowering garden.

McKay knew that in accepting invitations from white friends, he risked exposing them, as well as himself, to insults and humiliations. And although he was aware, when racially motivated rebuffs did occur, they almost invariably wounded and angered him. The hurt burned deepest on those occasions when the simplest human pleasures were spoiled by the sudden, unexpected raising of the color bar in public places. Once, for example, he accompanied Max Eastman and Eugen Boissevain on a leisurely automobile trip to various points in New Jersey, where they viewed the Manhattan skyline and enjoyed the summer countryside. Toward the end of the day, they decided to eat but could find no restaurant in New Jersey that would seat McKay. One place finally offered to serve them in the kitchen at a table reserved for the hired help during their breaks from work. For lack of a better alternative, they agreed and ate a miserable meal amid the heat, noise, and clatter of a busy commercial kitchen. For McKay, the experience not only spoiled the day's enjoyment, it made him extremely wary of venturing on any excursion that might conceivably lead to a similar incident. His white friends did not always understand his refusal of their invitations. "Sometimes they resented my attitude. For I did not always choose to give the reason. I did not always like to intrude the fact of my being a black problem among whites." His white friends were often unaware of the pervasiveness of racial barriers in their own society, and, McKay recalled, "in their happy ignorance they would lead one into the traps of insult." Such circumstances made really close friendships difficult to maintain. On segregation and discrimination in public places, McKay later wrote, "I think the persons who invented discrimination in public places to ostracize people of a different race or nation or color or religion are the direct descendants of medieval torturers. It is the most powerful instrument in the world that may be employed to prevent *rapprochement* and understanding between different groups of people. It is a cancer in the universal human body and poison to the individual soul."[35] For McKay the bitterness it engendered often left him silent before his white friends or, more perplexingly, ill-humored and spiteful. As Eastman remembered him during these years, "[Claude] was an aristocrat in the *Liberator* crowd, slightly aloof, as people of superior sensitivity have to be, but not priggish. Indeed his genial understanding and quick-witted hilarious laughter vastly promoted the spirit of equalitarian fellowship without which [the *Liberator*] would not have existed. Underneath these urbane qualities, Claude was a complex knot of tangled impulses out of which fits of unaccountably spiteful behavior would at times burst. But most of the time he was merely mischievous and altogether lovable." From the perspective of a lifetime, Eastman eventually concluded that "[McKay] was my best friend on the *Liberator*, and a good friend also of Crystal's."[36]

Another more casual acquaintance of McKay's, Alfred Tiala, socialized with him only in "three or four brief get-togethers in a Greenwich Village cafe named Three Steps Down." He also remembered McKay's air of detachment and reserve. Not being a close friend or an advocate of McKay's poetic genius, Tiala's observations provide an interesting contrast to Eastman's; Tiala's remarks, moreover, generally substantiate McKay's own account of his relation with most of his Greenwich Village associates. "To me, at least," wrote Tiala,

> he was a charming, very likable person. He struck me as being wistfully idealistic—not a bold, forward crusading type. . . . Among us white acquaintances of his I wonder if there was anyone in the position of a friend. We were merely on the fringe of his feelings—none of us were close to him. . . . It was as if he were probing as to how near to us he could come without being affronted. Perhaps the basis of it was an innate shyness.

Perhaps you can make something of the fact that personalities like Maxwell Anderson and Eugene O'Neill frequented the cafe Three Steps Down. Claude McKay had his lunches there and saw Anderson and O'Neill and others often. . . . Yet he had seemingly not become acquainted with them.

. . . McKay had a wistful, pleasant style; but at no time did I see him become exuberant or even joyous. He was quietly, pleasantly sombre on [every] occasion. . . . Perhaps it was I who caused him to deport as he did when with me.[37]

In the memory of those with whom he was closer, Claude always remained a much more dynamic presence. Most members of the *Liberator* staff, for example, came closer to Eastman's estimate of him than to Tiala's. The *Liberator* artists John Barber, Maurice Becker, and William Gropper, as well as the writer Joseph Freeman, all remembered him with affection.

In addition, as the solitary black editor on a predominantly white radical magazine, McKay's very presence lent credence to the staff's insistence that to a man, it was working for genuine racial equality and justice. In no sense did they treat McKay as an outsider. On the contrary, John Barber recalled that "it would be nearer the truth to point out that the whole lot of us liked Claude more than we ever liked each other." To Barber, he had a "wonderful personality and . . . limitless generosity. Yet there was nothing Pollyanna or humble about him. His acute critical sense and sharp knowledge of human nature and people made us only wish to be acceptable to him—to 'pass muster' so to speak and earn his approval. And all these qualities gave him great influence."[38] Maurice Becker also stressed McKay's cordial relations with the *Liberator* group: "As to the relations between the *Liberator* contributors and Claude McKay, there was never anything but the closest comradeship. Claude was on the office staff and whenever we others dropped in and time permitted, off we'd go to a cafeteria for a snack and spell of loafing. On several occasions we spent an evening at Claude's Harlem basement flat, and I am reminded that the white-haired Max Eastman and Claude once confronted one another on a tennis court in Croton."[39]

Perhaps the *Liberator* contributor closest to McKay was William Gropper, whose art Claude greatly admired. Gropper's political cartoons were vivid, forceful, and revealing. Unlike Robert Minor's larger-than-life statements, they combined political shrewdness with a touch of whimsical humor that revealed the fallible, human elements in every political situation. Gropper and McKay got along well together and saw a great deal of each other in 1921 and 1922. Gropper later recalled that "we went to many parties together, as well as poetry readings and meetings at the *Liberator*." He thought "Claude was special . . . a fine poet and very sensitive." He remembered that McKay had "many likes and dislikes" about both white and black people, "particularly [because] he had come from the West Indies and there were Negroes who seemed to feel different about West Indian Negroes, so Claude once explained to me, when one night at a party in Harlem it ended in a scrap. . . . I don't remember Claude having many Negro friends. He was at that time spending most of his time with white intellectuals. When he suffered isolation or loneliness, nobody was his people. . . . His poetry . . . challenged and stimulated everyone around him. He was definitely a great guy to know."[40]

Not everyone on the *Liberator* staff responded so positively to McKay. Robert Minor questioned his revolutionary zeal. McKay's acceptance of E. E. Cummings' poetry led Minor to observe that such tastes revealed McKay to be "more of a decadent than a social revolutionist." McKay's British West Indian sophistication, his often caustic wit, and perhaps his sexual preferences made him difficult for Minor to classify. In *A Long Way from Home,* McKay wrote that "Robert Minor said he could not visualize me as a real Negro. He thought of a Negro as of a rugged tree in the forest. Perhaps Minor had had Negro playmates like that in Texas and he could not imagine any other type."[41]

Another *Liberator* artist, Adolf Dehn, shied away from McKay for an even more personal reason. In *A Long Way from Home,* McKay wrote of his fascination with New York "as an eye-dazzling picture" and told of his endless exploration of it by ferry, train, and on foot. In particular, he remembered "some nocturnal wanderings with Adolf Dehn, the artist, spanning blocks upon blocks along the East River, and the vast space-filling feeling of the gigantic gas tanks."[42] Many years later Dehn also recalled their long walk together, and he, too, remembered that it had been a fine evening until toward the end, "when I was startled and disturbed to realize that [McKay] was indubitably making homosexual overtures to me. They were fairly delicate but became quite insistent. It took me a long time to get him to leave. This all took place on the waterfront so at least I was not in the position of getting him out of my small apartment where we had been earlier. He did not want to accept the simple fact that I was not interested in such activities. This all was done in a most friendly if a somewhat embarrassed manner on my part. My notion of him is that he was a most lecherous fellow with considerable charm and that it did not matter whether he took on man or woman." Dehn found McKay's attempted seduction so unsettling that it destroyed what might have otherwise been a good friendship. "No ill feeling existed between us as far as I know, but it did not allow for a continued friendship. We saw each other accidentally after that." Dehn did note, however, that the rest of "the *Liberator* crowd got along with [McKay] very well."[43]

McKay met many people in his capacity as an associate editor of the *Liberator*. Not surprisingly, only a few became really close friends. He did, however, solidify his relationship with Max and Crystal Eastman, and he also began fruitful friendships with James Weldon Johnson, Grace Campbell, and Arthur A. Schomburg, the black bibliophile. And despite the public disclosure of a private remark about certain members of the NAACP, McKay also valued Harrison's company. With these few special friends he maintained lasting contact.[44]

To be sure, he also developed other friendships while on the *Liberator*. Some were significant, but they did not endure for long. One such friendship was with the British IWW organizer Charles Ashleigh, who had been imprisoned in Chicago after World War I. The *Liberator* published several of his prison poems, appealed to its readers to contribute toward his release on bail, and eventually welcomed him to New York. There in 1921 he and McKay met and began an intense affair that lasted intermittently until the mid-1920s. Ashleigh eventually became a dedicated Communist. He never considered McKay a committed revolutionary, but he enjoyed his company, and in his old age fondly remembered their first dinner together in a New York restaurant.[45]

Another more casual acquaintance of McKay's in the 1920s was James Ivy, who subsequently became a skilled teacher of English, French, and Spanish, as well as an accomplished journalist and editor of the NAACP's *Crisis* magazine. In 1922, he was a college student at Virginia Union University in Richmond, visiting New York over the summer. One day in the Rand School's bookstore, he chanced upon a white youth named Donald Duff who had met McKay in Greenwich Village. In 1929, Ivy described his meeting with McKay:

> Claude was then living at . . . 23 East 14th Street. Duff knocked at room number eight. A mellow voice bade us enter. . . . Duff opened the door and ushered me into a small, neatly furnished room.
>
> There in one corner was McKay stretched out on an army cot. He wore a shirt open at the throat and trousers. The cot was littered with books and

magazines and manuscripts. He was courteous. His accent was British West Indian. In physical appearance he was well built, muscular, of average height, dark brown in complexion. Eyes, smiling, brown, and challenging. The head set off with a mop of rather heavy, long hair.

McKay must have responded positively to Ivy's alertness, intelligence, and curiosity, for they "immediately became friends." McKay invited Ivy to join him the next day for a meal at John's Italian Restaurant on the Lower East Side. "It was on this occasion," Ivy recalled, "that he told me of his London days." Ivy was not homosexual, but he was decidedly curious about sex and sexual behavior and would eventually collect a large library of erotica. He soon found out about McKay's marriage, but Claude would say little about it or about his relation with black women, beyond coyly remarking that "I'm all out of touch with the dusky beauties." Because Ivy was a student, McKay proudly showed him his old English composition papers from Kansas State; Ivy judged them "all quite good. Above the average for undergraduate papers." He also noted that McKay wrote out all his poems "in a very careful longhand" and then had them typed. While composing his verse, "he also [made] use of one of Haldeman-Julius' little rhyming dictionaries." [46] Ivy became another long-term friend and would see McKay often in the 1930s.

While establishing and extending his rather elaborate, if for the most part casual, network of friends and acquaintances, McKay continued to play a vital role on the *Liberator* staff. After joining it, he contributed occasional articles and book reviews, as well as a steady stream of poems. During these years, the style and content of his poetry matured rapidly, and he wrote his most significant American poetry. Like his earlier American verse, it was uneven in quality, often derivative, and sometimes just plain bad. By 1922, most of his verses were short, mostly conventionally rhymed and structured sonnets, whose unusual subject matter and passion alone gave them force, originality, and distinction. Yet, to a degree, they represented some loss of poetic imagination. For all its faults, his dialect verse had an originality of form, diction, rhythm, and subject matter absent in his sonnets and short lyrics.

On the other hand, the best of his American poems represented distinct advances in self-knowledge and in a more mature understanding of the black dilemma in Western culture. They were, in fact, fully realized expressions of the tragedy inherent in the Afro-American experience. They also powerfully focused on the principal themes he had first begun to develop in the dialect poems—the bittersweet brevity of love, the lost innocence of his Jamaican childhood, and the alienation, anger, and rebellion he felt in a world unfairly dominated by a white culture that refused to concede justice, humanity, and equality of human feelings to the black race. For all their obvious echoes of his English literary inheritance, McKay's *Liberator* sonnets sometimes stated profound truths about the black condition in American society that were not equaled in literature until James Baldwin's great prose essays of the 1950s and 1960s. Indeed, McKay's forceful expressions of despair and rebellion marked an important departure in American literature, for his angry rebelliousness laid bare for all to see a genuinely intolerable estrangement, shared in varying degrees by all black Americans. As McKay clearly revealed in such poems as "Outcast" and "In Bondage," blacks were alienated not only from the society that oppressed them but also from their own human potential and from the fullness of life itself.

> Something in me is lost, forever lost,
> Some vital thing has gone out of my heart,
> And I must walk the way of life a ghost
> Among the sons of earth, a thing apart.
>
> For I was born, far from my native clime,
> Under the white man's menace, out of time.

And in "In Bondage," he wrote:

> Somewhere I would be singing, far away.
> For life is greater than the thousand wars
> Men wage for it in their insatiate lust,
> And will remain like the eternal stars,
> When all that shines today is drift and dust
> But I am bound with you in your mean graves,
> O black men, simple slaves of ruthless slaves.[47]

The only alternative to such a living death was uncompromising resistance, a continuous exertion of human will against the forces of death. As McKay later expressed it:

> I stripped down harshly
> To the naked core of hatred
> Based on the essential wrong.[48]

Like W. E. B. Du Bois before him, McKay did not flinch from expressing his hatred:

> My being would be a skeleton, a shell,
> If this dark passion that fills my every mood,
> And makes my heaven in the white world's hell,
> Did not forever feed me vital blood.[49]

This was strong medicine, but it was not the whole story. McKay also recognized that he did not simply hate; he also loved America's liberating energy and vitality:

> . . . I will confess
> I love this cultured hell that tests my youth!
> Her vigor flows like tides into my blood,
> Giving me strength erect against her hate,
> Her bigness sweeps my being like a flood.[50]

This affinity for America and, more broadly, for Western culture derived from genuine feelings of kinship. Western culture had shaped him, and he felt for it a love that, because it was denied in return, placed him, symbolically at least, in the position of the speaker in "Mulatto," who could exclaim:

> There is a searing hate within my soul,
> A hate that only kin can feel for kin,
> A hate that makes me vigorous and whole,
> And spurs me on increasingly to win.
> Because I am my cruel father's child,
> My love of justice stirs me up to hate,
> A warring Ishmaelite, unreconciled,
> When falls the hour I shall not hesitate
> Into my father's heart to plunge the knife
> To gain the utmost freedom that is life.[51]

McKay's best poems in the years after World War I stand like concisely compressed essays on the black condition in the modern world. Sympathetically read, their continuity with later developments in black literature is clear.

McKay's adherence to the "classical" conventions of English poetry received much encouragement from his chief critic, mentor, and literary editor, Max Eastman. Though perhaps unfortunate, Eastman's influence was not sinister. McKay essentially agreed that "real" poetry adhered to Victorian poetic conventions, and that the modernists substituted novelty for discipline and incomprehensibility for beauty. More important, as McKay's chief editor and critic, Eastman apparently quite frequently changed McKay's poems for the better. That, at least, was McKay's opinion to the very end of his life. As late as 1945, he was sending poems to Eastman and admonishing him to "make any corrections you think necessary. . . . I should like to get your opinion and also see the mark of your blue pencil, for I am aware there is no more excellent judge." Eastman obliged, and McKay responded by exclaiming, "And the poems! They are wonderful to look at after you chop them up! That makes me think of the old days."[52] On his side, Eastman believed in McKay's poetic genius and died firm in the belief that Claude McKay was the greatest Afro-American poet.

Altogether, McKay published forty-two poems in the *Liberator*. The first appeared in April, 1919, and the last in August, 1923. His articles and book reviews numbered far less—only eleven appeared between June, 1921, and August, 1922. With a few exceptions, they can be broadly divided into two subject categories. One group expressed his political and social preoccupations; in the other he explored the great significance and potential of the black artistic developments occurring around him. In all his articles, he displayed critical acuity and a consistent maturity of style. In his first *Liberator* article, "How Black Sees Green and Red," he analyzed the international significance of the Sinn Fein revolution for Irish independence and gave his impression of the Irish. His last piece in August, 1922, was a review of T. S. Stribling's *Birthright*. In it, he confessed his growing doubts that American Communists could ever free themselves sufficiently from racial prejudices to win the black masses to their cause. In the fourteen months between these first and last *Liberator* articles, he also wrote, among other things, a review of the pioneering black musical, *Shuffle Along,* which appeared on Broadway in 1922, several other theater and book reviews, a commentary on Marcus Garvey as a "Negro Moses," and an impassioned denunciation of racial segregation in New York theaters.[53]

In "How Black Sees Green and Red," he displayed his familiarity with the British and Irish scene by using the Sinn Fein movement to illustrate a number of points. McKay loved the Irish. He considered them racially prejudiced, like other whites, but not hypocritical, like the Anglo-Saxons. He believed that Irish independence represented the first step in "the dissolution of the British Empire and the ushering in of an era of proletarian states, [which] will give England her proper proportional place in the political affairs of the world." At the same time, McKay had no illusions about Ireland's "bourgeois nationalists." For this reason, despite his admiration for Sinn Fein, McKay declared that "it is with the proletarian revolutionists of the world that my whole spirit revolts." Moreover, he added,

> the yearning of the American Negro especially, can only find expression and realization ín the class struggle. . . . For the Negro is in a peculiar position in America. In spite of a professional here and a businessman there, the maintenance of an all-white supremacy in the industrial and social life, as well as the governing bodies of the nation, places the entire

race alongside the lowest section of the white working class. They are struggling for identical things. They fight along different lines simply because they are not as class conscious and intelligent as the classes they are fighting. . . . The Negro must acquire class consciousness. And the white workers must accept him and work with him, whether they object to his color and morals or not. For his presence is a menacing reality.

In this regard, he now found Marcus Garvey's black nationalist leadership totally deficient, and in his article on him, McKay stressed that Garvey had repudiated "all the fundamentals of the black worker's struggle." Garvey, McKay wrote, "talks of Africa as if it were a little island in the Caribbean Sea. . . . He has never urged Negroes to organize in industrial unions."[54]

McKay's criticism of Garvey appeared only after the latter's federal indictment for alleged mail fraud. Like many black intellectuals, and especially most black socialists, McKay had earlier viewed Garvey's movement as an unprecedented opportunity for racial organization and advancement. Garvey, however, believed in the great-man theory of history. He would have nothing to do with ideas that conflicted with his basic belief that "the fundamental issue of life [is] the appeal of race to race . . . of clan to clan . . . of tribe to tribe, of observing the rule that self-preservation [is] the first law of nature." Others, such as Mussolini and Hitler, as well as members of the Ku Klux Klan in the United States, thought along similar lines. Such opinions meant only an intensification of racial antagonisms. "All who think broadly on social conditions," McKay declared, "are amazed at Garvey's ignorance and his intolerance of modern social ideas." At the same time, McKay admitted that Garvey was "beyond doubt a very energetic and quick witted mind, barb-wired by the imperial traditions of nineteenth-century England." And he had proven himself a "universal advertising manager" by becoming "the biggest popularizer of the Negro problem, especially among Negroes, since *Uncle Tom's Cabin*." Garvey's spirit, McKay concluded, was revolutionary, "but his intellect does not understand the significance of modern revolutionary developments." But then again, "maybe he chose not to understand" because "a resolute facing of facts would make puerile his beautiful schemes for the redemption . . . of Africa."[55]

If Garvey disappointed him, other developments in black American life provided encouragement. In particular, McKay saw in the new musical *Shuffle Along*, written and directed entirely by blacks, proof that black artists might soon break through "the screen of sneering bigotry put between them and life by the dominant race" and begin to express for all to see that zestful "warmth, color and laughter" in black communities that had "yet to be depicted by a true artist." McKay had special praise for Florence Mills, "the sparkling gold star of the show." And his review, together with Hugo Gellert's illustrations, caused "a sensation among the theatrical set in Harlem." McKay never forgot *Shuffle Along*. In *A Long Way from Home*, he stated that "it definitely showed the Negro groping, fumbling, and emerging in artistic group expression." Others have since concluded that *Shuffle Along* was indeed a milestone in black theater.[56]

As the sometime drama critic of the *Liberator*, McKay reviewed other productions in 1921 and 1922, notably Eugene O'Neill's *Emperor Jones* and the musical review *Chauve Souris*, which featured Russian entertainers, musicians, and themes. His most brilliant review by far, however, was his report in the May, 1922, *Liberator* of his experience at the Theatre Guild's presentation of Leonid Andreyev's *He Who Gets Slapped*. When the Theatre Guild tickets arrived at the *Liberator* offices, McKay elected himself "dramatic critic by acclamation" and invited along his friend William Gropper, whom he described as that "*Liberator* artist of the powerful punch and vindictive line, and master of the grotesque." On the appointed night, McKay arrived at the theater in high spirits. He keenly relished the prospect of sitting "in a free front-row parquet along with 'The Press,' instead of buying a ticket for the second balcony."[57]

When he and Gropper presented their stubs, however, the usher hurried off in search of the manager, who presently appeared and presented the startled pair with a new set of tickets for the rear balcony, where, according to Gropper, they were placed behind a post and "could neither see nor hear the performance." In his subsequent review of *He Who Gets Slapped* McKay rose to polemical heights that he never again equaled in his prose. "I had . . . come as a drama critic," he wrote, "a lover of the theatre, and a free soul."

> But I was abruptly reminded that all these things did not matter . . . the important fact, with which I was suddenly slapped in the face, was my color. I am a Negro. . . . I had come to see a tragic farce—and I found myself unwillingly the hero of one. As always in the world-embracing Anglo-Saxon circus, the intelligence, the sensibilities of the black clown were slapped without mercy.
>
> Poor painful blackface, intruding into the holy place of the whites. How like a spectre you haunt the pale devils! Always at their elbows, always darkly peering through the window, giving them no rest, no peace. How they burn up their energies trying to keep you out! How apologetic and uneasy they are, yes, even the best of them, poor devils, when you force an entrance, blackface, facetiously, incorrigibly smiling or disturbingly com-

posed. Shock them out of their complacency, blackface, make them uncomfortable, make them unhappy! Give them no peace, no rest. How can
they bear your presence, blackface, great unspeakable ghost of Western
civilization.[58]

McKay's last article in the August, 1922, *Liberator,* was super-
ficially a review of T. S. Stribling's novel *Birthright.* It was actually a
warning to his radical friends not to ignore "the ugly fact" that the
Negro's sufferings as a worker were relatively greater than those of
the white worker. He warned that without this recognition of the
Negro's special problems, "the pretty parlor talk of international
brotherhood" and "the radical shibboleth of class struggle" would be
insufficient to resolve the race problem. Above all, he warned that
radicals themselves were often prone to succumb to racism when it
suited their convenience. McKay stated that such articles as Morel's
"Outcry Against the Black Horror" not only aided the bourgeoisie in
pitting white against black "but also the ultranationalist Negro leaders, who, in their insistent appeal to the race prejudice of blacks
against whites declare that no class of white people will ever understand the black race." McKay then scored his main point:

> This racial question may be eventually the monkey wrench thrown into
> the machinery of the American revolutionary struggle. The Negro radical
> wants more than anything else to find in the working class movement a
> revolutionary attitude toward the Negroes different from the sympathetic
> interest of bourgeois philanthropists and capitalist politicians. And if the
> interest is not practially demonstrated, Negro leaders can hardly go to the
> ignorant black masses and show them why they should organize and
> work by the standard of the white workers. Karl Marx's economic theories
> are hard to digest, and Negroes . . . may find it easier to put their faith in
> the gospel of that other Jew, Jesus. . . . And in that event the black workers
> will lose—and the ruling classes will win.[59]

In large measure, McKay's remarks reflected the tensions on the
*Liberator* staff that by August, 1922, led him to resign his editorship.
During his first seven months with the *Liberator,* no serious problems developed. The magazine had sufficient money to meet its
monthly costs, a sizable readership, and a relatively unified editorial
staff. Then, in October, 1921, its bookkeeper, E. F. Mylius, embezzled
$4,500 from the *Liberator*'s operating funds and squandered it in
stock market speculations. The editors suddenly discovered they had
almost no money in the bank.[60]

For Eastman, who had earlier attempted to lessen his involvement
with the *Liberator,* it was the last straw. At a special staff meeting

a few weeks later, the increasingly dogmatic Michael Gold assailed his "lackadaisical" attitude and "remoteness from the suffering proletariat" and challenged his right to remain as editor. Instead of defending himself, Eastman quietly took the opportunity to tender his resignation and to announce plans for a trip to western Europe and Russia. He mischievously suggested that Gold himself assume the editorship of the magazine. An anxious discussion ensued and "in the small hours of the night," at Eastman's suggestion, it was finally agreed that Gold and Claude McKay would assume joint editorship of the *Liberator*.[61]

Eastman no doubt reasoned that McKay's sophistication and radical skepticism would balance Gold's tendency toward revolutionary extremism. Over the last year Gold had first suffered a nervous breakdown and had afterward rededicated himself with increased zeal to furthering his revolutionary convictions.[62] Eastman knew McKay possessed none of Gold's fanaticism. He hoped that McKay's "political intelligence" and "literary tastes" would balance Gold's strident, increasingly humorless Communist absolutism. In private, Eastman suspected that neither really had the patience and tact necessary to manage "the rather impractical bunch of creative geniuses that had gathered around [the magazine]. . . . They were both richly endowed with complexes." And, Eastman later wrote, "Claude looked upon Mike's tobacco-stained teeth, and his idea of [a proletariat literature] as the opposite of a poised loyalty to art and the proletariat."[63]

Nonetheless, beginning with the January, 1922, issue their names appeared as the new "executive editors" of the *Liberator*. For a brief while, ideological and temperamental differences were subordinated to the practical necessities that confronted them. Money had to be raised immediately. Appeals were made for contributors; a variety of *Liberator* forums, social affairs, and even a sporting evening were staged as fund-raisers. Eastman stayed around long enough to help them put out their first two issues before sailing for Europe in February. His departure hurt. No one else had his ability to extract generous contributions from wealthy liberals who seemed alternately sympathetic to and frightened by radical-bohemian literature and politics. With his relaxed, aristocratic charm, Eastman had consistently put them at ease. After his departure, the *Liberator* had to struggle as never before, but it survived, at least for a while.[64]

Along with everyone else on the staff, McKay did his bit as a fund-raiser. It was McKay's urging, for example, that induced his friend Grace Campbell to persuade "Chris Huiswoud, the only Negro basketball referee in the country, to feature two black and white basketball games and [a] dance for the *Liberator* at the New Star Casino on the 10th of March, [1922]." Apparently Huiswoud had some misgivings, for a *Liberator* editorial (probably by McKay) remarked that "Chris . . . notwithstanding a most top-lofty aloofness toward economic and class differences, is a real sport and takes a sporting interest in a magazine like the *Liberator*. All Liberators should make it their business and pack New Star Casino to the roof."[65]

McKay also made a special effort to attract good writers to the *Liberator*. Like most irreverent spirits of the day, he had a special fondness for the caustic humor of H. L. Mencken, who since World War I had edited *Smart Set*. He had once expressed to Mike Gold a willingness to contribute to the *Liberator,* and at the end of March, 1922, McKay informed Mencken that "anything" from him "at this time . . . would be a big help to us, for now that Max Eastman is away, we are finding it harder than ever to get good writing to keep up the standard of the magazine." Mencken responded with four pen-and-pencil sketches of eastern European radicals that he had acquired in the course of his editorial duties. In June, McKay thanked him but insisted that he still wanted an article. Lest Mencken hesitate because of ideological considerations, McKay pointed out that "our gang here hold divergent views on politics too—what holds us together is that we are all rebellious and have a vague idea of revolutionary change, however far away it may be." McKay went on to say that he and Eastman held "radically different" views from Gold and Minor, and that Floyd Dell and Charles Wood went off at yet another angle. *Liberator* contributors, moreover, included everyone from anarchists to the liberal bourgeoisie. "So," McKay concluded, "there is room for you even if you only want to say 'why my love of free expression, etc. makes me seem revolutionary to radicals though I am at heart a very old style Southern Gentleman.'"[66] McKay came closer to the truth than perhaps he realized. Mencken never wrote for the *Liberator,* and by the end of his life he revealed himself to be a political reactionary. He did answer McKay's letters, however, and the two corresponded periodically over the next three years.

One prospective contributor whose striking originality had caused "lively discussions" among the *Liberator* staff in December, 1921, was Jean Toomer, a young Afro-American author. Through the spring of 1922 he sent the magazine extracts from his as yet unpublished novel *Cane,* now generally recognized as a great work of eccentric genius.[67] McKay was intrigued by Toomer's stories, but along with the rest of the editorial staff, he initially decided against their publication. On December 6, 1921, he wrote to "Miss Toomer" that his story was "a little too long, not clear enough, and quite lacking in unity. Perhaps if you would send us a very short sketch that could hold the reader's attention all through, we might be able to use it." Through June, McKay persisted in thinking Toomer a woman. He liked the "bright local coloring and individual poetic power" of Toomer's stories but "none ever seemed to carry clear through from beginning to end on a high level." He nevertheless urged Toomer to continue to submit his pieces to the *Liberator* and agreed with him that the magazine would "always be a living force whilst it retains [a] free artistic spirit."[68]

In July, McKay finally learned Toomer's true gender and apologized for "my mistaking you for the other sex. But," he added, "it wasn't such a bad mistake if you are not anti-feminist." Eventually, in September and October, 1922, the *Liberator* published two stories and a poem by Toomer, but even then McKay accorded them only qualified approval: "I liked your poem in the September *Liberator*—the sketch not so particularly well in spite of its high points. Some day I hope I shall be able to talk to you about such things."[69]

By September, McKay's active participation in *Liberator* editorial decisions had ceased. Despite a real effort on his part to ignore Michael Gold's strident concentration within himself of all the world's proletarian anger, the two could not get along.

Michael Gold, born Irwin Granich, was a Jew who had grown up in the wretched tenements of New York's Lower East Side. His past quite clearly haunted him in complex and ambiguous ways. "We cling to the old culture [of capitalism]," he wrote, "and fight for it against ourselves. But it must die. The old ideals must die. . . . Let us fling all we are into the cauldron of the Revolution." Seeing no way to take the whole of his capitalist or his Jewish inheritance through the revolutionary struggle, Gold frantically fashioned for himself a self-image that would survive the upheavals to come. He became the class-conscious, street-tough child of the tenement. "Intellectuals have become bored with the primitive monotony of Life—with the deep truths and instincts," he declared. "The boy in the tenement must not learn of their art. He must stay in the tenement and create a new and truer one there." He must identify wholly with the masses, for "they are the eternal truth."[70]

Joseph Freeman remembered that Gold "affected dirty shirts, a big, black uncleaned Stetson with the brim of a sombrero; smoked stinking, twisted Italian three-cent cigars, and spat frequently and vigorously on the floor—whether that floor was covered by an expensive carpet in a rich aesthetic's studio or on the bare wooden floor of [his] . . . small office."[71]

To McKay such behavior seemed childish. When in June, 1922, word reached him that Gold, a former amateur boxer of repute, had strode through the Civic Club, a gathering place of liberal reformers, in his usual dress and with a noticeably aggressive manner, McKay remarked that he "didn't see any point in doing that to the pacifist Civic Club; that he might have gone instead to the Union League Club." The comment eventually reached Gold's ear, and he found McKay one evening at John's Italian Restaurant and challenged him to box. McKay shrugged and said he would, but he explained that their differences were actually intellectual and could not be settled by fighting. "So we laughed the matter off," McKay recalled, "and drank a bottle of dago red together. However, I saw clearly that our association could not continue." [72]

Shortly afterward, McKay resigned his post as executive editor and Joseph Freeman succeeded him. Gold wanted desperately for the *Liberator* to "express . . . the punch and the raw stuff of life and labor," and had earlier attacked Eastman for being "too much of an esthete, too Baudelaire-like in his poetic expression." McKay had sided with Eastman. He thought Gold too sentimentally enthralled by the idea of bringing forth in the pages of the *Liberator* a new literature produced by the proletariat. This preoccupation, McKay believed, undermined Gold's critical judgment. From the start, there had been little agreement between them. The six months of their joint editorship from January to June, 1922, provided everyone on the *Liberator* staff a chance to see their essential incompatibility. In fact, according to Eastman, McKay and Gold had eventually "announced" their differences to be irreconcilable and had "compelled the board of editors to choose between [them]." The other editors, partly because of Eastman's advice from abroad, chose Gold to carry on as executive editor. Only then, according to Eastman, did McKay resign. [73]

Eastman's account was essentially correct. McKay had no desire to work under Gold, and rather than remain as a disruptive force, he simply withdrew from all editorial work on the *Liberator*. Eastman later explained to McKay the reason for his recommendation that Gold continue as chief editor: "On the basis of the magazines you each put out, in spite of the superior reliability and delicacy of yours, I was in favor of Mike because his magazine had more 'pep.'" [74]

Like Eastman before him, though for different reasons, McKay did not find it too difficult to give up his *Liberator* responsibilities. In addition to his differences with Gold, McKay by June had also become disenchanted with what he considered the *Liberator* staff's myopic approach to the race question. With both the *Workers' Dreadnought* in London and the *Liberator* in New York, he had found a rare personal camaraderie, but he had also found that in general neither the British nor the American Left had the foresight regarding racial matters he thought essential if radicals were to win blacks to their cause. On the contrary, he found that far too many communists and socialists were themselves still afflicted with the racist phobias common to the age and that, when it suited their purposes, they did not hesitate to voice them.[75]

McKay actually functioned on two levels as a *Liberator* editor. On one level, he was simply an artist among equals and was accepted as such. There was always room for disagreements and arguments at staff meetings, and the *Liberator* often reflected the chaotic diversity of opinions current among its editors and writers. It was in this highly individualistic atmosphere that McKay debated with Gold and others about the relationship between art and revolution. On a strictly racial level, however, McKay was disadvantaged in such a freewheeling atmosphere. As the magazine's solitary black man, he brought a perspective on the racial question that the other staff members could share only up to a point. For McKay, the revolutionary's handling of the racial problem was necessarily of decisive importance, while to the other *Liberator* editors it was only one important problem among many. Because of their other preoccupations and also because their readership was overwhelmingly white (and potentially flighty where race was concerned), the white staff members sometimes questioned the amount of space devoted to racial matters. McKay never actually demanded more space on the subject than his fellow editors were willing to give, but their fearfulness where race was concerned annoyed him. He pointed out that since blacks constituted 10 percent of the nation's population, it would not be unfair to devote at least that amount of space in the *Liberator* to their problems. Even this seemed to some a proposal that, if carried out, would jeopardize the magazine's appeal to white readers. In short, McKay's position as a black man vitally concerned with pushing forward a black radical perspective on a predominantly white journal created for him problems that figured prominently as an unspoken though underlying reason for his willingness to leave the *Liberator* in June, 1922.[76]

Almost a year later, McKay voiced these racial considerations in a manuscript he was preparing for publication in the Soviet Union, and his frankness resulted in a heated correspondence with Max Eastman. Eastman felt that McKay had made his resignation appear to be the "direct result of a disagreement about the race question," that he had distorted "completely" the nature of such disagreements as did exist, and that he had demonstrated a highly emotional, sub-jective conception of "the Negro problem," instead of a "scientific" perspective on the class struggle. His accusations, Eastman ob-served, seemed to have been dictated "by some obscure motive of re-sentment." McKay replied that he had "no intention of letting the public think I withdrew . . . solely because of a disagreement over the race question." In any event, he reminded Eastman, their personal correspondence clearly showed he had long been preparing to leave the *Liberator.* "But," he stressed, "I want to state emphatically . . . that [Michael Gold] made the race story in the June *Liberator* the basis of his attack on me, and his opinion . . . and the discussions . . . by the *Liberator* group revealed to me that the group did not have a . . . comprehensive grasp of the Negro's place in the class struggle." McKay admitted that "the race matter was incidental to my quitting the executive work," but he had seen clearly that "the leading minds" of the *Liberator* understood little about the revolutionary implica-tions of the racial struggle in America or abroad. McKay stressed that Eastman was mistaken to think that the *Liberator* group had ever ar-rived at any agreement about its policy on race. "In fact," McKay de-clared, "as a group we never even discussed the labor movement seri-ously. My position on the *Liberator* I discussed seriously only with the radical Negro group in New York. . . . I tried to discuss the Irish and Indian questions with you once or twice, . . . but with little sym-pathy you said that they were national issues. I never once thought you grasped fully the class struggle significance of national and ra-cial problems. . . . I don't know why, my dear Max, but the atmo-sphere of the *Liberator* did not make for serious discussion on any of the real problems of Capitalist Society much less the Negro."[77]

McKay stated that in joining the *Liberator,* he had hoped "to fur-ther a solution of the Negro problem in the revolution." In criticism, Eastman replied he must have had other motives as well, "because I know that you are not a more simple person than others; rather you are more complex." In reply, McKay acknowledged that his job on the *Liberator* had secured him food and shelter. As to being complex, he pointed out that no black man in America could get anywhere if he were not complex. "And," he concluded, "I am complex enough to forgive your sneer at my saying that . . . I was 'moved by the desire to further a solution of the Negro problem in the revolution.'"[78]

If nothing else, their quarrel demonstrated the social, cultural, and ideological differences and misunderstandings that have often existed between even the closest white and black radicals in the United States. Probably as a consequence of their argument, McKay deleted from the published version of his manuscript all details relating to his resignation from the *Liberator* staff. Since the manuscript has been lost, their correspondence is all that remains of the deleted "chapter" from what became McKay's Russian-language book, *Negroes in America*.

In the spring of 1922, however, as his dispute with Michael Gold approached its inevitable climax, McKay's *Harlem Shadows* finally appeared. By far his most important book of poetry, it contained all the best poems he had written since his first arrival in the United States in 1912. There were seventy poems in *Harlem Shadows*. Thematically they could be about equally divided into three categories—nostalgic poems concerning Jamaica and nature, love poems, and poems bearing on his racial experience. Almost all the poems in his previous book, *Spring in New Hampshire*, were included in *Harlem Shadows*.

With its appearance, McKay was immediately acclaimed the best black poet since Paul Laurence Dunbar. The New York *Times* noted that McKay's efforts marked a clean break with the dialect tradition of Dunbar. It also pointed out McKay's preference for "the more conservative verse forms" and speculated that he was perhaps attempting to portray the spirit of the modern Negro "in a high and lofty manner." The reviewer concluded by stating that although "certain portions unravel into mere sentiment," McKay had by and large succeeded in his purpose.[79]

The most searching review was Robert Littel's in the *New Republic*. Littel considered McKay "a real poet, though by no means a great one. . . . A hospitality to echoes of poetry he has read has time and again obscured a direct sense of life and made rarer those lines of singular intensity which . . . reveal [his] naked force of character." Littel nevertheless praised McKay where he thought praise was due, and he was especially impressed by his protest poetry. In the same review, he also wrote about James Weldon Johnson's *Book of American Negro Poetry* and concluded that "if McKay and the other poets don't stir me unusually when they travel over the poetic roads so many others have traveled . . . they make me sit up and take notice when they write about their race and ours. They strike hard and pierce deep. It is not merely poetic emotion they express, but something fierce and constant, and icy cold, and white hot."[80]

Black reviewers were generally less reserved in their assessment of McKay's poetry. This was especially true of Walter White and James Weldon Johnson of the NAACP. White called McKay "without doubt the most talented and versatile of the new school of imaginative, emotional Negro poets." He concluded by boldly asserting that "Mr. McKay is not a great Negro poet—he is a great poet." James Weldon Johnson in the New York *Age* reaffirmed White's contention: "Mr. McKay is a real poet and a great poet. . . . No Negro has sung more beautifully of his race than McKay and no poet has ever equalled the power with which he expresses the bitterness that so often rises in the heart of the race. . . . The race ought to be proud of a poet capable of voicing it so fully. Such a voice is not found every day. . . . What he has achieved in this little volume sheds honor upon the whole race."[81]

In 1920, Hubert Harrison in a review of *Spring in New Hampshire* in the *Negro World* had already praised McKay's accomplishments and had lambasted the black press for having failed to recognize his talents. "Without any aid from Negro editors or publications," Harrison argued, "he made his way because white people who noted his gifts were eager to give him a chance while Negro editors, as usual, were either too blind to see or too mean-spirited to proclaim them to the world." In 1922, Harrison also reviewed *Harlem Shadows,* this time for the New York *World.* Perhaps because of McKay's angry letter back in January, it contained less fervent praise than his earlier review, though he concluded by asserting that "there can be no doubt that in range, technique and mastery of the medium of verse Claude McKay is the greatest living poet of Negro blood in America today."[82]

In Garvey's *Negro World,* a fellow West Indian, Hodge Kirnon, wrote perhaps the longest and most appreciative review of *Harlem Shadows.* Kirnon had long held the menial position of elevator operator at 291 Fifth Avenue, the location of Alfred Stieglitz's famous photographic studio and art gallery. Running an elevator had not prevented Kirnon from becoming a sensitive and skilled observer of the Harlem cultural scene. In his review of *Harlem Shadows,* he strove to point out McKay's real strengths as a poet. Kirnon praised McKay's simplicity, his "rare" balance of thought and emotion, and his "revelation of the spiritual isolation and loneliness which many of us—rich and poor, white and black—have felt quite often in the heart of the noise and bustle of this great city." As an immigrant, Kirnon had special words of praise for the poem "America," McKay's declaration of love for the vitality and strength he had found in the United States. For Kirnon, the poem expressed "in a most satisfactory manner what I have always felt and thought to be the main redeeming feature of America. And I daresay many other aliens like myself have felt and thought in like manner without ever giving [it] expression." In a letter, McKay thanked Kirnon for his review and emphasized that he appreciated the "real feeling" Kirnon had shown for his poetry. "I am so sick," he wrote, "of pretentious critics posturing about creative work which they haven't the understanding heart to comprehend."[83]

There were other black poets writing in 1922 whose work was in some ways more attuned than McKay's to the modernist trends in American poetry. The critic Clement Wood noted two in his review of *Harlem Shadows*. "Fenton Johnson and Anne Spencer among Negro poets," he observed, "have gone much further in the newer modes of singing." But McKay's verse still struck him as "modern in its directness and simplicity, its vigor and variety."[84]

McKay's sensitivity, his "naked force of character," and, above all, as James Weldon Johnson noted, his ability to voice "so fully . . . the bitterness that so often rises in the heart of [his] race," placed him in 1922 at the forefront of black American poets. If his style was in most respects anachronistic and sometimes clumsy, his essential message of alienation, anger, and rebellion was thoroughly modern. And while T. S. Eliot and James Joyce in 1922 were proclaiming in *The Waste Land* and *Ulysses* the bankruptcy of Western culture, McKay in the *Liberator* was passionately exhorting his people to live in the full knowledge that their days of triumph lay ahead:

> I cry my woe to the whirling world, but not in despair. For I understand the forces that doom the race into which I was born to lifelong discrimination and servitude. And I know that these forces are not eternal, they can be destroyed and will be destroyed. They are marked for destruction. Mesopotamia, Egypt, Greece, Carthage, Arabia, Babylonia, Tyre, Persia, Rome, Germania! The whole historical pageant of the human race unfolds before me in high consolation.
>
> Cherish your strength, my strong black brother. Be not dismayed because the struggle is hard and long, O, my warm, wonderful race. The fight is longer than a span of life; the test is great. Gird your loins, sharpen your tools! Time is on our side. Carry on the organizing and conserving of your forces, my dear brother, grim with determination, for a great purpose—for the Day![85]

With *Harlem Shadows*, McKay became in effect the pacesetter for a new generation of black American poets and novelists. As the 1920s progressed, they would move significantly beyond the genteel and the old dialect traditions of previous generations in their exploration of the black American experience. Jean Toomer's *Cane* was already finished and would be published in 1923. By the middle of the decade a cluster of even younger writers would appear. Langston Hughes, Countee Cullen, Nella Larsen, Rudolph Fisher, Eric Waldron, and Wallace Thurman would all contribute their diverse talents to the awakening of Harlem as the black literary and artistic capital of America.[86]

The ground for this harvest had been broken over a decade earlier when the NAACP and the National Urban League established their national offices in New York. They started monthly magazines that attracted young black writers and began to cultivate among white publishers, editors, and producers a receptivity to black art and artists. McKay was among the very first to take advantage of these new developments.[87] By the time Alain Locke formally introduced the "New Negro" in his famous anthology of 1925, McKay was far from Harlem and older by some ten years than the average young writer represented in Locke's volume.[88]

The July, 1922, *Liberator* announced that Claude McKay was "resigning as an executive officer of the *Liberator* to be free to write poetry and to see more of the world than is permitted to an office worker on a magazine." He would continue as a contributing editor, and his work would "have the same high place in the pages of the *Liberator* as heretofore." In fact, McKay's career with the *Liberator* was over; he published only one more article, "Birthright," his angry polemic against socialist shortsightedness concerning the Negro. It appeared in the August issue. A single poem entitled "Petrograd: May Day, 1923," appeared exactly a year later.[89]

When Eastman left the *Liberator* early in 1922, the remaining editors had promised him to turn the magazine over to the Workers' party if they could no longer keep it afloat. In November, 1922, a new financial crisis delayed the magazine's appearance for a month. When it reappeared in December, 1922, the *Liberator* announced it would "direct attention more deliberately than heretofore to the Workers' Party." Over the next year, party affairs and ideology dominated its pages. Finally, in 1924, the *Liberator* "combined with William Z. Foster's *Labor Herald* and with *Soviet Russia Pictorial* to form a regular propaganda organ called the *Communist Monthly*, owned by the American Communist Party and edited by its future leader, Earl Browder."[90]

Joseph Freeman, Robert Minor, and Michael Gold all became party members, subject to the regulation and discipline of the party executive and bureaucratic chain of command. As Daniel Aaron has observed, the Gold-McKay dispute in its larger significance thus represented the decisive battle between those on the *Liberator* who refused to subordinate their art wholly to revolutionary political considerations and those willing to shape their art to fit party policies.[91]

In alluding to McKay's position in the conflict, Joseph Freeman later stated that "Claude McKay's warm, sensuous, . . . heart swam in thoughtlessness; he was aggressively antirational on the principle that art comes exclusively from the emotions and that he was primarily an artist."[92] Freeman oversimplified McKay's position; he was less thoughtless and more rational than most supposed.

By the summer of 1922, McKay had worked almost three years with radical magazines in London and New York. And although he had grown impatient with and discouraged by the many obstacles to black and white revolutionary cooperation in Europe and America, the Soviet example still attracted him. It represented a fresh departure in the affairs of men. Its triumph promised a resolution to the Russian empire's centuries-old national and ethnic problems, and its leadership of the international Communist movement could not be ignored. McKay had wanted to visit the Soviet Union for several years. Jack Reed had urged him to come, and he had since read accounts of many who had made the journey. Having just published *Harlem Shadows* and without editorial responsibilities, McKay at last felt free to see for himself "the grand experiment" taking place in Russia.[93]

After leaving the *Liberator,* he loafed for a while with "a small circle of friends. We convived together," he later explained, "consuming synthetic gin." During this summer of relative inactivity, the unexpected reappearance of his wife, whom he had not seen in more than seven years, galvanized him into action and sealed his determination to visit the Soviet Union. Among other things, her sudden return made him acutely aware of how weary he had grown of the never-ending race consciousness that was part of life in the United States. He longed to find a freer atmosphere. As he recalled, he wished to "escape from the pit of sex and poverty, from domestic death, from the cul-de-sac of self-pity, from the hot syncopated fascination of Harlem, from the suffocating ghetto of color consciousness."[94]

Deciding to go was one thing. Actually getting there presented another set of problems. Despite the critical success of *Harlem Shadows*, it did not sell well enough for him to afford a trip to the Soviet Union. He had no influence within the emerging American Communist party, nor did he have any official invitation from the Soviet government. To finance his projected trip, friends once again had to come to his aid.

At the suggestion of James Weldon Johnson, McKay sent autographed copies of *Harlem Shadows* to "a select list of persons connected with the NAACP" and asked each for a five-dollar donation. In addition, Crystal Eastman appealed to friends of the *Liberator* on McKay's behalf. Between his black and white admirers—liberals, radicals, and bohemians—enough money was raised by September, 1922, for him to depart. He hoped to arrive in time to attend the Fourth Congress of the Third Communist International scheduled to begin in Moscow in November.[95]

McKay knew of course that once in the Soviet Union, he would be on his own, financially, so he asked H. L. Mencken to recommend him to the Baltimore *Sun* as a special correspondent. McKay explained that he wished to study the status of "the old-estate peasantry" and the Jews under the new Soviet regime and to compare their past and present conditions with those of southern Negroes in the United States. "I want to ask you," he concluded, "(if you consider my project commendable) to use your influence in getting me a commission from the *Sun* to do a series of special articles. Is there any chance?" There was none; despite Mencken's intercession, he got no commission from the *Sun* or from anyone else. He would have to take his chances that, once abroad, he could find an income.[96]

McKay left the United States around September 20. On the eve of his departure, James Weldon Johnson gave him a farewell party and invited prominent writers of both races. Years later, Johnson wrote McKay: "We often speak of that party back in '22. . . . Do you know that was the first getting together of the black and white literati on a purely social plane. Such parties are now common in New York, but I doubt any has been more representative. You remember there were present Heywood Broun, Ruth Hale, F. P. Adams, John Farrar, Carl Van Doren, Freda Kirchwey, Peggy Tucker, Roy Nash—on our side you, DuBois, Walter White, Jessie Fauset, [Arthur] Schomburg, J. Rosamond Johnson—I think that party started something."[97]

As he prepared to leave New York that fall, McKay could not have known all that would await him in Russia. Nor could he have foreseen that he would afterward spend the next twelve years in western Europe and North Africa. The night before his departure, he was nevertheless in a reflective mood. He had planned a last meal with his good friend Crystal Eastman, but after waiting half the evening for her arrival, he went out alone and dropped in at several of his favorite Harlem haunts where he drank "a farewell to the illegal bars" of Prohibition America. At one speakeasy, he ran into Hubert Harrison, and they had a drink together. But McKay did not tell him he was leaving the next day. Perhaps their relationship had not fully recovered from the incident that had caused McKay so much embarrassment, or as McKay later put it in *A Long Way from Home,* he may simply have refrained from mentioning his sailing to Harrison "or any of my few familiars" because "sentimental *adieux* embarrass me." Back home in the early morning hours, he found Crystal had, after all, dropped by and had left him a note—"Claude dear: I just dashed in to give you a hug and say goodbye—Bon Voyage, dear child!"[98] He slipped the note into his billfold and went to sleep.

Since his return from England in February, 1921, McKay had broadened his contacts with both black and white intellectuals in New York City and had, on the surface at least, secured his reputation as an important black poet and perceptive journalist and editor. On a more personal level, however, he remained in a state of transition. Although he was still a self-proclaimed revolutionary, he no longer trusted most of his comrades on the *Liberator*. They seemed to him increasingly committed to the emerging Communist party ideology at the expense of their artistic independence, and he knew them to be quite limited in their comprehension of the importance of blacks to the success of any revolutionary movement in the United States. Despite his continued commitment to communism, he still clung to his independence as a literary artist and openly proclaimed his belief that an artist should not subordinate his aesthetic freedom to his political convictions.

McKay's primary loyalties unquestionably lay with the black quest "to gain the utmost freedom that is life."[99] Socialism still seemed to him the theory that best explained the historic injustices under which all blacks lived, and Marxist communism still appeared to him the path for blacks and whites in their quest for justice. But by 1922, McKay had begun to question whether or not Marx's program for world history would automatically fulfill itself. In large part, he left for Russia in the hope that he could find there evidence that the equality, justice, freedom, and humane treatment of his fellow men he had envisioned under socialism was actually taking place. He already had his doubts.

# 6
# The Journey to Russia, 1922—1923

McKay began his epic journey around September 20, 1922, shortly before his thirty-second birthday. To conserve the modest funds he had collected from his friends, he signed as a stoker on a merchant ship bound for England and worked his way across the Atlantic. According to his subsequent description of life as a seaman in his first novel, *Home to Harlem,* he did not particularly enjoy his voyage. The ship he described "stank between sea and sky" and his fictional hero breathed relief at the thought of leaving it.[1]

After arriving in Liverpool in early October, McKay went directly to London, where he expected, through the intercession of his Communist friends, to secure a visa for Russia. At the International Socialist Club, he saw a number of old acquaintances, but several had already departed for the Soviet Union. A few had gone to stay; others had left to attend the Fourth Congress of the Third International scheduled to convene in November. The official delegation of the Communist Party of Great Britain offered McKay no aid. They remembered him as a former member of the quarrelsome Pankhurst group. One of their members, Arthur MacManus, told him that he should have secured the assistance of American Communists.

McKay did not let such rebuffs deter him. He learned that the former executive secretary of the Pankhurst group, Edgar Whitehead,
was currently working for the Comintern in Berlin as a liaison agent
and interpreter for the English-speaking radicals who were traveling
to Russia. McKay knew Whitehead well. In the past, they had together "waxed satirical about Communist orthodoxy and . . . had
often discussed the idea of a neo-radical magazine in which nothing
in the universe would be held sacred."[2]

McKay immediately left for Berlin. After a friendly reunion, Whitehead assured McKay he would get him to Russia in time to attend the
Fourth Congress. While waiting, McKay had a good time discovering
the wilder side of Berlin night life. His handsome face aroused interest wherever he went. He was especially welcome in the cabarets that
had "sprung up like mushrooms" since the end of the war. In the general confusion that followed the collapse of the monarchy and the
founding of Germany's new republican government, the cabarets
provided hedonistic relief from the economic uncertainty, political
unrest, and social turmoil that daily confronted the defeated, divided,
and embittered German populace. To McKay, the cabarets he visited
"seemed to express the ultimate in erotomania," where "youngsters
of both sexes . . . were methodically exploiting the nudist colony indoors." Such innovations, he concluded, were "more exciting than
the outdoor experiment." McKay also saw some of the new experi-
mental theater of the German expressionists. His introduction to
German cabaret and theater life must have been brief, however, because Whitehead soon escorted him before a Russian official for an
interview.[3]

McKay showed him a letter of recommendation from Crystal Eastman. He also explained that although he was not a member of any
official Communist party delegation traveling to Moscow, he nevertheless shared a belief in international communism and an enthusiasm for the accomplishments of the Russian Revolution. He wished
to attend the congress and to write about his visit for the black American press. McKay received his visa and soon traveled to the Baltic
port of Settin, where he boarded "an old potato boat" bound for Petrograd. Ironically, his companions on the voyage were a small group of
British Communists. Among them was his friend, the former IWW
organizer Charles Ashleigh, whom he had met the previous year in
New York.[4] From Petrograd, McKay went by train to Moscow and arrived there about a week before the Fourth Congress convened. It
was scheduled to begin November 5, 1922, and would last for a
month. Delegations were arriving from the Communist parties of all

the major nations, including the United States.[5] Once in Moscow, McKay still had to secure permission from Comintern authorities to attend the congress as an unofficial delegate-observer. But his right even to be in Russia, much less attend the congress, was immediately challenged by the American Communist delegation.

The American Communist party, long internally divided, had brought to Moscow for final settlement the bitterly disputed question of whether it should maintain or abolish its illegal, underground apparatus, which it had established after the Palmer raids back in 1919. Besides maintaining an old European conspiratorial revolutionary tradition, the underground party seemed to many still necessary in capitalist America. American radicals had suffered considerable persecution since World War I, and a majority of the American delegates at the Fourth Congress understandably favored a continuation of the underground organization. Opposing them was a smaller contingent representative of the Workers' Party of America, the open, legal arm of the underground party, which had been created only in December, 1921.[6]

McKay's position on the question was clear: the party could do more effective work if it organized openly and aggressively pursued its goals within the American labor movement. When asked by Rose Pastor Stokes, one of the leading defenders of the illegal party, what he thought about the matter, McKay stated flatly that there was no need for an underground party in the United States. By thus lining up with the minority delegates led by James P. Cannon, McKay incurred the wrath of the majority. Although Cannon's group eventually won the Comintern's support, the view of the majority prevailed before the congress started. They initiated a campaign to discredit McKay as a revolutionary and have him expelled from the Soviet Union.[7]

As representatives of the American Communist party, only they could recommend that he be seated as a delegate. This they refused to do. Instead they conspired to throw him out of the relatively comfortable Lux Hotel. With winter rapidly approaching, all McKay could find was a single room with broken windowpanes, furnished only with an army cot. It was in "a dilapidated house in a sinister *pereulok*," where many lived in worse circumstances. He immediately rushed out and bought two blankets and a pair of long felt boots that reached to his thighs, "the kind," he later reported, "that Russian peasants wear."[8] He also set out to counter the increasingly dangerous campaign the American delegates had launched against him.

After considerable uncertainty and tension, McKay finally, and quite suddenly, won the right to attend the congress as "a special delegate." His vindication resulted from two causes. In the first place, Sen Katayama, the leading Japanese Communist at the congress, had lived for years in the United States and had known McKay in New York. Katayama convinced Comintern officials that McKay spoke with authority about the potential role of blacks in the international Communist movement. In his younger days, Katayama had attended a small Christian college near Nashville. While there, he became familiar with the black side of the American racial dilemma. Although no student record survives, McKay later maintained that Katayama had also attended classes at Fisk University; perhaps he was an unofficial auditor. At any rate, unlike most Russian and American Communists, he was thoroughly familiar with American blacks.[9]

McKay had met him while working on the *Liberator*, and the two had gotten along well. Katayama had taken McKay to lunch in Oriental restaurants in New York. They had talked for many hours about the effect of communism on colonial peoples and national minorities and had almost certainly learned much from each other. Katayama was always friendly and exceedingly curious. His "was a sort of minute methodical curiosity" that McKay had never encountered before, and he remarked in *A Long Way from Home* that "like a permanent surprise he invaded my rooms at all hours and talked in his squeaky grandmotherly voice about Negro problems." McKay had been impressed: "He demonstrated a vast interest and sympathy for Negro racialists and their organizations. I liked Sen Katayama immensely." In Moscow, Katayama proved a real friend. As McKay put it, he was "*the* Japanese revolutionist" within the Comintern. As one of the elder statesmen of international communism, his position was secure. In 1922, Katayama occupied a place of authority within the Comintern and was a great favorite with Russian Communists. A word from him regarding McKay's seat at the Fourth Congress probably carried more weight than the ill will of the entire American delegation.[10]

McKay's second source of support was the people in the streets. His color, his unmistakable Negroid features, his unusually high, arching brows, and his bright smile and rollicking laughter, all made him instantly attractive to the crowds that gathered daily for the celebration of the Bolshevik Revolution's fifth anniversary, which coincided with the opening of the congress. Years later McKay still marveled at the warm, spontaneous reception he had received from the Russian masses, and he felt that curiosity about his color alone was not responsible for it: "But, no! I soon apprehended that this . . . was a different thing. Just a spontaneous upsurging of folk feeling. . . . The Bolsheviks . . . soon . . . perceived the trend of the general enthusiasm for me and decided to use it. And I was not averse to that." The crowd sometimes demonstrated its affection in novel ways. En route to the opening of the Fourth Congress, for example, McKay had trouble making his way through the dense crowds along the Tverskaya Boulevard, when suddenly he was picked up and tossed along by the people for an entire block. "The civilians started it. The soldiers imitated them. And the sailors followed the soldiers, tossing me higher than ever."[11] Such spontaneous displays of acceptance gave McKay great joy. He had not expected to see "crowds . . . happier and friendlier than the crowds of New York and London and Berlin." The country had been at war for years, and the people were poorly housed and clad. Yet, far from being despondent and drained by their ordeal, they were exultant and hopeful about the future. Max Eastman, who had previously arrived in Moscow for the Fourth Congress, also noted this happy mood among the people. Late in his life, he remarked that the unusually festive atmosphere that pervaded the land in 1922 probably owed much to the revival of the economy that was occurring under Lenin's New Economic Policy, which for a time allowed the return of capitalistic enterprise.[12]

Much lay in store for McKay in Russia, but after winning acceptance as a delegate, his first obligation was to attend the Fourth Congress. In *A Long Way from Home,* his account of his participation in the proceedings of the congress seems substantially accurate. In one way, however, it was misleading; just as he had failed to explain the full extent to which he had become involved in the politics of the British radical Left, so too, in his account of the Fourth Congress, he failed to acknowledge frankly that he spoke as both a black Communist and a black writer who desperately wanted the Comintern to understand the position and potential of blacks within the international Communist movement. By the time he got to Moscow, McKay had grown skeptical about the willingness or ability of his white comrades in England or America to embrace blacks as true equals within the movement. The Comintern provided him a platform to relate his experiences and explain his perspective, and he took full advantage of the opportunity; he had, in fact, come to Moscow primed to attack American Communists for their reluctance to deal with the race problem.

At the same time, he felt uncomfortable in his role as a black radical spokesman. He considered himself primarily a creative writer who happened to hold radical social views, and he denied repeatedly that he wished to become a disciplined, full-time party worker. Despite this fundamental ambivalence, the Comintern deemed his point of view important enough to be heard. Previous congresses had had no opportunity to hear blacks speak out on their relationship to communism. Although McKay had no prestige within the national parties of either the United States or Great Britain, the Comintern recognized the importance of "the Negro problem" and allowed him to speak his mind.[13]

Another Negro, Otto Huiswoud, was also present. He was an official American party delegate. A mulatto several shades lighter than McKay, Huiswoud attracted considerably less attention at the congress and in the streets, but he enjoyed the confidence of American Communists and shared with McKay the task of presenting the black perspective to the assembled delegates. He and McKay were the first blacks to discuss the American race problem before the Third International. Both happened to be West Indians, Huiswoud being a native of Dutch Guiana.[14]

Prior to the Fourth Congress, the Communist International's first substantial investigation of the American race problem had been in 1920 at its Second Congress, when John Reed of the American delegation presented two long papers on the Afro-American in the United States. He presented one before a committee discussing "national and colonial questions" and the other before the assembled congress. In both papers he declared that American blacks were primarily interested in winning equal rights as citizens of the United States. He advised Communists to participate in Negro movements for social and political equality and at the same time endeavor to make blacks aware of how futile were their strivings for advancement in a "bourgeois society." Reed minimized the importance of black nationalist movements and stated that blacks in the United States considered themselves "first of all, Americans." After Reed's report, the Second Congress decided to invite a group of black revolutionists to Russia. Reed actually sent McKay such an invitation in 1920, but nothing came of it.[15]

Some months after the Second Congress, Lenin admonished his American comrades not to neglect blacks in their infant party but to recognize them as "a strategically important element in Communist activity." Only then did American Communists attempt any systematic recruitment of Afro-Americans. Their efforts led in 1921 and 1922 to the first substantial influx of blacks into the party, primarily through Cyril Briggs's African Blood Brotherhood.[16] This influx, of course, coincided with McKay's association with the *Liberator* and with the brotherhood. Despite his later denials that he ever became a party member, McKay must have agreed with Briggs's strategy of merger with the Communist party. He certainly considered himself a part of the Communist movement in the United States, no matter how far removed he may have been from its political center.

In fact, the available evidence suggests that McKay's political activities within the African Blood Brotherhood may have been influential in moving that organization into the Communist orbit. In his introductory "Note" to McKay's book, *Negroes in America,* the Russian translator said that when he became an editor of the *Liberator,* McKay had taken "an active role in the [American] revolutionary movement and [had] applied all his efforts to creating a group of Negro revolutionaries in New York." This statement was made in the course of defending McKay's credentials as a revolutionary, and too much should not be read into it. Nevertheless, it indicates that McKay was very likely instrumental within the African Blood Brotherhood in promoting its merger with the Communist Party of America. Finally, in *Negroes in America,* McKay himself stated that during the course of the Fourth Congress, he had asked that his Communist party membership be transferred from the illegal, underground party to the legal Workers' party, which implied that he had joined the illegal party by 1921, before the Workers' party came into existence. Otto Huiswoud had entered the American party even earlier, in 1920. Two years later he was rewarded—he was appointed the first black American delegate to a Comintern congress. McKay's path had not been so easy or direct, but as it turned out, he achieved greater popularity, if not influence, at the congress.[17]

At the inaugural session of the congress, McKay entered "the vast Bolshoi auditorium" and saw the Danish author Martin Andersen Nexo waving to him from "the center front of the hall." As McKay started to make his way toward Nexo's seat, he suddenly became aware that the ushers had begun to move him along toward another destination: "At first I thought I was going to be conducted to the balcony, but instead I was ushered onto the platform to a seat beside Max Eastman and just behind Zinoviev [the Comintern's chairman]. It seems as if the curious interest of the crowd focused upon me had prompted Zinoviev to hoist me up there on the platform."[18]

Although McKay refused to speak on this occasion, despite everyone's urging, both he and Otto Huiswoud subsequently addressed the congress. Huiswoud spoke first. He maintained that the Second Congress had not adequately discussed the relationship between the race problem and colonialism. He then went on to outline the Afro-American and colonial questions in general Marxist terms before beginning his survey of black reformist and revolutionary activity in the United States. Among Afro-American organizations, he pointed out the NAACP as the most influential, with the Garvey organization and the African Blood Brotherhood running a poor second and third. He dismissed the National Urban League as a strikebreaking organization, and he lamented the black's inability to integrate American labor unions. He then mentioned the potentially important role of black newspapers in spreading Communist propaganda. Huiswoud ended his remarks by emphasizing the especially wretched conditions of Negroes in the South.[19]

McKay always felt inadequate as an orator and disliked the task. He therefore began his speech by declaring that he "would rather face a lynching stake in civilized America than try to make a speech before the most intellectual and critical audience in the world." He then apologetically explained that "my public speaking has been so bad that I have been told by my own people that I should never try to make speeches but stick to writing, and laughing." His poetry, he went on, and in particular one poem, "If We Must Die," had nonetheless propelled him forward as "one of the spokesmen of Negro radicalism in America to the detriment of my poetical temperament." After this deferential beginning, McKay went on to give a surprisingly strong, straightforward, and critical summary of the black relationship to the American Communist movement. Despite his limitations as a public speaker, he had, after all, concluded that "it would be an eternal shame if I did not say something on behalf of the members of my race" before the assembled revolutionaries of the world. Through the opportunity given to him by the Comintern to address its Fourth Congress, an honor had been extended to blacks everywhere. "My race on this occasion is honored, not because it is different from the white race and the yellow race, but [because it] is especially a race of toilers, hewers of wood and drawers of water, that belongs to the most oppressed, exploited, and suppressed section of the working class of the world." He noted that the Communist International was for the full emancipation of all workers, and that its commitment did not remain "solely on paper as the 15th Amendment to the Constitution of the United States [does]."[20]

Like Huiswoud, McKay spoke at length on "the international bourgeoisie's" efforts to create conflict between black and white workers in order to keep them both in slavery. Then, with characteristic frankness, McKay boldly switched his tone and declared that in the United States it had nevertheless been the "reformist bourgeoisie," not the Socialists and Communists, who had done the most to improve the Negro's social, political, and economic life:

The Socialists and Communists have fought very shy of [the race problem] because there is a great element of prejudice among the Socialists and Communists of America. They are not willing to face the Negro question. In associating with the comrades of America I have found demonstrations of prejudice on the various occasions when the White and Black comrades had to get together: and this is the greatest difficulty that the Communists of America have to overcome—the fact that they first have got to emancipate themselves from the ideas they entertain toward Negroes before they can be able to reach the Negroes with any kind of radical propaganda.

Theodore Draper has stated that McKay's accusation of racial prejudice within the American party was only "the first of many such complaints."[21]

Both McKay and Huiswoud agreed that Afro-Americans and colonial troops were used effectively by the Allied side in World War I, and could be used again if Communists failed to reach blacks with their message of international working-class solidarity. McKay in particular had long been concerned about the shameless exploitation by England and France of black colonial troops, and he concluded his speech by expressing the "hope" that "a few Negro Soldiers" would soon be included in "the Red Army and Navy of Russia" as "a symbol that the Negroes of the world will not be used by the international bourgeoisie in the final conflicts against the World Revolution."[22]

At the Fourth Congress, the Comintern for the first time formed a Negro Commission which consisted of Huiswoud, a few white Americans and Europeans, and some Asian party members. The commission's "Resolutions on the Negro Question," formally adopted by the Fourth Congress, represented the Comintern's "first real effort to state its position" regarding blacks. The resolutions noted the unrest that had developed among Afro-Americans and black colonials as a result of World War I. It then stated that "the history of the Negro in America fits him for an important role in the liberation struggle of the entire African race." A brief Marxist survey of the black's struggle against American oppression concluded that "the post-war industrialization of the Negro in the North and the spirit of revolt engendered by post-war persecutions and brutalities caused a spirit, which . . . places the American Negro . . . in the vanguard of the African struggle against oppression." The document ended by reminding blacks that their struggle was at base a struggle against capitalism and imperialism. It then outlined steps by which Communists could more effectively secure black support in the "proletariat struggle for freedom."[23]

"The Fourth Congress," Theodore Draper has written, "opened a period of Communist policy for the American Negro in which the international and especially the African aspect predominated."[24] McKay's precise role in hammering out this policy cannot be determined. His presence and his analysis of the black American situation had some influence on the Comintern's decision to set up a Negro Commission and to formulate resolutions on the topic. Besides addressing the congress, McKay also spoke with Leon Trotsky, who at the time seemed destined to succeed Lenin as the leader of the Soviet Communist party. Gravely ill, Lenin was only barely able to address the Fourth Congress. He was to die the next year.

McKay and Trotsky talked about the racial situation in the United States and about how best to combat the use of African troops by European colonial powers. McKay also told Trotsky of the antiblack propaganda the English socialists had used in their campaign against the French occupation of the Rhineland. Trotsky believed only class-conscious black activists could prevent European nations from using their black colonials in future European conflicts. He urged upon McKay the necessity for black Communists to organize within their own race to combat the evil effects of European colonialism. Their exchange of opinion was printed in *Pravda* and other leading papers. McKay also reprinted much of it in *Negroes in America*.[25]

In *A Long Way from Home*, McKay claimed that his remarks "about the Negroes of the South" and the tyranny under which they existed had "precipitated" the more extended discussion of "the Negro question" at the Fourth Congress, in which his friend Sen Katayama aggressively accused white American delegates of not understanding the racial problem in the United States. "It was an unforgettable experience to watch Katayama in conference. He was like a little brown bulldog with his jaws clamped on an object that he wouldn't let go." If nothing else, McKay exerted an influence on the deliberations through his friendship wih Katayama, who apparently shared his scorn of American Communists' approach to racial issues. "Think not," McKay wryly observed, "that it was just a revolutionary picnic and love feast in Moscow in the fifth year of Lenin['s rule]!"[26]

McKay's influence on the Fourth Congress' "Resolutions on the Negro Question" can, of course, be overestimated. Otto Huiswoud also received a respectful hearing at the congress, and he actually served as an official member of its Negro Commission. McKay and Huiswoud together represented the general perspective of several West Indian radicals in the United States, who after World War I contributed substantially to left-wing black thought. In this respect, the official stance of the Comintern regarding blacks in 1922 was in-

fluenced by West Indians, who were simultaneously much more nationalistic, class conscious, and international-minded than were
American-born blacks.

But there were certainly other, equally important factors that determined the Comintern's emphasis on the international aspects of
the Negro problem. Marxist-Leninist theory on the relationship between capitalism and imperialism would compel such emphasis. In
addition, the response of urban Negroes in the North to Garvey's
UNIA perhaps provided the Comintern with some hope of eventually
winning blacks to the Communist version of "universal improvement."

Within the United States, the Comintern's position made little
or no impression on Afro-American leadership. Aside from Garvey's
followers and the relative handful of black radical activists in the
United States, W. E. B. Du Bois was the only prominent black leader
who had made any sustained effort to build an international movement after World War I. In 1919, Du Bois had attempted to unite
black leaders from all countries into a Pan-African movement, whose
purpose was to work for an end to colonialism in Africa. Du Bois's
first Pan-African Congress met in 1919 while the Versailles peace
conference was in session. Several more Pan-African congresses met
in the early 1920s, but Du Bois's movement, at least in the short run,
accomplished little except to provide a precedent for later attempts at
Pan-African unity after World War II. The NAACP gave Du Bois only
grudging support from the first, and it soon quietly withdrew all
its aid. Du Bois's ambitious plans were not Communist-inspired or
-supported, but he did envision a socialist economy in Africa once
freedom had been attained.[27]

After the conclusion of the Fourth Congress in December, 1922,
McKay remained in Russia for six more months. During that time he
became something of a celebrity: "Never in my life did I feel prouder
of being an African, a black and made no mistake about it. . . . From
Moscow to Petrograd and from Petrograd to Moscow I went trium-
phantly from surprise to surprise, extravagantly feted on every side. I
was like a black ikon in the flesh. The famine had ended and the NEP
was flourishing, the people were simply happy. I was the first Negro
to arrive in Russia since the Revolution, and perhaps I was generally
regarded as an omen of good luck! Yes, that is exactly what it was. I
was like a black ikon."[28]

Besides being commissioned to write articles, poems, and stories
for the Soviet press, McKay was sent by Trotsky on a tour of Soviet
military installations, where he was elaborately toasted by the Red
army and navy. One memorable trip from Petrograd to the nearby

naval base at Kronstadt was made by plane during a snowstorm. The pilot lost his way in the blizzard but made a safe landing not far from his destination. McKay arrived at the Kronstadt airfield by automobile to discover that a contingent of sailors had been forced to wait for him in the cold. Such incidents embarrassed him.[29]

Surprisingly, McKay had time to meet many "non-partisan and anti-Bolsheviks." A year later he reported in the NAACP's *Crisis* magazine that "I spent many of my free evenings [in Moscow] at the Domino Cafe, a notorious den of the dilettante poets and writers." It was in such an atmosphere that McKay became acquainted with the poetry of Sergei Yesenin, who, in some of the most beautiful verses of the period, celebrated the peasants and soil of the old Russia now rapidly passing away. McKay felt a special affinity for Yesenin's poetry. But Yesenin, who drank heavily, was never able to accommodate himself to the Soviet regime, and eventually committed suicide in 1925.[30]

The correspondent Walter Duranty, who toured the Soviet Union shortly afterward, wrote that "the black man" about whom Yesenin had written in a late poem of that title had been Claude McKay. Duranty stated the two had known each other in Moscow. He may have heard stories about McKay's visit from writers in Moscow who had known of his interest in Yesenin. But McKay and Yesenin never met. Yesenin had left Russia with the dancer Isadora Duncan about the time McKay was leaving Germany for Petrograd.[31]

Who then was "the black man" who tortured Yesenin by his presence? All critics agree he was a symbolic figure who constantly reproached the poet for his failure to achieve the fulfillment of his artistic potential, for being untrue to himself by wrecking his health and destroying his poetic gift. During the last two years of his life, Yesenin suffered from hallucinations and other mental afflictions connected with alcoholism. Nobody but Duranty ever identified "the black man" as Claude McKay.[32]

Could it be possible, however, that Duranty's tale contained a germ of truth? Perhaps upon his return to Russia from America with Isadora Duncan, Yesenin had learned from friends about McKay's high regard for him. In his last remorseful months, Yesenin may have conjured in his mind an image of this strange black man, who had once sung his praises above all other Russian poets, now returned to haunt and reproach him for his failures. Although it is only speculation, Duranty may not have been entirely wrong in his assertion that Claude McKay was in this sense "the black man" of the famous poem.

Although McKay did not meet Yesenin, he did become conversant with the various literary schools and trends competing with one another in the relatively free literary atmosphere of Moscow and Petro-

grad in 1922 and 1923. Before going to the Soviet Union, he had assumed that the Bolsheviks had imposed "a strict literary censorship,"
but he soon found that "no such thing" existed. In Moscow and Petrograd, he encountered "Parnassians, Romantic Classicists, Formalists,
Proletarians, Futurists, and Imagists. A member of the last named
school," he informed the overly skeptical H. L. Mencken, "gave me a
copy of his latest book containing a creepy poem called: 'Leprous
Moscow' which [Maxwell] Bodenheim might have written about
New York, had he any vital power over the manipulation of words."[33]

During his seven months in Russia, McKay met an impressive
number of important literary figures. They included Korney Chukov-
sky, a leading critic and author of children's books; the novelists Boris
Pilnyak and Yevgeny Zamyatin; and the poet Vladimir Mayakovsky,
the leading proponent of a new proletarian drama. With the possible
exception of Mayakovsky, these writers all had serious reservations
about the new Bolshevik regime; in his conversations with them,
McKay must have heard much that tempered his enthusiasm for the
new government.[34]

Throughout his visit, McKay stressed that he was primarily a poet.
While accepting wholeheartedly the aims of international communism, he could never give himself wholly to political work within the
party. To some party members, it was a maddeningly naïve stance. For
the moment, however, the Comintern leaders accepted McKay on his
own terms and assiduously wooed him. Some probably appreciated
his candor. Trotsky, for one, was not totally alienated by McKay's position and probably even sympathized with it up to a point. In truth,
the leaders of the Russian Revolution in 1922 and 1923 did not demand that artists conform strictly to any ideological line.[35]

For his articles, stories, and poems in *Izvestia* and other Soviet
publications, McKay received fees well above those given to most Soviet writers. His literary activities, combined with public appearances, and his tour of Soviet military bases kept him constantly active. After his first perilous days in Moscow, McKay "awoke," as
he expressed it, "to find myself the center of pageantry in the grand
Byzantine city" of Moscow. "The photograph of my black face was
everywhere among the highest Soviet rulers, in the principal streets,
adorning the walls of the city. . . . I was installed in one of the most
comfortable and best heated hotels in Moscow. . . . Wherever I wanted
to go, there was a car at my disposal. Whatever I wanted to do I did.
And anything I felt like saying I said. For the first time in my life
I knew what it was to be a highly privileged personage. And in the
Fatherland of Communism! Didn't I enjoy it."[36]

The six months following the Fourth Congress proved hectic, exhilarating, and personally triumphant. Everywhere McKay received thunderous welcomes that left him wondering if, in truth, his actual achievements merited such receptions. "I felt that if I were to be a *bolshoi* as a literary artist in a foreign language, I should first make a signal achievement in my native adopted language, English." Such thoughts, as well as his aversion to practical politics, kept McKay from being swept completely off his feet and into the ranks of the self-lessly dedicated within the Third International. He still had to prove himself as a literary artist and went so far as to characterize his past literary production as "my trifling poems."[37]

McKay in Moscow adopted a peculiarly complex stance. He wished to support the Bolshevik government in the Soviet Union and the Third Communist International abroad while retaining his independence as a poet, writer, critic, and political analyst. He urged blacks to become class conscious and to ally themselves with the Communist cause, yet as a black participant in Communist party politics, he remained wary of Communist motives, understanding, and strategy about race relations, imperialism, and the importance of African and Asian nationalism. McKay made his position quite clear by the time he left the Soviet Union: he would remain an iconoclastic rebel and a poet. As ideological lines and bureaucratic standards of acceptance hardened within the Comintern after the death of Lenin, McKay would eventually have had no choice but to disassociate himself from involvement in the Communist movement. It was his good fortune that he did not have to make that choice while in the Soviet Union.[38]

By the end of the congress, even McKay's sharpest critics within the American delegation acknowledged his membership within their party. Zinoviev had at one point referred to him as "a non-party member." The Congress' daily newspaper, the *Bolshevik,* published Zinoviev's remarks. This prompted letters from both McKay and the chairman of the American delegation, Ludwig E. Katterfield (using the pseudonym G. Carr), which McKay later reprinted in the appendix of *Negroes in America.* In his letter of December 2, 1922, Katterfield informed the *Bolshevik* that "the words 'although he is not a communist' must be discarded." McKay, he pointed out, was a member of the Workers' party and spoke "in the name of the African Blood Brotherhood."[39]

The following day the *Bolshevik* printed McKay's more detailed statement, in which he declared himself a Communist and attempted to justify his request for a transfer from the secret Communist Party of America to the aboveground Workers' party. He did not obtain the transfer, he declared, because he was afraid of the danger involved in underground work. "In America," he observed, "it is much less dangerous to be a Communist than to be a Negro." He desired membership in a legal party because he was convinced that Communists could reach blacks only if the alliance were pursued openly and in the face of hostile white opposition. Black Communists would get nowhere by simply urging "solidarity with white workers" because blacks knew white workers as historically "their most bitter enemies." The black Communist's task was infinitely more complex.

> The Negro Communist must not only be an interpreter of the moods of his own people for white comrades . . . , but he must also be capable of establishing contact with white reformers and the petty bourgeois leaders of his own race. He must prod them to make greater and greater demands for the Negro masses and undermine their authority by making counter-demands. When the petty-bourgeois Negro leaders and white reformers defend such American taboos as mixed marriages and the right of Negroes freely and completely to meet with whites in social places and in private homes, Communists must boldly implement all these in theory and in practice. Similarly, Communists must fight so that competent Negro workers are allowed into powerful white unions on an equal basis. This struggle must be carried out against hostilely inclined and unenlightened white workers . . . who must be turned towards international class consciousness. . . . To go to the very heart of the Negro Question for Communists means to incur the violent anger of American public opinion in the North as well as the South.

If such an aggressive policy were adopted, McKay predicted that much violence directed against blacks might ensue, that even black and white Communists might "accidentally" find themselves in "opposing camps"; but that it would be a price worth paying if it helped "to move the large complacent mass of reactionary America to the universal ideal of internationalism." [40]

In *Negroes in America,* McKay took the articles he had written for the Soviet press and shaped them into a rough survey of black conditions in America. He elaborated on a Marxist interpretation of black American history that stressed the economic basis of race relations in the United States. The book included an extended discussion of the position of blacks within the American labor movement, the prospects for radical organization among blacks, and a critique of the Communist attitude and approach toward blacks since World War I. Against a historical backdrop of fundamental and consistent economic exploitation, McKay included chapters on the social and cultural ramifications of American race relations in which he pointed out the connections in American history between the black crusade for freedom and the women's crusade for equality. Although the book clearly suffered because of the feverish haste with which it was composed, McKay nevertheless managed to make a detailed statement of his fundamental view of black history and contemporary race relations in the United States. In the process, he also revealed a great deal about himself and his relation to the international Communist movement.

McKay viewed U.S. history from both a class and a racial perspective. Black Communists, he insisted, had a dual responsibility to interpret black consciousness to their white comrades and to communicate to blacks an understanding of their historic position as workers within the capitalist economies of the West. Above all, McKay hammered home the point that black acceptance of Marxism was vital to the success of the Communist movement in America. Communists would attract the black masses only if the party demonstrated in theory and practice that it accepted blacks as unquestioned equals in every area of life and displayed a willingness to confront the issue of race relations head on.

In his chapter entitled "Labor Leaders and Negroes," McKay claimed that only one American labor organization, the Industrial Workers of the World, had truly accepted blacks as equals in their organization and in their campaigns against American capital. The Workers' party, and certainly the illegal Communist Party of America, had yet to match the IWW's record.

McKay correctly observed that labor unions in America had lost membership since World War I. The postwar return to "normalcy" had placed them once again on the defensive after a period of wartime growth. Against the great unionization efforts of 1919, the large corporate interests had marshaled every resource, including black strikebreakers, to defeat union drives in major industries from steel to meatpacking. Labor strife between blacks and whites in the meatpacking industry had been a major contributing factor in the great Chicago riot of 1919. McKay wrote *Negroes in America* as an impassioned witness to the strife and bloodshed of workers who should have been allies. Having experienced such senseless strife, he insisted that blacks must be organized along class-conscious lines with or without whites if the American labor movement was ever to progress. In the absence of a radical spearhead of black and white laborers, the bourgeoisie in the United States imposed its paternalistic reforms and hired blacks where whites gave trouble, whether it was in the coal fields of West Virginia, the steel mills of Pittsburgh, or the stockyards of Chicago. Fear of black competition retarded the development of working-class consciousness among white American workers.[41]

In McKay's view, the situation for blacks and whites could have hardly been worse, and he stated flatly that "the question of Whites and Blacks is mainly a question of self-preservation for American labor. The sentiment of brotherhood can be completely discarded. . . . The American worker's movement finds itself at the crossroads. It must choose one of the following two paths: the organization of black workers separately or together with whites—or the defeat of both by the forces of the bourgeoisie."[42]

In the accomplishment of such organization, McKay had no faith in the traditional leadership of the black American community—its church spokesmen, middle-class reformists, businessmen, educators, and social workers. They had all failed to advance either themselves or their race within the American class structure, whose upper class seemed determined "to keep the Negro intelligentsia, as well as the masses, at the bottom."[43]

While providing this broadly generalized class analysis of American race relations, McKay also managed to include several important cultural phenomena within his Marxist framework. In his chapter "Negroes in Sports," for example, McKay argued persuasively that in the United States, sport was both a corporate business and an important symbolic expression of white supremacy. As befitted a poet, McKay also included chapters entitled "Negroes in Art and Music" and "Negroes in Literature." Black artists of all types, he noted, occupied a peculiarly lonely position in the United States; they were ignored by whites and misunderstood by black critics too insecure to encourage their talents. By and large, McKay concluded, "those who stay in the United States after flashing a first bright spark turn into mediocrities and thus find the place assigned to them."[44]

Despite such dismal conclusions, McKay ended on an optimistic note that indicated the direction he would shortly take in his own literary efforts. "Our age," he wrote, "is the age of Negro art. The slogan of the aesthetic art world is 'Return to the Primitive.' The Futurists and Impressionists are agreed in turning everything upside down in an attempt to achieve the wisdom of the primitive Negro."[45] Such an effort appealed enormously to McKay's romantic nature, and in his novels and short stories he would within the next decade confound the conservative critics of black art and literature by extolling the apparently aimless existence of "primitive" black drifters who existed on the fringes of urban life in America, Europe, and the Caribbean.

In his last chapter, entitled "Sex and Economics," McKay tried to explain in largely Marxist terms why the United States seemed so obsessively preoccupied with and fearful of black sexuality. According to McKay, this peculiarly American problem most likely began to manifest itself in the South, when its slaveholding oligarchy managed to isolate southern poor whites and black slaves from one another and to limit their possibilities for social intercourse and mutual work. As the distance between them widened, poor whites and blacks grew increasingly scornful of one another. "Thus," McKay concluded, "by the time of the Civil War, the Southern oligarchy owned not only the bodies of white workers and black slaves, but it had succeeded completely in controlling the psychology of both races. The sexual taboo is a form of black magic and splendidly served the aims and intentions of the master class." As far as McKay was concerned, the situation was not confined to the South but afflicted to varying degrees the entire nation. "In reality," he wrote, "the whole white American nation is, in a strange way, possessed by a Negro neurosis."[46] Whites in the North appeared particularly fascinated with black crime, and the publication of the gruesome details of southern lynchings held for the northern tabloid reader an enormous fascination. In effect, northerners shared to a large degree the old morbid and fearful curiosity about blacks so long exhibited by poor whites in the South.

Throughout *Negroes in America,* McKay displayed a generally well informed interest in American history and made some interesting comparisons between race relations in the United States, the Caribbean, and colonial Africa. He explained that while blacks and other colonial peoples generally received better treatment in France, England, and other European countries, these same countries generally engaged in ruthless economic exploitation of their African, Caribbean, and Asiatic territories.

*Negroes in America* cannot be counted among McKay's more polished prose works. It was hastily written under chaotic circumstances that did not allow him time to research his topics in any depth. For sources he relied heavily upon books, pamphlets, and journals he had brought with him from New York. McKay had had no idea he would write *Negroes in America* for the Soviet press when he left for Russia or that he could ever complete such a project from start to finish in only six months. And in its occasional hyperbole, misstatement of fact, questionable generalizations, and faulty organization it did betray the evidence of haste. On the other hand, McKay succeeded admirably in giving his Russian readers some idea of the historical complexity of American race relations, the peculiar position of blacks in the American labor force, the mutually antagonistic psychology of blacks and whites in America, and the urgent need of Communists to overcome the disruptive competition and deep-seated mutual enmity that existed between white and black workers.

The book bore the indelible stamp of McKay's particular passion for racial justice and his complex dissatisfaction with his American and British comrades. In joining the Communist movement, he had expected understanding and positive action on racial and colonial questions, and he urged upon his comrades his conviction that no Marxist revolution would ever occur and no satisfactory interracial reconciliation would ever take place in the United States if the racial question could not be faced and overcome by American Communists. His book was a challenge to action on the racial front. On its title page he quoted Whitman, "My call is the call to battle / I nourish active rebellion."[47] Increasingly, it seemed to him, Communists in the United States were letting their opportunities slide back into the grasp of a resurgent capitalism that understood only too well how to divide and continue to conquer. Certainly, he saw little evidence within the American movement that its members were eager to place near the top of their revolutionary agenda the winning of blacks to their cause.

McKay had, of course, come to Russia full of resentment against his colleagues on the *Liberator*. In his original draft of *Negroes in America,* he had voiced all his dissatisfaction with them; he had, moreover, chosen to concentrate on those disagreements between himself and the other editors that related to the racial issue in order to expose the lack of understanding of black concerns that prevailed even among otherwise deeply committed radicals such as those who ran the *Liberator*. Max Eastman strenuously objected to McKay's emphasis. He reminded McKay that his personal differences with Michael Gold and not disagreements over the racial problem had been the primary reason for his departure from the *Liberator*. Eastman also maintained that McKay had tried to introduce more black material than the other *Liberator* editors thought wise, but that their objections had been merely tactical. They did not wish to alienate a readership that was "practically entirely among whites" who were "full of peculiar ignorance and intolerance of the Negro."[48] Even McKay's proposal that they devote at least 10 percent of the magazine's contents to the race problem seemed to Eastman unsound.

McKay eventually deleted his section on the *Liberator*, but not before he wrote Eastman a blistering letter of rebuttal. Eastman's criticism, McKay claimed, had cast doubt on the motive and honesty of his *Liberator* account. He accordingly adopted a tone of aggrieved superiority. "I do not," he haughtily announced, "intend to argue with you about my motives and honesty—to prove or disprove anything, I am only attempting to enlighten you." McKay stated that Eastman was wrong to think that his remarks concerning the *Liberator* would leave the impression that his departure from the magazine had been because of a dispute over racial issues. He instead wished to show how difficult it was for American radicals to understand the importance of the race problem in the class struggle. McKay stressed that he had never arrived at any agreement with Eastman or the other editors regarding the *Liberator*'s policy on racial issues. McKay concluded that he thought it important to state explicitly "the truth that the leading minds of the *Liberator* did not, to me, have a comprehensive grasp of the Negro question." McKay had yet more to say. *Liberator* readers, he went on, far from being offended by the race material introduced into the magazine by him, had on the contrary sent him "letters of encouragement and appreciation." And in response to his article "He Who Gets Slapped," he said, "certain members of the Theatre Guild" had protested against their management's practices of discrimination. Eastman had asked McKay whether he was living in the practical, "scientific" era of Lenin or the age of Tom Paine. In reply, McKay stated that both Lenin and Paine had to be judged by what they accomplished in their own eras, and in a savage thrust that must have hurt, he told Eastman that "if you had in your whole body an ounce of the vitality that Paine had in his little finger, you with your wonderful opportunities, would not have missed the chances for great leadership in the class struggle that were yours in America."[49]

Eastman was appalled by McKay's letter. He denied that he had ever accused McKay of dishonesty or had disparaged his motives. He reminded McKay that when he joined the *Liberator,* he had been "like some of the rest of us," a poet eager to find the freedom to write his poems. Now he stood somewhat abashed before the "very solemnly consecrated political soul" that had somehow suddenly materialized in McKay. In reply, McKay stated:

> I have no more my "solemnly consecrated political soul" today than at the time when I first went to the *Liberator.* I still love to laugh, dance and wine and delight in pleasure. If you had seen me standing on street corners and selling red literature in London, you would not make such a funny remark. If you had seen me doing propaganda work among the colored soldiers you would modify your "opinion." And I never missed a single opportunity in enjoying living then as now. Do you think I was playing when twice in 1921 you saw colored men and women in the *Liberator* office discussing political and race problems with me—and you did not

like it from fear of the Department of Justice? You have been entirely deceived about me, Max. I suppose it is due to this everlasting infectious smile of mine.

Eastman feared their friendship had ended. In the heat of the argument, McKay may have thought so too. But upon reflection he decided, after all, not to antagonize his former comrades. In its published version, *Negroes in America* contained scarcely a mention of the *Liberator*. Still, McKay left the Soviet Union without reconciliation with Eastman, and the question of their future relationship remained unsettled.[50]

As had happened so often in the past, McKay was preparing to leave the scene of his book's publication. He would not capitalize on it or on his overwhelming personal reception in Russia. Just as he had previously done in Jamaica, the United States, and England, so in the Soviet Union he abandoned the field at the moment he seemed most assured of further successes. In the spring of 1923, he made a final trip from Moscow to Petrograd in preparation for departure.[51]

It had all been an exhilarating but exhausting experience. In Petrograd, McKay finally felt the strain. For the first time in his life, he had a tooth pulled. The painful extraction was performed under primitive conditions, but it was less ominous than the apparent paralytic stroke that for a time left one side of his face and neck without feeling. It was the first symptom of chronic hypertension. Although the paralysis soon passed, the underlying cause remained. Despite its seriousness, however, he soon threw himself into a last hectic round of social activities and public appearances.

McKay's visit was brought to a grand climax in Petrograd during the May Day celebration of 1923. "For hours," he later wrote, "I stood with Zinoviev and other Petrograd leaders in the reviewing stand in the Uritsky Square." That night McKay returned to the former palace of the late Grand Duke Alexander where he was staying and tried to sleep, but the throngs continued to march before his eyes. He finally sat down at the late Grand Duke's desk and penned a farewell poem to Russia. In the concluding stanza of "Petrograd: May Day, 1923," McKay caught some of the exultation he felt, not only on that particular day, but throughout his Russian adventure.

> Oh, Petrograd, oh proud triumphant city,
> The gateway to the strange, awakening East,
> Where warrior-workers wrestled without pity
> Against the power of magnate, monarch, priest—
> World fort of struggle, hold from day to day
> The flaming standards of the first day of May![52]

Shortly afterward, he left Petrograd for Germany. From there he went to France, where he strayed far from the Communist fold to embark upon a decade-long literary expatriation.

From 1919 to 1923, Claude McKay spent four intensely committed years as a poet, journalist, and black Communist radical of the literary Left. It was a momentous period that saw, among many other changes, the establishment of the world's first modern socialist state and the rebirth under its auspices of the international Communist movement.

From the moment the Bolsheviks seized power in Moscow in October, 1917, expectations of truly revolutionary changes spread around the world. Claude McKay had been among the thousands who saw in the bright banners of Red Russia a new hope. For him and for those few hundred black revolutionaries of his generation who had seen the vision, Marxist revolution, and specifically the kind demonstrated under Lenin's clear-sighted leadership, seemed to offer the only really practical and just resolution to the binding exploitation still experienced by the majority of black peoples the world over. From the first, therefore, McKay's vision was of a world revolution in which his people, whether in Africa, the Caribbean, or the United States, would participate as equals with all others in the remolding of their mutual fates.

McKay enjoyed a tremendous personal triumph in Russia, but his independence and his increasingly bitter disillusionment with the American and British Communist movements made his future place within international communism increasingly problematic, even as he enjoyed the rich fruits of his Soviet reception. The dream of a truly egalitarian socialist revolution nevertheless remained alive in McKay. In New York, London, and Moscow, he had participated intimately in a movement whose significance would not dim, even as he and it diverged in the years ahead.

Finally, it must be said: there was something in McKay's personality that made it impossible for him to accept success once he had achieved it. He had political success within his grasp in Moscow, but it seemed incompatible and somehow insignificant when compared with the purely literary success he sought. His poems seemed to him insufficiently important for the fame they had brought him. He felt the need to push on with his literary career, to prove himself—in a real sense, to start again, to quell the doubts, the fears, and the lonesome insecurity within by defining yet again what it meant to be black in the third decade of the turbulent and increasingly dangerous twentieth century.

# 7
# The Expatriate Years, 1923–1925: "Color Scheme"

In May, 1923, McKay left Petrograd for Hamburg, then went on to Berlin. During his trip to the Soviet Union, conditions in Germany had grown worse. After the Weimar Republic failed to meet the Allied reparations schedule, the French under Prime Minister Poincaré had seized the Ruhr Valley. As a result of this military occupation, the German mark had collapsed; rampant inflation threatened to ruin the German middle class and to plunge the nation into anarchy. This desperate situation was felt by McKay personally soon after his arrival in Berlin. After he had left New York in the fall of 1922, Eugen Boissevain had cabled him twenty-five dollars, payable in German marks. When McKay returned to Berlin in the summer of 1923 to collect his money, its dollar value had shrunk to only twenty-five cents.[1]

Socially, as well as economically, Berlin was more feverish than ever. McKay again made the rounds of the cabarets with Charles Ashleigh, who later remembered that Claude's bright-checked suits and happy smile made him popular everywhere. McKay was curious to see if the presence of French African colonial troops in the Ruhr had sparked racial prejudices among the Germans. He found no antiblack sentiment, only anger against the French and a heightening of political and class antagonisms among Germans themselves. From both the Right and the Left, extreme conservatives and radicals worked persistently to undermine the authority of the moderate Weimar government. The ground was being sown for the rise to power of Adolf Hitler's National Socialist party a decade later.[2]

Despite the pervasive economic and political instability, German art and literature thrived. No work captured the period's decadence and cynicism better than George Grosz's book of drawings, *Ecce Homo*, a sustained commentary on the baser qualities of human nature exhibited by the bourgeois establishment of postwar Berlin.[3] McKay had first sought Grosz out in Moscow after seeing his drawings in a Communist newspaper and learning that he was at the Fourth Congress. In Berlin, McKay took his personal copy of *Ecce Homo* to Grosz for autographing. A few weeks later he took the American artist Marsden Hartley to meet Grosz.

Besides Hartley, McKay encountered several other congenial Americans in Berlin, including Pierre Loving, the poet, who found McKay a room "exactly right to live and work in," and novelist Josephine Herbst, "who was very kind and helpful in a practical and also artistic way." Claude also met in Berlin for the first time the Afro-American philosopher Alain Locke. Although differences of temperament, taste, and aesthetic judgment would eventually drive them apart, they initially got along well together.[4]

McKay also happened upon the Indian Communist leader M. N. Roy, who invited him to contribute to his newspaper, which he was then editing in Berlin. McKay declined after a friend advised him not to get involved in the complicated affairs of the Indian Communists, who were in serious conflict with each other and with Moscow.[5] It was perhaps just as well he did not pursue his relations with Roy because he had other preoccupations. McKay had arrived in Germany still elated by his successes in Russia and determined to communicate his experiences to his fellow blacks in the United States. Before he left Petrograd, Zinoviev in a formal declaration had forcefully reminded McKay that the revolutionary government of the Soviet Union had acted promptly to solve its own ethnic and national minority problems by securing "to the smallest Republic entering the Union [of Soviet Socialist Republics] . . . a full and real equality, not in theory, but in practice." He charged McKay as an "American Negro guest at the Fourth Congress" to carry back the Comintern's message of unity with all workers of whatever race or nationality. Zinoviev emphasized the Third International's determination to foster world revolution and twice urged McKay to communicate its revolutionary message as well as its "fraternal greetings and best wishes to the Negro workers of America."[6]

McKay decided that the proper vehicle for his impressions of the Soviet Union was W. E. B. Du Bois's *Crisis* magazine. On July 8, 1923, he wrote Walter White at the NAACP from Berlin that he was "back out of Russia, after a great triumphal trip there"; he hoped to publish in the United States the book he had written in the Soviet Union and added, "I will do an article for the *Crisis*. Ask Du Bois if he wants it. Do they pay anything? You see, I must have money to live on while I am doing my impressions here." McKay also urged White to send him various NAACP pamphlets for "propaganda work" in Europe. After using them himself, he wished to forward them to Moscow for use by the Comintern.[7]

McKay also persisted in the hope that H. L. Mencken would either commission an article on Russia for his magazine or would help him place articles in other publications. From Berlin, he wrote the Sage of Baltimore a remarkably detailed six-page, typewritten letter in which he apprised Mencken of his reputation in Soviet literary circles, defended the justice of the Bolshevik Revolution, explained its historical background, surveyed the current Soviet literary scene, and urged Mencken to visit Russia and see for himself the transformations occurring there. After surveying the disintegration of the old order in Russia and the birth of the new, McKay concluded, "The Communist dictatorship in Soviet Russia is a ruthless aristocracy of brains. . . . I don't think [it] has any intellectual and practical comparison in history, except perhaps the period of the Holy Roman Empire." And, he continued, "Russia today is the nightmare of the competitive system, because with all her wonderful natural resources, she is beginning to challenge the bourgeois competitive system with a national labour cooperative." By contrast, he noted, "The American system is efficient . . . and its masters are competent, but as the greatest of the industrial nations, the forces of social disintegration interwoven in the fabric of America is far greater than the present-day problems of crumbling Europe. America has its Plutocracy, its Southern Oligarchy, its Western Farming Interests, its Labour Aristocracy, its Proletarian Mass, a great body of unassimilated foreign-born Labour in its Basic Industries, acute immigration problems, and a great body of Unassimilable Negroes. The outlook for America is certainly not at all Utopian. Its future is rosy as hell-fire."[*]

---

[*] Claude McKay to H. L. Mencken, July 17, 1923, © 1987 by Hope McKay Virtue, 1110 Olive Avenue, Long Beach, Calif. 90813, and used by her permission. This letter is in the H. L. Mencken Papers, Berg Collection, at the New York Public Library.

Mencken found McKay's letter "very interesting." He acknowledged that the Russian experiment was probably worth the effort,
if only because "it keeps the fear of God before the capitalists and
gives them bad dreams at night." He admitted, however, that he was
"unable to believe . . . in the principles underlying it." Capitalism,
Mencken maintained, was "based on ineradicable human appetites.
Every workman with an idea in his head is a secret capitalist."[8]

In his reply to Mencken, McKay did not elaborate upon his previous defense of the Bolshevik regime, but instead defined his personal
interest in it. In the process, he revealed his own elitism, his ambivalence toward the working classes, and his general idea of revolutionary change.

> Historically and imaginatively the collective force of the working class
> movement (its culture[,] its writers, artists, politicians and financial back-
> ers) interest me far more than the wellbeing of the average worker. . . . It
> seems to me that society always reaches a stage where the class that mo-
> nopolizes the administrative trust wallows so much in [consumption] and
> effeteness that the vigorous brains on the outside begin to organize and
> attack it in its many vulnerable parts and that it must ultimately collapse.
> Shorn of propaganda and romance the workers individually are not better
> to me than other people, but it happens that their social status gives re-
> formers and agitators their weapon against opponents—and I suppose it
> always will.

McKay regretted that Mencken during his own recent trip to Europe
had not seen for himself the great changes occurring in Russia.
"This reconstruction period," he wrote, "the flexibility of the people
and government in adapting themselves to the lightning changes is a
stimulating thing to see. In a couple more years it will have passed
altogether away."[9] Despite their exchange of ideas, Mencken refrained from publishing anything by McKay. Nor did he help him
place his work elsewhere. In fact, McKay had no luck in placing articles on his Russian experience with any white American publishers. His Russian book likewise remained unpublished in the
United States until 1979.

He had better luck with *Crisis*. Du Bois wanted his articles on
Russia and agreed to pay for them, so Claude set to work. Between
July and October, he produced a long account of his Russian trip,
which appeared in two installments in the December, 1923, and
January, 1924, issues, and one shorter article, which followed in Sep-
tember, 1924.[10]

The sale of these articles hardly sufficed to cover McKay's expenses while he remained in Berlin. British security agents believed

that McKay had brought with him out of Russia a large sum of Comintern money to be used by Communists for propaganda purposes among blacks. They were wrong. In the name of art and necessity, he accepted all handouts offered him. Among the American artists, writers, bohemian expatriates, and literary-conscious tourists and students in Berlin at the time, some knew of McKay's poetry. A few proved friendly and helpful. McKay fitted naturally into their milieu; when able, they were not averse to loaning him a few dollars or treating him to a meal or drinks. When he had the money, he returned the favor.

One day, to his amazement, he happened upon the formerly flamboyant Greenwich Village model, the Baroness von Freytag-Loringhoven, selling newspapers on a Berlin street corner. After her exotic postwar fling in New York, she had returned to Germany, where her reckless existence soon reduced her to penury. Claude took her to dinner and brought along a wealthy American student, who gave her a few American dollars. There was little else McKay could do. Like his former friend Michael, the petty thief, "poor brave Baroness von Freytag-Loringhoven" had become ensnared beyond redemption in her own excesses and the merciless environment of the day.[11]

Although often angrily frustrated by its too-frequent necessity, McKay had over the years become adept at cajoling funds from friends, acquaintances, and well-wishers. Like many other writers before and since, he justified the practice in the name of necessity. He simply could not advance his literary career if he had no leisure to write. And when freed from menial work, he could produce.

His articles for *Crisis*, for example, were certainly worth more than the little money he cadged from friends while writing them. In them, he not only provided his Afro-American readers with a detailed account of his adventures in Russia, he also forcefully admonished them that their own struggles for racial justice at home could no longer be divorced from the international changes wrought throughout the world by the Great War and the Bolshevik Revolution. With American money now dominant throughout western Europe, McKay believed it vital that blacks project their grievances onto the world stage. If they did not, he feared that American racial attitudes would follow the dollar throughout the world to reinforce the grip of European colonialism in Asia and Africa. On the other hand, if blacks made the effort to educate the average European about the realities of American race relations, they would find a sympathetic audience. "American Negroes," he observed, "are not as yet deeply permeated with the mass movement spirit and so fail to realize the importance of organized propaganda. It was Marcus Garvey's greatest contribution to the Negro movement; his pioneer work in that field is a feat that men of broader understanding and sounder ideas who will follow him must continue." [12]

Throughout the summer of 1923, money problems continued to bedevil McKay. In late August, he finally wrote Arthur A. Schomburg in New York with several requests: get a dozen copies of *Harlem Shadows* from Harcourt, Brace, send them to him in Berlin, and also collect any royalty payment due from Harcourt and send it, payable, of course, in American dollars. Also, Schomburg should contact Richard B. Moore, have him remove from storage twelve copies of *Spring in New Hampshire,* and send them on. McKay had previously written Moore, a fellow radical, but had received no answer. Finally, Schomburg was to send Benjamin Brawley's book on Negro literature and Carter Woodson's *Negro History,* both of which McKay needed as reference works in revising his Russian book. [13]

These were only the first of many demands he imposed on the long-suffering Schomburg over the next two years. Another letter, soon after, informed Schomburg that he simply had to have "the latest Negro Year Book! . . . even if you have to give your own . . . it is essential to my work." McKay acknowledged his demands were "expensive," but added, "I am working in my small way for the common cause and I hope we shall square up some day." By late September, he even sent Schomburg an essay and instructed him to place it for him with any paper, "white or colored—whilst the article is not tinkered with. This is a great task I am putting on you. But I am in a tight corner. . . . I can't go home to America now, for I haven't the money. Besides I don't want to—I want to stay abroad and write some things. But I am quite broke—want to go to Italy where it is warm and cannot. Frightfully cold here—and must have some money next month. I am depending on you to help me all you can." [14]

Schomburg did the best he could for McKay, whose demands, unfortunately, escalated with every favor granted. Like most Afro-Americans at the time, Schomburg had limited resources and many pressing commitments—to his job, his family, his book collection, his lodge, even his mistresses. "How are all your women and are you still carrying high your book collecting?" McKay inquired in one brief aside. [15] Still, Schomburg managed to meet a few of McKay's requests. He sent copies of *Harlem Shadows* but had trouble locating the trunk containing *Spring in New Hampshire.* Like most dedicated bibliophiles, he was loath to give away any of his own books.

In October, McKay finally left Berlin, "driven out," as he explained to Schomburg, "by the high prices, general disintegration and intolerance since [the] failure of [the German] passive resistance [campaign against the French in the Ruhr]." The intolerance he referred to was not racial prejudice directed against him, but the increasing political intolerance of the German Right against their moderate and radical opponents.[16] From Berlin, McKay journeyed to Paris, the mecca of American expatriates in the postwar years. There, despite the political factionalism, a greater measure of social and economic stability prevailed. Although the franc was not outlandishly devalued like the German mark, one could receive in Paris a favorable exchange for American dollars. It only remained for McKay to find the dollars.

By the time he reached Paris, however, he had another worry besides money—he was seriously ill. Until his Russian trip, McKay had never experienced any really serious illnesses. Just before he left Russia, he developed "a sort of deadness" in his left side, "and once," he explained in *A Long Way from Home,* "my face gradually became puffed up like an enormous chocolate souffle." Before he left Petrograd, he continued, "I became quite ill and had a tooth extracted for the first time in my life, under the most painful conditions." After arriving in Berlin, he still did not feel entirely well, and his summer there was punctuated by a series of "intermittent fevers and headaches." Eventually, during the first week of October as he prepared to leave Berlin for Paris, white pimples began to appear all over his body. After his arrival in Paris, a French specialist informed him he had syphilis and advised him to enter a hospital immediately; McKay followed the doctor's orders.[17]

His sickness embarrassed, dismayed, and depressed him. Fortunately, he had friends in Paris. The *Liberator* artist John Barber, who had the greatest admiration for McKay, was there. McKay had also become friendly in Moscow with a young French engineer, Pierre Vogein, who served as secretary to the French Communist delegation at the Fourth Congress. Vogein's fiancée, Fanny Rappaport, was a medical student attached to the hospital where Claude was admitted. Together, she and Pierre saw that McKay was well cared for during his hospitalization.[18]

He nevertheless fell into depression. After months of intense physical and mental activity in Russia and Germany, his illness jarred him into a recognition of his human vulnerability. The insidious nature of syphilis, its slow, silent destructiveness, especially appalled him. During his hospitalization, he wrote several uncharacteristically gloomy poems that directly reflected his depression. The best of them was entitled "The Desolate City." He later described it as "largely symbolic: a composite evocation of the clinic, my environment, condition and mood."

> My spirit is a pestilential city,
> With misery triumphant everywhere,
> Glutted with baffled hopes and human pity.[19]

McKay had good reason to be depressed. In 1923, syphilis was difficult to cure. Treatment consisted of measured doses of mercury or arsenic, whose side effects, as he would eventually discover, were almost as treacherous as the disease itself. His doctors assured him that his disease was in a relatively early stage and should respond well to treatment, and their optimistic prognosis seemed borne out by his subsequent progress. A year later he wrote Alain Locke, "The treatment in Paris went like magic; the doctors said the disease was only incipient and in six weeks my flesh was sound again. I am strong and look healthier than ever, but I must take treatment at intervals for about a year or two for the germs in the blood." In the same letter, McKay protested that he had not been careless in Berlin. "Although I went around to all sorts of places I was quite discriminating and had fewer affairs than you imagine! But the best of persons get caught sometimes."[20]

In November, 1923, McKay left the hospital with an essentially clean bill of health but with instructions to continue his medication awhile longer. Once again, he had to think about money. This time his friend John Barber came to his rescue and found him a job as a model in the well-known art school of André Lhote. For a while, at least, he had an income, though small, and could begin to enjoy Paris.[21]

"After . . . the high pressure propaganda spirit of new Russia" and the crisis atmosphere of Berlin, Paris was a relief. For the American artist of whatever race, Paris in the early 1920s possessed on an international scale the same attraction that Chicago and Greenwich Village had held for American provincials in the early decades of the twentieth century. The city had long been hospitable to artists and writers. "There in Paris," McKay later explained, "radicals, esthetes, painters and writers, pseudo-artists, bohemian tourists—all mixed tolerantly and congenially enough together." Although he sometimes found the small shopkeepers and waiters impertinent and dishonest, he soon understood that Paris offered artists freedom to pursue their own goals, no matter how unorthodox. Unlike London, it also had a

Claude McKay as he appeared in the frontispiece of *Spring in New Hampshire* (1920)

Claude McKay and Max Eastman in Moscow, 1922

Carl Cowl, a friend from McKay's *Liberator* days, became in the 1940s his last literary agent and literary executor.

Arthur A. Schomburg, the famed bibliophile, was one of several friends whose financial and personal assistance enabled McKay to pursue his literary career in the 1920s and 1930s.

The poet Countee Cullen, along with Harold and Ivie Jackman, became good friends with McKay in the 1930s.

Eulalie Imelda Lewars McKay, Claude McKay's wife

U'Theo McKay (*right*), discussing agricultural prices with his neighbors in Clarendon Parish in the 1930s

Hope McKay Virtue, Claude McKay's daughter, before the modern secondary school named in his honor. The school is near Sunny Ville, where the McKay family lived.

The road to Sunny Ville, Claude McKay's birthplace, Clarendon Parish, Jamaica

Photo by Wayne F. Cooper

stimulating night life available in separate ways to both the wealthy and the poor. If nothing else, one could, for the price of a few cups of coffee, spend a profitable evening engaged in conversation in one of the city's many small cafés.[22]

As an aspiring novelist and short-story writer, McKay had a keen interest in the new works of expatriate American writers in France. He read with admiration young Ernest Hemingway's recently published group of stories, *In Our Time,* but he refused to visit Gertrude Stein's famous salon. He had not been impressed by her treatment of black life in the story "Melanctha," and he remained unconvinced she had anything to offer him. "I never went," he explained, "because of my aversion to cults and disciples. I liked meeting people as persons, not as divinities in temples."[23]

McKay had more respect for James Joyce and his monumental novel, *Ulysses.* During McKay's sojourn in England, Frank Budgen had made him aware of Joyce's importance, and he admired the Irish writer's achievement. As he later wrote, "Joyce . . . is a seer and Olympian and was able to bring the life of two thousand years into the span of a day. If I were to label James Joyce I would say that he was (in the classic sense of the word) a great Decadent." As with

Stein, however, McKay had no fundamental sense that Joyce spoke directly to him, to his problems, his hopes, or his future. There was, he maintained, "no confusion, no doubt, no inquiry and speculation about the future in James Joyce."[24]

Only one great modern writer touched him profoundly, and he was not part of the Paris expatriate scene, though like McKay, he, too, was a restless traveler. That writer was D. H. Lawrence, with whom McKay felt a psychic kinship and for whom he had a profound and lasting admiration. While McKay recognized that *Ulysses* was "a bigger book than any one of Lawrence's books," he nevertheless "preferred Lawrence as a whole. I thought that D. H. Lawrence was more modern than James Joyce. In D. H. Lawrence I found confusion—all of the ferment and torment and turmoil, the hesitation and hate and alarm, the sexual inquietude and the incertitude of this age, and the psychic and romantic groping for a way out. . . . I loved . . . the Lawrentian language, which to me is the ripest and most voluptuous expression of English since Shakespeare." His friends in Paris thought he preferred Lawrence because he was a rebel, but McKay understood that Lawrence was not a social thinker "like Pushkin, William Morris, Tolstoy and Bernard Shaw."[25] For McKay, Lawrence's appeal lay instead in his compulsive and impassioned struggle to overcome the psychological traps that threatened to imprison and destroy man's direct appreciation of life and its mysteries in the modern age. In Lawrence, McKay found a constant personal struggle against the forces of suppression and death. McKay could relate on many levels to such a struggle.

After reading *Sons and Lovers,* in particular, he must have discovered in Lawrence a man whose fundamental parental loyalties, social background, and young manhood resembled his own. Like McKay, Lawrence had a mother with whom he closely identified, an emotionally distant father with whom he felt little kinship, and a psychological restlessness that drove him steadily toward artistic achievement and away from the marginal existence of his natal community. In his own life, of course, McKay faced the additional complicating factor of race. As he entered the expatriate world of white American artists and writers in the fall of 1923, he was acutely aware that their problems were only partly his own. As he summed it up in *A Long Way from Home,* the young expatriates he encountered in Europe had a variety of motives for living and working abroad. Some had fled America to enjoy what they considered the richer cultural life of Europe; others "were . . . harassed . . . by complicated problems of sex." In New York, McKay had not experienced their cultural or sexual inhibitions. He had, in fact, been stimulated by the vigorous spirit and the accelerated social pace of the industrial Northeast.[26]

At the same time, white racism, which poisoned the very well-springs of black life in America, hindered in innumerable ways his life as a man and an artist. The pervasive racial oppressiveness of the American environment caused McKay to dread the thought of returning to the United States. He wanted relief from the racial burdens imposed upon him within America. In comparing his own situation with those of his white fellow expatriates in Europe, McKay concluded:

> Color-consciousness was the fundamental of my restlessness. And it was something with which my fellow-expatriates could sympathize but which they could not altogether understand. For they were not black like me. Not being black and unable to see deep into the profundity of blackness, some even thought that I might have preferred to be white like them. They couldn't imagine that I had no desire merely to exchange my black problem for their white problem. For all their knowledge and sophistication, they couldn't understand the instinctive and animal and purely physical pride of a black person resolute in being himself and yet living a simple civilized life like themselves. Because their education in their white world had trained them to see a person of color either as an inferior or as an exotic.[27]

McKay knew he was neither. He was a writer eager to earn his way, and he had arrived in Paris determined to produce fiction that would sell. At the same time, he wished through his fiction to explore seriously his fundamental experiences as a black man in the modern, industrialized, white-dominated world of America and Europe. His arrival in Paris in the fall of 1923 had been noted in the Paris edition of the New York *Herald Tribune* by Eugene Jolas, who explained that McKay was intent upon capturing in fiction some of the essence of his rich experience in both Jamaica and America.[28]

Before he was well recovered from the shock of hospitalization for syphilis, however, he came down with another serious illness. In December, while "posing naked in Paris studios," McKay fell ill with a severe case of influenza. He spent the 1923 Christmas season in bed fighting desperately to regain his health. All the while he faced the possibility of eviction from his room because his rent was in arrears. Once again, friends rescued him. Louise Bryant, the widow of Jack Reed, had recently married William Bullitt, a wealthy Philadelphian; they were living in Paris. Through a mutual friend, she learned of McKay's latest illness and sent a doctor to look after him. Pierre Vogein also ministered to him, and an American acquaintance, Mrs.

Josephine Bennett of Brookwood Labor College, paid his rent and brought him fruit during his convalescence.[29]

Despite such generosity, McKay still had neither a regular income nor any luck in finding a publisher interested in his Russian experience. He remained dependent on the charity of friends and admirers. In his desperation, he sometimes assumed in his letters to them the tone of an aggrieved and quarrelsome child. On January 7, 1924, for instance, he appealed for a second time to an old radical acquaintance in Harlem. To Grace Campbell he wrote:

> You are just as bad as all American correspondents. They never answer letters. I had the bummest holiday in my life. I was down with the grippe for 10 days and only forced myself to get up on New Year's day. I suffer because I am not properly clothed to stand the winter. I am wondering if anything can be done over there to raise a little money to tide me over these bad times. I nearly got turned out of my little room but for Mrs. Bennett. . . . My life here is very unsatisfactory for a propagandist—cadging a meal off people who are not at all sympathetic to my social ideas. There is so much work to be done if I am helped a little.[*]

On the same day he exclaimed to A. A. Schomburg, who had not replied to his latest requests, "[I] am at a loss to know why you should have ditched a fellow like that. . . . I have been very ill confined to my room during the holidays and I am still unwell. Hoping you will drop a fellow even a post card—if nothing else."[30]

Such appeals eventually brought results. Schomburg finally sent McKay copies of Brawley's and Woodson's books, as well as clippings from the Afro-American newspapers and periodicals he requested. McKay had asked Grace Campbell in the name of Harlem's socialists to appeal to Eugen Boissevain or Dudley Field Malone for money. Campbell instead passed McKay's letter to Walter White, who in turn requested that his fellow workers at the NAACP contribute to McKay's relief. Joel Spingarn generously gave fifty dollars. By the end of January, White cabled one hundred dollars to McKay in Paris.[31]

Even before he received this sum, McKay's fortunes had begun to turn. Louise Bullitt not only supplied him with a doctor during his illness, she also agreed to help him financially. He had previously met her in New York after her return from Russia following Jack Reed's death. At that time, McKay had sympathized with her loss and told her of Reed's early invitation to him to visit the Soviet Union. Now, she listened to his hopes, read the few stories he had already written,

---

*Claude McKay to Grace Campbell, January 7, 1924, © 1987 by Hope McKay Virtue, 1110 Olive Avenue, Long Beach, Calif. 90813, and used by her permission. This letter is in the Walter White Papers, NAACP Collection, at the Library of Congress.

and urged him to continue in his efforts to produce marketable fiction. More important, she agreed that McKay should leave the cold damp of the Paris winter, and she gave him enough money to live for the next three months on the French Mediterranean coast. Toward the end of January, 1924, McKay left Paris.[32]

He went first to Marseilles for a brief visit to France's oldest seaport. Marseilles's oldest waterfront section, the decaying *vieux port,* especially fascinated McKay. There he encountered an ugly yet bewitching mélange of foreign sailors, international drifters, prostitutes, criminals, and *petit bourgeois* merchants—all scrambling frantically for a living in a small area that eventually came to symbolize for him the very condition of modern Western civilization. After a few days in Marseilles, McKay journeyed back up the French coast and visited a number of small towns. He finally settled in La Ciotat, a fishing and boatbuilding center on a fine bay located midway between Toulon and Marseilles. Although the town was picturesque, McKay's new quarters had no heat, and mornings and evenings were cold. Discomfitted but determined, he regularly attended to his writing, often wrapped from head to foot in the heavy blanket he had purchased during his first days in Moscow.

McKay shortly began to spend many of his spare hours in nearby Toulon, a naval center that lacked the ingrained sordidness of Marseilles's *vieux port.* Before long he made friends in Toulon with a sailor he called Lucien in *A Long Way from Home* but whom he once referred to as Leon in a letter to Alain Locke.[33] Lucien (or Leon) had a bohemian girlfriend named Marcelle, and McKay soon began to see the two of them on a regular basis. Through them, he discovered better quarters in Toulon and in April, 1924, he moved there from La Ciotat.

Lucien eventually introduced him to other sailors from his ship, and McKay seldom lacked company, especially on the weekends when Lucien and his friends were free. With Lucien and Marcelle, he explored the rugged Var countryside around Toulon, and in the evenings, he often frequented their favorite bars and dance halls.[34]

Shortly after his move to Toulon, McKay received word from Anna Davis, secretary of the Garland Fund in New York City, that its board of directors had heard of his plight and had decided to grant him a monthly stipend of fifty dollars so that he could complete his writing project. Freed at last from the prospect of absolute poverty, McKay proceeded to enjoy Toulon, his new friends, and his writing.[35]

Despite the personal difficulties he had encountered since leaving Russia, McKay had developed a clear idea of what he wanted to accomplish in fiction. He had long felt that black leaders in the United

States feared any realistic portrayals of Negro life that did not safely advance the cause of racial justice. As he had said earlier in his *Liberator* review of *Shuffle Along,* "The Negro critics can scarcely perceive and recognize true values through the screen of sneering bigotry put between them and life by the dominant race." As a consequence, only the most solidly respectable efforts received the unreserved approval of "the sensitive and pompous . . . black intelligentsia." All the while, McKay concluded, the black common folk continued to express themselves "with a zest that is yet to be depicted by a true artist." At long last, McKay felt sufficiently freed from the demands imposed upon him as an editor and radical activist to attempt a fictional rendering of "the warmth, color and laughter" he had found during his years in the workaday world of black Americans.[36]

Back in December, 1923, while still ill with "the grippe," McKay had explained to H. L. Mencken his expectations. "My plans, before I took ill, and they are still not much changed, was [sic] to do a series of prose sketches of my contacts in America, using the most significant things, yet, leaving no subject, however degraded, untouched. Much of the period 1914–1919 was spent in the so-called semi-underworld and should make interesting reading from the point of view I shall write from. I have the whole thing planned in my head and I see the scenes in a finer perspective from here."*

By the following May, he could report from Toulon to his various correspondents in the United States that he was already over halfway through his first novel. By the end of the summer, he had finished it and had decided to return to Paris, where he hoped to make contacts that would ease the way to its quick publication. His grant enabled him to live rather well for the moment, but it would run out by the year's end. Without a publisher's advance, he would again be penniless. This worried him, for despite every effort on his part to live moderately and take care of himself, he still occasionally suffered from headaches and dizziness. For several days in August, just before setting out for Paris, he experienced again, as once before in Russia, what appeared to be some sort of paralytic stroke that left him for a time numb along the left side of his face. These alarming symptoms increased his determination to get a good critical opinion of his novel and push for its earliest publication.[37]

*Claude McKay to H. L. Mencken, December 28, 1923, © 1987 by Hope McKay Virtue, 1110 Olive Avenue, Long Beach, Calif. 90813, and used by her permission. This letter is in the H. L. Mencken Papers, Berg Collection, at the New York Public Library.

McKay had every reason to believe he could find a publisher. For one thing, he was already a published author. In addition, Walter White wrote that "many changes" had come in the United States since he had left in 1922. The success of Roland Hayes in music and Paul Robeson in *The Emperor Jones* and *All God's Chillun Got Wings*, "coupled with the various novels, poems and other signs of an awakening artistic sense and articulacy on the part of the Negro have caused what seems to be a new day to set in." Publishers had become more receptive to works by black authors, and White himself had just published a novel, which, he confessed to McKay, he had written in only twelve days from start to finish.[38]

White and James Weldon Johnson at the NAACP, Alain Locke at Howard and Charles Johnson at the Urban League's *Opportunity* magazine, all encouraged the new literary awakening. They were articulate, educated men with numerous contacts in the white social, business, and literary circles of New York City. They saw the interest in black writers as beneficial to blacks in general. It seemed to them a positive step toward the eventual resolution of the country's racial problems. As James Weldon Johnson wrote in a private memorandum to Walter White, it had been his "long cherished belief . . . that the development of Negro art in the United States will not only mean a great deal to the Negro himself, but will provide the easiest and most effective approach to that whole question called the race question. It is the approach that offers the least friction." Alain Locke concurred and "confidently" predicted that the "recognition and removal of prejudice can most easily and tactfully be offset by the influence of art." Locke wrote Walter White from Europe in 1923 or 1924 that he had found great interest in black arts among such notable publishers and theater directors as Paul Guillaume in France and Max Reinhardt in Germany.[39]

For his part, McKay welcomed the new developments, but he advised White that black writers should be willing "to stand good straight-out criticism and not allow ourselves to be patronized as Negro artists in America." He also thought that black writers would only be hurt in the long run by "too much undiscriminating praise from Negro journals."[40] He naturally believed he had a positive role to play in these new developments, and he set out for Paris with high expectations.

McKay remained in Paris from late August, 1923, until January, 1924. During these six months he did his share of socializing, though probably no more than most American expatriates in Paris during the 1920s. Many of his experiences were, in fact, almost identical to the oft-told stories of his white counterparts. He visited Sylvia Beach's bookshop, Shakespeare and Company. He encountered Harold Stearns, the famous editor of *Civilization in America,* and witnessed his descent into hopeless alcoholism. And he met, too, a number of friends and acquaintances from New York who happened to be in Paris. Finally, he talked with a few publishers' representatives and made efforts to find a literary representative in London—all, it seemed, to no avail.[41]

Like their white counterparts, many black American writers of the period visited Paris. In the fall of 1924, Claude informed Walter White that he had encountered Miss Jessie Fauset, the novelist and literary editor of *Crisis,* on at least two occasions, but that he had decided to avoid her because she was too proper and schoolmarmish for his tastes. McKay also met Jean Toomer for the first time in Paris and told White that Toomer could accomplish more in fiction if he would not let his tendency toward mysticism interfere with his sense of reality.[42]

In Paris, McKay also met students and fellow travelers from Africa, the French West Indies, and North Africa. As in New York and London, he exchanged with them ideas and life histories. His first acquaintance with French-speaking blacks in France had, of course, begun during his first stay in Paris in 1923. One of these early encounters had, in fact, resulted in his last article for *Crisis,* which had appeared in April, 1924. In it, McKay told of meeting a Dahomean prince residing in Paris. His name was Kogo Tovalou Honenou, and his uncle, King Behanzin, had been deposed by the French colonial administration in Dahomey. After a sound French education in linguistics, law, and medicine, Honenou had emerged as a Parisian sophisticate. According to McKay, however, he had not forgotten his first responsibilities. Through the presidency of an association entitled the Amitié Franco-Dahoméenne, he tried to expose French colonial injustices in his native land. He understood little about the tragic absurdities of American race relations, and had once been bewildered when asked to leave a Paris café after his presence had been protested by a group of American tourists.[43]

McKay met other French West Indian and African blacks in the fall and winter of 1924, but he did not discuss them in *A Long Way from Home.* Even as late as 1937, he probably had little idea of the influence he had exerted upon the development of black French literature. Whether he ever knew it or not, however, some of his acquaintances were figures of primary importance in the establishment of black literature in French in the late 1920s and early 1930s.

Because of his personal contact with them and, above all, because of his poetry and future novels, McKay was eventually to be acknowledged by these writers as a catalytic influence in the development of their own works. As early as 1924 or 1925, McKay may have met Paulette Nardal from Martinique. It was she who, with her sister Jane, developed many of the seminal ideas eventually incorporated into the *Nègritude* movement of the 1930s and 1940s. At their Parisian literary salon in the 1920s, they actively propagated the belief that French-speaking black Africans and West Indians had to rediscover their folk cultures and affirm their intrinsic human values, just as American blacks were attempting to do in the United States. By the early 1930s, their home in Paris had become a regular meeting place for young French African and West Indian intellectuals. There they met visiting members of the new Afro-American literary elite from the United States.[44]

Claude McKay played a significant role in bringing the Nardal sisters into contact with the leaders of the Negro Renaissance in the 1920s. A brief note he once left for Alain Locke at a Paris hotel makes it plain that McKay was already acquainted with the Nardals. It was dated February 10, but the year, unfortunately, was omitted: it might have been as early as 1923 or as late as 1928. It read: "Mlle. Nardal is giving an 'afternoon' for her sister just arrived from a visit to Martinique and they are anxious to meet you. It is Sunday afternoon about 3 at Clumart and they told me to get hold of you. Unfortunately, I have forgotten the address at Clumart but if you call me tomorrow before noon I shall give it to you or you can get it at Sylvia Beach's bookshop Rue de l'Odeon."* Locke subsequently became an annual guest at the Nardals' gatherings. In his turn, he introduced them to the younger writers of the New Negro movement, including Countee Cullen, Langston Hughes, and Jean Toomer. In this way, young African and French West Indian writers such as Léopold Sedar Senghor from Senegal and Aimé Césaire of Martinique became acquainted with their black American contemporaries and began to read their works.[45]

In the 1930s, Senghor and Césaire through their poetry and criticism propounded a theory about black life and art that was to dominate French West African writing for several decades. The rhythm, emotion, and directness of black artistic endeavor, they believed, set

*Claude McKay to Alain Locke, February 10, [no year], © 1987 by Hope McKay Virtue, 1110 Olive Avenue, Long Beach, Calif. 90813, and used by her permission. This letter is in the Alain Locke Papers at Moorland-Spingarn Research Center, Howard University Library.

it apart from Western art. This complex of black artistic characteristics they called *Nègritude,* and the roots of their movement lay at least in part in the Harlem Renaissance.[46]

And, as they later acknowledged, Claude McKay's work in particular had a direct, galvanizing effect on their own development. Thus, even as he struggled to develop his own voice as a novelist, McKay's very presence in France influenced the direction of black Francophone literature: first through his contact with the Nardals, and finally with the publication of his second novel in 1929. His impact was of primary importance in the shaping of the *Nègritude* movement.[47]

In 1924, however, McKay could not have foreseen such a role for himself. His most immediate task was to survive long enough to get his first novel published. Of the writers he met in Paris that year, Sinclair Lewis proved the most helpful. Their meeting was arranged by Walter White, who had enjoyed Lewis' company in New York just before the famous author left for Europe. White mentioned that McKay was in France, and Lewis expressed a desire to meet him. White, who believed that McKay would surely benefit from Lewis' advice on the art of fiction, immediately urged McKay to see Lewis.[48]

They spent two evenings together, from which McKay derived three important benefits. He profited greatly from Lewis' unsparing criticism of his first novel; he received from Lewis an unspecified amount of money; and he convinced Lewis that he was indeed seriously engaged in the novelist's craft. Lewis subsequently recommended to the administrators of the Garland Fund that McKay's grant be extended.[49]

As his grant neared its expiration, McKay indicated to the fund's administrators that he needed more time and money to write a second draft of his novel. They were hesitant to give more. For one thing, they had only a vague idea of what McKay was trying to accomplish in Europe. They had, moreover, received reports from other sources that McKay appeared to be doing little work in Paris. McKay never knew for sure just who these sources were, though he suspected Pauline Rose, a Communist sympathizer he had met in Moscow and later encountered in Paris. He had earlier written White and others that Rose, an English Jew, was coming to the United States, and he had advised them that she could give them good firsthand information about conditions in Russia.[50]

He soon changed his mind about her reliability and informed Arthur Schomburg that she had proved to be "after all only a gossipy little kike" and had taken "back the stupidest and quite untrue stories about me to New York." Because of her, McKay claimed, his "allowance" was stopped "for three months" at the beginning of 1925.

In fact, by the time he met Lewis, he had already "gone beyond" the expiration date of his original grant. As he matter-of-factly informed White, "I am just now in low water again, but I've sent off three frantic begging letters. . . . I am not sure what's going to happen. I can only hope."[51]

Largely on the strength of Sinclair Lewis' recommendation, the Garland Fund finally agreed at the end of February, 1925, to extend McKay's aid for another six months through August, 1925. By then he had returned to Toulon and had begun the second draft of his novel, now entitled "Color Scheme." He worked hard to improve his book. As summer approached he became frantic to finish it and to send the manuscript to New York, where he hoped it would find a publisher before fall.[52]

While his expectations remained high, his strategy for placing the novel never went beyond an unreasonable reliance upon the well-meaning but inexperienced Arthur A. Schomburg. Walter White, whose personal acquaintance with New York publishers was infinitely greater than Schomburg's, informed McKay late in May that a new firm, Viking Press, had expressed great interest in his novel. White strongly advised him to send the manuscript directly to Viking. By the time McKay received this message, however, he had already sent the manuscript to Schomburg, with instructions to submit it initially to Alfred A. Knopf, then to Harcourt, Brace, and, if both failed to take it, to Boni and Liveright. He distrusted White's advice; he had never heard of Viking, knew nothing of the new firm's stability or reputation, and assumed it would never be able to distribute or promote his work as well as the firms he already knew.[53]

For an experienced author, McKay knew surprisingly little about publishing. In the past, he had relied upon well-placed and experienced friends and patrons to find a suitable publisher. Now that he found himself without such support, he turned naturally, if mistakenly, to his most sympathetic and reliable correspondent. Schomburg tried to follow McKay's instructions, but he was no literary agent. Nor did he possess Walter White's public relations skill or reputation as a promoter of black talents. McKay advised Schomburg to seek White's advice and assistance, but at the same time he indicated that White and "that N.A.A.C.P. crowd" might find "Color Scheme" shocking and even immoral. He told Schomburg that his novel was a frank satire in "black and white" that broke through the inhibitions that had constrained earlier Negro writers. "I make my

Negro characters yarn and backbite and fuck like people the world over," he exclaimed.[54]

McKay's ambivalence toward White and the NAACP had the effect of reinforcing Schomburg's own grievances against the organization and made him reluctant to seek Walter White's help. Before too long, McKay heard from Alain Locke that Schomburg understood he was not to let White know about "Color Scheme." This prompted from McKay yet another frantic letter to Schomburg in which he advised him that "Walter is really one of my best friends. Certainly you could not have said that to Locke. Did you?" He went on to warn Schomburg against "all backbiting gossip. But you must know," he concluded, "how the Negro black belts are just rotten-crazy with spiteful, nonsensical malice and if we get mixed up in that sea of shit we shall never be able to do any real revolutionary work along artistic or social lines."[55]

After mailing "Color Scheme" to Schomburg, McKay left Toulon and toured Arles and other cities in southern France. Then he went again to Marseilles. From there he decided to visit his sailor friend Lucien, who had been discharged from the navy in the winter of 1925. After his release, Lucien had gone home to St. Pierre, a small town near Brest in the province of Finistère. For some time, he had been urging McKay to visit him. His letters, full of praise for the seacoast and countryside of his native Brittany, finally persuaded McKay to accept his friend's invitation.[56]

As he waited for his train to depart Marseilles, McKay casually glanced out the window and saw Max Eastman sitting opposite him in another train that had just arrived. The two had begun corresponding again, but they had not seen each other since their quarrel in Russia. McKay hastily postponed his trip until the following evening, and they spent the intervening time talking.[57] Both were happy to renew their friendship. They had much to discuss. Eastman had remained in Russia much longer than McKay. While there, he had learned Russian and had found a wife, Eliena Krylenko, whom he now introduced to McKay. He had also collected from Leon Trotsky material for a biography. Before leaving the Soviet Union, Max had become aware of Joseph Stalin's systematic isolation of and triumph over Trotsky within the Communist party. Most important, he had received from Trotsky and others irrefutable evidence that Lenin on his deathbed had denounced Stalin's aggrandizement and had favored Trotsky as his successor. From Russia, Eastman eventually journeyed to Paris, where he wrote *Since Lenin Died*. It contained the sensational revelation of Lenin's "last testament" and provided details of Stalin's campaign to establish himself as the undisputed head of the Communist government of the Soviet Union.[58]

McKay had already read the book and had only recently written Eastman to congratulate him. Like Eastman, McKay still considered himself a communist, but Eastman's book confirmed what he already knew—that the international Communist movement, at least in the West, could only be hurt by submitting to Russian domination. By exposing the ruthless internal struggles within the Russian party, Eastman had, in McKay's opinion, "done more than anyone can imagine just now for the Proletarian movement—you are helping to lift the clumsy hand of Moscow off it." Well before most of his erstwhile comrades, including Eastman, McKay had realized the long-range implications that Russian dominance had for Communist movements in other lands. From Arles he had written Eastman that "something will have to be done."

> Personally I think the headquarters of the International should be removed from Russia if it could set up legally in another country. I feel about it that Russia has already had her Revolution—and that because so many of the Russian leaders of the International are connected with the Russian government, the International will always consciously or unconsciously be overinfluenced by Russian governmental politics internal and external—to the detriment of the proletarian movement. Wherever I look in the Communist International I see nothing but dry rot—the little leaders of Western Europe and America mere ventriloquists vying each with the other to repeat the words of Moscow. To me it seems bad for everybody all round and even worse for Russia. Fancy a great wonderful country like that using a ventriloquist show to scare the great lords of international capitalism.*

For McKay, submission to Moscow's will already meant the betrayal of the historic revolutionary struggles going on elsewhere in the world. He had accordingly ceased all active participation within the international Communist movement. He still considered himself a revolutionary, but he saw his dreams suborned, perverted, and destroyed by Stalin, who he perceived would be even more ruthlessly brutal in his drive to power than the czars he had helped topple. In 1925, in an unpublished poem dedicated to Max Eastman, he asked what "we who revolt" hoped to gain by ceaseless efforts to "teach the world's unthinking how to think . . . / of freer worlds." With words, they had worked to "forge golden things from mankind's dim de-

---

*Claude McKay to Max Eastman, [undated, 1925], © 1987 by Hope McKay Virtue, 1110 Olive Avenue, Long Beach, Calif. 90813, and used by her permission. This letter is in the Max Eastman Papers (private possession).

sires," but clearly their efforts "to clear the jungle growth around man's mind" had resulted only in "a new tyranny," whose pretensions, he prophesied, would result in unimaginable horrors.

> We shall see prancing tyrants in the place
> Of shattered kings, an unctious renegade
> Planting his foot on a broken mace,
> Posing a smith's hammer, a peasant's spade!
> And we shall see the thoughts we loved so well
> Twisted and torn and mangled into shapes
> More hideous than the fancied forms of hell,
> To strengthen the old tyranny of new-crowned apes.

Eastman had been the first revolutionary from the West to present an informed explanation of Stalin's rise and Trotsky's fall from power; his efforts to expose the wily Georgian's machinations within the Bolshevik power structure had been widely denounced by many former friends in the Third International. For the moment, he stood almost alone. In his poem, McKay emphatically declared himself in Eastman's corner, no matter the consequence. There could be no other alternative for the committed revolutionary.

> For tyranny eternal must be fought,
> Whether he dons a king's or peasant's dress.
> .  .  .  .  .  .  .  .  .  .  .  .  .  .  .  .  .  .  .
> Revolt with pennants streaming and flags unfurled!*

While eager to fight the new tyranny developing in Russia, McKay, unlike Eastman, placed no faith in Leon Trotsky, whom he considered to be intellectually brilliant but politically inept. In the remorseless winnowing of the Bolshevik political process, Trotsky had been overcome by Stalin, whose cunning seemed to make him better suited to dominate the highly centralized Bolshevik administrative machinery. McKay very early concluded that Trotsky had been ousted by a more able man. While giving Trotsky his due as an intellectual, he never considered joining his political movement.[59]

After his brief visit with the Eastmans, McKay journeyed first to Bordeaux to visit a West Indian friend. From there, he wrote to Lucien that he would soon see him. The answer he received stunned him: Lucien's parents wrote that their son had recently died of tuberculosis. They urged him to come anyway because Lucien to the end had talked enthusiastically of his impending visit; they wanted to welcome him in their son's stead. In all the time McKay had spent

*Claude McKay, "We Who Revolt (To Max Eastman)," © 1987 by Hope McKay Virtue, 1110 Olive Avenue, Long Beach, Calif. 90813, and used by her permission. This unpublished poem is in the Walter White Papers, NAACP Collection, at the Library of Congress.

with him, Lucien had never complained of ill health. Looking back upon their correspondence, he did remember that in one letter Lucien had mentioned he had fallen ill, but that "it was not serious." McKay could hardly comprehend what had happened. He had the strange sensation that he had been corresponding with a ghost. "All the time he was regularly writing those healthy letters . . . he was actually passing rapidly away."[60]

After a second invitation from Lucien's parents, McKay journeyed to St. Pierre. It was his first visit to a French *petit bourgeois* home. Lucien's father was a big, hearty artisan, open and friendly. McKay stayed in nearby Brest, but he often ate with Lucien's parents. He also met his late friend's older brother and two married sisters. The visit proved so successful that McKay spent the entire summer of 1925 exploring Finistère and getting to know "the Breton folk," whom he "liked more than any other of the French." No doubt his warmth and friendliness and the novelty of his visit provided some comfort for Lucien's family. And on McKay's side, the beauty of Finistère, especially the picturesque small seacoast towns, enabled him to better appreciate Lucien's love of the area and helped to distract him from his underlying anxieties about the fate of his novel and his future as a literary artist.[61]

At the end of July, McKay learned that Knopf had rejected his novel. Besides concluding that its literary quality was "uneven," their reader believed that should it ever appear in print its explicit sexual references would almost certainly be judged obscene by the courts. Although disappointed, McKay did not entirely lose hope. He had originally refrained from sending the manuscript to Walter White because he had wanted his work accepted on its intrinsic merits, not merely because it had the endorsement of NAACP officials. Partly for this reason, he had advised Schomburg to seek out H. L. Mencken, whose "standard of judgment," McKay believed, "would be entirely literary."[62] Schomburg did not contact Mencken. After hearing from Knopf, McKay himself finally wrote Mencken in the hope that "a word from you, if it should take you favorably, may make the route of the manuscript a little. easier." McKay explained that he had tried to restrain his language and to mask certain sexual references in French phrases. At the same time, he had "hewed hard to the line of sincerity" and had perhaps used "certain phrases [which] might still be too raw for the American public. The novel itself is a realistic comedy of life as I saw it among Negroes on the railroad and in Harlem. . . . I know the stuff is uneven . . . but it is a first novel on which I've worked hard indeed under unpleasant (to say the least) conditions and I should like to have it published so I may have the chance to continue writing." As usual, Mencken sent a kind reply but provided no help. By the late fall of 1925, McKay realized he would not get his novel published. After two years of effort, he had returned to where he had started—broke and unpublished as a novelist.[63]

From the fragmentary summaries of its plot found in his letters, one can only speculate about the overall quality of "Color Scheme." McKay himself finally concluded that it was not a successful novel and burned the manuscript.[64] Although he could not appreciate it at the time, the effort invested in "Color Scheme" had not been totally wasted. Aside from the hastily written short stories he had published in the Soviet Union, "Color Scheme" represented his first sustained attempt to utilize in fiction his American experiences. His Soviet stories had been slight and overtly propagandistic, concentrating directly on the very real problems of lynchings and racial discrimination.[65] "Color Scheme" was not so obviously didactic. In it, he focused instead on Harlem and the developing ghettos of the urban Northeast in an attempt to capture something of the essential health and vitality he had found among the black common folk during his years on the railroad and in New York City.

From his American correspondents, he had already learned that the white critic and novelist, Carl Van Vechten, was also hard at work upon a Harlem novel. McKay naturally wanted his to appear first. He feared that Van Vechten would steal his market. McKay believed, too, that as an insider his would be the more authentic portrait.[66] In "Color Scheme," he returned to the use of the salty, uninhibited colloquial language of "the common people." In his best Jamaican dialect poetry, he had quite early employed such language to good effect. Unfortunately, the literary censorship of the day in the United States inhibited McKay's natural tendency to use the everyday language of the streets. After "Color Scheme," he sometimes invented awkward verbal substitutes to replace what would otherwise have been a more vigorously realistic use of Afro-American language.[67]

With "Color Scheme," McKay began a decade-long effort to capture through fiction the fundamental ethos and character of black life as he had experienced it in the United States and the West Indies. Through a clarification of the essential identity of the black common folk and their culture, he sought to define their position in the modern industrialized world and to understand better the meaning of his own life. Although McKay aimed at a broad definition of black life, his fiction remained largely autobiographical. In this narrower sense, it can be read as progressive efforts to comprehend his individual experiences and to resolve the inner conflicts they had engendered.[68]

# 8
# The Expatriate Years, 1925–1929: *Home to Harlem* and *Banjo*

As the fall of 1925 approached, McKay had no time to consider all he had achieved in "Color Scheme." He had received his last monthly stipend from the Garland Fund without having found a publisher. He had endured both poverty and the personal humiliation of asking for charity from friends, and his letters began to register again tension, anger, and self-pity. To Walter White, he angrily exclaimed, "So there you are! I am in [a] hell of pecuniary fix! No, thanks, I don't expect you to help me personally and I['m] fed up with begging! . . . But my position is tragic. I am always working under the shadow of insecurity and it paralyses one's best efforts." White sympathized with McKay, but he could do little to help him. Between his duties with the NAACP and devotion to his own writing, White had all he could manage. Schomburg, too, had many personal responsibilities. But why, McKay echoed repeatedly, had they taken so long to answer his letters and inform him of their progress toward finding a publisher for his manuscript?[1]

Even as he bombarded White and Schomburg with such complaints, McKay began to write again and to turn toward others better situated to help him escape his latest impasse. Since arriving in 223

France, he had written one or two short stories, and he now began to write others. If "Color Scheme" could not be placed, perhaps he could sell a few stories and eventually publish them as a collection. Meanwhile, he took what little money he had and returned to the French Mediterranean.

The Eastmans had recently settled on Cap d'Antibes between Cannes and Nice, and McKay decided to visit them. He badly needed advice and guidance, and he trusted no one more than Max Eastman; above all, he considered him a first-rate editor. After the disastrous handling of "Color Scheme," Eastman's availability seemed providential.

McKay had left Brittany in September, 1925, full of despair and anxiety. Financially, his situation seemed hopeless. If only he had been in the United States, he might have had better luck. If circumstances did not improve quickly, he would go to Marseilles and try to get work on a ship bound for America. This prospect only deepened his anxieties. He was no longer as fit as he had been, and a job as a stoker on a merchant ship was physically demanding. He also seriously doubted that American immigration authorities would allow him to reenter the United States. Immigration laws had become more restrictive since 1922, and his radical past would count against him.[2]

When McKay arrived in Cap d'Antibes, he learned that the Eastmans might soon leave. Discouraged, he journeyed to Marseilles. While he was waiting there for a ship, McKay's luck changed. Eastman and Eliena decided to stay and wrote urging him to return, so he hastened back to Cap d'Antibes. Soon his mood lightened. Eastman read all his short stories. He meticulously pointed out those parts that needed improvement or that might prove censorable, and he encouraged McKay to continue along the lines he had already set for himself. To Walter White, McKay wrote, "I was discouraged and demoralized at first. But Max Eastman has put heart into me again to continue."[3]

McKay hoped White could find a journal that would accept his short stories. Failing a quick sale, he wanted White to find him an agent, for he was broke. He detested relying on the charity of friends and decided to look for work. For a while, he picked up a few dollars serving as "a valet" for a wealthy American. This job apparently lasted only a short while. It was hardly a position McKay relished.[4]

He tried his hand at other jobs. In the process, he left the Eastmans and moved into a room of his own in Nice. In May, 1926, he informed Alain Locke that "I have been doing everything to live—working as [a] domestic, on buildings, [as an] errand boy." Over the winter, he had also received checks from Boni and Liveright for several of his poems that they had included in their anthology of *Masses-Liberator* verse. From *Bookman*, he also received a small sum for his poem "Mulatto." [5]

McKay had originally sent "Mulatto" to Alain Locke for inclusion in his special Harlem edition of the *Survey Graphic*, which appeared in 1924, but Locke had declined because of its bitterly radical tone. This infuriated McKay, and he had hastened to condemn Locke for his timidity.

> You know of course that I am suicidally frank. Your letter has angered me. Your attitude is that of Booker T. Washington's in social reform[,] Roscoe C. Bruce in politics[,] and William Stanley Braithwaite in literature. It's a playing safe attitude—the ultimate reward of which are dry husks and ashes! . . . There are many white people who are longing and hoping for Negroes to show they have guts. I will show you by getting a white journal to take Mulatto. . . . No wonder the Negro movement is in such a bad way. No wonder Garvey remains strong despite his glaring defects. When Negro intellectuals like you take such a weak line. . . . Send me back *all* the things—and I do not care to be mentioned at all—don't want to—in the special Negro number of the Survey. I am not seeking mere notoriety and publicity. Principles mean something to my life.

McKay proceeded to warn Locke that if he published his other poems and omitted "Mulatto," "*you may count upon me as an intellectual enemy for life!*" He closed by admitting surprise at Locke's action, "yet not too much" because "you are a dyed-in-the-wool pussy-footing professor."[*]

Locke ignored McKay's protests and published several of his other poems in the *Survey Graphic*'s special edition devoted to Negro arts and letters. Among them was a two-part sonnet sequence entitled "The Negro Dancers." It had originally appeared in the *Liberator,* but McKay later omitted it from *Harlem Shadows* and intended to exclude it from all future collections. Locke's including the poem without any consultation frustrated and angered McKay. Locke used his *Survey Graphic* selections as the basis for his influential 1925 anthology, *The New Negro.*[6]

Meanwhile, McKay implored Locke to restore the original title of "The White House," which Locke had arbitrarily changed to "White Houses" in the *Survey Graphic*. Otherwise, McKay grudgingly for-

*Claude McKay to Alain Locke, October 7, 1924, © 1987 by Hope McKay Virtue, 1110 Olive Avenue, Long Beach, Calif. 90813, and used by her permission. This letter is in the Alain Locke Papers at Moorland-Spingarn Research Center, Howard University Library.

gave Locke his editorial indiscretions and errors. "How can I fight you from way over here?" he lamented. "How can I? So better let it be as it is. Tell me about yourself." By the spring of 1926, McKay had yet to see *The New Negro,* and he reminded Locke to send him a copy.[7]

Early in the spring of 1926, McKay found a job he actually liked. The Hollywood movie director Rex Ingram had only recently opened his own studio outside Nice. He hired McKay, first as an extra and then as a reader, summarizing novels that seemed likely material for conversion into motion pictures. Quite aside from this work, McKay's verse interested Ingram, who also held radical social views and wrote poetry.[8]

Although now nearly forgotten, the Irish-born Ingram in 1926 stood near the pinnacle of his profession. In 1921, he had made *The Four Horsemen of the Apocalypse,* in which Rudolph Valentino had first attracted the attention of the movie-going public. Ingram had moved to St. Augustine, just outside Nice, to escape the pressures of Hollywood and to gain greater control over his melodramas. He had quite early attracted to his new studios Max and Eliena Eastman, as well as several other curious American artists and writers in Cap d'Antibes. At least one, the magnificently bearded and broad-chested artist Waldo Peirce, had already been featured by Ingram in the role of Neptune rising from the sea in the film *Mare Nostrum.* With the approach of spring, Ingram again found several willing extras among the affable American expatriates. This time the Eastmans brought along their black radical friend and introduced him to the famous director.[9]

Thus, much to his delight, McKay found himself caught up in the wondrous world of silent-screen make-believe. Along with Eliena and several of her acquaintances, he suddenly became a dancer. They were probably all among the extras in *The Garden of Allah.* Everyone had such a good time that Eastman celebrated the event in a poem that he sent to Waldo Peirce, who had returned to New York City. "We need you Waldo, as the fifes the drums, / . . . We're all becoming movie stars." And "Claude," he noted, "[was] dancing ragtime and the Mumbo-Jum."[10]

For Eastman, it was all a blissful good time, but for McKay complications soon developed. The studio's general manager tried to limit his time in the film because he feared that a black man's presence, even as an extra, would be resented by American audiences. McKay also heard from French acquaintances on the set that many of Ingram's technical assistants objected to his presence. Still, after his abbreviated role as an extra, McKay stayed on as a reader. Ingram no doubt understood that McKay needed an income. Much to the envy of the more seriously ambitious actors and actresses among the extras, McKay occasionally dined with Ingram at his private table.

Despite his friendship with Ingram, McKay could not escape racist sniping that went on at the studios. One Italian in particular had acquired an outspoken prejudice against blacks during his years in the United States. He sought every opportunity to remind McKay that in America he would not be allowed to associate freely with whites as he was now doing in Nice. This person had charge of seating employees on buses that took them back to Nice after the day's work. He often kept McKay waiting until the last bus. One day Claude lost his temper and demanded an explanation. The Italian only goaded him by asking rhetorically if McKay wanted to box with him. McKay flew into a rage and exclaimed, "Look here, I won't defile my hands with your dirty Dago skin, but I'll cut your gut out!" Suiting action to words, he pulled a knife from his pocket and proceeded to chase his tormentor around the bus. In an instant, however, his sanity returned. He put his knife away, and in a scene worthy of a Jean Cocteau movie, a French acquaintance sped him away on a motorcycle. The incident shamed and embarrassed McKay. He knew the old stereotype about blacks fighting with knives would be confirmed in everyone's mind. He expected to be fired, but Ingram said nothing. "Rex Ingram's face revealed," McKay later claimed, "that he possessed an intuitive understanding of poets. He is Irish. He knew I had suffered enough from the incident."[11] McKay stayed on until the studio closed in the summer.

In spite of the anxiety he suffered over his future as a writer, McKay spent a good deal of time in Nice with people he enjoyed. The black American singer and actor Paul Robeson and his wife Essie were there for a while, and McKay passed at least two pleasant evenings with them. Mrs. Robeson, however, considered McKay's salty tongue and bohemian morals a harmful influence on her husband, and she did her best to limit their acquaintance. Besides the Robesons, McKay encountered several old friends in Nice. One was Charles Ashleigh, whom McKay one day met while on his way to buy some vegetables for a dinner he and a woman friend were preparing. McKay simply forgot the vegetables, the dinner, and the woman, and accompanied Ashleigh back to his hotel in nearby Cagnes, where they stayed for a week. McKay also saw from time to time in Nice and elsewhere in the Midi an unsavory East European whom he had first met in Berlin and whom he identified only as "Bull Frog" in *A Long*

*Way from Home*. Like his young friend Michael in New York, though on a larger, more sophisticated scale, Bull Frog extorted money from wealthy individuals whom he artfully manipulated into compromising situations. Most of his victims were aging widows. Although McKay did not approve of his character, he sometimes consented (no doubt for pay) to translate into fluent English letters Bull Frog had originally composed in French for his occasional English victim. Bull Frog preyed on the wealthy but also aspired to be accepted by them. His audacity intrigued McKay, who corresponded with him throughout his stay in France. Their infrequent literary collaboration was as close as McKay ever came to the life of an unabashed con man.[12]

One friend whom McKay genuinely treasured in Nice was Frank Harris, who was spending his last days there. McKay saw him frequently during the winter and spring of 1926. He respected Harris' spirit and tenacity in the face of old age and adversity, though he wondered if Harris had not over the years sometimes overstepped the bounds of honesty and truth in his efforts to keep himself financially solvent. One day Claude dared to question Harris about an old business deal in New York that McKay suggested had bordered on extortion. "He just exploded," McKay remembered, "with a mighty sermon about the artist and intellectual integrity. . . . Whatever he did he had reserved intact his intellectual integrity." His answer pleased McKay immensely. Harris, he concluded, "was aware that there was plenty of dross inseparable from the gold of life, and he embraced the whole."[13]

In the early summer of 1926, Rex Ingram closed his studio. McKay decided to finish his collection of short stories in Marseilles, where he could live more cheaply. As an encouraging farewell, Ingram generously provided McKay a free train ticket and a 600-franc bonus. With this sum, he could work comfortably on his fiction for the rest of the summer.

In Marseilles, McKay worked hard to revise and polish his stories. Louise Bryant Bullitt had promised to take his stories back to New York if he got them into shape before her departure.[14]

As usual, McKay's money did not last as long as he had hoped. Once in Marseilles, he began to socialize regularly with the black dockers, beached seamen, and other black residents of the *vieux port,* who composed a small, transient international community of black men from Senegal, South Africa, Dahomey, Morocco, the West Indies, and the United States. Few had much money, and McKay must have initially stood more than one round of drinks. The black dockers, however, had regular incomes, and they soon found McKay an occasional day's work helping to unload ships. Among the seamen, several were also musicians, who often were able to earn money and meals playing in the quarter's numerous cafés. Altogether, McKay found among the Africans, West Indians, and Afro-Americans of Marseilles a community of interests and a sense of kinship he had found nowhere else in Europe. One Senegalese had only recently acquired a bar on the waterfront with money he had saved working in the United States. Blacks from all over the world soon gathered regularly at his place, and McKay spent many hours there. Despite wide disparities of origin, language, and occupation, McKay found again in Marseilles companionship with fellow blacks, and "it was good to feel the strength and distinction of a group and the assurance of belonging to it." [15] His experiences in Marseilles during the summer of 1926 would eventually form the basis of his second novel, *Banjo*.

His most immediate task, however, was to make sure that his stories would be adequately revised before they were submitted to a publisher. He had already sent rough copies to Louise Bryant Bullitt back in March, and on June 24, he wrote imploring her either to return his stories with her comments and corrections or to shape them herself for submission to a publisher. In the letter, he poured out all the frustrations and anxieties that he had endured over the last year. When he had sent the stories to her in March, he declared, he had "just reached the end of my rope." He had ceased to write poetry "altogether" and had devoted all his time to the stories in the hope that he could "get in on the Negro Vogue" that was creating so much stir among New York publishers. He had tried to work "as a general servant" for a month and then "on a building," but "I found that work in France was very much more exacting than in America. I had no time to think, much less write. . . . I decided to try to write or starve." He omitted any mention of his work with Ingram or his current social activities in Marseilles. He instead expressed bitter disappointment that she had kept the stories for over three months when she had promised him before he left Nice that she would send them in a week.

> And here I am—hoping and waiting on them to help me—existing, trying to write in swarms of flies and bugs and filth, when, maybe, my stories corrected and sent to America might change my wretched situation a little. Just might—I don't know—but isn't it better to hope? . . . Marseilles is my last and cheapest stand. I don't want to be driven out of here by hunger and want as I was out of Cagnes, Nice, and Menton.

After all, the few things I manage to turn out are the only joy I have. Before I must leave Marseilles for God knows where I want to work out these stories. Otherwise I'll always carry along with me the haunting feeling of work uncompleted.*

Eleven years later in *A Long Way from Home*, McKay made no mention of the extreme anxiety and frustration under which he labored in Marseilles. In his memoir, he remembered only the relief and warm comradeship he found among his black companions there and his fascination with the mean but colorful atmosphere of the *vieux port*. One could conclude that his letter to Louise Bullitt was a calculated effort on his part to get a quick response, just another variant on the "begging letters" he had alluded to in one letter to Walter White.[16]

There was an element of deliberate calculation in such letters. At the same time, they revealed the impatient beseeching of a person who had never really outgrown his childhood dependence upon others. Thus, while he could genuinely enjoy Marseilles and the companionship he found there, he could also be utterly miserable, helpless, and dependent on friends to provide him reassurance and practical support.

Louise Bryant Bullitt did not let him down. She had been remarkably supportive of McKay ever since the winter of 1924, when she first provided the money for him to recuperate and write in the south of France. From time to time, she had continued to send him small amounts even as her personal life began to deteriorate.[17] Louise had never emotionally recovered from the death of John Reed. Although she had a child after her marriage to William Bullitt, their union was rapidly falling apart. She drank heavily, and he grew impatient with her reckless dissipation. He also distrusted her odd circle of bohemian friends. Even Louise became disillusioned by their incessant requests for money. Bullitt would soon divorce his wife, and Louise, her health utterly wrecked, would rapidly accelerate her downward spiral to premature death.[18]

Even as her own doom began to close around her, however, she continued to assist McKay. She returned his stories to him in Marseilles. After revising and polishing them, he managed to return them to her just before she left Paris for New York at the end of Au-

---

*Claude McKay to Louise Bryant Bullitt, June 24, 1926, © 1987 by Hope McKay Virtue, 1110 Olive Avenue, Long Beach, Calif. 90813, and used by her permission. This letter is in the Claude McKay Papers, James Weldon Johnson Collection of Negro Literature and Art, American Literature Collection, at the Beinecke Rare Book and Manuscript Library, Yale University.

gust. After placing his latest work in her care, McKay remembered in *A Long Way from Home,* he spent what remained of the summer enjoying himself. He swam almost daily; in the evenings, the *vieux port* provided a continuous spectacle, and McKay saw it all, including "men's fights and prostitutes' brawls, sailors robbed, civilian and police shooting." [19]

While he may, in fact, have relaxed and enjoyed Marseilles, McKay did not actually stop writing after he finished his short stories. On August 1, he wrote Schomburg, whom he hoped to see soon in Paris, that he was on "the last lap of [a new novel] (handwritten) and it will soon be finished. Then I must revise and rewrite." He had taken a new tack, he informed Schomburg. "There are no obviously naughty things in it." He wanted to have it ready for "the market immediately after my short stories are published." From the plot summary he provided Schomburg, McKay had, indeed, retreated to a safe and well-worn subject. The story concerned "an octoroon girl" in Harlem who in the process of choosing among a white man, a black businessman, and a near-white adventurer "is finally broken by inexorable circumstances." Despite his initial optimism about the story, he soon abandoned it altogether and decided that it had been a false start. [20]

Schomburg, who had spent the summer touring Europe, wanted to see McKay, and he unwisely suggested that he might commission Claude to produce a handwritten copy of *Harlem Shadows* so that McKay could afford to meet him in Paris. Claude lost no time accepting; the prospect of visiting Schomburg in Paris delighted him. "I am happy—like a kid—about it," he revealed. Schomburg, unfortunately, soon had second thoughts about the plan (he realized, too late, that he could not afford it). As a consequence, McKay's letters soon degenerated into a series of all too familiar "begging letters." On August 26, he wrote that because he thought Schomburg would pay him for a handwritten copy of *Harlem Shadows,* he had told Louise Bryant to keep the 1,000 francs she had promised him and to hire instead a typist to provide clean copies of his stories. Now he could not renew his *pension* at the beginning of September. "I have not a sou," he complained. "I am in the tightest corner, believe me, that I've ever been in since I came to Europe and I've been in very tight ones!" Two days later, Schomburg informed McKay that he would soon be leaving Paris and could not afford to see him or to send any money. McKay replied immediately. He felt "dreadfully disappointed." If only Schomburg could send him a little money, he would "always feel indebted" to him. "I feel I am going under just when I am on the point of success." He could not appeal to Louise Bryant again. She had al-

ready "done so much." Schomburg must do something before he
sailed. "And don't leave me in the lurch," Claude implored. Couldn't
Schomburg at least "find someone to lend me 100 dollars?" Perhaps
McKay had Louise in mind because he thoughtfully included her address in this final appeal to Schomburg.[21]

The well-meaning, ever-tolerant Schomburg simply lacked the resources to lift McKay out of his latest financial hole. Others did not. A
few weeks later, just as the cool dry winds of the northern mistral
swept over Marseilles, McKay received an invitation from Max and
Eliena to stay with them once again in Antibes. At about the same
time, he also received word from Louise that Harper and Brothers
had expressed interest in his short stories. She had previously shown
them to the leading American literary agent in Paris, William Aspenwall Bradley, and she strongly urged McKay to allow Bradley to represent him in any dealings with Harper. At long last, McKay's luck was
about to change. Louise had found in Bradley someone able and willing to manage his literary career.[22]

William Aspenwall Bradley had worked in New York as a writer
and editor before World War I, and during the war had served in
France as a captain in the United States Army. After the war, he had
remained in Paris and married a native Frenchwoman, Jenny Ser-
reyr. By 1926, he had established himself as the leading representative of American expatriate writers in Europe. His wife, a woman
of talent and great resourcefulness, maintained an influential and
well-known literary salon. By 1926, Bradley had acquired many distinguished clients, including Gertrude Stein, Natalie Barney, Louis
Bromfield, Katherine Anne Porter, Glenway Wescott, and Edith
Wharton. Louise Bryant had secured for McKay the most capable
American agent in Europe.[23]

In the early winter, Bradley visited McKay in Antibes and persuaded him to expand one of his short stories into a novel. Harper
wanted McKay's stories, but they preferred a novel. It would sell
better and would bring him more money and prestige. McKay readily
agreed to Bradley's suggestion. Both thought that "Home to Harlem,"
a story about a young black soldier's return to Harlem after World War
I, could easily serve as the basis for a novel about Harlem life in the
years just after the war. McKay had already written one Harlem
novel, "Color Scheme," and most of his other short stories dealt with
various aspects of life there. He felt confident that he could expand
Jake's adventures in "Home to Harlem" into a full-length novel.[24]

By February, 1927, he had finished the first two chapters. In a
letter to Bradley, McKay exuberantly reported that "I am having a pic-

nic doing it. Everything is clear and I see through the whole story
to the end. I ought to have the thing done by the end of March."
He added that "the background and most important settings" were
"coming quite naturally" from his other short stories. "I thank you
very much indeed," he concluded, "for giving me the right idea."[25] In
actuality, it took McKay slightly longer to finish than he anticipated.
He completed *Home to Harlem* at the end of May, but this scarcely
made any difference. He worked to the end with the relief and confidence that came with having a publisher, an adequate advance, and a
representative in whom he could confide and trust.

He had never before had a formal literary representative. He had
previously depended on patrons and editors for support and advice.
At the beginning of his new relationship with Bradley, its monetary
aspect made him nervous. Bradley asked him to sign an agreement
that McKay would retain him as his representative for the length of
his contract with Harper, which called for two more novels and a collection of short stories. Since he had negotiated the contract, Bradley
believed he should remain McKay's representative through its life.
McKay hesitated, then agreed, but he made clear to Bradley that he
expected more from their relationship than a simple business arrangement. In effect, McKay sought from Bradley the same kind of
unselfish support he had received in his earlier relationships with patrons and editors. To Bradley, he anxiously explained that "Louise
Bullitt had written that I should put myself entirely in your hands.
Therefore I knew that your interest in me was not that of a mere representative. If I thought so, I could not have written to you always as I
did, nor expected so much of you in other matters."[26]

Bradley liked McKay, whom he found generally friendly and
charming. Like other successful literary agents, he understood that
part of his job sometimes involved soothing temperamental egos. He
did not, therefore, take offense at McKay's condescension toward
"mere" literary representatives. On the contrary, he proceeded firmly
and ably to manage McKay's business affairs for the next six years.
On his side, McKay appreciated Bradley's role, but he always remained mildly rankled that Bradley should calmly skim from his income the literary agent's standard 10 percent.[27]

One of the first things McKay asked Bradley to do was recover the
short stories he had previously submitted to *Opportunity,* the monthly
magazine of the National Urban League. It had become one of the
chief promoters of the New Negro in literature and had begun to
sponsor an annual short-story competition for black writers. In 1926,
McKay had entered "Home to Harlem" in the *Opportunity* contest

and had sent the magazine other stories as well. After acquiring a publisher and an agent, McKay became concerned that *Opportunity* would publish all the stories without any remuneration.[28]

Since 1924, he had lost confidence in New York's black editors. It was not only Alain Locke; W. E. B. Du Bois had also disappointed him. After his illness in 1924, McKay had sent several poems to *Crisis*, along with a plea for money. Before he received any reply, his financial situation improved, and he immediately had second thoughts about the quality of the poems and asked Du Bois to return them. He received no reply, and *Crisis* in 1926 inexplicably published the poems without any explanation or remuneration. In the absence of his literary editor Jessie Fauset, Du Bois himself had apparently been responsible for this questionable decision. McKay reproved Du Bois, maintaining that Miss Fauset would not have done such a thing.[29]

After his experiences with Du Bois and Locke, he expected the worst from *Opportunity*. If its editor discovered that Harper planned to publish his stories, McKay believed that he might publish them first, "thinking," as McKay explained to Bradley, that "I am helpless over here." A formal request by Bradley for their return, McKay thought, would forestall such an occurrence. "I can do nothing with them," he complained. "Negro editors are in a class by themselves and do not follow any of the rules of journalistic decency."[30]

McKay's fears proved groundless. *Opportunity* returned his stories, and he maintained good relations with its editors over the next few years. In general, however, Du Bois and other blacks in positions of influence had grown wary of McKay. Du Bois could not understand why he did not simply "come home," especially if he were sick or starving in Europe. Walter White had ceased to write him with any frequency. McKay's repeated requests for favors even as he sniped at the NAACP could not have endeared him to White. Alain Locke had already smarted under McKay's rebukes, and he too ceased to write him. All were angered by McKay's opinion of them; they had questions of their own about his motives and goals. McKay reacted with anger. To Alain Locke, he exclaimed, "I am sorry that 'because of your much abused candor in the past' you dropped corresponding with me also! . . . Nobody in America writes to me now. I suppose I am in disgrace—a back number."[31]

Toward the end of May, 1927, McKay sent Bradley the last chapters of *Home to Harlem*. In composing the novel, McKay had drawn liberally for material from several other short stories he had written. At least one story, "He Also Loved," which related the total dependence of a pimp upon his prostitute, had been inserted in its entirety as a separate chapter in *Home to Harlem.* McKay also informed Bradley that the new novel was "in feeling . . . very much after the pattern of ["Color Scheme"]." In one vital respect, however, the two differed significantly. Ray, the central character in "Color Scheme," was an alienated black intellectual. In *Home to Harlem,* the central character, Jake, was an uneducated man of the people whose instinctive wholesomeness and vitality were emphasized throughout the book. In *Home to Harlem,* Ray appeared only as a contrast and complement to Jake. McKay cast Ray as a wandering Haitian intellectual whose education had instilled in him an awareness of the larger structure of society. He possessed powers of conceptualization and analysis that Jake lacked, but he also lacked Jake's spontaneity and confidence. McKay felt that bringing the two together strengthened the novel. In a sense they were two sides of one personality, each incomplete without the other. As McKay admitted to Bradley, "Ray . . . gives me a chance to let myself go a little." McKay named him after "a railroad pal" and he felt that without Ray he could not have gotten "the railroad scenes 'pat.'"[32]

McKay believed his treatment of Ray in "Color Scheme" had not been successful. "As the principal character," McKay explained to Bradley, "I don't think Ray stood up as well as he does in a secondary role. Maybe I was more interested in his ideas than in his life. I think I've found out how to get at him now." Even so, McKay recognized he could not develop Ray with the same objectivity as he did Jake. He feared that the intrusion of Ray's ideas distracted from "the main telling of the story." McKay still regretted the fate of "Color Scheme." At one point he declared to Bradley that "I am quite sure that if you had seen it, it would have turned out differently."[33]

Well before he submitted his last chapter of *Home to Harlem* to Bradley, McKay had already decided on the subject of his second novel. It was to be a fictional account of the black seamen, drifters, and dockers he had gotten to know in Marseilles during the summer of 1926. McKay saw a good story in their marginal existence amid the degradations of the *vieux port,* where the naked exploitation of man's sexual needs epitomized for him the corrupt greed at the heart of Western materialistic society. Marseilles both fascinated and repelled McKay, and he looked forward to rendering his impressions in fiction. In the early spring of 1927, he had returned there for a weekend to see how his black friends had fared over the winter. Time had taken its toll. "Their number," he reported to Bradley, "was diminished by about one-half. Two had died in hospital and three others, after being very ill in hospital were sent home by the American Consul. The guitar and banjo players were hired by some kind of traveling show, but a few remain rather sad, dirty and scantily-clothed, but hanging on to the beach all the same and having no desire to leave it."[34]

McKay again returned to Marseilles in May, shortly before he mailed Bradley the final chapters of *Home to Harlem*. He remained there for a year, writing the greater part of his picaresque novel *Banjo*. This took longer to write than *Home to Harlem*. It was a bigger novel with a different setting and atmosphere. Before composing *Home to Harlem*, McKay had already spent four years wrestling with Harlem material in "Color Scheme" and his short stories. *Banjo* required a similar, though shorter, period of gestation and experimentation. In the interval, McKay had his usual problems. His health continued to bother him: he suffered periodically from high blood pressure, severe headaches, and occasional pains in his arms and hands, and one summer night he fainted in a Marseilles café. All these problems encouraged moderation. He tried to drink and eat sensibly, and he sought a warm, sunlit room.[35]

Harper's advance for *Home to Harlem* had not exceeded five hundred dollars, and by the time McKay settled in Marseilles, little of it remained. He hoped that Harper would advance an equal amount for *Banjo*. In the meantime, he took a cheap, ill-lit, scarcely heated room on the Marseilles waterfront. The room faced away from the sea and proved as dismal and shut-in as an East Side tenement.[36]

McKay was soon explaining to Bradley that he had to have a regular income in order to do his best work. He also appealed once again to Louise Bryant Bullitt for help, and he urged Bradley to sell some of his short stories to magazines in the United States or Europe. For some months he lived from hand to mouth, and at one point almost decided to take a berth as a messman on a freighter bound for Singapore. Bradley, however, sent him small sums at critical junctures and encouraged him to continue writing. In November he visited McKay in Marseilles, interceded on his behalf with Mrs. Bullitt and others in Paris, and generally stayed in close contact with him through the fall and early winter. By February, 1928, Bradley secured another small advance from Harper and arranged to dole it out to McKay in monthly installments through the spring. After some searching, McKay found a large sunny room with a fireplace and settled down to complete *Banjo*.[37]

Meanwhile, in the early spring of 1928, *Home to Harlem* finally appeared. McKay had corrected proofs in early December and had been pleased to see that Eugene Saxton, his editor at Harper, had not "chopped it up" as badly as he had feared. While writing *Home to*

*Harlem,* McKay had stressed he wanted no trouble with censors and was willing to change or delete passages to conform to acceptable standards. Harper did change a few words here and there, but generally left McKay's phrasing untouched. Later in the winter, Saxton sent him a dummy of the dust jacket, and shortly thereafter *Home to Harlem* went on sale in American bookstores.[38]

By the spring of 1928, interest in black writing, art, and music had peaked in the United States, especially in New York, and *Home to Harlem,* assisted by a fair amount of publicity, began to sell at a rate far beyond everyone's expectations. In April, McKay mischievously reported to Bradley that "I see *Home to Harlem* like an impudent dog has [moved] right in among the best sellers in New York."[39] Its success spurred McKay to finish *Banjo.* By May, he had completed all except the last two chapters. By then, Marseilles had become oppressive to him; in the course of a year of struggle and work, the meaner aspects of the *vieux port* simply depressed him.

In February, one of the Nigerian seamen upon whom he was basing the character Taloufa in *Banjo* returned to Marseilles minus both feet. At the end of 1926, he had stowed away on a French ship bound for New York, but he had been discovered and locked in an unheated water closet during the crossing. In New York, immigration authorities had immediately hospitalized him. His feet had been frostbitten beyond recovery; his legs had to be amputated below the knees. In the ensuing publicity, a New York lawyer secured a settlement of $17,000. After the lawyer took his $5,000 fee, the British consul in New York forwarded $10,000 to the victim's Nigerian home. With the remaining $2,000, the rehabilitated seaman began a long voyage home that for some reason included a final stop in Marseilles. Two days before finally sailing for Africa, the double amputee was jailed by French authorities for having illegally embarked on the ship in 1926. McKay, the Senegalese bar owner, and others immediately protested. McKay in particular warned that as a writer he was in a position to make a *cause célèbre* of the case. After two weeks, the prisoner won his release and left for home. The incident reinforced McKay's growing contempt for French justice.[40] At the same time, he recognized a good story when he saw one and decided to make the episode the basis for his next novel.

By the spring of 1928, McKay had definitely had enough of Marseilles. A few black beachcombers had reappeared, but the *vieux port* no longer appeared as beguiling as it had during his first long summer there "when the franc was cheap and food and wine were cheaper." Now, he thought only of the need to "get out and away from this atmosphere that has become depressing [in order] to read [*Banjo*] over and make it better in perspective."[41]

Early in the summer, McKay left. He accompanied to Barcelona a West Indian boxer who had a bout there. The Spanish sporting crowd impressed him with its fair-minded appreciation of excellence, and Barcelona charmed him with its festivals. He decided to remain the whole summer. Spaniards, McKay quickly learned, lacked the brisk impersonality of French shopkeepers; on the weekends, there were dances in the streets. His spirits quickly lifted, and he settled down to complete his second novel. On August 24, 1928, he announced with relief to Bradley that "at last I have finished *Banjo,* three-hundred and seventy-odd pages, and I am fagged out." Still, it was not completely finished. He needed to rewrite and revise and that would take a while longer. McKay predicted he could finish his revisions in a month, but other things intervened to delay him. One was the death of an old friend. In the same letter to Bradley, he also noted that "I have just seen by the *Nation* that Crystal Eastman is dead. She was one of my best friends and I feel terribly down." Crystal had died prematurely in London of a chronic kidney disease. Her last years, McKay knew, had not been happy, but her death nevertheless came as a shock. He still remembered her as "big with primitive and exceptional gestures." And she had "imprinted on her mind," he believed, a "Book of Woman" that no one else could write. Now, he believed, "life" had been cheated of one of its elemental forces. He still carried in his billfold the farewell note she had written him six years earlier on the eve of his departure for Russia. He took it out, read it once again, and cried.[42]

Although Crystal's death saddened him, his personal fortunes remained on the upswing. *Home to Harlem* continued to sell well through the summer. White reviewers generally praised it, and it stirred loud controversy in the black press. Since his departure from the United States in the fall of 1922, the explosion of literary interest in things black had generated controversy as well as exhilaration and optimism. When *Home to Harlem* appeared, it immediately became the focus of a battle that had been raging in the black press since 1926 between members of the younger generation of writers and older racial leaders who had nourished them to maturity. It involved, as McKay had foreseen, questions of artistic freedom versus traditional preoccupations with racial advancement.

A whole new generation of young black poets, short-story writers, and novelists had emerged since McKay's *Harlem Shadows* in 1922. Langston Hughes, Countee Cullen, Jean Toomer, Zora Neale Hurston,

Nella Larsen, Rudolph Fisher, and Wallace Thurman were all about ten years younger than McKay, and between 1922 and 1928 they had begun to produce the kind of freer, more varied and self-assertive literature that had first been suggested by McKay's poetry after World War I. Langston Hughes, for example, had adapted Carl Sandburg's style to produce free-verse poems in which he attempted to capture in the rhythms of jazz and the blues, the life and spirit of the black common folk. Jean Toomer, Zora Neale Hurston, and Rudolph Fisher also embraced more directly their folk roots in the short stories they produced during these years. In 1928, four black novels besides McKay's appeared, by Rudolph Fisher, W. E. B. Du Bois, Nella Larsen, and Jessie Fauset.[43]

Du Bois, Fauset, Alain Locke, James Weldon Johnson, and Charles S. Johnson of *Opportunity* were leaders among the older generation, and they all served as anxious guardians of the New Negro movement. They had laid the basis for the younger writers' success by providing contacts with white publishers, critics, and editors. Du Bois, Fauset, and Charles S. Johnson had also promoted younger writers by publishing their works in *Crisis* and *Opportunity*. As men and women devoted primarily to the achievement of justice for blacks, they remained concerned that the new movement contribute to their larger aim: the end of legal segregation and the abolition of old discriminations based on race. As middle-class progressive leaders, they wanted to project a positive, even a heroic, image of blacks and black life. Some among them were embarrassed and ill at ease when a lively and imaginative young writer such as Langston Hughes chose to extol the virtues of the lowest and least enlightened elements within the black community. Nor, as Locke's handling of McKay's poetry proved, were they always comfortable with expressions of black bitterness. Equally alarming in their eyes were the well-meant but misguided enthusiasms of those white critics and admirers of Afro-Americans who, as the movement progressed, seemed bent upon locking blacks into a new version of an old stereotype, that of the primitive, joyful, happy-go-lucky "prancing nigger" of the old plantation myth. In the new version (the positive version, as it were), blacks became the repository of an elemental health that Europeans no longer possessed because of their bankrupt morality and excessively mechanistic civilization.[44]

Black music, dance, and the plastic arts of Africa, in particular, had a directness and vitality that inspired artists, writers, and critics in Europe and America to praise and emulation. This new appreciation of black arts and culture had begun in Europe before World War I and had influenced great artists such as Henri Matisse and Pablo Picasso.

By the 1920s, this appreciation had moved from fine arts to literature. To varying degrees and at various times, it inspired a host of white writers, including southern writers such as Julia Peterkin, DuBose Heyward, E. C. L. Adams, Roark Bradford, Clement Wood, Howard Odum, and Paul Green.[45]

In New York, the white critic and novelist Carl Van Vechten tried in every way possible to support the efforts of black writers in the 1920s. In 1926, when McKay was abandoning his efforts to find a publisher for "Color Scheme," Van Vechten had produced *Nigger Heaven,* his own novel of Harlem life. In it he included middle-class blacks striving for respectability as well as the new popular image of a black subculture that thrived instinctively in amoral abandonment of all middle-class pretensions. The result was a curious hybrid that pleased some white reviewers but no blacks except Van Vechten's loyal friends such as James Weldon Johnson, Langston Hughes, and Countee Cullen.[46]

In truth, the efforts of the black middle class to guide, if not control, the New Negro movement and to keep it safely within the bounds of their own preoccupations proved impossible. In the same year that Van Vechten's *Nigger Heaven* appeared, the youthful Langston Hughes announced to the world that his generation of black writers had passed beyond the genteel treatment of black life and intended to express their "individual dark-skinned selves without fear or shame." He went on to add that "we build our temples for tomorrow, strong as we know how, and we stand on top of the mountain, free within ourselves." While many older racial leaders stood aghast at such bold pronouncements, white literary sophisticates in New York, led by Van Vechten, plunged headlong into black Harlem for a refreshing immersion in black culture. Their interest was not restricted to abstract literary activities. Black song, dance, and sex had to be experienced in their native milieu to be truly appreciated. By the mid-1920s, whites were flocking to Harlem nightclubs and cabarets, and books by and about Negroes were actively sought by publishers.[47]

It was altogether an extraordinary phenomenon. Never before had black artists and writers had such opportunities to be seen, heard, and read. The "Negro Vogue" among whites quickly became so intertwined and confused with the serious efforts of black writers to define themselves, their art, and their relationship to their people that conservative black critics accused Langston Hughes and others of selling out to a jaded white audience who refused to recognize any aspect of black life not associated with exotic dance, jazz, cabarets, and bathtub gin. The Jazz Age had arrived, over black conservative protests.[48]

In the larger perspective, of course, as Nathan Huggins has insisted, the New Negro movement, and particularly its younger participants, were part of the American literary revolt against the genteel tradition, a revolt in which Claude McKay had begun to participate after 1914. Integral to this revolt was a search for new aesthetic forms and values. For better or worse, the Negro writer of the 1920s could not avoid the new image of black primitivism that whites thought they saw in Harlem. For both young black writers and their conservative critics, the question of how to deal with this image in their own works had become by 1928 a subject of serious controversy.[49]

*Home to Harlem* appeared in the midst of this debate and immediately became a focus of intense condemnation and intense praise. Conservative blacks greeted it with dismay, while the young—Langston Hughes chief among them—were overjoyed to find that McKay had given new life to their cause. In *Home to Harlem,* the working-class black man, far removed from the worries, frustrations, and thwarted ambitions of the educated middle classes, lived a life of positive self-affirmation unknown to those obsessed with the injustices imposed by white society. Although he knew that his life was narrowly restricted to segregated Black Belts and that his occupation was confined to menial tasks, within those confines he managed to keep his wits intact and never lost his ability to experience directly the elemental pleasures as well as the sorrows of life. He lived for the moment, unencumbered by any restraints except those imposed by his innate sense of elemental decency and good taste. With the exception of Ray, the sensitive and frustrated Haitian intellectual, there were no representatives of the black middle class. There were no black families either (except in the distant rural past), no really permanent relationships, and no overweening worldly ambitions.

The hero of *Home to Harlem,* Jake Brown, was, in effect, the natural man forever dear to pastoralists and their urban counterparts, the authors of picaresque novels. But Jake was no Don Quixote: his sense of the real was too firm. Neither was he a Tom Jones: he was no innocent. If anything, he embodied traditional black folk sense moved to the city. He was the product of a hard realism that expected and asked no favors. Yet he was not lacking in generosity. Above all, Jake accepted himself, trusted his native wit, and affirmed his worth by never violating with his actions his inborn sense of dignity. In essence, McKay agreed with those who argued that blacks were closer to nature and spiritually healthier than whites. The Jake Browns of the world, McKay maintained, were different from whites. They accepted their differences, even rejoiced in them, and desired only to remain themselves.[50]

In relating the story of Jake's desertion from a black work crew in wartime Brest and his postwar return via London to Harlem, McKay gave scarcely a hint that the black middle class and its leadership existed, much less counted, in Jake's vagabond life as an itinerant seaman, longshoreman, and railway chef. McKay instead sketched in a rogue's gallery of Harlem "low-life" characters. Love-starved "grass widows" and the "sweetmen" who alternately preyed and depended upon them, pimps and prostitutes, homosexuals and drug addicts, loan sharks and labor scabs, alcoholics, gamblers, sadomasochists, and corrupt cops—all were found in Home to Harlem. In 1928, the existence of such types in black communities, though privately acknowledged, was not publicly advertised in respectable Negro publications. Neither was black sensitivity to the various shades of skin complexion that characterized every black community. McKay readily acknowledged that such sensitivity existed and then proceeded to name in riotously sensual language all the rich shades of color found within the Harlem community. To those who believed in decorum and restraint and also to those whose first concern was always to project black grievances onto the national stage, Home to Harlem seemed a betrayal of racial trust and solidarity.[51]

The novel was, as McKay had intended it to be, a militant assertion of the artist's right and duty to discuss any aspect of black life that moved him to creative expression. Such right and duty encompassed even the endorsement of white stereotypes if they contained aspects of black existence vital to the black man's character and survival. McKay had obviously accepted the basic contentions of the new primitivism. But in creating Jake Brown, he created a real man and not a mere caricature embodying the current white image of the primitive Negro. In Home to Harlem, Jake moved through a real world that imposed upon him a marginal status as a worker and citizen, whether in the army in Brest, as a docker in London, or as a railroad employee in the northeastern United States.

McKay's Harlem was not the exotic neighborhood of Van Vechten's Nigger Heaven, but the Harlem he had known as a solitary young black workingman. It was the Harlem of the rural migrant whose family was elsewhere—in the Carolinas, Alabama, Georgia, or the islands of the Caribbean—and whose only pleasures were those he fashioned for himself in the hours between dusk and dawn after a long day on the road or at menial jobs in the city. It was the Harlem of the picaresque black wanderer, who found there "down home folks" like himself, trying as best they could to fashion their lives anew in an alien environment. They had scant material resources but great energy, imagination, and stamina. If they often reveled by night, they also toiled by day. Ultimately they questioned their solitary lives. Some knew perpetual defeat. Jake was the shining exception, the exemplar by which those who knew him could measure themselves. But not all could move unscathed through Harlem's "semi-underworld" as he could.[52]

Ray, the wandering intellectual, marveled at Jake's sure instinct for life. He himself was full of self-doubts, hesitations, and inhibitions. Above all, he rebelled against the idea of trying to raise a family in such an environment. He did not know what the future held, but he knew he needed time and freedom to think, observe, and write. The schoolboy ideas he had absorbed from his Victorian mentors had seemingly all been rendered invalid by the Great War and the Russian Revolution. He now had to fashion values of his own in order somehow to resolve the paralyzing ambivalences within himself. At the novel's conclusion, Ray signs aboard a merchant ship bound for Europe. In *Home to Harlem*, McKay had in fact written the first chapter of his own search for meaning and value. Despite all the brave assertions of black vitality and joy in the novel, it was a troubled book by an author whose own unresolved tensions and self-doubts were never far from the surface.[53]

To his contemporary critics and admirers, however, *Home to Harlem* was simply a confirmation of their own ideas about the direction taken by the New Negro movement. Back in 1925, Langston Hughes had informed McKay that "you are still the best of the colored poets and probably will be for the next century and for me you are the one and only." Shortly after *Home to Harlem* appeared, he wrote again, praising the book. "Undoubtedly," he stated, "it is the finest thing 'we've' done yet. . . . Your novel ought to give a second youth to the Negro Vogue." Its critics, he asserted, were "amusing and pathetic. . . . Everyone's talking about the book, and even those who dislike it say it's well written."[54]

Of the older generation, James Weldon Johnson alone remained warmly supportive of McKay. A literary artist himself, he did not shock easily. He had moved in black literary, musical, and theatrical circles in New York since the first decade of the century, and he welcomed the new white interest in black culture as a significant advance in American interracial understanding.[55] Since the winter of 1928 he had been urging McKay to return to the United States. "You ought to be here," he advised, "to take full advantage of the great wave of opportunity that Negro literary and other artists are now enjoying. In addition, we need you to give more strength and solidity to the movement." Before *Home to Harlem* appeared, he wrote for Harper a promotional sketch of McKay, and afterward he assured Claude that "I think you've written a wonderful book." They were to remain friends.[56]

Other black leaders were less positive in their assessments of *Home to Harlem.* W. E. B. Du Bois, for example, saw no merit in it. In his *Crisis* review, he summed up his reaction by saying that after reading *Home to Harlem,* he had felt distinctly unclean and in need of a bath. The review stung McKay. He respected Du Bois's long record of achievement as a racial leader. His *Souls of Black Folk* had been important in the development of McKay's own self-awareness. When he answered Du Bois's attack, therefore, his letter contained a note of anguish and regret as well as defiance. Du Bois, McKay asserted, had stepped "outside the limits of criticism" and had become "personal" in his attack on *Home to Harlem.* He had questioned McKay's motives, wondering publicly how far one could sink in search of money and popularity. He had, McKay maintained, brought his argument "down to the level of the fish market." Replying in kind, McKay said Du Bois understood nothing about aesthetics and was "not competent or qualified to pass judgment upon any work of art."[57]

As for his motive in writing *Home to Harlem,* McKay protested that he had since "boyhood" been "an artist in words" and had stuck to his vocation "in spite of the contrary forces and colors of life that I have had to contend against through various adventures, mistakes, successes, strength and weakness of body that the artist-soul, more or less, has to pass through." He sympathized with and pitied Du Bois for not understanding his motives because Du Bois had, after all, been forced by circumstances into the role of a racial propagandist and had been cut off "from contact with real life." Propaganda, McKay maintained, was "but a one-sided idea of life. Therefore," he wrote, "I should not be surprised when you mistake the art of life for nonsense and try to pass off propaganda as life in art!" McKay closed by asserting that "deep-sunk in depravity though he may be, the author of *Home to Harlem* prefers to remain unrepentant and unregenerate and he 'distinctly' is not grateful for any free baptism of grace in the cleansing pages of the *Crisis. . . .* Yours for more utter absence of restraint."[58]

Du Bois was not alone in questioning McKay's motives. One columnist for the Pittsburgh *Courier* compared McKay to Thomas Dixon, the notoriously racist author of *The Clansman,* who wrote "solely [for] shekels, shekels and still more shekels." William Ferris in a syndicated column also charged that McKay, driven by a desperate need for money, had finally gotten it by holding "up his own race to ridicule and contempt before the Caucasian world." Dewey Jones in the Chicago *Defender* concurred and lamented that "white people think we are buffoons, thugs and rotters anyway. Why should we waste so much time trying to prove it? That's what Claude McKay has done."[59]

Not all black reviewers questioned McKay's motives, but most did label *Home to Harlem* a black version of *Nigger Heaven.* At best, they said, both books were misguided; at worst, libelous. Almost all black critics pointed out that McKay's characters represented only a portion of Harlem's "many thousands," most of whom led quiet, respectable lives far from the saloons, cabarets, and gin mills depicted in *Home to Harlem.* The book, they charged, would only reconfirm in white minds all the old stereotypes regarding blacks.[60]

Such opinions were probably reinforced by the praise with which some white critics greeted the book. For instance, John R. Chamberlain in the New York *Times* betrayed an enthusiasm that verged on caricature: "[*Home to Harlem*] is beaten through with the rhythm of life that is a jazz rhythm . . . the real thing in rightness. . . . It is the real stuff, the lowdown on Harlem, the dope from the inside." Chamberlain's review was, in fact, more perceptive than such phrases indicated. He recognized that McKay had evoked "the things that he himself has actually experienced. His workers are not mere puppets; they are McKay recast to fit the story." But his review still contained enough to confirm the black critics' conviction that McKay's work seriously distorted the reality of black life in America. "If there is a moral or a point or whatever you want to call it to this novel," Chamberlain wrote, "it is the Negro is happiest when he makes no attempt to assimilate an alien white culture."[61] All white racists could applaud such sentiments, but McKay's black critics knew that America's racial dilemma could never be resolved so simply.

Chamberlain meant well. Others who praised *Home to Harlem* were more consciously racist. Louis Sherwin of the New York *Sun,* for example, prefaced his praise of the novel by avowing "a vast disesteem for the jig-chasing passion that has obsessed the literati of this village for the last few years." He found Negro spirituals to be only "ludicrous" versions of Methodist hymns, and "newly literate Ethiops . . . just as sophomoric and self-conscious as a parvenue . . . from

Iowa." In his view, however, McKay was "a superior craftsman" who had produced "far and away the best book I have ever read dealing with the African stepbrother and infinitely superior to any work by a white man on this subject."[62]

Not all whites were so laudatory in their condescension. A more respectable critic, Carl Van Doren, noted the episodic structure of the book and discounted it as a novel. He declared it instead a compilation of Harlem folklore. In a much more sympathetic review, Burton Rascoe agreed that *Home to Harlem* was "not a novel in the conventional sense," but he nevertheless thought it a book "to invoke pity and terror, which is the function of tragedy, and to that extent—that very great extent—it is beautiful." Like Chamberlain, Rascoe recognized that McKay wrote from intimate experience and deep conviction about "the lost generation of colored folk in the teeming Negro metropolis north of One Hundred and Tenth Street, New York." It was, he concluded, "the story not of the successful Negroes . . . [but] of the serving class . . . and all those who compensate for defeat . . . in the white man's world by a savage intensity among themselves at night."[63]

All reviewers agreed that McKay had written in vibrant, often poetic language and that his characters were vividly drawn. One note of praise that especially pleased Claude came from F. Scott Fitzgerald. McKay and Fitzgerald had met back in 1926 while McKay was staying with the Eastmans in Antibes. McKay had been in the kitchen preparing a meal when Fitzgerald arrived, and much to everyone's merriment he at first thought McKay was a servant. They subsequently enjoyed the evening together. After the publication of *Home to Harlem*, Fitzgerald wrote McKay that "[I] can't tell you how I enjoyed your book. . . . For me it was one of the two most worthy novels of the spring." Fitzgerald noted a "Zola-Lewis" influence in the railroad scenes, which stood in contrast to "the emotion of the purely Harlem scenes." Another well-known literary figure of the period, Dorothy Parker, also praised *Home to Harlem* as one of the more interesting novels of the season.[64]

After five years of struggle and pain, McKay rejoiced in such praise. To James Ivy, who had written to congratulate him and to remind him of their brief meeting years ago in Greenwich Village, McKay answered exultantly, "Oh yes I remember you all right and thanks for your letter. . . . The reviews in the big-boss press are great, all of them, and the book is selling in spite of its stark realism." As for his black critics, McKay dismissed them as "ignorant" in the ways of art and artists and simply "afraid of [the] white man's ridicule and mockery."[65]

In a brief essay in *McClure's*, McKay explained that *Home to Harlem* had grown out of his early experiences in New York. After he left Kansas, he wrote, "Harlem was my first positive reaction to American life." Once there, he had given himself "entirely up to getting deep down into . . . [the] rhythm [of Harlem life]." As a consequence, as he explained in a letter to James Weldon Johnson,

> I consider *Home to Harlem* a real proletarian novel, but I don't expect the nice radicals to see that it is, because they know very little about proletarian life and what they want of proletarian art is not proletarian life truthfully, realistically and artistically portrayed, but their own fake, soft-headed and wine-watered notions of the proletariat. With the Negro intelligentsia it is a different matter, but between the devil of Cracker prejudice and the deep sea of respectable white condescension I can certainly sympathize, though I cannot agree, with their dislike of the artistic exploitation of low-class Negro life. We must leave the appreciation of what we are doing to the emancipated Negro intelligentsia of the future, while we are sardonically aware now that only the intelligentsia of the superior race is developed enough to afford artistic truth.*

Writing for the *Amsterdam News,* the black journalist J. A. Rogers reported from France that McKay had told him that "it will take the Negro in America another thirty or forty years to see *Home to Harlem* in its true light—to appreciate it in the spirit in which I wrote it."[66]

Once again, as he had first done in his dialect poetry and again in his American verses during and after World War I, McKay had explored in *Home to Harlem* areas of the black experience that had seldom, if ever, been given such direct expression by a black artist. Like his poetry, *Home to Harlem* had stylistic flaws. It was loose and episodic, and it flirted dangerously with common white stereotypes of black life. As he had intended, however, it broke free from the restraints of respectable black caution to help open new areas of exploration for the black literary artist. As McKay had predicted to Alain Locke after the failure of "Color Scheme" in 1926, "I have difficulty enough in getting out a book, but when I do put it over it will be a book to wake the world up. Am I too boastful?"[67] As events proved, he was not.

Among younger black writers and critics, *Home to Harlem* aroused enthusiasm, but among established racial leaders (with the exception of James Weldon Johnson) it did little to enhance McKay's repu-

*Claude McKay to James Weldon Johnson, April 30, 1928, © 1987 by Hope McKay Virtue, 1110 Olive Avenue, Long Beach, Calif. 90813, and used by her permission. This letter is in the James Weldon Johnson Papers, James Weldon Johnson Collection of Negro Literature and Art, American Literature Collection, at the Beinecke Rare Book and Manuscript Library, Yale University.

tation or position. In 1928, when Harper submitted his name for consideration for the Harmon Foundation's Annual Awards for Distinguished Achievement Among Negroes, the hostility of the black establishment became evident. During the selection process, Walter White wrote confidentially that "*Home to Harlem* does not impress me as being as fine and as sincere an accomplishment as Mr. McKay is capable of. I do not mean by this to imply that I believe him guilty of intellectual or artistic dishonesty. I do know that he has suffered greatly within recent years from illness and poverty. It is out of this suffering that I believe the shortcomings of *Home to Harlem* emerged."[68]

Among the five final judges, there was only one black, the conservative critic and poet William Stanley Braithwaite. His first choice for the award was Nella Larsen for her novel *Quicksand*. His second choice was Jessie Fauset for *Plum Bun*, another novel; he bestowed upon McKay an honorable mention. One of the four white judges, the journalist W. D. Howe, did not include McKay on his list. The other three—the editor John C. Farrar and two university professors, Dorothy Scarborough of Columbia and J. Melvin Lee of New York University—chose McKay, who in early 1929 was duly awarded in absentia the Harmon Gold Award for literature. It included a cash prize of four hundred dollars. At the presentation ceremony in the AME Zion mother church in Harlem, James Weldon Johnson accepted it on McKay's behalf. But by their actions, White and Braithwaite gave notice that the black establishment generally did not appreciate McKay's accomplishments in *Home to Harlem*.[69]

For McKay, its success made all the aggravations of the previous five years worthwhile. In one letter to Bradley, written in early September, 1928, he reflected candidly on some of the reasons his success had been so long in arriving. "Yes," McKay agreed, "it was a hard struggle as you say, but I have never felt personally bitter about life for it, because I realize that most of it is the direct result of my own temperament. I had a number of easy chances which I let slip from temperamental reasons. However if I had not travelled that hard road I could not have come through with *Home to Harlem!*"[70]

While completing the final revisions of *Banjo*, McKay at last felt prosperous enough to embark upon a new adventure. He had always been curious about life in Africa, and his encounters in Marseilles with black and brown people from all parts of Africa had stirred his interest even more. Among the blacks he had chanced upon in the *vieux port* was a Martinique seaman who had a home in Casablanca and who sailed regularly between North Africa and various southern European ports. He insisted that of all the African ports and coun-

tries he had seen, Casablanca and Morocco were the best. He urged
McKay to visit him there. McKay had been in Barcelona three months
when he encountered the same seaman, who again invited him to
Casablanca. This time McKay accepted the invitation. His summer
in Barcelona had made him aware of Moorish influences upon Spanish history, architecture, and customs. His new-found appreciation of
Spain impelled him farther south.[71]

McKay left Barcelona in late August, shortly after he completed
his initial draft of *Banjo*. He went first to Nice, where he relaxed and
socialized for two weeks. In early September he returned to Spain,
and by way of Seville crossed over to the international city of Tangier,
where he lingered briefly before proceeding to Casablanca at the end
of September, 1928. McKay remained in Morocco for around seven
months. His acceptance of Moslems and Moslem customs proceeded
slowly at first, and then more rapidly as he got better acquainted with
the Moors.[72]

The Martinique seaman, he discovered, was one of several non-
Moslem blacks who had "gone native" to the extent of taking Moslem
wives and living together around an enclosed court in an old Arab
section of Casablanca, far removed from the modern European quarter of the city. Their adoption of Arab customs, however, stopped
short of complete integration. For example, they allowed their wives
to eat with them in McKay's presence, and they retained their French
citizenship, which enabled them to make "about six times what the
natives doing the same work got." McKay ruefully concluded that his
friend "was 'really' living white in Africa." In Casablanca, McKay
quickly became aware of some of the inequalities of French rule in
Morocco and of the restiveness of the native population under colonial domination. He wanted to see other cities in the interior that he
hoped would be less dominated by the European presence.[73]

Before setting off for Rabat, Fez, Marrakesh, and other towns in
Morocco, however, he assured Bradley that he would soon be receiving the completed manuscript of *Banjo*. During his journey to Casablanca, McKay explained, "I toted *Banjo* along with me, re-reading,
emendating and retyping and pasting all the time, and it is now almost as I want it. I shall send it off during this week."[74] True to his
word, McKay finished *Banjo* in Rabat and then plunged enthusiastically into the life around him.

To his surprise, he found that it reminded him in great ways and
small of his native island. On his first day in Casablanca, Morocco's
long historical connection with black West Africa had been brought
vividly home to McKay by a group of "Guinea sorcerors or Gueanoua,"
as they were called in Morocco. They were all black West Africans or

descendants of West Africans. He happened upon them near the home of the Martinique sailor. The Gueanoua were "exorcising a sick woman" and as they "danced and whirled like devils" before him, McKay realized with a shock that their performance duplicated almost exactly the trancelike dances of the Myal cults of Jamaica, which he had witnessed as a young man. He stood transfixed until a dancing woman threw herself "in a frenzy" upon him. Other participants informed him that he "was a strange spirit and a hindrance to the magic working." He left the scene with the feeling that he was in some unexpected ways much closer to home than he had been in a long time. At first he compared the Arabs of Morocco to the East Indians he had known in Jamaica. He admired their self-sufficiency but felt little kinship with them. He informed Bradley that he had never felt such distance with the Chinese minority in Jamaica, and he could not explain the reasons for his lack of intimate feeling for East Indians and Arabs.[75]

Such aloofness soon vanished. In Rabat, he began to see the native life more clearly as "a big tree with solid roots and spreading branches." By contrast, the city's European section seemed only "an imported garden, lovely and carefully tended," but black Africa's contributions to Moroccan history and culture left an even more indelible impression on him. He was surprised to discover that "even the illiterate Moor" was familiar with "the history and the poetry of Antar," one of the poets of the Arabian Pleiades and a child of a black slave mother. In the cafés he frequented, he often heard songs from Antar. Upon learning that he was a poet himself, his Moroccan acquaintances would sometimes exclaim that "our greatest poet, Antar, was a Negro." Since Antar was "as great in Arabian literature as Homer in Greek," McKay in later years bemoaned the black American's ignorance of him. Some of his verses seemed to speak directly to the Afro-American's own history and condition:

> I have borne the evils of fortune, till I have discovered its secret
>     meaning . . .
> I have met every peril in my bosom,
> And the world can cast no reproach on me for my complexion:
> My blackness has not diminished my glory.[76]

The black African element in Morocco's great age of Islamic conquest, too, stirred McKay. At Shellah he saw the tomb of "the Black Sultan, who, according to the native legend, was the greatest ruler of Morocco, having united all of North Africa under his rule, [and] conquered Spain." After visiting Marrakesh, he reported to Bradley that it was "still semi-savage with the Arabs always coming into the city from the . . . country and [blacks] from the Soudan and the Senegal bush."[77]

McKay seemed not at all upset by the lingering forms of slavery still practiced in Morocco in 1929. At Fez, where he finally made intimate contact with native Moroccans, he visited "an old medieval house with a wonderful court where young girls—blacks and Arabs—are actually sold—secretly. But it is not the white-slavery traffic, nor the old time Negro slavery. It is rather a way of getting a domestic servant or a slave wife."[78] McKay, perhaps, would not have been so complacent had he seen men, as well as women, on the auction block. As he viewed it, such surreptitious slave markets were hardly more than another example of the Arab male's complete dominance over his women.

In Fez, he enjoyed a reception among the Arabs comparable to the hospitality extended to him in Russia. He received countless invitations to Arab homes, enjoyed "many dens where they smoke the 'kiff,'" and in general had "such a great good time in the native town" that he temporarily abandoned his hotel, donned the local garb, and "went native."[79] As in Spain, he saw in Morocco a civilization vastly different from the bourgeois culture of France. In Morocco, especially, each of the different ethnic groups—Arab, Berber, black African, and Jew—managed somehow to retain internal community cohesiveness, dignity, and tradition, despite poverty, colonialism, and material backwardness. Each group had its place and function in the overall society, and McKay began to feel some such balance of ethnic groups would eventually be the answer to the race problem in the United States.

Morocco whetted his desire to see black Africa. In fact, Bradley secured from Harper an advance sufficient to finance such a trip, but at the last moment McKay decided to postpone it. By January, he had begun to worry about correcting the proofs of *Banjo*, which he was expecting soon. "Just now," he explained to Bradley, "I think it is more important to have 'Banjo' all right than to go on to West Africa." In addition, his North African journey had been more expensive than he had anticipated. To see Africa thoroughly would be even more costly. He concluded that it would be better to wait until he had digested his Moroccan experience and written about it before proceeding farther south. When he did go, he hoped to proceed from West Africa around the Cape all the way to Egypt and to write something significant. "This is a big programme," he admitted, "and I had better wait to see if it is realizable." His objective would be to convey "the human element from the American Negro's point of view." And in anticipation of *A Long Way from Home* almost a decade later, he revealed that he had already found in North Africa the kind of balance among diverse ethnic groups that in his opinion should hold the most interest for Afro-Americans. To Bradley, he confided that "I am sure I won't strike any other place like it of more interest to American readers from a sociological angle."[80]

McKay had found in North Africa the kind of cultural and ethnic pluralism in a colonial setting that he had first experienced on a smaller scale in Jamaica. In the decade just ahead, he would (rightly or wrongly) hold the North African example up as an ideal to be striven for by American blacks. In North Africa, ethnically diverse groups lived in what appeared to him a relatively harmonious and complementary balance. Instead of demanding integration, black Americans within the United States, McKay eventually concluded, would do better to strive for the kind of internal community cohesiveness and complementary functionalism he had observed in North Africa. The central importance of his North African experiences in the development of his thought made it easier for McKay to decide not to take his West African journey. Unfortunately, the opportunity to visit black Africa never arose again.[81]

Even if he had decided to go ahead with the trip, McKay might well have found his entry into West Africa blocked by colonial authorities. Before leaving Morocco, McKay discovered that his radical past had not been forgotten. In Fez, his constant association with Moroccans, including disaffected intellectuals, caused the French some concern. They had long been aware of McKay's Communist activities after World War I. Once in 1924 he had been questioned by the police in Toulon. In France, however, he had posed no threat to the government, and he had not been bothered. His presence in French North Africa was another matter. There, the French viewed his racial and political militancy as a definite threat. He was accordingly summoned before a French police official and in the presence of a British consul was advised to stop associating with the natives. McKay argued that he was neither a political propagandist nor an agitator. He emphasized that his Moroccan friends had not protested his company, and he knew that the British, who had legal jurisdiction over all British subjects in Morocco, could bring no charges against him because he had not violated any laws. The meeting ended in an uncomfortable standoff. Among his new Moroccan acquaintances, McKay had experienced a singular freedom from the obsessive racial consciousness that had dogged him since childhood. His encounter with the colonial authorities jarred him into a renewed awareness of his unusual position as an articulate black within the framework of Western imperialism. No matter how nonpolitical his life had become, he remained suspect.[82]

McKay eventually discovered that British colonial authorities distrusted him even more than the French did. On his return from Morocco, they refused him entry into Gibraltar. Despite his abandonment of communist politics, British security circles still considered him a dangerous character. Since his year in London, he had intensely disliked the British. Their actions in Gibraltar convinced him that they had encouraged his harassment by French authorities in Morocco.[83]

In January, 1929, McKay settled briefly in Tangier to await the page proofs of *Banjo*. When they arrived, he discovered that his prose had been heavily edited. Many words and phrases he had used to capture the rough atmosphere of Marseilles's old port had been deleted. The editors had substituted words and phrases McKay considered to be mere literary clichés that destroyed totally his artistic intent. As with *Home to Harlem,* he had given Eugene Saxton permission to alter passages that might bring censorship proceedings, but *Home to Harlem* had been accepted with few changes. McKay could not understand why *Banjo* had been revised so extensively. He had certainly not agreed beforehand to such substantial alterations, and he immediately decided to force Saxton to restore his manuscript to its original form. McKay wrote Bradley that he expected his total support. He would never accede to *Banjo*'s publication in its altered form and would consider all obligations to Harper at an end if they published it as it stood.[84] He then explained to Eugene Saxton why *Banjo* had to be cleansed of the editorial alterations:

> I am not a Jim Tully writing roughly and at random . . . I am a poet and have always striven conscientiously to find words to say exactly what I see and feel. I took a long time to write "Banjo" in the face of real difficulties, writing and re-writing to find the right words to render the atmosphere and the types that moved in it. . . . And then someone ups and wantonly compromises the character of my writing by replacing my personal words with cheap two- and three-syllabled stock words. . . .
>
> I prefer to be crude and ungrammatical and achieve a clean and clear expression thereby, rather than spill the sap of my thoughts into dead husks of words.*

*Claude McKay to Eugene Saxton, January 30, 1929, © 1987 by Hope McKay Virtue, 1110 Olive Avenue, Long Beach, Calif. 90813, and used by her permission. This letter is in the William Aspenwall Bradley Papers (private possession).

Harper made the corrections but at McKay's expense, and *Banjo* duly appeared in the late spring of 1929. Through reflection upon his life among the beached black seamen of Marseilles, he sought to make a significant statement about the status and condition of blacks in Western civilization. In the process, he once again endorsed the notion that ordinary, unlettered black folk enjoyed a more direct, vital, and realistic relationship to life than the educated of their race whose preoccupation with social advancement robbed them of spontaneity, happiness, and the direct appreciation of the world as it actually existed.[85]

McKay conceived and wrote *Banjo* in a more purely picaresque mode than *Home to Harlem*. Its subtitle, "A Story Without a Plot," indicated that it encompassed a season of random adventures. As in *Home to Harlem*, his characters existed precariously but with zest amid the bawdy residue of commerce and industry, this time in the *vieux port*, "the Ditch" of Marseilles, as the black seamen dubbed it. It provided a colorful, infamous setting full of easy sex, endless con games, and much misery for the unwary. In fact, the *vieux port* was known to all seamen and seasoned international travelers as a place where literally anything could be had—for a price.[86]

The novel's chief character, Lincoln Agrippa Daily, called "Banjo" because of his mastery of that instrument, was a more roguish version of Jake Brown in *Home to Harlem*. Like Jake, Banjo chanced upon Ray, the wandering Haitian intellectual, and a friendship quickly developed. McKay used it to present once again his own relationship to folk types such as Banjo, who moved through "the Ditch" with a sure confidence gained from years of living solely by his superior wit and intuition.

After several years of living and writing in Europe, Ray admired more than ever the free-spirited vagabondage of such a man as Banjo. Ray shared, he knew, something of Banjo's adventuresome, uninhibited spirit, his love of life, and the ability to rise above or descend into his surroundings. But Ray was burdened with the urge for self-expression, and in *Banjo*, years of hand-to-mouth living abroad had taken their toll. "Now," Ray felt, "he was always beholden. . . . He was always writing panhandling letters to his friends, and naturally he began to feel himself lacking in the free splendid spirit of his American days. More and more the urge to write was holding him with an enslaving grip and he was beginning to feel that any means of self-expression was justifiable. Not without compunction. For Tolstoy was his ideal of the artist . . . who balanced his creative work by a life lived out to its full illogical end." Such passages, of course, were pure autobiography, and *Banjo* contained many. Through the mouth of Ray, McKay reflected upon his own life, criticized the Afro-American elite, editorialized upon the significance of black folk culture, and condemned the overweening hypocrisy of European civilization in its treatment of black colonials. At the same time, he painted a grimly realistic picture of Marseilles and the black men he had known there.[87]

McKay's description of the *vieux port* was thorough, unsparing, and accurate. After reading *Banjo*, Rex Ingram wrote Claude a congratulatory letter. "You have certainly studied your subject well," Ingram said. "I know the quarter of Marseilles well and you have it to the life." During World War II, the *vieux port* became a center of French resistance activity. In retaliation, the Nazis mined the entire quarter, and demolished it as they evacuated the town toward the end of the war. Because it no longer exists, McKay's description of its congested alleyways, dark habitations, seedy bars, and sinister denizens has become for some French a classic evocation of the quarter as it was between the wars. As one French writer stated in his account of the *vieux port*'s fate, "Tout s'est effacé dans la poussière des explosions de dynamite. Nous refaisons souvent, par la pensée, nos promenades errantes dans la 'fosse' comme l'appelaient Ray, Malty, Banjo et Gingembre, ces personages de couleur du livre de Claude MacKay [*sic*]: *Banjo*"[88] (Everything was obliterated in the dust from exploding dynamite. In our thoughts we often wander again through the "ditch," as it was called by Ray, Malty, Banjo and Ginger, the people of color in Claude McKay's book *Banjo*).

Despite its apparent formlessness, *Banjo* had a loose structure that accurately reflected the black seamen's haphazard existence between jobs. In Part I, the seamen come together. The atmosphere of "the Ditch" is described, and the rhythm of their daily life is set. In Part II, Ray enters to share the stage with Banjo. Banjo collects a group about him who form a band that plays in various dives for drink, food, and small change. At the end of this long interlude, the band breaks up and the men drift off to look for work or new adventures. In Part III, they return briefly, but the life of "the Ditch" has become harder, its magic worn thin. Some grow ill; others sign aboard a new ship being fitted for a voyage to the Caribbean. All eventually go their separate ways.

Through their peregrinations about Marseilles and its environs, Banjo remains McKay's archtypical black vagabond, the natural man making his way by fair means or foul in an unnaturally harsh world. "I ain't got no head for remembering too much back, nor no tongue for long-suffering delivery. I'm just a right-there, right-here baby, yestiday and today and tomorrow and forevah. All right-there right-here for me now." To which his light brown companion, the West Indian Ginger, who held the record in the group for the longest time on the beach, replied, "Hallelujah! Lemme crown you. You done said a mou'ful a nigger stuff."

Not all his companions shared Banjo's healthy hedonism. Bugsy, for example, was consumed by a fierce hatred for all whites and was dominated by a quick pugnaciousness that he directed toward anyone who crossed him. After the group's breakup and later return to "the Ditch," they found Bugsy, who had fallen ill, dead in a dark fetid room. In death as in life, he greeted them wild-eyed, but cold and stiff. By contrast, the slow-witted, ineffectual Lonesome Blue had no defenses whatever against the dangers of "the Ditch." Consumed by syphilis, ragged, dirty, and listless, he passed up several opportunities to be sent home by the American consul. He had finally been given up as hopeless, even by his sympathetic companions, who shunned him in the hope that isolation and loneliness would drive him from Marseilles. Another, the sensitive young Goosey, had quit his ship in Marseilles after an altercation with one of its officers. He too was race-conscious to an extreme. While highly resentful of whites, he remained haunted by the fear that his fellow blacks on the beach, by their panhandling, drunkenness, and indiscriminate womanizing, confirmed all the old white stereotypes of Negroes.

Finally, there were the Senegalese, as all West Africans were called. Some were dockers. Some had lost their papers and passports to thieves and were officially listed as of "doubtful" nationality. They generally formed a separate group, somewhat apart from and a little strange to their West Indian and Afro-American fellows. But color brought them together, and from them Ray learned much about how carelessly Great Britain and France treated colonial workers. All the black seamen had been touched in one way or another by the Garvey movement, by radical agitation in Europe, and by the growing movements of anticolonial protest in West Africa, India, and the Middle East.[89]

*Banjo* contained, in effect, a rich mix of images, impressions, and messages that often tended to undermine, if not overwhelm, McKay's continuing insistence that the primitive, "natural" response to life of a man like Banjo revealed the essence of black life. Life for blacks was obviously more complicated, more varied, more rigorously challenging, and more problematic than Banjo could comprehend or cope with alone. To a considerable degree, his happy jazzing involved an individualistic evasion of hard problems that he, in fact, simply could not face. McKay nonetheless considered him the personification of blackness and black culture. Banjo had to be the starting point in any realistic self-definition because it had been the rhythm, music, dance, and fundamental durability of the Banjos and Jakes of the race who had given blacks in America the strength to rise above and to survive their harsh existence. In short, they had accepted themselves and had drawn enormous strength from such self-acceptance.[90]

In McKay's opinion, the black bourgeoisie hardly qualified as a true middle class because they lacked property, wealth, and power. To him they were only a pathetic imitation of the white American middle class. He regarded them as a tragically misguided and impotent intelligentsia. If they desired a genuine racial renaissance, Ray (read McKay) advised them that they "should study the Irish cultural and social movement . . . and read about the Russian peasants . . . and . . . their lowly, patient, hard-driven life, and the great Russian novelists who described it up to the time of the Russian Revolution." He also advised them "to learn all you can about Ghandi [sic] and what he is doing for the common hordes of India." In the meantime, they should not despise but should try to understand Banjo's "Hallelujah Jig."

> Lay off the coal, boy, and scrub you' hide,
>     jigaway . . . jigaway
> Bring me a clean suit and show some pride,
>     jigaway . . . jigaway.

McKay denied that any feelings of "superior condescension" lay behind Ray's "love [for] the environment of the common black drifters." Rather, "he loved it with the poetical enthusiasm of the vagabond black that he himself was. . . . Among them was never any of the hopeless, enervating talk of the chances of 'passing white' and the specter of the Future that were the common topics of the colored intelligentsia. Close association with the Jakes and Banjoes had been like participating in a common primitive birthright."[91]

McKay's critics were wrong to assume he could write in this vein merely for money, although as George Orwell once pointed out, money is always a motivation among writers of every race, nationality, and ideological persuasion. And McKay was not blind to the opportunities that lay at hand. As Banjo forthrightly declared at the beginning of his novel, "The American darky is the performing fool of the world today," and he ought to turn that situation to his own advantage.

Again, near its conclusion, he touched upon the theme from a slightly different direction. "The wul'," he declared, "ain't gone a'mourning forevah because [of the Great War's carnage]. Nosah. The wul' is jazzing to fohgit. . . . And Ise jest gwine on right along jazzing with the wul'." To the departing Goosey, whose hatred of whites was tempered only by his fear of their ridicule, he added, "I ain't swore off nothing like you." Blacks will find "white divilment" wherever they go, he counseled. "But we niggers am no angels, neither." Goosey would eventually learn, Banjo believed, "to know life" in its fullness just as he himself did.[92]

Many of those critics who had applauded *Home to Harlem* also welcomed *Banjo*. But some questioned McKay's easy acceptance of broad generalizations about the black man's "primitive vitality." As one noted, "He shares with his brothers of the Klan a dangerous proclivity to generalize—only he reverses the values. To him, the Negro is superior in all that appears important: a capacity to feel and enjoy, to be generous and expressive, to be warm and irresponsible, to live without shame and inner repression. . . . Are Negroes . . . the uninhibited children of joy that Claude McKay believes?" Another critic observed that McKay's easy characterizations failed to provide any true test of his characters, especially Ray. "We should like to see a novel devoted to Ray in which he would be forced to think and feel his way out of some real problem." Walter White in the New York *World* took issue with McKay's analysis of the Afro-American elite. He argued that McKay's animosity actually flowed from his black West Indian background where a wealthy class of mulattoes stood aloof from their black kinsmen. McKay wrongly believed, White asserted, that a similar situation prevailed among Afro-Americans. Despite this shortcoming, White conceded that "*Banjo* represents in some respects a growing power on the part of Mr. McKay in the selection and handling of his material." To many in the Afro-American press, *Banjo* only confirmed their earlier conclusions about McKay. In brief, they believed that he was simply pandering to vile white prejudices. As Aubrey Bowser in the New York *Amsterdam News* concluded, "He knows he is slurring his own people to please white readers."[93]

*Banjo* enjoyed some success in the United States; it sold well, though not as well as *Home to Harlem*. But it made an overwhelming impression on French West African students in France when it appeared there in translation late in 1929. In *Banjo*, McKay gave an unsparingly harsh account of French duplicity in its treatment of black colonials. Nor did assimilated black Frenchmen from the

West Indies escape his censure. In one chapter, Ray advised a young mulatto student from Martinique that because of his education he had learned to despise his own race. When he came to maturity he would realize "with a shock that you don't and can't belong to the white race. . . . And instead of accepting it proudly and manfully, most of you are soured and bitter about it—especially you mixed-bloods." He urged the student to look for his roots among his own people in Africa and America instead of merely accepting French culture as the ultimate achievement of human civilization. "'Getting down to our native roots and building up from our own people,' said Ray, 'is not savagery. It is culture.'"[94]

*Banjo* quickly became a bible of inspiration to such young black literary aspirants as Léopold Sedar Senghor, Aimé Césaire, and Léon Damas, who would shortly launch their own literary careers. Lilyan Kesteloot has emphasized that *Banjo*'s success did not stop with the first "triumvirate" of black writers. Ousmane Socé remembered that "Banjo was displayed in black-student bookshelves right next to a book by [the anthropologist] Delafosse," who was also writing sympathetically of African culture. In 1950, Joseph Zobel remembered in *La Rue Cases Nègres* that *Banjo* also aroused much discussion in Martinique. Finally, in 1956, Sembene Ousmane from Senegal wrote *Le docker noir,* a novel that Kesteloot believed "was more influenced by *Banjo* than by the novels of Richard Wright, to which *Le docker noir* is occasionally compared." In interviewing Senghor, Damas, and Césaire in the early 1960s, Kesteloot found they could "still cite entire chapters" of *Banjo.* "What struck me in this book," Césaire recalled, "is that for the first time Negroes were described truthfully, without inhibition or prejudice."[95]

Césaire and Senghor would eventually incorporate into their own works many of the ideas contained in *Banjo.* For them, too, blacks would possess a natural spontaneity and a direct emotional involvement with the world and with each other that Europeans had lost in the process of industrialization, mechanization, and urbanization. In essence, as Senghor remarked, "Claude McKay can be considered . . . as the veritable inventor of *Negritude* . . . not of the word . . . but of the values of *Negritude.*"[96] For young French West Africans and West Indians, McKay would not have to wait "thirty or forty years" for his aesthetic purposes in *Home to Harlem* and *Banjo* to be understood and appreciated.

By the time the first American reviews of *Banjo* appeared, McKay had returned to France. He had left Tangier in late February, 1929, and had made his way leisurely through Spain, viewing with appreciation the landmarks and monuments left from the great age of struggle between Moslem and Christian. He visited Granada, where he contemplated the Alhambra and considered its significance in Spanish and Islamic history. He also journeyed to Seville to see "the Giralda that legend attributed to the Black Sultan." Such reminders of the African and Islamic presence in Spain made McKay appreciate the deep-rooted significance of Spanish Catholicism. More than ever, he admired the Spanish above all of Europe's peoples. Their national character, he realized, had been forged out of a mighty struggle, and their friendliness, dignity, and pride of place were genuine.[97]

In Madrid, he lingered long enough to purchase two tailored suits and a new hat before proceeding by way of Marseilles and Nice to Paris. He remained in Paris from April until July, 1929, and while there he encountered many Afro-Americans prominent in the Negro Renaissance. McKay welcomed the chance to talk with them about the significance of all the new developments in black arts and letters that had occurred since he had left the United States in 1922. Above all, he wished to discover just where he stood in their eyes. Because *Home to Harlem* had been roundly denounced in the Afro-American press, he wondered what he could expect from his peers should he decide to return to the United States.[98]

James Weldon Johnson had recently urged that he return, but McKay had hesitated. Although his newly won notoriety as a novelist pleased him, it also made him wonder if there would ever be a place for him in the Afro-American community. He continued to insist that as a writer his role was to report truthfully his own experiences and convictions. Such independence, he believed, remained at odds with the Afro-American elite's drive to break down the barriers of segregation and social inequality in American society. His stay in Paris allowed him to renew some old personal acquaintances from Harlem, to meet other American blacks for the first time, and to gauge their attitude toward the New Negro movement and toward him.[99]

From a purely social point of view, McKay enjoyed himself. *Blackbirds,* a popular musical comedy from New York with an all-black cast, came to Paris while he was there, and McKay met the entire company. He also met in Paris several members of the early dramatic production of DuBose Heyward's *Porgy.*[100]

By 1929, black artists, writers, and musicians attracted as much attention in French literary circles as they did in New York. When William Aspenwall Bradley and his wife gave a party for the members of the *Blackbirds* cast, everyone present, including McKay, had "a grand gay time together, dancing and drinking champagne." McKay also met the Afro-American poet Countee Cullen in the spring of 1929. From the first, McKay and Cullen got along well together and remained friends. Cullen possessed none of McKay's mercurial irritability, and the two never quarreled. Years later, when McKay mentioned this fact to Cullen, he just laughed and pointed out that he never quarreled with anyone.[101]

By 1929, Alain Locke must have surely been more wary of McKay than Cullen ever had reason to be. McKay had long since lost all respect for Locke's critical acumen. Locke had refused to acknowledge any wrong in his editing of McKay's poems for the *Survey Graphic* in 1924 or for his inexcusable reprinting of them in *The New Negro* the following year. All this led to bitter exchanges in which McKay told Locke at one point that "there is no question but, that, in spite of your doctor's degree, you have not acted as a man of honor." McKay also stated that though he doubted Locke would understand, he had to explain that "I am a man and artist first of all. The imprisoning quality of my complexion has never yet, and never will, move me to bend to flunkeyism and intellectual imprisonment with the sorry millions that are likewise tinted." Locke deeply resented McKay's criticisms. Still, in their mutually condescending ways, they met cordially in Paris once again. Both were dressed in the latest fashion and when Locke exclaimed that their gloves were identical, McKay could not resist remarking, "Yes, but my hand is heavier than yours."[102] So much for their friendship.

McKay also met at this time Carl Van Vechten, Joel A. Rogers, and John Hope, president of Atlanta University, who, McKay duly noted in *A Long Way from Home*, looked even more "Nordic . . . than Walter White." Like White, however, he proved "affable" and invited McKay to visit Atlanta when he finally returned to the United States. As a fellow novelist and chronicler of Harlem night life, Carl Van Vechten intrigued McKay even more than had President Hope. Claude found the author of *Nigger Heaven* wholly at ease with him and definitely not patronizing, but the two still had trouble communicating during their one morning together in Paris. They were introduced after midnight at the Café de la Paix by a young black man described by McKay as "one of Mr. Van Vechten's Harlem Sheiks." Van Vechten had already had a few drinks. As a matter of course, he assumed McKay would drink with him. Claude, however, ordered a soft drink. He had good reason for abstaining. He still suffered from chronic high blood pressure and severe headaches, and a French doctor had recently warned him not to drink any alcoholic beverage, even wine. Van Vechten, who was already tipsy, naturally did not understand the situation. After a while, he excused himself to go to the men's room and never returned. McKay eventually paid both their bills and left. The two did not get together again until after McKay's return to New York in 1934. By then, Van Vechten had himself stopped drinking.[103]

The one person in Paris during the summer of 1929 who roundly condemned both McKay's and Van Vechten's novels of Harlem was the Jamaican-born writer and journalist, J. A. Rogers. He shared the opinion current in the Afro-American press that both men had catered to prurient white stereotypes of black sexuality. Neither Rogers nor McKay apparently took the other very seriously. McKay poked fun at Rogers' penchant for journalistic sensationalism; Rogers was sure McKay had sold his black soul to Mammon in writing *Home to Harlem*. Beneath their intellectual differences, an old Jamaican class difference also divided the two men. As a light-complexioned Jamaican, Rogers had very early become aware of McKay's rural prejudice against the island's mulatto gentry. Neither ever quite forgave the other the accident of his birth. A mutual friend, James Ivy, later remembered with great amusement how each would visit him in the 1930s and refer disparagingly to the other's complexion.[104]

Rogers' opinion of *Home to Harlem* was not shared by all blacks in Paris. Some among the *Blackbirds* cast warmly defended McKay's book. He listened with keen interest to all those who ventured any opinion about the Negro Renaissance and his place in it. Most were young and aspiring writers, artists, actors, or teachers. They tended to look upon McKay, now nearly forty, as at best a precursor of their movement. His two recent novels were welcome but late additions to the Harlem Renaissance. The egoism of the young did not disturb McKay. The apparent narrowness of their vision did. Many, he felt, had no clear understanding of the potential importance for their racial group of a genuine artistic renaissance. McKay understood the importance of cultural renaissance in European and Arabian history, and he had followed the more recent national revivals of Russian and Irish literature. The possibility of a Negro renaissance had "deeply stirred" him. This did not mean that his notions of a black renaissance were grandiose. As he put it, "My idea of a renaissance was one of talented persons of an ethnic or national group working individually or collectively in a common purpose and creating things that would be typical of their group." Among those American blacks in Paris in the spring of 1929, he met few who shared this vision. Their social pretensions, he felt, obscured from their view the larger artistic and cultural meanings potentially inherent in their activities. "I was surprised," he later wrote, "when I discovered that many of the talented Negroes regarded their renaissance more as an uplift organization and a vehicle to accelerate the pace and progress of smart Negro society." They were so flattered to be patronized by white, upper-class connoisseurs of the arts that they never realized that "perhaps such white individuals were searching for a social and artistic significance in Negro art which they could not find in their own society." Above all, they failed to understand that white interest in them as artists did not connote the social acceptance of blacks in all areas of white society. Moreover, the interest and support shown black artists in 1929 did not mean that they could expect such patronage indefinitely. They must learn to stand on their own feet and pursue their own ends, irrespective of the temporary white interest in the exotic aspects of Harlem night life.[105]

In effect, McKay felt the same kind of ambivalence toward the Afro-American elite in Paris that he had felt seven years before in New York City when he had first become acquainted with the NAACP's top leadership and Harlem's middle-class social set. He liked to socialize with them, but he knew their preoccupations with social advancement, particularly their relentless battle against the color line, conflicted with the central thrust of his writing. As a writer his main concern was with self-acceptance and the assertion of his race's positive existence in the immediate present. Whatever possibilities blacks had for advancement, as individuals or as a group, had to rest upon their present strengths. These, McKay firmly believed, showed themselves to best advantage in the Jake Browns and Lincoln Agrippa Dailys of the race, not in the socially ambitious elite, who he believed were futilely obsessed with winning acceptance from their white counterparts.

# 9
# The Expatriate Years, 1929–1934: *Gingertown* and *Banana Bottom*

Despite his underlying reservations, McKay had some good times in Paris with the cast of *Blackbirds,* with Countee Cullen, and with a pretty, young black socialite named Anita Thompson, who would eventually follow him to Tangier. During the latter part of his stay in Paris, however, he became nervous, irritable, and depressed. In *A Long Way from Home,* he maintained that Paris had always had this effect upon him. He could never work there; the city distracted him. In addition, his health was not good.[1]

All this may have been true, but there was yet another reason for McKay's unhappiness. To his dismay, he learned that his long-lost wife, residing again in New York, was seeking to "tie up" his royalties in a legal knot that would bind him once again to support her and their child, whom he had never seen. While not averse to aiding his daughter, he wished to do it on his own terms. To forestall legal proceedings, he invited his wife to visit him in Paris. When she arrived, they discussed their situation, and McKay somehow succeeded in averting a costly legal battle. But the emotional price to both was great. His wife left with the accumulated bitterness of many years, intensified by the realization that what little he could give her would not be worth a court fight to get. Even the money he advanced for their daughter Hope's support and education went to McKay's relatives in Jamaica. While her mother worked in New York City, Hope remained in Jamaica. Claude's family saw to it that Hope received a good education, and her maternal family, the Lewars, gave her the warmth and emotional support to overcome the bewildering sense of abandonment she sometimes felt in the absence of both her parents.[2]

McKay's traumatic confrontation with his wife left him nervous, distraught, and depressed. He began to drink again, which did not help. One night his old friend Louise Bryant Bullitt found him drunk and depressed in a café. She urged him to leave Paris and to go back to work. McKay heeded the advice. Louise's own deplorable condition probably served as warning enough. Since McKay had last seen her in 1925, Louise had lost her health, her beauty, and her husband and child. McKay was appalled by her decline. Besides drinking too much, she consorted with an unpleasant woman whom McKay detested. Still, Louise remained a friend, and he saw her often during his stay in Paris.[3]

Late in July he went to Antwerp for a brief vacation, but he returned to Paris, where he lingered until late August. Max Eastman had written earlier from the United States that he planned to arrive in August, and McKay wanted to see him. In the interval, he tried without success to write. The social distractions of Paris combined with chronic health problems—headaches, "sciatica" (in his arm and shoulders), and high blood pressure—defeated again his best efforts to concentrate.

In desperation, he went with a young medical student to Bilbao and then to San Sebastián in northeastern Spain. In Bilbao, he began another novel based on his experiences in Marseilles. It was an imaginative account of the stowaway African, his misfortune, and his return to Marseilles. Central to the story was the African's tempestuous affair with a spirited North African woman who in the end murders him in a fit of passionate rage. From San Sebastián, McKay went in September to Madrid; there he began to work in earnest on his story.[4]

Although he preferred Barcelona to the relative bleakness of Madrid, he nevertheless felt at ease in the "quiet lazy-moving existence" of the Spanish capital. As he explained to Bradley, he could work there, "being in harmony with it." His months in Paris, he found, had only increased his love of Spain. To Bradley he wrote, "It may be that I exaggerate but as soon as I crossed the border I felt as if I had escaped from a swarm of wasps to find myself among a people who can appreciate simple dignity when they meet with it, because dignity is a fundamental of their social life. . . . I am afraid I shall at last grow romantic about *some* country."[5]

In Madrid he read in the Paris edition of the New York *Herald* that Eastman was in Paris. McKay immediately sent a telegram only to find that he had already left for the United States. Eastman's letters announcing the dates of his stay in Paris had not caught up with McKay in time to enable him to see his old friend. McKay was bitterly disappointed. He still looked to Eastman for counsel, and he wanted to discuss with him "a thousand things—yourself, Eliena, and our old group, politics, prose, poetry." McKay had also wanted to talk with Eastman "intimately . . . about myself, my health. I am sure a talk with you would have done me lots and lots of good." Now, he concluded, "I'll have to wait until I come 'home' next year." He planned to return to the United States, he explained, "just for a few months to get material for a book on that damned thing called nigger society." He hastened to add, "I am sure I couldn't live there again. I saw enough of Americans white and colored this summer in Paris to know that if I have ever mused the thought of living in America again I was a fool. Still, I want to come back to establish right of residence."[6]

McKay remained in Spain until June, 1930. During that time he worked conscientiously on his new novel, at first called "The Jungle and the Bottoms." The Bradleys visited McKay in November, 1929, and again in December after he moved to Barcelona, where he "rested and played through the holidays." In January, 1930, he resumed work and "kept straight on knuckling down to the job." In March he allowed himself a weekend in Valencia, and thoroughly enjoyed the trip. "Valencia was lovely," he wrote Eastman, "with chubby orange trees full of fruit, fields upon fields of them and pickers and carriers and ships trading and sailing and the town has a fluffy creamy color that is very delicious."[7] Back in Barcelona, he soon finished the novel.

"The Jungle and the Bottoms" proved transitional in McKay's development as a novelist. Like *Home to Harlem* and *Banjo*, it dealt with working-class characters in an exotic "low-life" setting that emphasized the marginality of black existence in Western commercial society. Unlike his first two novels, however, "The Jungle and the Bottoms" was more conventionally plotted. It revolved around a character in many ways essentially different from Jake, Banjo, or Ray. Lafala, the handicapped African, was not a character McKay could completely understand. Despite Lafala's handicap, McKay failed to make him a very sympathetic character. In the end, his girlfriend, Zhima, first overshadows, then literally annihilates him in perhaps the most powerful single scene in all of McKay's fiction.

Throughout the novel's composition, McKay remained acutely aware that Lafala was not developing into an engaging character. "It's the girl Zhima," he explained to Bradley, "who runs away with the story and after that Malty," a West Indian character of modest good sense who had previously appeared in *Banjo*. By March, 1930, he informed Bradley that Lafala was "standing up strong on his own corks" but admitted that "the Arab girl is growing bigger than I ever dreamed and running away with the book and me."[8]

Bradley thought McKay should not include too many scenes reminiscent of *Banjo*. Although McKay initially called the city Dreamport, it clearly remained the Marseilles of *Banjo*. Bradley also advised McKay that he tended to editorialize too much through the mouth of Malty, who in "The Jungle and the Bottoms" replaced Ray as Claude's fictional alter ego. Bradley expressed concern that the book might include too much talk of race and race relations, but McKay rejected that notion. He believed all blacks, even "the happy-go-lucky Negro," often dwelt on racial matters. The topic, he explained, "came naturally" to "the talk and thought of Negroes, like their complexion, giving a peculiar and definite color to the human story." Such talk, he admitted, sometimes conflicted "with the picaresque story, but if I'm to go on as a writer my characters besides acting must think and talk some sense and if those characters are mainly Negroes, there will certainly be in their thinking and talking ideas peculiar to Negroes."[9]

Although he did not know it at the time, "The Jungle and the Bottoms" was to be McKay's last effort to sustain the picaresque mode he had first developed in *Home to Harlem* and *Banjo*. In June, he finished the book and sent it off to Eugene Saxton at Harper. He was not entirely comfortable with either its theme or its development, but he had worked hard to complete it and he hoped to see it succeed at least as well as his two previous novels. The great stock market crash of 1929 had already occurred in the United States the previous fall, but McKay as yet had no inkling of its consequences, either for himself or for the world. As the summer of 1930 approached, his main preoccupation remained, as it had for some time, his health. He decided to go to Berlin for a thorough medical examination. McKay knew his headaches, high blood pressure, and chronic pains in his arms were probably related to his old venereal infections and their treatments. From Berlin, he confided to Eastman that in the past he had contracted gonorrhea, as well as syphilis, and that perhaps his physical problems stemmed as much from overtreatment as from the diseases themselves. He had come to Berlin, he explained, because he had been assured by Spanish doctors that the German venereal-disease specialists and their medicines were the world's best.[10]

Since 1923, McKay had been haunted by his bout with syphilis and had remained fearful that he still harbored the dreaded spirochete. Because of this understandable fear, he had persisted in treating himself with the mercury-based medicines longer than he should have. In Berlin he placed himself under the care of "two specialists, one . . . a professor of the university faculty . . . said to be very good." They proceeded to draw fluid from McKay's spine and brain in search of a specific cause of his maladies. They found no evidence of syphilis. They concluded that he had indeed been "over-medicined"; his "continued head trouble—dizziness, heaviness and even lightness" was caused by the medicine he had consumed since 1923.[11]

Their diagnosis did not lead to a cure. McKay would still suffer periodically from alarmingly severe headaches, as well as occasional chest pains, backaches, and immobilizing pains in his arms (a condition he always described as sciatica). Still, in the summer of 1930 the knowledge that he was definitely free from syphilis made him so happy that he took an extended vacation. From Berlin, he traveled first to Luxembourg, where he stayed a month. From there, he proceeded in July and August to tour the Rhineland by boat and train. He visited "Strassburg . . . Baden, Heidelberg, Frankfurt, Mayence, Coblenz, Bonn, Treves, [and] Cologne."[12]

Finally, toward the end of the summer, he returned once again to Paris, where he talked with Eugene Saxton and Bradley about the status of his latest novel. Both men felt that "The Jungle and the Bottoms" required some rewriting before it would be acceptable for publication. Unlike his two previous works, it was not a picaresque tale, though its characters and setting were in many ways reminiscent of those in *Banjo*. Saxton apparently questioned the novel's overall coherence and unity. He may have also wondered if certain themes developed by McKay would be accepted by the American reading public. For in "The Jungle and the Bottoms," McKay frankly and sympathetically discussed for the first time the plight of homosexuals in Western society. In a fully developed substory inserted into the novel almost as an aside, McKay devoted an entire chapter to portraying the homosexual underworld of the docks in the person of gigantic "Big Blonde" and his effeminate young "page boy" lover. Their attempt to get service in a cheap waterfront café ends in a brawl, with Big Blonde pathetically bemoaning the seeming impossibility of people like themselves ever winning any respect. Whatever Saxton and Bradley may have felt about this particular chapter, both concurred that the novel could be set right without major revisions. McKay did not agree.[13]

In "The Jungle and the Bottoms," he had tried to create a carefully structured story "very different in style and mood from the preceding ones." He had intended the character studies of Ashima [also called Zhima] and Lafala in particular to be "more fully realized" than those in his first two novels. Above all, he sought to capture the emotional depth of their conflict. "As the book is a more serious attempt than the others and will set the tone for future work," he informed Bradley, "I should like to make it as perfect as I can."[14]

The more he considered its imperfections, however, the less enthusiastic he became about publishing it. By September, 1930, he had decided to set the book aside. He urged that Saxton accept instead his collection of short stories. As he explained to Max Eastman, "The Jungle and the Bottoms" remained too much after the mode of *Home to Harlem* and *Banjo*. He had grown tired of such "picaresque" tales. Because his contract called for a collection of short stories, he insisted upon their publication next, rather than a novel that he, Bradley, and Saxton thought not satisfactory. Despite his brave defenses of *Home to Harlem* and *Banjo*, his critics had obviously made some impression upon McKay. To Eastman, he confessed his eagerness to have his short stories published because "they will show that I am a writer of many moods and open the way for any book or any theme I may choose to write instead of my being taken solely as a writer of picaresque stories."[15]

Bradley and Saxton had no choice but to go along with McKay, though both warned that collected stories, even in the most prosperous of times, seldom brought their author any profit. Bradley in particular believed that McKay was making a grave mistake in substituting the stories in place of "The Jungle and the Bottoms," which, as he saw it, needed relatively few alterations to make it acceptable for publication. McKay remained adamant and soon tired of the discussion. Without announcing his destination, he abruptly left Paris in September, 1930, for Morocco. As he explained to Eastman, "I feel sure that the short stories will more than cover what they have already advanced, because they are good stories and I already have enough of a name that will help them sell. . . . I had about written myself dry on the picaresque stuff. . . . The six Harlem stories go much deeper into the life of the Harlem Negroes than *Home to Harlem* ever did."[16]

From Paris, McKay journeyed by way of Marseilles and Oran to

Fez, where a Moroccan friend whom he had met during his last trip
had promised him a native house where he could live and work. After
his arrival, however, the French colonial police informed him that the
president of the French Republic would soon be visiting Fez and he
would have to leave the city. "They said," McKay informed Bradley,
"they had information from the British authorities that I was a propagandist." McKay speculated that perhaps his criticism of French
civilization in *Banjo* also "had something to do with it!" He protested
that he was no propagandist and "was only interested in the simple
native life. Maybe," he concluded, "that is just what they are against."
The police were polite but firm. McKay got no help from the British
consul and in the end he departed Fez, "accompanied by a policeman," for the international city of Tangier. This experience, together
with his previous experiences in Morocco in 1928, caused McKay, as
he expressed it, "to see the French cock-eyed through a police veil."
The French police in Morocco, however, were at least courteous,
even as they ordered him to leave their colony.[17]

McKay had no illusions, of course, about the French as colonizers.
It was evident in Morocco that they treated their colonial subjects
badly. His own deepest resentments, however, remained directed toward the British, who he believed were behind all his French Moroccan troubles. The British had barred him from entering Gibraltar in
1929, and the French police now admitted that their information on
his past radical activities had come from British sources. Nothing
McKay said or did in protest seemed to alter his status in the eyes
of the British intelligence system. His protests to British consular
agents in Morocco, his letters to their superiors in the British government, and his personal appeal to George Lansbury to use his influence as a member of Parliament to stop the harassment he experienced both in French Morocco and Tangier—all had no effect.
"Technically," McKay reported to Bradley, "I can travel because my
passport is good, but I should like to have the police bar lifted because
it is embarrassing." Throughout his residence in Tangier, McKay's
movements and activities continued to be monitored.[18]

After seven years of wandering in Europe, McKay decided he must
settle in Morocco. Since he could not stay in Fez, Tangier might, after
all, be a better place to live and work. Although jointly administered
since World War I by several European nations (principally France,
Great Britain, and Spain), it remained geographically and historically
a part of Morocco, and directly across the Strait of Gibraltar lay Spain,
which McKay also loved. Together with its colonized majority of Arabs

and Berbers, Tangier had a substantial European community. Spanish, French, Italian, and British subjects—all jealously protected by their respective governments—made Tangier a center of international intrigue in North Africa. They also gave it a cosmopolitan flavor appropriate to an international city.[19]

McKay, however, chose to live as close as possible to the indigenous North Africans. He had recently turned forty and had begun to feel the need to sink roots in an environment and among people with whom he felt at ease. Although he had no compelling desire to return to Jamaica itself, he recognized among the people of Morocco a basic community existence, rooted in folk tradition, similar in some respects to the kind of environment he had known as a boy. "I need to settle down," he informed Max Eastman, "and no place has satisfied me since I left home as much as Morocco. There are many things in the life of the natives, their customs and supersititions, reminiscent of Jamaica." At the same time, he wrote Bradley that his next "'best seller' will be the Jamaican book—dealing with the religious customs and social life of the peasants. I am ripe for it as I am also feeling very religious now among the Moslems. . . . After my experience here the 'Jungle' seems rather thin and cheap. I am right in coming back here to feel that."[20]

In "The Jungle and the Bottoms," McKay had strained for a transition from the essentially rootless existence of vagabondage depicted in his first two novels toward a more substantial depiction of psychological realism. But as it turned out, both of his leading characters in that novel had remained mired in "the Ditch" he had so vividly described in *Banjo*. In Tangier, McKay succeeded at last in escaping his own sense of rootlessness. He successfully completed the transition he sought from purely picaresque fiction to a more psychologically satisfying depiction of black life rooted in the community of his youth.

He planned to include a few Jamaican tales in his volume of short stories, and shortly after settling in Tangier he began work on "The Agricultural Show." In it he recreated the "naive fresh manner" in which the mountain community of his childhood planned and organized their first agricultural show. The story was almost purely autobiographical, a quiet, evocative re-creation of the wonder and joy he had felt as a child following his older brother as he conceived and orchestrated one of his many community projects. For the critic and scholar Robert Bone, "The Agricultural Show" was "a pure specimen of [Harlem] Renaissance pastoral," illustrating perfectly one of the many uses that the black writers of the 1920s made of the strengths and virtues of their rapidly vanishing black rural heritage. Bone was right in thinking that for McKay "The Agricultural Show" was "a poetic vision, an expression of an inner need. McKay's Jamaican pastoral," he concluded, "with its images of racial harmony and social peace, is an objective correlative of the inner harmony that he so desperately seeks. Split and shredded by his contact with the Western world, he returns in his imagination to Jamaica in order to reconstitute his soul."[21]

In *Home to Harlem* and *Banjo,* Jake and Lincoln Agrippa Daily wandered far from the rural families and communities that nurtured them. Both novels reflected the fragmented world of the single, black male rural migrant in the cosmopolitan cities of the West. In both novels, the characters exist without the support of families and with only the most tenuous community ties. Both novels accurately reflected McKay's own spiritual vagabondage since leaving Jamaica. In Morocco, he experienced among the Moors the kind of deep-seated, traditional community self-sufficiency that he had known as a child in the hills of Jamaica. The experience enabled him to deal, finally, with the problems of family, community, and group values that he had not been able to explore fully in his first novels.[22]

From this perspective, the depression McKay experienced in Paris in 1929, his abandonment of "The Jungle and the Bottoms," and his flight from Paris in 1930 were understandable and necessary; both personal and artistic necessity impelled him to return to Morocco. The bohemian freedoms of Paris were no longer relevant to his needs. He sought instead a more traditional setting, one governed by ancient, preindustrial patterns and routines that would allow him to remember again the significance of his own black Jamaican heritage.[23]

After living awhile in Tangier proper, McKay rented a small cottage in January, 1931, "in an Arab village" just outside the city but still well within the Tangier international zone. His house had three rooms and a terrace from which he could view the ocean. After spending most of January fixing the place and settling into it, he began work in earnest on his volume of short stories. By spring the collection was virtually complete. It consisted of six Harlem stories he had begun in the mid-1920s, four more recent stories of Jamaican country life, and two concluding stories, one set in a Mediterranean port similar to Marseilles and the other in an Arab city resembling Tangier.[24]

Before he had finished the collection, however, McKay had a visitor, one whose presence for a while seemed to promise an end to the solitary existence he had led for so long. In Paris in 1929 he had become acquainted with Anita Thompson, a pretty, young Harlem socialite who had left the United States to enjoy the social freedom of life among the expatriates of Paris. In Paris, she had become involved with a young Dutch painter, Kristians Tonny, whom Gertrude Stein admired and encouraged. After arriving in Tangier, McKay received several letters from Anita. She complained she had grown tired of Paris and of Tonny, and wished to visit McKay in Tangier. She wanted to escape Paris to write an account of her adventures in America and Europe, and she believed that McKay could help her find a publisher. McKay was flattered by the idea, and he encouraged her to come. For about two or three weeks after her arrival, everything seemed idyllic. Anita liked Tangier, and McKay enjoyed introducing her to his friends. Everyone liked her: she was bright, witty, and beautiful—a delightful companion whose presence brightened McKay's life.[25] But trouble soon developed.

Anita sought more than a companion. According to McKay, she wanted a husband. He flatly rejected the idea. He already had a wife. One, he had learned, was more than enough. McKay's refusal even to entertain the idea of marriage led inevitably to quarrels. Anita should have married Tonny, he said; perhaps she would, she said, for Tonny was on his way to Tangier. Fine, he said. And their brief affair ended, with Anita moving with Tonny to another section of Tangier. McKay greeted this development with mingled pain and relief. He was contemptuous of Tonny, whom he scarcely knew. Anita told his Moroccan friends that McKay hated all whites. They cautiously inquired if it were true. To escape the gossip and settle his nerves, McKay "gave up the little house and went for a few months up in the mountain fastness of Xauen in Spanish Morocco."[26] In Xauen, McKay settled down and finished *Gingertown*, his volume of short stories.

Everywhere he went in Morocco, McKay quickly made friends and observed with sympathetic eyes the life around him. He loved the rich musical traditions of the country and spent many hours in cafés drinking exotically flavored tea, socializing, and listening to the native music. On the whole, he led a quiet, contemplative life. He tried to live moderately, for despite every precaution, his health remained precarious. He still suffered from all the old, frightening ailments that had plagued him intermittently since his return from the Soviet Union almost a decade before. Life sometimes seemed a succession of headaches, chest pains, nerve disorders of the upper extremities, and odd colds and other annoyances. Through it all, he tried to hew a moderate course that would allow him to continue writing. To W. A. Bradley, McKay wrote, "My illness is something terribly real. And for seven years past I have been living radically different from my old way of existence, almost solitary, so that I could conserve myself for a little creative work. My appearance may deceive, but one doesn't go shouting one is ill to all one's acquaintances all the time."[27]

Sometime in the early fall of 1931, McKay returned from Xauen to Tangier. He had sent *Gingertown* to his publisher, and he had already planned his novel of Jamaican hill country life through to the end. Before settling down to its completion, however, he once again had to find a suitable place to live. For the moment, he had sufficient money to invest in a comfortable house. Besides advances from Harper for *Gingertown* and his next book, he also received a few thousand francs for the French translations of *Home to Harlem* and *Banjo,* as well as occasional royalty checks. His income was not large but, for the moment at least, he had enough money to raise himself above the hand-to-mouth existence that he had known before the publication of *Home to Harlem* in 1928.

In keeping with his desire to live among the Moors, McKay again found a place in the countryside, well outside the European quarters of Tangier. Near the mouth of the Suani River, where it flowed into the Atlantic close to the boundary with Spanish Morocco, McKay found a cottage on over an acre of land, at least half suitable for gardening. Although the house was more than three miles from town and dilapidated, McKay jumped at the chance. The owner agreed that if McKay made it habitable, he could have it for two years for only 600 francs.

Claude set to work, and by December, 1931, he had transformed a leaky "old barn without doors" into a comfortable, if unpretentious, home. On December 1, he wrote Max Eastman

> I started repairing it after my return from Xauen and now it is very habitable, but I spent the best part of my assets making it so. However, I have faith in the place and myself. One half of the land is good truck garden soil and I have planted two sacks of potatoes and a little peas and carrots and turnips, so if the international crisis should get worse and the elements are not unfavorable to the garden I might in time be able to feed off my own place. As soon as I can manage I shall get a milking goat. The house is right on a river which divides it from the sea and at high tide when the sea rides up the river the water washes the foundations. It is deep enough for good bathing especially when the sea is high, with a little

stretch of sandy beach, and next summer I want to build a runway right into the water. The house is just about the size of yours at Antibes and planned almost the same way. It commands a most lovely view of the sea, the town of Tangier, and Spain on one side and on the other the mountains of the Spanish zone.*

At the time it seemed an ideal investment. After years of vagabond-age, he had finally put down roots in a beautiful land that promised refuge from the gathering clouds of international depression.[28]

McKay had worked hard since 1923 to establish himself as a creative writer, and he sensed that his next book would be his best. He had reason to feel confident. But unfortunately, while he had grown and matured as a novelist, the world that had supported his first efforts had collapsed. As incomes declined in the United States, readers bought fewer books and publishers reduced their lists. In addition, readers' interests shifted, which meant for McKay more lost readership and a precipitous decline in income. The Negro as the exotic primitive, happy in his poverty, had lost his appeal as white readers suddenly found themselves facing an economic abyss that threatened to plunge them into an acquaintance with poverty much harsher than any they had ever imagined.[29]

Despite his genuine understanding of world politics and economics, McKay never quite comprehended the impact of the Great Depression on his personal career. He tended to blame himself for the failure of his works to sell. In the fall of 1931, certainly, he simply could not foresee that his hard-won competence would not bring its own rewards in the decade ahead. While waiting for the publication of *Gingertown*, McKay ensconced himself in his new place and worked hard on his next novel, *Banana Bottom*. If *Gingertown* failed, as Saxton and Bradley feared it would, McKay wanted to be ready with a novel that could not fail to make money.[30]

In the early spring of 1932, *Gingertown* finally appeared and the reviews in both the black and white press were generally favorable. But as Bradley and Saxton had predicted, it had poor sales and made no money for either Harper or McKay. It could hardly have been published at a worse time. Depression had long since settled upon America; McKay very likely could not have made any money even if *Gingertown* had been an outstanding novel.[31]

Although reviewers still expressed enthusiasm for his work, a few

*Claude McKay to Max Eastman, December 1, 1931, © 1987 by Hope McKay Virtue, 1110 Olive Avenue, Long Beach, Calif. 90813, and used by her permission. This letter is in the Max Eastman Papers (private possession).

ventured some serious reservations that boded ill for his future as a novelist. Rudolph Fisher spoke perhaps for the younger generation of black writers in New York when he suggested in his *Herald Tribune* review that McKay seemed out of touch with Harlem as a locale and that "strange West-Indianisms" sometimes issued "from the mouths of American blacks" in the six Harlem stories that formed the first half of the book. Fisher maintained that these stories dealt with real problems, but they were only coincidentally set in Harlem. Although Fisher acknowledged that the stories in *Gingertown* possessed the same "robust vigor characteristic of all Mr. McKay's work," he strongly implied that their author had long ago lost touch with the distinctive characteristics of Harlem and the many changes that had occurred there since 1922.[32]

An anonymous reviewer for the New York *Times* had more praise for McKay, but he also intimated that the reading public had grown weary of tales of Harlem life. He condescendingly declared that McKay was "more of a genuine artist than most of the New Negro novelists. . . . Perhaps, however, no one can entirely escape the curse which over-dramatizing has laid upon Harlem as a subject for a serious writer. . . . Stories of the Black Belt always sound a trifle artificial." The best stories in *Gingertown*, the reviewer stated, were McKay's Jamaican stories. "[They] have an authenticity and a quality of acrid poignancy which are not matched in the Harlem stories. . . . In choosing less hackneyed subject matter Mr. McKay seems to cast off restraints. Even his prose, always good, is richer and more supple in the last half of the book."[33] McKay may have found encouragement in such praise, but the overall tone of the review indicated that black artists, particularly those who chose Harlem as their setting, were liable to get short shrift in the New York *Times*.

After the publication of *Gingertown*, McKay used his last assets to complete *Banana Bottom*. After only four years of relative prosperity, he again faced poverty. His future seemed to depend on the success of *Banana Bottom*, and he poured into its composition all his energy and creative resources. In June, 1932, he sent it to Harper. Saxton and everyone who saw it there liked the story.[34] To maintain hope for the future, McKay had to believe that *Banana Bottom* would sell much better than *Gingertown*. Still, it would not appear until the early spring of 1933; in the meantime, McKay had to exist in a limbo of nervous anticipation. He had never been patient with economic uncertainty, and he soon bombarded his friends with piteous wails. Fortunately for him, however, during the summer and fall of 1932, he entertained a succession of visitors whose encouragement and friendship helped him keep his anxieties under control. Pierre Vogein and his wife, Fanny Rappaport, now a physician, visited him from Paris. Vogein would continue to write Claude until the German occupation of France disrupted their correspondence. McKay also entertained another French visitor, Henri Cartier-Bresson, who eventually gained international fame as a photographer. Claude had been photographed in Paris in 1924 by the young American photographer Berenice Abbott, and he may well have met Cartier-Bresson there about the same time.[35]

McKay also welcomed into his home in 1932 several Americans. Some were visitors to Tangier, others lived there. The young American poet Charles Henri Ford for a while lived near McKay and became a frequent visitor. McKay later recalled that Ford caused a stir among his native friends. Some of the younger ones "said he looked wonderfully like the cinema portraits of Marlene Dietrich." One of the attractions of Tangier for McKay must have been its tolerance of homosexuals, though as usual he remained circumspect. Ford remembered that parties in McKay's home included native musicians, good food, and hashish. McKay, he recalled, always appeared reserved at such gatherings, older and plumper, more of an observer than a participant in the festivities.[36]

The writer, composer, and editor Paul Bowles, who eventually settled permanently in Tangier, knew Kristians Tonny and Anita Thompson. When he arrived in Tangier, in 1932, Bowles found the lovers' triangle far from settled. Anita, it seemed, would visit McKay for days at a time whenever she and Tonny quarreled. After existing alone for a while, Tonny "would swallow his pride and walk out to the house by the river to fetch her." One day Bowles and a friend, the American literary agent John Trounstine, accompanied a group to visit McKay. "We all went out to see McKay; he was plump and jolly, with a red fez on his head, and he was living exactly like a Moroccan. At one point with a clap of his hands he summoned his Moroccan dancing girl, not yet twelve, and bade her perform for us. Trounstine was displeased by the entire scene. He was not liking Morocco very much, in any case." The scene was perhaps less sinister than Trounstine imagined. In *A Long Way from Home*, McKay explained that when he moved into his new home he had "found a little brown native girl to take care of the house. She brought her mother along, so that she could look her own people in the face without flinching. There was also a boy on a bicycle to run errands . . . we all cultivated the garden and lived comfortably on twenty-five dollars each month."[37]

Whatever Trounstine's first impressions of McKay, sometime within the year he agreed to become his literary representative in New York. Ever since his disagreement with Bradley over "The Jungle and the Bottoms," McKay had been anxious to find a new agent. Bradley had represented him well, but McKay had begun to believe that as his agency had grown and prospered Bradley no longer had time for the intimate attention of earlier days. From long habit, McKay expected the kind of patron-client relationship he had known with Walter Jekyll, Frank Harris, and Max Eastman. To Eastman, always his confidant, McKay explained that "the thing is to find such a person as I chanced to find Bradley! . . . Bradley was excellent in his 'young' days, but since we knew him he has become quite a business man with a large office and well-staffed and he travels all the time [and] gives less time to individual matters."[38] Agents such as Bradley, McKay eventually discovered, were rare. Although he did not know it at the time, he would never again find his equivalent.

While McKay and Trounstine were establishing a temporary business relationship, Claude's acquaintance with Bowles took a different turn. Shortly after he met Bowles, McKay's house was burglarized and his passport stolen. McKay suspected that French or British agents were responsible. He guessed, correctly, that he had again become the object of official harassment. For reasons never entirely clear, he decided that Paul Bowles was responsible for the disappearance of his passport; McKay confronted Bowles. According to Bowles, "One evening he came around to the bedbug-infested Hotel Viena, where I lived, and demanded to see me. Because he was black and wore a fez on his head, and also because he was obviously in a state of great excitement, the Spanish proprietor refused to allow him past the desk in the courtyard. I came out onto the balcony and stood there while he shouted up imprecations and threats in his West Indian English, brandishing his cane at me, at the hotel employees and at the dueno, who forced him out into the street." Although he may have been mistaken in his conviction that Bowles was responsible for the theft of his passport, McKay had in fact divined the main outlines of the conspiracy against him. According to Bowles, an "opium eater" named Abdeslam ben Hadj Larbi, with whom he had become friendly, had shown an unusual interest in McKay. Larbi and another man, it turned out, had stolen McKay's passport and denounced him to the police as a Communist. At some point, Bowles's name had probably entered in their testimony. McKay guessed that, whether deliberately or inadvertently, Bowles had been the instigator of the affair. Bowles did remember in his autobiography that McKay had shown him a letter from Max Eastman announcing his intention to visit Tangier later in the year after first visiting Leon Trotsky on the Turkish island of Prinkipo. Perhaps Bowles had told Larbi of this letter, not realizing the latter's duplicity. After the burglary, McKay probably decided that he had erred in showing Bowles his Eastman correspondence. As it turned out, McKay eventually received a new passport but not before the chief English consul in Tangier had removed from it his right to travel in the territories of the British Empire.[39]

That McKay showed Eastman's letter to Bowles indicated the value he still placed upon his relationship with his old editor and radical colleague. Despite McKay's readiness to pinpoint weaknesses in Eastman's various positions on literature, science, and politics, he remained in McKay's eyes vastly superior to the other literary radicals he had known during his days with the *Liberator*. And through the summer of 1932, he looked forward to Eastman's visit with an almost childlike eagerness.[40]

In part, McKay remained loyal to Eastman simply because he admired Eastman's magnificent presence and aristocratic bearing. For McKay, Max epitomized the best of old Yankee culture. Also, Eastman continued to share with McKay fundamental intellectual assumptions about literature, politics, and life. Both had an unappeased craving for new experiences, both opposed most modernist trends in literature, and both remained (for the moment, at least) committed to the eventual triumph of socialism in Western society, despite their increasing inability to embrace the emerging Communist orthodoxy. The irony of the relationship was that McKay continued to defer to Eastman as his intellectual superior, even though his criticisms of Eastman's various positions on the Soviet Union, Leon Trotsky, and the question of literature versus science repeatedly revealed that McKay possessed a more subtle, flexible, and penetrating intellectual grasp of men and events. While Eastman often lacked McKay's subtlety, he dared (however awkwardly at times) to develop broad general positions that McKay fundamentally accepted, despite specific reservations. Whatever their intellectual differences, McKay still looked to Eastman for practical guidance and editorial assistance. He recognized that Eastman was something he was not, a technically proficient philosopher who thought in systematic conceptual patterns. No matter how superior McKay's occasional insights, he continued to look to Eastman as an intellectual father figure. To the end of his life, McKay continued to defer to Eastman's judgment in literary matters, though not always in political affairs.[41]

After a lengthy trip from Prinkipo through the Middle East and southern Europe, the Eastmans finally arrived in Tangier in the early fall of 1932. McKay proudly showed them his new home, and they spent many hours over the next week talking about all that had happened since they had last been together in 1927 on the French Riviera. McKay introduced the Eastmans to his Moroccan friends, showed them around Tangier, and accompanied them on short excursions to Tétouan and Ceuta. All too soon, however, Max and Eliena departed for home, and McKay suddenly found himself alone with his anxieties about the future.

Shortly after they left, he became ill and had to spend several days in bed. The Eastmans had brought over from Spain an old Ford convertible. McKay and Eliena had gone to Tétouan in it and had driven back with the windshield down. The doctor who treated McKay in Tangier speculated that he had become too "chilled . . . riding so much without a windshield." By now, of course, neither McKay nor his doctor could easily differentiate between some ordinary ailment and the aftereffects of his treatments for venereal disease. As McKay wrote Eastman, "The original sin they say (and scientifically too) is responsible for all sorts of complications." After McKay recovered from this latest illness, his doctor decided, probably as a precaution, to inject him with "a series of new kind of bismuth" used in the treatment of syphilis. Unless McKay had contracted the disease anew, such treatment could not have done him any good. In fact, it may have only added to his aches because, as he wrote Eastman, "one disquieting symptom was a severe spinal pain right over the small across the hip bones, which began with the first series and remains with me still. Otherwise I am not so bad." Fortunately, he could not afford to begin the second series of shots. He had likely already absorbed enough mercury, arsenic, and bismuth to have killed the average mortal.[42]

By the spring of 1933, McKay's prospects looked dim. Saxton and Trounstine wrote from New York that conditions in publishing remained bleak. McKay nevertheless continued to hope "all the same to make something [with the publication of *Banana Bottom*]—enough to give me a holiday of which I am badly in need." He decided to "write some Moorish pot-boilers for Trounstine . . . to make ends meet," and he also began a new novel about the black expatriate caravan abroad. But his funds were rapidly dwindling. By spring he had even pawned his typewriter. Without it, he felt deprived of a primary tool of his trade. He nonetheless continued to write. He had not yet reached rock bottom, but he did not have far to fall, should *Banana Bottom* fail.[43]

In April, his spirits lifted when Eastman sent his new three-volume translation of Trotsky's *History of the Russian Revolution*.

McKay thanked him profusely and wrote, "It is hot now. My flowers are gorgeous and I have already started bathing." It was the last cheerful message he would send Eastman from Tangier. *Banana Bottom* had been published in March, 1933, and early in May a letter from Trounstine confirmed McKay's worst fears. Sales were dismal. Like *Gingertown* before it, *Banana Bottom* would make no money. McKay had been forewarned, but he still found it hard to accept. "The news from Trounstine," he confessed to Eastman, "was like a knock-out blow, but I haven't taken the count." Although he realized that *Banana Bottom* had been "published at the very worst time possible," he blamed himself for failing to deliver what his public wanted. "There must be something lacking," he complained to Eastman. "Evidently my readers prefer my realism of rough slum life than of rural life. If so I can supply the need." [44]

Since January he had been rewriting "The Jungle and the Bottoms," now retitled "Savage Loving." He was hoping that Trounstine could place it with another publisher. Harper no longer wanted it and declined to sign McKay to another contract. They had already advanced him a thousand dollars on two financial failures and refused to commit themselves to what they perceived would be further losses. McKay's hopes now rested on Trounstine's resourcefulness in New York. At Claude's behest, Eastman offered Trounstine whatever assistance he could provide. McKay refused to believe all was lost. "I still have assets," he insisted. But his assets, he realized, were slim: an unpublished novel that everyone agreed had problems, plus a germ of another story about black Americans abroad. For the moment, providentially, he had a little money. The French publisher Reider had just sent him a check for a thousand francs for the rights to the French edition of *Banana Bottom*. Like everyone else who read it, their editors thought it a fine novel. [45]

American reviewers agreed unanimously that *Banana Bottom* was McKay's best. It told the story of a young black woman's successful efforts to reintegrate into the peasant culture of her youth. At the age of twelve she had been taken, with her parents' consent, by a Protestant missionary couple, the Reverend Craig and his wife, and sent to England for a formal education. In her twelfth year, the young heroine, Bita Plant, had been raped by a mentally unstable local musician; the missionary couple sought to prove that, with a proper education and upbringing, her life could be redeemed for the kind of Christian service they were trying to impose upon the semipagan Jamaican hill country peasants.

The novel begins with Bita's return to Jamaica as an accomplished pianist and highly literate, well-mannered young lady. However, she gradually realizes that she cannot fit herself into the narrow, self-righteous mold of the Craigs. With the help of a sympathetic English-man, Squire Gensir (the fictional equivalent of Walter Jekyll), she discovers her natural inclination is to embrace again the black folkways of her peasant childhood and to bring into their settled, steady rhythms her own heightened awareness and sensibilities. In-stead of marriage to a proper black clergyman, educated to disdain the folk life of the peasants, she chooses to marry her father's dray-man, Jubban, whose strength and reliability are emphasized by his total commitment to traditional farming. Around this plot, McKay created a lovely pastoral image of the Jamaican mountain culture he had known as a child at the turn of the century. It was a society com-plete within itself and fundamentally alien to the harshly moralistic world of Christian Europe that had, in its modern commercial mani-festation, so constricted the lives of his characters in *Banjo* and *Home to Harlem*. With the creation of *Banana Bottom*, McKay's pica-resque search for psychic unity and stability, begun with *Home to Harlem*, came full circle to rest again in the lost paradise of his pas-toral childhood.[46]

As Robert Bone has pointed out, it was not a unity that could be sustained in the real world. Even as McKay wrote *Banana Bottom*, the crisis of European and American capitalism was pressing in upon him and upon the island whose memory he revered. In 1933, his brother U'Theo wrote from Jamaica:

> At present we are going through a very severe depression the equal of which has not been experienced as far as the memory of living man recalls. Very heavy winds hit us in November followed by a drought that was [as] prolonged as it [was] intense. My earnings as a fruit agent has dropped about 90% and the immediate future shows little or no better prospects. . . . World conditions are not only appalling but very puzzling. It is rather a strange phenomenon that prices should fall so dramatically now, that there should be so much unemployment in spite of the terrible destruction caused by the Great War. And yet the world seems to be more given to sport than ever and life is not held as sacred as heretofore.[47]

Even as McKay wrote *Banana Bottom*, all his old ambivalences about Jamaica and the West Indies, in fact, remained with him. In one letter to Eastman he remarked that "those few islands belonging to Euro-pean nations in the New World are certainly a bastard forsaken lot."[48]

The financial failure of *Banana Bottom* placed McKay in an un-tenable position. Until his novels began to sell again, he needed to write something that would bring him ready cash. Journalistic essays seemed one obvious possibility. Since 1924, however, he had written only three. One was his discussion of *Home to Harlem* in *McClure's*.[49] The other two were written in 1932. One of these, for an anthology edited by Nancy Cunard, the shipping heiress, never appeared in print.

Throughout 1932, he had corresponded extensively with Cunard, whose introduction to black culture via jazz in Venice had resulted in her celebrated affair with an American black musician in defiance of her mother's outraged protests. In the course of her adventure across the color line, Cunard had published a pamphlet defending her actions entitled *Black Man and White Ladyship*. McKay later maintained that in it young Miss Cunard had simply seized upon "a Negro stick to beat the Cunard mother."[50] At any rate, during this love affair, Nancy Cunard conceived the idea of compiling a comprehensive anthology of essays describing all aspects of black culture.

She asked McKay if he would contribute. He agreed to submit an article, and when she wrote him of an impending trip to Jamaica, he also put her in touch with his brother U'Theo. She subsequently visited U'Theo in Frankfield and wrote McKay glowing reports of his hospitality. When Claude finally submitted his promised essay, along with a request for payment, the happy exchange came to an abrupt end. Cunard informed him that because of her commitment to black culture, her mother had stopped her generous allowance, and she could not afford to pay any of her contributors.[51]

McKay was not sympathetic. He replied that he would not write for free and demanded that his article be returned. He also advised U'Theo not to write anything for Miss Cunard. Claude's correspondence with her ended in acrimony. He wrote, "I have never had the itching vanity to appear in print just because it is a lovely thing, and I have refused many little magazines and Negro newspapers, feeling that my creative work should not be exploited shamelessly as my common labor has been because of the necessity of daily living." When Miss Cunard's giant tome finally appeared in 1934, it contained a photograph of U'Theo but nothing by Claude. His difficult personality, Miss Cunard hinted, had made cooperation impossible.[52]

McKay had written one significant article, "A Negro Writer to His Critics," for the *Herald Tribune Books* section in the spring of 1932. It said that the black artist could not be limited by the same constraints as black journalists and racial leaders, who tended to judge all black writing by its probable effect upon the advancement of the black race in the United States. Although such leaders performed absolutely essential functions, McKay believed they should not be the sole arbiters of black art. Their standards of what constituted black art tended to be conservative and censorious of all subject matter they judged might reveal Negroes in a less than favorable light. In his own career, McKay pointed out, his protest poetry had been condemned by a leading black critic as too angry and violent; his novels had been denounced as simply scandalous pandering to depraved white tastes. "Because Aframerican group life is possible only on a neutral and negative level," McKay observed, "our critics are apparently under the delusion that an Aframerican literature and art may be created out of evasion and insincerity."[53]

McKay stated that black artists could avoid neither the bitterness at the heart of black existence in America nor "the animal joy and sin and sorrow and dirt" that existed in the Black Belts of American cities, just "as they did in ghettos, slums, tenderloins and such like places all over the world." White and black critics should realize, McKay maintained, that "the spirituals and blues were not created out of sweet deceit":

> There is as much sublimated bitterness in them as there is humility, pathos and bewilderment. And if the Negro is a little bitter, the white man should be the last person in the world to accuse him of bitterness. For the feeling of bitterness is a natural part of the black man's birthright as the feeling of superiority is of the white man's. It matters not so much that one has had an experience of bitterness, but rather how one has developed out of it. To ask the Negro to render up his bitterness is asking him to part with his soul. For out of his bitterness he has bloomed and created his spirituals and conserved his racial attributes—his humor and ripe laughter and particular rhythm of life.[54]

"A Negro Writer to His Critics" was a significant statement of the black writer's position between the two world wars. But it did nothing to help the sales of *Gingertown* or *Banana Bottom*. White America was not listening, and not enough black Americans could afford either McKay's books or the Sunday *Herald Tribune*.

After the failure of *Banana Bottom*, McKay wanted to write more articles, but his confidence had been shaken. He complained to Max Eastman that "I just can't get the knack of journalese. Unless," he added significantly, "I had somebody to guide my hand." This statement clearly signaled that McKay was once again retreating to a familiar position: salvation from stress through a renewal of a client-patron relationship. Fortunately for him, Eastman was in a position to help. For the past several years, his lecture fees had enabled him to make a comfortable living, and he responded positively to McKay's appeals throughout the summer and fall of 1933.[55]

By the spring of 1933, Claude had been forced to dismiss his young servant girl and her mother. During one two-week period before the arrival of the thousand francs from Reider, he had lived on spiced tea and the potatoes he had grown in his garden. Life in the country had suddenly become very hard and lonely. He yearned for the liveliness of town. "However," he wrote Eastman, "when I am finished working I take long walks over the hills. And I have been swimming in the river since last month. . . . I don't think about my health at all—better *not* to in my state and so I am physically fit so to speak."[56]

Despite such small advantages, he felt increasingly that "I am jammed and damned here and can't budge." Among other things, he could no longer afford to maintain his subscriptions to the *Nation* and other American periodicals. This only increased his sense of isolation. In May, 1933, Eastman finally sent him a bundle of magazines. "I fell on them at once," McKay exclaimed. "It was like being among a roomful of New York intellectuals, and I didn't feel so terribly lonely anymore." If his situation in Tangier did not materially improve, McKay knew he must eventually leave, but "where to," he complained to Eastman, "with British agents after me. It's not persecution mania. I'm not that type as you know, but I knew they were following me—probably my house was broken into and my original passport taken by them. . . . Those dogs never come out in the open you know, but set others on to you."[57]

To contain his anxieties, McKay worked hard to complete the rewrite of "The Jungle and the Bottoms." At the end of May he sent it off to Trounstine via an American black woman, a tourist who had visited him as she passed through Tangier. To complete it, he explained to Eastman, "I worked in a fury like a nigger . . . with my head expanding and a fire in it as if it were going to blaze up—but I kept on[,] afraid and yet determined to finish." McKay admitted that the story was still "awful rough stuff but genuine." Maybe Trounstine could get a few dollars for it. In the meantime, he hoped Max was "trying to do something" for him. Among other things, McKay was applying for a Guggenheim Fellowship even though as a British subject and nonresident of the United States he doubted his eligibility. He was "groggy with work and anxiety," he reported to Eastman. He had never expected *Banana Bottom* to sell like *Home to Harlem,* "but I never guessed it would be a total failure—after two years steady working." The woman who had taken his latest version of "The Jungle and the Bottoms" had suggested that McKay deserved a grant because he was among the very few blacks steadily engaged in creative writing. McKay agreed. "If I could only get something to hold on to, some place to anchor," he exclaimed to Eastman. He wanted to start on a new series of stories and write some poetry, but he needed "some good news first."[58]

Good news never arrived. Trounstine could not place "Savage Loving." (This new title of "The Jungle and the Bottoms" was eventually changed to "Romance in Marseilles.") Neither could he find a magazine that would accept an article McKay sent him on the influence of the western Sudan on Moroccan history. To make matters worse, Trounstine, according to McKay, lacked Bradley's promptness and efficiency as a correspondent. Claude soon lost all confidence in Trounstine and began referring to him in his letters to Max as "a very neurotic and fussy sissy Jew," completely the opposite of "Bradley, [the] shrewd level-headed Yankee." He thanked Eliena for her praise of *Banana Bottom* but lamented that "I can't work up any enthusiasm for a book that cannot bring me in [enough] to buy a loaf of bread and soap to wash my black skin after one year's hard labor." Trounstine lacked the patience to deal with McKay and apparently returned barb for barb without any encouraging news. He "writes me the most pathetically discouraging letters," McKay noted, "that if I didn't still retain a little faith I'd jump in the river."[59]

To fight despair, McKay set to work on a new novel about black tourists and expatriates abroad that he had long been planning to write. He hoped to include in it all his experiences with the black Americans and West Indians he had encountered in France during the prosperous 1920s. He worried, however, that anything he might write would be misconstrued by the black bourgeoisie as insults. "They are all so touchy. And if I go back 'home' I'll have to live among them." He only wanted, he wrote Eastman, "to assemble the facts and get down to the truth. But that is just what these people can't stand. I don't mean to libel them for I like them as a group, but all they like is pretty painting."*

He nevertheless set to work and soon sent a few pages to Eastman for his criticism. After his rebellion against Bradley's tutelage, he once again voluntarily and with relief placed himself under Eastman's guidance. In the real solitude of his private life, McKay desperately needed someone he could depend upon to guide him through personal crises. It was the dependence of a child upon a father (or, in

---

*Claude McKay to Max Eastman, June 28, 1933, © 1987 by Hope McKay Virtue, 1110 Olive Avenue, Long Beach, Calif. 90813, and used by her permission. This letter is in the Max Eastman Papers (private possession).

McKay's case, an older brother), but he remained blind to the essential immaturity of this aspect of his character. In fact, he naïvely believed that the solution to his problems would be to find a reliable partner who could manage the vexing details of his everyday life. To Eastman, he wrote, "I wish I [were] neurotic and didn't know what was wrong with me. But the trouble is I do know. I ought to be closely attached to somebody, woman or even man, instead of being off at loose ends living lone-wolfishly. But I never can feel a sentimental attachment for the persons that attract me intellectually. And the types that stir up passion in me are no good for intimate attachment. . . . I can't get my mind and emotions in harmony together and concentrated on someone. That's my whole tragedy. I need somebody to look after me. But generally I appear so strong to people as if I don't need looking after." [60]

Besides Eastman, McKay also resumed his correspondence with James Weldon Johnson, who discussed with Eastman Claude's latest dilemma. Both agreed McKay would be better off back in the United States. Johnson suggested that Eastman solicit contributions from "literary friends" for Claude's return fare. "I feel deeply," Johnson wrote, "that we should not allow Claude's genius to be smothered by any conditions that we might be able to remove." [61]

McKay dreaded the possibility of returning permanently to the United States. He could no longer live there as an unknown laborer, "like in the old days before the *Liberator*." Among black Americans, he had become a famous author. As such, "I'll have to find myself among the 'Niggerati' as I hear they call themselves in Harlem. And I think it would be more losing than finding," he told Eastman. He would consider, however, a temporary return "at the right moment . . . when the new book is coming out." [62]

As the summer of 1933 advanced, however, it became obvious that McKay could not continue to function as a writer in Tangier. No one wanted to publish "Savage Loving," and Eastman had yet to see his uncompleted novel about black expatriation. McKay simply had no immediate prospects or money. For subsistence, he had to depend increasingly on a thin driblet of dollars from Eastman (and perhaps a few other friends). Under such conditions, he could not complete his novel. A move back to Spain or France would not improve his condition. The only alternative appeared to be a speedy return to the United States, where he had some possibilities for employment as a writer, teacher, or lecturer. [63]

Still, McKay lingered in Tangier, hoping to hear that Trounstine had found a publisher for "Savage Loving." "The terrible uncertainty," he explained to Eastman, "weighs me down and retards the writing of the [new] story." He would send the first chapter for Eastman's criticism. "I need something," he wrote, "a little lifting of the spirit to harden and encourage me to bring my writing up to standard and in tune to the mood of five years ago." Five years was not such a long time, but across the chasm of the Great Depression it was a great distance. His immediate task was to survive the chaotic terrain of the new reality. In fact, he could not go back "to the mood of five years ago."[64]

In August, 1933, McKay's lease on his riverfront cottage expired. He moved into town and piece by piece slowly sold most of his household furnishings in the native market. Before the move, McKay received from Eastman $144.50. He could have used the money to return to the United States, but he clung to the hope that his luck would turn, and he could go back to the United States on terms more to his liking—with a new book and brighter literary fortunes. To carry on, however, he needed not only money but Eastman's practical suggestions and close scrutiny of his work in progress. "For the fact is," he confessed, "that getting down again has shaken my confidence, not in my mental equipment, but in trying to live practically. . . . I won't be able to carry on with a sure hand until I hear from you or some other good critic that I am on the right track." Moving into town, "with its movement and noise . . . lifted somewhat" McKay's spirits, but it also cost him "nearly all" his capital. He longed for "a comeback, to surprise everybody and madden some" but admitted that "the atmosphere of anxiety in which I work is almost paralyzing."[65]

For a while, Alfred A. Knopf considered adding McKay to its list of authors, but decided against it. "Savage Loving" seemed crudely thrown together and strangely dated in depression-ridden New Deal America. McKay was too big a risk. By the end of September, he had had enough. The isolation and the tension of living from hand to mouth in Tangier at last made even America seem attractive. In early October, he wrote Eastman that he was again without "a sou." He had hoped James Weldon Johnson would raise some money for him, as Walter White had once done back in 1924. "But," McKay wryly commented, "he couldn't I suppose among Negroes, *they love me so much.*" Work, he observed, remained his only "safeguard," and he had continued writing his new novel of expatriate life in the hope that it would be complete by the time he arrived in the United States. In the meantime, he pleaded, "Do please write. I feel so lost."[66]

James Weldon Johnson may not have sent any money, but he

did write that an acquaintance in the U.S. State Department had informed him that McKay could return to the United States without any problems, provided friends vouched for him and that he had a minimal amount of money. "I feel very strongly," Johnson wrote, "that you ought to come and stay. New York is your market, and the United States is your field. Furthermore, we, the Negro writers, need you here." [67]

Armed with Johnson's reassurances and encouragement, McKay in October, 1933, began the process of getting the necessary visa from the U.S. consul in Tangier. It proved a time-consuming process. Among other things, he had to write to Jamaica for two copies of his birth certificate. They took several weeks to arrive. In the meantime, Eastman once again collected money for his return fare, over one hundred fifty dollars. Among those who contributed were Oswald Garrison Villard, Walter Lippman, and Joel Spingarn. [68]

Eastman's evaluation of the opening chapter of McKay's new novel was not positive, and in late October, Claude informed him that "as soon as I got your letter I stopped writing the new story." Since 1928, he had published three novels and a volume of short stories. He had also written and rewritten "The Jungle and the Bottoms," plus a handful of essays and unpublished poems. His early successes with *Home to Harlem* and *Banjo* had provided him with the impetus he needed to continue through to the completion of *Banana Bottom*. After its failure, however, McKay could no longer sustain the pace he had set over the last five years. To Eastman he wrote, "It was too much. To keep on writing like that one book after another! No creative writer can do it and the moment I stopped I felt better as if a great weight was lifted from me. And I feel better all over with the thought of a *voyage* and going '*home*.' Oh god, I haven't been out of this little international wasp's nest since you took me to Cuenta and it was beginning to get worse than a Black Belt." [69]

In late December, 1933, McKay left Tangier for Spain. From there he sailed in late January, 1934, for the United States. After twelve years abroad he was at last going back to Harlem. What exactly he would do there he did not know, but after a lifetime of controversy and struggle, he hoped to find a living that would lift him out of the demoralizing poverty he had experienced over the last two years. He had no assurances of a job or a publisher in New York City. He dreaded a return to the atmosphere of race relations in America. [70]

In the meantime, while his personal fortunes had declined, his work—particularly his recent novels—had inspired to action a whole new generation of black writers from French West Africa and the

West Indies. In 1931, the Nardal sisters began to publish in Paris their *Revue du Monde Noir*. They reprinted in its first issues poems by McKay and other Afro-Americans. In 1932, another French West Indian, Etienne Léro, also published an important manifesto, *Légitime Défense*, in which he quoted approvingly from McKay's *Banjo* and declared that in French West Indian writings "a stranger vainly searches . . . for an original or profound accent, the sensual imagination of the black man, the echo of the grudges or aspirations of an oppressed people." Léon Damas, Léopold Sedar Senghor, and Aimé Césaire would shortly follow with their own more fully developed doctrine of *Nègritude,* which in significant part, as they themselves acknowledged, could be traced directly to McKay's example in *Banjo.*[71]

As McKay made his midwinter crossing of the North Atlantic back to the United States, it remained to be seen if his achievements would ever be as warmly appreciated in his adopted country. After a decade of real achievement, he had come full circle once again. He would, in fact, have to begin anew the long and difficult process of finding for himself a place in the American and Afro-American literary worlds.

# 10
# The Search for Self-Definition, 1934–1937: *A Long Way from Home*

On Friday, February 1, 1934, Claude McKay returned to New York City on the SS *Magallenes* from Spain. From dockside, he went to Harlem and checked in at the YMCA on 135th Street. There young Henry Lee Moon interviewed him for the New York *Amsterdam News* and reported that "ten years of exile . . . have done something to the author of . . . *Home to Harlem*. A slightly corpulent, reserved individual with a cynical twinkle in his eye has replaced the young firebrand who once helped edit the *Liberator* . . . more than a decade ago." McKay had little to tell Moon about his plans for the future. He refused to comment "at all" on politics. When asked why he had returned, however, a "cynical twinkle" appeared in his eyes, and Moon recorded the following remark: "Well, the Negro intellectuals have been boasting for years that I could not come back. So maybe I . . . came back just to prove them wrong—as usual."[1] It was not a statement calculated to win friends, and Moon pointedly observed that McKay immediately left Harlem to spend the weekend with Max Eastman at Croton-on-Hudson.

Moon's article touched on almost all the central problems that faced McKay upon his return to the United States: his future live- 291 lihood, his relationship to Afro-American leaders, and his political stance in depression America. All these problems, as he would shortly discover, were interrelated, and they were to consume almost all his energies for the remainder of the decade.

Neither in his politics nor in his relationship to American Negro leaders was McKay in step with the times. As a consequence, he would receive little help from either the black elite or the various political groups inside and outside Harlem who could have used their influence to further his career. Not all McKay's difficulties, of course, involved politics or questions of racial strategy. There was the equally serious problem of convincing potential friends in high places that he was something more than an incorrigibly difficult personality. Although he was usually friendly and charming, his frankness, his occasional moodiness, and his tendency to lash out at friends when angry kept many potential allies at arm's length. As he well knew, this often hindered him in achieving his larger aims. But it was an ingrained habit, not easily broken, and as his interview with Moon suggested, he had returned to America with that aspect of his character honed to a fine edge. As he once remarked in a letter to Walter White, "You're lucky in making friends. You're so altogether charming and fine. I'm a son of a bitch. I like really well so few people, that those I can like, I prize dearly and I always feel happy when I can possibly like some new freak of God."[2]

In fairness to McKay, however, he had taken seriously James Weldon Johnson's insistence that his presence in the United States would strengthen the Afro-American literary community. He arrived determined to help revive the sagging fortunes of black writers in any way he could. Just where he would fit into the structure of Harlem life nevertheless remained a difficult question.

Harlem and America had changed radically from the hectic but relatively prosperous days McKay had known during World War I and in the early 1920s. The Great Depression had crippled the American business structure and had left the nation close to economic ruin. Roosevelt's New Deal, barely two years old, had begun to restore a measure of hope for the future, but full recovery remained a dream. During McKay's years abroad, black Harlem had expanded northward and to the east and west above 110th Street. But the old optimism of the postwar years, which had nurtured hopes of a great black metropolis in Manhattan, had been destroyed by the new realities. Harlem was desperately poor. As always, blacks, who had known little prosperity to begin with, suffered disproportionately more unemployment than whites and had much farther to go along the road to recovery.[3]

For the black writer, the depression had meant an end to the Negro Vogue. Fewer whites trekked uptown to spend their money for black entertainment. White patrons and downtown publishers no longer sought out black writers. And the black community itself had precious few resources to share with unemployed writers. The NAACP and the National Urban League could no longer afford the luxury of promoting new black writing with their old vigor. As their budgets declined, *Crisis* and *Opportunity* devoted less space to literary and artistic concerns. To many, it now seemed that the Negro Renaissance had been too intertwined with ephemeral white interests that had little to do with the realities of Afro-American life. By 1934, novels such as *Home to Harlem* and *Banjo,* which had celebrated the black man's primitive vitality in an increasingly mechanistic world, seemed dated and irrelevant.[4]

Like many of their white counterparts, black writers were increasingly attracted by revolutionary solutions to the harsh social conditions created by the collapse of capitalism. Even in more prosperous times, blacks could expect little from a system that considered them only inert pawns on its economic chessboard. The New Deal promised some relief but no solutions, beyond the salvaging and restoration of an economic system that had already proven itself inimical to black advancement.[5]

By the time McKay arrived in Harlem, the American Communist party had already begun to attract many young black intellectuals. It promised revolutionary action and the replacement of capitalism with a government patterned after the Union of Soviet Socialist Republics. Such a system promised blacks a nation of their own within the southern portion of the United States, a nation that would exist as an equal with other socialist republics in a new American union freed from all past discriminations based on race and class differences. The depression had given the American Communist party a new opportunity to build a mass party, and it had eagerly seized the chance to build a strong black contingent in Harlem and other northern Black Belts. While the party argued for the development of a black nation in the South, in the North it stressed the total assimilation of blacks and whites and the complete integration of all party activities both within and without the black ghettos of the urban North. No political group had ever embraced the black cause with such unabashed fervor and total commitment. Many intelligent young blacks were responding positively to the party's efforts to assist in innumerable community projects and self-help campaigns.[6]

To McKay, the new Communist influence in Harlem seemed even more cynically exploitive than the Republican domination of black

voters after the Civil War. Republicans had at least wielded actual political power within the American social system. During the Civil War
they had presided over the emancipation of blacks from slavery and
had afterward attempted for a while to grant blacks political equality
in the South. By contrast, McKay argued, the American Communist
party had nothing to offer blacks that they could not provide for
themselves through effective self-organization. Communists had
some potential, but little actual, political power within the American
social system. To make matters worse, the American Communist
party took orders from Moscow. In fact, it could not be said to have
any effective existence independent of Comintern direction. To
McKay, this placed black Communists in double jeopardy within the
American system. Not only were they subject to racist attacks, they
could also be viewed as agents of a foreign power. For blacks to ally
themselves wholeheartedly with any political party, much less a for-
eign-directed party, was, in McKay's view, next to insanity. Their long
devotion to the Republican party had only resulted in its cynical
abandonment of black interests. How much worse would it be, McKay
reasoned, to offer similar devotion to a party that existed, he was convinced, solely to further the interests of the new Soviet state? Finally,
McKay rejected as unrealistic the party's emphasis in the North on
complete social assimilation in all areas of life. Blacks, he insisted,
could never be wholly assimilated as individuals into every aspect of
white American life. He detested forced segregation but argued that
even if all legal barriers to integration fell, blacks would (and should)
still exist as a distinct racial and ethnic group in America. They
should, therefore, do all they could to achieve material wealth, political power, and truly meaningful equality as a powerful ethnic group
within the American nation.[7]

McKay developed his position while ironically aware that the Communist Party of America, in strenuously wooing and unreservedly
accepting blacks as equal partners in revolution, had at last adopted
the very position he himself had so vigorously promoted during his
visit to the Soviet Union in 1922–1923.[8] Since then, however, McKay,
the Soviet Union, and the course of international communism had
changed. As he saw it, the Soviet Union under Stalin was now building another great nation-state, and international communism under
Russian direction had become "a stuffed carcass" devoid of any life of
its own. With its demise as a coalition of independent parties, McKay
had given up on international communism. He still believed that socialism must eventually prevail in the world, but he abhorred the dictatorship that had emerged under Stalin. McKay no longer placed his

faith in the inevitability of Marxist revolution. As the decade advanced and he became more familiar with the influence of the Communist party in Harlem, his criticism would grow.

At the same time, his persistent criticism of the integrationist orientation of the NAACP won him few friends among the noncommunist black elite in Harlem. McKay's position regarding the response of black Americans to their situation within the United States stopped short of any espousal of black nationalism; he argued instead that black leaders should pay more attention to strengthening the black community and less to integration. He firmly believed that integration would benefit only the few whose education, ability, or circumstances would allow merger into the larger society. Exclusive concentration on the injustices they suffered under American racism, McKay believed, had created among blacks, especially black civil rights leaders, a near paralysis of community action for self-improvement because they feared that such action would only encourage the forces of segregation. As a consequence, blacks in large urban ghettos such as Harlem suffered unnecessarily from a lack of many essential community services. They allowed the continuous deterioration of their neighborhoods to occur because they had never developed a true spirit of communal self-help that characterized all other ethnic groups with whom he was familiar—his own family experiences in Jamaica and his later observation of Moslems, Christians, and Jews in North Africa. His beliefs on this subject eventually led him to defend the largely discredited program of Booker T. Washington at Tuskegee Institute.[9]

McKay's peculiar background as a child of the independent Jamaican peasantry, as a disillusioned veteran of early Communist agitation in the United States and England, and as an essentially independent poet and novelist in a decade devoted to group organization and action even among artists, brought him sharp conflict, severe poverty, and eventual isolation even as he attempted to carve a place for himself within the Afro-American community in Harlem.

Despite the undertones of hostility in Moon's article, prospects looked relatively bright for McKay during his first weeks back in the United States. He spoke before various local groups about his experiences abroad and reestablished contact or met for the first time such Harlem Renaissance personalities as Carl Van Vechten, Countee Cullen, Harold Jackman, and Bruce Nugent. Jackman, a local Harlem schoolteacher, wrote nothing himself, but he socialized with all the principals of the Negro Renaissance. They valued his company. He was tall, handsome, affable, well read, and supportive of all

his literary friends. Throughout the 1920s, he and McKay had corresponded, and they were to remain friends in the years ahead.[10]

Bruce Nugent was a young painter who also wrote, acted, danced,
and enjoyed an active social life. He frankly admitted that he was a
dilettante in all the arts save painting and that he enjoyed the role.
Along with Langston Hughes and Wallace Thurman he had helped
edit *Fire*, the short-lived literary magazine created for the younger
members of the Harlem Renaissance. Its first and only number in
1926 had been largely consumed by a real fire in the Harlem basement where it had been stored. Nugent came from a distinguished
light-colored family in Washington, D.C, and he won McKay's acceptance by one day remarking to him that the capital's famous "high
yellow" society had copied white society with "tragic fidelity."[11]

McKay also mingled with many others in the Harlem community
who had no literary or scholarly credentials. He enjoyed, for example,
the company of Darrell Campbell, "the 'exalted ruler'" of the local
Elks Club, as well as a number of women whom he chanced upon.
One came from McKay's boyhood home in upper Clarendon. They
had grown up together, and their fathers had been close friends and
"church officers." She had traveled a long way from those bucolic
days to become "pretty well fixed as a policy manipulator" in Harlem.
Fortunately for McKay, she remained "very sentimental about the old
association" and did her best to help him get settled. She was probably the same woman he described in *A Long Way from Home* as the
operator of an intimate speakeasy in 1922. Other women acquaintances also welcomed him back to Harlem. Most were simply friends
whom he saw occasionally. But romance sometimes resulted. As
McKay wrote Eastman in the spring of 1934, "Except for the old
head trouble I am all right. . . . I am all excited about a girl pal who
has the most perfect back."[12]

He had dreaded returning to the constant strain of interracial relations in America, but Harlem, he discovered, still possessed the old
ability to beguile and quicken his senses, even under the most dis-
tressing circumstances.

> Rich is the flavor of this Harlem street;
> The dusk over the dark-warm scene is tender,
> The murmuring of fruit-ripe throats is sweet
> And gladly to the tumult I surrender.[13]

While in Morocco he had applied for a Guggenheim Fellowship,
and he hoped after his return to get one. Others active in the Harlem
Renaissance had already enjoyed a Guggenheim, but McKay's application for a grant to write a study of the black African impact on

Moroccan life and history did not sufficiently impress the jury, and his request was refused. His prospects for other assistance, however, at first appeared good. Someone—perhaps President Hope at Atlanta University or James Weldon Johnson, who had connections with Fisk—assured him that he could spend at least a year as a college professor, provided a foundation could be persuaded to underwrite his salary. After weeks of waiting, that proposal, too, came to nothing.[14]

In the meantime, McKay had moved out of the Harlem YMCA and into a small efficiency apartment at 168 West 135th Street. He had no money other than what little he could scrounge from friends such as Eastman, Schomburg, and Darrell Campbell of the Elks. Their help proved insufficient to pay his rent, and in May, 1934, his landlord politely but firmly insisted he pay or leave. Faced with eviction, McKay had no choice but to find other quarters. For weeks, he lived precariously in rented rooms or with friends. In August he even accepted from an aged Negro gentleman a free room with a kitchenette. In return, McKay agreed to help the old man, a "Professor" Siefert, until noon each day to "shape up and write his researches" on ancient African history.[15] At the same time, he was himself trying to find a reliable literary agent. Upon his return, McKay had engaged Maxim Lieber as his agent, apparently on Eastman's recommendation. It soon became apparent to Claude that he could not work with Lieber, who did not seem to be promoting his work and work proposals with publishers and who was bluntly critical of McKay's style in *Home to Harlem* and *Banjo.* In exasperation, he dropped Lieber and in May, 1934, wrote to Harcourt, Brace and Company directly, asking if they would consider publishing a new, expanded edition of *Harlem Shadows,* which would contain a series of poems on cities and historic sites he had visited while abroad. Donald Brace himself replied that he was interested. He asked to see McKay's new poems in order to arrive at some final estimate of what contract terms they might be able to offer. As in the past, McKay hated the prospect of having to negotiate a contract himself. From May to August he repeatedly beseeched Eastman to recommend him to an agent more congenial than Lieber. McKay desperately needed someone who would get him as good a contract as Bradley, the trustworthy "Yankee," had done in the 1920s. Meanwhile, he continued to experience great difficulty in finding enough money for regular meals, much less the other necessities of daily life. As a result, he could never quite manage to collect, revise, and type his poems for submission to Harcourt, Brace. That opportunity for publication thus gradually slipped away.[16]

Although he was once again proving inept in the management of his own affairs (admittedly under the most trying of circumstances), McKay had been correct to conclude that Maxim Lieber lacked the proper empathy to represent him. Lieber was not only a member of the Communist party of the United States, he also served in 1934 as an integral part of a Soviet espionage ring in New York. McKay may have known of Lieber's party membership. In 1934, while making no secret of his disillusionment with communism, McKay had not yet developed that obsessive aversion to party members that eventually came with the conviction that they would use their influence to hinder or even sabotage the careers of those on the Left who disagreed with them politically. But he certainly had no knowledge of Lieber's employment as a Soviet agent. Lieber's role as a spy would later figure prominently in the Whittaker Chambers–Alger Hiss affair. [17]

Did Lieber purposely sabotage McKay's efforts to find a publisher in 1934? The circumstantial evidence contained in McKay's letters to Eastman suggests that Lieber disliked McKay's early novels, procrastinated in his search for a publisher, and generally discouraged his first attempts to find one after his return in 1934. This, at least, is what McKay concluded. While there is no evidence that Lieber deliberately subverted McKay's efforts to find a publisher, he clearly did not convince McKay that he was working hard in his behalf. McKay reported to Eastman that "Lieber told me that [Eugene] Saxton [at Harper] remarked to him that he thought the American public was not interested in Negro authors enough to justify publication [of either the poetry or "Romance in Marseilles"] and he thought the successes of the nineteen twenties were the result of a fad only! Lieber didn't want to tell me but finally did." [18]

In fairness to Lieber, it must be remembered that publishers were reluctant in 1934 to commit themselves to black authors, especially to someone such as McKay whose last two books had sold very poorly. Lieber may have simply concluded that McKay's was a hopeless case. But given his deep involvement in Comintern affairs, he may have also concluded that McKay's current political orientation made him doubly hopeless.

McKay, of course, refused to accept either judgment. Even as he labored to move his own career forward, he began in the spring and summer of 1934 to meet with other black authors in New York to discuss their common dilemma: how to revive and advance black writing, with or without white support. He had only contempt for those who believed that black writers had to depend solely on the pleasure of white publishers and a fickle white reading public. In his opinion, black writers, like all others, would inevitably continue to express themselves and to illuminate the life around them. They should not, therefore, throw their hands up in despair at the temporary loss of a portion of their readership. They had a larger duty to themselves, their ethnic group, and to the universal functions of literature, and should not despair at the abandonment of erstwhile allies and patrons.[19]

By midsummer, McKay and a small circle of his friends in Harlem had decided to establish a black literary magazine devoted to publishing the best Afro-American writing from whatever political or aesthetic perspective. Because of his prior experience, McKay seemed a logical choice to edit such a journal. He had, after all, conceived the idea. As he saw it, the new magazine would be a black version of the old *Masses* and *Liberator,* open to all who had something significant to say and who said it well. Like the *Liberator,* it would be a cooperative venture of its editors and contributors, but McKay wished to establish himself as the controlling force who, like Eastman on the *Liberator,* "could not be maneuvered out in case of a difference or a schism."[20]

McKay wrote a clear statement of his objectives in a circular letter entitled "For a Negro Magazine," which he mailed to prospective supporters and contributors in July and August, 1934. In the letter, he noted that many considered the Negro Renaissance to have been only part of a passing fad, "a mushroom growth" that had failed to send any "roots down in the soil of Negro life. But we believe," he wrote,

that any genuine artistic expression can transcend a fad; that the Negro's contribution to literature and art should have a permanent place in American life; that American life would be richer by such contribution; and that it should find an outlet and a receptive audience.

Therefore, our aim is to found a magazine to give expression to the literary and artistic aspirations of the Negro; to make such a magazine of national significance as an esthetic interpretation of Negro life, exploiting the Negro's racial background and his racial gifts and accomplishments.

We want to encourage Negroes to create artistically as an ethnological group irrespective of class and creed. We want to help the Negro as a writer and artist to free his mind of the shackles imposed upon it from outside as well as within his own racial group.

We mean to go forward in the vanguard of ideas, trends, thoughts and movements. But we are not demanding that the creative Negro should falsely accept nostrums and faiths that he does not understand.[21]

This was a clear statement of opposition to the currently fashionable insistence upon class consciousness in creative writing, and it was directed in particular against the Communist party's dictum that the writer's ultimate duty was to help advance through his writings class consciousness and proletarian revolution. Instead of such narrow political requirements, the letter put forth the following general standards, "to which," it stated, "we will hold our contributors":

SINCERITY OF PURPOSE
FRESHNESS AND KEENNESS OF PERCEPTION
ADEQUATE FORM OF EXPRESSION [22]

"For a Negro Magazine" clearly stated McKay's faith in the future of black literature. But circumstances made it impossible for him ever to realize his dream of founding the kind of magazine he envisioned. He simply had no money and no effective means of raising any. Even if money had been forthcoming, McKay lacked the administrative capacity to launch such a venture. As usual, he turned to Eastman for information about the proper way to install himself securely as editor. He even asked Eastman to provide precise information about the costs of producing such a magazine. In reality, neither McKay nor his associates had the money, time, or practical experience necessary to launch a magazine in the midst of the worst depression in the nation's history. [23]

For a while, however, McKay pursued the idea. He planned to name the magazine *Bambara,* after a large tribe of the western Sudan, famous for its fine masks and other objets d'art. And he supervised in early September at least one fund-raising affair that netted twenty-five dollars. More could have been realized, but Harold Jackman, who was supposed to have collected money at the door, "got tight and deserted his post at that late hour, when bohemian-minded people prefer to drop in at a party—and many just walked in." [24]

Before the event, Eastman gave McKay enough money to buy new clothes. He had in August written Max a letter that had clearly revealed his utter poverty. "I have so much work to do, trying to get my verses together and worrying about the magazine and hardly anybody helping me. I am desperately hungry most of the time, lacking even pennies to mail letters and go to the library where I am looking through old magazines for some poems." To make matters worse, having a place to stay depended on his "doing part time work writing history to prove that African Blacks were the founders of Civilization, for an eccentric old Negro who titles himself professor." As McKay explained to Eastman, he "wouldn't mind it so much if the old fool was not always butting in on me with senile talk about ancient African glory." [25]

It was a pathetic situation. Under such circumstances McKay

could not hope to start a magazine or even prepare his poems for consideration by Harcourt, Brace. "I thought," he told Eastman late in August, "I could get all the poems together and in their hands by September, but I can't even find time to type them, much less to overhaul them."[26]

The social success of the fund-raiser in September briefly encouraged McKay, but it did not materially improve either his situation or his plans for a magazine. He soon gave up the scheme as impractical (at least for the present) and began to search for a job—any kind of job—that would enable him to escape the harrowing uncertainties of his daily existence. He could not continue his ill-matched collaboration with the old "professor" and soon left for other quarters. Although he managed to dress decently and otherwise maintained a brave front, his only money came in driblets from friends. Eastman helped, as did Joel Spingarn, but neither they nor anyone else could provide McKay with a regular income.

It is difficult to imagine a white writer, even in the depths of the depression, with past accomplishments equal to McKay's and with similar ambitions, ability, and drive, who could not have found a publisher or, as a last resort, some kind of job on which he could have lived. Vast areas of employment and opportunity were effectively closed to McKay merely because he was a black male. When, for example, he went to a labor bureau for an unskilled job, he found they had openings only for black female domestic workers. Among the black establishment, he could find no help. His outspoken criticisms of Afro-American society now came back to haunt him. "Any of those colored places could have found me a place, even to address envelopes. But I have no pull, and I guess they are afraid of me," he concluded in one letter to Eastman.[27]

In desperation, he considered going on relief, but he had entered the country on the stipulation that he would not become a public charge. He refused the chance to apply under an alias. Late in October, 1934, he instead made arrangements to enter a work camp run by the city in upstate New York, sixty miles from Harlem. Camp Greycourt, as it was called, was located "upon a hill above the village of Greycourt between Monroe and Chester." It had formerly been a women's prison and consisted of a collection of stone buildings that had been converted the previous May to a place of rehabilitation for the down-and-out of the city's municipal lodging houses.[28]

The city official who recommended the place to McKay did so with the idea that he could work in the camp's administrative offices, help edit its newsletter, and in his spare time resume his writing. The idea appealed to McKay. Anything was better, he reasoned, than a continuation of the haphazard existence he had been leading in Harlem. To implement the plan, the official wrote to the commander of the camp and explained McKay's dilemma; McKay then went to a municipal lodging house and signed up with other down-and-outs as a day laborer. His pay and theirs would be a dollar a day with fifty cents deducted each day for room and board. After less than a year back in America, he had hit rock bottom. But at least he had something to do, a job of sorts, and that, he concluded, was a step in the right direction.[29]

Camp Greycourt, he quickly discovered, was more than a way station for the unemployed. It also served as a rehabilitation center for alcoholics. In fact, a majority of the seven hundred men there were alcoholics who had lost all ambition save the desire to drink. The place was, moreover, crowded. Even the director, Commander Clarke, had to share a room with someone. Many newcomers lived barracks-style. McKay's tiny cell consisted of two cots and a chair. Under such conditions, he was ashamed to ask for special privileges. The office where he worked was equally cramped.[30]

At first, McKay tried to make the best of it. He worked on the weekly newsletter for a while but soon decided he would have more free time if he transferred to the dining hall and served behind the counter with the breakfast crew. There he practiced once again some of the skills he had acquired on the railroad during World War I. Despite his efforts to adjust, his new environment depressed him and he began to bombard Eastman with long descriptions of the hopelessness of the place. He could find no solitude for creative work. The commander kept telling him that he, too, was a writer but had no time for creative work. This made McKay even more reluctant to discuss his own situation. "He dabbles in poetry," McKay wrote Eastman, "and prose too, bad stuff. One has to be wary with people who have the writing bug and can't get it off. They are the most capricious and cutting in the world." The commander also had "a vast contempt for Communists," whom he confused "with socialists, anarchists, and what not." He firmly believed, mistakenly in McKay's opinion, that the Communists had sent paid agitators to his camp. To make matters worse, McKay added, he "and ninety percent of the crew here are Irish, as moody and chameleon-like as Moors."[31]

At the camp, McKay here and there found a kindred soul, including a supervisor, a former globetrotter who had known in Europe some of the same people McKay had associated with in Paris. But in general, as McKay complained to Eastman, "this dreary camp *Grey-court*" was populated by hopeless alcoholics, "even the best ones—

the clerks, college men—bum drinkers, and the downfall of most of them is drinking . . . so the place is a kind of sanitorium." They were, moreover, "jealous of the slightest favor shown to one of their number . . . no working class pride here—no hope for a better life for workers." With few exceptions, they were, he reiterated, "the worst bums of the Bowery and municipal lodging house, chronic criminal dead souls. The railroad, freight boats, and Marseille were heavens in comparison."[32]

By December, he was frantic to leave. He had decided that his next project should be a memoir about his experiences abroad, and he rightly felt that for him Camp Greycourt was "such a waste of energy—nothing to gain by [the] experience. . . . I feel more and more like a caged wild animal."[33] His stay at the camp would make great material for a story, he admitted to Eastman, but not for him to write. He disliked suffering in both life and literature and had no urge to write about his stay there.

Through it all he never doubted that given the chance he could produce another book and find for it both a publisher and readers. As in the past, he had to find help, and he hammered Eastman incessantly with appeals that he find a way to assure him enough money for food and a place to stay in New York. McKay insisted that he was willing to work, even as a doorman, and he urged that Eastman ask Joel Spingarn to use his influence to find for him any position that would ensure him enough money to survive. McKay insisted that his creative urge was as strong as ever; he needed only the opportunity to produce. As he expressed it in one letter to Eastman: "I know what's wrong with me is birth pains—too many abortions, the lusty child is crying to be born—but needs the right doctor."[34] It was an apt metaphor. Someone had always been present with timely aid to resolve his practical problems, and he needed such assistance now more than ever.

Eastman wrote Spingarn, who answered that he was willing to assist, but he pointed out that he had over the years found McKay a difficult person to help. He remembered, too, that McKay had once dismissed him as a bourgeois philanthropist even as he was finding for him a publisher for *Harlem Shadows*. In reply, Eastman admitted that Claude's abrasive personality did make him a difficult person. But he said that something had to be done, nonetheless, to help McKay through his latest impasse.

Eastman inadvertently revealed Spingarn's misgivings to McKay, who immediately protested to both men that their opinions about him were wrong. He admitted to Eastman that he was "no angel" and that he did find it difficult to work as a part of a group. He was, he confessed, an introvert whom social-minded people had difficulty understanding. But McKay reminded Eastman that he had worked successfully on the *Liberator* and that he remained the only member of its staff who understood and supported Eastman's criticisms of contemporary Marxism. Above all, McKay pointed out that when given the opportunity he had always been a productive worker. His basic problem, he insisted, was not his personality (difficult though it may be) but his poverty. "People are not satisfied unless they can get you by the very guts and make you puke up your soul." [35] If he was to continue as a writer, he had to have the assistance of people in a position to support his efforts.

To Spingarn he wrote a more restrained and formal letter of apology for having offended him "back in 1921." He explained that "I had forgotten all about calling you any names." And he assured Spingarn that he had never intentionally been personally disrespectful to any man because he had different social and intellectual ideas and belonged to a different social class and practiced philanthropy "according to his lights." McKay explained that if he had known how Spingarn felt about his remark, "I should long ago have apologised to you—as I always do readily if I have done, as I am likely to do, something impulsive and wrong. And now at this long distance and late date I want to apologize. And I wish I had known before how you felt about it, when I was materially better off and could have said simply and frankly I was sorry and you might have found more grace in it than now when I am in such trouble." He went on to explain that what he needed was a job that would give him the means to find permanent lodgings, "a place, where my mind would be relieved of pressing harassment instead of this hectic confusion out of which nothing can take permanent form." When he agreed to go to Camp Greycourt he had not realized that it would be a place "planned intolerably to make the individual drink to the dregs the fact of his being a down-and-out ward—everything operated to deprive him of all feelings of individual decency and manhood. . . . It is altogether peonage—a trap." [36]

With Eastman's help, Claude left Camp Greycourt just before Christmas and spent the holidays with friends in Harlem. While he was there, Spingarn sent him enough money to get his typewriter out of hock and to live on while he continued to search for a more permanent solution to his troubles. Despite McKay's insistence that he would take any kind of work, neither Spingarn nor anyone else could help him find a job. As a world-famous author, he was in peculiarly difficult circumstances. Many people assumed he wanted an administrative position in publishing and would not be interested in menial work. McKay himself feared that black newspapers would splash his name across their front pages if they discovered him accepting any kind of welfare or work relief. And if he should accept a menial position, that, too, could be turned into unpleasant publicity.[37]

As 1934 ended and a new year began, McKay's problems were far from over. But he had at least escaped Camp Greycourt. As the new year advanced, his situation gradually improved. His friends never completely deserted him, and he had made some new ones since his return who also proved steadfast. Chief among the latter in 1935 was Selma Burke, a former nurse and currently an artist's model and art student, who had become friends with McKay soon after his return from abroad. After his return to Harlem from Camp Greycourt, their friendship rapidly deepened into a love affair that continued intermittently for the remainder of Claude's life.

With Selma, McKay almost met his match. Like him, she possessed great vigor, determination, and purpose, and one of her objectives in 1935 was to provide McKay a decent place to live. She herself had only a small income. Claude had none, and he had decided he could not ask Eastman for more favors. When Spingarn's gift began to run low, he refused to approach Max for more money. Eastman, however, knew that McKay had not found a permanent income, and he decided to give Selma enough money each month to help her pay for an apartment to share with Claude. McKay may have suspected she was receiving assistance from Eastman, but she never told him. Sometime in the late winter or early spring of 1935, they set up housekeeping together at 214 West Sixty-third Street in the old Hell's Kitchen area where Lincoln Center for the Performing Arts now stands.

Selma valued her new relationship. She respected McKay's accomplishments and his wide knowledge of European art and artists. She was herself studying to become a sculptor, and she learned much from McKay's intimate knowledge of European and African arts. His criticism of her work was sometimes unsparingly harsh. He would even occasionally destroy her clay models because he felt that they showed no distinction. Such actions might have unhinged a lesser being, but Selma possessed as much self-confidence as McKay did. She persisted in her work and eventually became an accomplished sculptor. After World War II, her head of Franklin Delano Roosevelt became the model for the profile on the new "Roosevelt" dime.[38]

On his side, McKay loved Selma and hoped their relationship

would last, but he soon grew restless and dissatisfied with their new intimacy. At base, he probably feared and resented Selma's strong personality and tremendous energy. As he once explained to Max Eastman, he possessed a quality of "unattachedness," a reserve that no one could break through. It made close relations difficult over any length of time. Claude demanded freedom from the ordinary tensions and routines that inevitably arose when two people shared a life. His attitude baffled Selma, despite her best efforts to understand him. Before too many weeks together, tensions appeared that led eventually to their separation in July, 1935.[39] The approximately six months they spent together, however, gave McKay the stability he needed to find an income, begin a new work, and to store up the energy to see it through to completion.

In the spring of 1935, at the suggestion of James Weldon Johnson, McKay had applied to the Julius Rosenwald Fund in Chicago for a grant to begin a memoir of his years abroad. While at Camp Greycourt, he had become convinced that an autobiographical work that concentrated on those years would be attractive to publishers. At the same time, it would also give him a chance to clarify his social, political, and artistic evolution and current convictions as a black writer. In Harlem, many believed that McKay had gone to Russia in 1922 with the American Communist delegation as a party member in good standing, only to quit the movement afterward for an undisciplined and irresponsible bohemian life in Paris and North Africa. Others thought he had become a follower of Leon Trotsky. Both views were wrong, and McKay was anxious to set the record straight. He hoped that by relating in detail the story of his years abroad, he could both produce an interesting narrative and clarify his real concerns as a man and a writer.

McKay had returned to the United States convinced that American blacks had much to learn from studying, as he had done, the lives of minority groups in Europe and North Africa, many of whom had survived and even flourished under conditions almost as bad as those that blacks had to endure in America. In his opinion, international communism had failed, and blacks should concentrate on strengthening their collective group life and promoting democratic government at home in order to be in a position to meet all eventualities. Whether they knew it or not, change was pressing in upon all Americans from both the extreme Left and the extreme Right. In Europe, Soviet-style communism and German and Italian fascism threatened to tear asunder all pretense at democracy. It was a dangerous world, and McKay feared that blacks lagged behind in comprehending the international forces that threatened them. He believed that socialist reform must eventually come and that blacks should prepare themselves for a vanguard role as an ethnic group within American society, or risk falling even further behind white America in all aspects of their collective existence. In McKay's view, collective group solidarity meant much more than the pursuit of integration by civil rights organizations. In his memoir, he wished to illustrate how he arrived at his convictions by relating in detail what he had learned during his years in Europe and North Africa.[40]

In late April and early May, 1935, McKay wrote Edwin R. Embree, the director of the Rosenwald Fund, two letters in which he set forth his objectives. McKay stated he had originally planned a fictional version of his years abroad but had discarded the idea because "certain items," namely, his relationship to international communism, required "direct and unveiled treatment. . . . There is an impression among intellectuals of the left," he explained, "that I was officially invited to Russia and later went back on my principles. In fact," he maintained, "I went into Russia with an independent spirit . . . and came out the same."[41]

In his book, he proposed to use his own experiences to illustrate what the American Negro could learn "from travelling, how he may use his experiences in perspective to see and understand more clearly and broadly the social and cultural position of the American Negro and also in adjusting himself to American life." At the core of the book, he planned to "place special emphasis on cultural and group relations."

> Because, what made the greatest impression upon me in Europe and in Africa was the importance of and the interest taken in group culture and group life. I noticed that whether it was in backward Brittany or Spain or advanced Germany or colonial Africa, that those people who had a strong sense of group consciousness possessed an unusual quality of dignity and assurance of living, even when they were terribly up against extreme exploitation and repression, and that that sense of group consciousness, whether it was regional or religious or working class was the raison d'etre of their social objectives.
>
> I want to use the foregoing as a theme in writing about the group spirit of the American Negro, to show how it could be given greater expression from within, if certain old problems were approached from a new attitude, such as Segregation, for example. However, this angle would be incidental to the whole. The book will not be an outline of a programme for the Negro. It will be primarily an impressionistic record of my observations.*

*Claude McKay to Edwin R. Embree, April 30, 1935, © 1987 by Hope McKay Virtue, 1110 Olive Avenue, Long Beach, Calif. 90813, and used by her permission. This letter is in the Julius Rosenwald Fund Archives at Fisk University Library.

McKay's application, assisted by strong letters of recommendation from James Weldon Johnson and Richard Moe, the director of the Guggenheim Foundation (he had been favorably impressed by McKay's Guggenheim application the previous year), persuaded Embree to approve a five-hundred-dollar Rosenwald grant for McKay in five monthly installments, starting June 26 and continuing until November, 1935. Embree admired McKay's past work, and in approving the grant, he departed from a firmly established practice of limiting such awards to students of unusual promise for advanced training in the professions. He expressed the hope that the five hundred dollars would allow McKay enough time to begin his new work and to find a publisher willing to advance him enough to complete it.[42]

McKay wasted no time getting started. His career seemed at last to be reviving. While searching for a permanent position and funds, he had also begun to write articles, and since February, 1935, two had been published in the *Nation*. In its editor, Freda Kirchwey, McKay found another friend. Her interest in him as a writer went back to the 1920s, and she would consistently encourage and support him throughout the 1930s and 1940s.[43]

In early February she published a short article by McKay entitled "There Goes God! The Story of Father Divine and His Angels," in which McKay briefly described Father Divine's cooperative movement. This slightly built, wizened little brown man from Sayville, Long Island, had captured the imagination of many in Harlem with his immodest claims to divinity and with his ability to provide his followers with relief from all their worldly troubles. Through his network of lodging houses, restaurants, and other cooperative ventures, he promised complete relief from sexual, family, and economic burdens. All his followers need do was abandon their old lives and devote themselves to him. He would provide clean, sexually segregated lodging, abundant food, and plenty of opportunity for emotional relief in the joyful worship of the Godhead embodied in his Divine Self. It was an audacious movement whose initial success, McKay believed, indicated both the desperation and the organizational potential inherent in Harlem's black masses. That such an incredible movement could make headway in Harlem only illustrated for McKay how little traditional black leaders were doing to meet the most basic communal needs of its population.[44]

Father Divine's movement was only the most successful of many cults and street-corner movements that engaged McKay's sympathetic attention. Almost from the moment he arrived in Harlem from North Africa, he had begun to study the numerous cults, occultists, and street-corner orators of Harlem. He was convinced they commanded more urgently than either the black elite or the Communists the attention of Harlem's largely unemployed poor black majority.[45]

McKay's second article for the *Nation* on April 3, 1935, dealt largely with another untutored but bold grass-roots leader who had since 1933 been stirring the Harlem population to action against the white, mostly Jewish merchants of 125th Street, the area's traditional retail shopping center. This article, "Harlem Runs Wild," described the rioting and looting of stores along 125th Street by Harlem residents on the night of March 19, 1935. McKay witnessed the rioting and in his article emphasized that it could not properly be called a race riot. The objects of the crowd's wrath were the stores and not white people as such, who "singly and in groups, walked the streets of Harlem without being molested." The explosion had been sparked by a rumor that a black child, caught shoplifting "a trifle," had been beaten by department store guards. The report proved false, but resentment against white merchants along 125th Street had been growing for the past two years, and the alleged incident sparked a night-long rampage. McKay praised the restraint of the police during the episode as "commendable in the highest degree: . . . In extreme cases, when they fired, it was into the air. Their restraint saved Harlem from becoming a shambles."[46]

In assessing the underlying causes of the riot, McKay discounted the influence of Communist agitation and emphasized instead the recent efforts by the Harlem community to force the larger merchants along 125th Street to hire black clerks. This movement, McKay pointed out, had not been initiated by either the Communists or by traditional black leadership; it had been started by a strange, turbaned black man "in gorgeous robes" who claimed Egyptian origin and called himself Sufi Abdul Hamid. In 1933, he had organized a Negro Industrial and Clerical Alliance that had begun to picket and boycott the large department stores on 125th Street, demanding clerical jobs for Harlem's unemployed blacks. Prior to the Sufi's appearance, blacks, amazingly enough, held no clerical positions in the stores there. From the beginning, his outlandish appearance and strong-arm tendencies led the black press and the established community leadership to denounce him as a labor racketeer, but he did succeed in persuading some of the smaller establishments along 125th Street to hire a few black clerks.

Finally, in the spring of 1934, the young Reverend Adam Clayton Powell, Jr., the pastor of Harlem's largest congregation, the Abyssinian Baptist Church, joined the Sufi on the picket line, and a new communitywide organization, the Citizens' League for Fair Play, was organized. For the first time, the black press also began to support the protesters. Soon larger stores capitulated and began to hire a few black clerks.

McKay emphasized, however, that the net gain for the community had been small. The Sufi was accused of anti-Semitism in the Jewish press and was charged in court with disorderly conduct and anti-Jewish invective. The charges were eventually dismissed, but the Sufi's organization was kicked out of the Citizens' League and his influence in Harlem was effectively curbed. These events, however, had not strengthened the movement. More dissension within the Citizens' League soon followed. According to McKay, internal quarrels over such questions as "whether the clerks employed should be light-skinned or dark-skinned" diminished its effectiveness at a time when the merchants themselves were growing stronger through organization and intrigue, in which charges of anti-Semitism continued to be leveled against various participants in the Citizens' League. Finally, in November, 1934, a unique court injunction had forbidden further boycotting by the league because it "was not a labor organization." As a result, even the small gains that had been made were gradually reversed as the merchants laid off most of the new clerks. The merchants maintained that business had suffered and the clerks were not needed. Thus, McKay argued, the movement had failed because of merchant solidarity, internal league disunity, and lack of real labor organization. As a consequence, McKay concluded, "the masses of Harlem remain disunited and helpless, while their would-be leaders wrangle and scheme and denounce one another to the whites. Each one is ambitious to wear the piebald mantle of Marcus Garvey. On Tuesday the crowds went crazy like the remnants of a defeated, abandoned, and hungry army. Their rioting was the gesture of despair of a bewildered, baffled, and disillusioned people."[47]

McKay's article on Father Divine was slight in comparison to his report on the Harlem riot and its background. But both articles helped to set the tone for many others, in which McKay proved himself a close, perceptive, and always controversial commentator upon many of the people and issues that agitated Harlem, New York, and the world in the 1930s.

In July, 1935, shortly after receiving the first of his five monthly Rosenwald installments, McKay left the apartment he shared with Selma and moved into a new one farther uptown on Seventh Avenue. He also found a new girlfriend and tried to isolate himself from the distractions of the past several months. On the weekends, he and

Selma had frequently visited the Eastmans at Croton-on-Hudson but that, too, stopped when McKay moved into his new place. He had a new agent named Laurence Roberts, he informed Eastman, and a friend (Pierre Vogein) had just arrived from Paris with two trunks loaded with his books, documents, and other personal effects. He was glad to be away from the Sixty-third Street area. He had already begun his new book. For the moment he did not need anyone. He was on his feet again.[48]

Through the summer and fall of 1935, McKay worked hard on his new manuscript. He also thought ahead to the day when his funds would be exhausted and began in the fall of 1935 to take steps to get on the payroll of the newly created Federal Writers' Project in New York City. At first, his efforts to join the FWP were delayed because he had not officially qualified for relief. By the time his grant expired in November, however, he had enough written to submit his manuscript to a publisher, Lee Furman, who thought well enough of the work to sign him to a contract and to advance him three hundred dollars in monthly installments. By the end of April, 1936, McKay had written his story through to the end of his Russian trip, but as he explained in a letter to Edwin Embree, he had so much material that he had not been able to finish the work before his advance expired. Furman had limited resources and could not give McKay another advance. Claude told Embree that he had completed all but "the French-Spanish section and the African section" of his memoir; he asked if the Rosenwald Fund could give him "another small grant" to finish the book. He explained that he had acquired "a small part time job," which prevented him from writing in the mornings when he worked best. "I find that my day is all broken up and returning home in the afternoon, it is rather difficult to get right into the regular rhythm of my creative writing."[49] Embree replied that he wished McKay every success but the Rosenwald Fund, he regretted, could not advance him any more money.

McKay may not have been entirely candid about his "small part time job." Since October he had been trying to join the Federal Writers' Project; by late April (certainly by the summer of 1936), he had qualified for the program and had been hired. For McKay, as for many other writers in the 1930s, the FWP became a refuge from destitution. For Claude in particular, it meant much more than mere relief; he could finish his autobiography and delve more deeply into the community life of Harlem than he would have ever been able to do as a solitary author existing upon the sufferance of friends, foundations, and publishers. Although it never paid him more than twenty-three dollars per week, his FWP salary enabled him to live and work in relative security for the next three years. During that time, he found enough leisure to complete a study of Harlem that had actually begun to take shape with his first articles on Father Divine and Sufi Abdul Hamid in 1935. During his years with the FWP, he also wrote several articles in which he clearly stated his position on a variety of interrelated contemporary issues ranging from communism and the Popular Front to the present and future of blacks within American society.[50]

In the summer and fall of 1936, however, McKay devoted himself to completing his autobiography. As he indicated in his letter to Embree, his new job required him to report daily to the FWP offices in the Port of New York Authority building on lower Eighth Avenue. This daily task eventually proved less onerous than McKay had first thought it would. After he signed in, his workday often consisted of briefly discussing his assignments with his administrative superiors and then returning home to work on his book. His supervisors had early decided that McKay had enough self-discipline and experience to choose for himself the specific topics he should research and develop. Like most blacks on the project, he concentrated on the contemporary history of New York's black population. Over the next three years, they collected a vast amount of material on Harlem, including dozens of biographical sketches on notable Harlemites from Sufi Abdul Hamid to Arthur Schomburg. McKay wrote a significant number of these sketches, which eventually wound up in the Schomburg Collection of Negro History and Literature on 135th Street in Harlem. By the middle of the summer, McKay had adjusted to his daily trip downtown. His FWP duties, he found, provided an interesting diversion from the isolation and concentration necessary to complete his primary task. By the summer, he was dividing his time almost exclusively between FWP duties and his autobiography.[51]

Not all his friends understood McKay's need for isolation, and their tendency to drop in unannounced or to send to his door strangers eager to meet a famous author led to misunderstandings and ill will. McKay sometimes tolerated such interruptions, but when his patience was gone he would castigate even his closest friends. Arthur Schomburg one day found himself on the receiving end of such a tirade. Embarrassed, hurt, and angered, Schomburg decided to have nothing further to do with him. Claude's animosity, of course, soon passed, and when he heard that Schomburg had declared their friendship at an end he hastened to write him an apology. "If I did offend you," he wrote, "I want to apologize before everybody, because

I didn't mean to; you are a friend of mine who has really befriended me and also I really like you yourself." McKay reminded Schomburg that no one knew better than he "the tight fix" he had been in since returning to the United States. Now that he had "a little chance" to recover lost ground, McKay explained, "I am working all day every day," both at home and "at the big library digging things up." Working hard while "existing on a shoe string with all my essential needs curtailed," he exclaimed, "makes me irritable enough. And I become more so when people crash in on me during my working hours, upsetting me and breaking the rhythm of my thought and arresting my writing—sometimes for hours." Even in his letter of apology McKay felt compelled, once he had brought the subject up, to expand upon his general grievance. "The people who callously intrude on creative workers certainly cannot have any appreciation of the difficulty of creative work. Evidently they think that because one provides humor and writes about the common people that he could do it standing on his head in the street with a crowd around. . . . For all their pretending they fundamentally think very little of the artist." Finally (in case, perhaps, Schomburg had begun to wonder about such an apology), McKay concluded by stating, "I want to come to see you and talk this over, but I won't if you remain angry. I may be crazy, but I bear no malice."* The two remained friends, but such incidents must have placed limits upon how far Schomburg could trust McKay's friendship.

Despite such difficulties, McKay persevered and by early September he had his manuscript ready to submit to his publisher. On September 11, 1936, he wrote Orrick Johns, the director of the New York City FWP, that he had completed his "new book, *A Long Way from Home*," and had "turned it in to the publisher." McKay had written Johns to request his next "creative work assignment." But he added that he would prefer "to continue under the old plan" until the government made clear whether a writer's creative work would belong "to himself or the government." Under the old assignment plan, McKay explained, he had sufficient time to complete his own work. He had concluded that it was "good" for a creative writer to "perform some kind of routine work," though he admitted that "the greatest difficulty for me was signing in [in] the morning, because I work better in the early morning and by signing in I lost the first half of the

*Claude McKay to A. A. Schomburg, August 20, 1935, © 1987 by Hope McKay Virtue, 1110 Olive Avenue, Long Beach, Calif. 90813, and used by her permission. This letter is in the Arthur A. Schomburg Papers, Schomburg Center for Research in Black Culture, at the New York Public Library.

day." Since that inconvenience would continue under the new, proposed creative writing assignment, it would be just as well for him to remain on routine assignments. "I like that research work," McKay concluded, "and I have been privileged to suggest the items I like to work on." [52]

Whatever McKay's initial misgivings about the new creative writing assignment proposed to him by Johns, he soon accepted it and became one of only a few writers on the New York project who were allowed to stay home and work on their own material. [53] This soon proved a boon because Lee Furman rushed McKay's manuscript through to the printer. By November, he had sent McKay the initial galleys for him to proofread. Over the next few weeks he worked closely with Furman to prepare the final proofs. By the end of the year, A Long Way from Home was ready for press.

In early January, McKay sat down to catch up on his correspondence. To James Ivy, he wrote that he had neglected answering his last letter because he had been busy with A Long Way from Home. He told Ivy that Lee Furman, his publisher, was the president of the Macauley Company but added that "he publishes the better kind of books under his own name." Both he and McKay had high hopes that A Long Way from Home would be a success. McKay also informed Ivy that while writing the book he had virtually curtailed his social life. "The necessity of working was greater than the desire to fool around." [54]

Despite his self-enforced isolation, McKay never lacked friends in Harlem, and after completing A Long Way from Home, he began to be more actively involved in the social and intellectual life of the Harlem community. In February his reemergence received a big boost with the appearance of A Long Way from Home. On May 4, 1937, Lee Furman hosted a reception and dinner for McKay at Sardi's for which invitations were extended to many of McKay's friends and acquaintances in Harlem and New York literary circles. After all he had experienced since his return to the United States, his dinner at Sardi's must have been for McKay a sweet triumph. He had dedicated A Long Way from Home "To All My Friends Everywhere," and truly, despite his occasional outbursts of ill temper and spite, he did appreciate them. They had, he realized, made it possible for him to continue his literary career. [55]

His friends were delighted to read his memoirs, but almost all found something to criticize. Max Eastman, for example, thought A Long Way from Home "in many places very noble and large spirited." He especially liked McKay's accounts of Frank Harris, his trip to

Russia, and his *Liberator* experiences. Eastman also appreciated Claude's "tribute to Crystal, which," he emphasized, "I mean to quote in my own autobiography." He labeled as false, however, McKay's assumptions that Eastman had been snubbed by Comintern officials and American Communist party delegates in 1922 even though, as McKay stated it, Eastman had been "as pure a Marxist as any of them." He had not been snubbed, Eastman asserted, and he was not then, nor had he ever been, an orthodox Marxist. Eastman went on to deny, too, McKay's further assumption that his alleged ill-treatment in 1922 had anything to do with his becoming a Trotskyist. Finally, Eastman also thought it callous of McKay to repeat the conversation they had had in Moscow about Lenin's exceedingly plain wife. He had remarked to McKay that Lenin, gravely ill at the time, might "get well if he had a pretty girl." Despite the embarrassment this printed remark now caused him, Eastman held no grudge against McKay. "It is no news to me," he told McKay, "that you are impish on occasion. . . . Friends are pretty scarce around my diggings these days and you have always been a precious one."[56]

Walter White was angrier about McKay's treatment of him. Although McKay made plain his admiration of White, he asserted that the fair-skinned White was "Negroid simply because he closely identifies with the Negro group—just as a Teuton becomes Moslem if he embraces Islam. White is whiter than many Europeans—even biologically." McKay devoted a page to the irony of White's complexion and the questions it raised about race definition. By contrast, he spent only a couple of paragraphs discussing White's dedicated service to the National Association for the Advancement of Colored People. To White, such treatment only revealed once more McKay's West Indian prejudice against mulattoes.[57]

Sylvia Pankhurst was another who resented her portrait. From England, she informed McKay that she considered his account of her relationship with the socialist editor and publisher George Lansbury libelous. McKay had written that in 1920 she had refused to print an article of his critical of Lansbury because she owed Lansbury twenty pounds and had borrowed paper from him on which to print the *Workers' Dreadnought.*[58]

Closer to home, Joel Spingarn wrote McKay a warm letter of appreciation. He had thoroughly enjoyed *A Long Way from Home,* he wrote, "and I owe you thanks for the hour or two of real enjoyment that this book has given me." Like others, however, Spingarn believed that McKay had erred in his specific remembrance of him. As he remembered it, he and McKay had differed about the NAACP, not about Spingarn's preference for McKay's racial poems over his non-racial ones, as McKay had stated in *A Long Way from Home*. "I am glad to see," Spingarn observed, "that the supreme contempt you felt for the Association then has been tempered by time."[59]

Spingarn's note prompted a warm letter of thanks from McKay in which, quite unintentionally, he once again managed to offend the aging and sensitive man. McKay wrote that he was "certain" he had not discussed the NAACP with Spingarn back in 1921–1922. They had instead differed over McKay's poetry. Spingarn had admired McKay's poems about the racial issue but had dismissed his other poems as at best "magazine verse." Spingarn had told him that in his opinion they were dominated by poetic clichés and vastly inferior to his poems of racial protest. As for the NAACP, McKay maintained, he had more respect for it while on the *Liberator* than he did currently. He and other black radicals, he assured Spingarn, had appreciated its indispensable role as a legal defender of black rights, even while criticizing its middle-class orientation. McKay told Spingarn that he only brought the matter up again because "I am trying to be intellectually honest with myself. Of course I am very proud to admit that from my experience I have changed some of my ideas. Three years of living in Africa were like three generations of experience. But that doesn't mean that I have arrived at the point of having faith in the old rotting bourgeois society. It means I am visualizing the new era of Labor and the Cooperative world as a progressive whole and not from a narrow and extreme radical point of view."[60]

McKay's letter was an honest statement of conviction. For Spingarn, however, it reopened old wounds. He had of late been ill and had no patience with what he mistakenly perceived as a veiled attack upon him. He replied that he remembered, among other things, that McKay had come asking his help "with arrogant manners." McKay quickly replied. "I feel very badly," he wrote, "that we should so completely misunderstand each other." He had sometimes, he admitted, been "impulsive and angry but never arrogant" in his relations with anyone. On the contrary, McKay protested, he was so "sensitive about correct and decent personal intercourse . . . that . . . I have been told I was too polite. For that reason people have often mistook [*sic*] my gentle ways for softness, thinking they could walk all over me." Mc-Kay added that he had already apologized once to Spingarn, and in *A Long Way from Home*, he had "made the utmost gesture of a public apology" by showing "that in spite of my rudeness, you found me a publisher." He had, moreover, never considered Spingarn a bourgeois person "in the French sense of Philistine, but in the radical sense of your being a man of wealth and naturally influenced by your position." And, he continued,

> Praise God I have never yet hated anyone merely for belonging to a different class or race. And I have real respect for the bourgeois who is honestly fighting to maintain the standards of his class, because he thinks they are the best for society as a whole, even though I am opposed to him. I am far and away removed from any blind radical hate and have no use for radical bigots; that is why I find myself in disagreement with Trotsky and against any form of dictatorship and am intellectually very lonely because I am not sincerely in sympathy with any of the radical factions. . . .
>
> I should like to feel that there was no unfriendliness between us. I rather think that in your contacts with Negroes you have met many who were insincere sycophants, just because they thought they could obtain a free mess of pottage by being sycophantic. Surely it should interest you that there is one who under the harshest circumstances has managed to maintain his individuality and integrity.*

There was a note of desperation in McKay's letter to Spingarn. He had written *A Long Way from Home* expressly to clear up the many misapprehensions that existed among both blacks and whites, radical and conservative, about his literary career and political beliefs. He had expected enmity from those who differed with him politically and artistically, but it hurt to find he had also antagonized his friends.[61]

In *A Long Way from Home,* McKay projected a very definite picture of himself as first and foremost a literary artist in the romantic mold. His first objective had always been to experience life directly in order to communicate the truth of his experience in his art. This urge for new experiences as nourishment for his creative expression is a theme sustained throughout *A Long Way from Home.* Whatever stifled man's potential to experience fully nature's free gifts, McKay rejected.

By defining himself simply as an independent, free-spirited poet, McKay avoided almost entirely any close examination of those deep inner motivations that had moved him to choose the particular paths he had taken from Jamaica to New York, to Moscow, to Paris, and to Tangier. By becoming simply The Poet, he avoided, above all, any real discussion of how deeply involved he had truly been, both

---

*Claude McKay to Joel Spingarn, March 12, 1937, © 1987 by Hope McKay Virtue, 1110 Olive Avenue, Long Beach, Calif. 90813, and used by her permission. This letter is in the Joel Spingarn Papers at the New York Public Library.

emotionally and intellectually, with communism between 1919 and 1923. As a consequence, *A Long Way from Home* became, as McKay intended it should be, a pleasantly impressionistic book, a seemingly effortless account of his travels and his encounters with the great and near-great of international communism and the literary world of Europe and America. Through it all, he portrayed himself as a black man intent upon remaining true to himself, yet accepting, too, the inescapable obligation to write truthfully about those qualities within himself and his race that both set blacks apart as unique and made them one with the rest of mankind. It was not a dishonest or ignoble goal; McKay had never been an introspective writer. But *A Long Way from Home* failed to convey the complexity of his life.

From a historical point of view, McKay's discussions of his early years in New York with the *Liberator,* his English experience, and his trip to Russia are full of interesting details and insights into the men and women he knew and the events he witnessed. But he actually revealed very little about his personal life in *A Long Way from Home*. The details of his early childhood and youth, his intimate personal relationships as an adult, his initial attraction to radicalism, his chronic health problems, and his reasons for turning away from communism after 1923—all are shrouded in hints, vague generalizations, and outright denials. His insistence that he was never a member of the Communist party was less than the whole truth, as was his assertion that his health problems after 1923 had been temporary. There was almost no discussion of his political thought after 1923, because as a free spirit he had remained essentially consistent in his political outlook. International communism had betrayed itself by becoming intolerantly sectarian and dogmatic. In responding to a recent attack on him in the *New Masses* for the alleged lack of class consciousness and class action in his poetry and novels, McKay asserted that his poems remained their own best defense against his critics and that in his novels he had, unlike most communists, written of the black proletariat from an intimate knowledge of their "inner lives." In *Home to Harlem,* Jake had in fact demonstrated class consciousness when he "refused to scab," and he had revealed an even higher sense of social propriety when he refused to pimp. "Perhaps," McKay mischievously concluded, "a higher sense than many of us critical scribblers."[62]

In *A Long Way from Home,* McKay had very largely achieved the kind of informal, direct, impressionistic book he had originally outlined in his letters to Edwin Embree in 1935. And Embree, for one, thought McKay had succeeded admirably. "The thing I liked best,"

Embree wrote, "was your cozy, companionable style. Amazingly you created the feeling not that you as a single individual were talking or writing, but that a group of us were having a free exchange—all discussing and telling tales and philosophizing together with a lot of give and take." He also liked McKay's "freedom from pathological infection" by either communism or color and race consciousness. McKay's "eclectic attitude" appealed to Embree. He believed that in *A Long Way from Home*, McKay resembled "both in style and attitude" his old friend Clarence Day. Embree explained that "Day used to like ideas while they were forming, but he seldom liked people's books. He said he liked eggs but couldn't stand roast chicken. He would have liked *A Long Way from Home;* it has so much egginess and so little of the formality and stolidness of a roast."[63]

In the midst of a decade in which fierce debates raged about the proper function of writers and artists in a world beset by perilous chaos and change, McKay in *A Long Way from Home* took what appeared to many a simple-minded and thoroughly outmoded position. To him, it was necessary for the poet to remain above the fray in order to hold fast to his immemorial function as an interpreter of reality to mortal men. Thus, he could assert that some sort of socialism must eventually triumph over the old capitalist system and that blacks had to develop a stronger group spirit in order to overcome their disadvantages, while at the same time disavowing any political role for himself either as a socialist or a black. He might dream of "a great modern Negro leader" who would guide blacks out of their confusion and inertia, but all he could give such a leader would be "a monument in verse."[64]

Such a position left McKay vulnerable to attack, and it soon came. In a review of *A Long Way from Home* in the *New Challenge,* a black quarterly with a decided leftist bent, Alain Locke hoisted McKay on one of his own petards by characterizing him as a "spiritual truant" and insincere and disloyal to every group with whom he had ever associated himself. Although an undoubted talent and a writer of great potential, by his unwillingness to avow loyalty to any racial leadership, political party, or even his expatriate friends in Europe, McKay had, in fact, revealed himself as the only "unabashed, 'Playboy of the Negro Renaissance.'" At the same time, McKay insisted that blacks should seek greater unity. Locke maintained:

> Even a fascinating style and the naivest egotism cannot cloak such inconsistency or condone such lack of common loyalty. . . . For a genius maturing in a decade of racial self-expression and enjoying the fruits of it all

and living into a decade of social issues and conflict and aware of that, to have repudiated all possible loyalties amounts to a self-imposed apostasy. McKay is after all the dark-skinned psychological twin of that same Frank Harris, whom he so cleverly portrays and caricatures; a versatile genius caught in the egocentric predicament of aesthetic vanity and exhibitionism. And so, he stands to date, the *enfant terrible* of the Negro Renaissance, where with a little loyalty and consistency he might have been at least its Villon and perhaps its Voltaire.[65]

Locke's incisive indictment would have been more honest and effective had he anywhere acknowledged in his review that McKay had singled him out for special criticism in *A Long Way from Home*. McKay had never forgiven Locke his editorial sins, and he described the fastidious Locke as "a perfect symbol of the Aframerican rococo in his personality," whose academic and pedestrian conception of art, together with his editorial arrogance, made him totally unfit to serve as a spokesman for the black arts in America.[66] Locke's failure in his review to acknowledge and answer directly this highly personal attack must have confirmed Claude's already low opinion of him, though for once Locke was direct and to the point in his criticism.

Taking up where Locke left off, the young black poet M. B. Tolson, in a well-written review of *A Long Way from Home*, diagnosed McKay's trouble from a leftist perspective. For Tolson, McKay's problem lay in his inability to understand "that Marxism can remove racial antagonisms. Therein lies the tragedy of McKay. . . . [He] failed to discover Marx's economic interpretation of racial prejudice." The political lessons McKay thought he had learned during World War I were being learned anew by a new generation of black writers. Most, including Tolson, were destined to follow essentially the same intellectual route McKay had taken. The greatest of these, Richard Wright, had already made his debut, and Tolson contrasted the disillusionment and "never-ending spiritual odyssey" of McKay with the confident self-assertiveness of young Richard Wright. "The essential difference between the unshakable loyalty of Richard Wright and the spiritual truancy of Claude McKay lies in [the] dramatic Marxist vision of Richard Wright."[67]

George Streator, another left-leaning black reviewer, took a different view. In the *New York Herald Tribune Books*, he called McKay a revolutionary poet and thinker but thought him highly prejudiced against mulattoes. He also accused McKay of dodging the draft during World War I by working on the railroad and insinuated that when racial rioting had broken out in 1919, McKay had gone to England for his safety. James Weldon Johnson had a ready explanation for Streator's curious review. In a letter of congratulations and praise for *A Long Way from Home,* Johnson wrote, "Probably you . . . have divined that [Streator's] attitude is in no small measure due to the realistic and common sense views that you express on Soviet Russia and Communism. You may confidently look forward to having all Marxian Negro brain-trusters coming down on you like a pile of bricks. These Negro near-Marxists are often quite amusing, if not ridiculous. You, of course, know many times more about Russia and Communism than all of them put together." [68]

Not all black critics panned *A Long Way from Home.* Henry Lee Moon, for example, gave it a polite, though by no means enthusiastic, review in the *New Republic.* The white press generally conceded that McKay wrote well and that his latest book was interesting, but *A Long Way from Home* generated few raves. It was simply a pleasant book, as easily forgotten as read. Some critics were troubled that McKay did not really delve deeply enough into the problem of blacks, especially black intellectuals and writers. As J. S. Balch of the St. Louis *Post-Dispatch* expressed it, "One might wish for less emphasis on the old conception of the poet as apart from other men. But who would quarrel with a book that runs as smoothly and absorbingly as good conversation over a glass of beer?" [69] Simple communication, McKay was discovering, did not necessarily lead to either understanding or reconciliation with one's fellow man.

# 11
## Looking Forward: The Search for Community, 1937–1940

Although McKay may have portrayed himself in *A Long Way from Home* as a poet "apart from other men," by 1937 he was trying desperately to communicate to his fellow blacks in New York his belief that they needed to improve radically the scope and quality of their group activities and communal life. As a member of the FWP in New York City, he had himself become actively involved in trying to direct a black writers' guild, composed largely of FWP workers in Harlem, toward a group commitment to foster a spirit of community improvement.

McKay had always thrived in a topsy-turvy environment, and his experiences in New York City with the FWP provided all the stimulation he needed to descend into the pit of public controversy. The New York FWP was by far the most faction-riven and turbulent of all the many projects around the country. Within it Communists, Trotskyists, anarchists, socialists, liberals, conservatives, reactionaries, nonpolitical idealists, and opportunistic cynics battled with each other and with the federal bureaucracy in a no-holds-barred effort to win positions of power and privilege within the FWP and the union that represented its workers. In this struggle, the Communists generally were the most united, if not the most numerous, and they controlled the writers' union on the project from its inception.[1]

McKay opposed neither the union nor the leading role of the Communists in it. He believed, however, that blacks on the project should have their own organization, and in the winter of 1937 he joined in Harlem a group of black FWP members who had formed a Communist-backed Negro Authors' Guild. His intention was to rally to himself those who believed as he did that blacks could do without Communist leadership. All proceeded quietly until midsummer. Then on July 9, 1937, one of the guild's members, Edward Bryant, sponsored for membership a white woman named Helen Boardman. McKay saw no necessity for white members in a Negro Authors' Guild and vehemently objected to the action, one which Communist party members and their "fellow-travelers" had made standard practice in all the groups they helped to organize in Harlem during the 1930s.[2]

McKay believed that blacks needed white allies, but he believed they also needed self-confidence and enough faith in one another to launch their own organizations in which they could plan and carry out community programs they themselves designed, free from the subtle inhibitions even the most sympathetic whites injected into black groups by their very presence. In his view, other minorities on the FWP were free from the pressure to integrate their particular ethnic organizations. He saw no reason why blacks should not enjoy a wholly black Negro Authors' Guild. In McKay's opinion, black churches, mortuaries, fraternal organizations, and barbershops hardly sufficed to meet the overwhelming problems confronting Harlem. Blacks needed to start thinking about organizing both locally and nationally for sustained communal self-improvement, and he hoped a Negro Authors' Guild might help to steer black thinking in that direction. He was determined, at any rate, to prevent the guild from becoming simply another experiment in racial integration.[3]

When Helen Boardman was presented to the group, only a few guild members were present. Any final decision, McKay argued, should be made at a later date. A week later, the group convened again, this time with most members in attendance. According to the New York *Amsterdam News*, McKay again "vociferously opposed" Boardman's membership. The discussion soon became so "acrimonious" that Boardman finally jumped up, yelled, "I resign! I resign!" and "left in a dither." Her supporters, however, insisted that she be retained as a member. They pointed out that the constitution of the guild forbade discrimination based on race. Neither side budged.

McKay was not alone. He had won to his side the guild's officers, as well as many of the rank and file. Finally, according to the *Amsterdam News*, "Ted Yates, the executive secretary, Ellen Tarry, the recording secretary, McKay, and others [snatched] up the minutes and other official data of the guild and [branded] those who voted for Miss Boardman's membership in it . . . a rump group." They then "left the meeting in a huff." According to the *Amsterdam News*, the guild had, in effect, been destroyed because of "the one man campaign" McKay had begun on July 9 when Boardman's "name first came up." [4]

McKay fully realized that Helen Boardman, a non-Communist long involved with black causes, had been well intentioned, and he immediately wrote to express his regrets that she had become "the goat" in the organizational difficulties of "our little Guild." He had wanted the guild to become part of a larger strategy he envisioned for "intensive group work and consolidation." Most blacks, he stated, would at first disagree with him. "But," he continued, "the Negro group badly needs self-confidence, self-reliance, and group unity in order that it may overcome the morbid fear of Segregation and take action to build itself upon a sound foundation." He emphasized his belief that blacks as a group were not facing their problems in a realistic, progressive manner. He feared, he concluded, that they would retard "radical" social progress and change in the United States if they did not overcome their obsession with integration as the sole solution to America's race problems. [5]

Like all his critics, Boardman replied by stating that McKay's ideas, if implemented, would lead to self-segregation, narrow ethnocentrism, and isolation. Boardman's conclusions enraged McKay. Among other things, he advised her to take her ideas to those Negroes who felt, as she did, that group unity meant segregation. "They prefer to remain guinea pigs for sentimental persons to praise and investigate. I am not a guinea pig." Why, he asked, did she have to work with Negro organizations? She should instead "start a movement against Anglo-Saxon arrogance." Boardman ended the exchange by concluding in her final letter to McKay that "I agree with you. Whatever kind of pig you may be, it is not a guinea pig." [6]

Over the next year, McKay worked assiduously to build another black writers' guild that would function along the lines he envisioned. To give his efforts the stamp of respectability, McKay sought the public endorsement of James Weldon Johnson. The retired executive secretary of the NAACP was a highly respected, essentially noncontroversial figure, and his own literary accomplishments made him especially acceptable to black writers.

Ever since his return from Europe, McKay had confided to Johnson all his hopes of becoming a useful contributor to Afro-American life and letters. As early as April, 1935, he had explained that "I am certain that Negroes will have to realize themselves as an organized group to get anything." While abroad, he continued, "I observed that people who were getting . . . anything were those who could realize the strength of their cultural group; their political demands were considered and determined by the force of their cultural grouping."[7] In the same letter, he asked Johnson for help and advice about how best to approach the problems of strengthening black group life.

Johnson understood McKay's concern and gave him his blessing, but he really did not share McKay's conviction that Afro-Americans had to reorient their basic goals and reconstitute themselves in any fundamental way as a group. Among prominent Afro-American leaders, only W. E. B. Du Bois had ideas similar to McKay's. Before McKay's return to the United States, Du Bois had suggested in *Crisis* that blacks had to retrench and try to establish an independent, cooperative group economy that would give them the economic power to survive the depression and the strength to demand better treatment in America. His espousal of such a plan had immediately been denounced by the NAACP's executive secretary, Walter White, and Du Bois had resigned as editor of *Crisis*.[8] In contrast to Du Bois, Johnson in 1934 published *Negro Americans, What Now?*, in which he basically advocated a continuance of the NAACP-sponsored civil rights approach to black problems.[9]

McKay read the book with great sympathy, but he wrote Johnson that it failed on two counts: 1) it did not stress sufficiently the Communist threat to Negro unity, and 2) it did not adequately discuss the Negro's stake in the labor movement. Labor, McKay reminded Johnson, was the most important class opposing capital. The old "rentier and investing class," McKay told him, had been squeezed out as effective forces by giant corporations and government inflation and tax measures. Blacks had to group themselves with either labor or capital, and it should be labor because most blacks were workers. McKay also told Johnson that he had read Du Bois's opinions "and wondered . . . if both of your views could not be reconciled in the interests of Negro unity and for a working program. . . . Du Bois makes it clear that he is opposed to Segregation where it means Discrimination." He added that he saw nothing wrong with black communities fighting for "New Deal money." They could use the profit that accrued to fight segregation.[10]

Johnson replied that he supported an integrated labor movement and opposed a segregated black union movement. It would lead to scabbing and "drive the wedge deeper between black and white labor." As to self-help, he was not opposed to blacks "taking the utmost advantage offered by imposed segregation," but he emphasized that Du Bois's idea of a separate, self-sufficient black economy simply could not be achieved.[11]

After the breakup of the Negro Authors' Guild in July, 1937, McKay wrote Johnson that earlier "the Communists tried the same trick on the Harlem Artists' Guild sending up artists from downtown to join," but they had not been allowed in by the all-black guild membership. Later, McKay contended, the Harlem Artists had won certain concessions for their members from the Federal Artists' Project that they probably could not have gotten as an integrated group. McKay asked Johnson to head his new writers' group "so it will be possible for all Negro writers who are sincerely group conscious and not communist crazy to pull around you."[12]

Although he could savagely attack them when provoked, McKay in 1937 could still view with humor the Communist party's efforts to manipulate black affairs in Harlem. "These are the days," he wrote Johnson, "when the black-red hand disguised tries to pull all the strings, even your pajamas."[13] Times had, indeed, changed from the days on the *Liberator* when battles had been fought openly and differences had often been tolerated where they could not be changed. "What I mainly dislike about the Communists of these times is their chicanery and intrigue," McKay complained to Johnson.[14]

In October, 1937, McKay wrote a circular letter for the creation of a new, "democratic association of Negro writers" and announced an organization meeting for November 1. He stressed that the committee for whom he spoke was "not thinking in terms of narrow sectarianism, but rather in universal aspects of group culture." By the end of the year, the new group was launched. From the beginning, McKay was its driving force, but a fairly large number of Harlem writers, journalists, and intellectuals attended one or more of its meetings and contributed to its discussions. Among them were James Weldon Johnson, Jessie Fauset, Countee Cullen, Henry Lee Moon, Gwendolyn Bennett, Ted Yates, Ellen Tarry, Arthur Schomburg, and Earl Brown. By and large, however, the new writers' guild had an irregular, fluctuating membership. Most attended only a few meetings. None had quite the same enthusiasm as McKay for an independent black writers' guild. He had hoped that such a group, meeting regularly once a month, would help its members "clarify" their thinking about the differences between literature and politics.

At the same time, he also envisioned them drawing closer to the problems of the black masses. He wanted them to solidify their literary traditions and work to improve their position in the world of letters. He did not want the organization to be politically oriented but to concentrate on the unique functions of literature in society, functions that he believed set it above mere politics. Politicians of every stripe, McKay believed, were ultimately pragmatists and/or opportunists. Artists were concerned with the quality of human values, whether moral, aesthetic, personal, or social, not with the simple mechanics of material existence.[15]

His objectives were fine. But modern writers of whatever race have seldom worked long together as equals, and those McKay brought together in Harlem proved no exception. By the spring of 1938, he had begun to doubt that it would be possible "to build up an organization of writers who are . . . infused with a group spirit." Real enthusiasm, he concluded, was not something that could be manufactured. To James Weldon Johnson, he wrote, "I always think of that letter you wrote to me abroad years ago, advising me to return and take part in the literary movement." He revealed that certain people had expressed doubts about his motives for organizing a writers' group. "Some people," he told Johnson, "think I am interested in a literary organization to use it to keep up my prestige, as my recent books were not good sellers. But in reality it was more your letter which gave birth to the idea." McKay expressed disappointment to find "many members of the old group mourning the good days past, instead of doing something to make the present day significant."[16]

Among those who encouraged McKay to continue was Countee Cullen. He enjoyed the meetings and McKay's friendship. Their correspondence throughout the late 1930s and 1940s contained on McKay's side none of the irritability, special pleading, or desperation that characterized so much of his correspondence. In his letters to Cullen, McKay always wrote as a relaxed, warm, and considerate friend.[17]

With the support of Cullen and a few others, the writers' group continued awhile longer. During the late spring and early summer of 1938, McKay and Cullen even began to see the possibility of realizing McKay's old dream of editing a literary magazine. In October, 1937, an organization calling itself the Universal Ethiopian Students' Association began a monthly magazine entitled the *African: A Journal of African Affairs*. It sought to expose the injustices committed by European imperialism in Africa, to inform readers about black problems in the United States, and to encourage American blacks to see their problems in broad, international perspective. It also sought to keep alive the strong black interest in the fate of Ethiopia, which only the year before had been overrun and occupied by Mussolini's armies. The magazine was antifascist, noncommunist, and concerned specifically with making blacks aware of the dangers they faced from fascism and traditional European imperialism and racism.[18]

It was the kind of journal McKay could support, and in the spring of 1938 he contributed to it an article about his experiences in Tangier. By then, the organization that controlled the magazine (McKay described them in one letter as former Garveyites) was experiencing the usual difficulties in publishing a new journal—namely, leadership, organizational, and financial problems. In April, 1938, McKay and Cullen began negotiating with the group to take over the editorship of the magazine. By the end of May, it appeared they had succeeded in obtaining the free hand they sought, and they announced to prospective supporters that they would begin in July to edit the magazine, renamed the *African: A Journal of Literary and Social Progress*. Their optimism proved premature. The Ethiopian Students' Association wavered, then reneged on their agreement, and McKay and Cullen soon withdrew from their involvement with the group. In a letter to McKay in late July, Cullen expressed regret about the failure of their efforts to take over the *African*, but he speculated that they would not in any case have been able to work with such "narrow-minded" people who only wanted to publish "propaganda."[19]

By the summer of 1938, McKay's role as the active leader of Harlem's most prestigious noncommunist black writers' guild had come to an end. It was probably just as well. McKay could be charming, witty, and incisive, but he was no leader of men. To have built his guild into the kind of permanent, influential cultural force he had envisioned would have taken a politician endowed with much more patience, practical resourcefulness, and, above all, financial means than McKay ever possessed. In the long run, what counted most, perhaps, was not that he failed to establish a permanent guild but that he made so great an effort.

Although his attempt as a practical organizer failed, the articles he began to write in 1937 remain as durable testimony to the consistency and integrity of the stands he took on a wide variety of public issues throughout the 1930s and beyond. In his articles, McKay always sought to disentangle rhetoric, whether of the Right or the Left, from the hard realities it usually obscured. In a decade beset by extreme partisanship on every side, McKay actually argued consistently for tolerance, moderation, and the defense of democratic freedoms. To many, however, the positions he took on specific issues seemed excessive. Even as a moderate, McKay almost always managed to stir heated controversy and extreme partisanship. Few appreciated the genuine personal disinterestedness with which he advanced his ideas. In fact, during his last years he was often much more perceptive and far-sighted than his critics realized.

While busily organizing his writers' group in 1937, McKay began to publish articles in which he spelled out the reasons for his anticommunism and his belief in the necessity for stronger black unity. He also commented upon the state of labor organization in Harlem.[20] As an old radical, McKay succeeded better in his articles than he had in his autobiography in explaining his opposition to the Communist party. Beginning in 1935, the emphasis within international communism had shifted from militant opposition to existing capitalist governments and non-Communist parties of all description, to a policy that emphasized a united front with all antifascist governments, parties, and individuals. The rise of nazism in Germany, combined with the existence of Italian fascism and the menace of Japanese expansion into Manchuria, caused Moscow to seek allies abroad in the hope of containing the threats the Soviet Union now faced in both Western Europe and Asia. Because the fascist threat to world peace was very real, many of all political persuasions welcomed Moscow's new policy.[21]

In the United States, the American Communist party had created a League of American Writers as part of its efforts to bring influential American writers into its united front against war and fascism. In July, 1937, the league held its second congress in New York, and McKay, who had been invited to participate at the opening session, found himself seated on the dais. The proceedings had hardly begun when he discovered himself in opposition to the keynote speaker, Earl Browder, the chairman of the Communist party of the United States. Although the Communists generally had sought non-Communist cooperation since 1935, their war against Trotskyists and other critics of the Soviet Union was unending. This led to serious consequences for its united front policy. By 1937, for example, the united front against Franco's counterrevolution in Spain was already being subverted by Communist efforts there to eliminate its left-wing foes within the forces loyal to the beleaguered republican government. Of more immediate concern to the liberals and non-Communists at the Second League Congress in New York, however, were the first trials of old Bolsheviks, which had recently occurred in Moscow itself. Their execution by Stalin's government had caused many to question the true nature of Soviet communism. To some, it seemed as bad as the emerging totalitarian regime in Germany. In May, the titular chairman of the League of American Writers, Waldo Frank, had called for a jury of Communists and socialists to investigate the assertion by Trotsky and others that the Moscow trials had been cynically staged in order to eliminate all possible rivals to Stalin within the Russian Communist party.[22]

For American Communist leaders, Frank's actions ended his usefulness in the League of American Writers, and at the opening session of its second congress he was denounced by Earl Browder. McKay thought such an attack was completely unjustified, and he reacted immediately. As Browder spoke, McKay left the stage and walked out of the meeting. Shortly afterward, he publicly stated his opposition to the League of American Writers in "An Open Letter to James Rorty," which appeared in the *Socialist Call*, July 17, 1937. Rorty had already denounced the league in the *Call*, but McKay maintained that mere statements of opposition were not enough. He believed that all American writers who valued independence and freedom of expression should be organized in a league of their own, and he urged Rorty to think about the steps necessary for the creation of such a league.

McKay rejected most emphatically Communist efforts to suppress all criticism of the Soviet Union by its Popular Front allies of the Left and center. Throughout human history, he asserted, critical opinion and the questioning of authority had been a prerequisite for progress in human affairs. The Soviet Union should welcome criticism, not try to quash it. Those writers who valued their historic role as independent critics and social commentators should make clear their opposition to all dictatorship, whether from the Right or the Left. McKay saw the situation presented by the League of American Writers as more than "merely a difference of tactics between radical factions." It had become "fundamentally a part of the great struggle between genuine democracy and dictatorship." McKay told Rorty that "more and more" the world's people were being forced to choose between dictatorship and democracy. "But because there exists on the left flank of bourgeois democracy a . . . proletarian dictatorship in Russia some liberal intellectuals argue that as Russia is a proletarian state they should suspend criticism of its mistakes and criticize only the fascist . . . maneuvers which menace the social progress of the world." Such people, McKay stated, were "either led or maneuvered by those who give their allegiance to the Comintern, who believe only in the principle of dictatorship and have nothing but contempt (which is sometimes concealed) for genuine workers' democracy. Such a situation naturally produces intellectual confusion." Since it was the scene of "perhaps the greatest social experiment in the history of the human race," McKay stoutly affirmed that "more than any the Soviet state stands in need of radical criticism and analysis." He then defined "independent intellectuals as the spiritual descendants of the prophets and skeptic philosophers, who always fearlessly opposed and criticized the priests, while the Communist and Fascist intellectuals, intolerant of criticism, stem straight from the scribes who always blindly and faithfully served the hierarchy of the priests." There could be no compromise between these two types of intellectuals, he avowed.

After having lived under Russian communism, Primo de Rivera's relatively mild dictatorship in prerepublican Spain, and a colonial dictatorship in North Africa, McKay stated that "in the intellectual sphere" he had found they all had "something in common . . . a feeling of fear among those who desired to think and express themselves independently." McKay concluded by affirming his belief in "*the social revolution and the triumph of workers' democracy, not workers' dictatorship.*" But he warned that "the scribes" were "highly organized" and could accomplish much. "Is it not possible," he asked Rorty, "to have an organization of independent writers?"[23]

McKay's open letter to Rorty in the *Call* marked only the first of several articles over the next three years in which he defined and clarified his objections to communism. Most appeared first in the *New Leader,* and they were often reprinted in the New York *Amsterdam News*. Among the many journals in New York in the 1930s that published former Communists and other radical socialists of anti-Stalinist persuasion, the weekly *New Leader* was perhaps the one most filled with contemporary news and rumors from the badly fragmented left-wing community in New York. On July 23, 1938, for example, it published an article that alleged that the Communist party had recently decided at a special meeting to drive all "Trotskyists" off the FWP in New York City. At the same meeting, the article said, party chieftains also "resolved to continue the present drive of the Communists to gain the favor of the Negroes working on the WPA." The article informed *New Leader* readers that "this is a pet project of the Communist Party and up to now they have met with the opposition of Claude McKay, Negro leader, who has fought vigorously against Communist domination of the Negroes on work relief. And so McKay was also denounced at the meeting and a drive against him and his activities was agreed on."[24]

This prompted an article from McKay in which he argued that it would have been more correct for the *New Leader* to have written that he had spoken out against "Communist persecution of non-Communist workers," rather than that he "fought against 'Communist domination of the Negroes on work relief.'" To have fought Communist domination he would have had to fight against "the union of the unemployed and the WPA workers and I stand by the principle of unionism. . . . More than any other group the Communists should be credited with the effective organizing of the unemployed and relief workers." He approved the Communist party's commitment to unionization and worker protection. What he adamantly opposed was "the basic political ideology of Communism." McKay proceeded to list his objections to Communist politics:

> (1) I reject absolutely the idea of government by dictatorship, which is the pillar of political communism. (2) I am intellectually against the Jesuitical tactics of the Communists: (a) Their professed conversion to the principles of Democracy which is obviously false since they defend the undemocratic regime in Russia and loudly laud its bloodiest acts; (b) Their skunking [sic] behind the smoke screen of People's Front and Collective security, supporting the indefensible imperialistic interests of European nations and deliberately trying to deceive the American people; (c) Their criminal slandering and persecution of their opponents, who remain faithful to the true traditions of radicalism and liberalism.

He was not, he said, as concerned about Communists dominating Negroes on work relief as he was about "the Communists capturing the entire colored group by cleverly controlling such organizations as the so-called National Negro Congress."[25] This was never a real fear, it might be noted, of established black leaders, though the NAACP had waged a losing battle earlier in the 1930s to retain control of the defense of the Scottsboro boys in Alabama.[26]

In several articles, McKay registered his scorn for the united front policy, which he maintained was being cleverly used by imperialist forces in France and by the Soviet Union to advance their own undemocratic policies abroad. Under Léon Blum's French Popular Front government, McKay charged, progressive nationalist and socialist movements in Morocco were ruthlessly suppressed while the forces of French reaction in North Africa were given a free hand to rule as they liked, all in the name of antifascism. "How cruel the delusion of the native intellectuals," McKay wrote in March, 1938, "who find themselves stripped by a People's Front Government of the few liberties which their Socialist and Communist supporters helped them to win.!"[27]

Over the next few years, McKay wrote several other perceptive articles on North Africa in which he never failed to discuss the harsh, reactionary nature of French colonial administration in the region. Long before Franz Fanon, McKay was pointing out the pernicious consequences of such rule for colonized and colonizer alike. In one article published in the *New Leader* in 1939, for example, McKay asserted that the Spanish republican government in the early 1930s might have adopted a more liberal regime in Spanish Morocco or might even have granted it independence if the French had not insisted upon the maintenance of the colonial status quo in North Africa. The consequences for Spain had been disastrous, for Spanish Morocco, like French North Africa, continued as a stronghold of reaction; it had been from there that General Francisco Franco in 1936 finally launched his fateful attack upon republican Spain.[28]

McKay saw the Spanish Civil War as a double tragedy. He ardently admired the Spanish people and passionately supported the young Moroccan intellectuals whom he had witnessed rejoicing with Spanish republicans in Morocco on the advent of republican rule in 1931. To William A. Bradley he had written that "I am very pleased . . . the way the Republic was put over and I admire the sanity and clear realism of the Spaniards and am more firmly convinced than ever that they are the first people of Europe and the most interesting."[29] Less than eight years later, both North African nationalists and Spanish republicans were besieged by reactionary forces thirsting for their annihilation.

In his articles written after 1937, McKay showed a clear recognition and understanding of the dangers to world peace presented by Italian and German totalitarianism, but its dangers disturbed him less than those that he perceived had arisen within the Soviet Union. In 1939, after the signing of the Nazi-Soviet Pact, he advanced his argument clearly and succinctly. Both the Nazi and the Communist dictatorships were built upon mass movements, but the former had openly "declared itself the enemy of progress, international culture, and labor as a liberating force." It was clearly retrogressive. "On the other hand the Communist dictatorship sets itself up as the high protector of labor and international culture, while it actually suppresses all criticism and progressive opposition and reduces labor to subservience to a ruling clique. The forces of progress may unite to struggle against Nazism even as they have eternally fought reaction. But against pharisaical Communist dictatorship they were hopelessly divided, disarmed and confused." The new alliance between nazism and Russian communism, McKay hoped, would help to reveal the truth about Stalin's Russia. And in Harlem, where "fellow-travelers were as numerous and noisy as the angels of Father Divine," Communist propaganda would no longer be as effective as in the past.[30]

As a black man and a colonial who lived daily with the consequences of European racism, McKay considered Hitler a kind of Frankenstein monster, spawned by European imperialism, who had at last turned to menace his creator. In McKay's view, Hitler threatened Europe with the same kind of domination it had long imposed upon non-Europeans. He could understand the anguish of German Jews who had been "dramatically and brutally" reduced to "an inferior" minority status in Nazi Germany, but in his articles on black-Jewish relations in the United States, he constantly reminded American blacks and American Jews that blacks had existed under a racist tyranny in the United States that in essence differed little from Hitler's persecution of German Jews.[31]

Ever since Sufi Abdul Hamid picketed merchants along 125th Street in the early 1930s, Jewish leaders in New York had been worried about the possibility that Harlem blacks might fall prey to anti-Semitism. McKay consistently denied that any such danger existed. He insisted there was no anti-Semitism in Harlem. Blacks had picketed Jewish merchants, McKay pointed out, because Jews happened to own many businesses in Harlem that exploited blacks, just as white businessmen did in all-black ghettos.[32]

In December, 1938, McKay in the *Amsterdam News* pointed to a recent appeal in the journal *Jewish Frontier* for closer cooperation between blacks and Jews in the United States. The article urged as a first step that both "minorities purge their ranks of all prejudice and intolerance." McKay agreed but went on to spell out what he believed to be the two major problems hindering closer black-Jewish cooperation.

First, according to McKay, Jews in fact constituted "an important unit of the white world which discriminates against colored people. . . . Jews control many theaters, apartment houses, hotels, restaurants, cabarets, newspapers, moving pictures and other establishments which discriminate against colored people." Second, blacks as a group would have to develop enough unity to confront forthrightly American Jews and demand they purge themselves of all discriminatory practices against blacks as a price for active black cooperation against the rising tide of anti-Semitism at home and abroad. "To stand together with the Jews, we Negroes must first be able to stand up on our feet! . . . Let us force our Negro leaders and organizations to take such a stand instead of mouthing sentimental piffle about anti-Semitism which does not exist among Negroes." McKay did not deny that resentments toward Jews existed among blacks, but he denied that these resentments had anything to do with traditional European anti-Semitism. At their core, they involved real issues of housing and control of retail trade and jobs in the Harlem community that too often pitted Jewish entrepreneurs against the community's black population. This, McKay maintained, was "a social and labor issue, that should not involve anti-Semitism. Jewish businessmen exploit Negroes exactly as they exploit Jewish workers and not especially because of the former's race. Three or four decades ago the Jewish workers were ruthlessly exploited in sweatshops by Jewish employers, until the Jewish workers organized and with agitation and strikes compelled their employers to give them better conditions."

On one issue, McKay in the 1930s definitely parted company with many Jewish leaders and groups, including the *Jewish Frontier*. He firmly opposed the Zionist policy of settling European Jews in Palestine. On this issue, as on all public issues he confronted in the 1930s, he was absolutely clear: "Personally I am as opposed to the Palestine policy of the Zionists as much as I am opposed to the anti-Jewish measures of Hitler. Upon this issue I stand with Oswald Garrison Villard's *Nation*, which is the most impressive anti-Nazi organ of opinion in the United States. If the Jews sincerely believe in majority rule and minority rights, then the Zionist attitude toward Palestine is untenable. Also it tends to confuse the issues and dilute the sympathy which the liberal and radical world feels for the persecuted Jews."[33]

McKay's opposition to the *Jewish Frontier*'s militant Jewish nationalism had not prevented him in October, 1937, from publishing in it a major public statement in advocacy of greater black self-help as opposed to a continued reliance upon integration as the major means of improving black existence in the United States. McKay had earlier in 1937 debated this subject over the radio in New York City with George Schuyler, the black journalist. His *Jewish Frontier* article in October represented a distillation of his radio presentation.[34]

If McKay had an obsession after 1934, it was his belief that since the days of Booker T. Washington, blacks in the United States had effectively abandoned any serious efforts toward community self-improvement. According to McKay, the black masses had been too long abandoned in their misery by leaders single-mindedly focused on integration as the solution, leaders who even secretly resented and feared black people as inferior and degraded. Indeed, McKay argued, the masses of blacks had for too long been a body without a head. Their leadership, he repeatedly insisted, had abandoned them for an "Uncle Tom," "Do-Nothing" policy of integration.[35]

McKay vehemently denied that he in any way supported forced segregation; he also denied with equal fervor that he advocated black nationalism. The former was inhumane, and the latter a waste of intellectual time and energy. He was no black Zionist.[36]

He did, however, admire and hold up for black emulation the many Jewish community institutions that had done so much to elevate the Jewish standard of living in New York City. Above all, he pointed to the "militant" United Hebrew Trades Association, which had done much to improve the lives of Jewish workers. McKay stressed that unless blacks organized to win a secure place for themselves as workers in the economic life of the nation, "integration" would remain a pipe dream.[37]

While arguing for greater group organization, McKay continued to report upon Harlem's grass-roots movements and to compare their inventiveness and direct approaches to practical problems with the general ineffectiveness of established black leadership. On October 16, 1937, for example, in an article for the *Nation* entitled "Labor Steps Out in Harlem," McKay surveyed the contemporary Harlem labor scene and compared it to the days of Sufi Abdul Hamid earlier in the decade. He noted that since the Harlem riots of 1935, the area had benefited by the creation of a Negro Labor Committee, headed by the old-line black socialist Frank Crosswaith, and by the organizing activities of the newly created Congress of Industrial Organizations (CIO). The Negro Labor Committee was an umbrella organization representing several established labor unions. Its purpose was "to remedy the acute problem of the Negro worker's relationship to organized labor through the existing unions." It worked closely with the CIO. Competing with both the Negro Labor Committee and the CIO for the allegiance of black workers in Harlem, McKay contended, was an all-black group, the Harlem Labor Union, led by a black soapbox orator and local Republican politician, Ira Kemp, whose orientation was, like the Sufi's before him, almost purely racial. McKay warned that such leaders still had a large potential following if organized labor could not deliver practical benefits to black workers. "There are," he warned, "many potential Harlem Labor Unions in the colored communities. . . . They will have to be reckoned with. For the Negro group will not remain contented with the white workers in the superior and the colored worker in the inferior position throughout the ranks of labor." Negro and white labor leaders would eventually have to act, he concluded, to place blacks in all job levels.[38]

McKay's persistent criticism of established black leadership did not go unnoticed in the black press. It made good reading and stirred controversy, which increased circulation. Among others, the Reverend Adam Clayton Powell, Jr., questioned McKay's assessment of the current labor scene, and George Schuyler sniped at McKay's emphasis on group solidarity. Without marshaling any contrary facts, Powell intimated in the *Amsterdam News* that McKay's survey of the Harlem labor scene was inaccurate, and Schuyler accused McKay of "wallowing in the black fascist trough."[39]

McKay's presentation of his case for "group survival" in the *Jewish Frontier* and his comments on Harlem labor for the *Nation* had both been forceful and clear, but at the same time restrained, well organized, and free from personal attacks on anyone. He did not appreciate either Powell's or Schuyler's penchant for name calling. In his rejoinders to them in the *Amsterdam News,* he exhibited scant patience with either. Powell he dismissed as a "political acrobat," an "opportunistic careerist," and a "loose-thinking would-be intellectual" who did not even understand his *Nation* article.[40]

To answer Schuyler, McKay simply consulted the "Schuyler dossier" of newspaper columns over the years and found numerous instances where he had in the past advocated the very things McKay stood for in 1937. "Today," McKay concluded, "he denounces his own brain child as black fascism. . . . Schuyler's inept attempt to slander me merely discredits himself." McKay closed by dismissing Schuyler and Powell together as the "Scribe" and the young "Pharisee," neither of whom would ever understand him.[41]

He summarized his own position: "My faith in the cause of social justice and a new social order broadly based on the dignity and democracy of labor has never wavered. But my intellect is not limited to the social interpretation of Marx and Lenin. It . . . finds its roots in the logic of the Greeks who actually used their brains to think, who approached social theories and problems with open minds; and from them extracted the genuine and rejected the spurious."[42]

From all this one should not conclude that McKay had no friends in Harlem or black America. In fact, he had many. James Weldon Johnson, for one, always respected McKay's efforts and provided encouragement and support. McKay idolized Johnson, whom he saw as the Afro-American equivalent of someone like Max Eastman. Like Eastman, Johnson was a man of varied talents, real sophistication, and many accomplishments who recognized McKay's genius and whom McKay in turn could accept as a kind of reassuring intellectual father figure, even though on some points he differed profoundly with him. After returning to the United States, McKay literally adopted Johnson as his father confessor, and the two men carried on a regular correspondence and often managed to see each other whenever Johnson was in New York City. Since his retirement as the executive secretary of the NAACP, Johnson had divided his time between Fisk University in Nashville, New York City, and various vacation spots in the Northeast. On June 26, 1938, he met an untimely death when a train struck his automobile at a railroad crossing in Wiscasset, Maine. His death shocked and grieved McKay and deprived him of the most prestigious supporter he had in black America.[43]

Others whom McKay saw frequently in the 1930s included Countee Cullen, James Ivy, Arthur Schomburg, Harold Jackman and his sister, Ivie, and Earl Brown, the editor of the New York *Amsterdam News*. McKay also knew almost all of Harlem's young artists, including Bruce Nugent, Romare Bearden, and Jacob Lawrence. On the FWP, McKay was on friendly terms with Ted Poston, Henry Lee Moon, and Ellen Tarry, the young Catholic author, whose friends within the church would play a decisive role in McKay's later years.[44]

Two men who joined the New York FWP around 1937 but with whom McKay never became friendly were Richard Wright and Ralph Ellison. Differences in ideology, age, and personality kept McKay from seeking their companionship. Wright was a member of the Communist party, and Ellison was his close friend. They could not see that McKay, an aging "spiritual truant" from earlier decades, had much to teach them, and he scornfully dismissed the possibility that any of the Communist party's black minions on the FWP had any real talent.[45]

Ironically, McKay was much closer in spirit to young artists such as Bearden, Selma Burke, and Lawrence than he was to most of the apprentice writers of the 1930s. He was friendly with young Dorothy West and had contributed a poem to her magazine, *Challenge,* in 1936. But by the time *A Long Way from Home* was published, her quarterly had reappeared as the *New Challenge,* a decidedly Left-leaning literary journal that featured, among other things, Locke's bitter review of McKay's autobiography and Richard Wright's "Blue Print for Negro Writing," in which he discounted the achievements of the Negro Renaissance generation.[46]

Although McKay's autobiography had been widely reviewed when it came out in 1937, it sold poorly. Shortly after its appearance, Lee Furman went out of business as an independent publisher. *A Long Way from Home* received very little promotion and soon disappeared from view. For the third time in five years, McKay had failed to make money on a soundly written book that a decade earlier might have brought him a handsome return. He still had, however, his FWP job. His articles also brought him a little additional money. And with one book achieved since his return, he felt his chances for a Guggenheim were better than they had been in 1934. In the fall of 1937, he again applied to the Guggenheim Foundation for a grant to write a novel of Harlem life. To Edwin Embree, he explained that no one had written a Harlem novel since *Home to Harlem* had been published in 1928, and he wished to write one "dealing with its numerous movements and different moods." He added that he had "accumulated some interesting material," and a grant would enable him to leave New York in order to write the novel in better perspective. He would be glad, he said, to give up his job with the FWP. "[Its] effect upon me," he complained, "is utterly demoralizing, acting like a brake against spontaneous expression." But he hastened to add that "this is no reflection on [the] WPA as a whole, which I regard as a great work and vastly beneficial, but my being on it as a *writer* works like a damper on my thinking." McKay felt that it was "just possible" that he might get a Guggenheim with his second application, since "every creative writer of any significance" had been granted one, except him. He asked Embree to help him find a distinguished university professor who might recommend him. He knew none but understood academic recommendations carried great weight in deciding among candidates.[47]

Embree tried to help, but McKay again failed to win a Guggenheim. He had asked at least ten individuals, including James Weldon Johnson and Edwin Embree, for recommendations. The others were mostly journalists and writers who had favorably reviewed his books or whom he knew and admired. They included Edmund Wilson, Lewis Gannett, John R. Chamberlain, Charles S. Johnson, Horace Gregory, Joseph Wood Krutch, and Benjamin Brawley of Howard University. His chances may have been hurt by those less candid than Lewis Gannett, who frankly told McKay that he would include in his recommendation that *A Long Way from Home* had disappointed him but that he still believed McKay a good writer who could do better work.[48]

There had begun to grow among some critics, black and white, a settled conviction that McKay had, after all, never quite lived up to his potential, or at least what *they* judged to be his potential. As a result, the best McKay could do in 1937 was to get a small grant of two hundred dollars from the Authors' Club of the Carnegie Fund. He continued with the FWP, where through most of 1937 he helped compile a series of short portraits of "famous or notorious Negroes who have lived more or less in New York." After failing to secure a Guggenheim, McKay in 1938 abandoned, at least temporarily, his plans for a novel and decided to do a factual portrait of Harlem, using all the rich material he had found on his own and through the FWP Harlem project. With the aid of a literary agent, Carlisle Smith, he got a small advance from E. P. Dutton and Company and set to work with the diligence characteristic of him whenever money and a firm contract presented themselves. He remained busy throughout 1938 and 1939, checking in whenever necessary with the FWP, socializing with friends, researching and writing his new book, and contributing numerous articles to the *New Leader,* the *American Mercury, Common Sense, Opportunity,* and the *Amsterdam News.* From the end of April through May, 1939, McKay had a regular weekly column in the *Amsterdam News.* At the same time, the Reverend Adam Clayton Powell, Jr., and the youthful Roy Wilkins of the NAACP also had columns in the paper, often on the same page as McKay's. Appropriately, Powell called his column "The Soapbox"; Wilkins called his "The Watchtower"; and McKay titled his "Looking Forward."[49]

Finally, in October, 1940, *Harlem: Negro Metropolis* appeared. At first, all seemed to go well. But trouble soon developed. Despite its adoption by the Book-of-the-Month Club as an alternate selection, it was neither as widely nor as favorably reviewed as *A Long Way from Home.* The comparative silence that greeted it in New York newspapers and journals particularly disturbed McKay. As usual, he had no money. He had counted on *Harlem* being a financial success, because sometime late in 1938 or in 1939 (the exact date is not clear), he had finally left the Federal Writers' Project. Although still in existence in 1940, it had been drastically reduced in personnel. McKay had no chance for any more government relief. On November 10, 1940, he requested that Edwin Embree write Dutton "and if possible give [him] some points on circulation among colored people." McKay explained that *Harlem* had been out "almost a month" and only the New York *Herald Tribune* had reviewed it. He feared "a kind of passive resistance against the book by New York reviewers." He did not believe it was because his book was bad. If that were the case, he would have "already been belabored." He feared instead a conspiracy of silence because of the book's contents. "From private reports," he wrote, "the opposition to the book comes from my detailed account of labor and Communist activities in Harlem . . . the last seven years. I could not honestly write about Harlem without reporting such activities."[50]

In *Harlem: Negro Metropolis,* McKay repeated and elaborated upon all the arguments he had previously made for a stronger emphasis by black leaders on community development and less emphasis upon integration as a panacea for black woes. In the process, he created a portrait of a desperately poor, crime-ridden, and demoralized community whose population, for lack of adequate leadership, constantly improvised religious, economic, and labor solutions that fell far short of coping with the actual problems. And in his last chapter, he charged that the Communist party's disproportionate influence within Harlem over the last decade had only confused and misled many of the black intelligentsia into supporting the Soviet Union and its foreign policy instead of working single-mindedly on behalf of the Afro-American population.

The core of McKay's concern in *Harlem,* as it had been since his return from North Africa in 1934, was his belief that the Afro-American's real problem in the United States was one of group adjustment, not integration. The general elevation of their living standards would allow blacks to view themselves as just another minority among a nation of minorities instead of as a people unhappily "living under an eternal grievance."[51] In essence, McKay desired that all Afro-Americans find what he had sought for himself during his long exile abroad, namely, "the instinctive and animal and purely physical pride of a black person resolute in being himself and yet living a simple civilized life" like everyone else.[52] Blacks in America could only achieve such freedom, McKay believed, through intensive and sustained community self-improvement. Why, McKay asked, did black neighborhoods inevitably turn into disease-ridden slums? In such communities, McKay explained, there was a lamentable "lack of community commerce among the residents" that was peculiar to blacks in the United States. Why? McKay blamed the lack of a fully developed community infrastructure not only on white America's forced ghettoization of blacks but also on the Afro-American's response to his condition. In effect, he wrote, "Negroes realize that they are segregated and . . . hate their community. . . . Thus in Negro communities there is a tacit evasion of direct social responsibility that is peculiar to them." To counter this condition, McKay maintained,

> The idea of the constructive development of Negro communities commercially, politically and culturally, should be actively prosecuted, in spite of intellectual opposition. The Negro minority has been compelled of necessity to create its own preachers, teachers, doctors and lawyers. If these were proportionately complemented by police officers, sheriffs and judges, principals of schools, landlords and businessmen, etc., the Negro community, instead of remaining un-American, would take on the social

aspect of its white counterpart. Undoubtedly this would result in the easing of the tension of the race problem and Negroes would begin to regard themselves more as one other American minority.

As it was, McKay continued, the "overwhelming majority of blacks . . . see the world divided as white humanity against colored humanity." In such a world view, the responsibility for all black problems is simply shifted onto whites. "Most of their social difficulties," McKay observed, "the setbacks in the struggle for existence, even congenital handicaps, are attributed to white malevolence. A perusal of the Negro Press attests this. It is a dismal, negative lamentation of prejudicial discriminations of the white world against the colored." McKay maintained that the black common folk had a better intuitive understanding of their community needs than did the educated elite. "Even white-collar movements . . . were initiated by the common people," he charged. "Unlike the Negro intelligentsia ineffectually fretting its soul away over a symbolic gesture, the inarticulate Negro masses realize that they have special community rights." Not surprisingly, the strongest chapters in *Harlem: Negro Metropolis* were those in which McKay examined in detail the phenomenon of Father Divine and the grass-roots labor movements of Sufi Abdul Hamid and Ira Kemp. He also included chapters entitled "The Occultists," "The Cultists," "The Business of Numbers," "The Business of Amusements," and "Marcus Aurelius Garvey." He had shorter chapters on the Harlem businessman and the Harlem politician, as well as descriptions and comparisons of the West Indians and Spanish in Harlem.[53] By and large, however, as McKay explained to Mrs. Catherine Latimer of the Schomburg Library, "My book is mainly about the popular movements of Harlem and so there is not much space given to the academic and cultural features."[54]

*Harlem: Negro Metropolis* was argumentative and frank in its anti-Communist bias, as well as in its attack upon conventional Negro leadership. At the same time, it was perceptive, engaging, thoughtful, and novel in its argument. It was a good book, and one that in many ways took up where *A Long Way from Home* left off. It clearly revealed that McKay had done an enormous amount of firsthand investigations of everything from Father Divine and his "Heavens" to obscure occult parlors in seedy tenements. His intimate acquaintance with all classes and minorities within Harlem, his careful study of the labor movement there, even his inside glimpses into Communist affairs, all were evidence of how completely he had researched his topics.

For all his understanding, McKay again failed to win much support within the black intellectual community. His analysis of the inner paralysis of black America was perceptive and largely true, but he failed to appreciate fully how thoroughly the problem of segregation versus integration had already been debated within the black community and how truly difficult it had been for black Americans ever to function as members of a normal community given the hostility of an overwhelmingly powerful white majority. He might have qualified his criticisms more if he had spent a lifetime, instead of just two or three months, in the high-pressure incubator of southern race relations. Then he might have been more ready to concede how truly monumental was the task faced by black leadership, whose people were trapped simultaneously by extreme discrimination, abject poverty, and limited educational resources. They were enclosed within a vicious circle where at least three elements—discrimination, poverty, and ignorance—fed upon and nourished one another. In all probability, no people similarly situated would have had the energy to concentrate upon more than one element of their imprisonment at a time. Once a single element of the triad fell, however, the way would be open for the destruction of the other two. Concentration on one of the elements did not mean abandoning the fight against the others. McKay argued with Booker T. Washington that the main attack should be on community poverty; the NAACP school of thought had chosen to concentrate on discrimination.[55]

In one way, Claude differed radically from both the NAACP and Washingtonian self-help schools. In discussing the problems of black Americans, he believed, as he had long ago told W. E. B. Du Bois, in the "utter absence of restraint."[56] There were no secrets within the black community too embarrassing to be discussed; McKay did not hold to the etiquette of American race relations. He did not believe in indirection, circumlocutions, or empty rhetoric. In public discussions of black problems, he did not speak one way to blacks and another way to whites. Even in 1940, therefore, his frank discussion of black problems and obsessions left some, including librarian Catherine Latimer, "almost" embarrassed.[57] For instance, he admitted frankly that blacks in Harlem used huge amounts of Vaseline to help straighten their hair. And he talked frankly and truthfully about the problems interracial sex had caused among black Communists. Black male leaders tended to marry only white women, a situation fiercely resented by black women members of the party who did not see white Communist leaders rushing to marry them. In general, McKay wrote, blacks might argue for the right of racial intermar-

riage, but in fact they were as opposed to it as were whites.[58] McKay's
candor might have gone largely unnoticed in the 1980s. In 1940, it
was startling to many black readers.

*Harlem* contained in essence the core argument later presented by
Harold Cruse in his *Crisis of the Negro Intellectual,* minus Cruse's
distortions of history, anti-Semitism, personal rancor, petty spite,
extreme tediousness, and essential lack of humor. As McKay told
Edwin Embree, his book "was a labor of love written from a deep desire to project the measure and manners, the mood and aspiration of
the entire Community."[59]

Predictably, not all in the black community recognized it as such.
The journalist Ted Poston, whom McKay had counted as a friend on
the FWP, condemned his arguments in two reviews for the *New Republic* and the *New Leader.* He considered McKay's book a bitter indictment of Negro intellectual leadership. McKay, he maintained,
failed to prove that the Negro masses desired segregation, which he
accused McKay of favoring, whether voluntarily or enforced. He also
said that contrary to McKay's denials, the Sufi was anti-Semitic, and
Ira Kemp, the organizer of the indigenous Harlem Labor Union, was
a labor racketeer who extracted money from helpless merchants and
from his rank and file.[60]

Roi Ottley in the *New York Times Book Review* repeated more emphatically the same charges. He said McKay emphasized the bizarre
personalities of Harlem's popular leaders but provided a weak analysis of their movements. He advocated "a fierce racialism" and supported uncritically both the growth of black businesses and independent black unions in Harlem, neither of which could get far in the
new age of "corporate control." McKay, Ottley concluded, was simply
a sour "penitent from the radical movement," who had "become one
of Harlem's most captious critics, allowing the deep undercurrents of
Negro life and their broad social import to escape him." His chosen
subjects needed "serious treatment and analysis." In short, Ottley
concluded, "McKay did not approach his subject with the thorough-
ness that it deserves."[61]

McKay got some good reviews from black reviewers, but they were
not printed in important organs of opinion. For example, Zora Neale
Hurston wrote in *Common Ground* that McKay

> know[s] what he is talking about. He knows what is really happening
> among the folks. . . . What is more, he fixes a well-travelled eye on the
> situation and thus achieves proportion. . . .
>     The author has done an amazing thing. He has been absolutely frank.
> He had spoken out about those things Negroes utter only when they are

breast to breast, but by tradition are forbidden to break a breath about when white ears are present. The book is as frank and open as twelve o'clock noon. For that reason it will not find favor among the large class of Negroes who plump for window-dressing for whites. Yet it is valuable to both races.[62]

Others also praised *Harlem* in personal letters, which McKay would have rather seen in print. A. Philip Randolph, whom McKay had praised extensively in his book for his herculean efforts in organizing the Brotherhood of Sleeping Car Porters (he even sympathized with Randolph's recent efforts to lead the Communist-inspired National Negro Congress), wrote McKay a warm letter of endorsement. It arrived in April, 1941, seven months after his book appeared. Randolph informed McKay that he agreed with his analysis in all its essentials. "As I see it," Randolph wrote, "the Negroes have a fight to wage for themselves, of themselves and by themselves." He assured McKay that "your description of the Sufi movement and other currents in Negro Harlem is brilliant, penetrating and constructive." Even before *Harlem: Negro Metropolis* appeared, Randolph had written McKay to praise him for his criticisms of the National Negro Congress and other Communist-front activities. As far as Randolph was concerned, McKay was "doing a most necessary and vital work . . . in helping to clarify these questions of ideological importance to the Negro."[63]

Another friend, the socialist Benjamin Stolberg, thought McKay's book "an important revaluation of American Negro life in its relation both to America and contemporary history." He conceded that its effect on him had been profound. He had always thought "that there must be no 'segregation' of any kind. But you have persuaded me that the Negro had better not wait until Kingdom Come before he does anything for himself." Stolberg also predicted that McKay's latest effort would not sit well with the established leaders of opinion. "You may be sure," he wrote, "that the intelligentsia of both races will ignore or knife your book. Partly, they are still scared of the Communist Party issue, whose fashionableness is dying slowly, and partly you have committed the moral sin of seeing through the Briefcase Brigade. That the Sufi, for all his absurdities, was closer to the masses than the Urban Leaguers or Mr. Walter White or Carl Van Vechten— that hurts. To deny that ideological fashion plates are 'leaders'— whatdyamean?"[64]

Despite such praise, *Harlem: Negro Metropolis* soon sank from sight. With its failure, McKay lost his last chance to reestablish himself as a popular and financially successful creative writer. He had since 1929 waged a valiant but losing fight for success. Time and the last energies of youth were now running out for him. He had less than a decade to live, and during that increasingly lonely time, his career, his accomplishments, and even his name went into an eclipse from which they have not yet fully emerged.

Essentially, McKay was advocating in the 1930s the development of "black power," a general term that only gained wide currency in the late 1960s, after it became evident that the achievement of abstract legal victories in the area of civil rights would not by themselves materially improve the position of Negroes in the United States. By then both McKay and his ideas lay buried and well-nigh forgotten by the black communities he had wished to serve.[65]

As an opponent of communism, a critic of Negro middle-class leadership, and an uncompromising advocate of cultural pluralism, McKay found himself in the 1930s almost completely isolated from the main currents of American opinion. He nevertheless developed in this period a clear, lucid journalistic style, and in his articles, essays, and two books composed between 1934 and 1940, he achieved some of his best writing, in both style and content. The positions he took on the great public issues of the 1930s were always clear, disinterested, principled, and consistently moderate. Privately, of course, it was a different matter. He had no patience with his critics, and when personally attacked, he returned barb for barb, often with devastating accuracy. Such quarrels did little to advance McKay's position among black leaders. In fact, whether justified or not, his reputation as a temperamental iconoclast had become a trap from which he could not escape. Unfortunately, his image as an irascible personality obscured the essential moderation and the truth of his public positions through the 1930s.

Broadly speaking, McKay tried to maintain throughout the 1930s the independent, left-wing stance he had first adopted as a *Liberator* editor after World War I. In this regard his position resembled George Orwell's in England.[66] Unlike the younger Orwell, however, McKay's greatest days as a creative writer were largely behind him by 1940. The failure of *Harlem: Negro Metropolis* left him bitter and more isolated than ever. He had failed to win the critical acceptance he needed either to make the book a success or to revitalize his career. He consequently found himself at the age of fifty with no position, no money, and no prospects. He had eight more years to live.

# 12
# Right Turn to Catholicism, 1940–1948

*Now faith is the substance of things hoped for, the evidence
of things not seen.* —Hebrews 11:1

For almost four years after the publication of *Harlem: Negro Metrop-olis*, McKay remained in New York City. He continued to write an oc-casional article, and he tried also to publish at least one more book-length manuscript. In the years since 1937, he had tinkered off and on with another novel, which he called "Harlem Glory." Like much of McKay's fiction, "Harlem Glory" consisted largely of thinly disguised autobiography. It related the fortunes of one Buster South, a black *bon vivant* who, like McKay, returned to Harlem and the Great Depression after a long European expatriation. Upon Buster's re-turn, he became involved in two quite different movements that were agitating the common people of Harlem. One was led by a self-proclaimed god, who called himself Glory Savior, McKay's fictional prototype of Father Divine. The other was directed by a gaudily at-tired Moslem of Afro-American origin known as Omar. Omar repre-sented Sufi Abdul Hamid, whose boycott in the early 1930s even-tually forced Harlem merchants to hire black clerks. In "Harlem Glory," the fictional Omar formed an organization called the Yeomen of Labor and began a similar campaign.[1]

In essence, "Harlem Glory" covered in fictional form much the 347 same ground that McKay surveyed so thoroughly in *Harlem: Negro Metropolis*. For that reason, perhaps, all his efforts to find a publisher after 1940 came to nothing, and he apparently never finished the story. In general, it represented no improvement over his factual survey in *Harlem*, but like all his fiction it had its moments of power and genuine insight. McKay observed, for instance, that the black intelligentsia tended to consider Omar and Glory Savior simply theatrical and unrealistic in their efforts to lead the Harlem masses. But for McKay there were profound lessons to be learned in the unfolding of their dramas. "The two movements of Glory Soul [*sic*] and of Omar respectively were like a two-faced mirror reflecting the strange unfathomed mind of the colored minority. Expressed in those movements were all its hidden confused reactions, its hopes and fetish fears, its Uncle Tom traditions, its desires, appetites, aspirations, its latent strength and obvious weakness." And in the person of Buster South, McKay also gave expression to the loneliness, frustration, shame, and anger he had experienced upon returning to Harlem, broke, after so many years abroad. "Buster felt . . . that everybody and everything in Harlem were against him. It was as if there were a conspiracy against him. The old crowd [was] mocking him. He felt it in their attitude, even though they were not all . . . offensive. . . . 'I guess they resented me all the time . . . and now I am out of luck they have a chance to show it. We Negroes are a lot of crabs in a barrel, pulling down anyone what's trying to climb out.'"[2]

In "Harlem Glory," Buster even left Harlem for a while and went, as McKay had, to a camp for the destitute in upstate New York. Like McKay, he left no stone unturned in trying to find a place for himself in depression-ridden New York. Buster even joined the local Elks Club in his restless search for a new start in America. Like all his other novels, "Harlem Glory," though unfinished, recorded McKay's efforts to reconcile himself with his black kinsmen, while at the same time portraying them, with all their shrewdness and confusion, in vivid, sweeping colors.

Despite all his best efforts, McKay had failed to establish himself securely in Harlem, and on the eve of America's entry into World War II, he remained as essentially broke and adrift as he had been upon his return to the United States in 1934. On November 5, 1941, the black poet Arna Bontemps wrote to his friend Langston Hughes that he had recently "met McKay and took him to dinner." Bontemps explained that McKay had been "all charm—the gentle, wistful poet." He noted that this had deprived him of seeing McKay's more outspoken side, though "he did . . . blast Stalin." Bontemps also described McKay's apartment "at 33 West 125th Street on the top floor" above an old storefront. "He has what looks like a typical Greenwich Village artist's roost of the more musty variety. Across the hall young [Romare] Bearden has a studio. There is a genuine bohemian note up there—like the old days. Even the international note of the Latin Quarter is struck. Claude has a Japanese friend who hangs around— a gray-haired oriental who wears corduroy slacks and talks 'art' very fluently. The place is warmed by an oil heater that smokes a bit. Claude looks well-fed and reasonably well-clothed, but he says he is terribly broke."[3]

About the time he was meeting Arna Bontemps, McKay published in the *New Leader* an article about black popular opinion on World War II and America's approaching involvement in it. He expressed the strong ambivalence and irony with which all blacks viewed the war against Nazi racism and Japanese imperialism. McKay pointed out that although black soapbox orators on Harlem street corners had no love for Hitler, who thought even less of them than he did the Jews, they were not eager to defend the British Empire. Their main concern remained their own abysmal situation in the United States, where in the South the majority of blacks still lived under state regimes that subjected them to a racist oppression that seemed to differ little from Hitler's national subjugation of German Jews.[4]

In his letters, McKay continued to express his concern that the Soviet Union represented a greater threat to civilization than did Hitler's Germany, which he never considered had much chance for victory. The Soviet Union, he reiterated, masked a refurbished Oriental despotism in the guise of a modern workers' state that divided and confused progressive forces in the West in a way that Hitler could never do.[5]

McKay recognized the injustices suffered by Jews under Hitler, but he continued to believe, rightly or wrongly, that blacks should concentrate on their own problems and not deliver their support unreservedly to American Jews in their fight against nazism unless they could see benefits for themselves at home. He would have been more sympathetic to the Jews' plight in Europe if he had had any idea of the unimaginable slaughter that awaited them (and many others) in Hitler's extermination camps.[6]

Early in 1942, McKay applied again for a Rosenwald Fund grant, this time to do a study of West Indian immigrants in New York City. "My purpose," he explained, "is to write a book about them, which is to be entitled, 'The Tropics in New York.'" Natives of the Caribbean, he estimated, constituted about one-third of Harlem's population and numbered about 100,000. He wished to explain their "native backgrounds" and "the customs and activities of the various island groups" in order to understand better "their contributions to the social, political and religious life of Harlem, showing them in their churches and clubs and in business. Also their particular forms of amusement, marriage customs and distinctive style of cuisine." McKay also planned to give some attention to the small groups from various parts of Africa who had settled in Harlem and other parts of New York. They would, he emphasized, all be studied as individual groups "(instead of persons) in their relationship and associations with the native American group of Negroes."[7]

It was a sound plan, and McKay seemed uniquely qualified to write such a study. He asked for fifteen hundred dollars. His dossier included good recommendations from Judge James S. Watson of the New York Municipal Court and librarian Ernestine Rose of the Schomburg Collection. Both felt, as Watson put it, that McKay was "highly qualified" to do the study. Other strong recommendations came from John Dewey, Louis Adamic, and Eugene Lyons. Dewey's letter was typical. "From both personal acquaintance and a knowledge of his published writings, I have no hesitation in recommending Mr. McKay highly. . . . I should want . . . to emphasize his fairness and independence of judgment as well as his power of work, of gathering and organizing information, and his very definite ability in literary presentation."[8]

These five recommendations were significantly qualified by a querulous evaluation of McKay made by Arna Bontemps, who had met McKay only briefly the previous October in New York. Their only other contact had been earlier in the summer of 1941 when Bontemps had offered McKay ten dollars for permission to reprint seven of his poems in an anthology for Harper. McKay had protested that Harper was a rich firm and could surely pay at least five dollars for each poem.[9] This incident, perhaps, combined with McKay's reputation for contentiousness, gave Bontemps the excuses he needed to kill McKay's chances of securing a second Rosenwald fellowship. Bontemps, himself a recent recipient of such a grant, wrote in an informal, initialed evaluation that

> Claude is an exasperating individual: a) he is sour and cantankerous; b) he never seems to do the writing of which he is capable.
>
> I doubt that the fellowship will help him, but one must admit a) that he is a gifted writer, at his best, b) that his references are of the best, c) that he projects a fascinating book, and d) that his talents are perfectly suited for this work.

But Claude has recently done a poor job on his book, "Harlem," failed in a re-write job on "They Knew Lincoln," and I doubt that he's putting much heart in his work. I hope I'm wrong. Maybe a fellowship will revive him. God knows he needs the money.[10]

It was an opinionated and spiteful attack, and it had its intended effect. In a brief sheet summarizing the judges' opinions of McKay's candidacy were the following remarks: "too old[;] we've helped this man once[;] He is a good writer but we have no further call[;] Bontemps says he is good but a fellowship wouldn't help him now."[11]

It was a callous dismissal and a sad commentary on the Rosenwald selection process. His opponents never understood or appreciated the nature of McKay's cantankerousness. He attacked directly, never indirectly; publicly, never obliquely behind one's back. And there were limits to how far he would go in his attacks upon his enemies. When, for instance, Benjamin Mandel had written in September, 1939, apparently to suggest that if McKay volunteered to testify against the Communists before the Dies Committee in Washington, he would get free publicity for his latest book and speed his citizenship process, McKay replied that he had nothing to tell that he had not already printed. He added that he could never do as Mandel had suggested for personal gain. "I am sure," he wrote, "that the real America would not think I was contributing anything to good citizenship by being a son-of-a-bitch." The following spring, on April 13, 1940, McKay received his final U.S. citizenship certificate without testifying before any committee.[12]

The Rosenwald Fund evaluation sheet had listed McKay as a freelance writer "and porter."[13] With no fellowship aid forthcoming, his literary prospects looked dim. He desperately needed a good job, but before he could find one, early in 1942, his health finally collapsed. Influenza, high blood pressure, heart disease, and poverty all threatened to kill him. Although he still had friends, black and white, he had grown weary of seeking their help, and he was too sick to look for work or other aid. Ellen Tarry, the young writer with whom he had worked on the FWP and the Negro Authors' Guild, found him extremely ill and alone in a wretched Harlem basement apartment.

Tarry happened to be a Catholic, and she sought for Claude the assistance of the young men and women at Friendship House, a Catholic lay organization on 135th Street in Harlem. They saw to it that he received medical aid and nursed him back onto his feet through the spring of 1942. McKay was grateful for the help, and he was especially impressed that they had extended their assistance without asking him to accept their religion.[14]

By 1942, McKay had grown disillusioned with what he liked to call all the modern "isms"—communism, socialism, liberalism, and conservatism. All political ideologies, it seemed to him, with their high-minded rhetoric, masked selfish, opportunistic motives. A romantic rebel from an early age, he had responded intuitively to those movements that seemed to promise a better, freer life for mankind. All had disappointed him. At the outbreak of World War I, the European agnostics and rationalists whom he had idolized in Jamaica all suddenly became rabid nationalists. And after the death of Lenin, it had become evident to him that a monstrous and overbearing dictatorship in the name of the proletariat—ruthless, efficient, and aggressively tyrannical—had imposed itself upon the Russian population in place of the decayed czarist regime that had been swept away during World War I.

Later, in Spain and in Morocco, he saw for the first time peoples whose religions still permeated deeply the fabric of their everyday lives. He had been impressed in Spain, above all, with the unassuming dignity Spaniards seemed to accord every man without regard to his station in life. In Spain and Morocco, he had felt strongly for the first time the need to become a part of a community of believers. While in England in 1920, George Bernard Shaw had lectured him upon the spiritual grandeur and beauty of Europe's cathedrals, and he had ever since made a point of visiting them during his travels. And even earlier, Frank Harris had preached to him the significance of Jesus' example. But only in Spain had he felt for the first time the full significance of Catholicism as a way of life and bedrock for an entire civilization.[15]

Finally, after failing miserably to find any secure place for himself with the American Negro community, McKay was more than ready for the helping hand extended to him by the young Catholic idealists of Friendship House. If he could find no refuge in the human community, he soon determined to seek it within the community of God.

Friendship House had been founded in Harlem in 1938 by Catherine de Hueck, a white Russian emigrée whose family had suffered severely during the Russian Revolution. After World War I, she lived first in Great Britain and then, from the early 1920s onward, in the United States and Canada. In Toronto in the early 1930s, she established in one of its poorest neighborhoods her first Friendship House. It provided a variety of "study Clubs and recreational facilities" for the youth in the vicinity. After she proved herself there, the church invited her to establish another Friendship House in Ottawa. And in 1938, "three eminent priests" in New York City, alarmed by "the ever-growing influence of Communism" in Harlem, invited her to establish there her first interracial Friendship House. As one who had herself endured considerable poverty and suffering, "the Baroness," as her devoted followers called her, believed that lay "Catholic Action" was absolutely necessary to counter the insidious spread of atheistic communism. She defined her "Catholic Action" movement as one with many aspects, "but all converge on one goal—to lead souls to God." And she explained, "It can do this by getting to the rock bottom of our ills, which are fundamentally neither political nor economic, but ethical and moral, by checking the greed and selfishness which are at the root of the trouble, and by establishing a society really based on Christian principles." She endorsed cooperative "back-to-the-land movements, . . . credit unions . . . family life . . . youth [and] labor [action] . . . and marriage." Above all, Catholics must seize the lead in alleviating human misery. For at the base of Catherine de Hueck's activism was a determined anticommunism. Communism meant militant atheism, and "no matter what form of Catholic Action is undertaken combatting atheism on all its main points must be included in the program." Before founding her first Friendship House, de Hueck had been asked by Archbishop Neil McNeil of Toronto "to . . . make a survey of the Communists' propaganda in Toronto and New York, whence Toronto took orders." As a consequence, "for a year, she lived with the Communists of Toronto, participating in all their activities as an observer, and often traveling to the U.S.A. to check some information or development." After submitting her report, she decided to launch on her own a Catholic Action movement and founded in Toronto the first Friendship House. She began it without official church funding, as an act of faith and Christian zeal, certain that financing would "come by praying and begging for it. Have not many movements in the Church started on Faith and prayer in past centuries! Why not ours?" Claude McKay could relate to such a movement.[16]

As soon as he was able, he began to visit Friendship House regularly. He particularly enjoyed the young people there, and he took seriously the Baroness' insistence that mankind's basic spirituality should not be allowed to succumb to either dialectical materialism or the rampant greed that lay at the heart of Western capitalism. As far as McKay was concerned, Protestantism had long ago sold its soul to Mammon. In a world beset by raging wars and empty rhetoric, the Roman Catholic church still stood as a bulwark against all the aggressive forces at loose in the world, forces that everywhere threatened "man's divinity" and the supreme "mystery" at the heart of human existence.[17]

All McKay's attempts at political and social moderation in the

1930s had only resulted in conflict, confusion, and further isolation. He had not found the community he sought in the world. By 1942, he began to wonder if he had not all along been seeking it in the wrong places.[18]

McKay never recovered from the illness that he first experienced in such acute form in 1942. His heart was irreparably diseased and the high blood pressure that had afflicted him for so long only complicated his problems. As in the past, he often suffered severe headaches and dizziness, now complicated by shortness of breath and extreme fatigue.[19]

Still, he had to make a living, and in the summer of 1942 he decided he should try to get a job with Elmer Davis' Office of War Information, a governmental agency devoted to explaining America's war efforts to the world. As he explained to Max Eastman in July, he was especially qualified to write and report upon North Africa and the Caribbean, and his wide travels would be a benefit on any project he might undertake. Eastman agreed that McKay was well qualified for such a job, but he took the occasion to point out to McKay that the "only reason" he did not have a responsible position already was that "you don't like people well enough to handle them and get along with them skillfully, as any kind of administrator must." Eastman went on to add that anyone could see that that was his basic problem.[20]

McKay disagreed and scolded Eastman, as he said, for lecturing "me like an old country parson preaching against liquor, while holding a flask on his hip. You should be aware that the chief reason why I have not had a job equal to my intellectual attainments is simply because I have no close academic associates nor college degree, and also I am a Negro. My racial group is even more than the white, narrow and hidebound about college qualifications. I know many persons in it who are not very capable, but have had good jobs because they were graduates of Harvard and Yale and Columbia. . . . I feel bitter, because your statement proves that after 23 years, you know very little about me; your impression is wrong."*

Eastman was surely right about McKay's basic impatience with people. Nonetheless, he apologized for criticizing him, and he sent Claude a strong letter of recommendation. "I knew that I had a disposition to give you semi-parental advice," Max confessed, "but it had not got through my head that it was distasteful to you. I will never do it again."[21]

*Claude McKay to Max Eastman, August 13, 1942, © 1987 by Hope McKay Virtue, 1110 Olive Avenue, Long Beach, Calif. 90813, and used by her permission. This letter is in the Max Eastman Papers (private possession).

For the next two months, McKay concentrated on getting the position he wanted with the Office of War Information. He was still sick much of the time and always broke. Friends gave him money from time to time, and he took an occasional temporary job. But he turned down a publisher's offer of a sizable advance for a book outline. To Harold Jackman's sister Ivie, a consistent friend during the 1940s, McKay explained, "I haven't been able to concentrate on a plot. It's quite impossible when one's mind is distracted. People can't realize the state of one's mind under such conditions, and the few I meet make me angry by telling me how happy I look. I suppose because I don't go around with a doleful face." He continued to see close friends, such as Ivie and Harold Jackman and Countee Cullen and his wife Ida. Besides enjoying their companionship, he depended upon them for loans and, above all, for solid letters of recommendation. Early in September, he reminded Ivie that "I sent your name as a sponsor on one of my applications and so if you are approached, please ballyhoo for me."[22]

His persistence paid off. On September 23, 1942, McKay was informed he had a job with the Office of War Information in New York City. He was relieved and happy. But he warned Ivie not to mention it to the others, "for I have only a temporary trial for a month," and he still had to be investigated by the FBI. Others like himself, he wrote, had been "fired after investigation." At first, everything seemed to go well, but suddenly, on February 16, 1943, he informed Ivie in another note that he had missed a theater engagement with her and other friends because "I had just lost my job and felt extremely down—no good for gay society." He had worked a little over three months, mostly (to judge from the available evidence) on radio scripts about American military actions and commanders in North Africa.[23]

McKay never explained just why he was fired, but he indicated that his superiors were constantly intriguing to hire their friends. He may well have been bumped to make way for someone's current favorite. Whatever the reason, it meant that he had to start another nerve-racking job search. In May he was still looking, while handicapped by a persistent cold. To Ivie Jackman he wrote on May 11, 1943, that his illness made him "a very miserable person, especially as I cannot stay in bed as I have so many things to attend to. So I am in the position of begging all my friends for help again. You remember I predicted it. One gratifying fact in the situation is that the Federal authorities have been busily investigating and Houseman and de Groot (the two responsible for getting me out) have been kicked out!" McKay tried hard to get another government position, "for which," he explained to Countee Cullen, "I am qualified and feel I could be honest to myself in doing." [24]

Another writing position never materialized, however, and in early June, McKay accepted a job as a riveter at the federal shipyard in Port Newark, across the river from New York City. For some reason, no physical examination was required, even though the work was laborious and the hours long. In no way was he physically able to bear the strain the job imposed on him, but he tried to make the best of it. He was tired of begging. [25] In mid-June he wrote to Mary Keating, one of his Catholic friends from Friendship House, and explained the situation.

> At present I am working in a war plant, long hours and monotonous and uncongenial work, but the pay is very good and I can purchase the necessary material things which I need. So I don't do any writing but I have wonderful stuff working in my head. And they'll blaze a trail when I finally get to writing and publishing them. However my health isn't the best. I never did quite get over that pleurisy following the influenza attack last year and I suffer from shortness of breath. This is not so helpful, for the work I do is strenuous."[*]

Friends had warned him against taking the position; their forebodings proved all too accurate. On June 25, 1943, he suffered a disabling stroke while on the job in Port Newark. Shortly afterward, a Harlem friend, Miss Vereda Pearson, a staff musician at the Harlem Recreation Center, described Claude's condition in a letter to Mary Keating. He had been "knocked off his feet on the job and the next day was partially blind." The stroke had affected the left side of his face. It also affected his gait when he walked. He was soon back on his feet, but Miss Pearson stressed that his physical appearance was deceiving. He looked fairly good. "But," Pearson wrote, "I want to impress on you the fact that Claude is really very ill. . . . Now if you notice carefully, you see that he does not walk normally, the left side of his face is dead, he can savor food only on the right side of his mouth and his eyes dance, so that he cannot read the newspaper." He did not immediately notify his closest black friends of his condition. To Countee Cullen, he later explained that he had not wanted to scare them. Freda Kirchwey and Max Eastman were soon told of McKay's condition, and they both helped. Kirchwey wired Edwin Embree of the Rosenwald Fund, who generously responded with two hundred

*Claude McKay to Mary Keating, June 14, 1943, © 1987 by Hope McKay Virtue, 1110 Olive Avenue, Long Beach, Calif. 90813, and used by her permission. This letter is in the Tom and Mary Keating Papers (private possession).

dollars to aid Claude during his recuperation. Eastman gave another fifty, and Mary and her husband, Tom Keating, offered McKay the use of their country cottage near New Milford, Connecticut, for the rest of the summer, or as soon as his doctors felt he could safely leave their care in New York City.[26]

At the end of July, McKay was allowed to leave for New Milford, and he stayed at the Keatings' place until the end of October. To Tom Keating, he confessed that the stroke had frightened him. "But," he added, "I couldn't blame the thing on Commies or anybody, it was God himself!"[27]

Even before his stroke, McKay had written to Mary Keating that "I wouldn't mind doing some work for the Roman Catholic setup. I have no sympathy with the Radicals, I feel estranged even from the Left Liberals, because they give me a sense of frustration and confusion. And as I think I wrote to you last year and said to the Baroness and as I have said to many people, I believe that the Catholic Church has a tremendously important role to play in the ending of this war and the reorganization of the world." In the same letter, written ten days before his stroke, McKay indicated that he might join the Catholic church and stated quite clearly what his reasons would be for taking such a step.

> I am quite aware that my act would be of more social than of religious meaning, if you can differentiate between both. I know for example, that the Communists are fighting me, that their influence is considerable among the colored intellectuals and that they go to great lengths to keep me out of their councils. Not that the colored intellectuals are against me! But they feel they cannot offend any powerful group of *whites* who claim to be friends of colored people! And so I would like to have the means and the weapons to fight back. While I was working for the government, and had to be investigated by the F.B.I. and the Civil Service Commission, I discovered that the Commies and their fellow travelers had done much to smear my character. In spite of that my reputation check was good. But it is not merely from personal but more from the broader social aspect that I feel I must fight the Communists. If I were drawn to the Church it would be as T. S. Eliot, who became an Anglo-Catholic from purely intellectual and social reasons.[28]

McKay, of course, never did anything for "purely intellectual and social reasons," and his conversion to Catholicism was not as calculating and deliberate as this passage might suggest. It reflected, nevertheless, the objective conditions, as he saw them, that impelled him toward the church.

Tom and Mary Keating had moved to Chicago since Claude had

first met them at Friendship House in the winter of 1942. And after his stroke, Vereda Pearson wrote Mary Keating urging her to do all she could to help Claude obtain the kind of responsible and intellectually challenging position he deserved. She added that "I know that Claude has a much larger following than he imagines—especially among his own people."[29]

In Chicago, the Keatings were associated with Bishop Bernard J. Sheil. His social activism and work among the youth of Chicago had made him well known among social reformers. The Keatings participated in many programs at his Catholic Youth Center, which Bishop Sheil had nourished into a thriving center of Catholic social, educational, and religious activities. They also worked with the Friendship House that Catherine de Hueck had recently established in Chicago.[30]

Pearson's letter led Mary Keating to speak to Bishop Sheil about Claude, who in August, 1943, while in Connecticut, indicated to her that he wanted to work in Chicago. At the end of October, he left Connecticut and returned to New York City, where he continued his correspondence with the Keatings. By then, he had already decided to join the church. He wanted first, however, to secure a job in Chicago. From Connecticut, he had sent Mary Keating biographical information to pass on to Bishop Sheil, but months dragged by before any definite word came from Chicago. [31]

In the interval, McKay battled to regain his health and fought off boredom by continuing a long cycle of sonnets he had begun to write while in Connecticut. They were much different from his previous poetry, less lyrical and more like satiric prose summaries of all the controversies he had had during the last decade. To Mary, he explained that he was glad to be writing them because "when I become a Catholic I'll bring along something and critics won't be able to say that I was finished when I joined."[32]

His "Cycle Manuscript" contained few really good poems, but they do provide a detailed summary of the disillusionment, bitterness, and ironic cynicism he felt toward Communists, liberals, black intellectuals, and the nation's myopic approach to black America. The first poem of the cycle well expressed his intent and may be the best, in strictly artistic terms, of the entire group.[33]

> These poems distilled from my experience,
> Exactly tell my feelings of today,
> The cruel and the vicious and the tense
> Conditions which have hedged my bitter way
> Of life. But though I suffered much I bore

My cross and lived to put my trouble in song
I stripped down harshly to the naked core
Of hatred based on the essential wrong!

But tomorrow, I may sing another tune,
No critic, white or black, can tie me down,
Maybe a fantasy of a fairy moon,
Or the thorns the soldiers weaved for Jesus' crown,
For I, a poet, can soar with unclipped wings,
From earth to heaven, while chanting of all things.*

After returning to New York from Connecticut in November, 1943, McKay spent the remainder of the year in and out of the hospital. Once again, friends contributed money for his support. On November 16, Freda Kirchwey wrote Edwin Embree to ask if he knew of any organization that might help McKay. Claude's prospects for recovery, she explained, were not good. "Max Eastman tells me that he will almost certainly not be able to work again. Both his heart and kidneys are affected and his blood pressure is very high. While the doctor believes he may survive for a good while, he seems to have little hope for actual recovery. This is all terribly sad and the situation is made worse by the fact that Claude has absolutely no source of income."[34]

When not in the hospital, McKay stayed at the 135th Street YMCA in Harlem and waited impatiently for word of a job in Chicago. For him, it was a "lonely . . . transitional period"; he missed the bright young Catholics he had met in 1942 and yearned "to talk to somebody" intelligent who had already gone through a religious conversion experience. To Mary Keating he wrote, "If I had had some friend like that, I'd have been a Catholic long ago."[35]

Finally, in early April, Bishop Sheil offered McKay a job as an advisor on Russian and Negro affairs. With much relief, McKay accepted it. By the middle of April, he was ready to leave for Chicago. To Mary Keating he wrote, "Now I am looking forward to seeing you and Tom and I hope it will be a happy meeting. New York has been so heaped upon me like a pyramid, I am happy to get away and from under." He was excited about the trip. "It is something," he wrote Keating, "I have wanted to do for a long time." Yet, it *was* "a leap of faith," and McKay had his fears. He well knew that with the world in upheaval few things remained certain. As he expressed it to Keating,

*Claude McKay, initial sonnet in the "Cycle Manuscript," © 1987 by Hope McKay Virtue, 1110 Olive Avenue, Long Beach, Calif. 90813, and used by her permission. The poems are in the Claude McKay Papers, James Weldon Johnson Collection of Negro Literature and Art, American Literature Collection, at the Beinecke Rare Book and Manuscript Library, Yale University.

"Everything in the world is changing so rapidly and ideas [are] so fluid that one can hardly hold on to them. And one doesn't know how much people are really interested in fixed principles today, because even those are being uprooted." Whatever his doubts and reservations, Claude had committed himself and there was no turning back. On April 15, 1944, he left for Chicago and a new life within the Roman Catholic church.[36]

Once in Chicago, McKay did not immediately enter the church, though he did begin to take instruction and to consult with a number of priests. In addition, he wrote Max Eastman several letters in which he revealed his spiritual travails, doubts, and hesitations. On June 1, 1944, he informed Eastman that he was "settling down" to his work, "doing a lot of reading and research, especially on Catholic work among Negroes, and I am also researching myself to discover how I can be a Catholic. Because if and when I take the step I want to be intellectually honest and sincere about it. From the social angle I am quite clear and determined. I know the Catholic Church is the one great organization which can check the Communists and probably lick them. But there is also the religious angle." McKay went on to call Eastman's attention to one other person close to the *Liberator* in the 1920s who had become a Catholic activist. She was Dorothy Day, editor of the socialist-pacifist *Catholic Worker*.[37]

Max would have none of it. Both his parents had been ministers. He remained a firm nonbeliever and considered the Catholic church a form of religious totalitarianism hardly distinguishable in its essence from the Bolshevik brand. He pleaded with McKay to stand fast in his agnosticism. "All these years, at such cost and with such heroism, you resisted the temptation to warp your mind and morals in order to join the Stalin church. Why warp it the other way now for the Catholics? Why not die firm, free and intelligent as you have lived? To see you go the way of Heywood Broun—so sick a finish, disproving, so far as you can, everything you've stood for—*handing the Stalinists just what they want*. Can nobody stand fast for the truth?"[38]

McKay loved Max, but he would not be deterred. There is a mystery to life, he reminded him, that grew the more one learned of life. Everyone felt it, and the common people, above all, accepted the reality of it and believed in God. McKay protested that he had always had, at bottom, a religious impulse, and it had grown stronger in Europe and Morocco. "By becoming a Catholic," he wrote, "I would merely be giving Religion the proper place it had in my nature and in man's nature. The Communists solve this problem by making a religion of Communism, or by becoming hypocrites."[39]

Later in the summer, McKay returned to the subject. He admitted that had he remained in Morocco he would have become a Moslem, or if he had resided in India or Japan he would have accepted other religions. But he was a child of the West, and he would become a Catholic as "an act of faith." As far as he was concerned, there was simply nowhere else to go. "I no longer think it is smart or enlightened to be a rationalist or an agnostic. I don't believe in Communism or National Socialism or Democracy as a solution to man's problems here on earth. The Catholic Church does not pretend to have any solution either, but it does provide an outlet for my mystical feelings and I do believe in the mystery of the symbol of the Mystical Body of Jesus Christ, through which all of humanity may be united in brotherly love." [40]

Two months later, McKay solemnly announced to Eastman that "on October 11, The Feast of the Maternity of the Blessed Virgin Mary, I was baptised into the Catholic (Roman) Faith." Ironically, in the same letter he raised again all his old intellectual doubts and hesitations and concluded that "'truth and mental integrity'" were simply "relative human things." Perhaps, he said, even the Marxists were right in concluding that "every human thought, emotion and action is determined by dialectical materialism." As for himself, he wrote, "I prefer the Catholic Church and its symbolic interpretation of the reality of Christ Crucified." For him, he confessed, it was "a new experience and, I suppose, the final stage of my hectic life. I am not the less a fighter." [41]

While taking his final steps toward church membership, McKay had also been integrating himself into the working life of the Catholic Youth Organization and the Sheil School, its education arm. Early in June, however, he had first to be admitted to a hospital for two weeks. While there, doctors discovered he had a greatly enlarged heart. It was, McKay wrote to Ivie Jackman, "as big as a balloon." [42] He congratulated her on hospitalizing a sick relative. "Christ knows, I am always glad to go into a hospital, where I can be taken care of," he added. McKay responded satisfactorily to his treatment and in July began to teach a night course on Negro literature at the Sheil School. When he came to the modern period and the Negro Renaissance, he started with Carl Van Vechten and "finished up with Richard Wright." McKay tried hard to minimize Wright's importance, but he could hardly avoid *Native Son*, Wright's hair-raising novel of the completely alienated and dehumanized black slum killer in Chicago named Bigger Thomas. "I pointed out," he explained to Ivie Jackman, "that Wright was an excellent writer of horror stories of the Edgar Allan Poe or King Kong order, but the white critics were practically destroying him when they tried to hoist him up as a Negro leader and say that Bigger Thomas was a symbol of the Negro race." He felt that Bigger was no more a symbol of the race than "the Negro characters created by Thomas Dixon . . . in the *Clansman* or the *Leopard's Spots*." [43]

It was ironic and sad that McKay, whose critics had compared him to Thomas Dixon after *Home to Harlem* and *Banjo,* should now link Wright's creation to the same white racist novelist of earlier decades. But he could not forgive Wright his association with the Communist party. In the fall, he had occasion to speak on trends in Negro litera- ture before a black church group in Chicago and was asked his opin- ion of *Native Son.* McKay conceded that Wright "was a very powerful writer," but again like his own critics in the 1920s, he argued that he "did not think [Wright's] book would help any a people struggling for- ward for a better life." Much to his surprise, his audience applauded his remarks. Wright was popular in Chicago, and McKay had ex- pected a different reaction. [44]

Wright's subject matter and approach in *Native Son* were alien to McKay, who had always presented lower-class blacks in a positive light as exemplars of health and vitality. If he had not remembered Wright's role as a Communist spokesman on the FWP, however, he would almost certainly have been less critical of him. As it was, old memories were stronger than critical sympathies. To Ivie Jackman he wrote:

> Did I tell you that I met [Wright] near the "Y" just before I left for Chicago and he wanted me to "have a bowl of soup" as he put it, but I declined. All I remember about him was that he was very rude, when he was an active Communist. You know, we were together on the Federal Writers Project and . . . he knew from which side his bread was buttered. I remember when Dorothy West was in a dither about changing her magazine and in- vited myself, Moon, Richard Wright and others down to her place. . . . Moon and I could scarcely get in a word for Richard Wright, according to the Communist formula was always talking. So the Communists got the magazine [*New Challenge*], as you may remember, and after publishing one number, killed it. For, of course, they couldn't make a Communist out of Dorothy.*

McKay's first year in Chicago was his happiest. In the fall, he lec- tured on Negro culture at the Sheil School and accepted numerous

---

*Claude McKay to Ivie Jackman, September 12, 1944, © 1987 by Hope McKay Vir- tue, 1110 Olive Avenue, Long Beach, Calif. 90813, and used by her permission. This letter is in the Ivie Jackman–Harold Jackman Papers at Trevor-Arnett Library, Atlanta University.

invitations to speak in Chicago and elsewhere in the Midwest. West Indians were not as common there as in the New York area, and audiences were charmed by McKay's Jamaican accent and gentle manners. He made a new set of friends at the Sheil School and at the CYO and the Chicago Friendship House. He also talked at length with Bishop Sheil about Russian communism, American race relations, and world affairs, and regularly prepared for him summaries of current articles in the popular press on radical politics, world affairs, and Negro problems.[45]

Some things did not change. He was, for example, still overly dependent upon friends for some of his most elemental needs. When he departed New York, he left his overcoat with the desk clerk at the Harlem "Y" and throughout the fall of 1944 he pestered Ivie Jackman to pick it up and mail it to him. Finally, on December 20, he wrote to her a frantic two-line note: "Have you heard nothing about my overcoat? I am freezing to death!" And in Chicago, he quickly became friends with a young Friendship House woman, Betty Britton, whom he called upon for countless errands and favors.[46]

In early December, 1944, he spoke at Marquette University in Milwaukee, and at the end of the month, he journeyed to Easton, Pennsylvania, for a retreat on Dorothy Day's nearby farm. From there he went to Morgantown to lecture at West Virginia University and then spent a few days in New York City before returning to Chicago. It was all too much. By the spring of 1945, he was ill again and had to spend a month in bed.[47]

For the rest of his life he was never long out of the hospital. He spent about half the summer of 1945 either in the hospital or recuperating at Catholic retreats such as St. Meinrad's Abbey in St. Meinrad, Indiana, near the Kentucky border. On August 30, he commented in a letter to Ivie Jackman that "I hardly ever see anybody of the Negro group, I am so buried among the Catholics." He worked at the CYO through the remainder of 1945 but he was so ill in the winter and spring of 1946 that it was decided he should leave for a warmer climate. In May, 1946, he left for Albuquerque, New Mexico, where he stayed until the fall. Like his mother before him, McKay now suffered severely from dropsy, a condition arising as a consequence of his heart disease and high blood pressure. It was characterized by excessive retention of body fluids around the heart, and it caused his abdomen to swell abnormally and to pressure his heart and other vital organs. Periodically his doctors would drain off the excess fluid, but it always returned. They could do nothing to alleviate the underlying causes. In August, 1946, he wrote Max Eastman that "the doctor thought I would be dead by now, but I am still alive."[48]

He was not only alive but busily at work on a new manuscript. He had never ceased trying to get the new poems of his "Cycle Manuscript" published, and since joining the church he had also written several new poems for Dorothy Day's *Catholic Worker*.[49] Once in Albuquerque, he completed a short memoir of his Jamaican childhood. It was his last sustained piece of work. He called it *My Green Hills of Jamaica,* and in it he returned one last time to the quiet, pastoral Eden of childhood memories.

The project had been suggested to him by Cedric Dover, an Anglo-Indian author and admirer in London. McKay had met Dover in the late 1930s in New York, and after the war they had begun corresponding. Dover had grown up in colonial India, and he and McKay so enjoyed sharing their memories of British colonial childhood that Dover eventually urged McKay to collaborate with him on a book. Each would simply write a memoir of his separate experiences in Jamaica and India and then would publish them together in one volume to be entitled "East Indian–West Indian."[50] In Albuquerque, McKay set to work and soon finished his memoir. To Max Eastman, he explained, "My new book is about my childhood in Jamaica which is a source of rich and inexhaustible material. I have such a rich field to write about that I don't have to mess myself up about contemporary personalities and events. I have had a hard time but I have also had some superb moments and in spite of my chronic illness I don't want to go sour on humanity, even after living in this awful land of the U.S.A. I still like to think of people with wonder and love as I did as a boy in Jamaica and the Catholic Church with its discipline and traditions and understanding of human nature is helping me a lot."[51] After McKay finished the text, a publisher suggested that he add a chapter to bring the reader up to date on his life.

What resulted was a long justification by McKay of his conversion to Catholicism. It never became a part of *My Green Hills*. Except for a short excerpt edited and published as an article by Cedric Dover after McKay's death, *My Green Hills* remained unpublished until 1981. The additional chapter, entitled "Right Turn to Catholicism," was really an elaboration of a prior statement by McKay, "On Becoming a Roman Catholic," which had appeared in the Catholic *Epistle* in the spring of 1945. It was not in any way an organic part of *My Green Hills,* but the two, when read together, nevertheless suggest that the seed of McKay's "right turn to Catholicism" lay in his troubled relationship with his father.[52]

In one episode of *My Green Hills,* the young Claude had acquired from an older brother, who was then teaching at a distant Catholic school, a colorful picture of some aspect of church life—perhaps it was a portrait of a saint or the Virgin Mary. At any rate, he liked its rich colors and put the picture on his bedroom wall, all the while quite unaware of its religious significance. When his father, the fiercely proper Baptist deacon, saw the picture, he ripped it off the wall and gave the bewildered youth a stern lecture on the evils of Catholic idolatry. Almost fifty years later, in "Right Turn to Catholicism," McKay made a point of declaring that all the evils of the modern world had their origins in the Protestant Reformation. "Agnosticism, Atheism, Modernism, Capitalism, State Socialism and State Communism were all children of the Pandora Box of Protestantism."[53] To some degree, at least, McKay's conversion to Catholicism can be considered a last act of rebellion against his sternly self-righteous father.

During his last year, McKay also collected his "Selected Poems," but he could not find a publisher for them. In searching for a suitable person to write an introduction to his poems, he did not choose either a Catholic or an American black. He chose instead the great philosopher of American pragmatism, John Dewey. Claude never considered a Catholic for the job and he adamantly declared that he wanted no American black to touch his poetry because none was "fit." Dewey, he knew, was an honorable man who would do him justice as a poet. To his literary agent, Carl Cowl, he wrote, "The last time I Saw Dr. Dewey was at a dinner for [Angelica] Balabanov and he and I and Carlo Tresca drank a bottle of wine together. And we talked about Trotsky who was in Mexico then."[54]

McKay stayed in Albuquerque until September, 1946. From there he traveled to San Diego, where at CYO expense he passed the winter and received almost constant medical care. In July, 1947, after months of treatment had succeeded in stabilizing (though not curing) his condition, he returned to Chicago to resume work with Bishop Sheil's CYO.[55]

His last year there was fraught with anxiety and ill health. He wanted desperately to find a publisher for *My Green Hills* and for his "Selected Poems," but Carl Cowl, his agent in New York, despite heroic efforts, could not find him a publisher. McKay blamed his old enemies, and he even grew suspicious that he had new ones within the Catholic church. To Cowl, he wrote, "You must understand that there is much opposition to my getting published! From Communists, . . . from literary cut-throats who were in high places in the New Deal . . . Negro leaders of the NAACP . . . the Urban League and . . . even certain groups of Catholics." Certain people within the

CYO, he declared in all sincerity, were even opening his mail, and he urged Cowl to be sure and seal all his letters. McKay had long been convinced that behind-the-scenes Communist influence had been used to wreck his chances for success in the 1930s, and he came to distrust those black and white liberals whom he considered soft on communism almost as much as he distrusted the Communists themselves. His distrust at times seemed to verge on paranoia.[56]

McKay had never been able to exist anywhere for long without making enemies, and as time passed he frankly expressed his dislike of certain individuals on the CYO and Friendship House staffs in Chicago. Although he hated gossip and personal spite, his outspokenness invited both, and when they came, his suspicion and distrust of those around him increased. He never lost the respect and trust of Bishop Sheil and most of those on the CYO staff, but he believed that in their eyes his prestige had slipped, at least in part because of his publishing difficulties. He felt he had become a burden, and when his doctor in the fall of 1947 suggested that he should leave again for a warmer climate, he rejected the notion. He could not ask the CYO to foot his bills another year. And so he stayed on in Chicago and worked as best he could.[57]

McKay's personality was so difficult a mixture of gentleness and impatience, of empathy and alienation, of sweetness and anger, that even his closest friends within the Catholic community soon recognized he caused problems for himself and others. His friend Mary Keating summed him up best, perhaps, when she wrote

Claude came to Friendship House and my first impression was that he was a shy amiable man. (He really wasn't. He was formidable in his opinions [and] incredibly cutting with people whose mind he did not respect. He was intellectual, opinionated and enormously blunt in an argument.) For some reason, Claude and I always got along . . . we never quarreled. We were never unkind to each other. I don't know why, either. He quarreled with most of his friends. I think he was a driven, unhappy genius, not at home in his times, nor in the world, and I sensed this, I guess.[58]

McKay felt no more at home in the postwar world than he had earlier in the 1930s and 1940s. With the death of Roosevelt, the Truman presidency, and the end of World War II, he looked upon the extension of American power around the world as almost as great a calamity as the spread of Communist power in Eastern Europe. He had no faith in the rhetoric of American democracy and was constantly reminding whoever would listen that "democracy was what you make it and not what you say it is."[59]

To Max Eastman, he declared that "I try to see things from the standpoint of right and wrong and when Soviet Russia is wrong I will say so. When the U.S. and Great Britain are wrong I will say so too, and the two latter in my mind are more often wrong than the Soviet nation. I am certainly never going to carry the torch for British colonialism or American imperialism abroad."[60] To McKay, the church appeared as a last refuge in an increasingly dehumanized world. Unlike many left-wing critics of communism, McKay in the final analysis refused to become an apologist for capitalist imperialism. Although he had become an American citizen in 1940, he could see no evidence after World War II that the United States had learned anything from the collapse of European colonialism. He feared American world dominance after World War II. In Dorothy Day's *Catholic Worker,* he wrote

> Europe and Africa and Asia wait
> The touted New Deal of the New World's hand!
> New systems will be built on race and hate,
> The Eagle and the Dollar will command.
> Oh Lord! My body, and my heart too, break—
> The tiger in his strength his thirst must slake![61]

To Max Eastman, who accused him of mouthing Stalinist slogans, McKay angrily retorted,

> Equality of white and brown people: bosh! You all ought to try to bring that about in America before going abroad to Asia, and even Africa, to try your experiments. . . . I have always thought that every Englishman and American is a dyed-in-the-wool hypocrite when it comes to seeing and facing other people's problems. In all my life I have never been a reactionary and I won't be one now, mouthing occasional pieces for the capitalist press, because I know one thing, the capitalists don't want me and I don't want anything of them. . . . I do not fear the Russian system will ever conquer America, but I do not care if it conquers the people of Asia or Africa. I do not think that mouthing goodwill the democracies have anything to offer such people. I should say to the so-called democracies of the United States and Great Britain: set your own house in order and try not to scare up a war against Soviet Russia.

McKay was not through. He went on to declare that he would rather his name "stand in history" beside Henry Wallace's as an opponent of the rapidly developing Cold War than with "the neo-reactionaries of the *New Leader.*" Still, Eastman should not think him "a partisan of Communism." He was a Catholic precisely because the church was "the foe of Communism," but he reminded Max that within the church, there was "a formidable left wing . . . because it can accommodate all, even you."[62]

In April of 1948, McKay's letters to his friends became less frantic. They assumed a quiet tone. He had no more accounts to settle. In a final letter to his literary agent and friend, Carl Cowl, who had endured from Claude several blistering attacks upon his competency, McKay wrote on April 9, 1948, to express thanks for all he had tried to do for him over the past year. And to Ellen Tarry on April 27, 1948, he concluded, "Now I think I have covered everything. Goodbye Tarry, till I hear from you again and God bless you."[63]

Not many people knew it, but McKay's daughter, Hope, had been in New York City for the past two years attending Columbia Teachers' College. Over the years, they had maintained a correspondence. He had always wanted to do more for her, but he seldom had any money. After she arrived in New York, he had asked Cowl to look out for her. In April, Claude and Hope were making plans to meet for the first time, but it never happened. In May he was hospitalized again, and on May 22, 1948, at the age of fifty-seven, Claude McKay died of congestive heart failure in the Alexian Brothers Hospital in Chicago. Death could not have come as a surprise, and surely he was ready. For had he not in the end truly become one with that company who had "all died in the faith, not having received the promises, but having seen them afar off, and [who] were persuaded of them, and embraced them, and confessed that they were strangers and pilgrims on the earth"?[64]

There have been many who have questioned the authenticity and sincerity of McKay's conversion. And certainly, in his letters to Keating, Eastman, and others, McKay indicated on various occasions that he was more convinced of the practical and political wisdom of his move to Catholicism than he was of his own spiritual conversion. In any event, however, he convinced himself and insisted to others that he had in fact become a Christian and a Catholic. All the while, of course, he never lost sight of the fact that for both himself and for the church, his conversion had practical benefits. Within the church, he found a job, medical care, and acceptance as an individual. In its turn, the church could hope that its significant new convert would influence through his example and his future writings other blacks and other intellectuals to take the same course. As McKay bluntly wrote to Carl Cowl in 1947, "It was a good thing I hooked up with the Catholics, intuitive, I guess, for they have certainly taken good care of me. You see they all want me to live, because they expect me to write more, which will redound to their credit."[65]

There was in this statement no deliberate deceit but considerable self-delusion. McKay had always needed someone who would "take care" of him, or at least the really practical monetary details of his life. In a real sense, the Roman Catholic church became the last and greatest of his patrons. In its bosom he found the means not only to live awhile longer but to die with some solace, dignity, and assurance that he had not labored wholly in vain. It is perhaps too easy for the nonbeliever to scorn such an end, but McKay accepted it as his culminating act of faith and affirmation. As difficult, tortured, and ambivalent as it was, he viewed his conversion as genuine, and that perhaps was what mattered most.

# Abbreviations

Frequently cited sources have been abbreviated as follows:

AASP   The Arthur A. Schomburg Papers. Schomburg Center for Research in Black Culture, New York Public Library, New York City, formerly the Arthur A. Schomburg Collection of Negro History and Literature.

ALP    Alain Locke Papers. Moorland-Spingarn Research Center, Howard University Library, Washington, D.C.

*ALWFH*   McKay, Claude. *A Long Way from Home*. New York, 1937.

*AN*   New York *Amsterdam News*, 1923–1948.

"ANP"   McKay, Claude. "A Negro Poet Writes." *Pearson's Magazine*, XXXIX (September, 1918), 275–76.

*B*    ———. *Banjo: A Story Without a Plot*. New York, 1929.

*BB*   ———. *Banana Bottom*. New York, 1933.

BBP    Betty Britton Papers. Private Possession.

"BJ"   McKay, Claude. "Boyhood in Jamaica." *Phylon*, XIII (Second Quarter, 1953), 134–46.

*CB*   ———. *Constab Ballads*. London, 1912.

| | |
|---|---|
| CCP | Countee Cullen Papers. Amistad Research Center, Dillard University Library, New Orleans. |
| CMP | Claude McKay Papers. James Weldon Johnson Collection of Negro Literature and Art, American Literature Collection, Beinecke Rare Book and Manuscript Library, Yale University, New Haven. |
| DMCP | Father Daniel Michael Cantwell Papers. Chicago Historical Society Library, Chicago. |
| FHP | Friendship House Papers. Chicago Historical Society Library, Chicago. |
| *G* | McKay, Claude. *Gingertown*. New York, 1932. |
| *H* | ———. *Harlem: Negro Metropolis*. New York, 1940. |
| HFP | Harmon Foundation Papers. Library of Congress, Washington, D.C. |
| "HG" | McKay, Claude. "Harlem Glory." Unpublished manuscript novel, in the Miscellaneous Claude McKay Papers. Schomburg Center for Research in Black Culture, New York Public Library, New York City. |
| HH | ———. *Home to Harlem*. New York, 1928. |
| HLMP | H. L. Mencken Papers. The Berg Collection, New York Public Library, New York City. |
| *HS* | McKay, Claude. *Harlem Shadows*. New York, 1922. |
| JIP | James Ivy Papers. Private Possession. |
| JP | Ivie Jackman–Harold Jackman Papers. Trevor-Arnett Library, Atlanta University, Atlanta. |
| JRFA | Julius Rosenwald Fund Archives. Fisk University Library, Nashville. |
| JTP | Jean Toomer Papers. Fisk University Library, Nashville. |
| JWJP | James Weldon Johnson Papers. James Weldon Johnson Collection of Negro Literature and Art, American Literature Collection, Beinecke Rare Book and Manuscript Library, Yale University, New Haven. |
| JWJP, NAACP | James Weldon Johnson Papers. NAACP Collection, Library of Congress, Washington, D.C. |
| KP | Tom and Mary Keating Papers. Private Possession. |
| *L* | *Liberator*, 1918–1923. |
| MEP | Max Eastman Papers. Private Possession. |

| | |
|---|---|
| *MGH* | McKay, Claude. *My Green Hills of Jamaica and Five Jamaican Short Stories*. Edited by Mervyn Morris. Kingston, 1979. |
| MMP | Miscellaneous Claude McKay Papers. Schomburg Center for Research in Black Culture, New York Public Library, New York City. |
| *NA* | McKay, Claude. *The Negroes in America*. Translated from the Russian by Robert J. Winter and edited by Alan L. McLeod. Port Washington, New York, 1979. This volume originally appeared in the Soviet Union as *Negry v Amerika*. Translated from the English by P. Okhrimenko. Moscow, 1923. |
| *NL* | *New Leader*, 1935–1944. |
| *PCM* | Cooper, Wayne F., ed. *The Passion of Claude McKay: Selected Poetry and Prose, 1912–1948*. New York, 1973. |
| "RHH" | McKay, Claude. "Review of *Home to Harlem*." In James Clarke, ed., "Significant Books Reviewed by Their Own Authors." *McClure's*, XL (June, 1928), 81. |
| "RM" | ———. "Romance in Marseilles." Unpublished manuscript novel, in the Miscellaneous Claude McKay Papers. Schomburg Center for Research in Black Culture, New York Public Library, New York City. |
| *SJ* | ———. *Songs of Jamaica*. Kingston, Jamaica, 1912. |
| *SNH* | ———. *Spring in New Hampshire and Other Poems*. London, 1920. |
| *SP* | ———. *Selected Poems of Claude McKay*. New York, 1953. |
| WABP | William Aspenwall Bradley Papers. Private Possession. |
| *WD* | *Workers' Dreadnought* (London), 1918–1923. |
| WSBP | William Stanley Braithwaite Papers. Houghton Library, Harvard University, Cambridge. |
| WWP, NAACP | Walter White Papers. NAACP Collection, Library of Congress, Washington, D.C. |

# Notes

*Chapter 1*

1. Claude McKay, "How Black Sees Green and Red," *Liberator*, IV (June, 1921), 17, 20–21, reprinted in *PCM*, 59, 61.

2. *MGH*, 23.

3. D. T. Edwards, "Small Farming in Jamaica: A Social Scientist's View," in David Lowenthal and Lambros Comitas (eds.), *Work and Family Life: West Indian Perspectives* (Garden City, N.Y., 1973), 27–28; Sidney W. Mintz and Douglas Hall, "The Origins of the Jamaican Internal Marketing System," in Sidney W. Mintz (ed.), *Papers in Caribbean Anthropology* (New Haven, 1960), 3–26, numbers 57–64 in *Yale University Publications in Anthropology*. Mintz and others in Caribbean anthropology do not define West Indian subsistence farmers as peasants in any historical European sense but as "a class (or classes) of rural landowners producing a large part of the products they consume, but also selling to (and buying from) wider markets, and dependent in various ways upon wider political and economic spheres of control. Caribbean peasantries are, in this view *reconstituted* peasantries, having begun other than as peasants—in slavery, as deserters or runaways, as plantation laborers, or whatever—and becoming peasants in some kind of resistant response to an externally imposed regime" (Sidney W. Mintz, *Caribbean Transformations* [Chicago, 1974], 132 [emphasis in original]).

4. The secondary material on the history of Jamaica from 1865 to 1938 makes it clear that the great poverty of the masses, the concentration of wealth in the hands of a few, cultural pluralism, and racism have been and remain persistent problems in Jamaica. Among others, see Orlando Patterson, *The Sociology of Slavery: An Analysis of the Origins, Development and Structure of Negro Slave Society in Jamaica* (London,

1967); Katrin Norris, *Jamaica: The Search for Identity* (London, 1962), 1–18; Samuel J. Hurwitz and Edith F. Hurwitz, *Jamaica: A Historical Portrait* (New York, 1971), 121–92; and M. G. Smith, "The Plural Framework of Jamaican Society," in Lambros Comitas and David Lowenthal (eds.), *Slaves, Freemen, Citizens: West Indian Perspectives* (Garden City, N.Y., 1973), 174–93. On the importation of Indian and Chinese laborers, see Noel Deerr, *The History of Sugar* (2 vols.; London, 1949–50), II, 388–401. The core of the Jewish population in Jamaica was of Sephardic origin. See W. Adolphe Roberts, *Jamaica: The Portrait of an Island* (New York, 1955), 153; Edward Braithwaite, *The Development of Creole Society in Jamaica, 1770–1820* (London, 1971), 136–37; and Philip D. Curtin, *Two Jamaicas: The Role of Ideas in a Tropical Colony, 1830–1865* (New York, 1970), 49–50. The Syrians in Jamaica and those elsewhere in the West Indies are of Lebanese origin. See Nellie Ammar, "They Come from the Middle East," *Jamaica Journal*, IV (March, 1970), 2–6; and David Lowenthal, *West Indian Societies* (New York, 1972), 208–10. For a succinct statement on the rebel tradition in Jamaican history, see Richard Price (ed.), *Maroon Societies: Rebel Slave Communities in the Americas* (Garden City, N.Y., 1973), 227–92. Finally, it should be noted that a most basic example of the diverging interests of the free colored and blacks in Jamaica concerned emancipation itself, which the slave owners among the free colored opposed. Free blacks, free colored, and the island's Jewish population all won political equality with the white population in 1830. In the short run, granting equality to blacks had little meaning; very few possessed enough property to qualify as voters or officeholders in the island's system of political representation. See M. C. Campbell, *The Dynamics of Change in a Slave Society: A Sociopolitical History of the Free Coloreds of Jamaica, 1800–1865* (Rutherford, N.J., 1976), 140–43.

5. Bernard Semmel, *Democracy vs. Empire: The Jamaica Riots of 1865 and the Governor Eyre Controversy* (Garden City, N.Y., 1969), 11–189. The Jamaican assembly voluntarily voted itself out of existence, in part because its white majority recognized that it would have been only a matter of time before their control over island affairs would pass to a new black and colored majority. They thus acceded to crown-colony rule because they felt that such a government would best protect their interests. The foundation for the reforms that occurred after 1866 is described by Vincent Marsala's *Sir John Peter Grant, Governor of Jamaica, 1866–1874: An Administrative History* (Kingston, 1972).

6. Max Eastman, "Introduction," in *HS*, xi–xii.

7. *MGH*, 10, 48–51, 61. McKay identified the Woolsey home as "Somerset House, a vast rambling barn of a place to which many additions had been made." Old "Mother Woolsey," about ninety in McKay's boyhood, had taught his mother her letters.

8. *Ibid.*, 59–60.

9. Interviews with M. E. McKay, Claude McKay's niece, September 1, 1978, at the McKay family home, Sunny Ville, Clarendon Parish, Jamaica, and with Hope McKay Virtue, Claude McKay's daughter, August 30, 1978, in Kingston, Jamaica. Unless otherwise noted, all interviews are by the author.

10. *MGH*, 12, 32–34, 41–42, 59–61.

11. Curtin, *Two Jamaicas*, 23–41, 158–77. For the persistence in Jamaican religion of African religious elements, see Martha W. Beckwith, *Black Roadways: A Study of Jamaican Folk Life* (Rpr. New York, 1969), 88–112. See also Leonard Tucker, *"Glorious Liberty": The Story of a Hundred Years' Work of the Jamaica Baptist Mission* (London, 1914), 85.

12. *MGH*, 12, 32–34, 41–42, 59–61.

13. *Ibid.*, 25. Interviews with M. E. McKay, September 1, 1978; Hope McKay Vir-

tue, August 30, 1978; and Edna McKay, Claude McKay's niece, September 2, 1978, in Kingston, Jamaica. See also the Reverend William Ellwood to the author, July 26, 1978, in possession of the recipient. Mr. Ellwood is a Jamaican Presbyterian minister with access to and familiarity with Presbyterian church records in Jamaica. Edward Bean Underhill toured upper Clarendon for the Baptist Missionary Society of England in 1861 and visited both Mt. Zion (the site of the future McKay family church) and Staceyville. At Mt. Zion, he found a "chapel . . . in a very unfinished state" and a small congregation, but at Staceyville he met a native minister presiding over a flourishing congregation in a substantial church. He also noted that "the nearer the sugar estates approached, the more emphatic were the complaints of the low morals of the population, and their degraded condition" (*The West Indies: Their Social and Religious Condition* [London, 1862], 445–49). Finally, see *ALWFH*, 36.

14. Philip Wright, *Knibb "The Notorious": Slaves' Missionary, 1803–1845* (London, 1973), 76–111, 167–68; Patterson, *The Sociology of Slavery*, 211–15; Curtin, *Two Jamaicas*, 86–89; James Watson and C. A. Woodkey (eds.), *Jamaica Congregational Churches: A History and a Memorial* (Guildford, England, 1901), 77–78.

15. The Reverend Gillet Chambers quoted in the Reverend R. A. L. Knight (ed.), *Liberty and Progress: A Short History of the Baptists in Jamaica* (Kingston, 1938), 82.

16. *MGH*, 48–49, 59–60. Here Claude stated that his mother died at the age of fifty-three. The inscription on her tombstone at Sunny Ville records only that she died in 1909. If Claude's statement is correct, she was born in 1856.

17. *Ibid.*, 60.

18. *Ibid.*

19. *Ibid.*, 58–61; Claude McKay to the editor of the *Nation*, May 23, 1947, in MMP; L. A. Thoywell-Henry (ed.), *Who's Who 1941–1946, Jamaica, British West Indies: An Illustrated Biographical Record of Outstanding Jamaicans and Others Connected with the Island* (Kingston, 1945), 444; M. E. McKay to Wayne Cooper, February 10, 1979, in possession of the recipient. McKay claimed September 15, 1889, as his birthday until 1920, when his sister, Rachel, wrote to remind him that he had actually been born on September 15, 1890. His family had apparently set his birthday back a year at some point so he would be eligible a year earlier than was legally permissible to become a student teaching assistant in his brother U'Theo's school. The clearest statement of the correct date of Claude McKay's birth is in McKay to Alain Locke, June 4, 1927, in ALP.

20. See the distinctions made by Douglas Hall between "peasants and rural labourers" and "small farmers" in *Free Jamaica, 1838–1865: An Economic History* (New Haven, 1959). The peasants and free laborers grew food for subsistence, the small farmers for export. On the varieties of contemporary Jamaican marriage patterns, see Edith Clarke, *My Mother Who Fathered Me: A Study of the Family in Three Selected Communities in Jamaica* (2nd ed.; London, 1966). For an excellent survey of the literature and scholarly debates on West Indian family patterns, see M. G. Smith's "Introduction" to Clarke's book (i–xliv). On McKay's prejudice against mulattoes, see Jean Wagner, *Les Poètes Nègres des Etats-Unis: Le Sentiment Racial et Religieux dans la Poésie de P. L. Dunbar à L. Hughes (1890–1940)* (Paris, 1963), 232. Wagner's book has been translated into English as *Black Poets of the United States: From Paul Laurence Dunbar to Langston Hughes*, trans. Kenneth Douglas (Urbana, 1973).

21. *ALWFH*, 11, 36–37. Hathaway is listed as among those Baptist missionary preachers who arrived in Jamaica in 1875 (Tucker, *"Glorious Liberty,"* 164).

22. *MGH*, 60; *ALWFH*, 36.

23. *MGH*, 60–61. On such practices as "informal . . . adjudication" and cooperative labor practices among peasants in Jamaica, see Smith, "The Plural Framework of Jamaican Society," in Comitas and Lowenthal (eds.), *Slaves, Freemen, Citizens,* 182–83.

24. *SJ,* 118; see also the poem "My Mountain Home," in *SJ,* 125. *MGH,* 58–59, 64. The major sources for insight into Claude McKay's childhood and youth are his own writings; all contain strong autobiographical elements. In several works, he deals almost exclusively with the world of his youth. Besides the two works cited above, these include his other volume of dialect poems (*CB*), several of his short stories (in *G*), and his last novel (*BB*). He also dealt with his early years in his autobiography (*ALWFH*). Many of his poems written after he left Jamaica are also essential for an understanding of his attitude toward his childhood. Finally, other references to these years can be found in his numerous articles and letters. What follows has been largely drawn from all these writings. The details in McKay's own accounts of his childhood and youth have been checked for discrepancies, and, wherever possible, they have also been compared to other contemporary Jamaican sources.

25. "BJ," 141; McKay's article "Boyhood in Jamaica" was excerpted from the then-unpublished manuscript of *MGH* by the Anglo-Indian scholar Cedric Dover and published in *Phylon* five years after McKay's death. Some of the passages in the article differ slightly from the corresponding passages in the manuscript copy of *MGH* currently in my possession. Dover may have used another copy of *MGH*, or he may have altered the text slightly while editing it. He and McKay both wrote memoirs of their respective childhoods in Jamaica and India and planned to publish them together in a book entitled *East Indian–West Indian.* Although both finished their respective halves, neither Dover nor McKay's literary executor could find an interested publisher. See also *MGH*, 12, 22.

26. *MGH*, 22.

27. *BB*, 7.

28. *MGH*, 61. In a translator's note to a book McKay wrote while in Russia in 1922–23, it is his mother, not his father, who is recalled as having been a splendid teller of "Negro folk tales." See the English version of "Original Translator's Note" by P. Okhrimenko in *NA*, xvi–xviii. The original English-language manuscript version by McKay has been lost.

29. *MGH*, 5, 10.

30. *Ibid.*, 5.

31. Claude McKay, "North & South," in *SP*, 20.

32. "ANP"; Okhrimenko, "Original Translator's Note," in *NA*, xv; *MGH*, 13, 20–22; *ALWFH*, 12.

33. *MGH*, 13. See also Thoywell-Henry (ed.), *Who's Who 1941–1946, Jamaica, British West Indies*, 444; and *Mico College: 125th Anniversary, 1836–1961* (Kingston, 1961), 7–22.

34. Madeline Kerr, *Personality and Conflict in Jamaica* (London, 1952), 74–84, 114–36.

35. Thoywell-Henry (ed.), *Who's Who 1941–1946, Jamaica, British West Indies*, 444. See also U'Theo McKay's obituary in the Kingston *Daily Gleaner*, June 17, 1949, p. 1.

36. *MGH*, 13, 20–22. In 1923, Okhrimenko's "Original Translator's Note" (in *NA*, xv) stated McKay returned after four years with U'Theo, who had taken "a position as a teacher in his native village." U'Theo's biographical sketches in the various editions of *Who's Who in Jamaica* do not mention that he ever taught in Sunny Ville or at Mt.

Zion, but one entry does list several nearby communities where he served as a teacher (L. A. Thoywell-Henry [ed.], *Who's Who and Why in Jamaica, 1939–1940* [Kingston, 1940], 137). Finally, McKay stated he spent his boyhood "in various villages with U'Theo" (*ALWFH*, 12).

37. *MGH*, 13–15.

38. *Ibid.*, 17–18; Kerr, *Personality and Conflict in Jamaica*, 42–46. See also McKay's early poem (1912), "Strokes of a Tamarind Switch," in *SJ*, 111–13. Agnes had a sorry end. She died young in a Kingston brothel. McKay memorialized her in one of his first published poems, "Agnes O' De Village Lane," in the Kingston *Daily Gleaner*, October 7, 1911, p. 6.

39. *MGH*, 15–16; *ALWFH*, 12.

40. Claude McKay, "On Becoming a Roman Catholic," quoted in Wagner, *Les Poètes Nègres des Etats-Unis*, 213.

41. *ALWFH*, 11–12.

42. *MGH*, 21–22. For an excellent history of the debate, see William Irvine, *Apes, Angels and Victorians: The Story of Darwin, Huxley and Evolution* (New York, 1955).

43. *MGH*, 19, 35–36.

44. *Ibid.*, 19.

45. William Gladstone on Mrs. Humphry Ward's novel, *Robert Elsmere*, quoted in Irvine, *Apes, Angels and Victorians*, 320. Mrs. Humphry Ward, Matthew Arnold's niece, was a Darwinist; she was among the novelists McKay read in Jamaica.

46. *ALWFH*, 11–12; *MGH*, 19.

47. U'Theo McKay to Claude McKay, March 1, 1929, in CMP.

48. U'Theo McKay to Claude McKay, April 26, 1929, in CMP.

49. *MGH*, 14–15.

50. *ALWFH*, 12.

51. Claude McKay, "Author's Word," in *HS*, xx.

52. "BJ," 137.

53. *MGH*, 18–19.

54. "ANP," 275–76.

55. *MGH*, 21–22.

56. *Ibid.*, 22–23.

57. *Ibid.*, 32–35. After Claude's return, his father engaged in a long bitter controversy with an English missionary pastor whom he had found to be a hypocrite. The elder McKay left Mt. Zion Church and took most of the congregation with him, and the preacher was finally forced out by other white Baptist pastors who feared he would bring discredit to them all. Afterward, McKay's father refused to shake the hand of the departing clergyman. Claude obviously admired his father's stance in the dispute. In *Banana Bottom*, his father's actions are ironically mirrored in the actions of an English mission preacher, Angus Craig, who in a similar dispute with a fellow pastor "never veiled his animosity by hypocrisy.... Friends... tried to bring about a reconciliation. But Angus Craig refused to stoop to a dirty reconciliation when his heart held a clean hatred" (*BB*, 25).

58. *MGH*, 22, 40–41.

59. *Ibid.*, 22–30, 62. See also McKay to Alain Locke, June 4, 1927, in ALP.

60. *MGH*, 44–45.

61. *Ibid.*

62. Claude McKay, "Old England," in *SJ*, 63.

63. *MGH*, 12.

64. *Ibid.*

65. Claude McKay, "Personal Notes on the History of Jamaica," in MMP.

66. Claude McKay, "The Agricultural Show," in *G*, 162–91. Robert Bone considers "The Agricultural Show" one of the most complete expressions of McKay's pastoral vision of Jamaica and "a pure specimen of [Harlem] Renaissance pastoral" (*Down Home: A History of Afro-American Short Fiction from Its Beginning to the End of the Harlem Renaissance* [New York, 1975], 167). Agricultural shows and choral singing were common occurrences throughout Jamaica in McKay's day, and both were frequently noted in the Kingston newspapers. For example, see Kingston *Daily Gleaner* throughout January, 1905.

67. See Kingston *Daily Gleaner*, January 24, 1905, p. 11, January 18, 1905, p. 10, February 17, 1905, p. 10, February 18, 1905, p. 6, February 22, 1905, p. 6, November 18, 1905, p. 6. What had begun in January as a call for moral regeneration in Jamaica ended by November in expressions of alarm when it was reported that Port Antonio on Jamaica's north coast was besieged with "street preachers." The revival spirit threatened to get out of hand.

68. *MGH*, 43.

69. *ALWFH*, 12. See also *MGH*, 43.

70. *MGH*, 43.

71. *Ibid.*, 51–52. See also "ANP," 275–76; Okhrimenko, "Original Translator's Note," in *NA*, xv; Walter Jekyll's "Preface," in *SJ*, 9; and Kingston *Daily Gleaner*, October 7, 1911, p. 6.

72. *MGH*, 53–58.

73. *Ibid.*, 55.

74. *Ibid.*, 57. In a feature story on McKay, his employer in Brown's Town was identified as a "Mr. Campbell." See Kingston *Daily Gleaner*, October 7, 1911, p. 6. In *MGH*, McKay referred to him only as "old Brenga."

75. *MGH*, 57.

76. *Ibid.*, 57–58.

77. Herbert Jekyll to Frank Cundall, March 16, 1929, in Frank Cundall Papers, West India Reference Library, Jamaica Institute, Kingston. Included in this letter was a brief account of Jekyll's life, which Cundall, the director of the Jamaica Institute, used in writing a retrospective appreciation of Walter Jekyll that appeared in the Kingston *Daily Gleaner*, August 19, 1929, n.p. See also the Jekyll obituary in Frank Cundall (ed.), *The Handbook of Jamaica for 1930* (Kingston, 1930), 557. Upon his death on March 22, 1876, Walter Jekyll's father left an estate valued at £140,000. To Walter was left "£300 per annum during the life or widowhood of [his] mother." At his mother's death or remarriage, he was to receive a total of £20,000 from his father's estate. See the *Times* (London), May 19, 1876, p. 10. Walter's brother, Sir Herbert, was a colonel in the Royal Engineers and a distinguished civil servant. See his obituary in the *Times* (London), September 30, 1932, p. 7. He left an estate valued at over £30,000. See the *Times* (London), January 24, 1933, p. 13. Walter Jekyll also had a distinguished older sister, Gertrude, one of England's leading landscape gardeners. She wrote over fourteen volumes on gardening and other subjects. See her obituary and an account of her funeral in the *Times* (London), December 10, 1932, p. 12, December 13, 1932, p. 17. See also Betty Massingham, *Miss Jekyll: Portrait of a Great Gardener* (London, 1966). See also Francesco Lamperti, *The Art of Singing According to Ancient Tradition and Personal Experiences*, trans. Walter Jekyll (London, 1884).

78. See Herbert Jekyll to Frank Cundall, March 16, 1929, in Cundall Papers. I have found no reference to Jekyll's friendship with Stevenson in any Stevenson biography.

79. *Ibid.*

80. *Ibid.* See also Herbert Jekyll to Frank Cundall, May 9, 1929, in Cundall Papers. After the outbreak of war in 1914, Boyle "rejoined his old regiment, the Honorable Artillery Company and he was killed in action on Feb. 7, 1917." See the notice of his memorial service in the *Times* (London), February 22, 1917, p. 9.

81. Walter Jekyll, *The Bible Untrustworthy: A Critical Comparison of Contradictory Passages in the Bible* (London, 1904; rpr. New York, 1966). Walter Jekyll also wrote *Guide to Hope Gardens* (Kingston, 1903).

82. Walter Jekyll, *Jamaican Song and Story: Annancy Stories, Digging Sings, Ring Tunes, and Dancing Tunes* (London, 1907; rpr. New York, 1966). As youngsters he and Gertrude had grown to love the country folk of Surrey, in a way perhaps not unlike the southern country gentlemen of the United States in the same period sometimes grew fond of their black agricultural laborers. Gertrude eventually wrote a valuable, detailed (though somewhat romanticized) account of Surrey country folk and their old ways of life. See Gertrude Jekyll, *Old West Surrey: Some Notes and Memoirs* (London, 1904; rpr. East Ardsley, Wakefield, Yorkshire, England, 1971). For McKay's account of Jekyll's interests, see *MGH*, 66–72, 76–79, 82.

83. This description of Jekyll is based on a number of partial descriptions. See *MGH*, 65–72; and *BB*, 71. McKay dedicated *Banana Bottom* to Jekyll's memory and in the "Author's Note" stated that "all the characters . . . are imaginary, excepting perhaps Squire Gensir," the fictional prototype of Jekyll (*BB*, frontispiece). It is reasonable to assume that his physical description of "Squire Gensir" did not deviate far from Jekyll's actual appearance. In connection with Jekyll's aristocratic bearing, see also Logan Pearsall Smith, *Reperusals and Re-Collections* (London, 1936), 60.

84. *ALWFH*, 13.

85. *MGH*, 58. McKay did not give up his apprenticeship immediately when he left Brown's Town. Arrangements were made for him to continue under a "Mr. Saunders" in Chapelton, but he did not work for him very long before giving up his apprenticeship permanently. See Kingston *Daily Gleaner*, October 7, 1911, p. 6.

86. *MGH*, 62–63. Gravestone inscription, Sunny Ville, Clarendon Parish, Jamaica.

87. Claude McKay, "Mother Dear," in *SJ*, 77–78.

88. Claude McKay, "Heritage," in *SP*, 29.

89. These poems were "The Harlem Dancer" and "Invocation," in *Seven Arts*, II (October, 1917), 741–42.

90. Claude McKay, "My Mother," in *SP*, 22. In *Banana Bottom*, the heroine's father, Jordan Plant, one of five brothers, after his own father's death, had returned alone "with his mother to the village of Banana Bottom, where she was born and where she had a lot of land. That lot he began cultivating and adding to until he became the most prosperous peasant of the village" (*BB*, 27). Thus, in McKay's fiction the son supplanted the father in real life.

91. *SP*, 22.

92. *MGH*, 66. In all likelihood, the poem was "Cotch Donkey," in *CB*, 46–47.

93. *MGH*, 67.

94. Interview with Louise Bennett, September 9, 1978, in her home at Gordon Town, Jamaica.

95. McKay's retention of his pronounced Jamaican accent was in large part deliberate. He had once found it useful during World War I and had decided then to make sure he retained and cultivated it in the United States. See *ALWFH*, 8–9.

96. *MGH*, 67.

97. *Ibid.*

98. *Ibid.* See also Okhrimenko's "Original Translator's Note," in *NA*, xv.

99. *MGH*, 67–68; Kingston *Daily Gleaner,* October 7, 1911, p. 6. In *MGH*, he stated that he joined with a friend whose company he enjoyed.

100. Marsala, *Sir John Peter Grant*, 42–43, 58–59.

101. Kingston *Daily Gleaner,* October 7, 1911, p. 6.

102. "ANP," 275–76.

103. *Ibid.*

104. Okhrimenko, "Original Translator's Note," in *NA*, xv; *ALWFH*, 14. For a recent account of the Rationalist Press Association, see Susan Budd, *Varieties of Unbelief: Atheists and Agnostics in English Society, 1850–1960* (London, 1977), 124–287.

105. *MGH*, 70. Like his earlier book on the Bible, Jekyll's translation of Schopenhauer had been published by Watts of the Rationalist Press Association. *The Wisdom of Schopenhauer as Revealed in Some of His Writings,* trans. Walter Jekyll (London, 1911).

106. *ALWFH*, 13.

107. *MGH*, 69.

108. *MGH*, 71–72.

109. Jekyll, *Jamaican Song and Story* (1966), 6.

110. The complicated question of parental influences upon the development of homosexual and heterosexual orientations in individuals has been reviewed by Marvin Siegelman in "Parental Background of Male Homosexuals and Heterosexuals," *Archives of Sexual Behavior,* III (1974), 3–18. He suspects that "disturbed parental relations are neither necessary nor sufficient conditions for homosexuality to emerge" (16). The question, however, is still much open to debate.

111. "ANP," 275–76. Edward Carpenter, *Homogenic Love and Its Place in a Free Society* (Manchester, 1894), *Love's Coming of Age: A Series of Papers on the Relations of the Sexes* (Manchester, 1896), and *Days with Walt Whitman, with Some Notes on His Life and Work* (London, 1906). See also Noel I. Garde, *From Jonathan to Gide: The Homosexual in History* (New York, 1964), 654–62, 671–73, 608–13; H. Montgomery Hyde, *The Love That Dared Not Speak Its Name: A Candid History of Homosexuality in Britain* (Boston, 1970), 90–170; and A. L. Rowse, *Homosexuals in History: A Study of Ambivalence in Society, Literature and the Arts* (New York, 1977), 158–60, 288–96.

112. U'Theo McKay to Claude McKay, April 26, 1929, in CMP. Information about Johnny Lyons came from an interview with Louise Bennett, September 9, 1978. Lyons died in 1976. Louise Bennett remembered quite clearly that Lyons always insisted that Walter Jekyll was the man whose name Robert Louis Stevenson used in his famous story.

113. Ronald Hyam, *Britain's Imperial Century, 1815–1914: A Study of Empire and Expansion* (London, 1976), 135–47.

114. *MGH*, 71.

115. *Ibid.*, 70.

116. Irvine, *Apes, Angels and Victorians,* 1–30; Raymond Williams, *Society and Culture, 1780–1950* (New York, 1958), 3–199, and *The Country and the City* (New York, 1973).

117. Hyam, *Britain's Imperial Century*, 135–47.

118. *BB*, 310.

119. Claude McKay, "Free," *CB*, 78. For McKay's account of Jekyll's role in securing his discharge from the constabulary, see *MGH*, 78–79.

120. *MGH*, 72.

121. Kingston *Daily Gleaner*, October 7, 1911, p. 6.

122. *MGH*, 78.

123. Max Eastman, "Biographical Note," in *SP*, 110.

124. *MGH*, 79, 82.

## Chapter 2

1. Claude McKay also had a third publication in 1912. Appended to *SJ* were six of the volume's love lyrics set to music. Late in the year these six arrangements were published separately as *Songs from Jamaica* (London, 1912).

2. Lloyd W. Brown, *West Indian Poetry* (New York, 1978), 19–62. In 1759, Francis Williams, a free black Jamaican (1700–1770), published in Latin "Ode to Governor Haldane." It was the first poem published by a black West Indian. Other predecessors to McKay in the West Indies discussed by Brown include the Guyanese poets Henry G. Dalton and Egbert Martin ("Leo"), who wrote in the last half of the nineteenth century. Among McKay's Jamaican contemporaries, the most notable poet was *Jamaica Times* editor Thomas MacDermot, whose gifts as a poet were limited. Brown has concluded that Claude McKay's "achievements place him well above everyone else" in the long span between 1760 and 1940.

3. *MGH*, 65–87; "BJ," 137, 142; Wagner, *Les Poètes Nègres des Etats-Unis*, 218–40; Brown, *West Indian Poetry*, 39–62; Ralph Glasgow Johnson, "The Poetry of Dunbar and McKay: A Study" (M.A. thesis, University of Pittsburgh, 1950); and Wayne Cooper, "Preface to the 1972 Edition," Claude McKay, *The Dialect Poetry of Claude McKay: "Songs of Jamaica" and "Constab Ballads"* (Rpr. 2 vols. in 1; Plainview, N.Y., 1972). McKay's dialect poetry served as one important source for Frederic G. Cassidy's *Jamaica Talk: Three Hundred Years of the English Language in Jamaica* (2nd ed.; London, 1971).

4. For example, *SJ* contained several poems that reflected McKay's experience in the constabulary.

5. Brown, *West Indian Poetry*, 41–52.

6. *SJ*, 63–65.

7. *SJ*, 63. See also Brown, *West Indian Poetry*, 42–43.

8. *SJ*, 55–58.

9. "My Native Land, My Home," in *SJ*, 84.

10. *SJ*, 13.

11. *SJ*, 13–14.

12. "King Banana," in *SJ*, 30–31. On the importance of bananas to small farmers in McKay's day, see Samuel J. Hurwitz and Edith F. Hurwitz, *Jamaica: A Historical Portrait* (New York, 1971), 165.

13. From "King Banana," in *SJ*, 30.

14. *SJ*, 30, 31.

15. From "Two-an'-Six," in *SJ*, 90–91.

16. *SJ*, 53–54.

17. Hurwitz and Hurwitz, *Jamaica*, 159, 161–62.

18. *Ibid.*, 160–61.

19. *CB*, 13.

20. *SJ*, 74–76.

21. H. G. DeLisser, *In Jamaica and Cuba* (Kingston, 1910), 86, 113. DeLisser pointed out that while the average peasant resented the government when in Jamaica, once he migrated to Central America or to the Canal Zone he took great pride in being a British subject.

22. For example, see "Quashie to Buccra," "Fetchin' Water," and "My Native Land, My Home," all in *SJ*, 13–14, 42–44, 84–85.

23. *CB*, 57–58.

24. *CB*, 7.

25. See "The Bobby to the Sneering Lady" and "A Labourer's Life Give Me," both in *CB*, 67, 71–72.

26. From "The Heart of a Constab," in *CB*, 63.

27. The quoted phrase is from "Fetchin' Water," in *SJ*, 42.

28. From "The Heart of a Constab," in *CB*, 63.

29. See "Papine Corner," "Pay-Day," and "Knutsford Park Races," all in *CB*, 40–42, 52–56, 59–61. On Louise Bennett, see Rex Nettleford's "Introduction" in Louise Bennett, *Jamaica Labrish* (Kingston, 1966), 9–24; and Brown, *West Indian Poetry*, 100–17.

30. Jekyll's publisher was the founder of the Rationalist Press Association, Charles A. Watts. For many years after 1899, Watts and Company published Rationalist Press Association materials. Jekyll's *Wisdom of Schopenhauer* was a superbly edited book, complete with a simply written introduction by Jekyll in which he clearly defined Schopenhauer's major philosophical terms and phrases. In addition, he also provided useful footnotes throughout the volume.

31. For a clear and concise discussion of Schopenhauer's philosophy, see Patrick Gardiner, *Schopenhauer* (Baltimore, 1967), 11–32, 124–86.

32. For a perceptive discussion of Schopenhauer's appeal to the young, see V. J. McGill, *Schopenhauer, Pessimist and Pagan* (Rpr. New York, 1971), 12–13.

33. *CB*, 76–77.

34. McGill, *Schopenhauer*, 29.

35. From "De Days Dat Are Gone," in *SJ*, 60.

36. From "A Labourer's Life Give Me," in *CB*, 71.

37. *SJ*, 97.

38. *MGH*, 86–87; the *Westminister Review*, quoted in Kingston *Daily Gleaner*, December 12, 1912, p. 6.

39. From "A Dream," in *SJ*, 98.

40. From "Strokes of the Tamarind Switch," in *SJ*, 111.

41. *CB*, 16. "Bennie's Departure" is the longest poem in either *Songs of Jamaica* or *Constab Ballads*. There is a shorter poem, "To Bennie," in *SJ*, 127. Aside from these two poems, nothing is known about McKay's companion or their relationship.

42. Raymond Williams, *The Country and the City* (New York, 1973), 200, 206–207, 209.

43. *MGH*, 78–79.

44. From Claude McKay, "Christmas in de Air," in *Jamaica Times*, December 16, 1911, p. 27.

45. See "The People's Parliament," in *Jamaica Times*, November 18, December 2, December 9, 1911, February 3 and March 9, 1912. Eventually the *Gleaner* also began to refer to its letters column as "The People's Parliament" but it was never on the front page.

46. *Jamaica Times*, April 1, 1911, p. 2.

47. *Ibid.*, July 20, 1912, p. 22.

48. M. E. McKay to Wayne Cooper, November 10, 1978, in possession of the recipient. Claude McKay noted that U'Theo had liked Olivier's book (*MGH*, 23).

49. *Jamaica Times*, January 13, 1912, p. 12.

50. *Ibid.*

51. See Kingston *Daily Gleaner*, January 8, 1912, p. 3. The *Gleaner* also summarized other reviews from abroad. Among the reviews thus noted was one from the *Literary Guide* of the Rationalist Press Association for January 1, 1912. The *Guide* proudly noted that McKay was a member of the RPA. Other journals whose reviews were quoted by the *Gleaner* included *Christian Commonwealth, Garden,* and *Gardening Illustrated.* The latter two reviews undoubtedly appeared because Gertrude Jekyll, Walter's eldest sister, was connected with them. In fact she may have written both reviews. Both ingenuously cataloged all the Jamaican flowers and plants McKay included in his poetry. The *Christian Commonwealth* reviewer, the Reverend W. Marwick, generously praised McKay, but deplored his anti-Christian stance. "It is to be hoped," Marwick wrote, "that he will be able to correct his rather crude views of the teaching of the City Temple pulpit, and of the value of Rationalism, with increased knowledge and experience of the real relation of Faith and Reason." See *Daily Gleaner*, January 13, 1912, p. 17, January 16, 1912, p. 13, February 19, 1912, p. 10, March 20, 1912, p. 14, April 30, 1912, p. 4. The *Gleaner* also reprinted excerpts from the English reviews of *Constab Ballads.* These included quotes from the Southampton *Times, Justice,* the *National Newsagent,* the Erith *Times,* and the *Westminister Review.* With the exception of the *Westminister Review,* which declined to recognize any genuine poetry in the volume, all these journals greeted *Constab Ballads* as an interesting curiosity of some poetic merit. See Kingston *Daily Gleaner*, November 20, 1912, p. 10, December 10, 1912, p. 6.

52. Claude McKay, "Peasants' Way O' Thinkin'," in Kingston *Daily Gleaner*, January 27, 1912, p. 8.

53. *Ibid.*

54. *Jamaica Times*, March 2, 1912, pp. 5, 10, 18.

55. *Ibid.*

56. *Ibid.* See also Kingston *Daily Gleaner*, February 24, 1912, pp. 1, 13, February 26, 1912, pp. 1, 14, February 28, 1912, pp. 1, 6, and February 29, 1912, p. 1.

57. Claude McKay, "Passive Resistance," in Kingston *Daily Gleaner*, April 6, 1912, n.p.

58. Claude McKay, "Gordon to the Oppressed Natives," in Kingston *Daily Gleaner*, May 3, 1912, p. 13. See the same poem in *Jamaica Times*, May 4, 1912, p. 20.

59. Jekyll's letter was apparently never published in the *Gleaner.* I could find no reference to this controversy in either the *Gleaner* or the *Jamaica Times.*

60. Kingston *Daily Gleaner*, October 21, 1911, p. 17.

61. *Jamaica Times*, March 9, 1912, p. 11.

62. Kingston *Daily Gleaner*, March 6, 1912.

63. *Jamaica Times*, March 30, 1912, p. 11.

64. *Ibid.*

65. Kingston *Daily Gleaner*, May 4, 1912, p. 6.

66. *Jamaica Times*, December 14, 1912, p. 49.

67. Kingston *Daily Gleaner*, October 13, 1911, p. 13.

68. *Jamaica Times*, February 13, 1912, p. 1, April 13, 1912, p. 11.

69. *MGH*, 79–82, 84–85; Kingston *Daily Gleaner*, April 11, 1912, p. 6, April 12, 1912, p. 6. The Tuskegee Conference was held April 17–19. Jamaica sent three delegates: J. R. Williams, Jamaica's Director of Education, who was white; the mulatto

principal of Titchfield School; and the black master of Old Harbour Elementary School, S. C. Thompson. See Kingston *Daily Gleaner,* May 1, 1912, p. 4.

70. *MGH,* 86.

71. *MGH,* 82, 85.

72. *Ibid.,* 84–85.

73. *Jamaica Times,* June 15, 1912, p. 11.

74. *Ibid.;* see also *MGH,* 45.

75. Interview with Louise Bennett, September 9, 1978.

76. *MGH,* 86–87.

77. *ALWFH,* 20; *BB,* 8.

78. *MGH,* 82–87; *Jamaica Times,* August 10, 1912, p. 23.

79. Hope McKay Virtue to Wayne Cooper, June 7, 1964, in possession of the recipient. Claude and Eulalie Imelda Lewars were married in 1914. Mrs. Virtue, their only child, now lives in California.

80. *MGH,* 83–84; *BB,* 73–86. On West Indian tea meetings, see Roger Abrahams, "The West Indian Tea Meeting: An Essay in Civilization," in Ann M. Pescatello (ed.), *Old Roots in New Lands: Historical and Anthropological Perspectives on Black Experiences in the Americas* (Westport, Conn., 1977), 173–208.

81. *MGH,* 84.

82. *Ibid.,* 85–86.

83. *Ibid.,* 87.

84. *Jamaica Times,* August 17, 1912, p. 1.

85. Kingston *Daily Gleaner,* August 5, 1912, p. 3.

86. From "De Days Dat Are Gone," in *SJ,* 60.

87. *Jamaica Times,* August 10, 1912, p. 23.

## Chapter 3

1. J. H. Parry and Philip Sherlock, *A Short History of the West Indies* (3rd ed.; New York, 1971), 155–58. See also the following articles on race and class in Jamaica and the West Indies: Marcus Garvey, "The Race Question in Jamaica (1916)"; C. V. D. Hadley, "Personality Patterns, Social Class, and Aggression in the British West Indies"; and Rex Nettleford, "National Identity and Attitudes to Race in Jamaica," all in David Lowenthal and Lambros Comitas (eds.), *Consequences of Class and Color: West Indian Perspectives* (Garden City, N.Y., 1973), 4–12, 13–34, 35–56.

2. C. Vann Woodward, *The Strange Career of Jim Crow* (2nd rev. ed.; New York, 1966), 3–95; Rayford W. Logan, *The Negro in American Life and Thought: The Nadir* (New York, 1954). On the castelike aspects of black-white relations in the United States, see Gunnar Myrdal, *An American Dilemma: The Negro Problem and Modern Democracy* (4th ed.; New York, 1944), 667–88.

3. For a relevant general description of lower-middle-class British West Indian personality patterns and their historical and social psychological determinants, see Hadley, "Personality Patterns, Social Class, and Aggression in the British West Indies," in Lowenthal and Comitas (eds.), *Consequences of Class and Color,* 13–34.

4. The varied black American opposition to Booker T. Washington's racial leadership has been discussed by a number of scholars. See August Meier, *Negro Thought in America, 1880–1915: Racial Ideologies in the Age of Booker T. Washington* (Ann Arbor, 1963), 161–278; and Louis Harlan, *Booker T. Washington: The Making of a Black Leader, 1856–1901* (New York, 1972), 304–24.

5. "ANP," 275–76.

6. *Ibid.*

7. Harlan, *Booker T. Washington*, 272–81.

8. Claude McKay, "In Memoriam: Booker T. Washington," was first printed in *PCM*, 116. As late as the 1930s, McKay would still cite Washington's work at Tuskegee as an example of what could be accomplished by black group effort. See Claude McKay, "For Group Survival," *Jewish Frontier*, IV (October, 1937), 19–26, reprinted in *PCM*, 234–39.

9. My thanks to Louis R. Harlan for this letter.

10. Student transcripts of Claude McKay from Kansas State, 1912–1914. My thanks to the Kansas State Registrar's Office and to Professor James C. Carey of the History Department of Kansas State for providing me with the complete transcripts.

11. "RHH." See also Claude McKay, "A Negro Writer to His Critics," *New York Herald Tribune Books*, March 6, 1932, reprinted in *PCM*, 132–39.

12. P. Okhrimenko, "Original Translator's Note," in *NA*.

13. Theodore Draper, *The Roots of American Communism* (New York, 1957), 41–44.

14. W. E. B. Du Bois, *The Souls of Black Folk* (Chicago, 1903); *ALWFH*, 109–10.

15. Du Bois, *The Souls of Black Folk*, 3–4.

16. Langston Hughes, *The Fight for Freedom: The Story of the NAACP* (New York, 1962), 203.

17. James Weldon Johnson, *Along This Way: The Autobiography of James Weldon Johnson* (New York, 1933), 203.

18. "RHH."

19. Student transcripts of Claude McKay.

20. *ALWFH*, 4.

21. Claude McKay to James Weldon Johnson, March 10, 1928, in CMP.

22. Countee Cullen (ed.), *Caroling Dusk: An Anthology of Negro Poetry* (New York, 1927), 82. McKay's daughter wrote that she had always understood that McKay received a $1,000 award from Kansas State upon his graduation in 1914 (Hope McKay Virtue to Wayne Cooper, June 7, 1964, in possession of the recipient). McKay, however, stated that he "quit college" (*ALWFH*, 4).

23. "ANP," 275–76.

24. Marriage license of Claude McKay and Eulalie I. Lewars, in CMP.

25. "RHH."

26. Gilbert Osofsky, *Harlem, The Making of a Ghetto: Negro New York, 1890–1930* (2nd ed.; New York, 1971), 110–11. For a historical survey of black neighborhoods in New York since 1865, see Seth Scheiner, *Negro Mecca: A History of the Negro in New York City, 1865–1920* (New York, 1965), 15–44. For a view of Harlem and Negro New York that reflects the hopefulness of Harlem residents around World War I, see James Weldon Johnson, *Black Manhattan* (New York, 1930).

27. For a detailed account of the early years of the NAACP, see Charles Flint Kellogg, *NAACP: A History of the National Association for the Advancement of Colored People (1909–1920)* (Baltimore, 1967).

28. Nancy Weiss, *The National Urban League, 1910–1940* (New York, 1974), 3–107.

29. James Weldon Johnson, "Brief Biography of Claude McKay" (Two-page statement, in Claude McKay file, HFP).

30. *Ibid.* In a letter to Johnson, McKay denied his restaurant venture had been on West Fifty-third Street (March 10, 1928, in JWJP). See McKay's statement about the restaurant he "managed" in Brooklyn, in *ALWFH*, 54.

31. *HH*, 35, 40.

32. *ALWFH,* 54.

33. "RHH."

34. "ANP," 275–76.

35. Claude McKay to James Weldon Johnson, March 10, 1928, Johnson to McKay, April 12, 1928, both in JWJP.

36. Hope McKay Virtue to Wayne Cooper, June 7, 1964, in possession of the recipient.

37. See "Truant," in *G,* 157–62.

38. This information regarding McKay's personal life was revealed to the author in conversations by several individuals who knew McKay after World War I. They included Carl Cowl, James Ivy, Dr. Fanny Rappaport-Vogein, and Charles Ashleigh. In addition, see Adolf Dehn to Wayne Cooper, January 14, 1964, in possession of the recipient.

39. *HH,* 57; for other examples, see "Romance," "The Snow Fairy," "Tormented," and "One Year After," all in *HS,* 73–74, 76–77, 82, 84–85.

40. "RM."

41. From "Truant," in *G,* 154.

42. "ANP," 275–76.

43. *ALWFH,* 4.

44. Henry May, *The End of American Innocence: A Study of the First Years of Our Own Time, 1912–1917* (Chicago, 1964), vii–xii, 3–120.

45. *Ibid.,* 219–329.

46. *Ibid.*

47. Clearly, black writers in general confronted in their developing literature during and after World War I problems much deeper and more complex than credited to them in Nathan Huggins, *Harlem Renaissance* (New York, 1971).

48. *ALWFH,* 4–5, 26–27.

49. For a good overview of Braithwaite's lengthy and unusual career, see Philip Butcher (ed.), *The William Stanley Braithwaite Reader* (Ann Arbor, 1972).

50. Claude McKay [Rhonda Hope] to William Braithwaite, January 11, 1916, in WSBP.

51. Claude McKay to William Stanley Braithwaite, September 29, 1918, *ibid.*

52. McKay [Rhonda Hope] to Braithwaite, January 11, 1916, *ibid.*

53. Claude McKay [Rhonda Hope] to William Braithwaite, February 15, 1916, *ibid.*

54. "Remorse," "My Ethiopian Maid," and "My Werther Days," all in WSBP.

55. "In Memoriam: Booker T. Washington" and "To the White Fiends," both *ibid.*

56. In 1937, McKay remembered only that Braithwaite had advised him "to write and send to the magazines only such poems as did not betray my racial identity." In fairness to Braithwaite, McKay might have remembered that he had initially voiced to Braithwaite his own concern that his poems on nonracial themes had elicited no interest among publishers and that he had shared at the time Braithwaite's concern that blacks not be judged solely on the basis of their race and racial concerns. *ALWFH,* 26–28.

57. *Ibid.,* 28.

58. Kellogg, *NAACP,* 4–64.

59. McKay to Braithwaite, September 29, 1918, in WSBP. See also Claude McKay, "Socialism and the Negro," *WD,* January 31, 1920.

60. Joel Spingarn, *Creative Criticism* (New York, 1917). See also Kellogg, *NAACP,* 61–283; Robert E. Spiller (ed.), *Literary History of the United States* (Rev. ed.; New

York, 1957), 1154–56; and B. Joyce Ross, *J. E. Spingarn and the Rise of the NAACP, 1911–1939* (New York, 1972).

61. *ALWFH*, 147.

62. From a *Seven Arts* editorial, written by Joel Oppenheim and quoted in May, *The End of American Innocence*, 325–26.

63. *ALWFH*, 26.

64. From Claude McKay, "Invocation," in *Seven Arts*, II (October, 1917), 741.

65. Richard Wright, *Black Boy: A Record of Childhood and Youth* (New York, 1945), 45; Ralph Ellison, *Invisible Man* (New York, 1952); James Baldwin, *Nobody Knows My Name: More Notes of a Native Son* (New York, 1961).

66. From Claude McKay, "The Harlem Dancer," in *Seven Arts*, II (October, 1917), 741.

67. May, *The End of American Innocence*, 392.

68. Bertrand Russell, "Is Nationalism Moribund?" *Seven Arts*, II (October, 1917), 687.

69. This poem obviously referred to the period immediately after the institution of Prohibition, but it was inspired by McKay's World War I railroad experiences. Untitled poem from Claude McKay's short story "Truant," in *G*, 159.

70. *HH*, 140.

71. From "Truant," in *G*, 144–45.

72. Claude McKay to Max Eastman, July 30, 1942, in *PCM*, 301–302.

73. *ALWFH*, 45–52.

74. *Ibid.*, 45, 50–52.

75. *Ibid.*, 49.

76. McKay, "A Negro Writer to His Critics," in *PCM*, 136–37.

77. Charles King to Claude McKay, April 5, 1928, in CMP.

78. *HH*, 79–80. In the chapter entitled "Myrtle Avenue," there also occurs a discussion about cocaine and its easy availability before World War I (*HH*, 35).

79. *ALWFH*, 30.

80. *Ibid.*, 3, 5–10. For an authoritative study of Harris, see Philippa Pullar, *Frank Harris: A Biography* (New York, 1976).

81. *ALWFH*, 9–10.

82. *Ibid.*, 18.

83. *Ibid.*, 21–22.

84. "ANP," 276.

85. Claude McKay to Max Eastman, October 16, 1944, in *PCM*, 305.

86. Okhrimenko, "Original Translator's Note," in *NA*. McKay reprinted in full a statement on the revolutionary aims of the IWW given to him in Moscow by William ("Big Bill") Haywood, the former IWW leader who had fled the United States in 1921 rather than accept a long jail sentence imposed upon him and other IWW leaders by a federal court in Chicago (*NA*, 29–33). Useful histories of the IWW include Melvyn Dubofsky's *We Shall Be All: A History of the I.W.W.* (Chicago, 1969); and Patrick Renshaw's *The Wobblies: The Story of Syndicalism in the United States* (Garden City, N.Y., 1967).

87. Philip S. Foner, *American Socialism and Black Americans: From the Age of Jackson to World War II* (Westport, Conn., 1977), 207–18.

88. *ALWFH*, 41–42.

89. Henry Miller, *Plexus* (New York, 1965), 560–61.

90. See Daniel Aaron, *Writers on the Left: Episodes in American Literary Com-*

*munism* (New York, 1961), 18; William L. O'Neill, *Echoes of Revolt: "The Masses,"*
*1911–1917* (Chicago, 1966), 17–24, and *The Last Romantic: A Life of Max Eastman*
(New York, 1979), 30–53; and May, *The End of American Innocence*, 314–17.

91. Quoted in Aaron, *Writers on the Left*, 21.

92. *Ibid.*, 41–113; O'Neill, *The Last Romantic*, 65–67, 72–81.

93. *ALWFH*, 28–29.

94. O'Neill, *The Last Romantic*, 37–38.

95. Claude McKay, "The Dominant White," in *L*, II (April, 1919), 20; *ALWFH*,
28–29, 39; O'Neill, *The Last Romantic*, 73.

96. See the biographical sketch of Crystal Eastman in Blanche Wiesen Cook
(ed.), *Crystal Eastman on Women and Revolution* (New York, 1978), 1–38.

97. *ALWFH*, 29–30.

98. *Ibid.*, 30.

99. O'Neill, *The Last Romantic*, 3–81.

100. *ALWFH*, 30–31; *PCM*, v, 300–16.

101. Max Eastman in the *Masses* and Joseph Freeman, quoted in Aaron, *Writers
on the Left*, 23. Freeman's autobiography provides many interesting parallels and con-
trasts to McKay's *A Long Way from Home*. Freeman, the son of Russian Jewish immigrants, grew up in New York City and attended Columbia University, but he shared
with McKay many of the same formative cultural influences, and their paths to communism were in many ways similar. Both had been indelibly influenced by English
literature and shared the same literary tastes. Both fell under the spell of the *Masses*
and Max Eastman, and both eventually shared the same disillusionment with communism, though Freeman remained in the party as a functionary until the late 1930s. See
Joseph Freeman, *An American Testament: A Narrative of Rebels and Romantics* (New
York, 1936).

102. O'Neill, *The Last Romantic*, 68–99. Max Eastman also very ably told his own
story of these years in *Love and Revolution: My Journey Through an Epoch* (New York,
1964), 3–166.

103. Max Eastman, quoted in Aaron, *Writers on the Left*, 42. On Eastman's early
years, see Max Eastman, *Enjoyment of Living* (New York, 1948); and O'Neill, *The
Last Romantic*, 3–53.

104. See McKay's letters to Eastman in *PCM*, 150–55, 307.

105. Claude McKay to Max Eastman, July 29, 1919, in *PCM*, 11.

106. O'Neill, *The Last Romantic*, 3–29. For the story of Max Eastman's second
marriage, see his own *Love and Revolution*, 644–51.

107. Throughout his life, Eastman consistently expressed admiration and respect
for McKay, whose friendship he valued. For examples, see Eastman's "Introduction" to
*HS*, ix–xviii; and Eastman, *Love and Revolution*, 72, 222–23, 467–68, 495. On Eastman's own doubts concerning his gift for poetry and his insistence upon McKay's vocation as poet, see respectively O'Neill, *The Last Romantic*, 246–48, 280–81, 296; and
*PCM*, 302. Finally, I would like to thank Carl Cowl, Claude McKay's literary executor,
for allowing me to hear the tape in his possession of Max Eastman's speech on Claude
McKay, delivered in 1952 at the New York Public Library's Schomburg Center in
Harlem. I also learned much about Eastman's loyalty to McKay's memory during the
several conversations I had with Eastman before his death in 1969. Eastman, who was
so frank about his own sexual life, remembered nothing about McKay's sexual preferences, even after an incredulous Carl Cowl (also present during this particular conversation) bluntly told Eastman he must have known of McKay's homosexuality.

108. A good summary of the unstable international climate in 1919 and its unbal-

ancing effect in the United States can be found in William M. Tuttle, Jr., *Race Riot: Chicago in the Red Summer of 1919* (New York, 1970), 1–50. See also Robert K. Murray, *Red Scare: A Study in National Hysteria, 1919–1920* (Minneapolis, 1955); and William Preston, Jr., *Aliens and Dissenters: Federal Suppression of Radicals, 1903–1933* (Cambridge, Mass., 1963).

109. Murray, *Red Scare.*
110. Tuttle, *Race Riot,* 3–31, 208–67.
111. *Ibid.,* 74–207.
112. *Ibid.,* 208–41.
113. *HH,* 140–41.
114. *ALWFH,* 31.
115. Tuttle, *Race Riot,* 208–41.
116. *HH,* 140.
117. Max Eastman, quoted in O'Neill, *The Last Romantic,* 37.
118. Claude McKay, "A Roman Holiday," in *L,* II (July, 1919), 21.
119. Claude McKay, "If We Must Die," *ibid.*
120. *ALWFH,* 21.
121. *Ibid.,* 31–32.
122. *Ibid.,* 31.
123. *Time,* September 27, 1971.
124. Claude McKay, "The Capitalist at Dinner," in *L,* II (July, 1919), 21.
125. Claude McKay, "The Little Peoples," *ibid.,* 20.

## Chapter 4

1. Max Eastman, "Claude McKay," *L,* II (July, 1919), 7.
2. W. A. Domingo in *Messenger,* September, 1919, quoted in Investigative Activities of the Department of Justice, Exhibit No. 10, "Radicalism and Sedition Among Negroes, As Reflected in Their Publications," *Senate Executive Documents,* 66th Cong., 1st Sess., No. 153, pp. 161–87, hereafter cited as U.S. Dept. of Justice, "Radicalism and Sedition Among Negroes."
3. Alain Locke (ed.), *The New Negro* (1925; rpr. New York, 1968), 4.
4. Edmund David Cronon, *Black Moses: The Story of Marcus Garvey and the Universal Negro Improvement Association* (Madison, Wis., 1955). See also Amy Jacques Garvey (ed.), *The Philosophy and Opinions of Marcus Garvey, Or Africa for the Africans* (2 vols.; rpr. New York, 1969); and John Henrik Clarke (ed.), *Marcus Garvey and the Vision of Africa* (New York, 1974).
5. *ALWFH,* 32.
6. *Ibid.,* 41–42, 55, 113; Philip S. Foner, *American Socialism and Black Americans: From the Age of Jackson to World War II* (Westport, Conn., 1977), 207–18, 266, 324. Several authors have devoted brief attention to black radicals in postwar New York. See especially James Weldon Johnson, *Black Manhattan* (New York, 1930), 246–51; and Theodore Draper, *American Communism and Soviet Russia: The Formative Period* (New York, 1960), 315–35. For an important, detailed autobiography of one black American radical who came of age during and after World War I, see Harry Haywood, *Black Bolshevik: The Autobiography of an Afro-American Communist* (Chicago, 1978). Two indispensable primary sources are government publications that resulted from the Red Scare of 1919: U.S. Dept. of Justice, "Radicalism and Sedition Among Negroes," 161–87; and New York (State) Legislature Joint Committee Investigating Seditious Activities, *Revolutionary Radicalism: Its History, Purpose and Tactics, with an Exposition and Discussion of the Steps Being Taken and Required to Curb It, Being*

the *Report of the Joint Legislative Committees Investigating Seditious Activities, Filed April 24, 1920 in the Senate of the State of New York* (4 vols.; Albany, N.Y., 1920), II, 1476–1520, hereafter cited as New York Legislature, *Revolutionary Radicalism.*

7. Jervis A. Anderson, *A. Philip Randolph: A Biographical Portrait* (New York, 1972); Theodore Kornweibel, Jr., *No Crystal Stair: Black Life and "The Messenger," 1917–1928* (Westport, Conn., 1975); Foner, *American Socialism and Black Americans,* 265–311.

8. Draper, *American Communism and Soviet Russia,* 322–26.

9. *Ibid.,* 325.

10. *Ibid.,* 326–53.

11. On W. A. Domingo, see *PCM,* 343–44. For information on Domingo, as well as the other Harlem socialists discussed here, I am indebted to Ben Waknin of New York City, whose work-in-progress contains a minutely detailed analysis of their individual personalities and thought. See also Kornweibel, *No Crystal Stair,* 3–104.

12. See Draper, *American Communism and Soviet Russia,* 322–53; Anderson, *A. Philip Randolph,* 68–150; Kornweibel, *No Crystal Stair,* 3–104; and *PCM,* 336, 343–44. For an extremely partisan, negative assessment of these early Harlem radicals, see Harold Cruse, *The Crisis of the Negro Intellectual from Its Origin to the Present Day* (New York, 1967).

13. By the mid-1930s, Afro-American charges that he had abandoned Harlem and black American efforts for racial advancement during the 1920s led McKay to defend his right to white as well as black friendships and impelled him to explain the reasons for his lengthy European expatriation after 1922. See *ALWFH,* 35–44, 237–354.

14. *Ibid.,* 39–42.

15. See "Old England," in *SJ,* 63; *ALWFH,* 60, 80; and C. K. Ogden, "Recent Verse," *Cambridge Magazine,* X (January-March, 1921), 115–17.

16. *ALWFH,* 66–72. See also Wayne Cooper and Robert C. Reinders, "A Black Briton Comes Home: Claude McKay in England, 1920," *Race,* IX (1967), 67–83.

17. *ALWFH,* 67.

18. *Ibid.*

19. *Ibid.;* Donald W. Klein and Anne B. Clark (eds.), *The Biographic Dictionary of Chinese Communism* (Cambridge, Mass., 1971), I, 204–19; Sidney Taylor (ed.), *The New Africans: A Guide to the Contemporary History of Emergent Africa and Its Leaders* (London, 1967), 370–73, 215–17.

20. *ALWFH,* 67–69.

21. *Ibid.,* 68. In *ALWFH,* McKay referred to it as "the International Club." Considering his disenchantment with international socialism in the 1930s, his omission of the word *Socialist* is understandable.

22. *Ibid.,* 68–69.

23. Claude McKay to Max Eastman, September 16, 1946, in *PCM,* 312. See the poem "Travail," in *WD,* January 10, 1920.

24. *ALWFH,* 69–70. Advertisements for the club's social activities appeared regularly in Sylvia Pankhurst's *WD.*

25. The literature on the British Labour party is large. For a compact summary of the party's evolution, see Henry Pelling, *A Short History of the Labour Party* (4th ed.; London, 1972). See Raymond Challinor, *The Origins of British Bolshevism* (London, 1977); Walter Kendall, *The Revolutionary Movement in Britain, 1900–1921: The Origins of British Communism* (London, 1969). See also Stanley Pierson, *British Socialists: The Journey from Fantasy to Politics* (Cambridge, Mass., 1979), 1–42, 253–350.

26. Challinor, *The Origins of British Bolshevism,* 160–66, 237–40, 195–283; Pierson, *British Socialists,* 270–91.

27. Challinor, *The Origins of British Bolshevism,* 87–215. Challinor, a Trotskyite, writes from a perspective sympathetic to the Socialist Labour Party.

28. The best portrait of Pankhurst and her organization is contained in David J. Mitchell's *The Fighting Pankhursts: A Study in Tenacity* (New York, 1967), 19–50, 80–110, 177–88, 239–63, 308–40. For other views on Sylvia Pankhurst and the Workers' Socialist Federation, see Challinor, *The Origins of British Bolshevism,* 168–69, 176, 220, 241; and Kendall, *The Revolutionary Movement in Britain,* 206–37.

29. *WD,* September 11, 1920.

30. Interview by Robert C. Reinders with Frank and Francine Budgen, August 18, 1966, in London. The artist, literary critic, and former revolutionary socialist, Frank Budgen, and his wife, Francine, both knew McKay well in 1920; they believed he first became acquainted with members of Pankhurst's organization at the International Socialist Club.

31. Claude McKay, "A Black Man Replies," *WD,* April 24, 1920. For the full story of Morel's campaign against the French and their use of black troops on the Rhine, see Robert C. Reinders, "Racialism on the Left: E. D. Morel and the 'Black Horror on the Rhine,'" *International Review of Social History,* CIII (First quarter, 1968), 1–28.

32. All the quotations are from Claude McKay, "A Black Man Replies." Before McKay's arrival in England, the *WD* had spoken out against outbreaks of white violence against blacks in London and had urged working-class tolerance of blacks in Great Britain. See especially the editorial commentary, "Stabbing Negroes in the London Dock Area," *WD,* June 7, 1919.

33. *ALWFH,* 74–76.

34. Between January and April 17, 1920, the following poems by Claude McKay appeared in *WD:* "Travail" and "Samson," January 10, 1920; "Song of the New Soldier and Worker," April 3, 1920; "Joy in the Woods," April 10, 1920; [pseud. Hugh Hope], "A Hero of the Wars," April 17, 1920. During the same period, the following articles also appeared in the *WD:* "Socialism and the Negro," January 31, 1920; "The Capitalist Way: Lettow-Vorbeck," February 7, 1920; "An International Money Crisis," February 14, 1920. On Sylvia Pankhurst's travels in the months prior to January, 1920, see Mitchell, *The Fighting Pankhursts,* 86–87.

35. See Reinders' interview with Frank and Francine Budgen. The Budgens believed that McKay had been introduced to the International Socialist Club by "Lillian Thring, a suffragette and friend of Sylvia Pankhurst." Crystal Eastman had preceded McKay in London the year before, and she may have suggested to him before he left New York that he look up Pankhurst and her group.

36. *ALWFH,* 76–77; Mitchell, *The Fighting Pankhursts,* 80–101.

37. Mitchell, *The Fighting Pankhursts,* 80–101.

38. *Ibid.;* see also Challinor, *The Origins of British Bolshevism,* 168–69, 150–256; and Kendall, *The Revolutionary Movement in Britain,* 187–257. Kendall wrote from a nonrevolutionary perspective. His account of the Russian role in the foundation of the Communist Party of Great Britain should be compared to Challinor's account, written from a critical socialist revolutionary perspective. Both Kendall and Challinor should be compared to more orthodox Communist party histories. In particular, see L. J. MacFarlane, *The British Communist Party: Its Origins and Development until 1929* (London, 1966), 30–126; and James Klugmann, *History of the Communist Party of Great Britain,* Vol. I, *Formation and Early Years, 1919–1924* (London, 1968).

39. *ALWFH,* 76–77.

40. McKay, "The Capitalist Way."

41. McKay, "Travail," in *WD.*

42. McKay, "Samson," *ibid.*

43. Claude McKay [Rhonda Hope] to William Stanley Braithwaite, January 11, February 15, 1916, both in WSBP.

44. Mitchell, *The Fighting Pankhursts,* 80–87.

45. Mitchell, in *The Fighting Pankhursts,* has a good deal to say about the use of pseudonyms by other writers on the *WD.*

46. McKay, "Socialism and the Negro." See Challinor, *The Origins of British Bolshevism,* 40–41, 158–59, 267–68, and *passim.* Harold Cruse believes the influence of black socialists on the Garvey movement was extremely pernicious, as they distracted blacks from greater concentration on primary community development (*The Crisis of the Negro Intellectual,* 44–63, 115–46). Ironically, McKay came close to advancing the same argument in the 1930s, at a time when the young Harold Cruse, just coming to maturity, looked to the American Communist party for leadership.

47. McKay, "Song of the New Soldier and Worker," in *WD.*

48. *ALWFH,* 86.

49. Ogden, "Recent Verse," 116–17.

50. *Ibid.,* 117. On Ogden's World War I coverage of the international press in *Cambridge Magazine,* see Margaret Cole's comments in the *Times* (London), March 29, 1957, p. 13. See also P. Sargent Florence and J. R. L. Anderson (eds.), *C. K. Ogden: A Collective Memoir* (London, 1977), 13–55, 56–81.

51. See "Poems: Claude McKay," *Cambridge Magazine,* X (Summer, 1920), 55–58.

52. Brown, *West Indian Poetry,* 19–62.

53. Kendall, *The Revolutionary Movement in Britain,* 196–219; Mitchell, *The Fighting Pankhursts,* 94–95; Challinor, *The Origins of British Bolshevism,* 252–53. The *Workers' Dreadnought* reported upon the formation and aims of the Communist Party (BSTI) in its issues of June 26 and July 3, 1920.

54. Mitchell, *The Fighting Pankhursts,* 88–93. Lenin and the Third Communist International were endeavoring to bring antiparliamentarians in Germany and Italy, as well as in Great Britain, into line with the Third International's new policy of left-wing European unity under Russian leadership. To this end, Lenin in his famous pamphlet, *Left Wing Communism: An Infantile Sickness,* attacked Sylvia Pankhurst and another British Communist, William Gallacher, as romantic, unscientific, and ineffectual participants in the new Communist internationalism. McKay counted Gallacher, as well as Pankhurst, a friend. See *ALWFH,* 64.

55. *ALWFH,* 76. For more on Comrade Vie, see Kendall, *The Revolutionary Movement in Britain,* 243, 246–49.

56. See Claude McKay [Hugh Hope], "Re-Affirmation," in *WD,* July 3, 1920. For a good survey of revolutionary events in Europe during 1919, see David J. Mitchell, *1919: Red Mirage* (New York, 1970). The following list of articles gives some idea of the range of topics discussed in the *WD:* Shapurji Saklatvala, "Coal and Iron," February 14, 1920; Louis C. Fraina, "The American White Terror and the Communist Party," February 28, 1920; [Editorial], "An African Protests," June 21, 1919; [Editorial], "The Colour Bar," January 10, 1920; and Herman Gorter, "Ireland: The Achilles Heel of England," May 8, 1920.

57. Claude McKay [Ness Edwards], "Some Thoughts on Tactics," *WD,* July 24, 1920. This was McKay's first use of the pseudonym Ness Edwards. He did not use it again until October 28, 1920, when in "Revolutionary Mass Action," he argued that the increased use of labor-saving technology in industry actually meant less profit for

the capitalist in the long run because machinery in itself could not compensate for the actual "surplus value" of the human labor displaced by technology. This argument was challenged and Ness Edwards responded (November 18, 1920) with a short recapitulation of his views, entitled "A Debate." McKay used the pseudonym C. E. Edwards more frequently in the *WD*. My suspicion is that he reserved Ness Edwards for his few ventures into the realm of pure Marxist theory. It is also possible that Ness Edwards may have been a joint effort by McKay and Comrade Vie, Erkki Veltheim. These articles have the imprint of McKay's style, but they are much more theoretical than most of his work. Another possibility, of course, remains: the short editorial criticisms that appear after Ness Edwards first two articles could have been written by Veltheim as a part of his efforts to help McKay be "more effectively radical." See also "Editorial Afterword," *WD*, July 24, 1920; and Claude McKay [Hugh Hope], "Communism and the Local Councils of Action," *WD*, September 25, 1920.

58. Claude McKay [C. E. Edwards], "The Revolution in Currency," *WD*, October 2, 1920.

59. See Claude McKay [Hugh Hope], "Review of *First Principles of Working Class Education* by James Clunie," *WD*, September 11, 1920; Claude McKay [Hugh Hope], "The Leader of the Bristol Revolutionaries," *WD*, August 7, 1920. On the Unity Conference, see Kendall, *The Revolutionary Movement in Britain*, 207–209, 211–12.

60. Claude McKay [Hugh Hope], "The Leader of the Bristol Revolutionaries." For a good brief summary of the way the British government dealt with labor's demands after World War I, see Charles Loch Mowat, *Britain Between the Wars, 1918–1940* (Chicago, 1955), 17–46. Mowat's retrospective views on the British government's reactionary stance toward labor after World War I generally accords with the criticism of the British Left at the time, though Mowat states his views in less extreme language.

61. Claude McKay [Our Special Correspondent], "Official Labor at Portsmouth," *WD*, September 18, 1920. McKay later discussed this article at length in *ALWFH*, 79–82.

62. *ALWFH*, 79. McKay did note the conclusion of the lumberyard strike in *WD*. See Claude McKay [C. E. Edwards], "End of Strike in Saw-Mills," *WD*, September 11, 1920. On Pankhurst's relation to William Lansbury, the lumber merchant, see Mitchell, *The Fighting Pankhursts*, 44, 109.

63. Mitchell, *The Fighting Pankhursts*, 89–95; Kendall, *The Revolutionary Movement in Britain*, 212, 232, 237.

64. David Springhall [R.000 (Stoker) HMS *Reliance*], "From the Lower Deck," *WD*, September 4, 1920; David Springhall [S.000 (Gunner) HMS *Lucie*], "With the Red Navy in the Baltic," *WD*, September 25, 1920; David Springhall [S.000 (Gunner) HMS *Hunter*], "Discontent on the Lower Deck," *WD*, October 16, 1920.

65. [Editorial], "A Communist on Trial," *WD*, November 6, 1920.

66. *ALWFH*, 76. The historian Walter Kendall, who examined Sylvia Pankhurst's papers at the International Institute of Social History in Amsterdam for his *Revolutionary Movement in Britain*, stated that he suspected "an article [by Claude McKay] helped send Sylvia Pankhurst to jail in 1920" (Walter Kendall to Robert C. Reinders, June 3, 1966, in my possession).

67. Claude McKay [Leon Lopez], "The Yellow Peril and the Dockers," *WD*, October 16, 1920.

68. *ALWFH*, 82–83.

69. *Ibid.*, 83–84. McKay's account has been confirmed and expanded upon by Kendall, *The Revolutionary Movement in Britain*, 246–58. Veltheim, who was born in Hollola, Finland, was only twenty-two years old at the time of his arrest.

70. *ALWFH*, 86.

71. Kendall, *The Revolutionary Movement in Britain*, 248–49.

72. From "A Communist on Trial."

73. *ALWFH*, 64–65.

74. I. A. Richards' "Preface" to *SNH;* I. A. Richards to Robert C. Reinders, May 19, 1966, in my possession.

75. *ALWFH*, 86–87.

76. McKay was characteristically vague about just who raised the money for his return to the United States. "An English friend," he wrote, "an I.W.W. who lived in America (I think he had been deported thence), undertook to find a group of friends to put up the fare to get me back there" (*ALWFH*, 87). The "English friend" was never further identified.

77. See also Charles Loch Mowat's interpretation of post–World War I England in his critical history, *Britain Between the Wars*, 1–142.

78. *ALWFH*, 61–64.

79. *Ibid.*, 71.

80. "Poets and Poetry," *Spectator*, CXXV (October 23, 1920), 539–40, quoted in *ALWFH*, 88. In his notice of *SNH* in the January-March, 1921, issue of *Cambridge Magazine*, C. K. Ogden confirmed that, with a single exception, "only one of the score or more journals on which the public depends for literary information has done more than briefly indicate that a 'nigger minstrel' or 'an overseas nigger' has issued some verses." The one exception, Ogden noted, was the *Westminster Review*, which gave McKay's verse its warm endorsement. See Ogden, "Recent Verse," 117.

81. See also *PCM*, 193–293.

82. Cooper and Reinders, "A Black Briton Comes Home," 83. See also Henry Pelling, *The British Communist Party: A Historical Profile* (London, 1958), 50, 93, 109, 111, 125–26.

83. Frank Budgen, *James Joyce and the Making of Ulysses* (Rpr. Bloomington, 1960).

84. Interview by Reinders with Frank and Francine Budgen.

85. *ALWFH*, 87.

86. Mitchell, *The Fighting Pankhursts*, 323, see also 102–10, 239–66, 308–40.

87. From "Flame-Heart," in *SNH*, 30.

88. "Exhortation" first appeared as "To Ethiopia," in *L*, III (February, 1920), 7. On the Hampstead School of African Socialism, see Cooper and Reinders, "A Black Briton Comes Home," 80.

## Chapter 5

1. Interview by Robert C. Reinders with Frank and Francine Budgen, August 18, 1966, in London. The Budgens remembered that McKay had seemed especially fond of Max and Crystal Eastman. During his sojourn in England, McKay contributed the following poems to the *L*: "To Ethiopia" and "Home Thoughts," III (February, 1920), 7, 19; "Mother," III (March, 1920), 24; and "The Tropics in New York," III (May, 1920), 48.

2. *ALWFH*, 96.

3. *MGH*, 48–50.

4. *ALWFH*, 97.

5. Max Eastman, "Editorials," *L*, IV (March, 1921), 1. See also Max Eastman, *Love and Revolution: My Journey Through an Epoch* (New York, 1964), 220–25; and *ALWFH*, 97.

6. Eastman, *Love and Revolution*, 225.

7. *ALWFH*, 97. See also Claude McKay to Max Eastman, April 3, 1923, in *PCM*, 83–84.

8. *ALWFH*, 99.

9. The *Liberator* published many firsthand accounts of Russian affairs, including those by John Reed, who unfortunately died shortly before McKay joined the magazine's editorial staff. See John Reed, "Soviet Russia Now," *L*, III (December, 1920), 9–11, and IV (January, 1921), 14–17; Boris Reinstein, "On Duty in Russia: A Letter from Boris Reinstein," *L*, IV (February, 1921), 16–17. For an authoritative discussion of the *Liberator*'s new revolutionary seriousness and the tensions it produced, see Aaron, *Writers on the Left*, 91–95. On Eastman's politics between 1918 and 1922, see William L. O'Neill, *The Last Romantic: A Life of Max Eastman* (New York, 1979), 82–99.

10. Eastman, *Love and Revolution*, 216–17, 224–25. See also Eastman, "To John Reed," Boardman Robinson, "A Memory," and John Reed, "The Dead and the Living: From a Letter Written by John Reed," all in *L*, IV (February, 1921), 15, 17, 20. See also Louise Bryant, "In Memory," *L*, IV (July, 1921), 24. For more on John Reed, see Granville Hicks, *John Reed: The Making of a Revolutionary* (New York, 1936); Richard O'Connor and Dale L. Walker, *The Lost Revolutionary: A Biography of John Reed* (New York, 1967); and Robert A. Rosenstone, *Romantic Revolutionary: A Biography of John Reed* (New York, 1975).

11. *ALWFH*, 130–31; Eastman, "Editorials."

12. *ALWFH*, 99–102, 104.

13. Clare Sheridan, *My American Diary* (New York, 1922).

14. *ALWFH*, 103–104. For example, see E. E. Cummings, "Maison," and "Libation," both in *L*, IV (July, 1921), 17, 24. See also Eastman, *Love and Revolution*, 139–40.

15. Max Eastman discusses his relationship with Deshon in detail in *Love and Revolution*, 7–11, and *passim*.

16. Charlie Chaplin, *My Trip Abroad* (New York, 1922), 31–33, and *My Autobiography* (New York, 1964), 285.

17. *ALWFH*, 117–19.

18. The importance of interracial contact in launching and promoting the Harlem Renaissance has been discussed by Hugh M. Gloster, *Negro Voices in American Fiction* (Chapel Hill, 1948), 106–11.

19. Claude McKay to William Stanley Braithwaite, December 15, 1920, in WSBP.

20. *ALWFH*, 147–48, 98.

21. *Ibid.*, 108–15, 147–48. See also Claude McKay to Arthur A. Schomburg, July 17, 1925, in *PCM*, 141–42.

22. *ALWFH*, 111–12. McKay dedicated his last book to the memory of Johnson. See *H*.

23. Claude McKay, "Letter to the Editors," *Crisis*, XXV (July, 1921), 102. See also W. E. B. Du Bois, *Dusk of Dawn: An Essay Toward an Autobiography of a Race Concept* (New York, 1940), 234–35, *The Autobiography of W. E. B. Du Bois: A Soliloquy on Viewing My Life From the Last Decade of Its First Century* (New York, 1968), 289, and "Editorial [Reply to Claude McKay]," *Crisis*, XXV (July, 1921), 102–104.

24. *ALWFH*, 108–15, 147–48. See also Charles F. Cooney, "Walter White and the Harlem Renaissance," *Journal of Negro History*, LVII (July, 1972), 231–40.

25. See *ALWFH*, 64–65, 110–11, 113–14. See also Claude McKay to Arthur A. Schomburg, July 17, 1925, and [undated, 1925], both in *PCM*, 141–43. McKay's deep-

seated antipathy to light-complexioned, middle-class Negroes has been discussed by Ellen Tarry in *The Third Door: An Autobiography of an American Negro Woman* (New York, 1955), 129; and in Wagner, *Black Poets in the United States,* 216. This topic was also brought up by Carl Cowl, James Ivy, and Bruce Nugent—all former friends of McKay's—in conversations with me over an extended period in the 1960s and 1970s. For more on the life of Walter White, see *A Man Called White: The Autobiography of Walter White* (New York, 1948); and Poppy Cannon, *A Gentle Knight: My Husband, Walter White* (New York, 1956). See also James Weldon Johnson, *Along This Way: The Autobiography of James Weldon Johnson* (New York, 1933), 64–65.

26. *PCM,* 193–299.

27. See especially James Weldon Johnson, "What the Negro Is Doing for Himself," *L,* I (March, 1918), 32–33; and Mary White Ovington, "Bogalusa," *L,* III (January, 1920), 31–33.

28. *ALWFH,* 109.

29. Claude McKay to Max Eastman, May 18, 1923, in *PCM,* 89. McKay did not mention Eastman's concern in *ALWFH* but remembered that when he found the group in the *Liberator* office, he had jokingly remarked, "Ah, you conspirators" (*ALWFH,* 109).

30. Theodore Kornweibel, Jr., *No Crystal Stair: Black Life and "The Messenger," 1917–1928* (Westport, Conn., 1975), 3–41; Draper, *American Communism and Soviet Russia,* 322–26.

31. *ALWFH,* 153. Earlier statements in other publications contradict McKay's contention in *ALWFH* that "I was not a member of the Communist Party." In particular, see *NA,* ix, xviii, 88–90.

32. *ALWFH,* 114–15; *PCM,* 234–63. For a view of West Indian–Afro-American relations during this period, see Ira DeA. Reid, *The Negro Immigrant: His Background, Characteristics, and Social Adjustments, 1899–1937* (New York, 1939).

33. *ALWFH,* 113–14. See also Philip S. Foner, *American Socialism and Black Americans: From the Age of Jackson to World War II* (Westport, Conn., 1977), 208–19.

34. See also Claude McKay to James Weldon Johnson, February 3, 1922, in JWJP, NAACP. Identical copies of this letter and the one to Harrison were also sent to Walter White.

35. *ALWFH,* 130–35.

36. Eastman, *Love and Revolution,* 222.

37. Alfred Tiala to Wayne Cooper, February 7, 1964, in possession of the recipient.

38. John Barber to Wayne Cooper, May 18, 1964, in possession of the recipient.

39. Maurice Becker to Wayne Cooper, May 14, 1964, in possession of the recipient.

40. All the quotations are taken from William Gropper to Wayne Cooper, January 14, 1964, in possession of the recipient.

41. *ALWFH,* 103–109.

42. *Ibid.,* 133.

43. Adolf Dehn to Wayne Cooper, January 14, 1964, in possession of the recipient.

44. *ALWFH,* 109. See also *H,* 139–42.

45. Interview with Charles Ashleigh, October 22, 1972, in Brighton, England. Ashleigh was living in retirement there and had recounted his experiences in a long unpublished autobiography. In the late 1960s and early 1970s, he was frequently consulted by young radical students from the nearby University of Sussex. They found in him a living link to early British Communists and the American Industrial Workers of the World. Ashleigh remained in the Communist party through the entire Stalinist period, working mainly as a journalist in Paris for English Communist periodicals.

46. James W. Ivy, "Claude McKay's Remarkable Career," Pittsburgh *Courier, Illustrated Feature Section,* February 2, 1929, p. 7.

47. *SP,* 39–41.

48. From an unpublished poem by Claude McKay, first quoted in Wagner, *Black Poets of the United States,* 231. The quotation is from the first poem in McKay's "Cycle Manuscript," a collection of fifty sonnets in CMP.

49. From "The White City," in *SP,* 7.

50. From "American," *ibid.,* 59.

51. From "Mulatto," in *PCM,* 126.

52. Claude McKay to Max Eastman, January 26, March 21, 1945, both in *PCM,* 307, 309.

53. See Claude McKay, "How Black Sees Green and Red," *L,* IV (June, 1921), 17, 20–21, "Birthright," *L,* V (August, 1922), 15–16, "A Negro Extravaganza [A review of *Shuffle Along,* a musical by Noble Sissle and Eubie Blake]," *L,* IV (December, 1921), 24–26. For a listing of McKay's *Liberator* articles and reviews, see *PCM,* 353.

54. McKay, "How Black Sees Green and Red," reprinted in *PCM,* 59–62; Claude McKay, "Garvey as a Negro Moses," *L,* V (April, 1922), 9, reprinted in *PCM,* 65–69.

55. Garvey quoted in Edmund David Cronon, *Black Moses: The Story of Marcus Garvey and the Universal Negro Improvement Association* (Madison, Wis., 1955), 152; McKay, "Garvey as a Negro Moses," in *PCM,* 67–69.

56. McKay, "A Negro Extravaganza," reprinted in *PCM,* 62–63; *ALWFH,* 142; see also Helen Armstead Johnson, "*Shuffle Along:* Keynote of the Harlem Renaissance," in Errol Hill (ed.), *The Theatre of Black Americans,* Vol. I, *Roots and Rituals/The Image Makers* (Englewood Cliffs, N.J., 1980), 126–35.

57. Claude McKay, "He Who Gets Slapped," *L,* V (May, 1922), 24–25, reprinted in *PCM,* 69–73. See also Claude McKay, "A Black Star [Review of O'Neill's *Emperor Jones*]," *L,* IV (August, 1921), 25, and "What Is Lacking in the Theatre? [Review of *Chauve Souris*]," *L,* V (March, 1922), 20–21.

58. William Gropper to Wayne Cooper, January 14, 1964, in possession of the recipient. See also *PCM,* 69–73. McKay, "He Who Gets Slapped," in *PCM,* 70–72.

59. McKay, "Birthright," reprinted in *PCM,* 73–76. See also Robert C. Reinders, "Racialism on the Left: E. D. Morel and the 'Black Horror on the Rhine,'" *International Review of Social History,* CIII (First quarter, 1968), 1–28.

60. For the details of this story, see *L,* IV (December, 1921), 7; Eastman, *Love and Revolution,* 262–65; and *ALWFH,* 137–38.

61. Eastman, *Love and Revolution,* 268–69.

62. *Ibid.,* 266–67. See also the editorial note, "To Our Friends," in *L,* IV (February, 1921), 14, in which it was announced that "Michael Gold, formerly a contributor and lately made a Contributing Editor of the *Liberator,* has suffered a serious nervous breakdown. Those interested in contributing to his recovery can send money to the *Liberator.*" For McKay's account of his appointment as co-editor with Gold, see *ALWFH,* 138–39.

63. Eastman, *Love and Revolution,* 269.

64. Aaron, *Writers on the Left,* 25.

65. "*Liberator* News," *L,* V (March, 1922), n.p. On the financial condition of the *Liberator* and the various efforts that had been initiated to save the magazine, see "To Our Friends," *L,* V (February, 1922), n.p.

66. Claude McKay to H. L. Mencken, March 31, June 1, 1922, both in HLMP. See Douglas C. Stenerson, *H. L. Mencken: Iconoclast From Baltimore* (Chicago, 1971); and Charles A. Fecher, *Mencken: A Study of His Thought* (New York, 1978).

67. Claude McKay to Jean Toomer, June 27, 1922, in JTP; Robert Bone, *The Negro Novel in America* (Rev. ed.; New Haven, 1965), 80–89, and *Down Home*, 204–38. See also Darwin Turner, *In a Minor Chord: Three Afro-American Writers and Their Search for Identity* (Carbondale, Ill., 1971), 1–59.

68. Claude McKay to Jean Toomer, December 6, 1921, June 27, 1922, both in JTP.

69. McKay to Toomer, July 11, 1922, *ibid.* Toomer's *Liberator* contributions for September, 1922, were the story "Carma" and the poem "Georgia Dusk." On the same page as "Georgia Dusk" there also appeared another poem, "To My Mother" by Louis Ginsberg, the father of Allen Ginsberg, the premier poet of the Beat Generation. Toomer's story "Becky" appeared in *L*, V (October, 1922), 30.

70. Michael Gold, "Toward Proletarian Art," *L*, IV (February, 1921), 20–24.

71. Joseph Freeman, *An American Testament: A Narrative of Rebels and Romantics* (New York, 1936), 256. Michael Gold's *Jews Without Money* (New York, 1930) is the story of his childhood.

72. *ALWFH*, 140–41.

73. *ALWFH*, 138–41; Max Eastman to Claude McKay, [spring, 1923], in *PCM*, 78–79.

74. Eastman to McKay, [spring, 1923], in *PCM*, 78–79.

75. *PCM*, 20–21, 78–90.

76. *Ibid.*

77. Eastman to McKay, [spring, 1923], McKay to Eastman, April 3, 1923, both *ibid.*, 78–82, 82–83.

78. Eastman to McKay, [spring, 1923], McKay to Eastman, April 3, 1923, both *ibid.*, 79, 84.

79. "Review of *Harlem Shadows*," *New York Times Book Review*, May 14, 1922, p. 17.

80. Robert Littel, "Review of *Harlem Shadows* and James Weldon Johnson, ed., *The Book of American Negro Poetry*," *New Republic*, XXVI (July 12, 1922), 196.

81. Walter White, "Review of *Harlem Shadows* and *The Book of American Negro Poetry*," *Bookman*, V (July, 1922), 531; James Weldon Johnson in the New York *Age* (May 20, 1922), quoted in Ralph Glasgow Johnson, "The Poetry of Dunbar and McKay: A Study" (M.A. thesis, University of Pittsburgh, 1950), 29.

82. Hubert Harrison, "The Poetry of Claude McKay," [*Negro World*], n.d., and "Review of *Harlem Shadows*," New York *World*, n.d., both clippings found among the papers of Hodge Kirnon, private possession.

83. Hodge Kirnon, "Claude McKay's *Harlem Shadows*: An Appreciation," *Negro World*, May 26, 1922, n.p., clipping, and Claude McKay to Hodge Kirnon, June 7, [1922], both *ibid.*

84. Clement Wood, "A Man's Song: Review of *Harlem Shadows*," New York *Evening Post*, October 25, 1922, n.p., clipping in the McKay Folder in the Schomburg Center for Research in Black Culture, New York Public Library.

85. McKay, "He Who Gets Slapped," 25.

86. The historiography of the New Negro or Harlem Renaissance period is large, varied, complex, and controversial. For a variety of statements concerning its importance and meaning, see Gloster, *Negro Voices in American Fiction;* Arna Bontemps (ed.), *The Harlem Renaissance Remembered: Essays Edited With a Memoir* (New York, 1972); Abraham Chapman, "The Harlem Renaissance in Literary History," *CLA Journal*, II (September, 1967), 38–58; S. P. Fullinwider, *The Mind and Mood of Black America: 20th Century Thought* (Homewood, Ill., 1969); Charles I. Glicksberg, "The

Negro Cult of the Primitive," *Antioch Review*, IV (March, 1946), 50; Bone, *Down Home*, 170–272; and Nathan Huggins, *Harlem Renaissance* (New York, 1971).

87. See especially Cooney, "Walter White and the Harlem Renaissance," 231–40; Eugene Levy, *James Weldon Johnson: Black Leader, Black Voice* (Chicago, 1973), 310–11; and Gloster, *Negro Voices in American Fiction*, 101–15.

88. Alain Locke (ed.), *The New Negro* (1925; rpr. New York, 1968).

89. "*Liberator* News," *L*, V (July, 1922), 27; Claude McKay, "Petrograd: May Day, 1923," *L*, VI (August, 1923), 10.

90. [Editorial] "We Haven't Cracked Under the Strain," *L*, V (November-December, 1922), n.p.; Eastman, *Love and Revolution*, 271.

91. Aaron, *Writers on the Left*, 95.

92. Freeman, *An American Testament*, 257.

93. *ALWFH*, 150, 206.

94. *Ibid.*, 149–50.

95. *Ibid.*, 150–54.

96. Claude McKay to H. L. Mencken, July 3, 1922, August 2, [1922], both in HLMP.

97. James Weldon Johnson to Claude McKay, August 21, 1930, in CMP.

98. *ALWFH*, 154.

99. From "Mulatto," in *Bookman*, LXXII (September, 1925), 67, reprinted in *PCM*, 126.

## Chapter 6

1. *HH*, 1; *ALWFH*, 154; Claude McKay to Jean Toomer, September 12, 1922, in JTP.

2. *ALWFH*, 155–56.

3. *Ibid.*, 156–57. Interview with Charles Ashleigh, October 22, 1972, in Brighton, England.

4. Interview with Charles Ashleigh, October 22, 1972; *ALWFH*, 156–57.

5. *ALWFH*, 157; Draper, *The Roots of American Communism*, 382. *The Roots of American Communism* is still the best analysis of the early history of the Communist party in the United States. See also Draper, *American Communism and Soviet Russia*.

6. *ALWFH*, 156–57; Draper, *The Roots of American Communism*, 327–95. On the legal persecution of American leftists, see William Preston, Jr., *Aliens and Dissenters: Federal Suppression of Radicals, 1903–1933* (Cambridge, Mass., 1963).

7. *ALWFH*, 160–62.

8. *Ibid.*, 162, 164.

9. *Ibid.*, 164–66. On Katayama's life, see Hyman Kublin, *Asian Revolutionary: The Life of Sen Katayama* (Princeton, N.J., 1964), 1–112, and *passim*. Although Kublin discounts Katayama as any kind of expert on American blacks or American race relations, McKay's testimony in *ALWFH* clearly suggests a keener awareness of and interest in American blacks than Kublin concedes.

10. *ALWFH*, 164–66.

11. *Ibid.*, 167–68. McKay told this story in "Soviet Russia and the Negro," *Crisis*, XXVII (December, 1923–January, 1924), 61–65, 114–18, reprinted in *PCM*, 95–106.

12. *ALWFH*, 159; Max Eastman, *Love and Revolution: My Journey Through an Epoch* (New York, 1964), 318.

13. *ALWFH*, 172–84; Draper, *Roots of American Communism*, 387; Draper, *American Communism and Soviet Russia*, 78, 321, 327, 335, 340.

14. Draper discusses Huiswoud in *Roots of American Communism*, 387, and more fully in *American Communism and Soviet Russia*, 313, 320, 322, 326–27, 350, 353, 404, 425–26. McKay had very little to say about Huiswoud in *ALWFH*, where he identified him only as "the mulatto delegate, who had previously high-hatted me" (*ALWFH*, 71). Huiswoud's party name in Moscow was "Billings."

15. Draper, *American Communism and Soviet Russia*, 319–22; *ALWFH*, 253.

16. Draper, *American Communism and Soviet Russia*, 322–32.

17. P. Okhrimenko, "Original Translator's Note," in *NA*, xviii; Draper, *American Communism and Soviet Russia*, 320. Shortly before his death, Cyril Briggs, the founder of the African Blood Brotherhood, exchanged letters with me. I also interviewed Briggs during a visit to New York in early July, 1965. In a letter to me, June 29, 1965, Briggs states that he and McKay "were very good friends and saw each other quite often." In person, Briggs told me that he remembered McKay had been a member of his African Blood Brotherhood and had become a party member, along with himself and others in the group.

18. *ALWFH*, 172.

19. This summary of Huiswoud's speech was taken from *Protokoll des Vierten Kongresses der Kommunistischen International* (Hamburg, 1923), 692–97.

20. Claude McKay, "Speech to the Fourth Congress of the Third Communist International," in *PCM*, 91–95.

21. Claude McKay, "Report on the Negro Question," *International Press Correspondence*, III (January 5, 1923), 16–17. Huiswoud's speech also appeared in this Comintern publication. Draper, *American Communism and Soviet Russia*, 327.

22. McKay, "Speech to the Fourth Congress of the Third Communist International," in *PCM*, 95.

23. Draper, *American Communism and Soviet Russia*, 327; "Resolutions on the Negro Question," *Resolutions and Theses of the Fourth Congress of the Communist International* (London, 1923), 84–85.

24. Draper, *American Communism and Soviet Russia*, 328–29.

25. *NA*, 6–10. See also *ALWFH*, 207–10.

26. *ALWFH*, 180.

27. On Du Bois, the Pan-African Congress, and the Pan-African idea, see Colin Legum, *Pan-Africanism: A Short Political Guide* (New York, 1962).

28. *ALWFH*, 168.

29. *Ibid.*, 213–16.

30. McKay, "Soviet Russia and the Negro," in *PCM*, 102; *ALWFH*, 188. On Yesenin's life, see Frances DeGraaf, *Sergej Esenin: A Biographical Sketch* (The Hague, 1966); Gordon McVay, *Esenin: A Life* (London, 1976); and Constantin V. Ponomareff, *Sergej Esenin* (Boston, 1978).

31. *ALWFH*, 188; Walter Duranty, *I Write As I Please* (New York, 1935), 238; Gordon McVay, *Isadora and Esenin* (Ann Arbor, Mich., 1980), 59–103.

32. McVay, *Esenin*, 307.

33. Claude McKay to H. L. Mencken, July 17, 1923, in HLMP.

34. McKay, "Soviet Russia and the Negro," in *PCM*, 102; *ALWFH*, 106. On these early Soviet literary figures, see Marc Slonim, *Soviet Russian Literature: Writers and Problems, 1917–1977* (2nd rev. ed.; New York, 1977); and Gleb Struve, *Russian Literature Under Lenin and Stalin, 1917–1953* (Norman, Okla., 1971).

35. *ALWFH*, 159, 173, 177. See also Adam B. Ulam, *The Bolsheviks: The Intellectual and Political History of the Triumph of Communism in Russia* (New York, 1968),

231–33, 449–51; and Leon Trotsky, *Literature and Revolution* (Rpr. New York, 1957), 215–27. Trotsky wrote this book in 1924.

36. *ALWFH,* 170–71, 185–205, 209–17.

37. *Ibid.,* 186; *NA,* 3. All citations in this chapter from McKay's *NA* are from the 1979 English-language edition, translated by Robert J. Winter and edited by Alan L. McLeod (Port Washington, N.Y., 1979). See also their English-language edition of Claude McKay's *Sudom Lincha* (Moscow, 1925), which is entitled in translation *Trial by Lynching: Stories About Negro Life in North America* (Mysore, India, 1977). This volume consists of several short stories McKay wrote while in Russia and published in the Soviet press.

38. *ALWFH,* 168–71; McKay, "Soviet Russia and the Negro," in *PCM,* 105; Claude McKay to Walter White, July 8, 1923, in WWP, NAACP.

39. Okhrimenko, "Original Translator's Note," in *NA,* xviii; Ludwig E. Katterfield [G. Carr] to editor of the *Bolshevik,* December 2, 1922, reprinted in *NA,* 88.

40. Claude McKay to editor of the *Bolshevik,* December 3, 1922, reprinted in *NA,* 89–90.

41. *NA,* 29–33, 33–36, 44.

42. *Ibid.*

43. *Ibid.,* 18.

44. *Ibid.,* 61, 63.

45. *Ibid.*

46. *Ibid.,* 75, 79, 81.

47. *Ibid.,* 10–11.

48. Max Eastman to Claude McKay, [spring, 1923], in *PCM,* 80.

49. Claude McKay to Max Eastman, April 3, 1923, *ibid.,* 82–85.

50. Max Eastman to Claude McKay, April 12, 1923, McKay to Eastman, May 18, 1923, and [May, 1923], all *ibid.,* 88, 89, 90.

51. *ALWFH,* 222–25.

52. *Ibid.,* 223, 225.

## Chapter 7

1. *ALWFH,* 237–38.

2. Interview with Charles Ashleigh, October 22, 1972, in Brighton, England; *ALWFH,* 237–40; see also Otto Friedrich, *Before the Deluge: A Portrait of Berlin in the 1920s* (New York, 1972), 112–60.

3. George Grosz, *Ecce Homo* (Berlin, 1923; rpr. New York, 1966). The American edition has an introduction by Henry Miller. On Grosz's social and historical significance, see Friedrich, *Before the Deluge,* 167–69; and Beth Irwin Lewis, *George Grosz: Art and Politics in the Weimar Republic* (Madison, Wis., 1971). George Grosz left Germany for New York during the Nazi era. See George Grosz, *A Little Yes and a Big No: The Autobiography of George Grosz,* trans. Lola Sachs Dorin (New York, 1946).

4. *ALWFH,* 240–41, 312. By the time McKay published *ALWFH,* he had grown critical of Locke; his first impressions had been more favorable. See Claude McKay to A. A. Schomburg, August 20, 1923, in AASP.

5. *ALWFH,* 242–43.

6. All the quotations are from Zinoviev's farewell letter to McKay, May 8, 1923, in WWP, NAACP.

7. Claude McKay to Walter White, July 8, 1923, *ibid.*

8. H. L. Mencken to Claude McKay, August 3, 1923, copy in MEP.

9. Claude McKay to H. L. Mencken, September 5, 1923, in HLMP.

10. See respectively Claude McKay, "Soviet Russia and the Negro," *Crisis*, XXVII (December, 1923–January, 1924), 61–65, 114–18, and "A Moscow Lady," *Crisis*, XXVIII (September, 1924), 225–28.

11. *ALWFH*, 241–42.

12. McKay, "Soviet Russia and the Negro," reprinted in *PCM*, 96, 98.

13. McKay to Schomburg, August 20, 1923, in AASP.

14. Claude McKay to A. A. Schomburg, [summer, 1923], September 25, 1923, both *ibid.*

15. McKay to Schomburg, August 20, 1923, *ibid.*

16. Claude McKay to A. A. Schomburg, [October] 7, [1923], *ibid.; ALWFH*, 239. McKay denied that he encountered any intolerance based on race in Germany.

17. *ALWFH*, 231. McKay did not reveal the nature of his illness in *ALWFH*, but he spoke more frankly in letters to friends. See Claude McKay to Alain Locke, May 1, 1924, in ALP; and Claude McKay to Max Eastman, December 1, 1930, in MEP. More detailed information about McKay's hospitalization was obtained in conversations with Dr. Fanny Rappaport-Vogein in Paris in the fall of 1972, and in a June 19, 1965, interview in Merion Station, Pa., with *Liberator* artist John Barber, who was in Paris in the fall of 1923 and helped McKay during his hospitalization.

18. Interview with Fanny Rappaport-Vogein, October, 1972.

19. *ALWFH*, 231.

20. McKay to Locke, May 1, 1924, in ALP.

21. Interview with John Barber, June 19, 1965; John Barber to Wayne Cooper, June 21, 1965, in possession of the recipient. See also *ALWFH*, 253.

22. *ALWFH*, 243. See also McKay to Schomburg, [October] 7, [1923], in AASP; and Claude McKay to H. L. Mencken, May 1, 1924, in HLMP. The importance of Paris in the development of modern art and literature is ably described by Roger Shattuck, *The Banquet Years: The Arts in France, 1885–1918* (Garden City, N.Y., 1961). American expatriates in Paris created a large literature of reminiscences that, in its turn, has inspired several histories. See, for example, Howard Greenfeld, *They Came to Paris* (New York, 1975); and George Wickes, *Americans in Paris* (Garden City, N.Y., 1969). One of the better memoirs is Samuel Putnam's *Paris Was Our Mistress: Memoirs of a Lost and Found Generation* (New York, 1947).

23. *ALWFH*, 248. See Gertrude Stein, "Melanctha: Each One as She May," in Carl Van Vechten (ed.), *Selected Writings of Gertrude Stein* (New York, 1962), 337–458.

24. *ALWFH*, 247–48.

25. *Ibid.*

26. *Ibid.*, 243; D. H. Lawrence, *Sons and Lovers* (New York, 1958). *Sons and Lovers* first appeared in 1913. For the great variety of critical approaches over the years, see Ernest Warnock Tedlock (ed.), *D. H. Lawrence and "Sons and Lovers": Sources and Criticism* (New York, 1965). There are several general scholarly works on the American expatriate experience, but none is wholly satisfactory. See Harold T. McCarthy, *The Expatriate Perspective: American Novelists and the Idea of America* (Rutherford, N.J., 1974); Ishbel Ross, *The Expatriates* (New York, 1970); and Ernest Penney Earnest, *Expatriates and Patriots: American Artists, Scholars, and Writers in Europe* (Durham, N.C., 1968).

27. *ALWFH*, 245.

28. *Ibid.*, 226; Hugh D. Ford (ed.), *The Left Bank Revisited: Selections from the Paris "Tribune," 1917–1934* (University Park, Pa., 1972), 100.

29. *ALWFH,* 253–54.

30. *Ibid.;* Claude McKay to A. A. Schomburg, January 7, 1924, in AASP.

31. Claude McKay to A. A. Schomburg, May 20, 19[24], in AASP; Walter White to Claude McKay, January 25, 1924, in WWP, NAACP.

32. Claude McKay to A. A. Schomburg, [undated fragment, *ca.* February, 1924], in AASP. See also *ALWFH,* 253–54.

33. *ALWFH,* 254–56; McKay to Locke, May 1, 1924, in ALP.

34. *ALWFH,* 255–56.

35. *Ibid.,* 257. The Garland Fund, also known as the American Fund for Personal Service, was established after World War I by Charles Garland, a young Harvard graduate. According to Joseph Freeman, Garland "celebrated his majority by dedicating his paternal inheritance to the service of the radical cause" (Freeman quoted in Aaron, *Writers on the Left,* 100). McKay's grant came out of the Garland "Personal Service Fund," which was described on its stationery as "for individuals working creatively for society along radical lines." Its list of officers included Roger Baldwin, Anna N. Davis, Charles Garland, and A. J. Muste. Its correspondence with McKay survives, at least in part, in CMP.

36. *NA,* 61–64; "A Negro Extravaganza," in *PCM,* 63.

37. Claude McKay to A. A. Schomburg, February 4, June 16, and August 14, 1924, all in AASP. See also Claude McKay to Walter White, December 4, 1924, White to McKay, September 12, 1923, both in WWP, NAACP; Claude McKay to Max Eastman, September 3, 1943, in *PCM,* 303–304; and Claude McKay to James Weldon Johnson, July 29, 1930, in JWJP; and *ALWFH,* 257.

38. Walter White to Claude McKay, August 15, 1924, in WWP, NAACP. White's novel was *The Fire in the Flint* (New York, 1924).

39. James Weldon Johnson to Walter White, April 13, 1923, Alain Locke to Walter White [*ca.* December, 1923–January, 1924], both in WWP, NAACP.

40. Claude McKay to Walter White, December 4, 1924, *ibid.*

41. *ALWFH,* 257–59.

42. Claude McKay to Walter White, December 15, 4, 1924, both in WWP, NAACP.

43. Claude McKay, "What Is and What Isn't," *Crisis,* XVIII (April, 1924), 257–62. See also the biographical sketch of Kojo Tovalou Honenou by Eslanda Goode Robeson, the wife of Paul Robeson, in "Black Paris," *Challenge,* I (January, 1936), 12–18. Her article, written over a decade later, confirms and elaborates the facts first noted by McKay in his *Crisis* article of April, 1924.

44. On the importance of the Nardal sisters in the development of modern French African and West Indian literature, see Jacques Louis Hymans, *Leopold Sedar Senghor: An Intellectual Biography* (Edinburgh, 1971), 23–24, 36–44, 274–78. See also the biographical sketch of Paulette Nardal by Robeson in "Black Paris," *Challenge,* I (June, 1936), 9–12.

45. Hymans, *Leopold Sedar Senghor,* 23–24, 54. See also Lilyan Kesteloot, *Black Writers in French: A Literary History of Negritude,* trans. Ellen Conroy Kennedy (Philadelphia, 1974), 56–57.

46. Kesteloot, *Black Writers in French,* 56–74; Hymans, *Leopold Sedar Senghor,* 53–59.

47. Hymans, *Leopold Sedar Senghor,* 54; Kesteloot, *Black Writers in French,* 72–73.

48. See Walter White to Sinclair Lewis, October 15, 1924, Lewis to White, November 12, 1924, and Walter White to Claude McKay, November 6, 1924, all in WWP,

NAACP. See also Charles F. Cooney, "Walter White and the Harlem Renaissance," *Journal of Negro History*, LVII (July, 1972), 231–40; David Levering Lewis, *When Harlem Was in Vogue* (New York, 1981), 140–41; and *ALWFH*, 259.

49. *ALWFH*, 59. See also Sinclair Lewis to Roger Baldwin, January 19, 1925, in CMP.

50. Roger Baldwin to Claude McKay, February 21, 1925, in CMP; Claude McKay to Walter White, January 8, 1925, in WWP, NAACP. See also undated note from Claude McKay to A. A. Schomburg, in AASP.

51. Claude McKay to A. A. Schomburg, April 28, 1925, in AASP; McKay to White, December 4, 1924, in WWP, NAACP.

52. Personal Service Fund [Anna Davis] to Claude McKay, February 24, 1925, Personal Service Fund [Roger Baldwin] to Sinclair Lewis, [*ca.* January, 1925], and Sinclair Lewis to Roger Baldwin, January 19, 1925, all in CMP.

53. Walter White to Claude McKay, May 20, 1925, in WWP, NAACP; Claude McKay to A. A. Schomburg, April 28, June 3, and July 22, 1925, all in AASP. See also McKay to White, June 15, 1925, White to McKay, July 8, 1925, both in WWP, NAACP. Viking was definitely interested in seeing McKay's manuscript. See George Oppenheimer to Walter White, May 25, 1925, in WWP, NAACP. See also Walter White to A. A. Schomburg, July 23, 1925, in AASP.

54. Claude McKay to A. A. Schomburg, [summer, 1925], July 17, April 28, 1925, all in AASP.

55. Claude McKay to A. A. Schomburg, [undated, 1925]. This letter and others to Schomburg have been reprinted in *PCM*, 139–43.

56. *ALWFH*, 260–62.

57. *Ibid.* See also Max Eastman, *Love and Revolution: My Journey Through an Epoch* (New York, 1964), 467–68.

58. Eastman, *Love and Revolution*, 336–43, 408–15, 419–27, 442–55. See also William L. O'Neill, *The Last Romantic: A Life of Max Eastman* (New York, 1979), 106–109. Finally, see Max Eastman, *Since Lenin Died* (1925; rpr. Westport, Conn., 1973).

59. The poem is dated "Paris, 1925." On the criticism and isolation of Eastman following the publication of *Since Lenin Died*, see Eastman, *Love and Revolution*, 442–56; and O'Neill, *The Last Romantic*, 106–13. McKay to Eastman [undated, 1925], June 27, 1930, May 9, 1934, all in MEP.

60. *ALWFH*, 261–64.

61. *Ibid.*

62. See Claude McKay to A. A. Schomburg, August 3, 1925, in AASP; Claude McKay to H. L. Mencken, August 2, 1925, in HLMP; and Claude McKay to Walter White, [*ca.* August, 1925], August 4, September 7, 1925, all in WWP, NAACP. See also McKay to Schomburg, [spring or summer, 1925], August 3, 1925, both in AASP.

63. McKay to Mencken, August 2, 1925, in HLMP; Claude McKay to Walter White, September 7, [1925], September 25, October 15, 1925, all WWP, NAACP. See also Claude McKay to Alain Locke, October 7, 1924, in ALP; and Claude McKay to A. A. Schomburg, October 15, 1925, in AASP.

64. Claude McKay to William Aspenwall Bradley, April 15, 1927, in WABP.

65. See A. L. McLeod's introduction to Robert Winter's retranslation into English of these three early stories in Claude McKay, *Trial by Lynching: Stories About Negro Life in North America* (Mysore, India, 1977), iii–viii.

66. McKay to White, August 4, 1925, in WWP, NAACP.

67. Claude McKay to William Aspenwall Bradley, May 23, 1927, in WABP.

68. On the importance of an autobiographical element in black fiction in general, see Roger Rosenblatt, *Black Fiction* (Cambridge, Mass., 1974).

## Chapter 8

1. Claude McKay to Walter White, September 7, [1925], October 15, November 25, 1925, all in WWP, NAACP. See also Claude McKay to A. A. Schomburg, September 9, [1925], October 15, 1925, both in AASP.

2. Claude McKay to Walter White, June 15, August 4, 1925, August 25, [1925], September 7, [1925], all in WWP, NAACP. See also McKay to Schomburg, October 15, 1925, in AASP.

3. Claude McKay to Walter White, September 25, October 15, 1925, both in WWP, NAACP.

4. *ALWFH,* 265. Claude McKay to Alain Locke, May 1, 1926, in ALP; Claude McKay to Louise Bryant, June 24, 1926, in CMP.

5. Claude McKay to Alain Locke, January 2, May 1, 1926, both in ALP. See also Claude McKay to Walter White, November 25, 1925, in WWP, NAACP; and John Farrar [editor of *Bookman*] to Claude McKay, January 28, 1928, in CMP.

6. Alain Locke (ed.), *The New Negro* (1925; rpr. New York, 1968), 133–35, 214–15; Alain Locke, (ed.), "Harlem: Mecca of the New Negro," *Survey Graphic,* VI (March, 1925), 621–724. See also Claude McKay to Alain Locke, August 1, 1926, in *PCM,* 143–44.

7. Claude McKay to Alain Locke, [undated, 1925], January 2, May 1, 1926, all in ALP. After the publication of *The New Negro,* Walter White informed Locke that Arthur Spingarn had found "170 mistakes" in the bibliography "alone. He stated further," White added, "that there was hardly a page that did not have five to ten errors in it." White advised Locke to correct the errors in future editions. Walter White to Alain Locke, February 26, 1926, in WWP, NAACP.

8. McKay to Locke, May 1, 1926, in ALP. See also *ALWFH,* 272, 274.

9. *ALWFH,* 272; see also Max Eastman, *Love and Revolution: My Journey Through an Epoch* (New York, 1964), 470.

10. Eastman, *Love and Revolution,* 470.

11. *ALWFH,* 272–76.

12. Interview with Charles Ashleigh, October 22, 1972, in Brighton, England; McKay to White, November 25, 1925, in WWP, NAACP; *ALWFH,* 265–68, 212, 288–91. My thanks to Professor Andrew Buni of Boston College for information on Essie Robeson's reaction to Claude McKay.

13. Philippa Pullar, *Frank Harris: A Biography* (New York, 1976), 369–413; *ALWFH,* 124–29, 265–71.

14. *ALWFH,* 128–29.

15. *Ibid.,* 277, 278–91. See also McKay's fictional portrait of Marseilles, in *B.*

16. Claude McKay to Walter White, December 4, 1924, in WWP, NAACP.

17. See, for example, Louise Bryant Bullitt to Claude McKay, February 14, [1926], in the Miscellaneous McKay Correspondence in the Schomburg Center. See also Bullitt to McKay, September 23, October 8, 1926, both in CMP.

18. There is a great need for a more thorough and precise description of Louise Bryant's last years. See Barbara Gelb, *So Short a Time: A Biography of John Reed and Louise Bryant* (1973; rpr. New York, 1981), 231–36.

19. *ALWFH,* 281–82.

20. Claude McKay to A. A. Schomburg, August 1, 1926, in AASP.

21. *Ibid.;* Claude McKay to A. A. Schomburg, August 26, 28, 1926, both in AASP.

22. *ALWFH*, 282. See also Bullitt to McKay, October 8, December 18, 26, 1926, [January?, 1927], January 8, 1927, all in CMP. There is no doubt that Louise Bryant's assistance at this point was crucial to McKay's success. When *HH* finally appeared in the spring of 1928, McKay dedicated it "To My Friend Louise Bryant."

23. For an authoritative biographical sketch of Bradley, see Karen L. Rood, "William Aspenwall Bradley (8 February 1878–10 January 1939)," in *Dictionary of Literary Biography* (Detroit, 1980), IV, 56–58.

24. *ALWFH*, 282.

25. Claude McKay to W. A. Bradley, February 7, 1927, in WABP.

26. Claude McKay to W. A. Bradley, April 15, 1927, in WABP.

27. Bradley's letters to McKay in CMP fully reveal the dispassionate, thoroughly competent manner in which Bradley managed McKay's affairs. Claude McKay to Max Eastman, December 1, 1930, in MEP.

28. Claude McKay to Alain Locke, August 1, 1926, in ALP, also in *PCM*, 143–44.

29. Claude McKay to W. E. B. Du Bois, June 18, 1928, in *PCM*, 149–50.

30. Claude McKay to W. A. Bradley, May 23, 1929, in WABP.

31. W. E. B. Du Bois to Claude McKay, March 16, 1927, in CMP; Walter White to Pauline Rose, [February, 1924], Walter White to A. A. Schomburg, August 27, 1925, Walter White to Langston Hughes, December 18, 1926, and McKay to White, November 25, 1925, all in WWP, NAACP; see also Claude McKay to Alain Locke, July 27, 1926, in ALP. For an example of McKay's aspersions on NAACP officials during this period, see Claude McKay to A. A. Schomburg, July 17, 1925, in *PCM*, 141–42.

32. McKay to Bradley, April 15, May 23, 1927, both in WABP.

33. McKay to Bradley, June 4, May 23, April 15, 1927, all *ibid.*

34. Claude McKay to W. A. Bradley, March 11, 1927, *ibid.*

35. McKay to Bradley, April 15, [April 24], May 14, 23, October 1, 1927, all *ibid.* McKay's social relations during this period and throughout most of his adult life, of course, often led him to bars, and he probably often drank more than someone with his health problems should have. There is no evidence, however, to suggest that McKay was ever an alcoholic or drank more than the average literary expatriate of the period for whom the consumption of alcohol seemed to be a necessity.

36. Claude McKay to W. A. Bradley, November 25, 1927, in WABP.

37. Claude McKay to W. A. Bradley, July 3, October 24, November 3, 25, December 3, 19, 31, 1927, January 18, February 10, 1928, all *ibid.*

38. McKay to Bradley, May 23, December 12, 1927, [February, 1928], all *ibid.*

39. Claude McKay to W. A. Bradley, April 12, 1928, *ibid.* See also Walter White to Claude McKay, July 14, 1927, Walter White to Eugene Saxton, July 14, 1927, Anonymous [James Weldon Johnson?] to Walter White, February 25, March 5, 1928, all in WWP, NAACP.

40. Claude McKay to W. A. Bradley, February 10, 1928, in WABP. See also Claude McKay to the director of the Fabre Company shipping line in Marseilles, January 13, 1928, in CMP. The company apparently dropped the charges after the African, whom McKay identified as Nelson Simeon Dede, agreed to pay his fare. See also Claude McKay to James Ivy, September 20, 1929, in *PCM*, 147–48; and *B*, 256–79.

41. McKay to Bradley, May 14, 25, 1928, both in WABP.

42. Claude McKay to W. A. Bradley, August 24, 1928, *ibid.*; *ALWFH*, 154–55.

43. Langston Hughes, *The Weary Blues* (New York, 1926), and *Fine Clothes To the Jew* (New York, 1927); Rudolph Fisher, *The Walls of Jericho* (New York, 1928); Nella Larsen, *Quicksand* (New York, 1928); and Jessie R. Fauset, *Plum Bun* (New York, 1928). On Hughes's poetry, see Wagner, *Black Poets of the United States*, 385–474; on the black short stories of the period, see Bone, *Down Home*, 107–58, 204–35.

44. Bone, *The Negro Novel in America*, 51–108, and *Down Home*, 107–38. Langston Hughes discussed the older generation's reaction to his early poetry in his autobiography, *The Big Sea* (New York, 1940), 265–72. A leading spirit in this new primitivism was, of course, Carl Van Vechten, whose novel, *Nigger Heaven*, precipitated a lively debate in the black press. For a conservative, scholarly black assessment of this white Negro Vogue, see Hugh M. Gloster, *Negro Voices in American Fiction* (Chapel Hill, 1948), 104–10, 157–71. See also Carl Van Vechten, *Nigger Heaven* (New York, 1926).

45. See Robert Goldwater, *Primitivism in Modern Art* (New York, 1966). See also Roger Shattuck, *The Banquet Years: The Arts in France, 1885–1918* (Garden City, N.Y., 1961), 47–79, and *passim*.

46. See James Weldon Johnson's review of *Nigger Heaven*, "Romance and Tragedy in Harlem," *Opportunity*, IV (October, 1926), 316–17, 330; and Hughes, *The Big Sea*, 268–72. For a summary of Afro-American critical reactions to *Nigger Heaven*, see Gloster, *Negro Voices in American Fiction*, 157–63.

47. Langston Hughes, "The Negro Artist and the Racial Mountain," *Nation*, CXXII (June, 1926), 692–94; Edward Lueders, *Carl Van Vechten* (New York, 1965), 34–35, 95–106. See also Leon D. Coleman, "The Contributions of Carl Van Vechten to the Negro Renaissance, 1920–1930" (Ph.D. dissertation, University of Minnesota, 1969); and Bruce Kellner, *Carl Van Vechten and the Irreverent Decades* (Norman, Okla., 1968).

48. Gloster, *Negro Voices in American Fiction*, 157–72.

49. Nathan Huggins, *Harlem Renaissance* (New York, 1971), 12–51.

50. The relation of the picaresque to the pastoral themes of Harlem Renaissance writers is discussed by Robert Bone in *Down Home*, 118–24; McKay's *HH* and *B* both support this view, as does his essay "A Negro Writer to His Critics," in *PCM*, 132–39. McKay's conviction that black common folk generally had a positive view of themselves has recently been reasserted by the black anthropologist John Langston Gwaltney in *Drylongso: A Self-Portrait of Black America* (New York, 1980).

51. Gloster, *Negro Voices in American Fiction*, 163–70.

52. Some did not appreciate Jake's good fortune and natural grace. At the end of *HH*, for instance, Jake and his girl are forced to leave Harlem for Chicago after Jake's friend Zeddy, in a fit of jealous anger, loudly proclaims in a bar that Jake had deserted the American army in France (*HH*, 172–73).

53. *Ibid.*, 119–21, 139–45.

54. Langston Hughes to Claude McKay, July 25, 1925, March 5, 1928, [April 21, 1928], all in CMP.

55. Eugene Levy, *James Weldon Johnson: Black Leader, Black Voice* (Chicago, 1973), 75–98, 297–322.

56. James Weldon Johnson to Claude McKay, January 26, April 12, 1928, both in CMP.

57. W. E. B. Du Bois, "The Browsing Reader: Review of *Home to Harlem*," *Crisis*, XXXV (June, 1928), 202; *ALWFH*, 109, 110.

58. Claude McKay to W. E. B. Du Bois, June 18, 1928, in *PCM*, 150.

59. "Book Chat," Pittsburgh *Courier*, March 17, 1928; William H. Ferris, "Ferris Scores Obscenity in Our Literature," Pittsburgh *Courier*, March 21, 1928; and Dewey R. Jones, "The Bookshelf: More 'Nigger Heaven' [Review of *Home to Harlem*]," Chicago *Defender*, March 17, 1928.

60. George W. Jacobs, "New Yorker Flays McKay's Book, *Home to Harlem*," Pittsburgh *Courier*, April 7, 1928; E. C. Williams, "*Nigger Heaven; Home to Harlem*—Authors, Greedy Filth Mongerers, Declares Howard Librarian," New York *News*, May 19,

1928; Thomas W. Young, "Harlem's Prodigal Son [Review of *Home to Harlem*]," Norfolk *Journal and Guide*, April 21, 1928.

61. John R. Chamberlain, "When Spring Comes to Harlem: Claude McKay's Novel Gives a Glowing Picture of the Negro Quarter [Review of *Home to Harlem*]," *New York Times Book Review*, March 11, 1928.

62. Louis Sherwin, "The African in Harlem [Review of *Home to Harlem*]," New York *Sun*, March 24, 1928.

63. Carl Van Doren, "Review of *Home to Harlem*," *Nation*, CXXVI (March 28, 1928), 35; Burton Rascoe, "The Seamy Side [Review of *Home to Harlem*]," *Bookman*, LXVII (April, 1928), 183.

64. Eastman, *Love and Revolution*, 468; F. Scott Fitzgerald to Claude McKay, May 25, 1928, in CMP; Dorothy Parker, "Review of *Home to Harlem*," in *The Portable Dorothy Parker* (New York, 1973), 352.

65. Claude McKay to James Ivy, May 20, 1928, in *PCM*, 145–46.

66. "RHH"; J. A. Rogers, "Ahead of Its Time: McKay Defends Book, *Home to Harlem*," *AN*, April 10, 1929.

67. McKay to Locke, May 1, 1926, in ALP.

68. Walter White to George E. Haynes, September 20, 1928, in Box 25, HFP.

69. See the Judges' Ranking and James Weldon Johnson's summary of McKay's life and the award program in Box 27, HFP.

70. Claude McKay to W. A. Bradley, September 7, 1928, in WABP.

71. *ALWFH*, 295, 396. See also Claude McKay to W. A. Bradley, October 1, 1928, in WABP.

72. McKay to Bradley, September 7, October 1, November 2, 21, 1928, all in WABP.

73. McKay to Bradley, September 7, October 1, November 2, 21, 1928, all *ibid.*; *ALWFH*, 297–98, 398; Claude McKay to James Ivy, September 20, 1929, in *PCM*, 147–48.

74. McKay to Bradley, October 1, 1928, in WABP.

75. *ALWFH*, 296–97; McKay to Bradley, October 1, 1928, in WABP.

76. *ALWFH*, 89–91, 298.

77. *Ibid.*, 298; Claude McKay to W. A. Bradley, March 25, 1929, in WABP.

78. McKay to Bradley, November 2, 1928, in WABP.

79. *Ibid.*; *ALWFH*, 299.

80. Claude McKay to W. A. Bradley, January 1, 1929, in WABP.

81. *ALWFH*, 342–54; *PCM*, 234–39, 289–94.

82. *ALWFH*, 260–61, 300–305.

83. McKay to Bradley, March 25, 1929, December 10, 14, 1930, all in WABP; McKay to Eastman, December 30, 1930, in MEP. See also *ALWFH*, 308.

84. McKay to Bradley, January 30, 1929, in WABP.

85. Claude McKay to W. A. Bradley, March 18, 1930, *ibid.*; *B*, 320–24.

86. For a recent book that suggests that Marseilles may have changed little since McKay's sojourn there (despite the great physical damage wrought upon the waterfront by World War II), see M. F. K. Fisher, *A Considerable Town* (New York, 1978).

87. *B*, 65, 68, 114–32, 188–98, 256–68, 301–26.

88. Rex Ingram to Claude McKay, [*ca*. 1929], in CMP; Pierre Guerre, *Marseille*, photographs by J. P. Trosset (Paris, 1962), 11.

89. The story line and quotations are from *B*, 33, 83–92, 177–78, 235–43, 259, 301–26.

90. See McKay, "A Negro Writer to His Critics," in *PCM*, 132–39.

91. *B*, 116–17, 201, 315, 320–24.

92. *Ibid.*, 14, 304–305.

93. Freda Kirchwey, Review of *Banjo*, in *Nation*, CXXVII (May 22, 1929), 614, 619; Review of *Banjo*, in *New York Times Book Review*, May 12, 1929, p. 8; Walter White, Review of *Banjo*, in New York *World*, June 9, 1929; Aubrey Bowser, Review of *Banjo*, in *AN*, May 8, 1929.

94. *B*, 200–201.

95. Kesteloot, *Black Writers in French*, 72–73.

96. Hymans, *Leopold Sedar Senghor*, 54.

97. Claude McKay to W. A. Bradley, March 14, 25, 1929, both in WABP. See also *ALWFH*, 307–309.

98. *ALWFH*, 306–307.

99. *Ibid.*, 306–23. Johnson had actually been working since 1928 to persuade McKay to return and had even contacted a friend in the U.S. Department of State to find out the precise steps needed to facilitate his reentry into the United States. See James Weldon Johnson to Claude McKay, January 26, February 27, April 12, May 19, 1929, all in CMP. See also McKay to Johnson, March 10, 1928, April 30, February 1, September 1, 1929, all in CMP.

100. *ALWFH*, 311–12. See also Claude McKay to James Ivy, September 20, 1929, in *PCM*, 147–48.

101. *ALWFH*, 312–15. The anecdote about McKay's later conversation with Cullen was told to me by Cullen's widow, Ida Cullen Cooper.

102. Claude McKay to Alain Locke, June 4, April 18, 1927, both in ALP; *ALWFH*, 312. See also Locke to McKay, [spring, 1927], carbon copy in ALP, in which he said he was as "dumb-struck" by McKay's attitude "as you seem to be by mine." Locke bided his time and in 1937 wrote a sweeping condemnation of McKay on the occasion of the publication of *ALWFH*. See Alain Locke, "Spiritual Truant" [Review of *A Long Way from Home*]," *New Challenge*, II (Fall, 1937), 81–85.

103. *ALWFH*, 312, 318–20.

104. See Rogers, "Ahead of Its Time." In *ALWFH*, McKay devoted three pages to Rogers but identified him only as "a prominent Afro-American journalist" (*ALWFH*, 315–18).

105. *ALWFH*, 311–23.

## Chapter 9

1. *ALWFH*, 230, 235, 311–12, 314–15, 324, 328–31; Claude McKay to W. A. Bradley, July 25, 1929, in WABP; Claude McKay to James Ivy, September 20, 1929, in *PCM*, 147; Paul Bowles, *Without Stopping: An Autobiography* (New York, 1972), 129–30, 147–49. In *ALWFH*, McKay did not identify Anita Thompson but instead called her Carmina. In a marginal note in his personal copy of *ALWFH*, James Ivy identified Carmina as "Anita Thompson, a gorgeous brown if there ever was one!" See also Claude McKay to Max Eastman, December 7, 1929, December 1, 1930, July 19, 1931, all in MEP. In one letter to W. A. Bradley, McKay himself specified that Anita Thompson had joined him in Tangier (May 15, 1931, in WABP).

2. Claude McKay to W. A. Bradley, June 17, 1929, Bradley to McKay, June 25, 1929, both in WABP; interview with Hope McKay Virtue, August 30, 1978, in Kingston, Jamaica.

3. *ALWFH*, 309–11, 324–25; Claude McKay to W. A. Bradley, July 5, October 2, 1929, both in WABP.

4. McKay to Eastman, December 7, 1929, in MEP. A manuscript copy of "Romance in Marseilles," which was never published, is in the Schomburg Center.

5. McKay to Bradley, October 2, 1929, in WABP.

6. All the quotations are from McKay to Eastman, December 7, 1929, in MEP.

7. Claude McKay to Max Eastman, June 27, 1930, *ibid.*

8. Claude McKay to W. A. Bradley, December 21, 1929, March 18, 1930, both in WABP.

9. McKay to Bradley, December 21, 1929, *ibid.*

10. Claude McKay to W. A. Bradley, June 25, 1930, *ibid.;* McKay to Eastman, June 27, 1930, in MEP; Claude McKay to James Ivy, February 21, August 1, 1930, both in JIP.

11. Claude McKay to W. A. Bradley, July 4, 1930, in WABP; McKay to Eastman, December 1, 1930, in MEP.

12. McKay to Eastman, December 1, 1930, in MEP.

13. *Ibid.* See also Claude McKay to W. A. Bradley, August 28, December 25, 1930, both in WABP.

14. McKay to Bradley, August 28, 1930, in WABP.

15. Claude McKay to W. A. Bradley, September 18, 19, 29, 1930, all *ibid.;* see also McKay to Eastman, December 1, 1930, in MEP.

16. W. A. Bradley to Claude McKay, December 25, 1930, in WABP; Claude McKay to Max Eastman, July 19, 1931, in MEP.

17. Claude McKay to W. A. Bradley, December 10, 1930, in WABP.

18. Claude McKay to James Ivy, September 20, 1929, in *PCM,* 147–48; McKay to Bradley, December 10, 14, 25, 1930, D. Postgate to Claude McKay, December 18, 1930, all in WABP.

19. McKay to Bradley, December 10, 1930, in WABP. See also McKay to Eastman, December 1, 1930, in MEP. On Tangier between the wars, see Lawdom Vaidon, *Tangier: A Different View* (Metuchen, N.J., 1977), 192–229; and Aleko E. Lilius, *Turbulent Tangier* (London, 1956). Vaidon's book is an informal but detailed social history that emphasizes the changing relationships of the city's different ethnic and national communities over the years. Both Vaidon and Lilius also point out that Tangier was especially attractive to homosexuals from the 1920s onward.

20. McKay to Eastman, December 1, 1930, in MEP; Claude McKay to W. A. Bradley, January 25, 1931, in WABP.

21. McKay to Bradley, December 14, 1930, in WABP. See also "The Agricultural Show," in *G,* 163–91. Bone, *Down Home,* 167–68.

22. *HH,* 139–45; *B,* 301–26; McKay to Eastman, December 1, 1930, in MEP; McKay to Bradley, January 25, 1931, in WABP.

23. McKay to Eastman, December 1, 1930, in MEP; McKay to Bradley, January 25, 1931, in WABP; see also Bone, *Down Home,* 167–70.

24. McKay to Bradley, January 25, 1931, in WABP; *G, passim.*

25. *ALWFH,* 324–32; Bowles, *Without Stopping,* 129–37, and *passim;* Claude McKay to W. A. Bradley, May 15, July 14, 1931, both in WABP; Claude McKay to Max Eastman, July 19, 1931, in MEP; *ALWFH,* 328–30.

26. *ALWFH,* 329–31. See also McKay to Bradley, May 15, 1931, in WABP; and McKay to Eastman, July 19, 1931, in MEP. *ALWFH,* 331–32.

27. *ALWFH,* 331–32; McKay to Bradley, May 15, 1931, in WABP.

28. Claude McKay to W. A. Bradley, February 16, 1931, in WABP. See also *ALWFH,* 331–33; and Bowles, *Without Stopping,* 147–48.

29. Claude McKay to W. A. Bradley, January 25, 1931, in WABP; Cass Canfield, *Up*

*and Down and Around: A Publisher Recollects the Time of His Life* (New York, 1971), 109–10.

30. McKay to Eastman, December 1, 1930, July 19, December 1, 1931, June 6, 1932, May 24, April 21, 1933, [May, 1933], all in MEP. See also McKay to Bradley, January 25, 1931, in WABP.

31. In *ALWFH*, McKay wrote almost nothing about his hopes and expectations regarding *G* or *BB*. He scarcely mentioned the impact of the Great Depression upon his own fortunes. See *ALWFH*, 324–39.

32. Rudolph Fisher, "White, High Yellow, Black [Review of *Gingertown*]," *New York Herald Tribune Books,* March 27, 1932, p. 3.

33. "Negro Life [Review of *Gingertown*]," New York *Times,* April 3, 1932, p. 7.

34. McKay to Eastman, [May, 1933], in MEP.

35. *ALWFH,* 334. See also Pierre Vogein's letters to Claude McKay in CMP. *ALWFH,* 335–36. There is a photograph of McKay by Berenice Abbott in *PCM.*

36. *ALWFH,* 338; interview with Charles Henri Ford, June 5, 1972, in New York City.

37. Bowles, *Without Stopping,* 147–48; *ALWFH,* 331.

38. McKay to Eastman, July 19, 1931, January 27, 1933, both in MEP.

39. Bowles, *Without Stopping,* 148–49; McKay to Eastman, [May, 1933], in MEP.

40. Claude McKay to Max Eastman, April 25, 1932, in *PCM,* 152. See also McKay to Eastman, July 19, December 1, 1931, both in MEP.

41. See Claude McKay to Max Eastman, January 26, February 3, March 21, 1945, September 16, 1946, all in *PCM,* 307–14.

42. *ALWFH,* 334; Claude McKay to Max Eastman, January 27, 1933, in MEP.

43. McKay to Eastman, January 27, April 21, June 18, 28, 1933, all in MEP. McKay started the novel on black expatriates, but there is no evidence that he wrote any Moroccan potboilers.

44. McKay to Eastman, April 21, 1933, [May, 1933], both *ibid.*

45. McKay to Eastman, [May, 1933]. See also McKay to Eastman, July 19, 1931, January 27, April 21, May 24, 1933, all *ibid.*

46. *BB,* 1–13, 312–13; Richard Priebe, "The Search for Community in the Novels of Claude McKay," *Studies in Black Literature,* III (Summer, 1972), 22–30; Kenneth Ramchand, "The Road to *Banana Bottom,*" in M. G. Cook (ed.), *Modern Black Novelists: A Collection of Critical Essays* (Englewood Cliffs, N.J., 1971), 188–209; Mervyn Morris, "Contending Values: The Prose Fiction of Claude McKay," *Jamaica Journal,* IX, Nos. 2, 3 (1975), 36–42, 52.

47. Bone, *Down Home,* 170; U'Theo McKay to Claude McKay, May 23, 1933, in CMP.

48. Claude McKay to Max Eastman, June 18, 1932, in MEP.

49. "RHH." This piece, it will be recalled, appeared in June, 1928, after the publication of *HH.*

50. *ALWFH,* 344. On Cunard's affair, see Ernest B. Speck, "Henry Crowder: Nancy Cunard's 'Tree,'" *Lost Generation Journal,* VI (Summer, 1979), 6–8. See also Hugh Ford (ed.), *Nancy Cunard: Brave Poet, Indomitable Rebel, 1896–1965* (Philadelphia, 1968); and Anne Chisholm, *Nancy Cunard, A Biography* (New York, 1979).

51. Nancy Cunard to Claude McKay, June 17, 1933, in CMP. There are about a dozen letters from Cunard to McKay in CMP.

52. Claude McKay to Nancy Cunard, January 25, 1933, in CMP; Nancy Cunard (ed.), *Negro Anthology* (London, 1934).

53. Claude McKay, "A Negro Writer to His Critics," in *PCM,* 134–35.

54. *Ibid.*

55. McKay to Eastman, [May, 1933], in MEP; Max Eastman, *Love and Revolution: My Journey Through an Epoch* (New York, 1964), 611.

56. McKay to Eastman, [May, 1933], in MEP.

57. *Ibid.*

58. McKay to Eastman, May 24, 1933, *ibid.*

59. Claude McKay to Max Eastman, July 5, September 7, June 20, June 21, [1933], June 28, 1933, all *ibid.*

60. McKay to Eastman, June 28, 1933, *ibid.*

61. James Weldon Johnson to Max Eastman, June 3, 1933, in JWJP.

62. McKay to Eastman, June 28, 1933, in MEP.

63. Claude McKay to Max Eastman, July 15, 23, August 19, September 7, 21, October 5, 20, 1933, all *ibid.*

64. McKay to Eastman, July 5, 1933, *ibid.*

65. McKay to Eastman, July 23, September 7, 1933, both *ibid.*

66. Alfred A. Knopf to Carl Van Vechten, quoted in David Levering Lewis, *When Harlem Was in Vogue* (New York, 1981), 296. Part of McKay's problem at this juncture was the fact that "Savage Loving" was poorly written. See John Trounstine to Max Eastman, July 27, 1933, in MEP. McKay to Eastman, October 5, 1933, in MEP.

67. James Weldon Johnson to Claude McKay, September 30, 1933, in CMP.

68. Claude McKay to Max Eastman, October 30, 1933, in MEP. Letters containing contributions from Oswald Garrison Villard's secretary and Walter Lippman's family are in MEP. McKay in a letter to Joel Spingarn thanked him for his contribution (April 12, 1934, in JSP).

69. McKay to Eastman, October 20, 1933, in MEP.

70. Henry Lee Moon, "Claude McKay Comes Home to Harlem After Spending Ten-Year Exile on 2 Continents," *AN*, February 7, 1934; Claude McKay, "Note of Harlem," *Modern Monthly*, VIII (July, 1934), 368.

71. Hymans, *Leopold Sedar Senghor*, 35, 54, 275. See also Kesteloot, *Black Writers in French*, 56, 66–74, 304–305.

## Chapter 10

1. Henry Lee Moon, "Claude McKay Comes Home to Harlem After Spending Ten-Year Exile on 2 Continents," *AN*, February 7, 1934.

2. Claude McKay to Walter White, December 4, 1924, in WWP, NAACP.

3. For a compilation of articles on various aspects of Afro-American life during the New Deal years, see Bernard Sternsher (ed.), *The Negro in Depression and War: Prelude to Revolution, 1930–1945* (Chicago, 1969).

4. James O. Young, *Black Writers of the Thirties* (Baton Rouge, 1973).

5. Barton J. Bernstein, "The New Deal: The Conservative Achievements of Liberal Reform," in Barton J. Bernstein (ed.), *Towards a New Past: Dissenting Essays in American History* (New York, 1968).

6. See Mark D. Naison, "The Communist Party in Harlem, 1928–1936" (Ph.D. dissertation, Columbia University, 1976), "Historical Notes on Blacks and American Communism: The Harlem Experience," *Science and Society*, XLII (Fall, 1978), 324–43, and "Communism and Black Nationalism in the Depression: The Case of Harlem," *Journal of Ethnic Studies*, II (Summer, 1974), 27–33.

7. *PCM*, 193–300.

8. Claude McKay to Max Eastman, December 19, 1934, *ibid.*, 213.

9. Claude McKay to Max Eastman, May 9, 1934, *ibid.,* 198; see also *PCM,* 232–49, 300–14; and *ALWFH,* 342–54.

10. See especially Harold Jackman to Claude McKay, June 3, 1927, in CMP. Jackman tells McKay something of his life.

11. Interviews with Bruce Nugent at various dates between 1968 and 1978, in New York City. See also Langston Hughes, *The Big Sea* (New York, 1940), 235–36.

12. Claude McKay to Max Eastman, May 15, September 11, 1934, both in MEP; McKay to Eastman, November 10, 1934, in *PCM,* 207.

13. Claude McKay, "Note of Harlem," reprinted in Wagner, *Les Poètes Nègres des Etats-Unis,* 582–83.

14. James Weldon Johnson to Claude McKay, January 9, April 16, 1934, both in CMP; Claude McKay to Max Eastman, June 20, 1933, May 9, 1934, both in MEP; Claude McKay to Joel Spingarn, April 12, May 30, June 8, 1934, all in JSP.

15. See Claude McKay to Max Eastman, August 24, October 25, 1934, both in *PCM,* 199, 203–204; John W. Walker to Claude McKay, May 10, 1934, in CMP; and McKay to Eastman, August 12, 1934, in MEP.

16. Donald C. Brace to Claude McKay, July 12, 1934, Claude McKay to Max Eastman, August 12, 24, 25, 1934, [November, 1934], all in MEP. Several of these letters are included in *PCM,* 197–208.

17. Allen Weinstein, *Perjury: The Hiss-Chambers Case* (New York, 1978), 113, 127–30, 148–49, 157n, 316–17, 322–24, 404, 525, and *passim.* For McKay's dissatisfaction with Lieber, see McKay to Eastman, May 9, July 11, August 12, 24, 1934, all in MEP.

18. McKay to Eastman, November 10, 1934, in *PCM,* 206–208.

19. Claude McKay, "For a Negro Magazine," [summer, 1934], in *PCM,* 201.

20. McKay to Eastman, July 11, 1934, in *PCM,* 198–99.

21. McKay, "For a Negro Magazine," in *PCM,* 201–203.

22. *Ibid.;* on the Communist party's literary activities in the 1930s, see Aaron, *Writers on the Left,* 161–268.

23. McKay to Eastman, July 11, 1934, in *PCM,* 198–99.

24. McKay to Eastman, September 11, 1934, *ibid.,* 200–201.

25. McKay to Eastman, August 24, 1934, *ibid.,* 199.

26. McKay to Eastman, August 25, 1934, in MEP.

27. McKay to Eastman, October 25, November 3, 1934, both in *PCM,* 203–205.

28. McKay to Eastman, October 25, November 10, 1934, both *ibid.,* 203–204, 206–208.

29. McKay to Eastman, October 25, December 19, 1934, both *ibid.,* 203–204, 213.

30. McKay to Eastman, October 25, November 3, 1934, both *ibid.,* 203–206.

31. McKay to Eastman, October 25, November 3, and December 3, 1934, all *ibid.,* 204–205, 209–11.

32. McKay to Eastman, October 25, November 3, and December 3, 1934, all *ibid.,* 204–205, 210.

33. McKay to Eastman, November 10, 1934, *ibid.,* 206.

34. McKay to Eastman, November 3, December 3, 1934, both *ibid.,* 206, 209–11.

35. Claude McKay to Max Eastman, December 19, 1934, *ibid.,* 212–14. For McKay's past criticisms of Spingarn, see *PCM,* 141–42; and *ALWFH,* 147.

36. Claude McKay to Joel Spingarn, December 18, 1934, in JSP.

37. Claude McKay to Joel Spingarn, December 24, 31, 1934, both *ibid.;* McKay to Eastman, October 25, 1934, in *PCM,* 203.

38. The information in the preceding paragraphs is based on interviews with Selma Burke, 1966, in New Hope, Pa.; Carl Cowl, 1965–1980, in New York City; and Hope McKay Virtue, August 30, 1978, in Kingston, Jamaica.

39. McKay to Eastman, December 19, 1934, in *PCM*, 213; McKay to Eastman, April 30, July 1, 1935, both in MEP.

40. McKay to Eastman, October 25, 1934, in *PCM*, 204; James Weldon Johnson to Claude McKay, April 20, 1935, in CMP; Claude McKay to Edwin R. Embree, April 30, 1935, in JRFA.

41. Claude McKay to Edwin R. Embree, May 10, 1935, in JRFA.

42. James Weldon Johnson to Edwin R. Embree, May 11, 1935, Edwin R. Embree to Claude McKay, May 7, June 18, and July 18, 1935, Dorothy A. Elridge to Claude McKay, June 26, 1935, all in JRFA. Elridge was an employee of the Julius Rosenwald Fund.

43. Freda Kirchwey had a distinguished career as an editor and journalist at the *Nation* and other journals.

44. Claude McKay, "There Goes God! The Story of Father Divine and His Angels," *Nation*, CXL (February 6, 1935), 151–53.

45. *H*, 32–85.

46. Claude McKay, "Harlem Runs Wild," *Nation*, CXL (April 3, 1935), 382–83, reprinted in *PCM*, 239–43.

47. *Ibid*.

48. Claude McKay to Max Eastman, [1935], in MEP.

49. Claude McKay to Edwin R. Embree, March 31, 1936, in JRFA.

50. Henry G. Alsberg to Claude McKay, October 25, 1935, in CMP. Alsberg was the head of the New York City branch of the Federal Writers' Project. A fair number of letters to and from Claude McKay and various FWP officials survive in CMP. For more on the FWP, see Jerre Mangione, *The Dream and the Deal: The Federal Writers Project* (Boston, 1972); and *PCM*, 226–99, 352–55.

51. See the letters from the various officials of the New York FWP to Claude McKay, November 13, 1935, July 7, September 11, December 21, 1936, January 5, March 13, 1937, all in CMP. See also Mangione, *The Dream and the Deal*, 155–90, 260–63; the FWP materials on microfilm at the Arthur A. Schomburg Collection, New York Public Library; and Claude McKay to Orrick Johns, September 11, 1936, in MMP. Johns at the time was director of the New York City FWP.

52. Claude McKay to Orrick Johns, September 11, 1936, in MMP.

53. Mangione, *The Dream and the Deal*, 245.

54. Claude McKay to James Ivy, January 4, 1937, in JIP.

55. See James W. Watson to David Frederick McCord, May 12, 1937, in CMP.

56. Max Eastman to Claude McKay, April 27, 1937, copy in MMP.

57. *ALWFH*, 110–11. White's anger was later reported by McKay to Max Eastman in a letter dated August 28, 1946, in *PCM*, 311.

58. Laurence Roberts to Claude McKay, June 4, 1937, in CMP. See also *ALWFH*, 78–79.

59. Joel Spingarn to Claude McKay, February 24, 1937, in CMP.

60. Claude McKay to Joel Spingarn, March 7, 1937, in JSP.

61. Claude McKay to Joel Spingarn, March 12, 1937, in JSP; see also Claude McKay to Max Eastman, August 28, 1946, in *PCM*, 311.

62. *ALWFH*, 226, 228.

63. Edwin R. Embree to Claude McKay, March 8, 1937, in CMP.

64. *ALWFH*, 354.

65. Alain Locke, "Spiritual Truant [Review of *A Long Way from Home*]," *New Challenge,* II (Fall, 1937), 81, 83–84.

66. *ALWFH,* 312–14.

67. M. B. Tolson, "Caviar and Cabbage: Claude McKay, Black Ulysses [Review of *A Long Way from Home*]," [undated clipping, 1937], in Claude McKay Clippings Folder, Trevor-Arnett Library, Atlanta University, Atlanta.

68. James Weldon Johnson to Claude McKay, March 26, 1937, in CMP. See George Streator, "Revolutionary in Color [Review of *A Long Way from Home*]," *New York Herald Tribune Books,* March 14, 1937.

69. Henry Lee Moon, "Review of *A Long Way from Home*," *New Republic,* XC (April 28, 1937), 364–65; J. S. Balch, "Review of *A Long Way from Home*," St. Louis *Post-Dispatch,* March 21, 1937, n.p., in Clippings Folder, CMP.

## Chapter 11

1. In his general history of the FWP, Jerre Mangione has devoted a long chapter entitled "Manhattan Hotbed" to the New York division. See *The Dream and the Deal,* 155–90.

2. "Writers Fail to Agree on Membership," *AN,* July 24, 1937. On the practice of Communist integration in the 1930s, see Naison, "Historical Notes on Blacks and American Communism," 325.

3. Claude McKay to James Weldon Johnson, January 9, August 22, 1937, both in JWJP.

4. "Writers Fail to Agree on Membership," *AN.*

5. Claude McKay to Helen Boardman, July 17, 1937, in CMP.

6. Helen Boardman to Claude McKay, [July, 1937], McKay to Boardman, July 27, 1937, Boardman to McKay, September 4, 1937, all *ibid.*

7. Claude McKay to James Weldon Johnson, April 15, 1935, in JWJP.

8. James Weldon Johnson to Claude McKay, May 27, 1935, in CMP. The articles in question have all been reprinted in Julius Lester (ed.), *The Thought and Writings of W. E. B. Du Bois: The Seventh Son* (2 vols.; New York, 1971), II, 231–57.

9. James Weldon Johnson, *Negro Americans, What Now?* (New York, 1934).

10. Claude McKay to James Weldon Johnson, May 16, 1935, in JWJP.

11. Johnson to McKay, May 27, 1935, in CMP.

12. McKay to Johnson, August 22, November 28, 1937, both in JWJP.

13. McKay to Johnson, November 28, 1937, in JWJP. See also Naison, "Historical Notes on Blacks and American Communism," 339.

14. Claude McKay to James Weldon Johnson, February 5, 1938, in JWJP.

15. Claude McKay, [circular letter for the creation of a Negro Writers' Guild], October 23, 1937, in *PCM,* 232–34; Claude McKay to James Weldon Johnson, August 10, 22, September 18, 26, November 28, 1937, February 21, 1938, all in JWJP. See also Claude McKay to Countee Cullen, August 12, September 9, 13, November 8, 1937, all in CCP.

16. Claude McKay to James Weldon Johnson, April 2, 1938, in JWJP.

17. See the McKay-Cullen correspondence in CCP.

18. Perhaps because it fell outside the usual political categories of Right and Left in the 1930s and because its existence was brief, the *African* has received almost no attention from students of recent Harlem history.

19. See Claude McKay to Alain Locke, May 14, 1938, in ALP; and Countee Cullen to Claude McKay, July 24, 1938, in CMP.

20. Claude McKay, "An Open Letter to James Rorty," *Socialist Call,* July 17, 1937,

p. 8, "For Group Survival," *Jewish Frontier,* IV (October, 1937), 19–26, and "Labor Steps Out in Harlem," *Nation,* CXLV (October 16, 1937), 399–402, all reprinted in *PCM,* 226–28, 234–39, 243–49.

21.  The literature on the Popular Front is extensive. For the purposes of this study, Daniel Aaron's account of its implementation on the cultural-literary front in the United States is central. See his *Writers on the Left,* 280–92, 356–60. See also John T. Marcus, *French Socialism in the Crisis Years, 1933–1936: Fascism and the French Left* (New York, 1958).

22.  Aaron, *Writers on the Left,* 280–308, 359–443; Hugh Thomas, *The Spanish Civil War* (New York, 1977), 522–23.

23.  McKay, "An Open Letter to James Rorty," in *PCM,* 226–28.

24.  Douglas Blaufarb, "Communist Party Members Ordered to Drive Trotskyists off WPA," *NL,* July 23, 1938. In the 1930s, the *NL* was a weekly newspaper. It later became a monthly magazine. In the process, it followed a classic path from a socialist journal in opposition to the Communist party on the Left to a fervid supporter of all Cold War measures taken by the U.S. government after World War II to contain Soviet power.

25.  Claude McKay, "Negro Author Sees Disaster If the Communist Party Gains Control of Negro Workers," *NL,* September 10, 1938, p. 5, reprinted as "Communism and the Negro," in *PCM,* 228–29.

26.  See Hugh T. Murray, "The NAACP Versus the Communist Party: The Scottsboro Rape Cases, 1931–1932," in Bernard Sternsher (ed.), *The Negro in Depression and War: Prelude to Revolution, 1930–1945* (Chicago, 1969), 267–81. The standard treatment of the Scottsboro case is Dan T. Carter's *Scottsboro: A Tragedy of the American South* (Baton Rouge, 1969). When McKay criticized James Weldon Johnson for not adequately discussing the Communist threat of domination over American blacks in *Negro Americans, What Now?,* Johnson simply replied that he did not think the United States would become communistic but he did believe that blacks should support *all* movements for a planned economy. See McKay to Johnson, May 16, 1935, in JWJP; and Johnson to McKay, May 27, 1935, in CMP.

27.  Claude McKay, "Dynamite in Africa: Are the 'Popular Fronts' Suppressing Colonial Independence?" *Common Sense,* VII (March, 1938), 11.

28.  Claude McKay, "Native Liberation Might Have Stopped the Franco Revolt," *NL,* February 18, 1939, reprinted as "North Africa and the Spanish Civil War," in *PCM,* 285–89.

29.  Claude McKay to W. A. Bradley, May 15, 1931, in WABP. On the Spanish Civil War, see Thomas' exhaustive treatment, *The Spanish Civil War.*

30.  Claude McKay, "Pact Exploded Communist Propaganda Among Negroes," *NL,* September 23, 1939, pp. 4–7. This article was an important summation of McKay's social views in the 1930s.

31.  *PCM,* 238, 258, 278–80, 295.

32.  Claude McKay, "Everybody's Doing It: Anti-Semitic Propaganda Fails to Attract Negroes; Harlemites Face Problems of All Other Slum Dwellers," *NL,* May 20, 1939, pp. 5–6, reprinted as "Anti-Semitism and the Negro," in *PCM,* 257–61.

33.  All the quotations from both the *Jewish Frontier* article and McKay's response to it are in Claude McKay, "Claude McKay Tells of Jews," *AN,* December 24, 1938, clipping in Claude McKay Clippings Folder, Trevor-Arnett Library, Atlanta University, Atlanta. The situation McKay describes, of course, was more true of New York City than elsewhere in the United States, where Jews generally constituted a tiny minority, even among businessmen.

34. McKay, "For Group Survival," in *PCM*, 234–39. McKay debated Schuyler in the spring of 1937 on radio station WEVD in New York City.

35. *Ibid.*; see also *H*, 89, 183–84, and *passim*.

36. McKay, "For Group Survival," in *PCM*, 234–39; see also *PCM*, 251–52.

37. McKay, "For Group Survival," in *PCM*, 236–39.

38. McKay, "Labor Steps Out in Harlem," in *PCM*, 243–49.

39. Adam Clayton Powell, Jr., "Soapbox," *AN*, October 30, 1937, p. 13; Schuyler quoted in Claude McKay, "Negro Extinction or Survival: A Reply to George S. Schuyler," in *PCM*, 253. Schuyler had a regular column in the Pittsburgh *Courier*, which was syndicated in other black newspapers across the country.

40. Claude McKay, "Claude McKay vs. Powell," *AN*, November 6, 1937, p. 4, reprinted as "On Adam Clayton Powell, Jr.: A Response," in *PCM*, 250–52.

41. Claude McKay, "McKay Says Schuyler Is Writing Nonsense," *AN*, November 20, 1937, p. 12, reprinted as "Negro Extinction or Survival," in *PCM*, 253–57 (quotation on p. 256).

42. McKay, "On Adam Clayton Powell, Jr.," in *PCM*, 252.

43. James Weldon Johnson to Claude McKay, November 15, 1937, in CMP; McKay to Johnson, January 9, 1937, in JWJP. An account of Johnson's fatal accident, in which his wife was seriously injured, can be found in Eugene Levy, *James Weldon Johnson: Black Leader, Black Voice* (Chicago, 1973). See also Max Eastman to Claude McKay, July 5, 1938, in CMP. In his grief, McKay had apparently tried frantically to contact Eastman to insist that he attend Johnson's funeral services in New York. But Eastman was in the American Southwest at the time, and he wrote to express his regrets and to tell McKay why he had missed the funeral.

44. A fairly extensive McKay correspondence exists with all these people except Earl Brown, who once explained in a telephone interview with me that he had great respect for McKay in the 1930s. Besides accepting his work for publication in the *AN*, he several times invited McKay to dinner with his family. Also see Ellen Tarry, *The Third Door: An Autobiography of an American Negro Woman* (New York, 1955), 187.

45. *PCM*, 228. On Wright and Ellison's association with the FWP, see Mangione, *The Dream and the Deal*, 245–56.

46. Claude McKay, "Honeymoon," *Challenge*, I (January, 1936), 18, and *New Challenge*, II (Fall, 1937), 53–65, 81–85.

47. Claude McKay to Claire Lennard, January 31, 1947, in CMP; Claude McKay to Edwin R. Embree, August 15, 1937, March 23, 1938, both in JRFA.

48. Claude McKay to Edwin R. Embree, August 15, 1937, in JRFA. Letters regarding recommendations for a Guggenheim are in CMP. See also the penciled outline of Gannett's answer to McKay's request on the margin of Claude McKay to Lewis Gannett, October 2, 1937, in Lewis Gannett Papers, Houghton Library, Harvard University.

49. H. L. Lederer [Authors' Club, Carnegie Fund] to Claude McKay, October 15, 1937, in CMP; Claude McKay to James Weldon Johnson, December 17, 1937, in JWJP; Carlisle Smith to Claude McKay, May 1, 25, 27, July 8, September 11, 1940, all in CMP. Four "Looking Forward" columns appeared in *AN*: on May 13, 20, 27, and April 22, 1939.

50. Claude McKay to Edwin R. Embree, November 10, 1940, in JRFA. In December, 1940, the Book-of-the-Month Club newsletter contained a review of *H* by Dorothy Canfield and listed it as an alternate selection for the month. Claude McKay to Howard C. Anderson, December 3, 1940, in CMP. The last days of the FWP are chronicled by Mangione in *The Dream and the Deal*, 329–48.

51. *H*, 32–85, 89, 101–16, 218–62, and *passim*.

52. *ALWFH*, 245.

53. *H*, 28–116, 143–80, 183–84, 260–61.

54. Claude McKay to Catherine Latimer, July 3, 1940, in MMP.

55. For a helpful discussion of black ideologies, see August Meier, Elliott Rudwick, and Francis L. Broderick (eds.), *Black Protest Thought in the Twentieth Century* (Indianapolis, 1971); and August Meier, *Negro Thought in America, 1880–1915: Racial Ideologies in the Age of Booker T. Washington* (Ann Arbor, Mich., 1963).

56. Claude McKay to W. E. B. Du Bois, June 18, 1928, in W. E. B. Du Bois Papers, University of Massachusetts, Amherst.

57. Catherine Latimer in *Library Journal*, quoted in an E. P. Dutton press release, in CMP.

58. *H*, 99, 233–34.

59. McKay to Embree, November 10, 1940, in JRFA. See also Cruse, *The Crisis of the Negro Intellectual*, 1–10, and *passim*.

60. Ted Poston, "Review of *Harlem: Negro Metropolis*," *New Republic*, CIII (November 25, 1940), 732.

61. Roi Ottley, "Review of *Harlem: Negro Metropolis*," *New York Times Book Review*, November 24, 1940, p. 5.

62. Zora Neale Hurston, "Review of *Harlem: Negro Metropolis*," *Common Ground*, I (Winter, 1941), 95–96.

63. A. Philip Randolph to Claude McKay, April 4, 1941, June 4, 1940, both in CMP.

64. Benjamin Stolberg to Claude McKay, December 17, 1940, in CMP.

65. On "black power," see Martin Duberman, "Black Power in America," *Partisan Review*, XXXV (Winter, 1968), 34–68; and Meier, Rudwick, and Broderick (eds.), *Black Protest Thought in the Twentieth Century*, liii, 469–629.

66. Like McKay, Orwell in the 1930s tried to view the course of Communist politics from a sympathetic left-wing perspective, but he became increasingly disillusioned as the decade advanced. See George Orwell, *The Road to Wigan Pier* (London, 1937), and *Homage to Catalonia* (London, 1938).

*Chapter 12*

1. There is a copy of "HG" in MMP. See the excerpt from "HG" in *PCM*, 187–90.

2. "HG," in MMP.

3. Arna Bontemps to Langston Hughes, November 5, 1941, in Charles H. Nichols (ed.), *Arna Bontemps–Langston Hughes Letters, 1925–1967* (New York, 1980), 94.

4. Claude McKay, "Negroes Are Anti-Nazi, but Fight Anglo-U.S. Discrimination. Soap-Boxers in Harlem Typify Negro Resentments," *NL*, October 25, 1941, p. 4, reprinted as "Nazism vs. Democracy: Some Harlem Soapbox Opinions," in *PCM*, 277–80.

5. Claude McKay to Max Eastman, July 28, 1941, July 17, 1944, both in MEP.

6. Claude McKay, "Author Assails Negro Congress for Message Sent to Washington on Jews," *NL*, November 25, 1938, p. 11; Claude McKay to Max Eastman, May 4, 1944, in MEP.

7. From Claude McKay's grant proposal, which he included in a letter to William C. Haygood, January 3, 1942, in JRFA. Haygood was a Rosenwald Fund executive.

8. James S. Watson to William C. Haygood, February 16, 1942, Ernestine Rose to Haygood, February 10, 1942, John Dewey to Haygood, February 3, 1942, all in JRFA. John Dewey had met McKay through Max Eastman, and had high praise for *H*. See Dewey to McKay, November 29, 1940, in CMP.

9. Claude McKay to Arna Bontemps, July 18, 1941, in JP.

10. Initialed note from Arna Bontemps ("A.B.") to [JRFA grant committee], [1942], in JRFA.

11. Grant committee, Claude McKay evaluation sheet (anonymous comments), in JRFA.

12. Claude McKay to Benjamin Mandel, September 28, 1939, and U.S. Citizenship Certification, both in CMP. See also the summary of the FBI interview with Claude McKay, September 11, 1947, a copy of which was given to me by Ben Waknin of New York City. In the interview, McKay recapitulated much of the information he had already published in *ALWFH,* and he directed the FBI only to well-known anti-Communists, who he believed might be willing to talk with the FBI. As for himself, the report stated that "McKay was somewhat reluctant to discuss his past activities and stated that he had no desire to discuss individual Communists as he did not care to get anyone in trouble." In the interview, McKay stated that he never joined the Communist party but did join the IWW in 1919. My thanks to Ben Waknin for passing this interview on.

13. Grant committee evaluation sheet (anonymous comments), in JRFA.

14. Ellen Tarry, *The Third Door: An Autobiography of an American Negro Woman* (New York, 1955), 187; interview with Ellen Tarry in the mid-1960s. See also Claude McKay to Max Eastman, August 13, 1942, in *PCM,* 301.

15. Claude McKay, "Right Turn to Catholicism" (Typescript, in MMP); *ALWFH,* 24–25, 62–63, 65.

16. Most of the information in the above paragraphs and in the discussion of Catherine de Hueck and Friendship House is taken from a pamphlet by Catherine de Hueck, *The Story of Friendship House* [New York, *ca.* 1939], in FHP.

17. See the poem, "St. Isaacs Church, Petrograd," in *SP,* 84; see also Claude McKay to Max Eastman, June 30, 1944, in MEP; and McKay, "Right Turn to Catholicism," in MMP.

18. Claude McKay to Tom Keating, June 29, 1942, and Claude McKay to Mary Keating, June 14, 1943, both in KP.

19. McKay to Tom Keating, June 29, 1942, McKay to Mary Keating, June 14, 1943, both in KP; see also Ivie Jackman to Claude McKay, November 17, 1942, in JP.

20. Claude McKay to Max Eastman, July 30, 1942, in *PCM,* 300; Eastman to McKay, August 6, 1942, in CMP.

21. Max Eastman to Claude McKay, August 21, 1942, in MEP. See also Max Eastman to Elmer Davis, August 5, 1942, in CMP.

22. Claude McKay to Ivie Jackman, September 11, 1942, in JP.

23. Claude McKay to Ivie Jackman, September 24, 1942, February 16, 1943, both *ibid.* In JP, there is a radio script by Claude McKay on Rear Admiral Henry K. Hewitt, USN, done for the Office of War Information. Hewitt was the commander of U.S. naval forces in the Mediterranean during the North African campaign.

24. Claude McKay to Mary Keating, March 25, 1944, in KP; Claude McKay to Ivie Jackman, May 11, 1943, in JP; Claude McKay to Countee Cullen, April 14, [1943], in CCP.

25. Claude McKay to Max Eastman, September 3, 1943, in MEP.

26. Vereda Pearson to Mary Keating, [summer, 1943], in KP; Claude McKay to Countee Cullen, July 25, 1943, in CCP; telegram from Freda Kirchwey to Edwin R. Embree, July 7, [1943], telegram from Embree to Kirchwey, July 8, 1943, both in JRFA. See also Claude McKay to Max Eastman, September 3, 1943, in *PCM,* 303.

27. Claude McKay to Tom Keating, August 8, 1943, in KP.

28. Claude McKay to Mary Keating, June 14, 1943, *ibid.*

29. Vereda Pearson to Mary Keating, July 1, 1943, *ibid.*

30. Roger L. Treat, *Bishop Sheil and the CYO* (New York, 1951); Mary Keating to Wayne Cooper, March 4, 1964, in possession of the recipient; interview with Tom and Mary Keating, October 14, 1976, in Chicago.

31. Claude McKay to Tom and Mary Keating, August 8, McKay to Mary Keating, September 16, October 11, 1943, all in KP.

32. McKay to Mary Keating, September 16, 1943, in KP.

33. This group of sonnets, known as the "Cycle Manuscript," consists of approximately fifty-five poems. Few ever appeared in print. Various drafts and carbons are in CMP.

34. Freda Kirchwey to Edwin R. Embree, November 16, 1943, in JRFA.

35. Claude McKay to Mary Keating, March 25, 1944, in KP.

36. Telegrams from Mary Keating to Claude McKay, March 30, April 12, 1944, Claude McKay to Bishop Bernard J. Sheil, April 6, 1944, Claude McKay to Mary Keating, [April, 1944], April 11, 1944, all in KP. In an earlier letter to her, Claude wrote that "most of the people I know here try to discourage me [from going to Chicago]. But they don't understand; I'll be having my hands and mind on something there, which I haven't here" (Claude McKay to Mary Keating, April 6, 1944, *ibid.*). See also Claude McKay to Ivie Jackman, April 14, 1944, in JP.

37. See Claude McKay to Father Daniel Michael Cantwell, in DMCP. See also Claude McKay to Max Eastman, June 1, 1944, in MEP.

38. Max Eastman to Claude McKay, June 7, 1944, in MEP.

39. Claude McKay to Max Eastman, June 30, 1944, *ibid.*

40. Claude McKay to Max Eastman, August 16, 1944, *ibid.*

41. Claude McKay to Max Eastman, October 16, 1944, in *PCM*, 304–305.

42. Claude McKay to Ivie Jackman, June 23, 1944, in JP.

43. Claude McKay to Ivie Jackman, July 15, 1944, *ibid.*

44. Claude McKay to Ivie Jackman, October 27, 1944, *ibid.*

45. Claude McKay to Ivie Jackman, September 12, 1944, *ibid.;* see also Claude McKay to Ivie Jackman, November 21, 1944, Claude McKay to Harold Jackman, May 9, 1944, both *ibid.;* and Claude McKay to Max Eastman, May 4, June 1, both in MEP. There are a few "Reports to [Bishop] Bernard J. Sheil" from McKay in CMP. They consist mostly of newspaper clippings and summaries and contain almost no analysis by McKay. He did, however, give his opinion to Sheil in personal conversations.

46. Claude McKay to Ivie Jackman, April 14, October 27, November 21, December 6, 20, 1944, all in JP. See also BBP. Through conversation, correspondence, and by providing leads and introductions to others who knew McKay in Chicago, Betty Britton has supplied much information about McKay's life in Chicago and his association with the CYO. Her collection of letters from Claude McKay to her from 1944 to 1948 give additional insight into his Chicago experience. My thanks to her.

47. Claude McKay to Ivie Jackman, December 6, 1944, January 4, May 1, 1945, all in JP.

48. Claude McKay to Ivie Jackman, August 30, 1945, June 3, 1946, both *ibid.* See also Claude McKay to Max Eastman, August 7, 1946, in *PCM*, 309–10.

49. Claude McKay to Mary Keating, March 25, 1944, in KP; Claude McKay to Ivie Jackman, October 27, 1944, in JP; Claude McKay to Max Eastman, November 28, 1944, in *PCM*, 306; Claude McKay to Betty Britton, September 1, 1946, in BBP. Between January, 1945, and July, 1947, McKay published twelve poems in Dorothy Day's *Catholic Worker.* Dorothy Day (1897–1980) was the cofounder with Peter Maurin of

the Catholic Worker movement and editor of the *Catholic Worker*. McKay had first met her in Greenwich Village during the *Liberator* period before she had converted to Catholicism. Her movement and paper have been consistently Christian, socialist, and pacifist. On Dorothy Day, see Dorothy Day, *The Long Loneliness: An Autobiography* (New York, 1981); and William Miller, *Dorothy Day and the Catholic Worker Movement* (New York, 1973), and *Dorothy Day: A Biography* (New York, 1981).

50. The idea of a joint publication entitled "East Indian–West Indian" continued after McKay's death when Dover, having completed his autobiographical piece, joined with Carl Cowl, McKay's last literary agent and his literary executor, in an attempt to find a publisher for the proposed volumes. They never succeeded. See correspondence between Cedric Dover and Carl Cowl, copies in my possession.

51. Claude McKay to Max Eastman, August 28, 1946, in *PCM*, 311.

52. Claude McKay to Carl Cowl, February 20, April 9, June 10, July 21, 28, 1947, all in CMP; Claude McKay, "On Becoming a Roman Catholic," *Epistle*, II (Spring, 1945), 43–45. In *MGH*, Claude's attitude toward his father had softened, but he still differentiated sharply between his parents' personalities; he still identified with his mother.

53. See *MGH*, 41–42; McKay, "Right Turn to Catholicism," in MMP.

54. Claude McKay to Carl Cowl, February 12, March 11, July 9, 21, 28, 1947, all in CMP.

55. Claude McKay to Ivie Jackman, November 29, 1947, in JP.

56. Claude McKay to Carl Cowl, February 13, 1948, in CMP; Mary Keating to Wayne Cooper, March 4, 1964, in possession of the recipient.

57. Mary Keating to Wayne Cooper, March 4, 1964, in possession of the recipient. See also Claude McKay to Betty Britton, November 29, 1945, May 8, 1947, both in BBP; and Claude McKay to Carl Cowl, September 30, November 1, 1947, both in CMP.

58. Mary Keating to Wayne Cooper, March 4, 1964, in possession of the recipient.

59. McKay, "Right Turn to Catholicism," in MMP.

60. Claude McKay to Max Eastman, August 28, 1946, in *PCM*, 311.

61. Claude McKay, "Tiger," *Catholic Worker*, XII (January, 1946), 3, reprinted in *SP*, 47.

62. Claude McKay to Max Eastman, September 16, 1946, in *PCM*, 313.

63. Claude McKay to Carl Cowl, April 9, 1948, Claude McKay to Ellen Tarry, April 27, 1948, both in CMP.

64. Hebrews 11:13; Claude McKay to Carl Cowl, March 1, 1947, in CMP; obituary, New York *Herald Tribune*, May 24, 1948.

65. Claude McKay to Carl Cowl, March 11, 1947, in CMP. Two retrospective views of McKay during his final years as a Catholic come to almost totally opposite conclusions regarding the sincerity of his religious convictions. See Ammon Hennacy to Wayne Cooper, April 19, 1969, in possession of the recipient; and Reverend Samuel J. Mathews, S.S.J., "Tribute to Claude McKay," *Colored Harvest*, XXXVI (July-August, 1948), 14–15.

# Essay on Sources

$F$or comprehensive bibliographies of Claude McKay's published works, interested readers should consult *PCM*, 349–58, and Wayne Cooper, "Stranger and Pilgrim: The Life of Claude McKay, 1890–1948" (Ph.D. dissertation, Rutgers University, 1982). For more extended discussions of unpublished as well as published material, see also Sister M. James Conroy, "Claude McKay: Negro Poet and Novelist" (Ph.D. dissertation, Notre Dame University, 1968); Phyllis Martin Lang, "Claude McKay: The Later Years, 1934–1948" (Ph.D. dissertation, University of Illinois, 1972); and Tyrone Tillery, "Claude McKay: Man and Symbol of the Harlem Renaissance" (Ph.D. dissertation, Kent State University, 1981).

Claude McKay's unpublished letters and manuscripts are widely scattered among manuscript libraries and private holdings, but most of his unpublished work is accessible to the diligent researcher. A central collection of his letters and unpublished poetry and prose can be found in the Harold Jackman, Langston Hughes, James Weldon Johnson, and Claude McKay papers in the Beinecke Rare Book and Manuscript Library, Yale University, New Haven. The Claude McKay Papers in the Beinecke Library consist mainly of those papers and  425 books in his possession at his death. In addition, the Jackman, Hughes, and Johnson papers all contain important McKay correspondence. The reader should also consult the other manuscript collections cited in the list of abbreviations for this book, all of which contain significant correspondence. In addition, some, such as the James Weldon Johnson and Walter White personal correspondence in the NAACP Collection at the Library of Congress and the William Stanley Braithwaite Papers in the Houghton Library, Harvard University, contain a few significant unpublished McKay poems. Of the private collections consulted, the most extensive and important were the Max Eastman and the William Aspenwall Bradley papers. The Eastman-McKay correspondence extends from 1919 until 1948, and the Bradley Papers contain invaluable information for that period in the 1920s and early 1930s when McKay was abroad writing his novels and short stories.

Students of McKay's letters should not be put off by his numerous "begging letters." Even when hard pressed for money and other favors, McKay revealed much about his times, his work, and himself in his letters. They collectively remain by far the most important of his unpublished works. And for the industrious scholar, there undoubtedly remain other significant caches of McKay's letters awaiting discovery.

In addition to those individuals who allowed me access to their personal correspondence with McKay, certain scholars, in particular Alan L. McLeod, Ben Waknin, Paul White, and Louis Harlan, shared with me the rich background materials, manuscripts, and letters they discovered in their research on Claude McKay and related topics. Many other individuals shared with me their memories and opinions of McKay in oral interviews, telephone conversations, and letters. They included Charles Ashleigh, John Barber, Romare Beardon, Maurice Becker, Louise Bennett, Mrs. William Aspenwall Bradley, Cyril Briggs, Betty Britton, Earl Brown, Frank and Francine Budgen, Selma Burke, Glen Carrington, Ida Cullen Cooper, Carl Cowl, Adolf Dehn, W. A. Domingo, Max Eastman, Reverend William Ellwood, Charles Henri Ford, William Gropper, Ammon Hennacy, James Ivy, Tom and Mary Keating, Walter Kendall, Edna McKay, M. E. McKay, Reverend Samuel J. Mathews, Richard B. Moore, Bruce Nugent, Dr. Fanny Rappaport-Vogein, I. A. Richards, Alfred Tiala, and Hope McKay Virtue. Of these, the generous cooperation of Hope McKay Virtue, Claude McKay's daughter, and of Carl Cowl, the executor of his literary estate, was most vital. Others from the above list who were particularly helpful and encouraging were Bruce Nugent,

Betty Britton, Mrs. W. A. Bradley, and the late Max Eastman and John Barber. These individuals not only shared with me their knowledge of Claude McKay, they also provided by their friendship and encouragement the kind of authoritative confirmation of the significance of my subject that every scholar needs who ventures into largely unexplored territory.

Useful also as background material were the Friendship House Papers in the Chicago Historical Society Library and the Frank Cundall Papers and the abundant secondary material in the West India Reference Library, Jamaica Institute, Kingston, Jamaica. Among the most useful secondary materials in the West India Reference Library were two newspapers, the Kingston *Daily Gleaner* and the *Jamaica Times,* both of which in 1911 and 1912 carried important poems by Claude McKay, news items about him, and reviews of his dialect verse. Finally, the New York Public Library and Schomburg Center for Research in Black Culture in Harlem provided a wealth of secondary material relating to McKay's times. The Schomburg Center also had the New York *Amsterdam News* and other periodicals that carried McKay's articles and poems in the 1930s and 1940s.

My research into the life of Claude McKay largely coincided with the growth of a diverse body of critical commentary on McKay. West Indian critics have commented ably on Claude McKay's Jamaican poetry and novels. The following, for example, assess McKay's role as a pioneer in the development of modern West Indian literature: Lloyd W. Brown, *West Indian Poetry* (New York, 1978); Kenneth Ramchand, *The West Indian Novel and Its Background* (New York, 1970); Mervyn Morris, "Contending Values: The Prose Fiction of Claude McKay," *Jamaica Journal,* IX, Nos. 2, 3 (1975), 36–42, 52; and Rupert Lewis and Maureen Lewis, "Claude McKay's Jamaica," *Caribbean Quarterly,* XXIII, Nos. 2, 3 (1977), 38–53. One should also see Mervyn Morris' introduction to Claude McKay's *My Green Hills of Jamaica and Five Jamaican Short Stories,* ed. Mervyn Morris (Kingston and Port of Spain, 1979). The most critical of these writers have been Rupert Lewis and Maureen Lewis, who felt that McKay's assessment of the Jamaica of his young manhood was severely limited by a basically middle-class perspective that lacked a well-defined class consciousness.

The best assessments of McKay's relationship to post–World War I radicalism remain Theodore Draper's two volumes, *American Communism and Soviet Russia: The Formative Period* (New York, 1960), and *The Roots of American Communism* (New York, 1957); and Daniel Aaron's *Writers on the Left: Episodes in American Literary*

*Communism* (New York, 1961). McKay's relationship to English communism after World War I is discussed in Walter Kendall, *The Revolutionary Movement in Britain, 1900–1921: The Origins of British Communism* (London, 1969).

McKay's relationship to the Harlem Renaissance has been examined at greater length than any other aspect of his career, and critics have varied widely in their assessment of his place in it and in Afro-American literary history in general. The French Catholic scholar, Jean Wagner, for example, argues in his monumental analysis, *Les Poètes Nègres des Etats-Unis: Le Sentiment Racial et Religieux dans la Poésie de P. L. Dunbar à L. Hughes (1890–1940)* (Paris, 1963), translated by Kenneth Douglas as *Black Poets of the United States: From Paul Laurence Dunbar to Langston Hughes* (Urbana, 1973), that McKay achieved a greater spirituality and universality of appeal in his poetry than the other poets of the Harlem Renaissance. By contrast, George Kent, in *Blackness and the Adventure of Western Culture* (Chicago, 1972), praises McKay for helping to prepare the ground for the emergence of a self-consciously independent black literature. In further contrast, Robert Bone in his two important analyses of black fiction, *The Negro Novel in America* (Rev. ed.; New Haven, 1965), and *Down Home: A History of Afro-American Short Fiction from Its Beginnings to the End of the Harlem Renaissance* (New York, 1975), considers McKay a significant literary force in his time but concludes that he achieved only modest artistic success as a novelist and short-story writer. The Harlem Renaissance and McKay's role in it are both subjected to a highly negative cultural analysis in Harold Cruse's *The Crisis of the Negro Intellectual from Its Origin to the Present Day* (New York, 1967). Finally, James R. Giles, in his *Claude McKay* (Boston, 1976) for Twayne's U.S. Author Series, has attempted a balanced assessment of McKay's literary achievements and limitations. Giles concludes that McKay was a major figure in the development of Afro-American literature because of his contributions to modern Afro-American protest themes in his poetry and also because his assertion in his novels of a black cultural independence strongly foreshadowed later developments in Afro-American art. But Giles, too, concludes that McKay's work as a whole was uneven and that his ultimate impact as a writer was certainly greater than the sum of his individual works.

One of the most controversial features found in McKay's works, and particularly in his novels, is his use of the ideas of primitivism to contrast the basic health and vitality of black folk cultures with the unhealthy materialism of Western civilization. His attachment to primitivism and the problems it presented in his work and his life have been discussed by Michael B. Stoff, "Claude McKay and the Cult of Primitivism," in Arna Bontemps (ed.), *The Harlem Renaissance Remembered: Essays edited with a Memoir* (New York, 1972), 126–46.

Partial background for understanding McKay in the 1930s can be acquired from the following: Jerre Mangione, *The Dream and the Deal: The Federal Writers Project* (Boston, 1972); Allen Weinstein, *Perjury: The Hiss-Chambers Case* (New York, 1978); and Mark D. Naison, "Communism and Black Nationalism in the Depression: The Case of Harlem," *Journal of Ethnic Studies,* II (Summer, 1974), 27–33, "Historical Notes on Blacks and American Communism: The Harlem Experience," *Science and Society,* XLII (Fall, 1978), 324–43, and *Communists in Harlem During the Depression* (Urbana, 1983).

McKay's influence on the *Nègritude* movement is ably recounted in Lilyan Kesteloot's *Black Writers in French: A Literary History of Negritude,* trans. Ellen Conroy Kennedy (Philadelphia, 1974); and in Jacques Louis Hymans' *Leopold Sedar Senghor: An Intellectual Biography* (Edinburgh, 1971).

# Index

## DATE DUE

| | | | |
|---|---|---|---|
| | | | |
| | | | |
| | | | |
| | | | |
| | | | |
| | | | |
| | | | |
| | | | |
| | | | |
| | | | |
| | | | |
| | | | |
| | | | |

921      Cooper
MCKAY      Claude McKay.

16.95                    63182